AQA
A-level

Business

 **Third Edition**

John Wolinski and
Gwen Coates

Approval message from AQA

This textbook has been approved by AQA for use with our qualification. This means that we have checked that it broadly covers the specification and we are satisfied with the overall quality. Full details of our approval process can be found on our website.

We approve textbooks because we know how important it is for teachers and students to have the right resources to support their teaching and learning. However, the publisher is ultimately responsible for the editorial content and quality of this book.

Please note that when teaching the _____ Business course, you must refer to AQA's specification as your _____. While this book has been written to match the specifica _____ plete coverage of every aspect of the course.

A wide range of other useful resourc _____ relevant subject pages of our website: www.aqa.org.uk.

Every effort has been made to trace all copyright holders, but if any have been inadvertently overlooked the Publishers will be pleased to make the necessary arrangements at the first opportunity. Although every effort has been made to ensure that website addresses are correct at time of going to press, Hodder Education cannot be held responsible for the content of any website mentioned in this book. It is sometimes possible to find a relocated web page by typing in the address of the home page for a website in the URL window of your browser.

Hachette UK's policy is to use papers that are natural, renewable and recyclable products and made from wood grown in sustainable forests. The logging and manufacturing processes are expected to conform to the environmental regulations of the country of origin.

Orders: please contact Bookpoint Ltd, 130 Milton Park, Abingdon, Oxon OX14 4SB.
Telephone: +44 (0)1235 827720. Fax: +44 (0)1235 400454. Lines are open 9.00a.m.–5.00p.m., Monday to Saturday, with a 24-hour message answering service. Visit our website at www.hoddereducation.co.uk

Cover photo © Rawpixel - Fotolia

Illustrations by Integra Software Services Pvt. Ltd., Pondicherry, India.

Typeset in 11/13 pt ITC Berkeley Oldstyle by Integra Software Services Pvt. Ltd., Pondicherry, India

Printed in Italy

A catalogue record for this title is available from the British Library

ISBN 978 14718 36091

Contents

Introduction

This textbook has been written specifically to meet the needs of students during the first year of AQA A-level Business. It is also intended to provide all of the materials needed for those taking the AQA AS Business qualification. It provides comprehensive coverage of the subject content of the AQA AS specification, section by section, as it is laid out in the specification document. These sections are those that the AQA scheme of work suggests are covered during the first year of the A-level Business course.

Up-to-date examples and illustrations from actual businesses and situations are used throughout the book in order to help you to recognise the dynamic and changing nature of business and its relevance to society.

Structure

This book follows the order of the AQA AS business (7131*) specification. (*7131 is the AQA code used to describe the AS award). The AS material represents the first year of the overall A-level award (coded as 7132.)

The AS specification is divided into six sections, each of which is split into further parts – shown by the individual chapters in this book. The sections and chapters are summarised below:

- **Section 1: What is business? Chapters 1–3**

  This section examines the purpose of business, the different forms of business and the external factors that influence their activities.

- **Section 2: Managers, leadership and decision making. Chapters 4–6**

  This section looks at management and leadership, decision making and the role and importance of stakeholders.

- **Section 3: Decision making to improve marketing performance. Chapters 7–10**
- **Section 4: Decision making to improve operational performance. Chapters 11–15**
- **Section 5: Decision making to improve financial performance. Chapters 16–19**
- **Section 6: Decision making to improve human resource performance. Chapters 20–24**

Sections 3 to 6 study the actions of a business's four main functional areas: marketing, operations management, finance and people/human resource management. These four sections explain how each of these functional areas contribute to improving the performance of a business.

Special features

This book contains several special features designed to aid your understanding of the requirements of the AQA AS Business course and the first year of the AQA A-level Business course.

Key terms

These are clear, concise definitions of the main terms needed for the course. Every term in the AQA specification is included as a key term to enable you to develop a sound understanding of the concepts that are essential learning.

Author advice

Both authors have over 30 years' experience of teaching and have used this to provide snippets of advice that will help you to improve your understanding of topics that may provide certain challenges and to help you avoid potential pitfalls.

Fact files

Topical examples from the world of business are included at regular intervals to help you develop your understanding and application skills by showing how the business ideas you have studied can be applied to real-life situations. The fact files will also increase your awareness of current developments and practices.

Did you know?

These boxes are placed throughout the book; they provide useful insights into the ideas and concepts covered in the course and their use in businesses. The comments will help you to improve your understanding of business activities.

What do you think?

On occasions, facts or comments on business activity are presented in the form of a challenge – what do you think? There is often a range of possible solutions to business problems or many differing consequences to an action. These boxes will get you thinking about possible alternative solutions or consequences.

Practice exercises and case studies

In the 24 chapters of this book, there are 62 different practice exercises that are provided to help you check your understanding of the topics you have covered in each chapter. Many of the questions in these exercises are geared towards assisting you in revising and testing your knowledge and understanding of the topics covered. Other questions will enable you to test your application skills, particularly where calculations are involved. Some questions will also test higher-level skills, such as analysis and evaluation.

In the book there are also 54 case studies to provide further practice of answering questions. Most of these case studies are based on real-life businesses and provide background information that is intended to help you to:

- develop further your understanding of the business world
- practise and develop your skills.

For shorter chapters the practice exercises and case studies are placed at the end of the chapter. This is to allow your understanding of the chapter contents to be tested immediately after completing the topics. However, some longer chapters cover a great deal of material and have been divided into identifiable topic areas. Consequently, some of the practice exercises and case studies in these chapters have been placed throughout the chapter, at the point at which a particular topic area has been completed. As a result, you will be able to test your understanding immediately after completing that topic rather than waiting until the end of the chapter.

Assessment skills

Hierarchy of skills

Every mark that is awarded on an AS or A-level paper is given for the demonstration of a skill. The following four skills are tested:

- **Knowledge and understanding** – demonstrating knowledge and understanding of the specified content of the course, such as knowing the definition of a business term or stating the advantage of a particular method.
- **Application** – relating or applying your knowledge and understanding to a specific organisation or situation. An example might be advising a business to target a particular segment of consumers, based on recognising the most relevant consumers for that organisation.
- **Analysis** – using business theory to develop a line of thought in relation to the solution of a business problem. An example might be showing how improvements in the quality of a product may cause cash-flow problems in the short term but lead to more satisfied customers, and therefore more sales revenue, in the long run.
- **Evaluation** – making a judgement by weighing up the evidence provided and, possibly, recognising the strength, quality and reliability of the evidence before making a decision.

All questions are marked according to this hierarchy of skills, with knowledge being the easiest and evaluation being the most difficult.

Command words

To help you recognise the highest level of skill required in a question certain command words will be used. Some key command words are:

- **Calculate**: Work out the value of something, such as the percentage of labour turnover.
- **Describe**: Set out the characteristics of certain data, such as a trend in sales value.
- **Explain**: Set out purposes or reasons, such as the factors influencing a decision to expand capacity.

- **Analyse**: Separate information into components and identify their characteristics, such as showing how financial incentives for staff may affect motivation.
- **Evaluate**: Judge from available evidence, such as weighing up the pros and cons of a particular marketing strategy.
- **Justify**: Support a case with evidence, such as studying two possible options for a business and showing why a particular option is better than an alternative option.
- **To what extent**: By how much or how many, such as studying a business that is aiming to increase profits and assessing the degree to which a decision to decrease price might improve (or worsen) the business's profitability.

Assessment of AQA AS Business

The **scheme of assessment** describes the format of the examinations and the methods of assessment – the AS course is assessed 100 per cent by examinations. For the AS qualification students take TWO examination papers. **Both papers are based on ALL of the AS specification.** This means a topic from a specific chapter might be tested in Paper 1 or Paper 2 of the AS level. The essential difference between the two papers is the style of assessment.

AS Paper 1: 90 minutes. Maximum marks: 80. All questions are compulsory

AS Paper 1 consists of three sections:

- Section A – Multiple-choice questions. 10 questions. Total: 10 marks
- Section B – Short-answer questions. Approximately four questions. Total: 20 marks
- Section C – Data response question 1. One 9-mark analysis question and one 16-mark evaluation question. Total: 25 marks. Data response question 2. One 9-mark analysis question and one 16-mark evaluation question. Total: 25 marks

AS Paper 2: 90 minutes. Maximum marks: 80. All questions are compulsory

AS Paper 2 consists of approximately eight questions based on a single case study.

The format of the questions set may vary but will be based on the following:

- Two or three short questions, requiring data interpretation or explanation of a concept. Total: 10 marks
- Two analysis questions of 9 marks. Total: 18 marks
- Three evaluation questions of 16 or 20 marks. Total: 52 marks

Assessment of AQA A-level Business

The assessment of A-level Business takes place at the end of two years. Details of the methods of assessment will be provided in the Year 2 version of this book. The format of the examinations and the methods of assessment at A-level are similar to the style used for the AS course, with the addition of essays. The A-level is assessed 100 per cent by examinations.

For the A-level qualification students take THREE examination papers, each of which must be sat at the end of the course and each of which is weighted as one-third of the A-level qualification. **All three papers are based on ALL elements of the A-level specification**. The essential difference between the three papers is the style of assessment. The paper structures are as follows:

A-level Paper 1: Multiple-choice, short answer questions and essays. 2 hours. Maximum marks: 100

- Multiple-choice questions (15 marks); Short answer and analysis questions, approximately six questions (35 marks) and two essays (50 marks)

A-level Paper 2: Data response questions. 2 hours. Maximum marks: 100

- Three articles, each with a set of approximately three data response questions, one of which will be based largely on numerate data only. There will be some short/calculation questions but each article is likely to have at least one analysis question and one evaluation question. Approximately nine individual questions in total.

A-level Paper 3: Case Study. 2 hours. Maximum marks: 100

- Approximately six questions based on a single case study. About two questions will require analysis; four questions will require evaluation skills.

Study advice

Keep up to date

This book contains many topical examples for you to use, but business is constantly changing. Although a textbook provides you with the theory, reading newspapers, magazines and internet articles will help you to keep pace with changes. One thing is guaranteed: the business environment will have changed between the beginning and the end of your course, so there is no substitute for keeping an eye on the latest business news.

Build your own business studies dictionary

As you progress through this book, build up your own glossary/dictionary of terms. This will ease your revision and help to ensure that you can define terms clearly. Knowing the exact meaning of terms will also allow you to write relevantly on the other, non-definition questions.

Read each chapter thoroughly

On completion of each topic, make sure that you have read each page of the relevant section or chapter and use the questions at the end of each section or chapter to test yourself. If you adopt this approach for every topic in the book, your revision will be just that: revising what you have already learned rather than learning material for the first time.

Complete the practice exercises and case studies

Tackle the practice exercises and case studies in each chapter, even if not asked to do so by your teacher. Completion of these exercises and case studies will help you to check that you have understood the basic ideas in the chapters. It will also help you to develop the best approach to answering business questions.

Develop your communication and data-handling skills

There is no need to have studied GCSE Business before starting the AS course; the AQA AS and A-level specifications assume that you have no prior understanding of the subject. However, the courses do expect you to have already developed certain skills during your general GCSE programme. These skills are communication and the ability to use, prepare and interpret business data. You should be able to understand and apply averages (the mean, median and mode); prepare and interpret tables, graphs, histograms, bar charts and pie charts; and use index numbers.

Focus on the higher-level skills

It is tempting to focus chiefly on the facts when you are revising. Remember, the really high marks are given for the depth of your answers. Include scope for this in your revision so that you are able to earn marks for analysis and evaluation. Try to think of ways to apply your learning. For example, as people become richer they buy more products, but some firms (those making luxuries) will probably benefit more than those providing necessities.

Read the Chief Examiner's report

This report will alert you to the strengths and weaknesses shown by previous students and will help you to refine your approach. Along with previous examination papers and mark schemes, these reports are available in PDF format from the AQA website (www.aqa.org.uk).

We wish you well in your studies and examinations, and hope that this book helps to provide you with the understanding needed to succeed. Good luck!

Acknowledgements

The authors would like to express their thanks to numerous individuals who have contributed to the completion of this book.

John wishes to thank all of his family for their tolerance and support during the writing of this book.

Gwen is grateful to John and Jessica, both of whom are always calm, relaxed and supportive, allowing her the time and space to complete this work.

1

Understanding the nature and purpose of business

This chapter provides an understanding of the nature and purpose of business. It is split into two parts. The first part examines why businesses exist by focusing on business objectives. It explains the terms 'business mission' and 'business objectives' and considers the relationship between a business's mission and its objectives. It discusses why businesses formally identify their mission and why they set objectives. It concludes by identifying and discussing the most common business objectives, including profit, growth, survival, cash-flow and social and ethical objectives. The second part examines the measurement and importance of profit. In examining the measurement of profit, it includes explanations of revenue (also known as turnover and sales), fixed costs, variable costs and total costs.

Why businesses exist

Businesses exist essentially to provide goods and services for their customers. Customers could be in the UK or abroad, they might be individuals, other businesses or government departments. If a business can meet the needs of its customers in terms of the cost and quality of the goods or services it provides, it is likely to be successful and to survive in the longer term.

Most businesses, even the very largest, will have begun in a small way, often being set up by a single individual or a small group of individuals. Individuals who have a business idea that they develop by setting up a new business and encouraging it to grow are known as **entrepreneurs**. They take the risk and reap the subsequent profits that come with success or bear the losses that come with failure. The initial motivation for setting up a business varies. Some individuals decide to set up in business because they have a talent or skill they wish to use to provide goods and services that they believe will sell. Others may have spotted a gap in the market that they feel they can fill, either by using their own skills or building a business that will allow them to cater for the needs they have identified.

Once a business has been established, its owners and managers will need to make sure that the business is able to cover its costs and make a reasonable profit if it is to survive. However, the owners may wish the business to do more than survive. For example, they may want the business to grow larger, to dominate the market or to diversify into making or selling different products and services. They may wish the business to contribute to the community in which it is based, for example by funding community sporting facilities, or they may wish to ensure the raw materials it uses are from sustainable sources. This discussion illustrates the fact that all businesses, no matter how small or large, are likely to have a purpose or a mission and objectives or goals they wish to achieve.

Relationship between mission and objectives

The **mission** of a business is its essential purpose or intentions. It is sometimes stated in terms of the main aim or aims of a business. The mission of a business is usually stated in qualitative rather than numerical terms. A **mission statement** is the means of communicating to key stakeholders (i.e. individuals or groups with an interest in the business such as shareholders, employees, suppliers and customers) what the organisation is doing and what it ought to be doing.

Business objectives are designed to enable a business to achieve its aims or mission. They can be set at corporate (or company-wide) level and at functional (or departmental or divisional) level. **Corporate objectives** govern the objectives set by each department or division of a business.

(Unless otherwise stated, business objectives in this chapter will focus on corporate objectives. **Functional objectives** in relation to marketing, operation finance and human resources will be discussed in detail in Chapters 7, 11, 16 and 20 respectively.)

Before an organisation can set its business objectives, it must have a clear understanding of its overall purpose, i.e. its mission. This is because the mission or corporate aims of a business will determine the way in which it is intended the business will develop, which in turn will provide a clear focus from which the business objectives can be set. The fact file below on Disney and the case study on Sainsbury's later in this chapter illustrate the relationship between mission and objectives.

Key terms

Mission An organisation's aims or long-term intentions, its ultimate purpose; a business mission is sometimes the same as its corporate aims.

Mission statement A qualitative statement of an organisation's aims that uses language intended to motivate employees and convince customers, suppliers and those outside the firm of its sincerity and commitment.

Key terms

Business objectives Goals that must be achieved in order to realise the stated aims of an organisation, department or individual team. Business objectives tend to be medium to long term. They can be corporate or functional objectives.

Corporate objectives Goals of the whole organisation rather than of different elements of the organisation. They are set in order to co-ordinate the activities of, give a sense of direction to, and guide the actions of the whole organisation. They are dictated by the mission or corporate aims of an organisation.

Functional objectives Goals of each of the functional areas of a business (including marketing, finance, operations and human resources). They are designed to ensure that the business achieves its corporate objectives and thus its overall aims or mission. Like corporate objectives, functional objectives are set in order to co-ordinate the activities of, give a sense of direction to, and guide the actions of a division or department.

Fact file

Disney's mission and business objectives

Disney's mission is to provide quality entertainment for the whole family. Disney's main business objectives include: 'to be one of the world's leading producers and providers of entertainment and information, using its portfolio of brands to differentiate its content, services and consumer products'; 'to maximise earnings and cash flow, and to allocate capital toward growth initiatives that will drive long-term shareholder value.' This illustrates how a broad mission is being translated into more specific business objectives. In this case the objectives indicate how the business will try to achieve its basic purpose of meeting the entertainment needs of its customers, while at the same time generating earnings that will allow the business to grow and to satisfy its shareholders.

Source: adapted from information on Disney's website, www.disney.com, May 2014

Fact file

Examples of the mission of a range of different businesses

Microsoft's mission is 'to enable people and businesses throughout the world to realize their full potential' and to do this by 'striving to create technology that is accessible to everyone—of all ages and abilities'.

BT's mission is 'a total dedication to the quality of service and experience their customers receive.'

ASDA's mission is 'To be the UK's best-value retailer exceeding customer needs every day'.

McDonald's mission is: 'To be our customers' favourite place and way to eat and drink'.

H&M's mission is 'to offer fashion and quality at the best price'.

Toni and Guy's mission is 'to grow the best, most profitable and most creative hairdressing company on the planet, where people love to work and clients love to be.'

Waterstones' mission is 'to be the leading bookseller on the high street and online, providing customers with the widest choice, great value and expert advice from a team passionate about bookselling'.

Source: adapted from information on each of the organisations' websites, May 2014

Why businesses formally identify their business mission

If a business is small, employing, say, 50 people, all the employees are likely to know exactly what the business does and will have a reasonable idea of what its goals are. In a large business employing thousands or even tens of thousands of people, this is unlikely to be the case. A large national business may make a range of quite different products and have factories and offices located across the UK or, in the case of a multi-national business, in countries around the world. There is no reason to expect a manager from a manufacturing division in Scotland to share a sense of mission with the board of directors, who are hundreds of miles away in the head office in London, or with the human resource manager of a retailing division in the USA. So, for a large business, a mission statement is useful for defining what the business is trying to do in a way that all staff can understand and identify with. Formally stating the business mission or main aims of the business provides a common purpose for everyone to identify with and work towards, and a collective view that helps to build team spirit and encourage commitment.

Why businesses set objectives

Business objectives are set in order to co-ordinate business activity and give a sense of direction to, and guide the actions of, the organisation as a whole. They act as a focus for decision making and effort, and as a yardstick against which success or failure can be measured. Appropriate business objectives encourage a sense of common purpose among the workforce. This makes it much easier to co-ordinate actions and to create a team spirit, which in turn is likely to lead to improvements in efficiency and a more productive and motivated staff. This idea of objectives encouraging people to work towards a common purpose is supported by Dave Packard, co-founder of Hewlett Packard, who suggests that 'It is necessary that people work together in unison toward common objectives and avoid working at cross purposes at all levels if the ultimate in efficiency and achievement is to be obtained.'

To be effective, broadly stated corporate business objectives need to be translated into objectives that can be used as clear targets to achieve. This is particularly the case for functional objectives that need to be set in such a way as to ensure that each section of a business is working towards the same goals so that the overall corporate objectives, aims and mission can be achieved. The use of SMART business objectives assists this process. SMART business objectives are objectives that are:

- **S**pecific – clearly and easily defined.
- **M**easurable – quantifiable (e.g. to increase market share from 15 per cent to 20 per cent within the next two years).
- **A**greed – managers and subordinates are involved in setting the targets.
- **R**ealistic – achievable and not in conflict with other objectives.
- **T**ime bound – based on an explicit timescale (e.g. to open 20 new stores within the next year).

Being specific, measurable and timed enables the business to assess the extent to which objectives have been achieved and to ensure that staff are clear about what it is they are trying to do and have a clear sense of direction. Being realistic means objectives are more likely to motivate staff and provide them with a realistic level of challenge. Being agreed by the whole workforce means objectives are much more likely to be achieved than if they were simply imposed by managers.

Business objectives form the basis for decisions on **strategy**. Strategies are the medium- to long-term plans that will allow a business to achieve its objectives. Such plans include details about what is to be done and the financial, production and personnel resources required to implement the plans.

4

Author advice

Some business texts suggest an alternative explanation of SMART, with the 'A' standing for 'achievable' and the 'R' for 'relevant'. Don't let this confuse you – objectives being 'achievable' and 'relevant' essentially mean that they are 'realistic'.

Author advice

When assessing the effectiveness of objectives of a business, always try to use the SMART criteria. Try to think about the sort of problems a business might face if its objectives are not SMART.

Key term

Strategy The medium- to long-term plans through which an organisation intends to achieve its objectives.

Did you know?

Small businesses are unlikely to write down their business mission and objectives, or even consider them formally, although they are likely to be tacitly understood. Even if business mission and objectives are not written down, it is still important for employees to know what the business is striving to achieve and to share the vision.

There is no single business objective to which every firm should aspire or that guarantees success. However, as long as clear objectives are derived from a well-understood mission or aims, and as long as these objectives are pursued with appropriate and well-resourced strategies, business success is more likely.

Common business objectives

Business objectives vary depending on the size of the business and its legal structure. For example, the main objective of a corner shop may simply be to survive, whereas a multinational business may be more concerned with promoting its corporate image and growing larger.

Some common business objectives are described below.

Profit

Profit maximisation is often cited as the most important business objective, but in practice firms are more likely to aim for a level of profit that satisfies the owners of the business. In order to achieve this overall objective, appropriate functional objectives will be needed, for example, effective marketing in order to increase sales, minimising costs in order to improve profit margins (the difference between revenue and costs for each item sold), effective utilisation of capacity and improving staff productivity by reducing staff turnover and staff absenteeism.

The measurement and importance of profit is explained in the second part of this chapter. Business objectives related to profit will be influenced by many factors, such as the level of competition in the market, the existence of spare capacity, the efficiency of the business, the state of the economy and the demand for the product.

Growth

Growth may relate to increasing market share, sales turnover (the value or volume of sales), number of outlets or number of business areas. Growth may be linked to another objective – to become the market leader in terms of sales value, sales volume or profits, for example. Business growth can be achieved by increasing the size of the existing business or by takeovers of, and mergers with, other businesses.

In order to achieve the overall objective of growth, appropriate functional objectives might include increasing market share, retaining profit in the business in order to finance growth, increasing capacity by expanding the number of sites, recruiting more staff and improving training provision. Growth is less likely to be an important objective for small businesses that value their independence.

External factors, such as the size of the market, the level of competition and the state of the economy, as well as the financial health of a business are likely to influence the attainment of business objectives related to growth.

Survival

Although most businesses wish to do more than simply survive, survival is a key objective for many small or new businesses, especially if they are operating in highly competitive markets. Survival is even more significant during periods of uncertainty and difficult economic conditions. When incomes are falling and demand is weak, many businesses will aim to survive until trading conditions improve and they can focus more positively on objectives related to profit and growth. Functional objectives that will assist a business's survival might include:

- achieving minimum levels of sales and sales revenue to ensure costs are met and market share is retained
- maintaining appropriate levels of stock in order to meet demand but not to tie money up in goods and materials whose value may be declining
- maintaining the required number of experienced or well-trained staff to meet production needs and to be prepared for when the market picks up.

Cash flow

A business must ensure that it has sufficient cash flowing into the business in order to cover the amount it must pay out in any period. Maintaining a healthy **cash flow** is therefore vital for all businesses. Even profitable firms can be vulnerable if they fail to manage their cash flow properly. For example a car repair business may give its customers three months to pay their bills but is only given two months before it must pay its tyre suppliers. If there is insufficient cash to pay its tyre suppliers on time, suppliers may refuse to provide tyres, which will mean the car repairer is unable to carry on its business. This might happen even though the business has plenty of customers and the potential to be profitable.

Social and ethical objectives

Social and ethical objectives are clearly evident in non-profit organisations such as charities, which are set up with the sole purpose of achieving particular social or ethical objectives. For example, Shelter's key objective is 'To relieve hardship and distress among homeless people and among those in need who are living in adverse housing conditions'. The Big Issues' main objective is to connect 'vendors with the vital support and solutions that enable them to rebuild their lives and journey away from homelessness.' Commercial or for-profit organisations are also likely to have social and ethical objectives. The case study on Sainsbury's later in this chapter provides examples of social, ethical and environmental objectives related to youth activity, animal welfare, community involvement, Fairtrade and packaging. Such objectives often enhance brand image and reputation and therefore sales and profits.

> ### Key term
> **Cash flow** The amounts of money flowing into and out of a business over a period of time.

Fact file

Social objectives

H&M's social and ethical objectives involve bringing about 'long-term improvement for people and the environment – in the supply chain, the garment lifecycle and the communities in which we are active.'

McDonald's social objectives include leading and supporting a range of community activities including litter-picking patrols, charity events and local football matches. In the case of the latter they have for many years supported 'initiatives to encourage young people into football through helping to train coaches and volunteers for local clubs.'

Source: adapted from information on each organisation's website

In addition to the above common business objectives, other business objectives include:

- **diversification**: this is where a business moves into the production or sale of different goods and services. A firm might wish to diversify in order to spread risk by reducing its dependency on a single market or product. Diversifying might also be a means of achieving growth and increasing profits. Functional objectives that will support a business wishing to diversify might include the development of niche markets, raising additional finance via appropriate and cost-effective sources, achieving cost savings where the processes used by different elements of the business are similar, and ensuring effective communication between different production sites.
- **market standing**: depending on the organisation, this might involve being seen as the most innovative and progressive organisation, a leader in technology or the best retailer. It is linked to corporate image and an organisation's reputation. Achieving an appropriate corporate image is likely to assist with the achievement of other objectives, such as growth and profit. The nature of this objective will vary according to the target market. For example, a different corporate image will benefit the company if the target market requires products that are 'cheap and cheerful' than if the target market is influenced by an exclusive image and high prices.
- **meeting the needs of other stakeholders**: other than social and ethical objectives, the objectives mentioned above tend to benefit the business owners or shareholders. However, businesses also place a high value on meeting the needs of other stakeholder groups, such as customers, workers and the local community, which in turn will enhance its reputation.

Author advice

In practice, many of the terms introduced in this chapter are used interchangeably. Some companies refer to their 'vision' or 'core purpose' or 'values' rather than mission; others use the terms 'aims' and 'mission' interchangeably. A goal is another term for an objective and in many cases the term 'aims' is substituted for 'objectives'. The term 'targets' is often used instead of objectives, although in other situations the term 'targets' is used for narrow, very specifically focused objectives, often at the level of department, team or even individual.

The important concept to understand is that there is a hierarchy with mission or broad corporate aims or goals at the top, which are then translated into more specific corporate or company-wide objectives, which are in turn translated into specific functional or departmental objectives (for marketing, production, operations, finance and human resources).

Figure 1.1 provides a hierarchy indicating the order in which mission and objectives should be set and thus how they influence each other. This order of objective setting will encourage a logical and co-ordinated approach to planning activities and is more likely to enable the organisation to achieve its goals.

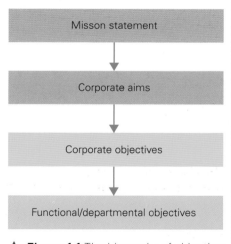

▲ **Figure 1.1** The hierarchy of objective setting within an organisation

Practice exercise 1

Total: 45 marks

1 Explain one reason for businesses to exist. *(4 marks)*

2 What does the term 'mission' mean for a business? *(3 marks)*

3 What are business objectives? *(4 marks)*

4 Explain the relationship between mission and objectives. *(4 marks)*

5 When might survival be an important business objective? *(4 marks)*

6 Analyse the reasons why growth is an important objective for a newly established estate agency operating in a competitive market. *(8 marks)*

7 Analyse why social and ethical objectives might contribute to the achievement of profit and growth-related objectives for a fashion retailer. *(8 marks)*

8 What does the mnemonic SMART stand for in relation to objectives? *(5 marks)*

9 Which of the following objectives is more likely to be a SMART objective?
   a) 'To increase sales by 3 per cent over the next 18 months.'
   b) 'To improve market share in the near future.'
   c) 'To expand the business to cover more areas of the UK.' *(1 mark)*

10 Explain why there is a hierarchy of objectives in most organisations. *(4 marks)*

Case study: Sainsbury PLC

Sainsbury's vision or mission is to be 'the most trusted retailer where people love to work and shop'. To achieve this they have five broad business objectives:

Objective	Progress so far ...
• Great food: the quality and value of their food, combined with strong ethical standards and supplier 1 relationships, help customers to 'live well for less'	• Own brand sales growing faster than brands and accounting for half of food sales • £1 in every £5 spent on fresh fruit and vegetables in UK supermarkets is spent at Sainsbury's, suggesting customers trust the quality, integrity and provenance of the goods
• Compelling general merchandise and clothing: offering customers high street quality and style at supermarket prices	• Sales of general merchandise and clothing growing at more than twice the rate of food; general merchandise sales (excluding fashion) topping £1 billion for the first time • The TU clothing brand is now the seventh largest in the UK market by volume and has risen to twelfth place by value; childrenswear is now sixth in the market by volume, with sales having grown by over 20 per cent year-on-year
• Complementary channels and services: a mix of supermarkets, convenience stores and online sales	• Sainsbury's Bank delivered its fifth consecutive year of profit growth • Convenience stores have delivered sales growth of over 17 per cent year-on-year and online grocery orders exceed 190,000 a week, with an annual turnover of nearly £1 billion
• Developing new businesses: this is an important part of the long-term strategy for the future	• Expanding pharmacy provision with 270 in-store pharmacies • New customers for Sainsbury's Energy (providing gas and electricity) increased by 83 per cent
• Growing space and creating property value: a clearly defined strategy for growing space in terms of new supermarkets, adding space to existing stores through extensions and new convenience stores	• Sainsbury's has added 14 supermarkets, 97 convenience stores and eight extensions to its property portfolio – in line with its target of around 5 per cent gross space growth

Social, ethical and environmental objectives are included in Sainsbury's 20x20 Sustainability Plan. This involves 20 areas of social, environmental and ethical activity that it hopes to achieve by 2020. Examples of these objectives and the company's progress so far include the following:

Objective	Progress so far ...
• Active youth: By 2020, 20 million children will be encouraged to enjoy physical activity	• £10 million package pledges to Sainsbury's School Games over three years • £136 million worth of Active Kids equipment donated since 2005
• Animal welfare: By 2020, all meat, poultry, eggs, game and dairy products will be sourced from suppliers who adhere to independent higher welfare standards	• UK's largest retailer of RSPCA Freedom Food, accounting for over 60 per cent of all Freedom Food sales • Leading retailer of cage-free fresh eggs and first major retailer to use cage-free eggs as ingredients in all own-brand products
• Community investment: By 2020, over £400 million will have been donated to charitable causes	• £51.3 million invested in charities and communities by Sainsbury's, its colleagues, customers and suppliers • Record £11.5 million raised for Comic Relief in 2013, the largest amount ever donated from any partner
• Fairly traded: By 2020, sales of fairly traded products will hit £1 billion.	• Sainsbury's claims to be the world's largest Fairtrade retailer, accounting for £1 in every £4 spent on Fairtrade products in the UK
• Packaging: By 2020, own packaging will have been reduced by a half compared to 2005	• New smaller carrier bags introduced in convenience stores in March 2013, saved 125,000 kg plastic and 68,000 kg carbon in 2013/14 • Helping customers reduce food waste via amended 'display until' and 'freeze by' labelling

Questions

Total: 45 marks

1 Analyse why a business such as Sainsbury's might set social and ethical objectives.

(9 marks)

2 Evaluate the benefits to a company of having detailed business objectives.

(16 marks)

3 To what extent does the case study illustrate the importance to a business of ensuring a clear relationship between mission and objectives?

(20 marks)

Source: adapted from information on Sainsbury's website, www.j-sainsbury.co.uk, May 2014

> ### Key terms
>
> **Price** The amount paid by a consumer to purchase one unit of a product.
>
> **Total revenue** (or **turnover** or **sales revenue**) The income received from an organisation's activities.
>
> Total revenue = price per unit × quantity of units sold
>
> (For example, if price is £5 and 10 units are sold then total revenue is £5 × 10 = £50)

Measurement and importance of profit

Revenue and price

Setting a **price** is a difficult task. Typically, a business must set a price that is high enough to cover the costs of making goods or providing a service and leave a surplus that is profit. However, a high price will mean a smaller number of customers are likely to buy the product. The business must find the ideal selling price – the one that helps it to make the most profit.

Total revenue

Total revenue may also be described by the following terms:

● income
● revenue
● sales revenue
● sales turnover
● turnover.

Total revenue (TR) can be calculated by multiplying the average selling price (p) by the quantity sold (q):

$$TR = p \times q$$

For example, if the selling price is £8 and 5 items are sold, total revenue is £40.

Similarly, if TR = £48 and the selling price = £4, the quantity sold is £48 ÷ £4 = 12 units.

Also, if TR = £60 and the quantity sold is 10 units, the selling price is £6 (£60 ÷ 10).

If two of the variables in the equation $TR = p \times q$ are known, the third can be calculated.

Effect of changes in sales volume on total revenue

When asked to look at the effect of a change in sales volume on total revenue, you should assume that the selling price remains unchanged, regardless of sales volume. Therefore, if sales volume doubles, total revenue will double; if sales volume falls by 10 per cent, total revenue will fall by 10 per cent. In both cases, the selling price will stay the same.

This is an oversimplification of what actually happens in real life, but it is helpful to firms because it allows them to make fairly accurate predictions about how total revenue will change as sales volume changes. In turn, this will assist them in making logical business decisions. In Chapter 8, the section on price elasticity of demand will provide an insight on how total revenue might change in a different way as sales volume rises.

Costs

Some functional areas of a business, such as operations and human resource management, can contribute to the achievement of rising profits by reducing costs. If more efficient methods can be introduced, the business can increase profit by cutting down on staff or reducing the amount of wastage on the production line. However, the business must be careful that these cost savings do not reduce the quality of the good or service. If this is reduced, total revenue may be affected as customers will be less likely to buy the products.

Costs are therefore a major factor in determining the overall success of a firm, as measured by its profit. Organisations need to understand their costs if they wish to improve their profit.

Classifying costs

Costs are classified as **fixed**, **variable** and **total**. There are two principal reasons for classifying costs:

- **To assess the impact of changes in output on the costs of production**: a firm can compare additional revenue from an increase in sales volume to see if it exceeds the extra costs incurred. Regardless of its current profit level, a firm aiming to make a profit should increase sales volume if the extra revenue exceeds the additional costs of increasing output.
- **To calculate the costs of making a particular product in a multi-product company**: it can be difficult to work out whether it is worthwhile making a product. It is easy to calculate the sales income of a product, but many costs (e.g. office rent, canteen facilities) are not specific to any single product made by a firm.

Costs and output

A company can use the link between costs and output to calculate the financial *implications* of changing its level of output.

In reality, it is impossible to predict the exact change in each and every cost, so general classifications of costs into fixed, variable and total costs, are used to *estimate* the likely effect of output changes on individual costs.

▲ A production line

▲ The cost of office rent and equipment isn't specific to any one product a company makes

Key terms

Fixed costs Costs that do not vary directly with output in the short run (e.g. rent).

Variable costs Costs that vary directly with output in the short run (e.g. raw materials).

Total costs (TC) The sum of fixed costs and variable costs.

11

If there is an $x\%$ rise in output, it is assumed that:

- fixed costs do not change
- variable costs change by the same percentage as the change in output (a rise of $x\%$ in this case).

Again, this is an oversimplification of what happens in real life, but it does enable firms to make reasonably accurate predictions about how costs will change as output changes, enabling them to make logical business decisions.

Table 1.1 shows how firms classify the costs they incur into fixed and variable costs. The logic behind these choices is that the costs of items in the first column are not affected by small changes in output. These fixed costs will, however, change in the long run if large increases in output are required. For example, if there were a significant increase in output, new machinery (a fixed cost) would have to be installed. The variable costs (shown in the second column) will change if output changes, even if it is only by a small amount.

▼ **Table 1.1** Classification of costs by output

Fixed costs	Variable costs
Machinery	Raw materials
Rent and rates	Wages of operatives/direct labour
Salaries	Power
Administration	
Vehicles	
Marketing	
Lighting and heating	

Note that a distinction is made between **wages** (paid to operatives who make the product) and **salaries** (paid to staff who are not directly involved in production). Similarly, power to drive the machinery is a variable cost, while office lighting and heating are fixed (not related to output).

Semi-variable costs are costs that combine elements of fixed and variable costs. A worker may be paid a set wage plus a bonus for each item produced. The set wage would be a fixed cost and the bonus a variable cost.

Effect of changes in output on costs

When asked to look at the effect of a change in output on costs, you should assume that total variable costs change by the same percentage as output. If output doubles, total variable costs will double; if output falls by 10 per cent, total variable costs will fall by 10 per cent. In both cases, the fixed costs will stay the same.

For example, let us assume that output is 1,000 units, fixed costs are £5,000 and total variable costs are £6,000. Therefore, total costs are £11,000. The fixed costs will not change if output changes. The variable costs of £6,000 will increase, but by how much? To calculate this we need to know the variable cost per unit. If 1,000 units cost £6,000 in variable costs, this is £6 per unit (£6,000 ÷ 1,000 units). If 1 more unit is produced, it will increase variable costs by £6 (to £6,006). If 50 more units are produced, variable costs will increase by £300 (50 × £6) to £6,300 (1,050 × £6). Fixed costs will stay at £5,000.

1 What happens to total costs if output doubles from 1,000 units to 2,000 units?
2 What happens to total costs if output falls by 10 per cent from 1,000 units to 900 units?

(Answers on page 539.)

Table 1.2 shows the link between monthly costs and output for a magazine producer. It illustrates why the magazine producer wants high monthly sales. If only 20,000 magazines are sold, the fixed costs are high as a percentage of total costs. However, if sales quadruple to 80,000 magazines, total costs increase by less than double (from £70,000 to £130,000) and the fixed costs are a much lower percentage of the total costs.

▼ **Table 1.2** Monthly costs and output for a magazine producer

Units of output (000s)	Fixed costs (£000s)	Total variable costs (£000s)	Total costs (£000s)
0	50	0	50
20	50	20	70
40	50	40	90
60	50	60	110
80	50	80	130
100	50	100	150
120	50	120	170

Fact file

Forecasting costs

In planning a business, it is vital that costs are forecast accurately because sudden changes in costs can affect future decisions.

In 2012 raw material costs were relatively stable, with an average price rise of 2 per cent for raw material prices in the UK. However, this increase was not spread evenly across all materials. Tobacco and alcohol ingredients rose by 6.6 per cent and food prices rose by 3 per cent in 2012, in sharp contrast to paper products which fell in price by 0.9 per cent.

For financial planning it is also important to anticipate changes in costs accurately. At the beginning of 2012 petroleum prices were forecast to increase by 5 per cent per annum to £1.40 per litre; surprisingly they fell by 1.2 per cent in 2012.

Figure 1.2 shows the volatility of petrol prices in recent years. The overall rise in price has proved to be a major problem for many firms, because it has made financial planning very difficult. Incorrect forecasting may mean that a business does not achieve the results that it needs to succeed (although it can also lead to larger than expected profits if costs are underestimated).

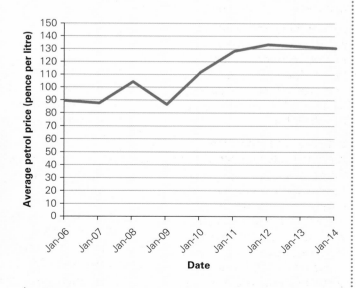

▲ **Figure 1.2** UK petroleum prices, January 2006 – January 2014 Source: ONS

Relationship between costs and price

In many industries, increases in costs, such as raw materials and labour, are 'passed on' to the consumer in the form of higher prices. Although business theory suggests that higher prices will lead to a fall in the quantity demanded (and possibly in sales revenue), demand is less likely to fall if every business is increasing its prices. This is likely to happen when costs are increasing, because all firms will be affected in a similar way and they will all be trying to maintain a profit margin (the difference between the selling price of an item and the cost of making or buying that item).

Profit

Profit is a prime objective of most firms and put simply, profit = total revenue − total costs.

In effect, there are two ways of improving profit:

- increase sales revenue
- decrease costs.

A combination of both is the ideal way of achieving additional profit.

Measuring profit

The calculation of profit described above only shows the actual profit being made. A business will want to choose the most profitable level of output and/or want to assess how changes in output and sales might affect profit. Table 1.3 takes the costs of the magazine producer in Table 1.2 and adds data on revenue and profit. In the table it is assumed that the selling price for the magazine is £2.

▼ **Table 1.3** Monthly revenue, costs and profit for a magazine producer

Units of output (000s)	Total revenue (£000s)	Total costs (£000s)	Profit (£000s)
0	0	50	(50)*
20	40	70	(30)*
40	80	90	(10)*
60	120	110	10
80	160	130	30
100	200	150	50
120	240	170	70

Profit = total revenue minus total costs

* Figures in brackets show a loss.

Table 1.3 shows that a loss of £10,000 is made if 40,000 magazines are sold, but a profit of £50,000 is made if 100,000 magazines are sold.

Importance of profit

Profit is important for a number of reasons. Some key reasons are outlined below.

- **Profit is a reward.** Business owners take a risk when using their money to purchase shares or take ownership of a business. To compensate for the risk that they have taken, business owners are entitled to the profits made by the business. Every six months, public limited companies usually pay a dividend to their shareholders. This dividend payment represents the share of the profits allocated to shareholders. Some shareholders depend on the dividend payment as a source of income, particularly retired people who rely on their shares to provide a steady flow of money. These shareholders may have a greater interest in making sure that a high dividend is paid. Without this opportunity to earn a reward it is unlikely that people would invest in businesses. In practice, profits are not always given to owners as dividends. Many businesses retain some of their profits so that they can buy more resources in order to make more profit in future years. In this way, owners are still being rewarded, but are waiting to receive some of those rewards.

- **Profit is a motivator**. For owners of businesses, profit is a motivator. Sole traders are entitled to all of the profits from their businesses, while many private limited companies will be owned by the people running the business. In many companies there are profit-sharing schemes, in which staff are given incentives to work effectively by receiving a share of the profit made. The John Lewis Partnership uses this type of incentive to reward its employees.

- **Profit is a measure of success**. It is possible to assess the performance of a business by comparing its profits to those of other companies, particularly its competitors. However, before using profit to measure success it is important to examine the business's objectives, as some businesses give profit a lower priority than others.

- **Profit is a guide for future investment**. The efficiency of different sectors of the economy can be analysed by observing where profits are high and where they are low. Prospective investors can use changes in profit levels as a guide to those markets where it is becoming easier to make profit and those where losses are more likely. In this way scarce resources are constantly moved away from unprofitable activities towards profitable activities. In general, it can be assumed that the latter activities are a more accurate reflection of what consumers want businesses to be producing.

- **Profit is a source of finance**. In order to fund expansion plans and capital investment, the company directors will wish to keep some of the profits in the business. This avoids the need to pay interest on borrowed money or to sell more shares in order to finance expansion. Retained (or 'ploughed-back') profits increase the assets of a business and should therefore increase the value of the company. Furthermore, retained profits should help the business to increase its future profits (and thus increase future dividends). In the UK, this is the main source of capital for established businesses, because it is very cost-effective and convenient. It does not have to be repaid and does not require payment of interest. Consequently, shareholders often support requests to increase the level of retained profit. In practice, most firms will strike a balance between paying dividends and retaining profits.

- **Profit is attractive to stakeholders**. A profitable business will find it easier to establish links with people and other organisations. For example, workers will be eager to apply for a job in a profitable company; customers will be more likely to want to purchase products from a successful company; and suppliers will be keen to obtain contracts with a business that is making a profit, as they will be a reliable customer in the future.

Practice exercise 2

A textile manufacturer sells 400 shirts at a price of £15 each. Raw material costs are £4 per shirt and wages are £5.55 per shirt. The costs of producing the 400 shirts are shown in Table 1.4.

▼ **Table 1.4** Costs for a textile manufacturer

Item	Cost (£)	Item	Cost (£)
Raw materials	1,600	Heating/lighting	60
Marketing costs	120	Property/rent	400
Power	80	Wages	2,220

1 Calculate the profit made from selling 400 shirts. *(4 marks)*

2 The retailers that buy the shirts have said that they will buy 600 shirts if the price is reduced to £13. Calculate the profit made if the textile manufacturer increases output and sales to 600 shirts, with the selling price at £13 per unit. *(6 marks)*

3 Using quantitative and qualitative factors, advise the manufacturer on whether it should charge a price of £13 or £15. *(10 marks)*

Practice exercise 3

1 Which of the following is a variable cost?
   a) Advertising expenditure
   b) Office equipment
   c) Stationery supplies
   d) Wages *(1 mark)*

2 Which of the following is a fixed cost?
   a) Direct labour
   b) Power
   c) Property rent
   d) Raw materials *(1 mark)*

Output level	Sales revenue	Fixed costs	Variable costs	Total costs	Profit
0	0				
1					
2					
3	75				
4		20			
5					
6			90		

3 The table above shows some costs and revenue data at different levels of output.
   a) What are the total fixed costs? *(2 marks)*
   b) What is the selling price of the product? *(2 marks)*
   c) What are the variable costs per unit? *(2 marks)*
   d) Using the above information, complete the table by filling in the gaps. *(6 marks)*

Case study: Gnomes United

Gnomes United is a small garden centre in Colchester. The owner, Jim Tavare, has successfully increased sales in recent years by widening the range of products and services offered. A total of 70 per cent of the garden centre's revenue comes from the sale of plants and garden tools, but the opening last year of a nearby superstore led to a sharp reduction in sales of these items. Sales of plants have fully recovered, owing to quality problems at the superstore, but sales of garden tools are still low. Market research among his customers has led Jim to realise that the sale of garden tools in his garden centre is important, because customers see them as an essential element of any garden centre. Furthermore, Jim remembers how sales of plants at his cousin Jack's garden centre in Ipswich fell sharply when Jack decided to stop selling garden tools.

Sales records show that relatively few garden tools are bought in the run-up to Christmas.

Last year Jim experimented with selling some Christmas products, such as decorations, because many customers visit the centre once a year to buy their Christmas trees. The restaurant at the garden centre enjoys a boom time in the month before Christmas, and Jim's research shows that about 20 per cent of his customers first came to the garden centre to buy Christmas products and have come back since for other products.

Jim is wondering whether to stock Christmas tree lights this year – an item that he has not previously sold. He has asked 50 customers and they seem to be keen on the idea. Their responses have led him to conclude that he will sell 200 boxes in December. A standard box of lights will sell for £24.99. The lights will cost £16.50 to buy from the supplier. To cope with the increased work, Jim estimates that he will need to increase the number of part-time hours worked by 4 hours in total, at a rate of £7.25 per hour. This estimate is based on asking the owners of three other local garden centres.

Questions

Total: 35 marks

1 Name two other terms that also mean 'revenue'. *(2 marks)*

2 Jim is wondering whether to expand the restaurant at the garden centre. This will lead to 8,000 more customers a year and increase his revenue by £60,000 per annum. However, his variable costs are £2.20 per customer and he will incur extra fixed costs of £15,000. He estimates that the space needed will cut his profit on plant sales by £20,000 per annum. Use calculations to show whether expanding his restaurant will improve his overall level of profit. *(6 marks)*

3 Based on the figures in the case study, calculate the extra profit that Jim hopes to make from the Christmas tree lights. *(6 marks)*

4 Analyse one reason why it would be difficult to estimate the effect of stocking Christmas tree lights on the number of part-time hours needed. *(5 marks)*

5 Evaluate the other factors that Jim should consider before deciding whether to stock the Christmas tree lights. *(16 marks)*

2

Understanding different business forms

This chapter focuses on different business forms. It begins with an explanation of the difference between private and public sector organisations. Private sector organisations are then considered in detail. The important concepts of unincorporated and incorporated businesses and of unlimited and limited liability are introduced first. Then private sector for-profit organisations are considered, including sole traders, partnerships, private limited companies and public limited companies. In relation to limited companies, consideration is given to ordinary share capital, market capitalisation and dividends. In addition, in relation to limited companies, the role of shareholders and why they invest, and the influences on share price and the significance of share price changes are discussed. A summary of the range of non-profit organisations in the private sector, such as charities and mutual societies, is included. The chapter concludes with a discussion of the effects of ownership on an organisation's mission, objectives, decisions and performance.

Different forms of business

A range of different forms of business exist, ranging from very small one-man operations to multinational corporations. Some business forms are set up in order to make profits for their owners and others are established to pursue community or charitable aims. Some business forms operate in the public or governmental sector and others in the private sector. Different business forms are supported by different legal structures that influence how they operate, how they can be financed, what their responsibilities are and what their objectives are.

Private sector organisations are owned, financed and run by private individuals. Organisations in the private sector range from the smallest sole trader business to huge multinational businesses. Although most private sector organisations aim to make a profit, a large number of organisations in the private sector are **non-profit organisations**, including charities and mutual societies.

Public sector organisations (also known as state-owned or government organisations) are owned and operated by the government, whether at national, regional or local level. These organisations mainly provide essential services, including education, health care, police services, refuse collection and street lighting. They are usually provided free at the point of delivery and financed from taxation, for example education and health care. The main aim of public sector organisations is to provide services that would be difficult for individuals to provide for themselves, such as street lighting, or that are deemed essential for all and which some people might not be able to afford to purchase from private sector organisations, such as education or health care.

Private sector organisations

The range of business forms (or legal structures) in the for-profit private sector is illustrated in Figure 2.1. Each of these business forms is considered in this section and their relative advantages and disadvantages are summarised in Table 2.1. A range of business forms that cater for non-profit private sector organisations are considered later in this chapter.

Two important classifications to understand when considering different business forms in the private sector are unincorporated and incorporated businesses, and limited and unlimited liability.

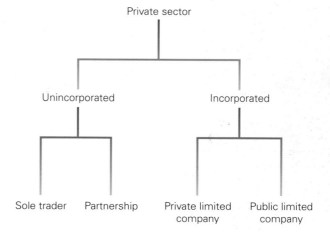

▲ **Figure 2.1** Legal structures of business in the for-profit private sector

Unincorporated and incorporated businesses

The distinction between **unincorporated** and **incorporated businesses** can be demonstrated by the following example, where Tesco is an incorporated business and Robinson's is an unincorporated business.

If you have a part-time job with Tesco plc, your employer, with whom you have a contract of employment, is Tesco and not the shareholders (owners) of Tesco. If, however, you have a part-time job with Robinson's, the local newsagent, which happens to be run as a sole trader by the owner, Mary Robinson, then your employer is the individual who owns the business, Mary Robinson. Similarly, if you had an accident on the premises of Tesco and were advised to sue, then you would sue Tesco plc, not the shareholders (owners) of Tesco. If, however, you had an accident on the premises of Robinson's newsagent, you would sue Mary Robinson, the owner.

Key terms

Unincorporated business There is no distinction in law between the individual owner and the business itself. The identity of the business and the owner is the same. Such businesses tend to be sole traders or partnerships.

Incorporated business This has a legal identity that is separate from the individual owners. As a result, these organisations can own assets, owe money and enter into contracts in their own right. Such businesses include private limited companies and public limited companies.

Unlimited and limited liability

Unlimited liability is a characteristic of businesses that are unincorporated, meaning that there is no distinction in law between the owners and the business. If the debts of the business are greater than the personal assets of the owners, they may be forced into bankruptcy. The main types of business with unlimited liability are sole traders and partnerships.

In contrast, if a business with **limited liability** goes into liquidation because it cannot pay its debts, the shareholders (owners) have no responsibility for further payments as long as they have paid in full for the shares they have purchased; their personal assets cannot be used to pay the debts of the business. Legally, such a business has 'died' and so its debts 'die' with it.

Limited liability is a feature of incorporated businesses, where the identity of the owners and the business are separate in law. The main types of business with limited liability are private limited companies and public limited companies. Limiting the amount of shareholders' liability is an important factor in encouraging people to invest because it ensures they know the extent of the risk they face.

Sole trader

A **sole trader** usually has little capital for expansion and is heavily reliant on the owner's personal commitment to make the business a success. Because of its unincorporated status, if the business is unsuccessful, there is no protection from limited liability because the finances of the business are inseparable from those of the owner. Sole traders are most commonly found in the provision of local services, for example newsagents, plumbers and hairdressers.

▲ A sole trader

Fact file

Partnerships

Partnerships are not included in the AQA specification but they are another form of business in the UK.

A partnership is a form of business in which two or more people operate for the common goal of making a profit.

There are three main types of partnership:

- An ordinary partnership: partners normally have unlimited liability. A partnership agreement sets out the rights and responsibilities of the partners and how profits will be allocated, but in the absence of an agreement, profits are shared equally among all partners. A partnership allows more capital to be used in the business than is the case with a sole trader and enables the pressures of running the business to be shared, although the partners' ability to raise finance remains rather limited.
- A limited partnership: at least one partner assumes responsibility for managing and running the business and has unlimited liability. At least one partner contributes finance, receives a dividend and has limited liability, but has no involvement in the management or running of the business.
- A limited liability partnership (LLP): designed for professional or trading partnerships. This type of partnership allows partners who are actively involved in the business to limit their liability. At least two partners (known as 'designated members') have additional legal responsibilities. LLPs lose the privacy enjoyed by general partnerships in relation to their financial affairs and must register with Companies House, like private and public limited companies.

Private limited company

Public limited companies are often the most high-profile business organisations but the significance of **private limited companies** should not be ignored. Most companies are privately owned and they contribute enormously to the economy.

Key term

Private limited company A small-to medium-sized business that is usually run by the family or the small group of individuals who own it.

- A private limited company can keep its affairs reasonably private and thus the owners can determine their own objectives without the pressure to achieve short-term profit that is so common for public limited companies.
- Private companies are funded by shares that cannot be sold without the agreement of the other shareholders, which means that their shares cannot be traded on the Stock Exchange.
- The share capital of private companies may be less than £50,000, although many have much higher levels of share capital.
- Private limited companies generally tend to be limited in size.
- A private limited company must have 'ltd' after the company name to warn people that its owners (shareholders) have limited liability.

Fact file

Changing legal structure to suit the circumstances

Samantha Hale has run her sports products business, Advance Performance UK, as a sole-trading operation, a partnership and a limited company. Samantha started selling sports products in 1996, operating from home. She didn't need outside funding, so being a sole trader seemed the simplest option. When she decided to get retail premises, things grew quickly and the expense of stocking and marketing the shop meant a strain on cash flow. A few months into having the shop, she formed a partnership with her, then, husband, who had a business coaching athletes. Doing that meant that they were able to offset the initial 'start-up' losses from the shop against the profits from the coaching side of the business.

When her marriage and business partnership collapsed, she changed the business to a limited company in order to protect her personal assets.

Samantha won East of England Business Woman Entrepreneur of the Year in 2008, BT Business Essence of the Entrepreneur in 2009 and the Peterborough Evening Telegraph Retail Business Award in 2009 and 2010. Advance Performance UK now has two highly successful Running and Triathlon stores, one in Peterborough and one in Cambridge.

Source: adapted from www.businesslink.gov.uk and www.advanceperformance.co.uk

Fact file

UK's biggest private limited companies

Each year *The Sunday Times* publishes Top Track 100, a league table compiled by research company Fast Track that ranks Britain's 100 private limited companies with the largest sales revenue. Typical Top Track 100 companies have sales between £700 million and £2.5 billion, are owned and run by established families and entrepreneurs or owned by private equity companies and managed by senior executives, and have between 500 and 20,000 staff.

The top five companies in the 2013 Top Track 100 league table (with ranked position in brackets) are:

- Alliance Boots – retailer and pharmaceutical wholesaler (1)
- Ineos – chemicals manufacturer (2)
- Greenergy – fuel supplier (3)
- John Lewis Partnership – food and general retailer (4)
- Swire – conglomerate (5).

The ownership of these companies varies, for example:

- 45 per cent of shares in Alliance Boots are owned by Walgreens, an American drugstore chain
- 75 per cent of shares in Ineos are owned by Jim Radcliffe, the founder and chairman
- 35 per cent of shares in Greenergy are owned by Tesco

- 100 per cent of shares in John Lewis Partnership are owned by employees
- 67 per cent of shares in Swire are owned by members of the Swire family

Other well-known businesses in the 2013 league table include:

- Virgin Atlantic – airline and tour operator (12)
- JCB – construction equipment manufacturer (14)
- Arcadia – fashion retailer (15)
- Iceland – frozen food retailer (16)
- Thames Water – water services provider (23)
- Specsavers – optical and hearing retailer (24)
- New Look – fashion retailer (30)
- Clarks – shoe retailer and wholesaler (31)
- United Biscuits – branded snack manufacturer (32)
- Phones 4U – mobile telephone retailer (38)
- Findus Group – food producer (39)
- Matalan – value retailer (42)
- River Island – fashion retailer (49)
- Dyson – appliance manufacturer (51)
- Formula One – motor racing administrator (62)
- Virgin Trains – train operator (66)
- Poundland – discount retailer (76)
- Odeon and UCI Cinemas – cinema operator (86)
- Harrods – department store operator (94)
- House of Fraser – department store operator (95).

Source: adapted from www.fastrack.co.uk (2014)

Key term

Public limited company A business with limited liability, share capital of over £50,000, at least two shareholders, two directors, a qualified company secretary and, usually, a wide spread of shareholders. It has 'plc' after the company name.

▲ Pizza Express is one company that has reverted from public to private limited company status

Public limited company

The shares of **public limited companies** are traded on the Stock Exchange, which enables these businesses to raise finance more easily. Private limited companies sometimes change to public limited companies, usually to obtain extra funds for growth. However, 'going public' has its disadvantages:

- It involves a loss of control, as the business moves away from the ownership and support of a family or close-knit group of individuals and becomes responsible to shareholders, including institutional investors.
- It subjects the business to constant scrutiny by the financial press.
- It may cause the business to focus on short-term profits for shareholders and maintaining share prices in order to avoid takeover pressure, which detracts from long-term decision making.

These disadvantages are such that a number of large, successful private limited companies resist becoming public limited companies, while other successful public limited companies revert to private limited company status. The number of public limited companies listed on the London Stock Exchange has declined from over 2,000 in 1998 to just over 1,000 in March 2014. Well-known companies that have reverted from public to private limited company status include Arcadia, Selfridges, New Look and Pizza Express.

Few of the companies that ceased trading as public limited companies did so because of financial failure. Most chose to go private for a number

Author advice

As both private limited companies and public limited companies are incorporated businesses and have limited liability, make sure you are clear on the distinction between them and do not confuse them when you answer questions on this topic.

of reasons, including the excessive cost of meeting the regulatory requirements for public limited companies, the continual dissection of public limited companies' performance by market analysts, and the relative privacy of the private limited company structure. A sharp rise in the amount of capital available to private companies is a major reason for the decline in the number of companies becoming public limited companies. Another key advantage of joining the stock market – share liquidity – has also become less persuasive and, indeed, is sometimes regarded as unnecessarily risky because predators can easily snap up shares and put pressure on management to make changes it may not agree with.

Author advice

Ensure that you understand the effect that becoming a public limited company with a quotation on the Stock Exchange can have on a company, as this can be a crucial factor for a company that wants to grow.

Did you know?

Institutional investors are pension funds, insurance companies, banks and other financial organisations that invest huge sums of money in the shares of public limited companies quoted on the Stock Exchange. They invest on behalf of others, for example, investing the funds employees pay into their pensions. Institutional investors are by far the largest group of investors in company shares and therefore have huge influence on companies. Critics suggest that it is pressure from institutional investors seeking to maximise their funds and profits that forces businesses to focus on short-term profits (known as short-termism) rather than on long-term performance.

Fact file

Stock Exchange listings

When a public limited company wishes to raise finance, it does this by issuing (selling) shares to the public. This is done by an **IPO (initial public offering)**, which is the first sale of shares by a private company to the public. IPOs are issued by smaller, younger companies seeking the capital to expand or by large privately owned companies wishing to become public limited companies. Once shares have been issued in this way, the owners can sell them on the **Stock Exchange**. The Stock Exchange is therefore a market where second-hand shares (i.e. shares that have already been issued to the original shareholders) of public limited companies can be bought and sold. The public limited company itself is not involved in stock exchange trading, but will just change its records so that any dividends due on the shares are paid to new owners. The Stock

Exchange assists companies in raising finance because people are more reluctant to buy shares if they cannot easily offload them when required.

▲ The London Stock Exchange

Fact file

Private equity firms

In recent years, private equity takeovers have played an important part in UK business. **Private equity firms** are made up of private investors who take over a company and work closely with the managers to turn the business around. Their aim is to make it profitable and then sell it. Therefore, they look for businesses that are undervalued and can be improved. Private equity firms often buy public limited companies, convert them into private limited companies, improve them and then sell them back to the public.

When public limited companies are listed on the Stock Exchange, managers often find that investors are interested only in short-term rewards. This can make it difficult to invest in longer-term projects or take risks. Radical or innovative decisions may be shelved in favour of more conservative choices. Reporting to many different investors also takes up a lot of management time. When a private equity company takes over a public limited company, it often empowers the managers to run the business and make the right decisions, even if they are risky or take years to pay off. The private equity firm is closely involved in the running of the business and in developing the right strategy.

However, private equity takeovers are usually financed by debts, so they carry a high risk. Some private equity firms have been accused of being asset strippers – buying a company to squeeze out whatever profit they can get before selling it on. In general, private equity is perceived as representing the short-term interest of between two and five years – quite different from the longer-term perspective taken by most family-based private limited companies.

▼ **Table 2.1** Advantages and disadvantages of different legal structures

Structure	Advantages	Disadvantages
Sole trader	<ul><li>easy and cheap to set up</li><li>few legal formalities</li><li>able to respond quickly to changes in circumstances</li><li>owner takes all the profit and hence there is good motivation</li><li>independence</li><li>more privacy than other legal structures, as financial details do not have to be published</li></ul>	<ul><li>unlimited liability</li><li>limited collateral to support applications for loans</li><li>limited capital for investment and expansion</li><li>difficulties when the owner wishes to go on holiday or is ill</li><li>limited skills as the owner needs to be a 'jack of all trades'</li></ul>
Private limited company	<ul><li>limited liability and the business has a separate legal identity</li><li>access to more capital than unincorporated businesses</li><li>more privacy than a plc, as it is only required to divulge a limited amount of financial information</li><li>more flexible than a plc</li></ul>	<ul><li>shares are less attractive, as they cannot be traded on the Stock Exchange and hence could be difficult to sell</li><li>less flexible if expansion needs finance, which is more difficult to raise than for a plc</li><li>there are more legal formalities than for an unincorporated business</li></ul>
Public limited company	<ul><li>limited liability and the business has a separate legal identity</li><li>easier to raise finance as a result of its Stock Exchange listing</li><li>greater scope for new investment</li><li>can gain positive publicity as a result of trading on the Stock Exchange</li><li>suppliers tend to be more willing to offer credit to public limited companies</li></ul>	<ul><li>must publish a great deal of financial information about its performance</li><li>greater scrutiny of activities</li><li>significant administrative expenses</li><li>founders of the firm may lose control if their shareholding falls below 51 per cent</li><li>a stock exchange listing means pressure from investors may lead to more emphasis on short-term financial results, rather than long-term performance</li></ul>

Ordinary share capital

Ordinary share capital is a term used in relation to private and public limited companies. Ordinary shares are also known as **risk capital** or **equity capital**. A shareholder owning 1 per cent of a company's ordinary shares receives 1 per cent of any profit given to ordinary shareholders as dividend and gets 1 per cent of the votes at the **annual general meeting (AGM)**. There is no guaranteed level of **dividend** and sometimes no dividend at all is paid. This is because people who are owed money by the business must be paid first and even in profitable years, profits may be ploughed back into the business to finance further improvements rather than distributed to shareholders. (More detail on ordinary share capital is provided in Chapter 18 Making financial decisions: sources of finance.) Because ordinary shareholders are usually given one vote for each share, ownership of 51 per cent of the shares in a company guarantees overall control of that company.

Fact file

Lloyds Bank and dividend payments

In the first quarter of 2014, Lloyds Banking Group's pre-tax profits improved by over 20 per cent. This was a result of falling costs due to job cuts and its withdrawal from many of its international businesses. The improved profit strengthened the bank's plan to pay its first dividend since it was rescued during the financial crisis.

Before the financial crisis Lloyds had a record of being one of the highest dividend paying shares in Britain, paying out just over half of its profits in dividends in 2005 and 2006. Following the financial crisis, the government pumped in £20 billion to keep Lloyds afloat, giving the British taxpayer a 41 per cent stake in the business. The Group has not paid a dividend on shares since the financial crisis.

Market capitalisation

Market capitalisation (or market cap) is the total value of the issued ordinary shares of a public limited company. It is calculated by multiplying the current market price of an individual share by the number of issued ordinary shares. For example, if a company has issued 25 million ordinary shares and the current market price of its ordinary shares is £10, the company's market capitalisation is £250 million (25,000,000 × £10 per share). Market capitalisation is therefore influenced by the number of shares issued and the market price of shares. Market capitalisation is often used as an indication of investors' opinion of a company's net worth or its overall value.

The value of ordinary share capital uses the price of shares at the time they were first issued – i.e. the value that initial investors paid for them, not the current market price, which is the value used in market capitalisation.

For example, if a company issues 100,000 ordinary shares at £2 each in May 2014, its ordinary share capital will be £200,000. By December 2014, its share price, as quoted on the Stock Exchange might be £5 each. Assuming all shares were sold and are fully paid up, its market capitalisation will therefore be £500,000 but its share capital is still £200,000.

Key term

Market capitalisation The value of outstanding shares in a public limited company. Outstanding shares are the total of all ordinary shares issued and fully paid up. Market capitalisation is calculated by multiplying the total outstanding shares by the current market price of an individual share.

Note: the value of a public limited company's ordinary share capital is not the same as its market capitalisation.

25

Role of shareholders and why they invest

Shareholders are the owners of companies. A small business may have just one shareholder – the founder – while a public company may have many thousands of individual and institutional shareholders. People invest in shares for a variety of reasons:

- To provide financial support for a business and to be involved in the running of a business. Shareholders of private limited companies will usually have this motivation.
- To gain control of a business, which they can do by buying up 51 per cent of shares. This may happen to a public limited company because its shares are traded on the Stock Exchange.
- By trading on the Stock Exchange, the company's shares are available for anyone to buy for the regular dividend they will receive, provided the company makes a profit and decides to distribute a portion of this to shareholders.
- To make a capital gain, i.e. to profit from the price at which they buy a share and the price at which they sell it at a later date.

Fact file

Shares in Royal Mail

Since making its debut on the London Stock Exchange in October 2013, the price of shares in Royal Mail has risen strongly. Experts suggested there were two compelling reasons to hold on to the shares:

1 Royal Mail paid out its first dividend in July 2014, nine months after issue. For those who bought shares when they were first issued at 330p per share, the dividend paid in July meant an annual return on their investment per share of over 6 per cent.

2 The company was viewed as a solid long-term bet because demand for parcels was expected to boom rather than decline and thus share price was expected to continue to rise.

Fact file

The Channel Tunnel

Groupe Eurotunnel, also known as the Eurotunnel Group, is a company listed on the Paris and London stock exchanges. Its core business is the operation of the cross-Channel Fixed Link (i.e. the Channel Tunnel). Its share capital of €220 million is made up of 550 million fully paid up ordinary shares with a nominal value of €0.40. Its share price in March 2013 was €6.5 and in March 2014, it was €8.55. Market capitalisation in March 2014 was therefore approximately €4.7 billion (number of fully paid up ordinary shares × current share price). Dividends per share have increased in each of the last four years from €0.04 in 2010 to €0.15 in 2013.

▲ Eurostar train at Waterloo Station

This data indicates the type of return on investment an average shareholder might gain. An investor buying shares in March 2013, when share prices were €6.5 and selling them in March 2014 would have made a capital gain of just over €2 per share (i.e. a capital gain of 31.5 per cent on their original investment – €2.05 increase in share price as a percentage of the initial share price of €6.5). In terms of dividends, an investor buying a share in March 2013 at €6.5 received a dividend of €0.15 at the end of the year, giving a return of 2.3 per cent (i.e. the dividend of €0.15 as a percentage of the share price paid of €6.5).

Source: adapted from Group Eurotunnel Annual Review and Corporate Social Responsibility Report 2013

Did you know?

There is no statutory requirement to hold an **annual general meeting** if the company is a private limited company, however the shareholders may request that one is held or the directors may call an annual general meeting if desired. Under the terms of the Companies Act 2006, public companies must hold an annual general meeting.

Shareholders have a number of important functions and have certain rights.

- One of the primary reasons for shareholders is to provide finance for a business. Issuing shares enables a business to raise funds for expansion or development. In return, the company's founders give up part ownership to new shareholders.
- The majority shareholder, i.e. the one that owns at least 51 per cent of ordinary shares will be in a position to influence the decisions taken by the organisation's management.
- Although the majority of shareholders in a public limited company do not play a major role in running the company, they do have a right to vote on resolutions at annual general meetings. These might include who sits on the board of directors, whether a proposed merger should go through or whether the level of directors' bonuses is appropriate. (Note: directors are also likely to be shareholders.)
- Shareholders have the right to inspect the company's books and records.
- Shareholders have a right to receive a portion of any dividends the company declares. If the company liquidates, they have the right to a share of the proceeds. However, creditors, bondholders and preferred shareholders have precedence over ordinary shareholders in the event of liquidation.

Influences on share price and the significance of share price changes

Key term

Share price The price of a single share in a company; share prices are usually determined by the supply and demand for shares.

Did you know?

Stocks and stockholders are American terms for shares and shareholders. The term 'stock' is used widely in other related terms, including stockbrokers (people who offer advice and buy and sell shares for clients), the Stock Exchange and the stock market.

The price at which ordinary shares trade will have nothing to do with their original value, but will be determined mainly by market forces i.e. by supply and demand. If more people want to buy a share (demand) than want to sell it (supply), then the price moves up. Conversely, if more people want to sell a share than want to buy it, there would be greater supply than demand, and the price would fall. In addition to market forces, the extent to which prices in general increase over time (known as the inflation rate) will influence **share prices**, particularly over the very long term.

Many factors influence the supply and demand for shares. Some of the main factors are as follows:

- **State of the economy**: if economic conditions are good and are expected to continue, investors tend to feel confident. Companies are more likely to perform well, make larger profits and thus are more likely to pay higher dividends. Under such circumstances, demand for shares tends to rise and thus share prices increase. However, if economic conditions are difficult, investors may feel nervous. They may worry that a company's profitability will decline and this will tend to reduce the demand for shares, which may cause share prices to fall.

- **Performance of the company**: if a company is performing well and is expected to continue to do well, its share price is likely to rise. When a company reports good profits, investors have more confidence in it and there is more demand for its shares, which increase in price. Conversely when a company reports lower profits, investors lose confidence in the company and sell their shares, which is likely to lead to a reduction in their price.
- **Competition in the market**: this is closely linked to the above point because how well a business responds to the threat of competition in the market in which it operates will influence how well it performs overall and, in particular, its profitability.
- **Proposed takeovers**: a takeover is when one company makes an offer to take control of another company by buying enough shares to ensure it has the power to influence policy, make decisions and elect directors. Shareholders in the company being targeted for a takeover usually receive an offer to buy their shares (either for cash or for shares or a combination of both) from the company planning the takeover. They can accept or reject the offer. The prospect of a takeover can influence the price of shares and will reflect whether investors think the takeover bid is likely to succeed. The potential and actual impact of takeover bids on share prices is the focus of regular discussions in the financial press.
- **Investors' expectations and their response to rumours**: when people see that others are selling their shares in a particular company for whatever reason – perhaps because they have heard a rumour that it is struggling and in danger of going into liquidation – more people will want to 'get on the bandwagon' and sell their shares. This will cause an increase in supply of these shares and with little demand for them, the price of the shares will fall, perhaps significantly, as people are desperate to get rid of them before their price falls even further. A similar process in the opposite direction happened to internet companies in the dotcom bubble period. Shares in these companies were tremendously popular and plenty of people wanted to buy them, but the number of shares on the market was limited to those issued by the companies in the first place. In order to get shares, the price was bid up. People saw these share prices rising and more people wanted to own them, pushing prices still further.

Although average share prices show a long-term upward trend, individual share prices are extremely volatile and can change rapidly. This is why for individual savers, investment in shares should be viewed as a long-term activity over many years.

Choosing a form of business and changing business form in the private sector

A number of factors affect the choice of business form or legal structure in the private sector. These have been discussed within the previous sections about each type of business organisation. To summarise, they include:

- the need for finance in order to expand
- the size of the business and the level and type of investment required

▲ A non-profit organisation

- the need for limited liability
- the degree of control desired by the original owners
- the nature of the business and its objectives
- the level of risk involved.

For example, a manufacturing business requiring heavy investment in plant and equipment before anything can be sold may need limited liability in order to raise sufficient funds. On the other hand, a business that requires much less investment and therefore very little borrowing will involve relatively little financial risk and so there may be no need for limited liability. In other cases, image might be vitally important and the word 'ltd' after a name may add status and 'plc' even more so.

Non-profit organisations

Non-profit organisations do not have a defined structure and such organisations can take many different business forms. These organisations are also known as the third sector (because they are not part of the for-profit private sector or the public sector). This sector includes voluntary and community organisations, charities, social enterprises, pressure groups, trade unions, co-operatives, mutual societies and trusts.

Although non-profit organisations vary, they share the following common characteristics:

- They are non-governmental organisations.
- They have a governing body responsible for managing their affairs.
- They are value driven and have social, environmental, community, welfare or cultural aims and objectives.
- They are usually established for purposes other than financial gain, with any profits or surpluses being reinvested in the organisation in order to further its objectives.
- Many use volunteer staff in addition to paid employees.
- These organisations may make profit, but their objective is not to maximise profit for their shareholders and owners. They can operate under a number of different legal structures, including charities, trusts, mutuals and companies limited by guarantee.

Apart from the distinguishing feature that non-profit organisations do not distribute profits to their owners, many such organisations have much in common with for-profit organisations. For example, while some non-profit organisations use only volunteers as employees and as managers and directors, any sufficiently large non-profit organisation is likely to require a permanent staff of paid employees, including highly skilled managers and directors. Many large non-profit organisations wish to accomplish their objectives in the same way as for-profit enterprises, so the same business tactics and management techniques as in the for-profit sector are used.

Fact file

Industrial and Provident Societies (IPS)

Industrial and Provident Societies (IPS) are incorporated organisations whose members benefit from limited liability. These types of organisations are often known as **mutual societies**. An IPS is owned and democratically controlled by its employees and members. A mutual exists with the purpose of raising funds from its members or customers, which can then be used to provide common services to all members of the organisation or society. Examples of this type of organisation in the UK are co-operative societies, mutual insurance companies and building societies. Instead of having shareholders, building societies have members who collectively own the business and are also its customers. Members have the right to vote for directors regardless of how much or how little money they have with the society.

Did you know?

The 1980s and 1990s saw many long-established building societies 'demutualise' by converting to, or merging with, banks, which are public limited companies. As a result there are now fewer than 50 building societies. The largest is Nationwide Building Society.

Did you know?

Community Interest Companies

The Companies Act 2006 introduced a new form of organisation known as a **Community Interest Company**. These are limited companies with special additional features and are created for use by people who want to conduct a business or other activity for community benefit, rather than private advantage. The assets and profits of these companies are intended to be used for the public good.

Fact file

Companies limited by guarantee

Non-profit organisations can be unincorporated or incorporated. In the UK, many non-profit organisations are incorporated as companies limited by guarantee rather than limited by shares. The organisations do not have shares or shareholders, but benefit from being incorporated, which includes limited liability for its members and being able to enter into contracts and purchase property in its own name. The profits of the company (known as the trading surplus) must be invested in achieving the goals of the company and must not be distributed to the company's members. By taking up limited liability status, a charity limits the liability of its management or trustees in respect of any financial losses that it may sustain. The directors of the organisation give a nominal guarantee (usually of £1), and are not personally liable for any losses beyond that amount. Examples of non-profit organisations that are companies limited by guarantee include: Shelter, the charity that helps homeless people; AQA, your examining board; and Amnesty International, the human rights campaigning organisation.

Effects of ownership on mission, objectives, decisions and performance

Just as a variety of factors affect the choice of business form, so the choice of business form influences the ownership of a business. This in turn influences the organisation's mission and objectives and its decision-making processes and ultimately will have an impact on its performance.

The mission and objectives of public sector organisations are generally focused on meeting social needs and providing essential services. For example, the mission of a Midlands-based teaching hospital is 'We will be a leading centre in healthcare driven by excellence in patient experience, research, teaching and education'. Decision making in public sector organisations will reflect a focus on meeting social needs and providing essential services. As a result, sometimes activities that are not profitable to provide, such as local libraries, are nevertheless still funded in some areas because the local authorities have judged that the benefits offered to the local population outweigh the costs of providing them. These organisations may not have to return maximum profits to shareholders, but they do have to provide good value for money for citizens. As a result, just as in the private sector, strong leadership of public sector organisations is essential to ensure effective decision making, tight financial management and efficiently-run operations.

The mission and objectives of non-profit organisations, although not focused on maximising profits for their owners or members, will be focused on generating sufficient profit or surpluses to reinvest in their particular

▲ A public sector organisation

field of interest. Examples of mission statements of non-profit organisations already mentioned in this chapter include:

> Shelter: 'Shelter believes everyone should have a home. Our work won't stop until there's a home for everyone.'

> Nationwide Building Society: 'We exist solely for the benefit of our members. We help them and their families meet their financial needs in a sustainable, responsible and secure way.'

As for all organisations, non-profit organisations need strong leadership and well-trained staff to ensure their operations are as efficient as possible to enable them to perform effectively and achieve their objectives.

Apart from non-profit organisations, most private sector organisations aim to make maximum profit for their owners. However, this is not the only objective as the following extracts from mission statements illustrate:

> JCB: 'We will support our world-class products by providing superior customer care. Our care extends to the environment and the community.'

> Tesco: '... to create value for customers to earn their lifetime loyalty'.

> Google: '... to organise the world's information and make it universally accessible and useful'.

Although for-profit private sector organisations must ensure they make sufficient profits to reinvest in their businesses and to satisfy their owners, they may also pursue other objectives, such as promoting long-term growth or developing a strong reputation for environmental and ethical standards.

In the case of sole traders, partnership and private limited companies, their owners usually have a significant role in the management and leadership of the business. When these businesses begin to expand, their ownership often changes and this can have significant effects on the mission and objectives of a business and how it makes decisions. A sole trader that expands by becoming a partnership may benefit from additional expertise and finance but the original owner will have to take the views and expectations of partners into account, which requires a very different approach to decision making. The eventual impact on the performance of the business will depend on how well these changes are planned for and handled. Similarly, bringing new shareholders into a small private limited company can add further expertise and increase the finance available, but new shareholders may not have the same values and aims as the original owners. The proportion of shares held by the original owners may decline and they may ultimately lose overall control of the business. As a result, the original mission of the business may change considerably. As mentioned above, how these changes impact on the performance of the business will depend on how well a change in ownership is planned for and how well the change is managed.

In public limited companies, the vast majority of owners of the company, the shareholders, are not involved in the management and leadership of the company, which can lead to tension. Shareholders may want the business to pursue strategies that bring short-term gains to profits and to share prices, while managers and leaders may prefer to pursue strategies that lead to the longer-term success of a company, which may mean lower profits in the short and medium term. More discussion of this point about the 'divorce of ownership and control' will be covered in Chapter 18.

Practice exercise 1

Total: 60 marks

1 Explain the implications for someone starting a business without having limited liability. *(4 marks)*

2 Explain one advantage and one disadvantage of a sole trader as compared with a partnership. *(6 marks)*

3 Distinguish between a private limited company and a public limited company. *(6 marks)*

4 Explain one advantage and one disadvantage of a private limited company over a public limited company. *(6 marks)*

5 Which one of the following business forms is likely to be most suitable for a non-profit organisation?
   a) Sole trader
   b) Public limited company
   c) Private company limited by guarantee *(1 mark)*

6 Company A has 5 million ordinary shares that were issued at a price of £5 each. The current market price of each share is £50.
   a) Calculate Company A's market capitalisation and explain why this differs from its ordinary share capital. *(7 marks)*
   b) Explain two reasons why people might decide to invest in shares. *(6 marks)*
   c) Identify and explain two factors that might influence the price of shares. *(6 marks)*

7 Identify and explain three factors that are likely to influence the choice of a company's legal structure. *(9 marks)*

8 Identify and explain three effects of different business ownership on a company's mission and its objectives *(9 marks)*

Case study: Staying private

A number of large, high-profile, public limited companies have made the decision to revert back to private limited company status in order to reduce media scrutiny and pressure and the accompanying emphasis on short-termism. Other expanding companies have made the decision to remain as private limited companies.

William Timpson opened his first shoe shop in 1865. In 1912, W M Timpson became a private limited company and converted to a public limited company in 1929. It was eventually bought by United Drapery Stores (UDS), a retail conglomerate, which was in turn acquired by Hanson Trust, a multi-industry conglomerate, in 1983. At this point, the Timpson family bought the company back and focused on shoe repairs rather than shoe sales. In 2003, the family-owned shoe repairer bought the Minit Group, which owned Sketchley cleaners, Supasnaps and Mister Minit. In 2009, it bought Max Spielmann photo stores, based mainly in the north of England. This was complemented by its acquisition early in 2013 of Snappy Snaps, the franchise photo chain based mainly in London and the South East.

Timpson now controls more than 900 retail outlets nationwide.

John Timpson, the group's chairman, is the great grandson of the original founder of the business, William Timpson. John Timpson is quoted as saying, 'We only have one firm plan, which is that we will not float the business. We think staying private is the best way to run the business.' He says that most months he is approached by bankers keen to buy shares in the business and help it expand. His response is that he prefers to fund expansion from cash flow, that is, from money generated within the business. He says he would never float the business and 'would hate going around the City having shareholders telling me what to do.'

Source: adapted from an article in the *Financial Times*, May 2003 and web sites www.timpson.co.uk and www.timpson.co.uk/blog (2014)

Unit 1 What is business?

32

Questions

1 At various times in its history, Timpson has been a sole trader, a private limited company and a public limited company. Evaluate how appropriate the sole trader and public limited company business forms might have been as the business grew and developed. *(20 marks)*

2 For some of its history, Timpson was a public limited company. Analyse the factors that might influence the share price of a public limited company in a similar market to Timpson and evaluate the factors that would persuade an investor to buy shares in a company like Timpson. *(20 marks)*

3 Discuss the factors that John Timpson might have taken into account in judging that 'staying private is the best way to run the business'. *(20 marks)*

3

Understanding that businesses operate within an external environment

This chapter explains that businesses operate within an external environment and that changes in the external environment affect business. It focuses specifically on how certain factors in the external environment affect business costs and the demand for goods and services. The factors considered are: competition, incomes, interest rates, demographic factors, and environmental issues and fair trade.

External environment

Although much of your study of business is concerned with the internal operations of a business, it is also vital to understand and appreciate that all business takes place within a much wider context than the business itself. This context is known as the external environment and is illustrated in Figure 3.1.

At the centre of the diagram in Figure 3.1 is the business. The middle ring of the diagram indicates the external competitive environment a business operates in. The extent and nature of this competition varies from industry to industry. The outer ring of the diagram is the general external business environment in which a business operates. This involves the broader influences that affect all businesses. These influences are often referred to using the mnemonic PESTLE, which is an aide memoire for the factors that affect business:

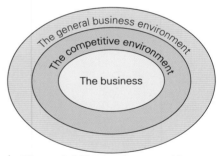

▲ **Figure 3.1** The business and its external environment

Political

Economic

Social

Technological

Legal

Environmental

Table 3.1 lists the PESTLE factors and provides examples of the issues that might affect business. Full coverage of the impact on business of each element of PESTLE is provided in your Year 2 textbook.

▼ **Table 3.1** PESTLE factors

PESTLE category	Examples of issues that might affect business
Political factors	• government economic policies • government social policies • extent of government intervention
Economic factors	• business cycle • income levels • interest rates • exchange rates • level of inflation • level of unemployment • membership of the EU
Social factors	• demographic factors • ethical issues • impact of pressure groups • influence of different stakeholders • changing lifestyles
Technological factors	• new products • new processes • impact of change • costs of change
Legal factors	• legislation
Environmental factors	• environmental issues and fair trade

As well as competition as a factor in the external environment that influences business costs and the demand for goods and services, this chapter focuses on some of the factors from the PESTLE model, including:

● whether the economy is growing and incomes are rising or whether the economy is moving into a recession and incomes are falling
● the impact of changes in interest rates
● changes in the make-up of the population of a country (known as demographics), for example whether there are larger proportions of young or old people
● how environmental issues, including fair trade considerations, affect the type of products demanded and the way they are produced.

Influence of the external environment on business costs and the demand for goods and services

Costs

Costs are a major factor in determining the overall success of a firm, as measured by its profit. Organisations need to understand their costs, and what influences them, if they wish to improve their profit. As explained in Chapter 1, business costs are made up of fixed and variable costs. The price of a product reflects these costs and the profit margin added. It is clear therefore that any factor that changes costs will also result in a change in the price of a product and/or the profit margin.

> **Key terms**
>
> **Demand** The amount of a product (i.e. a good or a service) that consumers are willing and able to buy at any given price over a period of time.

Factors influencing demand for a product

It is important for a business to understand the nature of the demand for its products and how this demand is affected by different factors.

Factors influencing **demand** vary according to the good or service that is being considered. However, there are a number of factors that influence the demand for most goods and services and these are described below.

Price

As the price of a product rises, the demand for it will usually fall. This is partly because consumers will think more carefully about whether the product is required, but also because alternative products will appear more attractive in comparison with the initial product.

For products that are necessities and have no close alternatives (substitutes), an increase in the price will make little difference to the quantity demanded. In contrast, if the product is not a necessity and has many close substitutes, an increase in the price can lead to a dramatic fall in the quantity demanded. The extent to which the price influences the demand for a product is known as the price elasticity of demand. This is considered in more detail in Chapter 8. The same logic applies to a fall in price – a fall in price will lead to a rise in demand. The degree of change in demand will depend on factors such as the level of necessity and the existence or non-existence of close substitutes.

Tastes and fashion

Over time, fashion and people's tastes change. Such changes affect the demand for products and services. Changes in work patterns tend to mean that fewer families sit down in the evening for a traditionally produced family meal, often because of a lack of time. Consequently, people are now more likely to buy takeaway meals or convenience food, as opposed to ingredients for meals that take time to prepare. In contrast, people now tend to spend more time shopping and are therefore more likely to spend time relaxing in a coffee shop or restaurant while on a shopping trip.

Some items, notably (but not exclusively) clothing, are also prone to swings in demand, according to what is perceived to be fashionable at the time. As a result, businesses in these industries must keep a close eye on the latest consumer trends in order to cater for changes in demand. Good market research can be the key to success in such cases.

Price of other goods

Sometimes, the demand for a product can be influenced by the price of a totally different product. This occurs in two instances – when the product is a substitute or complementary.

- **Substitutes**: these are goods that are close alternatives to a particular product. If the price of the substitute increases, the original product will appear to be much better value for money in comparison and demand for it will increase. Similarly, a fall in the price of a substitute will lead to a fall in demand for the original product.

- **Complements**: complementary products are ones that are used alongside each other, such as fish and chips, or shampoo and conditioner. If the demand for one of these products increases, the demand for the complement will also increase and vice versa. For example, if fish becomes more expensive, people will be less likely to buy it, so the demand for chips will fall, even though the price of chips remains the same.

Marketing and advertising

Successful marketing and promotion can have a major impact on the demand for a good or service. The creation of a strong brand can lead to consumers being prepared to pay a higher price for a product, as well as purchasing more of it. This means the business can increase its sales volume, its value added and its sales value. (Marketing is dealt with in detail in Chapters 7–10.)

Seasonal factors

The time of year has a significant impact on demand. Products such as porridge and ice cream experience huge fluctuations in demand between summer and winter. Businesses may try to overcome these fluctuations by providing a range of goods (e.g. a clothing store will change its stock according to the season) so that demand is more evenly spread throughout the year. However, it is difficult to ensure that there are no seasonal fluctuations in demand.

Government action

The government can influence demand for a product in a number of ways.

To encourage demand, it can subsidise a product to reduce the price the consumer pays but if it wishes to reduce the demand for a product, the government can do this through taxation. For example, cigarettes are taxed heavily and this leads to a much higher price. Alternatively, the government can introduce its own advertising campaign to encourage the purchase of particular products, for example, health-related advertising to encourage people to purchase and eat at least five portions of fruit and vegetables per day. The government may also use advertising to discourage purchase of particular products, for example all cigarette packets carry health warnings. The government can introduce legislation (laws) to restrict the advertising or use of a product or to ban it altogether.

Other factors that influence the demand for goods and services include competition, incomes, interest rates, demographic factors, and environmental issues and fair trade. These are all factors in the external environment of a business that influence business costs and the demand for goods and services. Each of these factors is discussed in detail in the next section of this chapter.

Costs and demand

Costs and demand are inextricably linked. For example, a rise in costs is likely, but not certain, to lead to an increase in price. Depending on the nature of the product, the quantity demanded may fall as a result. Similarly, a fall in costs may lead to a fall in price, which in turn may lead to a rise in quantity demanded. Chapter 8 provides a detailed explanation of the influence of price on the demand for different types of product.

The rest of this chapter looks at five key factors in the external environment and considers how each one influences business costs and the demand for goods and services. The five factors are: competition, incomes, interest rates, demographic factors, and environmental issues and fair trade.

Competition

Almost all businesses operate in competition with other businesses, whether this is Apple and Samsung competing for customers at a national and international level, Sainsbury's competing with Asda for customers at a local and national level or two local hairdressers competing for clients in a single town. Competition is usually between firms supplying the same products, but it can be broader. For example, British Gas competes not just with other suppliers in the gas provision market but also with the suppliers of other types of fuel, including coal, electricity and oil. Similarly, *The Guardian* competes not just with other newspapers but also with other news sources, including internet sites, radio and television.

The demand for a firm's goods and services will be influenced by the strategies of its competitors. For example, competitors may reduce the price of their products, introduce new products or increase the popularity of their existing products by effective marketing. These actions will lead to a decrease in demand for a rival firm's products. The reverse also applies. Ineffective actions by competitors may help a firm to benefit from an increase in demand for its products.

Competition is generally regarded as being positive, particularly in bringing benefits to customers. The advantages of competition are based on the fact that, in order to gain market share, firms need to offer customers products that are the cheapest or the best quality, or products that are of good quality and are reasonably priced. This usually means that firms try to improve the:

- efficiency of their operations
- cost-effectiveness of their operations
- quality of the goods and services they provide.

However, there are also disadvantages associated with competition.

- When competition between firms is based solely on price, product quality is often sacrificed. The pursuit of low costs can lead to decisions about production that may have ethical implications. For example, a firm may be able to sell its goods at very low prices because it manufactures them in very low wage economies overseas. (See the fact file about Nike on page 56.) Even firms whose products are not low priced may move their production sites abroad to take advantage of low labour costs in order to compete more effectively.
- Huge resources, for example in relation to marketing, are devoted to competing with other firms, but it can be argued that these resources could be spent on developing cheaper or better products.
- Intense competition can result in some businesses being forced out of the market, leading to the economic and human consequences of

Did you know?

The managing director of Waterman Pens is famously quoted as saying: 'We are not in the market for pens, but executive gifts.', thus redefining the company's competitors as Dunhill and Rolex, rather than Parker and Bic.

redundancy and unemployment. In the period from Christmas 2012 to March 2013, the following large retailing businesses closed: Blockbusters, Jessops, Comet and HMV – although both Jessops and HMV were later rescued. (See fact files on Blockbusters and Jessops below and the case study on HMV on page 57.)

- The competitive process often means that successful businesses take over, or merge with, unsuccessful ones. This in turn leads to the existence of a smaller number of larger and larger businesses and in the end less competition. The motor vehicle industry is an example of where successful businesses have gradually taken over less successful ones, leading to a few, very large, motor vehicle manufacturers.

Fact file

Blockbuster

In November 2013, Blockbuster, the video rental franchise business, closed. Competition from new products in the market, including the rise of Netflix, mail-order DVDs, video-on-demand and streaming services online, meant demand for Blockbuster's products declined such that the business was no longer viable.

Fact file

Jessops

In January 2013, Jessops, the camera specialist, closed its 187 stores, resulting in 1,370 jobs being lost. The business had been in operation for 78 years. The main reason for its failure was the relevance of the business in a declining market where developing technology means consumers no longer want dedicated cameras, favouring instead multipurpose devices such as smartphones.

Jessops tried to respond to the shift in technology and consumer behaviour by refreshing its stores to give customers a more interactive experience, training staff to provide advice and information and offering products other than cameras, such as a personalised printing service, own-brand accessories and photography courses.

None of these initiatives worked because they were not solutions to the problem. Jessops was trying to bring people back to cameras, rather than accepting that many people don't need cameras anymore. Another problem was that consumers were moving to online sales and advice. Jessops had too many stores for the market and was not moving sufficiently into the online business.

In March 2013, two months after closing, Peter Jones, of Dragon's Den, bought the brand from the administrator PwC. Mr Jones is intent on re-establishing Jessops as a multi-channel retailer with a national high street presence. Products are sold online and in-store at the same price. The presence of high street stores will facilitate what Mr Jones sees as an increasing demand for a 'collect-in-store model' – which, he says, people want with technical products.

Did you know?

Administration is a rescue mechanism for businesses that become insolvent. It is an alternative to liquidation. A company that 'goes into administration' is allowed to continue trading. An administrator will be in charge of its operations and will work on behalf of the creditors, trying to find options other than liquidation. Options include selling the business to new owners or separating the business into different elements that can be sold and closing down those that cannot.

Jessops (see fact file above) and HMV (see case study on page 57) both went into administration and were eventually sold to new owners.

Fact file

Low-cost airlines

In 1967, a small interstate aircraft carrier named Southwest Airlines was launched. It made its first flight in 1971 shuttling passengers between the Texan cities of Houston, Dallas and San Antonio for fares as low as $20 one-way. Southwest started a low fares and no frills format that was later replicated by Michael O'Leary of Ryanair and Stelios Haji-Ioannou of easyJet.

O'Leary was inspired by what he saw at Southwest and, as a result, Ryanair, a small Irish airline, was reborn as a low-cost carrier offering passengers cheap, no-frills flights to secondary airports in Europe. Stelios's easyJet started by advertising flights to Edinburgh and Glasgow that were 'as cheap as a pair of jeans'.

These low-cost airlines are now major corporate players. Willie Walsh, the chief executive of International Airlines Group, owner of British Airways and Iberia, has admitted that most national flag-carriers (the large airlines like British Airways) simply underestimated their budget rivals. Over the past 15 years, budget airlines, in general, have gained 40 per cent of intra-Europe air travel revenues. This has been possible because low-cost airlines have a unit cost advantage on the national flag-carriers of around 35 per cent.

However, at the end of 2013, O'Leary admitted that his resolutely no-frills approach at Ryanair may have run its course. As a result, Ryanair is beginning to move away from its no-frills approach by allocating seating and providing better customer service – something that has proved highly successful at easyJet, which introduced speedy boarding, more flexible fares, guaranteed seats and better food in 2012. Ryanair and easyJet together still account for only 20 per cent of the overall European short-haul market, highlighting a significant opportunity to gain further market share from struggling large national flag-carriers.

▲ easyJet is a low-cost airline

Source: adapted from an article by Nathalie Thomas in *The Telegraph*, 16 November 2013

Determinants of competitiveness and their impact on costs and demand

Almost all businesses operate in markets where there is competition from other businesses. As a result, the success of any one business depends on how competitive it is, i.e. its ability to match or surpass the popularity of products offered by its competitors. The main determinants of competitiveness and how they affect costs or demand or both are identified and explained below.

Investment in new equipment and technology

Machinery and computers can improve the speed, reliability and quality of products, meaning that labour and other costs can be reduced as a result. Businesses that fail to adopt new processes that are being widely introduced in the industry in which they operate are likely to have higher costs and thus become uncompetitive.

Improvements to operational procedures

Improvements to areas such as factory layout, the location of the organisation, stock control and the processes used in the factory or outlet can all reduce unit costs. Businesses that fail to focus on the quality of their operational procedures may find their costs and therefore their prices are too high compared to their competitors.

Effectiveness of the marketing mix

A well-planned marketing mix, suited to the needs of the business, can greatly improve competitiveness and therefore the ability to gain sales in the face of competition. Businesses that fail to adopt a well-co-ordinated and effective marketing mix to promote their products are likely to suffer reduced demand as customers turn to more persuasive competitors. (The marketing mix is covered in detail in Chapter 10.)

Innovation through investment in research and development

The pace of change requires companies to update and broaden their product range constantly. Product life cycles are becoming shorter and new ideas must be incorporated into products in order to stay ahead of the market. (The product life cycle is covered in detail in Chapter 10.) Businesses that fail to update their products in line with those of their competitors are likely to lose sales. See the fact files on Blockbusters and Jessops above and the case study on HMV on page 57.

Financial planning and control

Careful financial planning and control can help reduce costs and improve a firm's competitiveness. A well-organised finance department can ensure that clear targets are set, challenging managers to improve their efficiency. Effective monitoring of progress towards meeting targets can also improve efficiency by making sure that any problems are quickly detected and rectified. Businesses that fail to ensure tight financial planning and control are likely to experience rising costs over time and reductions in their profitability.

Incentive schemes for staff

Motivated staff work more effectively, take on more responsibility and identify more closely with the aims of the organisation. A workforce that is rewarded and motivated will contribute towards a successful business in terms of improved efficiency, leading to lower costs, higher quality goods and services and increased demand. A business that fails to reward and motivate its staff is likely have higher labour turnover and higher costs as employees move to what they see as 'better' employers. (Motivation is covered in Chapter 23.)

Quality procedures

Effective quality procedures can both reduce the unit cost of production by improving the efficiency of the process and improve the quality of the product itself. Improved quality is likely to enhance the reputation of the product in the eyes of consumers and can help the business to increase sales volume. Lower unit costs and improved quality and reputation might enable a firm to increase its selling price without losing demand, leading to greater profits. Businesses that have poor quality procedures in comparison to their competitors can quickly develop a reputation for poor quality products and lose sales.

Staff skills, education and training

Highly skilled employees will be more productive, thereby reducing the cost of the goods produced or services offered. Well-trained staff are more likely to identify innovative ways of making a product and be able to produce high-quality products and identify defective ones, thereby preventing flawed products from reaching the consumer. In businesses that provide services this may increase customer loyalty and encourage additional demand. A well-educated workforce tends to be more flexible and adaptable. In the modern business world, where change is becoming increasingly rapid, this can be a significant asset for a business that is trying to stay ahead of its competitors. Businesses that fail to ensure their employees are appropriately trained and skilled are likely to incur higher costs than their competitors and may lose custom to them.

Enterprise

The entrepreneurial skills of the owners and their desire to become their own bosses create a culture of independence, hard work and flexibility, which helps to supply the needs of larger organisations as well as providing alternative products and services. Often such entrepreneurial competitors take established businesses by surprise and quickly begin to eat into their markets, causing the demand for the products of established firms to decline. (See the fact file on low-cost airlines on page 40 for an example of entrepreneurial competitors.)

Although the determinants of competitiveness considered here, concern internal aspects of a firm's operations, they indicate how individual firms by improving their competitivenes, can become negative features of the external environment of their rivals. They also indicate how a firm faced with increasing competition can respond to lessen this negative impact.

Incomes

The effect of a change in income on business costs is likely to be minor in comparison to the significant and direct impact such a change will have on the demand for goods and services. The extent of the impact on the demand for goods and services will depend on the nature of the goods and services in question.

Effect of changing levels of income on business costs

If incomes increase because the national wage level increases, for example because the national minimum wage rates increase or because there is a general increase in wage rates across most industrial sectors as the economy grows, then business costs will increase. This is because wages and salaries are a major element of business costs. The further impact of an increase in costs will vary depending on the nature of goods and services. Where a business judges that it can maintain its profit margin and pass the increased costs on to customers, the price of goods may rise. Where a business judges that by increasing prices, demand may fall too much, it may decide to keep prices stable and reduce its profit margin instead.

Economists say that wages are 'sticky', that is, there is usually severe resistance to any attempts to cut them. However, during a recession when demand is falling, firms are closing and unemployment is rising, average incomes are likely to fall. A fall in incomes, while having a negative effect on demand, may enable firms to cut their wage bills because employees may be prepared to work for lower wages and salaries in order to help their firm stay in business. See the fact file below on average wage movements for more details.

Fact file

Average wage movements in the UK

Office for National Statistics (ONS) data show that wage growth was highest in the 1970s and 1980s, when it went up by an average of 2.9 per cent a year. This annual wage growth slowed to 1.5 per cent in the 1990s, then to 1.2 per cent in the 2000s. Data since the beginning of 2010 indicates that real wages have fallen by 2.2 per cent annually up to 2013. By the third quarter of 2013, they showed a drop of 1.5 per cent compared with the same period a year earlier.

The ONS said that the response to the fall in productivity during the recession of 2008 and 2009 was the main reason for the fall in wages. If a firm's output falls, it will respond by reducing either the level of wages or the number of people employed in order to maintain its viability. Many firms seem to have held on to staff by asking them to work shorter hours, therefore putting downward pressure on wages. For example, during the last recession, JCB, maker of bright yellow diggers for building sites, needed to cut jobs because of falling demand. In negotiation with trade unions, about 2,500 staff agreed to a 4-day week and a £50-a-week pay cut. ONS data also suggests that the changing composition of the UK workforce may have had an impact on real wages, particularly the shift from higher paid workers in the manufacturing sector (where average weekly wages in 2010 were £524) towards lower paid workers in the services industries (where average weekly wages in 2010 were £437).

Source: www.ons.gov.uk

Effect of rising income on the demand for goods and services

As consumers' incomes increase, their overall demand for products is likely to rise and the pattern of their demand for different products is likely to change. A rise in income is likely to lead to an increase in demand for luxury products because people are now able to afford those products that were previously too expensive. A rise in income may not affect the demand for a range of essential products, such as bread, milk and salt. However, some products, known as inferior products, may suffer a fall in demand when incomes rise because people are able to substitute better quality products for them. Such products include cheaper cuts of meat and cheap and low quality clothing. (Chapter 8 includes an explanation of the impact of changes in income on the demand for different types of products.)

As demand for goods and services increases, businesses may need to employ more people in order to meet demand. The labour market is said to 'tighten' because fewer people are looking for work. This makes it more difficult for firms to recruit suitably skilled or qualified individuals. The existing workforce and potential applicants have more bargaining power and firms may be forced to increase wages for existing workers and to offer substantially higher wages in order to attract new workers. This leads to increased costs and possibly prices, affecting demand and competitiveness.

Increasing demand may lead to a shortage of stock and prices may rise. However, if the increased demand is expected to be maintained in the longer term, it may provide opportunities for a business to consider expansion.

Effect of falling incomes on the demand for goods and services

When incomes fall, the demand for luxury items will fall, the demand for essential items will remain more or less the same and the demand for inferior products is likely to increase. Falling incomes are likely to have the following additional consequences.

- Because demand is falling, excess stock may eventually lead to reduced prices and the business may need to reduce levels of output. This is likely to lead to lower profits or even losses and workers being laid off. Businesses may have to close. On the other hand, firms producing inferior goods may benefit because consumers switch from luxury items to low-priced alternatives. These firms may need to increase output and employ more people.

- As demand falls, cost-saving strategies may be introduced. For example, a firm may decide to cut its training budget or it may consider rationalisation. Rationalisation means reorganising the business in order to increase its efficiency, for example, by delayering (removing layers of management and supervisory staff) or, in a multi-site business, closing a factory or the administrative or finance departments in each site and creating a single, centralised department. Another alternative is to outsource work to countries where labour costs are much cheaper. For example, Dyson moved the production of its vacuum cleaners from the UK to Malaysia, where production costs were 30 per cent lower.

- Many of these strategies to cope with reduced demand due to falling incomes may lead to a firm becoming uncompetitive, which compounds the impact on demand for the firm's products.

Interest rates

Interest rates can be looked at in two ways – as the cost of borrowing money and as the return for lending money. They are also an important tool of government economic policy. By influencing the cost of borrowing and the reward for lending, the government can influence spending in the economy and therefore the rate of inflation (the rate at which the general price level is rising), the level of employment, the rate of exchange (of pounds sterling with other currencies) and the level of exports and imports.

Fact file

Since 1997, the control of interest rates in the UK has been the responsibility of the Monetary Policy Committee (MPC) of the Bank of England. The MPC is responsible for maintaining price stability in the UK. It meets monthly to consider interest rate changes and is free to decide the level of interest rate (known as the bank rate) necessary to meet the target for inflation set by the government, which is currently 2 per cent or less. The bank rate was reduced to 0.5 per cent in 2009 in order to encourage spending and combat the effects of recession in the economy (low income, low demand and rising unemployment) and, at the time of writing (July 2014), is expected to remain at that level until early in 2015. Figure 3.2 illustrates how interest rates have changed over recent years and how they are expected to change in the near future.

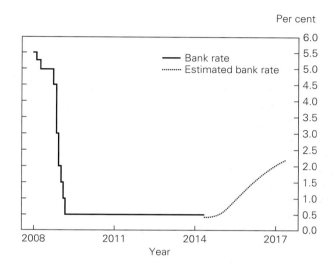

▲ **Figure 3.2** Bank rate (2008–2017) Source: Bank of England and Bloomberg

Did you know?

The interest rates charged for bank loans, mortgages and credit card purchases and those paid to savers are not the same as the bank rate set by the Bank of England. They are usually a few percentage points above the bank rate but they are influenced by the bank rate. This means that when the bank rate rises, interest rates generally will rise and when the bank rate falls, interest rates generally will fall. Figure 3.2 indicates that, given the current and expected state of the economy, interest rates are expected to begin to rise from 2015.

Did you know?

Disposable income is income left for spending after taxes have been deducted from gross income. **Discretionary income** is disposable income less all the regular bills that must be paid, including rent, mortgage, bank loans, credit card payments, utilities, transport and food. Discretionary income is therefore income available to spend on luxury or non-essential goods and services. If an individual has a mortgage, a bank loan and a credit card, an increase in interest rates will mean their repayments for each of these will increase. As a result, they will have less discretionary income available to spend on other goods and services.

Effect of a change in interest rates on business costs

Changes in interest rates affect business costs because interest payments are an element of most business's fixed costs.

A fall in interest rates is likely to lead to a fall in business costs.

- A fall in the interest payments on loans will have a beneficial effect on firms that are highly geared, i.e. a firm with extensive long-term loan commitments (a high proportion of capital employed in the form of long-term loans) because fixed costs for these firms will fall. This in turn will reduce unit costs and the level of sales a firm needs to make in order to cover all its costs and begin to make a profit (known as the breakeven point). It may also make it possible to introduce price cuts and therefore adopt a more competitive strategy in the market. Alternatively, it can have potentially favourable effects on profits because as unit costs fall, profit margins will rise, unless price is reduced.
- The increase in overall demand for both consumer and capital goods that results from a fall in interest rates may lead firms to consider expanding production. As a consequence, more employees may be needed, leading to increased competition in the labour market. This in turn might create skill shortages in certain areas, resulting in increasing wage costs.

A rise in interest rates is likely to lead to a rise in business costs.

- A rise in the interest payments on loans will have a negative effect on firms that have a large amount of long-term loans (highly geared firms) because their fixed costs will rise. This in turn will increase their unit costs and the level of sales that must be reached in order to make a profit (the breakeven point). Prices may have to rise, which may mean firms are less competitive or profit margins may have to fall.

Did you know?

Unless otherwise stated, when analysing the implications of a change in interest rates on business costs, assume all other factors are constant. For example, in the above analysis, a fall in interest rates is said to lead to a fall in business costs, which at a simple level is the case because interest payments will fall. However, whether business costs overall fall depends on what other things are happening at the same time – for instance, energy costs and taxation rates might be rising and these increases might outweigh any reduction in costs due to the fall in interest payments. The same point should be taken into account when analysing the impact of any single factor on a business situation.

Effect of a change in interest rates on the demand for goods and services

Changes in interest rates affect demand for goods and services because the cost of borrowing money will change, which affects people's ability to buy products, particularly expensive products such as houses and flats, holidays, cars, TVs, washing machines and other 'white goods'. It also affects their spending on other products because it affects their discretionary income. As well as affecting consumers' demand for goods and services, changes in interest rates affect the demand by firms for capital goods.

A fall in interest rates is likely to lead to an increase in demand for consumer goods and for capital goods.

- Saving money is less attractive because less interest is received. This may mean that people prefer to spend rather than save, causing demand for consumer goods to increase.
- Mortgage payments and other loan and credit repayments will fall, meaning that homeowners will have more discretionary income, which they may spend on more consumer goods.
- The cost of goods bought on credit will fall. In particular, this will affect expensive, durable items such as cars, furniture and electrical goods, and luxuries such as holidays, the demand for which tends to rise when people have more income to spend (in this case more discretionary income).
- Because it becomes cheaper to purchase expensive capital equipment on credit, firms may bring forward planned future investment or actually increase the level of investment. This is because the return on projects is likely to exceed interest payments that must be made on borrowed funds or that could be received by investing the firm's own funds elsewhere. The rise in demand for capital goods such as machinery is because firms become more confident of the future and the demand for their products.

A rise in interest rates is likely to lead to a fall in demand for goods and services.

- Saving money is more attractive because more interest is received. This may mean that people prefer to save rather than spend, causing demand for consumer goods to fall.
- Mortgage payments and other loan and credit repayments will rise, meaning that homeowners will have less discretionary income to spend.
- The cost of goods bought on credit will rise. In particular, this will affect expensive, durable items, demand for which tends to fall when people have less income to spend (in this case less discretionary income).
- Because it becomes more expensive to purchase expensive capital equipment on credit, firms might delay any plans they have for investment or may decrease their current level of investment. This is because the return on projects is likely to be less than interest payments that must be made on borrowed funds or that could be received by investing the firm's own funds elsewhere. The fall in demand for capital goods is because firms are no longer confident of the future and the demand for their products.

Fact file

Index numbers

Many pieces of information, particularly sales records and economic data, are presented as index numbers. The use of index numbers simplifies comparisons between the different items over time. To demonstrate this, consider which of the products in Table 3.2 has experienced the fastest rate of growth in sales.

▼ **Table 3.2** Volume of product sales (units)

| | Year | | | Change from |
	2011	2012	2013	2011 to 2013
Product A	150	285	345	+195
Product B	600	780	990	+390
Product C	250	225	215	−35
Product D	40	70	120	+80
Product E	80	100	128	+48

Sales of product C have declined, so it is clear that this has been the most disappointing product.

Sales of product B have increased by the greatest number, but does this mean that it has performed better than product A?

Product A has more than doubled its sales in the two years, but product B has less than doubled its sales. In this respect, product A has performed better than product B if the firm's main objective is growth.

Index numbers are used to make it easier to compare numbers that would otherwise be difficult to compare. They are constructed as follows:

- A base year is selected. The sales volume (or value) in this year is given an index number of 100 (a figure from which it is easy to calculate percentage changes).
- Figures in later years are calculated as a percentage of the base-year figure.
- The index number is calculated as follows:

$$\text{index number} = \frac{\text{actual sales volume in selected year}}{\text{actual sales volume in base year}} \times 100$$

Thus sales of product A were 150 units in 2011 and 285 units in 2012. The index number for 2012 is therefore:

$$\frac{285}{150} \times 100 = 190$$

Similarly, the index number for product A in 2013 is:

$$\frac{345}{150} \times 100 = 230$$

This shows the percentage growth in sales between the base year and the year being studied. For product A, growth between 2011 and 2013 has been from 100 to 230, an increase of 130. As a percentage, this is:

$$\frac{130}{100} \times 100 = 130\%$$

Completing the calculations for all of the products in years 2011, 2012 and 2013 gives the results detailed in Table 3.3.

▼ **Table 3.3** Index number of product sales

| | Year | | |
	2011	2012	2013
Product A	100	190	230
Product B	100	130	165
Product C	100	90	86
Product D	100	175	300
Product E	100	125	160
Base year (2011) = 100.			

At a glance it can be seen that product A has grown much faster than product B. It also shows that product D has had the fastest growth rate, and that the growth rate of product E is only slightly less than that of product B (although it was much less in terms of volume).

Index numbers are used where it is more important to compare percentage growth rates than the actual volume of change. They can be used to calculate and compare information on the business cycle, exchange rates, inflation and unemployment.

Practice exercise 1

Year	GDP at 2011 prices £ millions	Index number of GDP Base year: 2004 = 100
2004	1507191	100.0
2005	1549491	102.8
2006	1596628	105.9
2007	1637432	108.6
2008	1631995	108.3
2009	1561646	103.6
2010	1591494	105.6
2011	1617677	107.3
2012	1628338	108.0
2013	1656498	109.9

1 What was the % change in GDP between 2004 and 2005? *(2 marks)*

2 What was the % change in GDP between 2007 and 2008? *(2 marks)*

3 What is meant by the term 'index number'? *(3 marks)*

4 Based on this data, has the UK economy recovered from the recession? *(4 marks)*

5 Analyse the implications of this data for UK retailers of household goods, such as electrical appliances and furniture. *(9 marks)*

Demographic factors

Demographic factors are related to changes in the characteristics of the population of a country.

The UK population has grown in recent years and alongside this overall increase there have been changes to the geographical spread of the population, its ethnic balance, the size of households and the age distribution of the population.

Demographic factors and their effect on business costs

The effect of demographic factors on business costs is relatively small in comparison to their effect on the demand for goods and services. Below are examples of how demographic factors might affect business costs:

● The number of people aged 65 and over who are working has doubled in the past two decades. Research shows that older workers generally have lower levels of labour turnover, have fewer accidents, are more punctual and have lower levels of absence from work due to short-term sickness than younger workers. This evidence suggests that employing older workers may enable firms to reduce their costs and improve their

> **Key term**
>
> **Demographics** The characteristics of human populations and population groups; it includes analyses of a range of elements including migration trends, birth and death rates, trends in age, ethnicity and gender, levels of education, marital status and size of family.

▲ Most people are now expected to work beyond 65

performance. B&Q, the DIY chain, is known to employ a significant proportion of older people on its staff because of the benefits they provide. Research suggests that businesses benefit most from a mixed-age workforce. McDonald's employs over 1,000 workers aged 60 and over and reports 20 per cent higher performance in outlets that employ those over 60 in a multi-generational workforce.

- The opposite of the above is that because people are living longer and pension ages have been pushed back, there is now an expectation that most workers will work well beyond their sixty-fifth birthday. This may lead to increased costs if older workers suffer from chronic illnesses that require them to be off work for long periods of time or their general mental and physical fitness slows their work rate and reduces their productivity.

- The increase in the proportion of women in the workforce, which has been growing since the early part of the last century, has been accompanied by more employment legislation to protect their rights and to promote equality of opportunity. Maternity leave and related maternity payments are one example of this, which has over the last 40–50 years increased the general wage costs of business. The provision of crèches to enable women to return to work soon after giving birth is another example of further costs for business – but presumably costs that are balanced by the benefits the business gets from being able to retain skilled female workers.

- Some commentators suggest that the employment of migrant workers, for example those from Eastern Europe, allows businesses to reduce their wage costs and thus become more competitive. There is little evidence to support this in the regulated employment sector where minimum wage regulations make it difficult for legitimate employers to pay wages below these rates. The fact file below on the views of London businesses, gives some insight into this issue.

Fact file

How business in London views migrant workers

The London Chamber of Commerce and Industry (LCCI) carried out a survey of 144 London businesses in November 2013. The survey explored the attitudes of businesses to the employment of migrant workers. A majority of the businesses surveyed (52 per cent) employed migrant workers, 10 per cent of them having a workforce composed of over 60 per cent of migrant workers. The survey asked businesses about why they employed migrant workers. Businesses said that migrant workers enlarge the pool of workers they had to select from. A majority (58 per cent) said skills gaps were the main reason – that migrant workers had relevant skills that were not always available in the indigenous population. Just over a quarter of businesses (26 per cent) said they employed migrant workers because they had a better work ethic or better attitudes to work – being prepared to work longer hours, to work outside core hours and generally to be more flexible. Just over a fifth (21 per cent) said migrant workers were more productive. Nine per cent said employing migrant workers meant lower wage costs.

Source: 'Let them come: EU migration and London's economy', London Chamber of Commerce and Industry, December 2013

Demographic factors and their effect on the demand for goods and services

The fact that the population has grown in recent years has led to an increase in overall demand for goods and services. Changes in the size and significance of different demographic groups are having a significant impact on the pattern of demand for goods and services. The ageing population and changing ethnic make-up of the UK are two of the most influential demographic factors influencing the demand for consumer goods and services.

Ageing population

Analysts suggest that over the next ten years, two-thirds of all retail spending growth will come from those aged 55 and over. The rising influence of this age group is likely to result in increasing demand for the categories of goods and services they favour. These include health-related, DIY and home maintenance products, and, for the well-off, leisure cruises (an area of the holiday market that has grown significantly as a result of the increase in demand from this older age group), compared to clothing, beer and soft drinks which are products favoured by a more youthful market.

Ethnically diverse population

Approximately 15 per cent of the UK population was not born in the UK. Approximately one-third of migrants entering the UK move to London. Half of the babies born in London are now born to non-indigenous UK mothers. These demographic characteristics suggest that the pattern of demand for goods and services, particularly in London and other urban areas where migrant populations tend to settle, will be strongly influenced by their needs. Immigration has led to the growth in sales of products such as Indian and Eastern European food in UK supermarkets and, in areas of concentrated minority ethnic populations, specialist shops that cater for their needs, for example halal butchers, shops selling saris and other Asian clothing and hairdressers catering for the needs of black and Asian customers.

Size of household

Households are getting smaller. The number of one-person households in England is forecast to increase, single parent households are forecast to continue to rise, and the number of one-child households is growing. These demographic characteristics lead to an increasing demand for smaller pack sizes, for example in relation to foodstuffs and household goods. The growing numbers of individuals living alone is leading to an increase in the building of flats rather than family houses.

Geographical shifts

A shift in the geographical spread of the population to the southeast of England is leading to an increase in demand for housing and for other goods and services in this area. It has, for example, led to an increase in the number of supermarkets in the southeast of England.

Demographic change can be perceived by businesses as either an opportunity or a threat. For example, businesses that take note of the changes in demographic trends will ensure that the goods and services they offer meet the needs of an ageing population and an ethnically diverse population. Those businesses that ignore these trends are less likely to be successful. Demographic change happens slowly and can be anticipated, analysed and understood. This is illustrated by data in the fact file that includes predictions of changes to age groups in the population up to 2035. This is a fundamental difference between the effect on business

Fact file

UK demographic age group changes

The UK population is growing and projected to rise to 73.2 million by 2035. The number of children aged 16 and under is projected to increase by 12 per cent to 13 million or just under 18 per cent of the population by 2035. At the same time, the proportion of 15–29-year-olds is forecast to decline to 17 per cent.

Over the next ten years, 37 per cent of the UK population will be over 50. By 2030, the number aged 65 or older is projected to reach 15.5 million, growing 43 per cent on its level in 2012, compared to an expansion of only 13 per cent in the population as a whole. Those aged over 85 are expected to rise by 101 per cent by 2030.

Source: adapted from data in The KPMG/Ipsos Retail Think Tank, July 2013.

of demographic factors and the effect of other factors in the external environment already considered (competition, income, interest rates), which tend to happen much faster and cannot always be predicted and prepared for to the same extent.

Environmental issues and fair trade

Environmental sustainability and concern about environmental issues involves making decisions and taking actions that take into account the need to protect the natural world and preserve the capability of the environment to support all forms of life.

Business activity can potentially cause damage to all areas of the environment. Some of the common environmental concerns include:

- damaging rainforests and woodlands through logging and agricultural clearing
- polluting and over-fishing of oceans, rivers and lakes
- polluting the atmosphere through the burning of fossil fuels
- damaging prime agricultural and cultivated land through the use of unsustainable farming practices.

Consideration of environmental issues can be an opportunity or a threat for a business. It can add to business costs and thus make a firm less competitive but it can also lead to improved reputation among consumers, making a business more competitive and thus leading to increased demand.

Environmental issues that affect business costs

Businesses face dilemmas about low-cost production versus environmentally responsible production. For example, firms have choices about whether to use finite resources such as coal and oil, or to use renewable resources. In many cases, the finite resources are cheaper, but their continued use will deplete supplies and may also cause additional environmental damage.

Another environmental choice involves waste and by-products generated by production processes. Gases may be released from large chimneys into the environment, liquid waste may be pumped into rivers and solid waste is likely to be taken away and buried in landfill sites. Each of these methods of disposal is harmful to the environment. The safe disposal of waste is often expensive and the alternative – changing methods of production in order to reduce waste – may be even more costly. Although governments may tax or fine firms that pollute the environment, it might be cheaper for a firm to pay the fines and continue polluting than to find a better way to dispose of its waste.

In general, engaging in environmentally responsible production is likely to lead to an increase in business costs. This may in turn reduce profit margins unless the business is able to pass the increased costs on to consumers in the form of higher prices. However, there are instances where taking a more environmentally responsible approach can lead to a reduction in costs. For example, becoming more energy efficient is likely to save a significant amount on energy costs in the longer term.

Fact file

Electrical waste

The Waste Electrical and Electronic Equipment (WEEE) Directive came into force in January 2007 and was updated with the WEEE Regulations 2013, which came into force on 1 January 2014. The Directive requires manufacturers to recycle all unwanted electronic appliances. The legislation aims both to reduce the amount of electrical and electronic equipment being produced and to encourage everyone to reuse, recycle and recover it.

Every year an estimated 2 million tonnes of WEEE items are discarded by householders and companies in the UK. WEEE includes most products that have a plug or need a battery. Large household appliances (e.g. ovens, fridges, washing machines) make up over 40 per cent of WEEE but there are large volumes of other equipment such as IT equipment (mainly computers), TVs (over 2 million discarded each year), small household appliances (e.g. kettles and hair dryers), electrical tools, digital watches, electronic toys and medical devices.

The exact treatment of WEEE can vary enormously according to the category of WEEE and technology that is used. Some treatment facilities utilise large-scale shredding technologies, while others use a disassembly process, which can be either manual or automated.

Retailers and distributors have three ways of being compliant with WEEE Regulations:

1 Joining the distributor take-back scheme (DTS): a scheme that assists in funding a network of collection facilities where consumers can dispose of their household WEEE free of charge for environmentally sound treatment and recycling.

2 Offering in-store take back: where retailers and distributors must accept free of charge an item of household WEEE equivalent to the new item of household EEE sold to the consumer, irrespective of when and where the original item brought for disposal was originally purchased.

3 Providing an alternative free take-back service, which is available and accessible to customers. WEEE deposited at such facilities must be managed in accordance with the Regulations and other waste management legislation and local planning requirements.

Industry sources suggest that the Directive is likely to lead to increased business costs because:

● businesses producing electrical and electronic equipment may need to improve product design to make it easier to dismantle, recycle and reuse equipment
● producers are expected to meet the cost of the collection systems noted above and the processing of WEEE.

Environmental issues that affect the demand for goods and services

A good reputation in relation to environmental issues can act as a positive marketing tool that encourages consumers to choose one brand over another. As a result, many firms have spent time and money building up a 'green' image as an integral part of their marketing strategy. In addition to increased sales and possibly stronger brand loyalty, a 'green' firm may be able to charge a higher price for its products. Many different products, from shampoos to coffee to banks, trade on the environment as their USP (unique selling point). However, the quality of products must be at least as good as non-green products in order to attract additional demand.

It is not always the case that consumers will favour environmentally friendly or ethically sound businesses. Very cheap prices are sometimes the result of very low labour and production costs, which in turn may be the result of operating in environmentally or ethically questionable circumstances. Nike has focused on tackling the difficult issues of ensuring environmentally friendly practices in its supply chain, overcoming its poor reputation and declining demand that developed in the 1990s as a result of unethical standards in the manufacture of its products. (See the fact file on Nike on page 56 for more detail.)

Fact file

The Greener Electronics Guide

'The Greener Electronics Guide', compiled by Greenpeace, aims to persuade the electronics industry to take responsibility for the entire life cycle of its products, to face up to the problems of e-waste and to take on the challenge of tackling climate change. First launched in 2006, the guide ranks the leaders of mobile phone, computer, television and games console markets according to their policies and practices on toxic chemicals, recycling and energy.

The guide has been a key driving force in getting many companies to make significant improvements to their environmental policies. The current top ten businesses are, in order: WIPRO (an Indian electronics company), HP, Nokia, Acer, Dell, Apple, Samsung, Sony, Lenovo and Philips.

The guide is aimed at consumers and the technology sector in general. It indicates the extent to which a 'green' approach to production can influence demand for products, with surveys by the Consumer Electronics Association regularly showing that consumers want and are willing to pay for green electronics.

Source: adapted from information on www.greenpeace.org

Fact file

'Fairtrade' or 'fair trade'

'Fairtrade' is an accreditation labelling system which certifies that products bearing the Fairtrade mark meet a range of specific criteria. 'Fair trade' expresses a rather wider vision of development, covering a much wider range of products than can be certified and embracing campaigning and awareness raising activity, as well as trading in food products.

Fair trade works to benefit small-scale farmers and workers in developing countries through trade rather than aid, in order to enable them to maintain their livelihoods and reach their potential. Products with the Fairtrade mark have been produced by small-scale farmer organisations or plantations that meet Fairtrade social, economic and environmental standards. The standards include protection of workers' rights and the environment, payment of the Fairtrade Minimum Price and an additional Fairtrade Premium to invest in business or community projects. Stocking fair trade products or using fair trade products in the production of other products is one way a business can demonstrate its ethical and environmentally sustainable credentials.

Fair trade sales have doubled year-on-year since 2003. There are now over 4,500 products with the Fairtrade mark, many of them available in stores on local high streets or shopping centres. As well as Oxfam, most major supermarkets stock Fairtrade products; Cadbury's uses Fairtrade chocolate in many of its products and Starbucks and Pret A Manger use Fairtrade coffee. Boots, Neal's Yard Remedies and Lush stock Fairtrade beauty products or use Fairtrade ingredients in their products. Laura Ashley, Marks and Spencer, Monsoon, Warehouse, Top Shop, Debenhams and Topman stock clothing that uses Fairtrade cotton.

Fact file

Why Fairtrade products make good business sense – even in the hotel business

Increasing numbers of hotels supply customers with Fairtrade products – including food and beverages, toiletries, bedroom and bathroom linen and flowers.

Key elements of the business case for using Fairtrade products in the hotel industry are described below.

- Recognition of the Fairtrade mark is higher than for any other consumer label and, according to surveys, consumers have a high level of trust in products that carry a Fairtrade logo. As a result, it is likely that both new and returning guests may feel that by staying at a hotel that uses Fairtrade products they are making a moral or ethically 'right' choice. According to an April 2012 Tripadvisor.com survey, 71 per cent of surveyed travellers said they planned to make more eco-friendly travel choices.
- Given that costs and quality are equivalent, offering Fairtrade products can be a good way of differentiating a business from its competitors.
- It's not just guests who may be happier with Fairtrade products. Staff, both current and potential, may be as well. Companies have found that the more they invest in sustainability, the prouder staff feel – so helping with recruitment and retention of the brightest and best staff.

The Green House Hotel, Bournemouth is an example of a hotel that has made a thorough commitment to Fairtrade and environmentally sustainable principles. Full details on its green principles are at www.thegreenhousehotel.co.uk

Source: adapted from an article by Holly Tuppen at www.greenhotelier.org, 28 February 2013

Fact file

M&S and its environmental Plan A

M&S's Plan A programme has environmental, ethical and social principles at its heart and involves a fundamental review of all the retailer's business processes. The programme aims to reduce the retailer's environmental impact while trading ethically and helping consumers become healthier.

The financial benefits from Plan A are the result of modest gains accumulating in various areas of the business, often the result of making relatively simple efficiencies.

Some aspects of Plan A cost M&S more, for example sourcing Fairtrade products, but any extra expenditure is covered in other areas, so that higher costs for certain products are subsidised by savings elsewhere in the business. The overall cost to the consumer is zero.

In relation to its supply chain, M&S is working with factory owners in Bangladesh to ensure workers there are paid enough to support themselves. Although that leads to higher wage costs, it also improves the productivity of those factories and this fact has released the cash to pay the workers more.

Source: Adapted from an article in *Marketing Week*, 'The new CSR: this time it's profitable', by Michael Barnett, 14 April 2011

Fact file

Nike's reputation

In the 1990s, Nike, like many businesses, outsourced its manufacturing in order to produce its products at a fraction of the cost of producing them in the United States. At the time, Nike insisted that employment conditions in its contractors' factories were not its responsibility. Nike's view was that without an in-house manufacturing facility, the company could not be held responsible for the actions of independent contractors. Nike had a code of conduct for its contractors about safety standards, environmental regulation and worker insurance. Suppliers were required to certify that they were following the code and local regulations. But, there was no effort by Nike to assess if contractors complied with the code.

Eventually, Nike's factories came under attack for their workplace practices, including the use of child labour. Nike's reputation was severely damaged by stories of abuse. Demand for its products fell. Its profits began to fall and in 1998 it was forced to lay off workers. In a May 1998 speech, Nike's CEO admitted that, 'the Nike product has become synonymous with slave wages, forced overtime, and arbitrary abuse.' Since then Nike's policies on contractors and the monitoring of local factories have been completely transformed and it now has a more collaborative approach to reforms, sharing workplace and human resource best practices.

Source: adapted from an article in Forbes online business magazine, 'Building sustainable and ethical supply chains', 3 September 2012, www.forbes.com

Practice exercise 2   *Total: 70 marks*

1 Explain each of the following terms:
   a) interest rates   *(3 marks)*
   b) demographic factors   *(3 marks)*
   c) environmental issues.   *(3 marks)*

2 Explain one example of how competition might affect business costs and one example of how competition might affect the demand for goods and services.   *(8 marks)*

3 Explain one example of how a change in income levels might affect business costs and one example of how a change in income levels might affect the demand for goods and services.   *(6 marks)*

4 Identify and explain three different ways in which a fall in interest rates is likely to affect the demand for goods and services.   *(9 marks)*

5 Explain two ways in which a rise in interest rates might affect business costs.   *(6 marks)*

6 Identify three examples of demographic changes and explain how these might affect the demand for goods and services or business costs.   *(9 marks)*

7 Why might a business be able to respond to demographic change more effectively than it might to changes in competition, income and interest rates?   *(4 marks)*

8 Explain two examples of how a business that adopts an environmentally friendly approach to its operations might incur additional costs.   *(6 marks)*

9 Why might adopting an environmentally friendly approach have a positive effect on the demand for a firm's products?   *(5 marks)*

10 What is meant by the term 'fair trade'?   *(3 marks)*

11 Why might an individual firm decide to include fair trade products in its business?   *(5 marks)*

Case study: HMV's failure to keep pace with competition

HMV, founded in 1921, collapsed into administration in January 2013 after struggling to compete against cut-price supermarket offers and internet downloads. At the time of its collapse, it employed 4,123 staff in 223 stores. It was rescued shortly after its collapse by the restructuring firm, Hilco, saving 2,643 high street jobs and 141 stores.

In the 1980s, HMV was the most high profile record retailer (records made of vinyl) and the advent of CDs and then computer games and DVDs ensured its profits kept on increasing.

HMV expanded around the world – the USA, France, Germany, Canada, Japan. In 1986, it opened the world's largest record store in Oxford Street. The opening ceremony included Bob Geldof and Michael Hutchence, tens of thousands of people attended and Oxford Street was closed. Liaising with the police for all new store openings in the 1980s and through most of the 1990s was essential, such was the pull of HMV and the music stars it could attract for a new store opening or personal appearance.

HMV continued to expand throughout the 1990s. It bought the book chain Dillons and Waterstones and in 2002 floated on the stock market for a £1bn valuation and a share price of £1.92. In contrast, in January 2013, just before it closed down, the company was valued at £15m and its share price was just above £0.03p.

Shortly after the 2002 float, consultants were asked to review the company and identify opportunities and threats. The three greatest threats identified were: online retailers, downloadable music and supermarkets discounting loss leader product. The managing director at the time dismissed these threats as rubbish. 'I accept that supermarkets are a thorn in our side but not for the serious music, games or film buyer and as for the other two, I don't ever see them being a real threat, downloadable music is just a fad and people will always want the atmosphere and experience of a music store rather than online shopping.' This seems a quite extraordinary response given later developments but, to put these views into context, the dotcom bubble had just burst and many people were mistaking this stock market meltdown for an internet meltdown.

Given its success in the 1980s and 1990s, HMV was exceptionally well placed to exploit the internet and take advantage of social media because of the power of the brand, its heritage in music, its unrivalled access to content from film, game and music companies. Right to the end of its life, the HMV brand was very strong. HMV had been a presence on the high street since 1921.

Most commentators agree that HMV's inability to compete with online retailers such as Amazon, as well as supermarkets such as Tesco and Sainsbury's, led to its demise. Retail experts suggested that HMV's brand strength meant that if it had gone online ten or 15 years ago it could have built up a real presence and taken on the likes of Amazon on their own territory. The fact is it remained tied to the high street, with its soaring rents and declining footfall.

Since January 2013, Hilco has successfully restructured HMV, leading to improved turnover and profits.

Source: adapted from articles by: Philip Beeching in *The Guardian*, 15 January 2013; Sarah Butler and Rupert Neate in *The Guardian*, 5 April 2013; and www.designweek.co.uk, 15 January 2013

Questions

(30 marks)

1 To what extent does the case study suggest that the effects of competition on HMV's costs and the demand for its products led to its eventual closure? *(15 marks)*

2 Identify and explain the possible changes HMV could have introduced, in order to remain competitive, and what impact these might have had on its costs and the demand for its products. *(15 marks)*

Practice exercise 3

(15 marks)

Look back at the following fact files in this chapter: 'Jessops', 'Low-cost airlines', 'Why Fairtrade makes good business sense – even in the hotel business', 'M&S and its environmental Plan A' and 'Nike's reputation'.

1 Evaluate the extent to which factors, other than competition, in the external environment of these businesses had an impact on their costs and the demand for their goods and services.

(15 marks)

4

Understanding management, leadership and decision making

This chapter explains what managers do, including setting objectives, analysing, leading, making decisions and reviewing. It considers types of management and leadership styles and the theories behind them, including the Tannenbaum Schmidt continuum and Blake Mouton grid. You will consider influences on the various management and leadership styles and review their effectiveness.

What managers do

Business managers perform a wide range of activities and have many different responsibilities, depending on the nature of business they are involved in. However, there are common elements to the role of a manager in any business context. These include setting objectives, analysing, leading, making decisions and reviewing. Each of these elements is considered from many different perspectives throughout the chapters of this book.

- Setting objectives, including the reasons why objectives are set and common business objectives, were considered in Chapter 1. Chapters 7, 11, 16 and 20 consider the value of setting objectives, and the nature of the objectives, set in relation to the functional areas of marketing, operations, finance and human resources, respectively.
- Analysing data or information is an important function of managers. Analysing the likely impact on costs and demand of changes to various external factors was considered in Chapter 3. Managers in different functional areas will need to analyse and interpret data in order to determine appropriate strategies. For example a marketing manager will need to analyse and interpret marketing data before deciding what marketing strategies to pursue. This type of analysis is covered for each functional area in later chapters.
- Leading staff is a crucial aspect of a manager's role. The content of the rest of this chapter focuses on different management and leadership styles, the influences on these styles and how effective they are in different situations.
- Making decisions is an essential aspect of a manager's role and is considered in most chapters in this book. Chapter 5 focuses formally on management decision making. In addition, later in the book, decision

making and the influences on decision making are considered in relation to each of the functional areas of marketing, operations, finance and human resources.

- Reviewing the impact of strategies and actions to determine whether they have been successful or need to be adjusted is a key element of a manager's role and is considered in relation to each of the functional areas in later chapters.

Managers and leaders

The distinction between managers and leaders is sometimes seen as the difference between being risk averse and risk seeking. Managers are thought to be relatively risk averse, seeking to avoid conflict where possible and to run a 'happy ship'. Leaders, on the other hand, are thought to be risk seeking. When pursuing their vision, leaders are assumed to consider it natural to encounter problems and hurdles that must be overcome along the way. They are therefore comfortable with risk, see options that others avoid as potential opportunities for advantage, and will happily break rules in order to get things done. The saying that 'Leaders seize opportunities and managers avert threats' reflects this distinction.

Despite the distinction between managers and leaders noted above, it is not the case that one role is more important than the other – in order to run a successful business both management and leadership are required. The risks taken by highly successful entrepreneurs, such as Alan Sugar or Richard Branson, have created important opportunities for their businesses. However, such opportunities will have required the skills of managers lower down the business hierarchy (who will in turn be leaders in their own areas) to turn such opportunities into tangible results.

Management skills can be seen as a subset of leadership skills. People who want to lead but not manage may have wonderful ideas, but without the ability to plan and oversee the necessary work, their ideas are not going to be realised – at least not by them. If their ideas are implemented, it will be done by another leader who has well-developed management skills. However, while management skills may be a subset of the skills required in a strong leader, the reverse is not necessarily true. There are many people who are very skilled at implementing someone else's vision but who are not leaders themselves and never could be. Thus in most large organisations, **management** and **leadership** are interdependent and leaders must work effectively with managers in order for the organisation to successfully achieve its objectives.

What do you think?

Consider the people you know who are in management/ leadership roles. This could be at your school or college or, if you have a part-time job, in your workplace. Are they managers or leaders and what distinguishes those you judge to be managers from those you judge to be leaders?

Key terms

Leadership Deciding on the direction for a business or a department or functional area, setting objectives that reflect this, and inspiring and motivating staff to achieve these objectives.

Management Getting things done by planning, organising and co-ordinating people and resources.

Author advice

In most large organisations there is a clear distinction between senior managers and middle managers. In most cases, senior managers, for example, marketing and finance directors, work directly with the chief executive or managing director, that is, the overall leader of the organisation. It is this group that is often defined as the 'leaders'. However, in practice, leadership occurs at all levels, so in a large organisation or branch, for example, departmental managers are actually middle managers in the context of the business as a whole, but in their branch or department they are leaders.

Fact file

Transactional and transformational relationships

Some experts suggest that managers have subordinates but leaders have followers. In this context, managers have a position of authority vested in them by the organisation and their subordinates work for them and largely do as they are told. Managers and workers therefore have what is known as a transactional relationship: that is, the manager tells the subordinate what to do and the subordinate does this because they have been promised a reward (their wage or salary) for doing so. Of course, managers are subordinates too and are paid to get things done, often within tight constraints of time and money. They therefore naturally pass on this focus on work to their own subordinates.

On the other hand, leaders do not have subordinates, other than those who are also managers. Although leaders have followers, telling people what to do will not inspire them to follow. In order to get people to follow them, leaders need to appeal to them and show them how following them will lead to benefits. Charismatic leaders find it easier to attract people to their cause. As a part of their persuasion they typically promise transformational benefits. For example, their followers will receive not just extrinsic rewards, such as wages and salaries, but intrinsic benefits, such as somehow becoming better people. Leaders realise the importance of enthusing others to work towards their vision.

Types of management and leadership styles

Management and leadership styles are concerned with the manner and approach of the head of an organisation or department towards his or her staff. A manager or leader's manner will affect the leader's personal relationships with employees. For example, some leaders will inspire loyalty, some respect and some fear. Management and leadership style will dictate the extent to which delegation takes place and whether employees are consulted on important decisions.

Fact file

Steve Jobs

Steve Jobs, the co-founder of Apple, was seen as an inspirational leader of one of the most successful companies ever created. He inspired his followers, both staff and customers, and yet he was not known to be a particularly good manager of people, being often regarded as arrogant and dictatorial.

Jobs had three qualities that great leaders often have: a clear vision; a passion for the company, its products and its people; and an ability to inspire trust. Jobs not only had a vision, he made sure that employees in the company bought into that vision. Employees trusted Jobs because he demonstrated his competence in many areas, especially product design.

In his biography of Steve Jobs, Walter Isaacson says that Steve Jobs' first act when he came back to Apple was how to define the values of his company. He did this with two words: 'think different'.

Isaacson identified a number of key business lessons that illustrate Steve Jobs' leadership:

- There are two ways to run a business: focus on profits or focus on products. Jobs focused on the products, knowing that the profits would follow. He considered simplicity, functionality, and consumer appeal before cost efficiency, sales volume, or even profit. This attention to detail was integral to the success of Apple, which, in June 2014, had the third largest market capitalisation of companies in the world.

- Business leaders must have intuition and foresight. Jobs is said to have asked, 'How do people know what they want until we show them?' The result of such intuition and foresight are evident in Apple products such as the iPad.

- Focus and single mindedness. Isaacson relates the story of an Apple retreat (residential training session) some years ago where employees came up with ten projects for the company to work on in the future. Jobs deleted seven items from the list, leaving three: the iPod, the iPhone and the iPad – the appeal and impact of these products supports Jobs' judgement.

- A good leader drives people to do things they don't think they can do. 'Don't be afraid. You can do it,' was a mantra repeated by Jobs to his partners.

Source: adapted from the biography, *Steve Jobs* by Walter Isaacson

▲ Steve Jobs

Four main categories of management and leadership style are used widely for purposes of analysis: authoritarian (also known as autocratic or dictatorial), paternalistic, democratic and laissez-faire.

McGregor's Theory X and Theory Y management and leadership styles

Douglas McGregor was an American psychologist who conducted research into the attitudes of managers to workers. In his book *The Human Side of Enterprise* (first published in 1960), he suggested that managers' approaches to workers can be grouped into two types, known as Theory X and Theory Y.

McGregor found that the majority of managers assumed their workers did not enjoy work, did not want to work and were motivated primarily by money; he termed this type of management approach Theory X and noted that it was likely to be self-fulfilling. In general, a Theory X manager assumes that workers:

● are lazy, dislike work and are motivated by money
● need to be supervised and controlled or they will underperform
● have no wish or ability to help make decisions or take on responsibility
● are not interested in the needs of the organisation and lack ambition.

This is an authoritarian approach in which the manager tells workers what to do and supervises them doing it. Such an approach can be useful in a crisis situation or in organisations with many constantly changing or part-time workers, who need clear instructions and clear supervision.

The alternative, minority view that emerged from McGregor's research was that managers assumed workers enjoyed work, wanted to contribute their ideas and wished to gain satisfaction from employment. He termed this a Theory Y approach. In general a Theory Y manager assumes that:

● workers have many different needs, enjoy work and seek satisfaction from it
● workers will organise themselves and take responsibility if they are trusted to do so

- poor performance is likely to be due to boring or monotonous work or poor management
- workers wish to, and should, contribute to decisions.

This is a democratic approach in which the manager delegates responsibility and authority and therefore involves staff much more in decision making.

Authoritarian management and leadership

With authoritarian management and leadership styles, power, control and decision making are retained at the top of an organisation and communication with the rest of the workforce tends to be one-way and top-down. Authoritarian leadership is also known as autocratic or dictatorial leadership. This style of management and leadership links to the 'produce or perish' leader in the Blake Mouton grid (discussed later in this chapter).

Most decisions are made by leaders, who give out orders rather than consulting the workforce or delegating responsibility further down the hierarchy. Authoritarian leaders usually employ formal systems with strict controls.

This style of management and leadership may happen because leaders have little confidence in the ability of their staff or because leaders are simply unable to, or prefer not to, relinquish power and control. It may, however, reflect significant pressures on an organisation that force leaders to make rapid and difficult decisions. In crisis or emergency situations, authoritarian approaches may be the most effective, with clear lines of authority resulting in quick decisions. However, it can cause frustration and resentment because the system is so dependent on the leader and because of the non-participation of workers in the decision-making process.

Authoritarian leaders use McGregor's Theory X approach, using rewards for good behaviour and performance and penalties for bad performance. This type of leadership reflects the ideas of F W Taylor, whose work on motivation is considered in Chapter 23.

Paternalistic management and leadership

Paternalistic management and leadership is a management and leadership style in which employees are consulted but decision making remains firmly at the top. It is essentially an approach where leaders decide what is best for their employees. As its name implies, this style is similar to the approach that parents take with their children. The workforce is treated as a family – there is close supervision, but real attempts are made to gain the respect and acceptance of employees and decisions are intended to be in the best interests of employees. In organisations with this type of leadership style, workers usually recognise that leaders are trying to support their needs. This is really a type of authoritarian management and leadership style, but with leaders trying to look after what they perceive to be the needs of their subordinates. Leaders are likely to explain the reasons for their decisions and may consult staff before making them, but delegation is unlikely to be encouraged.

This type of leadership reflects Elton Mayo's work on human relations and the lower- and middle-level needs of Maslow's hierarchy of human needs (considered in Chapter 23).

Democratic management and leadership

Democratic management and leadership is a management and leadership style involving two-way communication and considerable delegation.

A democratic management and leadership style follows McGregor's Theory Y approach. Two-way communication provides opportunities for the workforce to be fully involved in the decision-making process. A democratic leadership style means running a business or a department on the basis of decisions agreed by the majority. Democratic leaders not only delegate, but also consult others about their views and take these into account before making a decision. In some situations this can mean actually voting on issues, but it is more likely to mean that leaders delegate a great deal, discuss issues, act on advice and explain the reasons for decisions.

The major advantage of democratic leadership is that the participation of workers in decision making allows input from people with relevant skills and knowledge, which may lead to improved morale and better-quality decisions. However, the decision-making process might be slower because of the need to consult and discuss and there might be concern as to where power lies and whether loss of management control is a danger.

This type of leadership is related to Maslow's higher-level needs and Herzberg's motivators, both of which are covered in Chapter 23.

Laissez-faire management and leadership

Laissez-faire management and leadership is a management and leadership style that abdicates responsibility and essentially takes a 'hands-off' approach. It is an approach where the leader has minimal input in the decision-making process and essentially leaves the running of the business to the staff. The term comes from the French for 'leave alone' or 'let be'. Delegation occurs in the sense that decisions are left to people lower down the hierarchy, but such delegation may lack focus and co-ordination. This style may arise as a result of poor or weak leadership and a failure to provide the framework necessary for a successful democratic approach. However, in some organisations there may be a conscious decision to give staff the maximum scope to use their initiative and demonstrate their capabilities. How effective it is depends on the staff themselves – some may love the freedom to use their initiative and to be creative, while others may hate the unstructured nature of their jobs.

This can be an effective style when employees are highly skilled, experienced and educated, when they take pride in their work and have the drive to do it successfully on their own. The style is less effective when it makes employees feel insecure, when leaders fail to provide regular feedback to employees on how well they are doing, and when leaders themselves do not understand their responsibilities and are hoping that employees can cover for them.

The next two theories of management and leadership – Tannenbaum and Schmidt's continuum of leadership and the Blake Mouton grid – make reference to some of the management and leadership styles already discussed in this chapter, including authoritarian and democratic management and leadership and McGregor's Theory X and Theory Y styles.

Fact file

Warren Buffett's laissez-faire approach to management and leadership

A laissez-faire approach to management and leadership is often seen as a negative approach. But this is not always the case.

Warren Buffett, the Chief Executive Officer (CEO) of Berkshire Hathaway Inc., is one of the world's wealthiest people and known to be one of the most successful investors. Berkshire Hathaway Inc. is an American multinational conglomerate holding company. It owns a diverse range of businesses including confectionery, transport, utilities and newspaper publishing. In acquiring firms, some it wholly owns, such as Dairy Queen, Fruit of the Loom and Netjets, and some it owns a proportion of, for example, it owns half of Heinz and has minority holdings in American Express, The Coca-Cola Company and IBM. The company has been in existence for almost 50 years and during that time its average annual growth in book value has been just under 20 per cent, compared to an average of just under 10 per cent for other major companies. It is among the ten largest companies in the world.

Buffett is known to use a 'hands-off' or laissez-faire management and leadership style, which is said to be highly effective. By allowing the managers of companies he acquires to retain full autonomy, he has created an atmosphere where his employees feel confident and motivated by their independence. In Berkshire Hathaway's 2010 Annual Report, Buffett states, 'We tend to let our many subsidiaries operate on their own, without our supervising and monitoring them to any degree. Most managers use the independence we grant them magnificently, by maintaining an owner-oriented attitude'.

This is an example of where, with highly motivated and skilled employees, or in this case, managers, who value the autonomy they are given, a laissez-faire approach to management and leadership can work.

Tannenbaum and Schmidt's continuum of leadership

The Tannenbaum and Schmidt continuum is a simple model of leadership that shows the relationship between the level of freedom in relation to decision making that a manager chooses to give to a team of workers and the level of authority retained by the manager. As the team's freedom increases, so the manager's authority decreases. The Tannenbaum and Schmidt continuum was the focus of an article by R Tannenbaum and W Schmidt, first published in the *Harvard Business Review* in 1958. The article was called 'How to choose a leadership pattern'. The continuum was updated in 1973.

Tannenbaum and Schmidt identified seven levels of 'varying control by the manager and freedom for the team' (known as 'delegated freedom') (see below). At one extreme, the manager-oriented position illustrates an authoritarian or Theory X style of management and leadership, while at the other extreme, the subordinate-oriented position illustrates a democratic or Theory Y style. This is illustrated by Figure 4.1.

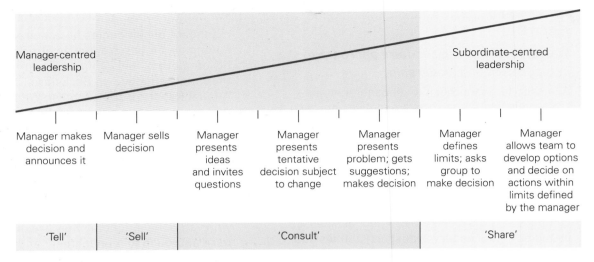

Manager-centred leadership

Subordinate-centred leadership

| Manager makes decision and announces it | Manager sells decision | Manager presents ideas and invites questions | Manager presents tentative decision subject to change | Manager presents problem; gets suggestions; makes decision | Manager defines limits; asks group to make decision | Manager allows team to develop options and decide on actions within limits defined by the manager |

| 'Tell' | 'Sell' | 'Consult' | 'Share' |

▲ **Figure 4.1** Tannenbaum and Schmidt's continuum of leadership

Level 1 The manager makes the decision and 'tells' the team the decision

The team plays no active part in making the decision. The manager has the problem, has made the decision and expects the team to carry out orders. Such an approach may be needed when a team is new, inexperienced or weak, but will be less appropriate as a team becomes more cohesive, skilled and committed to the aims of the organisation.

Level 2 The manager makes the decision and then explains or 'sells' the decision to the team

The manager explains or 'sells' the reasons for the decision and particularly the benefits the team will derive from the decision. In so doing the manager is seen by the team to recognise their importance and to have some concern for them. With this approach, the manager is still in control, but wants the team to understand why they are doing what the manager wants.

Level 3 The manager makes the decision, presents the decision to the team, provides background ideas that led to the decision and invites questions or 'consults' the team

The team is invited to ask questions and discuss with the manager the rationale behind the decision. This more participative approach enables the team to understand the reasons for the decision. Such an approach is likely to be more motivating for the team than levels 1 or 2. The manager is still in control and still makes the decision, but now checks it out with the team. If the team are not ready for more responsibility, they are unlikely to have many questions or comments but, if they are ready for more responsibility, the manager is providing them with an opportunity to discuss their ideas.

Level 4 The manager suggests a provisional decision, invites discussion about it by 'consulting' the team and then makes the decision

This approach enables the team to influence the manager's final decision. Because this approach acknowledges that the team has something to contribute to the decision-making process, it is more motivating for the team than the previous level.

Level 5 The manager presents the problem, 'consults' the team by getting them to make suggestions and then makes the decision

The team's high level of influence in the decision-making process in this approach would be most appropriate when the team has more detailed knowledge or experience of the issues than the manager. Because of this high level of involvement in the decision-making process, this approach is likely to be more motivating and provide more freedom than the previous level. Although in this situation, the team 'owns' the problem and are encouraged to come up with the solution, the manager makes the final decision.

Level 6 The manager explains the situation, identifies any limitations on the decision to be made and asks the team to come up with the decision; the manager 'shares' the problem with the team

The manager has effectively delegated responsibility for the decision to the team but still has some control over the process and any potential risks because of the limitations set. The manager may or may not choose to be a part of the team making the decision. This approach is likely to be more motivating for the team than any previous level. The degree of decision-making freedom given to the team means they must be skilled and experienced at working well together. The manager gives the team responsibility for finding the answers and making the decision. The final decision may still be the manager's but the team have had a high level of influence over it.

Level 7 The manager allows the team to identify the problem, develop the options and make the decision within any limits set; the manager 'shares' the problem with the team

This approach is at the opposite end of the continuum to level 1 – the team at level 7 is effectively doing what the manager did at level 1. In this approach, the manager indicates to the team that he or she will support the decision made by the team and help the team to implement it. The manager may or may not be part of the team, and if he or she is a member of the team, will have no more authority than anyone else in the team. The approach in level 7 is potentially the most motivating of all, but is also potentially the most risky. For this approach to be effective, the team must be experienced, skilled and capable in terms of investigating options, making and implementing decisions and reviewing outcomes.

The seven levels of control and freedom correspond broadly to a team's level of development. When a team is new, unmotivated and unskilled, managers are likely to use a style on the left-hand side of the continuum. As a team develops its decision-making skills, managers should be able to relinquish their control and the area of freedom for subordinates should increase. When a team is motivated and skilled, the style is likely to be on the right-hand side.

The particular style to use will depend on:

- the experience and skills of the manager and the level of confidence the manager has in the team
- the skills and commitment of the workforce and whether the organisation has a culture of delegation so that workers are used to taking responsibility rather than following orders
- the particular situation, for example, whether the problem is urgent or high risk or routine or relatively unimportant; the particular culture of the organisation and the style of decision making that are dominant or expected.

The continuum is a useful model because it illustrates the fact that more traditional ideas of management and leadership styles, such as the autocratic and democratic labels discussed earlier in this chapter, tend to be too black and white and that leadership practices in real-life situations lie somewhere between the two extremes and vary depending on the context.

Blake Mouton grid

Some managers and leaders are very production- or task-oriented – they simply want to get things done and lead their teams by setting and enforcing tight schedules. Others are very people-oriented – they want their teams to be happy and lead by making people and their needs the priority. Others are a combination of these two extremes.

In 1964, Robert Blake and Jane Mouton developed a managerial/leadership grid. Their grid is based on two aspects of managers' or leaders' behaviour:

- **Concern for people** – the degree to which a manager or leader considers the needs and interests of team members when deciding how best to accomplish a task.
- **Concern for production** – the degree to which a manager or leader emphasises organisational efficiency and high productivity when deciding how best to accomplish a task.

The grid plots the degree to which managers and leaders are people-oriented or production/task-oriented. The model identifies five different management and leadership styles based on the balance of concern for people and production. Figure 4.2 illustrates the grid and where each of the different management and leadership styles is positioned.

The characteristics of each of the identified management and leadership styles are as follows:

- **Impoverished (also known as Indifferent) leadership style** – low concern for production/low concern for people. This type of leader is ineffective, has little regard for creating systems for getting the job done or for creating a work environment that is satisfying and motivating for the team. As a result, team members are likely to demonstrate a high degree of dissatisfaction, there is unlikely to be much harmony within the team and there is likely to be high labour turnover. Overall, this style of management and leadership is likely to result in inefficient operations for an organisation.

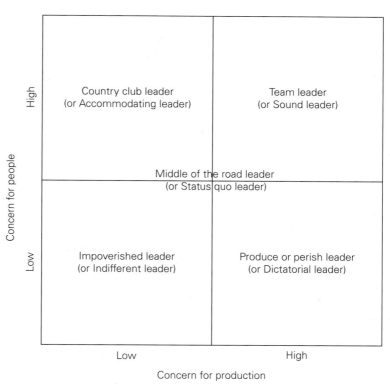

▲ **Figure 4.2** The Blake Mouton grid

- **Country club (also known as Accommodating) leadership style** – high concern for people/low concern for production. This type of leader is most concerned about the needs and feelings of members of their team. They operate under the assumption that as long as team members are happy and secure then they will work hard. As a result, the work environment tends to be very relaxed, team members are likely to be happy and there is likely to be good harmony within the team. However, production tends to suffer because productivity is low due to lack of direction and control.
- **Produce or perish (also known as Dictatorial) leadership style** – high concern for production/low concern for people. This type of leader tends to be authoritarian and display Theory X characteristics. They are likely to have strict work rules, policies and procedures, and view punishment as the most effective means of motivating their team. Team members are likely to experience high levels of dissatisfaction and conflict is likely to occur. High levels of labour turnover are likely to result. If production does improve, peak performance is likely to be short lived and unsustainable.
- **Middle-of-the-road (also known as Status quo) leadership style** – medium concern for production/medium concern for people. This type of leader appears to provide a balance of the two competing concerns for people and for production. At first this might appear to be an ideal compromise. However, by compromising, neither production nor people needs are fully met. As a result, there may be harmony in their team but team members are unlikely to be particularly happy or particularly dissatisfied. Leaders who use this style settle for average performance.

Author advice

The following two leadership and management styles have been added to the original Blake Mouton model but they do not change the important ideas of the original model:

● **Opportunistic leadership style** – this could occur in any of the original five positions. Opportunistic leaders seek any position that will be of benefit to them and so will adopt any style that will increase the likelihood of reaching their own objectives. These leaders see 'the end as justifying the means'.

● **Paternalistic leadership style** – this style can occur at either the Country club or Produce or perish position, i.e. at either extreme. These leaders will praise and reward employees for good performance but will discourage any thinking that is contrary to their own.

● **Team (also known as Sound) leadership style** – high concern for production/high concern for people. According to the Blake Mouton model, this is the best management and leadership style. These leaders stress production needs and the needs of people equally highly. The assumption is that in this situation, team members understand the organisation's purpose, are committed to it and have a stake in its success. As a result, employees' needs and production needs coincide. This creates a highly cohesive team environment based on trust and respect, which leads to high satisfaction and motivation. As a result, labour turnover is low, the organisation attracts highly skilled employees and efficiency and productively are high. The characteristics of this leadership style are very similar to those of McGregor's Theory Y style.

The Blake Mouton grid is a practical and useful framework that helps managers and leaders think about their management and leadership style. By plotting 'concern for production' against 'concern for people', the grid highlights how placing too much emphasis on one area at the expense of the other leads to low overall productivity. The model proposes that when both people and production concerns are high, employee engagement and productivity increase accordingly. The model allows an analysis of leadership style that involves more than the black and white models of Theory X and Y or the authoritarian/democratic theories. Despite the value of the grid model, it takes no account of the context in which leadership occurs, such as how internal and external constraints affect a business. For example, although the Team leadership style is seen to be the 'best' style, this isn't always the most effective approach in every situation. While the benefits of democratic and participative management are widely accepted, there are times that call for more attention in one area than another. If a business is involved in a significant change situation, such as a complex merger, it can be acceptable to place a higher emphasis on people than on production. Similarly, if a business is experiencing a severe fall in sales due to aggressive competition in the market, people concerns may be less important, at least in the short term, until greater sales have been achieved.

Fact file

'Team-based' versus 'them and us' styles

Increasingly, firms are employing workers in teams. This is resulting in significant changes to the role of managers and leaders. They are seen more as facilitators and supporters than as supervisors and are there to help teams of employees fulfil their potential and meet company objectives. For this changing role to be effective, managers, leaders and employees must have trust and confidence in each other's abilities and be focused on meeting company objectives. To gain this trust, managers and leaders need to delegate responsibility to workers to enable them to take full control of their own work. Level 7 of the Tannenbaum Schmidt continuum is an example of this. This is a major move away from the more traditional 'them and us' approach. In the latter approach, managers and leaders did not communicate regularly with workers — their job was to instruct and closely supervise workers, who obediently carried out tasks without question.

Some organisations try to overcome 'them and us' differences by treating all staff equally. For example, all employees, at whatever level of the organisation, may be known as 'associates' or 'colleagues'. This emphasises the idea of the whole organisation being a team. This is usually linked to a move away from traditional hierarchies and their focus on status.

Summary of the influences on management and leadership styles

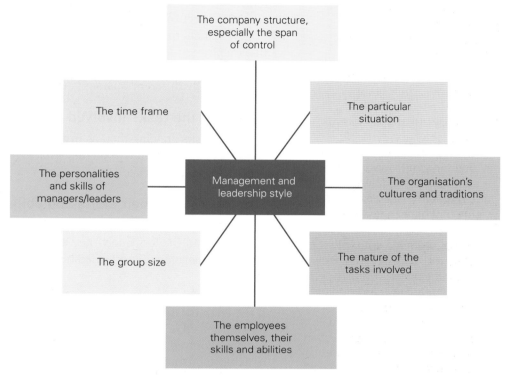

▲ **Figure 4.3** Influences on choice of leadership style

Figure 4.3 identifies a broad range of influences on leadership style. Many of these influences have already been discussed in relation to the various management and leadership styles considered in this chapter. The examples below illustrate these influences further but the examples are not exhaustive and there are many more that might be considered.

Company structure and especially the span of control

This concerns the number of layers of management and the extent to which decision making is delegated further down the organisation. This is dealt with in more detail in Chapter 22.

Particular situation

While most of the influences identified in Figure 4.3 are internal factors, the particular situation concerned could include external factors, such as the influence of the competitive market in which the business operates or whether a rival firm is attempting a takeover. If a crisis occurs, such as a natural disaster, or if dangerous faults are found in a product, an authoritarian leadership style that is very task-oriented may emerge to ensure urgent action is taken that is co-ordinated and tightly focused. In a stable situation, with well-trained, skilled and experienced staff, a democratic style of leadership is likely to be best in order to maintain or enhance the motivation and goodwill of employees and thus encourage them to maximise their performance. The situation that a business is faced with is therefore likely to be a major influence on leadership style.

Organisational culture and traditions

The culture of an organisation affects, and is affected by, the style of leadership, which in turn is a major influence on the degree and effectiveness of delegation and consultation. The culture of an organisation will also affect the amount of resistance to change and therefore the ability of new leaders to impose their style or decisions on subordinates. The fact file 'Inspiration-led versus aspiration-led businesses' provides an example of how different types of management and leadership styles influence and are influenced by different business cultures.

Nature of the tasks involved

Whether tasks are classified as urgent, essential, optional, can wait, simple, complex, risky or safe will dictate what type of management and leadership style is most appropriate.

Employees and their skills and abilities

The more skilled and experienced employees are, the more autonomy they will want and the less likely they are to work well under an authoritarian style of management and leadership.

Group size

If the team is large, and particularly if it is large and unskilled or inexperienced, a more authoritarian style of management and leadership may be required to ensure employees are well organised and co-ordinated to achieve business objectives.

Personalities and skills of managers and leaders

These will dictate the extent to which they are able to demonstrate appropriate leadership skills. Someone with poor interpersonal skills is less likely to be a good democratic leader and is more likely to focus on tasks rather than on relationships with people.

Time frame

In emergency situations, when time is crucial, an authoritarian style may be more effective in ensuring that everyone is focused on the goal and completing the most appropriate tasks to achieve the deadline.

Summary of the effectiveness of different styles of management and leadership

An appropriate leadership style is vitally important if an organisation is to be successful. However, there is no particular style of management and leadership that is the most effective in every situation. A very task-oriented, authoritarian approach, used with highly skilled and experienced staff, in normal circumstances is likely to alienate staff and prove unsuccessful in terms of achieving business objectives. Equally, a very democratic or even laissez-faire style of management and leadership in an emergency situation, or where workers are inexperienced and unskilled, is likely to lead to real problems because workers need clear guidance and deadlines in order to function efficiently.

There are a few key qualities that are often evident in great leaders. These include a clear vision; a passion for the organisation, its products and its people; and an ability to inspire trust. The fact files on Steve Jobs and Warren Buffett indicate the importance of these qualities in their leadership of Apple and Berkshire Hathaway, respectively. However, in most cases, the most appropriate leadership style is 'situational', i.e. it depends on the context. A style that might work under some circumstances might not work in others. There are no 'universal' leadership characteristics that are most appropriate for all situations and contexts. Steve Jobs' leadership style and his genius in design were key ingredients in Apple's success but might not have been as successful in other organisations. Equally Warren Buffett's laissez-faire approach would not be successful in organisations where managers and leaders who are left to run his companies are not sufficiently skilled or motivated.

Practice exercise 1

Total: 65 marks

1 Which of the following activities is not included in the main role of a manager?
   a) Setting objectives
   b) Analysing data
   c) Promoting products
   d) Making decisions
   e) Reviewing   *(1 mark)*

2 Distinguish between leadership and management.   *(6 marks)*

3 Outline the main characteristics of:
   a) an authoritarian management and leadership style   *(4 marks)*
   b) a paternalistic management and leadership style   *(4 marks)*
   c) a democratic management and leadership style   *(4 marks)*
   d) a laissez-faire leadership style.   *(4 marks)*

4 Contrast the management and leadership characteristics of McGregor's Theory X and Theory
   Y managers.   *(6 marks)*

5 Contrast the management and leadership styles indicated in the two extremes
   (level 1 and level 7) of the Tannenbaum Schmidt continuum.   *(6 marks)*

6 Which of the following leadership styles is not on the Mouton Blake grid?
   a) Country club leader
   b) Team leader
   c) Produce or perish leader
   d) Laissez-faire leader   *(1 mark)*

7 In the Blake Mouton grid, why is the Middle of the road leader not judged to be the best
   management and leadership style for an organisation?   *(4 marks)*

8 Use two different examples to explain the 'particular situation' as an influence on management
   and leadership style.   *(6 marks)*

9 Apart from the 'particular situation', identify four other influences on the type of management
   and leadership style adopted in any organisation.   *(4 marks)*

10 Is it possible to say that one leadership style is more effective than another? Justify your view.   *(15 marks)*

Practice exercise 2

1 Refer to the fact files on Steve Jobs and Warren Buffett. Evidence indicates that the leadership styles of both men have been highly effective in bringing about success for their companies. Does this mean that their particular styles are the ones all managers and leaders should copy in order to ensure the success of their organisations? Justify your view. *(15 marks)*

2 Business A is a medium-sized manufacturing business with a relatively inexperienced and low skilled workforce. It is losing sales because of strong competition and may have to make job cuts unless significant changes are made to its operations and procedures. Business B is a small and relatively new IT business. The owner employs a team of young, highly skilled, very motivated graduates who pride themselves on their creativity and commitment to the business. The business is doing very well and the owner wants it to grow steadily while retaining its innovative approaches. For each business, explain the leadership style you would recommend should be used and evaluate why the two businesses should use different leadership styles. *(15 marks)*

5

Understanding management decision making

This chapter focuses on the value of decision making based on data (scientific decision making) and on intuition. The role of risks, rewards, uncertainty and opportunity cost in decision making is considered. The discussion of scientific decision making includes an explanation of decision trees, how to interpret them and how to calculate expected value and net gains. Evaluation of the use and value of decision trees in decision making is provided. The chapter concludes with an analysis of influences on decision making, including a consideration of mission, objectives, ethics, the external environment and resource constraints.

Value of decision making based on data (scientific decision making) and on intuition

Decision making in any business is very important and takes place at every level of the organisation. A number of different approaches to decision making are used, ranging from scientific to intuitive approaches.

Decision making based on data

Scientific decision making involves using a systematic process for making decisions in an objective manner. Such a procedure eliminates the practice of decisions being made on the basis of intuition or a hunch and removes, as far as possible, bias and subjectivity by ensuring that decisions are made on the basis of well-researched, factual evidence. It therefore reduces risk because decisions are based on hard data, and it allows actions to be reviewed and the most effective course of action to be decided. This does not mean that the decisions made will always be the right ones. Scientific decision making can be criticised as being a rather slow process that lacks creativity and which therefore may fail to lead to innovative and different approaches.

A scientific decision-making model similar to that in Figure 5.1 is widely used. The model can be explained by reference to the following hypothetical decision. Assume that a firm is faced with falling demand for its existing product. It wishes to cut production of that product and to build up

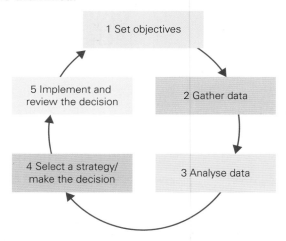

Key term

Scientific decision making A logical and research-based approach to decision making.

production of an alternative product aimed at a different market. The alternative product could be produced in a factory abroad, which would mean closing down one of its existing factories and making the workforce redundant. The steps in the decision-making process are as follows:

- **Set objectives**: the firm must set objectives in relation to what it wants to achieve and where it wants to be within a given time scale, ensuring that this fits well with its corporate mission statement. In relation to the decision, the firm wants production to take place in the most cost-effective location, taking account of long-term training costs, infrastructure costs and building up relationships with customers, suppliers and distributors, etc.
- **Gather data**: data on costs, demand, location, available workforce and reputation will be needed and may be gathered through primary and secondary research methods.
- **Analyse data**: data that have been gathered need to be analysed in order to provide a recommendation. Various quantitative decision-making techniques or tools are available to do this. One of these techniques is decision trees, which is considered later in this chapter.
- **Select a strategy**: the decision as to which strategy to pursue should be made on the basis of the recommendations that emerge from the data analysis.
- **Implement and review the decision**: implementation will itself involve numerous decisions on tactical and operational issues. Reviewing the decision involves looking at how well the outcome has succeeded in achieving the initial objective. For example, if the decision was to maintain production at home but it transpires that unit costs are too high and so competitiveness is reduced, the decision not to move abroad may need to be re-examined.

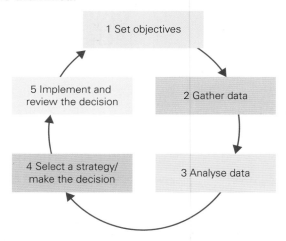

▲ **Figure 5.1** Scientific decision-making model

Benefits of using a scientific approach to decision making

The scientific approach offers the following benefits:

- It provides a clear sense of direction. By emphasising the need to set objectives, it ensures that people involved in the decision-making process are aiming for the same goals. SMART (specific, measurable, agreed, reasonable and timed) objectives will help the firm to make decisions that match the aims of the organisation.
- Decisions are based on business logic, involving comparisons between alternative approaches and between pros and cons.

- It is likely that more than one person will be involved in the process, which will reduce the possibility of bias.
- A scientific approach ensures that decisions are monitored continually and reviewed. Although this will not prevent mistakes, it should limit their impact because problems can be identified quickly.
- A major advantage of a scientific approach is its flexibility. At any stage in making a decision, the process can be reviewed and changed if circumstances require.
- If all decisions are based on rational thinking, overall success is more probable.
- It is easier to defend a policy that has been developed on the basis of good planning and in co-operation with other managers than one that is based solely on one person's intuition or gut feeling.

Decision making based on intuition

Intuitive approaches to decision making involve individuals making decisions on the basis of a 'hunch' or feeling or instinct. This approach is more likely to be used by small businesses that are owned by a single individual or small group. If the individual or group has a great deal of experience and expertise, this approach may be appropriate and may lead to more creative and innovative decision making. However, such decisions are not always informed by evidence and will often involve a level of, mostly unintended, bias and subjectivity, leading to inappropriate or ill-judged outcomes. Some examples of this approach include deciding to site a factory in a location that is not appropriate but is linked to the owner's childhood; deciding to change the bonus system for all employees because a new system works well for a particular group of employees, even though there is no evidence to suggest that all groups of employees are motivated by the same things; and deciding not to upgrade the IT system because everyone understands the current system and changes to IT systems always seem to create major problems for organisations.

The case studies on HMV in Chapter 3 and on J.C. Penney at the end of this chapter illustrate poorly judged decisions based on individual views and **intuition** rather than on data and evidence.

Key term

Intuition The ability to understand something without the need for conscious reasoning; similar to 'hunch'; a gut feeling held by a manager that is based not on scientific decision making but on the personal views of the manager.

Fact file

Red or Dead – an example of decision making based on 'gut instinct'

Wayne Hemingway and his wife Geraldine founded the Red or Dead fashion house in 1982 by sheer chance: 'We ran out of money one weekend so we emptied our clothes on to Camden Market. We took a load of money and that was it. It was like a lot of good things, you just fall into it. Absolutely no planning – never has been any planning – but sometimes you've just got to follow your nose ...We've never done any kind of market research, the market research has always just been in our mind ...You should always follow what your gut instinct tells you ...we had more successes than failures and that's what it's all about.' The business became an internationally renowned brand in the 1990s, winning British Fashion Council's Street Style of the Year Award three times. The Hemingways sold Red or Dead in 1999.

Source: www.startups.co.uk and www.hemingwaydesign.co.uk

Benefits of using an approach to decision making based on intuition

In general, intuition or hunches are used because of problems involved in using a scientific approach to decision making.

- A scientific approach requires a large collection of data and regular gathering of information to control and review decisions. This can be an expensive process and is hard to justify if there is very little risk involved.
- Following a scientific approach to decision making is time consuming. The constant checking and monitoring means that decisions may be delayed.
- The data collected in a scientific approach to decision making might be flawed. The information may be dated or the original sampling may have a bias. Customers may have just changed their minds.
- Invariably, scientific decisions are based on past information. Decisions may be better if they rely on the instincts of a manager who has a 'qualitative' understanding of the market and can anticipate a change in the trend.

Fact file

Knut Eicke and his hunches

German multi-millionaire Knut Eicke made a lot of money from hunches. His insurance company, Sir Huckleberry Insurance, offered the usual insurance policies but also provided the world's quirkiest alternatives. Based on a hunch, Knut started offering weird insurance policies against eventualities such as 'choking on pretzels', 'injuries from falling over at a beer festival' and 'being fired from work for playing computer games'. According to Knut, 'insurance against abduction by aliens was the big seller'. For additional premiums, people could also gain compensation for being whisked off to Mars (a payout of £2,500 for a policy that cost less than £20 per annum). Knut did not believe that scientific decision making would have revealed this opportunity. Knut never paid out on the alien abduction policy! But it was a big seller as a novelty gift. (The company was founded in 1985 and registered in the Netherlands. It no longer exists.)

Source: adapted from an article on www.thisismoney.co.uk, 31 March 2004.

Fact file

The Body Shop

The Body Shop was set up on a hunch because, according to its founder, Anita Roddick: 'We had no money – I was trying to pay the bills by doing what I was interested in. If I'd had a shedload of money, I'd have done everything wrong – marketing, focus groups, although they are more important now [that the business has grown].'

Source: www.startups.co.uk.

Choosing between scientific decision making and decision making based on intuition

The following factors are critical in deciding which approach to use.

- **Speed of the decision**: where quick decisions are required, there may be insufficient time to analyse the situation and so intuition and hunches may be followed. If time is not an issue, a more scientific (but slower) approach can be adopted.
- **Information available**: where detailed data are not available, intuition and hunches are more likely to be used. However, if data are held, a more scientific decision is possible.
- **Size of the business**: as a rule, in smaller businesses, leaders are more likely to make decisions on the basis of intuition and hunches. Larger

firms have established approaches to decision making that are used by each department. Furthermore, larger firms face more complicated decisions that need a more scientific approach.

- **Predictability of the situation**: in an unpredictable situation, the use of intuition and hunches may be the best approach. However, if past data are reliable indicators of future changes, a scientific approach is ideal.
- **Character of the person or culture of the company**: an entrepreneurial risk taker is more likely to use intuition and hunches. A manager (or business) that tries to avoid risk or blame is more likely to use a scientific approach to justify any decisions.

Role of risks, rewards, uncertainty and opportunity cost in decision making

Most decisions cannot be taken with 100 per cent certainty of the outcome. The fact that decisions are rarely based on perfect information means that some risk is usually present. This could be because the business has limited information on which to base the decision or because the outcome of the decision is uncertain. For example, launching a new product in a new market will be risky, especially if a firm has no experience of selling in that market and if, despite market research, it is unsure about how consumers will react. A given level of risk is not a bad thing if it is balanced by acceptable rewards. Most successful businesses have had to take risks in order to succeed, such as entering a new market in order to gain first-mover advantages.

In order to make well-judged decisions, an understanding of risks, rewards, uncertainty and opportunity cost is necessary.

Risks

Most decision making involves an element of risk. For example, the decision to open another sales outlet in a different part of town may involve huge additional costs but may not generate the expected sales; a new approach to marketing a particular product may actually turn customers away from the product.

Rewards

Business decisions are usually taken in the expectation of some form of reward or benefit for the business. For instance, a new employee incentive scheme is expected to result in increased productivity; a new IT system is expected to reduce costs by increasing efficiency.

Uncertainty

Just because a particular project is risky does not mean that a decision to pursue it should not be made. The increased risks involved may also mean greater potential rewards are available. However, careful analysis of the balance of risks and rewards should be carried out and any areas of uncertainty should be fully explored. For example, if a decision has to be made about opening an additional store in a different part of town to an existing store owned by the same business, market research might be used to establish if there is likely to be demand in that particular area or if the new store might just 'cannibalise' custom from the existing store. The case study on J.C. Penney at the end of this chapter provides an illustration

---

Did you know?

First mover advantages are advantages that a business achieves by being the first to enter a new market. These include developing customer loyalty and brand recognition before other competitors move into the market and gaining control of key resources that businesses entering the market later are unable to obtain.

of how failure to test market a new strategy in a few stores, and therefore reduce uncertainty about the impact of the new strategy on the market, led to a significant fall in sales revenue. The fact file on the Met Office on page 87 shows how data on weather conditions can be linked to a business's own data on market conditions in order to reduce uncertainty and so help to clarify the risks involved in planning outdoor events.

Opportunity cost

Key term

Opportunity cost The 'real cost' of taking a particular action or the next best alternative foregone, i.e. the next best thing that you could have chosen but did not.

Opportunity cost is the real cost of a decision in terms of the next best alternative. Every decision has an opportunity cost. For example, the time you have available in the evenings and at weekends is limited and you may have to choose between going out with friends or, say, revising a business topic for a class test. The 'real cost', as opposed to the monetary cost, of spending an evening out with friends may be your failure to understand the business topic and your resulting low marks in the test. Alternatively, the 'real cost' of an evening spent revising could be the missed opportunity to attend a concert. Resources, including time and money, are scarce, so choosing to pursue one thing inevitably results in foregoing something else. The opportunity cost of opening a new store in another part of town is the potentially higher return that could have been made by investing the money elsewhere.

Scientific decision making is more likely to formally take into account risks, rewards, uncertainty and opportunity cost. However, this does not mean that scientific decision making is always the best approach. There are many examples of very successful businesses that started because their entrepreneurial owners used intuition and gut instinct to come up with an idea and get started – see the fact files on the Red or Dead fashion label and The Body Shop above. However, once a business is very large, the risks that result from ill-judged decisions are much greater and scientific decision making becomes much more important.

Marketing model

The marketing model is an example of how the principles of scientific decision making can be applied to marketing decisions. The model is not dissimilar to the generic scientific approach provided above and can also be applied more generally to assist managers in planning and executing strategy.

The marketing model involves five stages:

1 Setting marketing objectives
2 Gathering the data needed to decide on a strategy
3 Assessing alternative marketing strategies and implementing the favoured choice
4 Planning and implementing the marketing mix (see Chapter 10) in accordance with the marketing strategy
5 Controlling and reviewing the outcome of marketing decisions

An essential element of the marketing model is the existence of constraints. Internal factors (strengths and weaknesses) and external factors (opportunities and threats) are continually monitored at every stage in order to assess their impact. These factors can lead to changes at any stage of the model. For example, feedback gained from stage 2 may help a firm to recognise that its objectives are unrealistic and so stage 1 may be modified. Similarly, control and review (stage 5) might indicate that the wrong strategy had been chosen (stage 3) or that the marketing mix had been implemented incorrectly (stage 4). For these reasons, the marketing model is often represented as a circle surrounded by constraints, to emphasise that marketing decisions do not always follow a set of routine stages (see Figure 5.2).

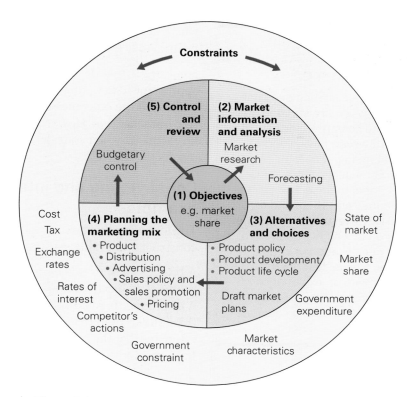

▲ **Figure 5.2** The marketing model

Practice exercise 1

Total: 30 marks

1 Distinguish between scientific decision making and decision making based on intuition and hunches. *(6 marks)*

2 Which of the following are not key stages in the decision-making process?
a) Setting objectives
b) Gathering data
c) Analysing data
d) Recording data *(1 mark)*

3 Explain two benefits of using scientific decision making. *(6 marks)*

4 Explain one reason for basing decisions on intuition. *(4 marks)*

5 Briefly explain how risks, rewards and uncertainty are likely to be a feature of any decision. *(6 marks)*

6 Define the term 'opportunity cost'. *(2 marks)*

7 Why is opportunity cost an important element of any decision? *(5 marks)*

Decision trees

Decision tree analysis is a model or tool to assist businesses in their decision-making processes. Decision tree analysis is usually applied to problems where numerical data are available and for which the probability of different consequences and the financial outcomes of decisions can be estimated.

Decision tree analysis provides a pictorial approach to decision making – the diagram used resembles the branches of a tree. It maps out the different options available, the possible outcomes of these options and the points where decisions have to be made. Calculations based on the decision tree can be used to determine the best option for a business to select.

Some argue that decision making is most effective when a quantitative approach is taken: that is, when the information on which decisions are based and the outcomes of decisions are expressed as numbers. A decision tree does just this. However, as with all quantitative models, caution must be exercised when considering the nature of the information used and the results themselves.

Constructing and interpreting a decision tree: an example

The following business scenario will be used to demonstrate how to construct and evaluate a simple decision tree.

A business wishes to invest in a new plant in order to extend its range of products. It has to decide whether to use the new plant to make product A or product B. Making product A will require a much higher investment (£7 million) than that required for product B (£2 million), but the business estimates that the financial returns look higher for product A than product B. Doing nothing is also an option. Its estimates are as follows:

- If product A is produced and demand is high, the payoff will be £16 million. However, if demand is low, the payoff will only be £6 million. The probability of a high demand for product A is 0.7 and that of a low demand is 0.3.
- If product B is produced and demand is high, the payoff will be £12 million. However, if demand is low, the payoff will only be £4 million. The probability of a high demand for product B is 0.6 and that of a low demand is 0.4.

Constructing the decision tree

1 Start with a small square, to represent the decision, towards the left of your sheet of paper.

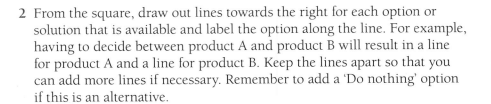

2 From the square, draw out lines towards the right for each option or solution that is available and label the option along the line. For example, having to decide between product A and product B will result in a line for product A and a line for product B. Keep the lines apart so that you can add more lines if necessary. Remember to add a 'Do nothing' option if this is an alternative.

3 At the end of each line, consider the results. If the result of taking that decision is uncertain, draw a small circle. For example, if production of product A may result in high or low demand, this is an uncertain outcome. If, on the other hand, the result of a particular option is not uncertain, as is the case with the option 'do nothing', extend the line to the far right. Insert the financial outcome (payoff) of any certain, final outcome.

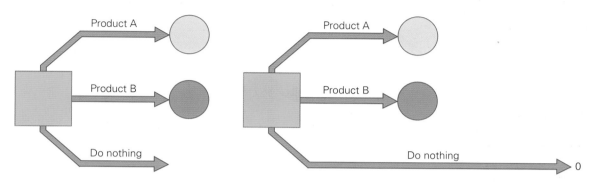

4 From any circle(s), draw lines to the right representing possible outcomes and above each line label the outcome (for example, success or failure, high or low demand). Review your tree diagram and see if there are any options or outcomes that you have missed. If so, draw them in.

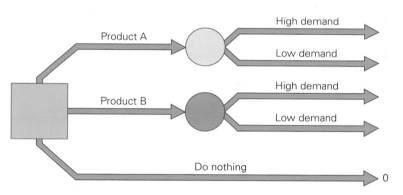

Interpreting the decision tree

This is where you work out which option is financially better.

5 At the end of the line, insert the financial result (payoff) of each outcome.

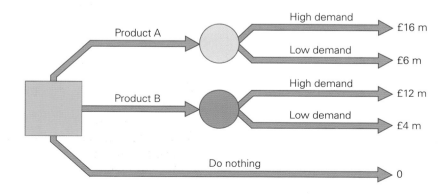

6 Note the probability of each outcome occurring immediately below the line showing that outcome. This will be calculated by considering data on similar events in the past and what experts and forecasts predict. If percentages are being used, the total for each option must add to 100 per cent; if decimals or fractions are used, the total for each option must add to 1.

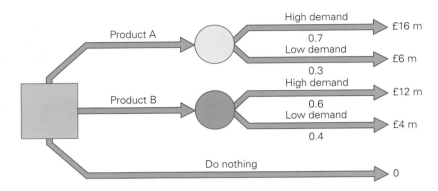

7 If there is a cost involved in selecting a particular option, note this under the line labelled with the option.

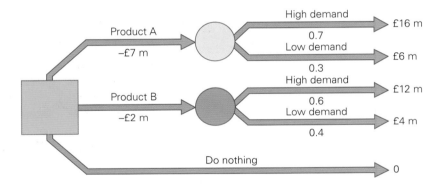

Calculating expected value and net gains

8 Calculate the expected values (EV) (also known as the expected monetary values – EMV) for each outcome and option. Start on the right-hand side of the decision tree. First calculate the **expected value** of the uncertain outcomes by multiplying the value of the outcome by its probability. Then add the expected values of all the uncertain outcomes of a particular option. Subtract any cost of that option. This gives you a value that represents the benefit of that particular decision or option, known as the **net gain** (also known as the net expected value).

Product A:	High demand:	expected value	$0.7 \times £16m =$	£11.2m
	Low demand:	expected value	$0.3 \times £6m =$	£1.8m (+)
		Total expected value		£13.0m
	Cost			£7.0m (–)
	Net gain			£6.0m

Key terms

Expected value The monetary value of an outcome of a decision; calculated by multiplying the expected monetary value of the outcome by the probability of that outcome occurring.

Net gain The value to be gained from making a particular decision; calculated by adding together the expected value of each possible outcome of a decision and deducting the costs associated with the decision.

Product B:	High demand:	expected value	$0.6 \times £12m =$	£7.2m
	Low demand:	expected value	$0.4 \times £4m =$	£1.6m (+)
		Total expected value		£8.8m
	Cost			£2.0m (−)
	Net gain			£6.8m

9 When you have calculated the net gains of each option, add them to the diagram and cross through any rejected decisions with two small diagonal lines, leaving untouched the line representing the decision that provides the largest financial benefit.

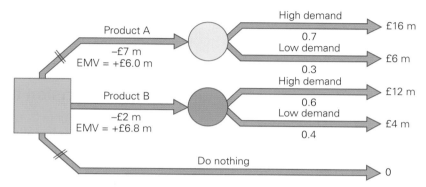

10 Taking into account your decision tree and any non-quantitative (qualitative) factors (discussed later in the chapter) that might be important, make a final decision on the best approach for the business to take. In our example, if quantitative factors only were taken into consideration, product B would be produced, as it has the highest net gain. However, the relatively narrow difference between £6.0 million and £6.8 million means that qualitative factors will probably be very important in the final decision.

Use and value of decision trees in decision making

Evaluating decision trees

Once the quantitative analysis using a decision tree has been completed, consider the following questions:

- How reliable are the figures used? For example, how were the estimated costs, probabilities and financial returns arrived at? Who provided them? When? What was their original purpose?
- What market research has been done and how effective is this?
- Are there other non-quantifiable factors that might affect the decision? For example: Are competitors likely to enter the market? Is the economy heading for a recession? What will be the impact on the brand image? Will employees' morale be adversely affected?

Benefits of using decision trees

Decision tree analysis is a useful tool when choosing between several options. It provides an effective structure within which to set out the options available and to investigate the possible outcomes of choosing those options. It also helps to form a balanced picture of the risks and rewards associated with each option.

One of the advantages of decision tree analysis over other decision-making tools is that it takes into account uncertainty and risk and tries to quantify these by estimating the probability of a particular outcome occurring. This estimation may be based on past experience, market research or informed guesswork.

By highlighting the issue of uncertainty, decision trees emphasise the fact that every decision can result in a range of possible outcomes, meaning that this type of analysis encourages managers to make more carefully considered decisions. In addition, using a quantitative approach should ensure a more objective decision-making process than the 'gut reaction' type of decision making based on intuition.

When faced with a number of different options, a business will usually want to choose the option that gives the highest financial return. When the outcome of each option is uncertain, decision trees can be used to help reach a decision that balances risk and financial return.

Limitations of decision trees

As with all quantitative models, caution must be exercised when considering the nature of the information used. For example, the figures used might be biased or may have been manipulated in order to gain a particular outcome. It is therefore important to consider who produced the figures and to assess their objectivity.

Decision trees are least useful when decisions do not involve clear-cut alternatives, when there are many individuals involved in the decision-making process, when circumstances are very uncertain or changing rapidly, and when completely new or one-off situations exist. In the last two instances, it would be almost impossible to estimate in any realistic or reliable way the probability of a particular outcome occurring.

Because of these disadvantages, decision tree analysis should only be part of the decision-making process. Other non-quantitative factors should be taken into account before a final decision is made.

Table 5.1 summarises the main advantages and disadvantages of using decision trees.

▼ **Table 5.1** Advantages and disadvantages of decision trees

Advantages	Disadvantages
• Set out the problem clearly and encourage a logical approach to decision making.	• Ignore the constantly changing nature of the business environment.
• Encourage careful consideration of all alternatives and thus the opportunity costs involved.	• Difficult to get accurate and realistic data in order to estimate probabilities.
• Encourage a quantitative approach that may improve the results and also means that the process can be computerised.	• Quite easy for management bias to influence the estimates of probabilities and financial returns, and for managers to manipulate the data.
• Take risks and rewards into account when making decisions and encourage a quantitative assessment of such risk.	• Less useful in relation to completely new decisions or problems and one-off strategic decisions or problems.
• Useful when similar scenarios have occurred before, so that realistic estimates of probabilities and financial returns can be made, thus reducing uncertainty.	• Few decisions can be made on a purely objective basis; most include a subjective element based on managerial experience and intuition.
• Useful when making tactical or routine decisions rather than strategic decisions.	• May lead to managers taking less account of important qualitative issues.

Fact file

'What if?' or sensitivity analysis

'What if?' or sensitivity analysis can be applied to decision trees by changing either the estimated probabilities of options or the estimated financial returns of outcomes. This type of analysis can be used to answer questions such as: 'How small does the probability of the most optimistic outcome need to be before the other option gives a greater net gain?'

This more detailed analysis helps to reduce the risks involved in the decision-making process by providing a thorough review of each possible outcome, from the most optimistic to the most pessimistic. Sophisticated computer packages are available for this kind of complex procedure that are able to produce tree diagrams and an array of 'what if?' solutions, once the data have been input.

By using data such as those provided by the Met Office (see fact file below), businesses can estimate probabilities such as the chances of bad weather and their likely financial outcome.

Fact file

Weather sensitivity analysis

Weather sensitivity analysis is a specialised service designed to uncover and quantify the precise relationship between the weather and a business's performance. This comprehensive resource from the Met Office offers a valuable insight into how weather affects consumer behaviour and demand for products or services. A firm's historical sales and marketing data are gathered along with specific weather data provided by the Met Office. This collated information is analysed and a report produced that documents the effects of the weather on a particular industry and the correlation between sales performance and specific weather activity.

The benefits of this system to firms are that it helps them to:

- understand the types of weather that have most impact on their business
- ensure availability of products and services to meet customer demand
- control costs and protect their infrastructure
- plan the timing of promotional activity
- manage inventories and stock levels effectively
- deploy staff and other resources effectively
- schedule maintenance work.

Source: Met Office website (www.metoffice.gov.uk).

Influences on decision making

Some decisions are short term, some long term. Some decisions are functional and tactical in nature, while others are corporate and strategic. All decisions are influenced by a range of internal and external factors. The AQA specification identifies the following influences: mission, objectives, ethics, the external environment and resource constraints. Each of these is discussed on the next page:

Tactical versus strategic decisions

Strategic decisions concern the general direction and overall policy of a business and are likely to influence its performance. These decisions have significant long-term effects on a business and therefore require detailed consideration and approval at senior management level. They can be high risk because the outcomes are unknown and will remain so for some time.

Strategic decisions often involve moving into new areas of activity, which are likely to require additional resources, new procedures and retraining. Strategic decisions might concern whether a business should consider expansion by acquisition or organic (internal) growth in order to achieve its corporate goal of, say, market dominance. They might concern how a business will compete in a way that distinguishes it from its competitors – for example, on the basis of quality and uniqueness or in terms of cost leadership and low prices.

Tactical decisions, on the other hand, tend to be short to medium term and are concerned with specific areas or functions of the business rather than overall policy. Unlike strategic decisions, tactical decisions are calculated and their outcome is more predictable. For example, if a product's sales are below target, a business may make tactical decisions to remedy this by cutting the price of the product and/or running a sales promotion. Tactical decisions may be used to implement strategic decisions and are usually made by middle management.

Mission

The mission of a business is its essential purpose or intentions. Chapter 1, which considers mission in detail, indicates that 'formally stating the business mission or main aims of a business provides a common purpose for everyone to identify with and work towards, and a collective view that helps to build team spirit and encourage commitment'. In this sense, the mission of a business will influence the type of decisions that are made. H&M's mission 'to offer fashion and quality at the best price' will be a constant influence on all decisions about the production and marketing of its goods.

Objectives

Objectives are designed to enable a business to achieve its aims or mission. They can be set at corporate (company-wide) level and at functional (departmental or divisional) level. Chapter 1 discusses business objectives in general and Chapters 7, 11, 16 and 20, cover respectively, marketing, operational, financial and human resource objectives. Chapter 1 indicates that objectives act as a focus for decision making and as a yardstick against which success or failure can be measured. For example, if the main business objective is profit maximisation, then decisions will tend be focused on reducing costs and increasing prices. If social and ethical objectives are important, then decision making might focus less on achieving the lowest cost, or greatest revenue and profit, and more on the needs of the workforce, local community or the environmental impact of any actions taken.

Ethics

Ethical issues were mentioned in the discussion in Chapter 3 on environmental issues and fair trade.

A decision made on ethical grounds might reject the most profitable solution for a business in favour of one that provides greater benefit to society as a whole, or to particular groups of stakeholders (i.e. groups of people who have a particular interest in the business, such as shareholders, the local community, customers and employees). Such decision making is likely to distinguish a business that is behaving ethically from one focused on profit.

On the other hand, a business may adopt a seemingly ethical position, for example, a production, marketing or investment strategy that promotes environmental or social principles, because it is popular with consumers and is likely to lead to increased sales. Whether this is a reflection of the business adopting a 'real' ethical position or a 'perceived' one (that is as a public relations (PR) exercise) to gain consumer loyalty and increase sales is debatable.

External environment

The external environment and its impact on business costs and the demand for goods and services were discussed in Chapter 3. That discussion indicates very clearly that the external environment is a major influence on decision making in business. Changes in economic policy, such as an increase in interest rates, will influence business decisions about whether to delay expansion plans because the costs of finance become too high and consumers' discretionary income falls. On the other hand, improving economic growth may mean incomes are rising, which in turn might cause a business to look more favourably on plans for expansion if it believes higher incomes will mean more sales. Environmental factors might influence decisions about which method of waste disposal to adopt. Demographic trends may influence decisions about what mix of products a business should provide in order to take advantage of, for example, the growing number of elderly people in the population. The actions of competitors will also be a significant influence on decision making. If a competitor brings out a new product, reduces the price of its existing products or establishes a new sales outlet nearby, each of these actions will influence the decisions a business makes about its own product, pricing and location strategies.

Resource constraints

Resources include financial, human and physical resources. Each type of resource is discussed in later chapters of this book. The fact that all resources are scarce relative to their demand has a huge influence on a business's plans and thus on its decisions. Resource constraints, or the fact that resources are limited or scarce, mean that every decision about how to deploy these limited resources will involve a consideration of opportunity cost.

- **Financial resources**: if a company is unable to generate sufficient financial resources, this will affect its decision making. For example, decisions about expansion or diversification will depend on the business having sufficient funds, or access to funds, to support these developments. Limited financial resources will mean a business must choose between alternatives – whether to allocate a larger budget to the marketing activities or to improving the quality of its production facilities.

Key term

Ethics The set of moral values held by an individual or group or organisation.

What do you think?

Can a business be considered ethical if it makes production decisions that are environmentally friendly because it knows this will increase its market share at the expense of a competitor rather than because it judges that this is the best thing to do to protect the environment?

Are consumers acting ethically when they buy very cheap clothing that may be produced by child labour in developing countries?

Refer to the case study on Dyson at the end of this chapter. Was Dyson's decision to move the manufacturing plant to Malaysia ethical?

- **Human resources**: the availability of human resources will influence an organisation's decision making – whether sufficient trained employees are available within a company or whether there is a sufficient number of qualified and skilled people interested or available to apply for jobs. Both situations will influence the ability of a business to pursue developments. For example, whether a business decides to introduce a particularly complex piece of computer software might depend on whether it has sufficient trained staff, whether it will be able to recruit trained and experienced individuals or provide appropriate training for unskilled, but otherwise suitable staff.
- **Physical resources**: if a business is considering expansion or the re-siting of a plant in another area, much will depend on the availability of suitable sites at an affordable price.

Other factors influencing decision making

Other factors influencing decision making include the relative power of stakeholders and the culture of an organisation. Both of these are considered briefly below.

Relative power of stakeholders

Stakeholders are examined in detail in Chapter 6. The relative power of individual stakeholder groups and their influence on decision making depends on the nature of the business.

- In some small family businesses, the interests of shareholders may be the major influence on decision making.
- For organisations whose location has a major impact on the local environment, local communities or environmental pressure groups may be powerful stakeholders and influence decision making.
- For businesses in highly competitive markets, customers will be powerful stakeholders and their needs will be a major influence on decision making.
- In businesses that are dependent on a highly skilled but hard to find workforce, employees may be powerful stakeholders who exert significant influence on the decision-making process.

Culture

Culture is often described as 'the way that we do things around here', meaning the type of behaviour that is considered acceptable or unacceptable.

Every business has its own unique culture based on the values of the founders, senior management and core people who built and direct the business. At the simplest level, it is possible to distinguish between a 'them and us' culture in a business where strict divisions exist between management and workers, and a more equitable culture in a business that tries to reduce barriers, with emphasis being placed on teamwork and more equal treatment of all. Over time, the culture of a business may change as new owners and senior managers try to impose their own styles and preferences or because of changing marketplace conditions. The case study of J.C. Penney at the end of this chapter indicates a situation where a new leader tried unsuccessfully to change the culture of a business. Culture therefore has a major influence on decision-making processes in a business, particularly in relation to how it responds to changes in the external environment. For example, the culture of a business will influence how resistant to change it is and thus the level of risk it is prepared to take in terms of decision making.

Practice exercise 2

Total: 50 marks

1 What is a decision tree? (*3 marks*)

2 Explain three advantages of using decision trees in a business context. (*9 marks*)

3 Explain two disadvantages of using decision trees in a business context. (*6 marks*)

4 If the probability of success is 0.6, what is the probability of failure and why? (*2 marks*)

5 A particular outcome has a 40% chance of earning £40,000 and a 60% chance of earning £100,000. What is its expected value? (*4 marks*)

6 Outline two situations where decision trees are likely to be a valuable tool. (*6 marks*)

7 Outline one situation where decision trees are unlikely to be useful. (*4 marks*)

8 Analyse two ways in which each of the following factors are likely to influence a firm's corporate decision making:
   a) ethics (*8 marks*)
   b) resource constraints (*8 marks*)

Case study: Lynne Lilley crafts

Lynne Lilley has been making crafts in her small studio in Skipton for approximately ten years. Her products include handmade greeting cards, beeswax candles, pottery and potpourri, most of which she makes herself and which she sells to local customers and visiting tourists. The studio is rented and she employs another person on a part-time basis to assist at weekends and during holiday periods. Profit over the years has been reasonable, but during the last few years costs, particularly rent, have started to rise. Skipton, a market town in Yorkshire, attracts many visitors and there have been more businesses setting up in competition with Lynne. As a result of the increased competition, cost increases cannot be passed on to customers through higher prices and so Lynne has found her profit falling steadily. Lynne believes she has two options available to her – to continue as she is at present or to move to cheaper premises.

If she continues as she is, she envisages three possible outcomes: there is a 30 per cent chance of a downturn in the economy, resulting in a loss of £10,000; there is a 40 per cent chance that the economy will stay the same, resulting in a profit of £30,000; and there is a 30 per cent chance of an upturn in the economy, resulting in a £40,000 profit.

Lynne could move to premises in a less prominent area of the town where rents are much cheaper. She has built a good reputation and therefore assumes that local customers will still find her, but she realises that she would be less accessible for the tourist trade. Lynne believes it would cost £4,000 to refurbish the premises she is considering and to cover the cost of advertising that would be needed to alert tourists to the presence of the new premises. Again, she faces three possible outcomes: a downturn in the economy, the economy staying the same or an upturn in the economy.

Each of these outcomes has the same probability of occurring as described above, but the expected values are different: if there was a downturn in the economy she would expect profits of £5,000; if the economic situation stayed the same she would expect profits of £35,000; if there was an upturn in the economy she would expect profits of £50,000.

Questions

1 Draw the decision tree and calculate the expected value and net gain of each option. *(9 marks)*

2 On the basis of your calculations, which option should Lynne choose and why? *(2 marks)*

3 Consider how useful decision tree analysis is in helping Lynne to make her decision. *(9 marks)*

Case study: Decision making at Dyson

It took five years and 5,127 prototypes for James Dyson to come up with his first bagless cleaner, which started selling in Japan in 1986. Since then, the Dyson business has expanded so that its products sell in over 65 countries, 85 per cent of products being sold outside of the UK.

Within two-and-a-half years of its introduction to the English market, the Dyson vacuum cleaner became England's bestseller. What lies behind the success of the Dyson cleaners, especially given that they are anything but cheap? A Dyson costs more than twice as much as most rival models. Moreover, the marketing campaign for the cleaners has stayed decidedly low-key. According to James Dyson, superior technology explains its popularity. Because there is no bag or filter to clog, his cleaners stay powerful. 'They maintain constant, maximum suction,' he says. 'All the time it's working to full efficiency, cleaning your home.'

The company enjoys strong brand loyalty thanks to its quality products that are positioned at the high end of the market. Tim Calkin, a US professor of marketing, said that Dyson succeeded by bringing something new and innovative to a market that had focused exclusively on price. 'They certainly have set themselves up as a superior vacuum cleaner,' says Calkin. 'They've almost made it an aspirational purchase; people who buy Dysons really like them. People take pride in their vacuum when they own a Dyson.'

Dyson shifted production of its vacuum cleaners from England to Malaysia in 2002, resulting in a loss of 865 manufacturing jobs. Mr Dyson said he had been forced to move the manufacturing business abroad because production costs were 30 per cent lower in Malaysia compared to England. He also cited the fact that both component suppliers and some of the cleaners' biggest markets were based in the region. Production of Dyson's washing machines also moved to Asia. The company continues to develop the technology in England, where about 1,000 engineers are employed in research and development. The move to Malaysia boosted profits and allowed the company to grow and expand in the USA, where it became market leader in just two years.

Source: adapted from articles in Business Week (www.businessweek.com) April 2005, BBC News (www.bbc.co.uk) July 2014 and www.dyson.com, July 2014.

Questions

1 How might factors in the external environment have influenced Dyson in its decisions about how to price and market its products and to locate its manufacturing processes in Malaysia? *(15 marks)*

2 Assess the extent to which a scientific decision-making model might have benefited Dyson in deciding on its production move from England to Malaysia. *(15 marks)*

Case study: Decision making at J.C. Penney

J.C. Penney Company Inc. (also known as JCPenney or Penney's) is a chain of American mid-range department stores that has been in existence for over a hundred years. The company operates over 1,000 department stores across America.

In June 2011, Ron Johnson became the chief operating officer (COO) of JCPenney. Prior to that, from January 2000 to November 2011, he was Senior Vice President of retail operations at Apple, where he pioneered the concept of the Apple retail stores. In April 2013 he was fired from JCPenney.

When Johnson announced his vision for JCPenney in January 2012, its shares rose by 24 per cent. He was ambitious to introduce new brands and a new pricing policy.

During his time at JCPenney:
- the company spent nearly $1 billion in 17 months, which reduced its cash balance from $1.8 billion to $930 million
- sales revenue fell by 25 per cent in 2012
- the company's market capitalisation fell by nearly 50 per cent.

The authors of a Forbes article on Ron Johnson's time at JCPenney suggest that leaders like Johnson are given a special name at Amazon: they're called HiPPOs, which stands for 'highest paid person's opinion'. HiPPOs, they say, are 'leaders who are so self-assured that they need neither other's ideas nor data to affirm the correctness of their instinctual beliefs. Relying on their experience ..., they are quick to shoot down contradictory positions and dismissive of underling's input.'

When introducing changes, Johnson used his intuition and trusted his gut instinct, rather than the data that was presented to him. He was reportedly shown the results of focus group meetings that indicated clearly that consumers, the traditional core of whom were elderly, had strong preferences for discounts, something JCPenney had always provided

in the past. Ignoring this, Johnson introduced a fixed pricing approach for all products, similar to the approach he introduced at Apple. Analysts suggest that this decision was a major cause of the 25 per cent decline in sales revenue. When customers didn't react positively to the fixed price approach and the disappearance of discounts, Johnson didn't consider the new policies were at fault but that customers needed to be educated about the new strategy.

The authors of the Forbes article suggest that Johnson not only ignored existing data but was also convinced that he didn't need new information to validate his strategy. He ignored suggestions by experienced staff at the company to test-market the changes in a small number of stores before rolling them out across America. The reason he gave for his decision was that Apple had never test-marketed when developing its store network. The results of test-marketing might have indicated that the new strategy was not going down well with customers.

Transforming a large company requires vision, conviction in one's beliefs and perseverance. The authors of the Forbes article suggest that despite his vision and conviction, Johnson's ultimate downfall was his inability to listen to others – whether employee feedback or data on customer preferences and trends. Johnson's defence was that the company needed quick results and that if he hadn't taken a strong position against discounting, he would not have been able to introduce the new brands.

Amazon, by contrast, has fostered a culture of experimentation in which leaders at all levels are encouraged to test ideas in the marketplace and then let data – not senior leaders' or HiPPO's opinions and intuition – guide the decision making about whether to implement ideas.

Source: adapted from information in 'What happens when a HiPPO runs your company?' by Chris Derose and Noel Tichy, www.forbes.com, 15 April 2013

Questions

Total: (50 marks)

1 Under what circumstances might decision making based on intuition benefit a business? *(9 marks)*

2 Assess how Ron Johnson's strategy of introducing new approaches at JCPenney might have benefited from a more scientific decision-making approach? *(16 marks)*

3 Discuss the value of different approaches to decision making that are available to an organisation. *(25 marks)*

6

Understanding the role and importance of stakeholders

This chapter considers the role and importance of stakeholders. It highlights why an organisation should take into account stakeholders' needs when making decisions. The needs of different groups of stakeholders are identified and the implications of possible overlap and conflict of these needs are analysed. Stakeholder mapping as a means of identifying and analysing the power and interest of different stakeholder groups is explained. The way in which information derived from stakeholder mapping can be used to determine how to manage relationships between different groups of stakeholders is discussed. Potential influences on the relationship with stakeholders are summarised. The chapter concludes with a discussion about the importance of managing the relationship with different stakeholders and how this might include using communication and consultation.

Stakeholders, as their name implies, have a stake in an organisation — something to risk and therefore something to gain or lose as a result of an organisation's activity. A **stakeholder** can have a negative or positive impact on an organisation and its activities.

Key term

Stakeholder An individual or group or other institution with a direct interest in the activities and performance of an organisation or in a project to be undertaken by that organisation.

Author advice

In this context, a project might mean the transfer of a business's operations to another location, the introduction of a new ICT system across an organisation, the move from a centralised, national organisational structure to a decentralised, regional structure, the closure of a factory, or any other business strategy that involves change and affects stakeholders.

For a business, its main stakeholders are likely to be its shareholders, employees, customers, suppliers, financiers, the local community and the government. Figure 6.1 illustrates the stakeholder groups that might have an interest in a football club such as Manchester United. If a business is planning a particular project, for example, the transfer of operations to a new location or the closure of one of its factories, stakeholders are likely to also include trades unions, different groups of employees and managers, the local council and the media.

```
        Manager and the
        management team

Suppliers              Customers/supporters

Creditors                  Employees of
                          Manchester United

Local                      Government
community

    Shareholders     Media
```

▲ **Figure 6.1** Manchester United's stakeholder groups

Stakeholders can be divided into:

- internal stakeholders, such as business owners, shareholders, employees, managers, trades union representatives and members of works councils. This group of stakeholders are closely connected to the organisation and their needs are likely to have a strong influence on how the organisation is run
- external stakeholders, such as customers, competitors, suppliers, central and local government agencies and regulators, **pressure groups**, investors, bankers, creditors, professional and trade associations, the local community and the media. External stakeholders have diverse needs and varying levels of influence on an organisation's ability to meet its objectives. This group includes stakeholders who, although external to the organisation, have a contractual relationship with it, such as customers, suppliers and investors. These latter groups are sometimes known as 'connected stakeholders'.

An alternative classification divides stakeholders into:

- **primary stakeholders**: those who are directly involved and affected, either positively or negatively, by an organisation's actions. These people will have the power to influence and shape decisions. (Primary stakeholders could be internal or external stakeholders)
- **secondary stakeholders**: the 'intermediaries', that is, persons or organisations who are indirectly affected by an organisation's actions. (Secondary stakeholders could be internal or external stakeholders)
- **key stakeholders**: can be either primary or secondary stakeholders but will have significant influence upon or importance within an organisation.

Considering stakeholders' needs when making decisions

Each group of stakeholders has different needs in relation to an organisation and its activities and these needs will influence the decisions the organisation makes. Depending on the context, some groups of stakeholders will be more powerful than others and their needs are likely to be more influential. The following examples illustrate the potential power of groups of stakeholders in different contexts and why it is important for organisations to consider their needs when making decisions.

- In small family-owned businesses, the needs and interests of shareholders may be the major influence on decision making. In such a business, there is likely to be a small number of shareholders, each with a substantial shareholding. Should any of these shareholders feel that a particular strategy or development does not meet their needs sufficiently (because it is unlikely to lead to high or frequent dividend payments, for example), they may vote against it and stop further developments.
- For organisations whose location has a major impact on the local environment, local communities or environmental pressure groups may be powerful stakeholders and influence decision making. Should these stakeholders feel that an organisation is polluting the local environment, they may take action in the form of a protest or boycott, which could disrupt the organisation's activities and plans.
- For businesses in highly competitive markets, customers will be powerful stakeholders and their needs – which are likely to include fair prices and good quality products – will be a major influence on decision making. Any decisions that ignore their needs are likely to lead to reduced sales and profits.
- In businesses dependent on highly skilled, specialist workers, these employees may be powerful stakeholders, particularly if they are hard to find. Their needs, which might include high levels of pay, good working conditions and a say in decision making, will exert significant influence on the decision-making process. If decisions fail to take account of their needs, they are likely to leave the organisation, damaging its ability to operate effectively.

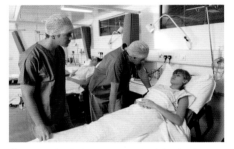

▲ Stakeholders of the NHS include patients and doctors

Fact file

Stakeholders and the NHS

As public consultation becomes an increasingly important element in public health policy, it becomes ever more crucial for decision makers to understand who is affected by the decisions and actions they take and who has the power to influence their outcome – that is, to understand their stakeholders. The requirement to engage stakeholders in public sector organisational strategy and project design is a key priority in government policy within the NHS. Stakeholder engagement is about ensuring stakeholders' views, needs and ideas shape strategies and projects. For example, a local health and well-being strategy may be developed by involving:

- internal stakeholders who participate in the co-ordination, funding, resourcing and publication of the strategy. They include the local health and well-being partnership, the local Primary Care Trust and the local authority.
- external stakeholders who are engaged in contributing their views and experiences in addressing the issues that are important to them as patients, service users, carers and members of the local community.

In each of the examples above, it can be seen that a failure to consider the needs of the main group of stakeholders when making decisions can have serious negative consequences for an organisation. Successful modern businesses must therefore prove as effective at managing their stakeholders as they are at managing their markets or their financial position.

Overlap and conflict of stakeholder needs

The things that stakeholders look for from an organisation are called stakeholder needs or expectations or objectives. As an organisation's survival depends, to a large extent, on support from its stakeholders, how and to what extent it can satisfy their needs and help meet their objectives is crucial. What makes the task difficult to accomplish is the fact that, on some occasions, different groups of stakeholders share common needs, while on other occasions their needs conflict. Table 6.1 summarises the possible needs of particular stakeholder groups in relation to the activities of a business.

▼ **Table 6.1** Examples of stakeholder needs

Internal stakeholder group	Needs
Shareholders	• high profit levels, which will in turn allow high dividends • a positive corporate image and long-term growth in order to encourage share prices to rise
Employees	• job security • good working conditions • high levels of pay • promotional opportunities • to be consulted about changes that might affect them
Managers	• high status • high pay • high bonuses • job security • to further the interests of their departments and functions as well as their own careers
Trades unions:	• to be consulted and to take an active part in the decision-making process in order to ensure policies and strategies benefit their members
External stakeholder groups	**Needs**
Customers	• high quality products at fair prices • good service • wide choice
Suppliers	• regular orders • fair prices • prompt payment • advance notification of any changes
Banks and investors	• full and prompt repayment of loans plus interest
Local community	• local employment opportunities • socially responsible activities that benefit the local community
Environmental pressure groups	• business activity to have a neutral or beneficial impact on the environment
Government	**central government:** • efficient use of resources • provide employment and training • comply with legislation on consumer protection, competition policy, employment, health and safety and environmental considerations **local government:** • same as central government and make a positive contribution to the local community • be consulted, for example on plans for expansion

Common or overlapping needs

All stakeholders of a business, except its direct competitors, have much to gain from it being a prosperous and successful business. For example, the closure of a car manufacturing business affects not only the employees of that business, whose job security and livelihood are dependent on its success, but also the suppliers of parts, the dealers and small servicing outlets specialising in the cars made in that factory. The shareholders who have bought shares in the business stand to lose some or all of their money. The directors and managers may lose the privileges associated with their present position if the business fails and may be forced to look for alternative employment. With a change of job come the problems and costs associated with having to relocate their homes and families. The closure is also likely to be detrimental to the local economy.

The above example illustrates the fact that, although different groups of stakeholders have different needs in relation to a business, in general, all stakeholders have something in common – their needs can usually be fulfilled only if the business is sufficiently prosperous and successful.

Sometimes the needs of different groups of stakeholders overlap, as shown in Table 6.1. For example, employees and managers have similar needs in relation to job security, pay and working conditions; the local community and pressure groups have similar needs in relation to business activity and its impact on the local environment; and shareholders and banks and investors may have overlapping needs in that they want a business that is financially sound so that it can provide shareholders with decent dividends and repay loans owed to banks.

Conflicting needs

The needs of different stakeholder groups often conflict. For example, workers are likely to want good pay and conditions and job security. If a business wishes to close one of its factories, their job security will be threatened and, with the support of their trades unions, they may go on strike. Strike action will damage the business – its reputation, productive capacity, sales and profits. Shareholders' needs and objectives are likely to be linked to high dividends and growth in the value of their shareholdings. They may see the factory closure as a way to make the business more efficient. Their needs and objectives are likely to be negatively affected because of the impact of striking workers.

The business world includes many situations where a conflict of interest arises. The directors of a public limited company are appointed to manage, co-ordinate and make a profit. If they fail at any of these, they may be voted out by the shareholders at the next annual general meeting. The nature of their job requires them to adopt a view on what is going on both inside and outside the company and over the short and long term. However, most employees of a company are there to carry out specific tasks. It is often difficult for them to see things from the directors' point of view. This does not mean that directors are always right and the employees are always wrong, but it does present a potential source of conflict. Even within a particular stakeholder group, there may be conflicting needs. For example, some customers will favour low prices over good quality, while others will favour quality over price; some employees will prefer job security and reasonable wages while others want high wages and may be prepared to leave an organisation if their needs are not met. Table 6.2 illustrates some typical examples of conflict between the needs of different groups of stakeholders.

▼ **Table 6.2** Typical examples of stakeholder conflicts

Stakeholder group	Conflict
Employees versus managers	Job security and high wages, which may increase costs *versus* high bonuses paid as a result of improved cost efficiency
Customers versus shareholders	Good quality products and low prices, which may reduce profits *versus* high profits and high dividends
Local community or pressure groups versus shareholders	Reduction in the adverse impact of business activity on the environment, which may incur high costs *versus* low costs leading to high profits and dividends

'Win–lose' or 'win–win'

Because a firm may not be able to meet the needs of all stakeholder groups, it has to set priorities and is therefore likely to encounter conflict. For example, if a firm helps the local community, fewer funds will be available for shareholders. Conversely, if more rewards are directed towards the owners (shareholders), less are available for employees. This analysis takes a 'win–lose' approach to the situation: that is, it views the company as having a fixed pot of benefits to share out among all groups; if one group gains more, another group gains less.

An alternative approach is that of 'win–win'. According to this analysis, a firm can, by its actions, cause the pot of benefits to grow so that all groups gain more. For example, better conditions and rewards for employees, although reducing rewards for shareholders in the short run, may increase them in the long run. This occurs because increased staff loyalty and motivation might result in better quality work, which in turn might increase consumer loyalty and enhance the firm's reputation. Pursuing this analysis further, it might lead to a need for less marketing expenditure in order to achieve the same or a higher level of sales and therefore profit.

Stakeholder mapping

The extent to which different stakeholder groups are able to influence business decisions depends on a range of factors, including their power over, and their interest in, the activities of a business. In 1991, Aubrey L Mendelow developed a framework or matrix, known as stakeholder mapping, to help analyse stakeholder power and interest and to help manage stakeholders' conflicting needs and objectives.

The process involves placing stakeholders into a matrix, with their position dependent on their relative power and interest in relation to a particular project being undertaken by a business. Mendelow's power–interest matrix is provided in Figure 6.2.

Power \ Level of interest	Low	High
Low	**A: Minimal effort**	**B: Keep informed**
High	**C: Keep satisfied**	**D: Key players**

▲ **Figure 6.2** Mendelow's power–interest matrix: an example of stakeholder mapping

> **Did you know?**
>
> Stakeholder mappings by other business writers use slightly different variables to Mendelow's power and interest ones. For example, some grids use the level of influence and interest; some use power and impact. Despite these slight differences, they are essentially the same in that they try to establish the influence different groups of stakeholders will have on an organisation's activities.

In making decisions about where to place stakeholders in the matrix, the following issues need to be taken into account.

- How interested different groups of stakeholders are to influence an organisation's choice of strategies by taking some sort of action. Stakeholders' level of interest is likely to be high if, for example:
  - as managers, they have made a significant personal, financial or career investment in what the business does
  - there are few alternatives – whether in terms of jobs for employees, customers for suppliers or suppliers for customers
  - in the case of local councils or government regulators, they may be called to account for failing to monitor the particular business activity.
- The extent to which stakeholders have the power to impose their own needs or objectives on an organisation. This depends upon factors such as:
  - their status, in terms of their place in the organisational hierarchy, their relative pay, their reputation in the organisation and their social standing
  - their claim on resources in terms of the size of their budgets and the number and levels of staff employed (for managers); the volume of business transacted with them (for suppliers and customers); or the percentage of workers they speak on behalf of (for trades unions)
  - the extent to which they are formally represented in the decision-making process.

The various sections of a stakeholder map indicate the amount of effort a business needs to put into meeting the needs of stakeholders. The example of a factory closure illustrates this.

It is important to recognise that a stakeholder map is not static. Changing events may mean that stakeholders can move into different quadrants of the map with consequent changes to the list of the most influential stakeholders.

Stakeholder mapping example: a factory closure

The following example of a business's decision to close one of its factories illustrates how the use of stakeholder mapping can help it to identify and manage its stakeholders. Figure 6.3 is an example of a Mendelow power–interest matrix used to map stakeholders' power and interest in relation to this particular project.

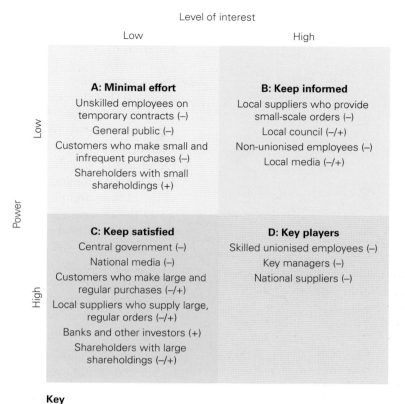

Level of interest

	Low	High
Low (Power)	**A: Minimal effort** Unskilled employees on temporary contracts (–) General public (–) Customers who make small and infrequent purchases (–) Shareholders with small shareholdings (+)	**B: Keep informed** Local suppliers who provide small-scale orders (–) Local council (–/+) Non-unionised employees (–) Local media (–/+)
High (Power)	**C: Keep satisfied** Central government (–) National media (–) Customers who make large and regular purchases (–/+) Local suppliers who supply large, regular orders (–/+) Banks and other investors (+) Shareholders with large shareholdings (–/+)	**D: Key players** Skilled unionised employees (–) Key managers (–) National suppliers (–)

Key

(–) Negative view of factory closure
(+) Positive view of factory closure
(–/+) Ambivalent view, recognising arguments on both sides

▲ **Figure 6.3** Mendelow's power–interest matrix: an example of stakeholder mapping for a business intending to close one of its factories

Having identified which quadrant each group of stakeholders best fits, strategies to deal with each group can then be developed in order to ensure that the project (factory closure) proceeds smoothly and stakeholder dissatisfaction is minimised/support is maximised. Below are examples of potential strategies.

- **Quadrant A**: the relative lack of interest and power of stakeholders in quadrant A means they are more likely than other groups to accept what they are told, so **minimal effort** needs to be devoted to managing their expectations. Possible actions: not to reappoint unskilled employees on temporary contracts but to provide them with limited redundancy support; other stakeholders may be informed of the intended closure but information and communication need not be regular or detailed.

- **Quadrant B**: stakeholders in quadrant B are interested in the project but lack power in relation to it. If the strategy is presented as rational, this may stop opponents of the project in quadrant B joining forces with more powerful dissenters in quadrants C and D. Rational explanations might include the fact that without this factory closure, the whole business might collapse or because another factory is expanding and taking on more employees. If there is evidence of consultation about the project, this might also satisfy stakeholders in quadrant B. Possible actions: brief all groups in this quadrant on the reasonableness of the case for closure and of the provisions being made for the redundant staff. Advance notice and **keeping these groups informed** will give them more time to adjust to the idea of the planned closure and so reduce their dissatisfaction.

- **Quadrant C**: stakeholders in quadrant C have power but relatively little interest in the closure of the factory. It is important to **keep these groups satisfied** in order to avoid them gaining more interest and shifting into quadrant D. Possible actions: inform them of the likely outcomes of the strategy well in advance, for example, reassure the government and suppliers that the closure will result in a more efficient firm that is able to compete worldwide. A similar message may reassure banks, investors and large shareholders, particularly if it is backed up with a positive short-term dividend forecast.
- **Quadrant D**: stakeholders in quadrant D are **key players** because they have both power and interest. As a result, they could be major supporters of the closure and play a large part in its success, or, if they are unhappy about the closure, they have the power and interest to make it very difficult for the business. Possible actions: extensive communication is needed to assure stakeholders that the change is necessary, followed by consultation and discussion about how to implement the change; fully involve the unions in determining the redundancy provision for employees; key managers should be involved in deciding, for example, the basis on which early retirements should be handled and how redeployment should be managed.

Given that time and resources are always limited, once stakeholders have been identified, judgements about how much effort to put into meeting their needs and objectives in relation to the project must be made. In this example, the major considerations for the business are likely to be:

- the negative attitudes of skilled, unionised employees, key managers and national suppliers, each group of which are key players in quadrant D
- the ambivalent attitude of large shareholders, suppliers and customers who need to be kept satisfied in quadrant C
- the potentially negative interventions of national media and central government in quadrant C
- the possible increase in the power of local councils and local media presently in quadrant B.

Managing the relationship with these groups of stakeholders will be crucial to the success of the project. It might involve, for example, taking action to shift the views of skilled unionised employees, who are likely to be made redundant, from quadrant D to C or B through generous payoffs, thus reducing the possibility of them going on strike and disrupting plans.

Influences on the relationship with stakeholders

There are a range of potential influences on the relationship a business has with its stakeholders. All have been considered in previous discussions in this chapter. Influences include the extent to which stakeholders:

- have status and power within or outside the organisation and in relation to the project under consideration; this includes social, economic or political status as well as positions of authority within the formal hierarchy of an organisation
- control resources relevant to the project being considered; this includes the control of relevant budgets and manpower within an organisation

- are involved in the decision-making process within the organisation or in other organisations in relation to the project (other organisations could include planning and regulatory authorities)
- have specialist expertise, knowledge and skills related to the project under consideration
- have needs and objectives that are similar to, or conflict with, those of other stakeholders and those of the organisation
- co-operate with or actively work against other stakeholders and the organisation
- are internal or external to the organisation or are direct or indirect stakeholders.

Influences on the relationship with stakeholders also include whether a business adopts a traditional shareholder approach or a stakeholder approach to their relationship. These are discussed below.

Traditional view: shareholder approach or shareholder value perspective

Traditionally, companies were established by their owners to meet the needs of those owners. Company aims and objectives were therefore dominated by the needs and objectives of shareholders (the owners), which were essentially to make profit for them. From this perspective, managers are seen as responsible solely to the owners of the company (i.e. to the shareholders), who employ the managers to run the company on their behalf. Everything managers do should be for the direct interest of shareholders and their aim should be to maximise shareholder value by striving for short-term rewards, such as profit and dividends.

Alternative view: stakeholder approach or stakeholder value perspective

Over time, companies have come to be seen more as networks of different groups – employees, suppliers, shareholders, external interest groups and customers – all co-operating to create mutually beneficial results. Companies have also been encouraged by government and pressure groups to meet the wider needs of society by taking into account the **externalities** arising from their decisions. This perspective emphasises the requirement to consider,

Key term

Externalities Costs and benefits that occur as a result of a firm's activities, but which are not recorded in its accounts. For example pollution and congestion may be caused by a firm's activities, but the costs are borne by the local community and not by the firm.

What do you think?

R. Edward Freeman, a professor of business administration in the USA, is an important authority on stakeholder theory. He is best known for his book, *Strategic Management: A Stakeholder Approach*, first published in 1984 and reissued in 2010. His view of the stakeholder/shareholder issue is as follows:

'Every business creates, and sometimes destroys, value for customers, suppliers, employees, communities and financiers. The idea that business is about maximising profits for shareholders is outdated and doesn't work very well, as the recent global financial crisis has taught us. The task of executives is to create as much value as possible for stakeholders without resorting to trade-offs. Great companies endure because they manage to get stakeholder interests aligned in the same direction.'

Source: Ed Freeman on Stakeholder Management, http://redwardfreeman.com

1 To what extent do you agree with this view?

2 If a business is failing, should short-term profits and survival become more important objectives than its obligations to other stakeholder groups? Try to explain the reasoning behind your answer.

and try to meet, the needs and objectives of wider groups of individuals who have an interest in a company. It takes the view that companies benefit from co-operation with their stakeholder groups and from incorporating the needs of all stakeholders into the decision-making process.

Managing the relationship with different stakeholders

Successfully managed organisations understand the contribution that positive relationships with stakeholders can make. Stakeholder relations management aims to influence stakeholder attitudes, decisions and actions for the mutual benefit of the organisation and its stakeholders. Poor stakeholder management can easily cause a project to fail. However, if stakeholder management is effective, stakeholders may become allies and so help to bring about a project's success. Assessing the expectations of stakeholders enables an organisation to gauge how well different stakeholder groups will support or try to prevent certain activities. Understanding this will enable an organisation to more effectively manage the relationship between different groups of stakeholders and, in particular, to resolve conflicts between those with competing needs and objectives.

Managing relationships with different stakeholders can involve a range of different approaches, as described below.

1 Cyert and March, in their book, *A Behavioural Theory of the Firm* (1963), identified four ways of managing relationships with stakeholders, particularly in relation to resolving conflicting needs and objectives:

- Satisficing – this involves negotiations between key stakeholders to arrive at an acceptable compromise. The strategy is usually the one that keeps all, or at least the most powerful, stakeholders happy.
- Sequential attention – this is when management focus on stakeholder needs in turn. For example, in a situation where budget cuts mean pay rises have to be limited, one group of workers may receive a pay rise one year, with a clear message that it will not be their 'turn' again for a few years and so they should not expect any further increases. Stakeholders are thus kept happy by taking turns to get their needs met and objectives realised.
- Side payments – these are used where a stakeholder's primary needs and objectives cannot be met so they are compensated in some other way. For example, a local community may object to a new factory being built on a site that will cause pollution, noise and extra traffic. The firm concerned may continue to build the factory but try to appease the community by also building local sports facilities.
- Exercise of power – this is when a deadlock is resolved by a senior figure forcing through a decision simply based on the power they possess.

2 Stakeholder mapping, such as Mendelow's power–interest matrix (considered earlier in this chapter) can help managers classify stakeholders according to their power and interest and make recommendations about how to manage different groups in relation to this.

3 Mission statements, considered in Chapter 1, describe the broad direction organisations follow and summarise the essential values of organisations. As such, by communicating key organisational values and priorities, a mission statement should help to resolve some of the conflicts between different stakeholder groups' expectations of a business.

4 Corporate social responsibility or ethics. One way for an organisation to view the ethical dilemmas it faces is to see them as stakeholder conflicts. For example, pollution concerns could be expressed as the conflict between trying to make more money for shareholders (e.g. by not spending money to reduce pollution) versus the impact on the wider community. Clear guidance on ethical approaches and improvements to the way an organisation manages its corporate social responsibility will help resolve such ethical conflicts. Social auditing, also known as corporate social responsibility reporting, is the process by which a business attempts to assess the impact of the entire range of its activities on stakeholders and society in general.

Benefits of effective communication and consultation with stakeholders

- The viewpoints of the main stakeholders can help shape a project at an early stage. Not only does this make it more likely that stakeholders will support the project, their input can also improve the quality of the project.
- Gaining support from powerful stakeholders can help win more resources. This makes it more likely that a project will be successful.
- By communicating with stakeholders early and often, stakeholders are more likely to know what is being done and understand the benefits of a project. This means they can provide active support when necessary.
- Managing stakeholder relations effectively allows a business to anticipate public reaction to a project and build into its plans actions that will win public support.

Information needs to be tailored to effectively communicate and consult with, and sufficiently inform, different stakeholder groups. Equally, the amount of time and effort spent on communication and consultation with different stakeholder groups will depend on the cost and the level of influence of the stakeholder. Some will require simple and infrequent updates; others will require regular, detailed and frequent communications.

Communication and consultation channels

Common communications and consultation channels between organisations and their stakeholders in relation to a particular project include:

- formal consultations with external and internal stakeholders, where views are submitted and taken into account in the planning and implementation stages
- formal meetings with powerful stakeholders
- informal meetings with interested groups of stakeholders
- newsletters to disseminate information to stakeholders on a project's progress

Author advice

Remember that limited resources and opportunity costs are fundamental issues to consider when discussing how to manage relationships with stakeholders.

- website information, including regular updates about a project's progress
- individual briefings for stakeholders with high levels of power and interest
- tours and demonstrations for interested stakeholders
- public forums if a project involves local community stakeholders
- media releases that report on significant project milestones
- advertisements and information displays in newspapers, magazines and notice boards, including visual representations of a project's progress in public places, where appropriate.

Fact file

Stakeholder analysis

Stakeholder analysis involves the identification of a project's key stakeholders, an assessment of their interests and needs and the ways in which these interests and needs affect a project and its viability.

Using Mendelow's power–interest approach, stakeholder analysis involves the following stages:

1 identify all relevant stakeholders

2 assess the nature of each stakeholder's influence in terms of their power and interest in relation to a project

3 construct a power–interest matrix and map stakeholders into the appropriate quadrant depending on the level of their influence

4 monitor and manage stakeholder relationships by ensuring appropriate action is taken in terms of

stakeholders' levels of influence and the extent to which their needs (in common, overlapping or conflicting) might influence their behaviour.

The benefits of undertaking stakeholder analysis before and during the implementation of a project are that it helps with the identification of:

- stakeholders' needs and objectives
- mechanisms to influence stakeholders
- potential risks, including possible coalitions and conflicts between different stakeholder groups
- key stakeholders to keep informed about a project as it develops
- negative stakeholders and their potential adverse effects on a project.

All of this should help a business achieve its aims and ensure the success of its project, while also meeting the needs of each stakeholder group as far as possible.

What do you think?

The BBC's move to Salford

In 2013, the BBC successfully relocated part of its operations to Salford in the north west of England. It recruited staff with expertise in managing relocations, set up a project team that developed and implemented plans for the move and maintained good communications with its various stakeholders. The move from London to Salford required the transfer of 1,500 job roles, indicating the importance of employees as key stakeholders to manage in this relocation process. The BBC's target was to relocate 30 per cent of existing staff from London to Salford, with new recruitment filling the rest of the jobs. In the event, 38 per cent of existing staff from London relocated. To encourage sufficient staff to move, some of the allowances the BBC offered as incentives and to compensate relocating staff and minimise redundancy costs were more generous than would normally be offered. For example, the 'remote location allowance' covered the cost of renting property in Salford and travelling to and from London for two years. This allowed staff who were unable to, or unwilling to, commit to moving permanently to Salford to keep their homes in the south east.

1 In relation to the relocation, do you think the BBC's offer of a generous 'remote location allowance' was an effective way to manage the relationship with one of its key stakeholder groups – its employees? Explain the reasoning behind your answer.

Practice exercise 1

Total: 70 marks

1 Distinguish between the terms 'shareholder' and 'stakeholder'. *(4 marks)*

2 Which of the following is not an internal stakeholder?
   a) Shareholders **c)** Managers
   b) Employees **d)** Customers *(1 mark)*

3 Which of the following is not an external stakeholder?
   a) Customers **c)** Banks and investors
   b) Suppliers **d)** Shareholders *(1 mark)*

4 Using the examples of two different stakeholder groups, explain why a business should consider stakeholders' needs when making decisions. *(6 marks)*

5 Which of the following is least likely to be one of the employees' needs or objectives in relation to a business?
   a) Low prices
   b) Job security
   c) High wages
   d) Good working conditions
   e) Opportunities to be consulted about decisions *(1 mark)*

6 'Stakeholder groups often have needs in common or that overlap.' Use two examples to explain this statement. *(6 marks)*

7 Identify and explain two examples of stakeholder needs that conflict. *(6 marks)*

8 Distinguish between the traditional shareholder approach and the alternative stakeholder approach in relation to the objectives of a business. *(8 marks)*

9 Distinguish between the 'win–lose' approach and the 'win–win' approach to meeting stakeholder needs. *(6 marks)*

10 Explain one purpose of stakeholder mapping. *(4 marks)*

11 Which two of the following elements form the two axes of Mendelow's stakeholder mapping matrix?
   a) Influence **d)** Interest
   b) Power **e)** Control
   c) Impact *(2 marks)*

12 Identify the key approach to stakeholders in each of the four quadrants of Mendelow's stakeholder mapping matrix. *(4 marks)*

13 Explain two key influences on the relationship of a business with its stakeholders. *(6 marks)*

14 Explain two ways in which a business might attempt to manage the relationship between different stakeholders. *(6 marks)*

15 Why might communication and consultation be important in this process? *(6 marks)*

16 Give three examples of channels to use for communicating and consulting with stakeholders about a project. *(3 marks)*

Case study: Tesco plc

Tesco's core purpose is, 'We make what matters better, together'. Tesco believe this is a clear and simple statement of what it does and what it represents. It reflects the fact that businesses must increasingly demonstrate a purpose that is more than just profit and must adapt to a culture where 'making what matters better' is more important than a culture where 'more is better'. Tesco notes that it wants to 'always do the right thing, to inspire and to earn trust and loyalty' from all of its stakeholders.

Tesco's values help it and its stakeholders to put this core purpose into practice. Its values are:

- 'No one tries harder for customers', which involves: understanding customers; being first to meet their needs; acting responsibly for their communities
- 'We treat people how they want to be treated', which involves: working as a team; trusting and respecting each other; listening, supporting and saying thank you; sharing knowledge and experience
- 'We use our scale for good', which involves: creating new opportunities for millions of young people around the world; helping and encouraging colleagues and customers to live healthier lives

and through this helping to tackle the global obesity crisis; leading in reducing food waste.

Tesco indicates that its values ensure that all its stakeholders understand what is important – about how they work together as a team and how customers are at the centre of what they do. It suggests that these are universal values that have helped guide stakeholders as Tesco has grown and entered new markets and new countries. For Tesco, engaging with the different groups of stakeholders that influence, or are affected by, its business is fundamental to its values.

Tesco has a wide range of stakeholders, with many different needs and expectations, and these sometimes conflict. Tesco acknowledges that it cannot be all things to all people, but can assure all stakeholders that it has listened to them and taken their views into account when balancing different considerations.

The table below shows the main issues raised by Tesco's various stakeholder groups and the process through which Tesco engages with them.

Stakeholder group	Needs and objectives in relation to Tesco	Engagement with stakeholders
Customers	<ul><li>Good shopping trip</li><li>Good neighbour</li><li>Operate fairly and honestly</li><li>Provide a good choice of products, including sustainable, healthy and affordable options</li></ul>	<ul><li>Customer Question Time (CQT) meetings help to identify and respond to changing customer needs.</li><li>CQTs are used to develop Customer and Community Plans. These plans are used to improve levels of customer satisfaction.</li></ul>
Employees	<ul><li>Fair pay and conditions</li><li>Interesting job</li><li>Managers who help</li><li>To be treated with respect</li><li>Opportunities to get on</li><li>Safe and healthy workplace</li></ul>	<ul><li>Staff give anonymous feedback through the annual Staff Viewpoint survey</li></ul>
Communities	<ul><li>Good neighbour</li><li>More employment</li><li>Support for local causes and initiatives</li></ul>	<ul><li>Community initiatives</li><li>Public consultations and exhibitions</li><li>Leaflets</li><li>Focus groups</li><li>Consumer panels</li><li>Work with community groups, including charities</li></ul>
Suppliers	<ul><li>To be treated fairly and honestly</li><li>Long-term relationships, opportunities for growth and shared customer insight</li></ul>	<ul><li>Application of core value is: 'We treat people how they want to be treated';</li><li>Use of annual Supplier Viewpoint survey</li></ul>
Government and regulators	<ul><li>Legal compliance</li><li>Stable, family-friendly job opportunities</li><li>Good quality training</li><li>Timely payment of all taxes</li></ul>	<ul><li>Engaging with governments and officials on a range of policy issues that affect Tesco and the communities in which it operates.</li></ul>

➤➤➤

Tesco is the largest supermarket business in the UK with a market share of 29 per cent. Its market share has been falling gradually in recent years (from just over 31 per cent in 2011). This decline is despite spending over £1 billion on store upgrades and price cuts in order to compete with supermarkets such as Aldi and Lidl. Industry experts suggest that Tesco is not the only major supermarket struggling to tackle rapid change in the industry as a result of the rise of discounters such as Aldi, Lidl and Poundland, as well as the increase in online shopping. The whole industry is seeing the impact of a reduction in spending power since the recession of 2008, with consumer spending not reflecting the benefits of lower inflation or the economic recovery. Following the news of a 3.8 per cent fall in sales during the three months to 24 May 2014 compared to the same period in 2013, the value of Tesco's shares fell by 1.3 per cent to 293.5p.

Source: adapted from information on www.tesco.com and news items during June 2014

Questions

Total: 70 marks

1 Analyse how stakeholder mapping might assist Tesco in achieving success in relation to its operations and their impact on its stakeholders. *(9 marks)*

2 Analyse the different ways Tesco attempts to manage the relationship with its stakeholders. *(9 marks)*

3 Assess the extent to which different stakeholder groups have needs and objectives in common or that overlap and how this could benefit Tesco. *(16 marks)*

4 Assess the potential conflict of needs and objectives among Tesco's stakeholders and the possible impact on Tesco and its stakeholders of such conflict. *(16 marks)*

5 Tesco's core purpose and values suggest it takes a stakeholder rather than a shareholder approach. Discuss the relative benefits of such an approach to the company and to its various stakeholders compared to a more traditional shareholder approach. *(20 marks)*

7

Setting marketing objectives

This chapter outlines the purpose of marketing and examines the marketing objectives that provide direction to organisations in their efforts to achieve success. Various key marketing objectives are considered, together with their benefits and limitations. The chapter concludes with an examination of the key influences on marketing objectives and decisions.

Purpose of marketing

The purpose of **marketing** is to meet the needs of customers and the organisation. The definition provided in the key term also provides an introduction to the purposes of marketing.

> **Key term**
>
> **Marketing** The anticipating and satisfying of customers' wants in a way that delights the consumer and also meets the needs of the organisation.

Anticipating customers' wants

The first stage of marketing is to conduct market research in order to discover the wants of customers and the factors that influence those wants. Detailed analysis of market research and the need for a business to understand its markets is provided in Chapters 8 and 9.

Satisfying customers' wants in a way that delights customers

An organisation will decide on suitable marketing techniques to ensure that customers are delighted. The approach used by organisations to achieve this aim is known as the marketing mix (also known as the '7 Ps' – product, price, promotion, place (distribution), people, process and physical environment (physical evidence)). The marketing mix is examined in detail in Chapter 10. Organisations can use the marketing mix in order to achieve their marketing objectives.

Meeting the needs of the organisation

Ultimately, marketing is intended to enable a business to satisfy its own wants. In Chapter 1 we examined the business's mission and business objectives (the goals and specific targets of the organisation as a whole). Having decided on its corporate (business) objectives, the organisation will then decide on suitable aims and objectives for its marketing activities or the marketing department in order to achieve its business objectives.

Author advice

Make sure you understand the distinction between a market and an individual firm or business.

A market is a place where buyers and sellers meet. In this respect, the market refers to generic goods or services, such as bicycles, breakfast cereals, hairdressing and travel agencies.

Individual firms will each operate *within* a market, trying to sell their particular brands of goods and services. Thus Kellogg's operates largely within the breakfast cereals market and will aim to improve the performance of its own cereals, such as Corn Flakes. The success of Corn Flakes will impact upon the success of competitors' breakfast cereals, such as Weetabix.

Marketing objectives

Key term

Marketing objectives The goals of the marketing function in an organisation.

A business's **marketing objectives** are the goals of the marketing department or function. These goals must be consistent with the goals of the organisation as a whole. For example, one of Sainsbury's business objectives is to ensure that its supplies are purchased from suppliers that behave ethically. In order to achieve this objective, Sainsbury's has set itself a marketing objective to ensure that, by 2020, all of the fish it sells will be independently certified as sustainable, so that supplies for future generations are not threatened.

Marketing objectives depend on the aims and priorities of an organisation and can be categorised in a number of ways, as described below.

Sales volume and sales value

These measures both show the size of a business, based on its level of sales.

Size can be measured by **sales volume** or **sales value**.

Put simply, *value = volume x average price*.

For example, if a '99p store' sells 100,000 items at 99p each, then its sales volume is 100,000 items and its sales value is £99,000.

A business will often consider success to be the achievement of a certain level of sales, usually a larger figure than their current level. Marketing objectives based on sales volume and sales value may be expressed in terms of:

Key terms

Sales volume Measures the number of items sold or produced (such as the number of televisions sold).

Sales value Measures the financial worth of the items sold (e.g. £30 million of televisions).

- a specific level of sales volume (e.g. Premier Inn UK trying to achieve sales volume based on having 75,000 hotel rooms by 2018)
- a specific level of sales value (e.g. Volkswagen aiming to achieve global sales of €200 billion in 2014).

The value of using sales volume as a marketing objective is that it is easy to measure and understand and is useful for comparisons. For example, car sales are usually measured by sales volume because the sale of a certain number of cars is easy to picture and compare. However, it is of limited value as it does not take into account the income received. Table 7.2 (page 121) shows that Mercedes Benz just overtook Peugeot in terms of sales volume of cars in the UK in 2013. However, this disguises the fact that the average Mercedes Benz has a much higher price than a typical Peugeot; thus the sales value of Mercedes Benz cars is considerably higher than the sales value of Peugeot cars.

Sales value is much more useful than sales volume when comparing multi-product firms such as clothing retailers. Retailers such as Fat Face and Gap sell a wide range of products with significant differences in price. Some clothing retailers, such as Debenhams and M&S, also earn significant income from non-clothing items. Consequently, sales value is usually a popular way of setting marketing objectives for such firms. Although sales value can be difficult to visualise it is much easier to use when comparing businesses whose products have different price levels.

Market size

Many markets are measured by *volume* because it is easier for people to identify with an item than with a sum of money. For example, in the car market it is easier to picture 2.5 million cars being sold than a value of £30 billion. However, in some markets (e.g. hair care products, dog food and deodorants) there are many different products with huge variations in price. In these cases, it is easier to measure the market in terms of the *value* of goods sold.

The **market size** indicates the potential sales for a firm. A large market size provides a greater opportunity for an individual business to achieve high sales volume or sales value, and so most businesses will wish to operate within a sizeable market. For example, the UK car market earns revenue of over £30 billion a year: a car manufacturer can therefore earn huge revenue, even if it is only small in comparison with its competitors. However, market size influences the level of competition and so firms in large markets may struggle to compete. A business may prefer to operate in a small market with few or no competitors, as competition in large markets can often drive down prices.

Market size is important to a business, but it is rarely used as a marketing objective because a single company will only form a part of a given market and therefore it has little value as a marketing objective. However, for a monopoly, where there is only one firm in the market, an increase in market size does guarantee an increase in sales for the monopolist (i.e. the firm that has the monopoly). The usefulness of market size lies in its role as an indicator of the maximum *potential* sales for a firm in a particular market.

Key term

Market size The volume of sales of a product (e.g. the number of computers sold) or the value of sales of a product (e.g. the total revenue from computer sales).

Author advice

Note that market size can increase as a result of extra sales of goods or through businesses persuading customers to pay higher prices. Trainers, tablets and other markets with premium brands are good examples of this latter point. If the average price rises by 10 per cent and sales volume stays the same, the market size has increased by 10 per cent in terms of sales value.

Key term

Market growth The percentage change in sales (volume or value) of a generic product or service, over a period of time. For example, market growth of bicycles in general, rather than a specific make of bicycle.

Market growth

The percentage **market growth** for a particular year is calculated as follows:

$$\frac{\text{Market size in year} - \text{Market size in previous year}}{\text{Market size in previous year}} \times 100 = \text{Market growth (\%)}$$

Although market growth is usually a factor that is outside the immediate control of an individual business, businesses will try to identify markets that will increase in size in the future. A business that is active in a market that has potential for fast growth is likely to benefit from this growth and therefore achieve a rapid increase in its sales volume and sales value. As a consequence, firms will often have the identification of markets with the potential for growth as one of their marketing objectives. For example, Nokia was originally a Finnish paper mill, but it identified the potential market for mobile phones in the early stages of market growth. As the use of mobile phones increased rapidly, Nokia benefited from this expansion, building a business with a market value that reached €100 billion in 2007. As recently as 2012, Nokia was the world's leading handset producer.

Large businesses, particularly those that dominate a market, may also see market growth as a target, because growth in the market within which they operate should automatically lead to growth in their own sales. By encouraging the development of a 'coffee culture', companies such as Costa and Starbucks have benefited greatly from the rapid expansion of people using coffee shops in the UK. This market has doubled in size in the last six years and is ten times larger than it was 15 years ago. Costa, whose market share exceeds 40 per cent, has been the major beneficiary of this growth.

Fact file

The future of coffee

Allegra Strategies, the leading analyst company for the UK coffee market, forecasts continued growth for the UK coffee market. At present the branded (specialist) coffee chain market size, by value, exceeds £2.6 billion, through over 5,531 outlets. In 2013 market growth was 9.3 per cent by value and 5.9 per cent by volume of coffee shops. By 2018 the branded coffee shop segment is forecast to exceed £4.1 billion, with 7,000 coffee shops. In the UK it is estimated that the market could sustain 9,500 branded coffee shops.

Source: http://www.fdin.org.uk/2014/01/uk-coffee-shop-market-demonstrates-strong-sales-growth/

Table 7.2 (page 121) shows that the volume of car sales increased by 10.8 per cent between 2012 and 2013. Expanding markets are likely to lead to rising sales for an individual manufacturer, but they also encourage competition. This can mean that small firms have to spend a lot of money to compete.

In declining markets, there is less scope for increased sales, but competition is likely to be less fierce. Although the car market grew by over 10 per cent in 2013, the market size is still 12.2 per cent lower than it was at its peak in 2003. Cars are often purchased on credit and fears of unemployment and recession or slowing economic growth make people more cautious. In the decade from 2003 to 2013 this was a market in which businesses expected sales to fall. Consequently, marketing objectives for car manufacturers were more likely to focus on limiting their decline or maintaining their share of the market.

Factors influencing market growth

Market growth is largely outside the control of individual firms. However, a business should be aware of the factors that influence growth, so that it can predict future trends and make sure that it is taking advantage of the potential for growth in certain markets (or avoiding the problems faced in declining markets). Some of the key factors that influence market growth are described below.

- **Economic growth**: if a country's wealth is growing by 3 per cent per annum, then sales are likely to rise in any given market.
- **The nature of the product**: markets dealing with luxury products, such as jewellery or investments, tend to grow more rapidly when economic growth is high, but often suffer more severe cutbacks when people are worried about their living standards.
- **Changes in taste**: as lifestyles change, new products become more popular while others decline. This is a factor that firms can influence through good marketing.
- **Social changes**: the way in which people live may influence product sales. A greater tendency to stay at home will assist sales of digital televisions, while longer working hours have led to fewer people preparing their own meals, thus increasing sales of convenience food and takeaway meals.
- **Fashion**: recent television programmes highlighting home cooking, garden design and do-it-yourself are likely to influence the number of people pursuing those activities. Note how the market for home cooking is being increased by this factor but reduced by the previous influence.

As with market size, market growth has limited value as a marketing objective, although it does show those markets that are growing. Successful businesses are often those that identify a market trend before other businesses, as this enables them to gain 'first mover' advantage. 'Early adopters' (consumers who are keen to be the first to buy new products) will often pay high prices for new, innovative products or services, enabling those firms that anticipate new or high growth markets to take advantage. If the market continues to grow, these firms will have built up expertise and brand loyalty and so they are likely to be more competitive than their rivals.

Sales growth

The percentage **sales growth** for a firm/product in a particular year is calculated as follows:

$$\frac{\text{Sales in that year} - \text{Sales in previous year}}{\text{Sales in previous year}} \times 100 = \text{Sales growth} \, (\%)$$

In general, a business will wish to increase its sales, but during difficult trading conditions, such as a recession, its objective may be to maintain current size or limit a decline in sales.

Marketing objectives based on sales growth may be expressed in terms of:

- a given increase in the level of sales volume (e.g. Audi aiming to increase UK sales by at least 8,000 cars in 2014, in order to record annual UK sales of 150,000 cars for the first time)
- a given increase in sales value (e.g. Restaurant Group TRG, owners of Frankie and Benny's, aiming to increase sales value by £60 million in 2014)
- a percentage rise in sales volume (e.g. Huawei targeting a 50 per cent increase in global sales of its smartphones in 2014)
- a percentage rise in sales value (e.g. Costa trying to achieve a 100 per cent rise in its sales revenue between 2014 and 2018).

Source: adapted from www.audi.co.uk; www.trgplc.com; www.huawei.com; Costa from Whitbread Annual Review 2014.

The value of sales growth as a marketing objective is similar to sales volume and sales value, especially as targets for sales volume and sales value are usually expressed in terms of a percentage growth in sales. However, as with market growth, its achievement is likely to be influenced by external factors as well as the firm's own efforts.

Market share

Market share is usually measured as a percentage, calculated by the formula:

Marketing objectives based on market share are expressed in terms of:

$$\text{Market share} = \frac{\text{Sales of one product or brand or company}}{\text{Total sales in the market}} \times 100$$

- a target percentage market share (e.g. Ford targeting a 14 per cent share of the UK car market)
- market leadership or a certain position in the market (e.g. ASDA and Sainsbury's fighting to be the second largest supermarket in the UK)
- a target aimed towards a particular aspect of the market (e.g. increasing market share of sales to males or teenagers).

Market share is an excellent measure of a company's success because it compares a firm's sales with those of its competitors. A company's market share can increase only if the company is performing better than some of its rivals. Because market share is the best comparison of a company or brand's performance in comparison to its competitors, it is a very popular measure of success and therefore a popular marketing objective.

The market leader is the company with the largest market share. Being the market leader is often a key marketing objective of a business.

In 2013 Peugeot's car sales increased by 6.0 per cent (see Table 7.2, page 121). However, because total sales in the car market rose more rapidly (by 10.8 per cent), Peugeot's market share fell slightly (from 4.9 per cent to 4.7 per cent).

Many analysts believe that market share is an excellent measure of marketing performance and therefore it is often used by firms as a marketing objective. Other measures, such as sales volume and sales value, can be influenced by external factors. In periods when the economy is growing, sales volume may be increasing because consumers are willing to spend more on most products and so achieving a higher sales volume may not be a result of more skilled marketing by the business. Similarly, if inflation is high then sales value will increase. If prices are rising by 10 per cent in a market, an increase in sales value of 7 per cent means that fewer products are being sold. Market share overcomes these issues. An increase in market share usually means that a business is out-performing its rivals, usually by taking customers away from competitors but sometimes by proving to be more attractive to new customers when the market is growing.

However, market share may not always be a reliable indicator of success. It can be very difficult to define 'a market'. Companies such as Unilever and Samsung trade in many different markets and some markets are difficult to define. Supermarkets, for instance, are continually broadening their product range and stocking 'non-grocery' items. Consequently, it can be difficult to measure the size of a market accurately. Another weakness of market share occurs if a market is declining. A firm's market share may grow simply because competitors have left the market and its sales are just falling more slowly than sales of other firms in the market.

Fact file

Decline of UK newspapers

In the UK the two daily newspapers with the highest market share, measured by printed copies, are *The Sun* and the *Daily Mail*. Between 2000 and 2013, *The Sun* increased its market share from 28 per cent to 29 per cent and the *Daily Mail* increased its market share from 18 per cent to 23 per cent. However, do these figures show success? Because market size has declined, the average daily readership of *The Sun* has fallen from 3.6 million in 2000 to 2.4 million in 2013. *Daily Mail* readership has fallen from 2.4 million to 1.8 million. Furthermore, are these figures reliable measures of the newspaper market? As more consumers opt to use online newspapers and other sources of news information, the market becomes more difficult to measure.

Source: ABC (Audit Bureau of Circulations)

Fact file

UK supermarkets

Table 7.1 below shows the sales value and market share of groceries for UK supermarkets in 2013 and 2014.

▼ **Table 7.1** Sales value and market share of groceries for UK supermarkets, 2013 and 2014

Supermarket	12 weeks to 31 March 2013		12 weeks to 30 March 2014		% change in sales
	Sales (£m)	%	Sales (£m)	%	
Tesco	7,385	29.7	7,166	28.6	−3.0
Asda	4,389	17.6	4,367	17.4	−0.5
Sainsbury's	4,204	16.9	4,133	16.5	−1.7
Morrisons	2,892	11.6	2,782	11.1	−3.8
Co-operative	1,549	6.2	1,534	6.1	−1.0
Waitrose	1,195	4.8	1,249	5.0	4.5
Aldi	848	3.4	1,147	4.6	35.3
Lidl	731	2.9	857	3.4	17.2
Others	*1,719*	*6.9*	*1,816*	*7.3*	*5.6*
TOTAL	**24,906**	**100.0**	**25,051**	**100.0**	**+ 0.6%**

Source: Kantar WorldPanel, May 2014 – Market Share Total Till Roll

This table is based on value rather than volume and can be used to illustrate most of the marketing objectives that we have considered so far in this chapter.

- **Market size**: in terms of value, the market size was £25,051 million in the 12 weeks to 30 March 2014.
- **Market growth**: the market size grew from £24,906 million in 2013 to £25,051 million 2014, an increase of 0.6 per cent.
- **Sales value**: each company's sales value is shown; in 2014 Asda's sales were £4,367 million, while sales at Lidl were £857 million.
- **Sales growth**: Asda's sales value fell slightly, by 0.5 per cent; Lidl's sales rose by 17.2 per cent and Aldi's sales rose by 35.3 per cent over the year, a spectacular achievement. This period was very unusual as the five largest supermarkets all experienced a decline in sales value at a time when the market was growing, albeit very slowly.
- **Market share**: there were noticeable shifts, with the discount retailers (Aldi and Lidl) recording increases in market share. Waitrose, the most upmarket supermarket, also gained market share. These changes showed that customers were moving away from the middle-ground retailers, particularly towards retailers offering lower prices.

Fact file

Measuring brand loyalty: Net Promoter Score (NPS)

A commonly used measure of brand loyalty is the Net Promoter Score (NPS). Companies using it include Apple, British Gas, Expedia and John Lewis. Customers complete one question: 'How likely are you to recommend our company (product) to a colleague or friend?' Answers use a 10-point scale, from '0 = Not at all likely' to '10 = Extremely likely'.

Respondents are classified according to their answers:

9–10 are 'Promoters'

7–8 are 'Passives'

0–6 are 'Detractors'

The NPS = percentage of promoters *minus* percentage of detractors.

Therefore, if 62 per cent of respondents give 9–10, 24 per cent give 7–8, and 14 per cent give 0–6, the NPS = 62 – 14 = 48.

Scores can vary from *minus* 100 to 100. A positive score of 50 is considered to be excellent.

Brand loyalty

Businesses will want to increase **brand loyalty** because it will enable them to:

- gain regular repeat purchases from loyal customers
- spend less money on promotions and advertising, as customers do not need further persuasion
- charge higher prices as loyal customers will be less concerned about the price of the product or brand.

Some examples of ways in which businesses have attempted to improve or secure brand loyalty are:

- O_2 acquiring naming rights to the O_2 Arena to widen its appeal to potential customers and increase brand loyalty
- McDonald's aiming to maintain the golden arches as the most widely recognised corporate logo in the world
- Specsavers aiming for a set percentage of 'repeat' customers
- Lush being able to set a premium price in comparison with other soap retailers.

Brand loyalty is an important marketing objective because high brand loyalty enables a business to sell more and charge higher prices. However, it is very difficult to measure objectively. Organisations such as Forbes, Interbrand and Brand Finance provide league tables showing which brands have the greatest value. In 2014, all three organisations placed Apple as the world's most valuable brand, but the subjective nature of these tables is shown by the fact that the three different organisations did not agree on the second most valuable brand in the world. Microsoft, Google and Samsung were the three brands in second place. In the UK, Brand Finance identified Vodafone, HSBC and Tesco as the three UK companies with the most valuable brand names.

Author advice

Marketing objectives are not static. They change as a business develops. They also change in response to both internal and external circumstances. This is not just a one-way process. Feedback from staff involved with organising the company's marketing tactics will be used to advise the directors. Feedback from staff can help the senior managers or shareholders to agree more realistic objectives.

Other marketing objectives

Market positioning

This is concerned with a company's decision to appeal to particular market segments or to try to attract new market segments. Examples include:

- rugby league trying to appeal to more market segments by targeting females, spreading its geographical base from its northern roots by awarding franchises to teams in London, Wales and France, and switching the playing season from the winter to the summer, arguably to avoid direct competition with the football season
- Starbucks targeting younger age groups
- BT bidding to show more Premiership football in order to increase its appeal to young male sports fans who would otherwise mainly watch Sky.

Innovation/increase in product range

Examples include:

- Ben & Jerry's introducing unusual flavours and names of ice cream in order to maintain its reputation for individuality
- Samsung and Apple introducing new tablets and phones to penetrate new markets and to enhance their reputations for innovation and design
- EE trying to achieve growth in its sales from fourth-generation (4G) products
- BBC and ITV both aiming to increase the availability of their programmes through the internet.

Security/survival

Examples include:

- W.H. Smith reducing its dependence on sales of newspapers in response to a significant fall in sales of printed newspapers in recent years (a market decline of 50 per cent since 2000).
- HMV introducing a mobile app to reposition itself for music downloading rather than direct sales of CDs and DVDs.
- Marks and Spencer trying to make sure that its general merchandise (clothing) sales, which fell by 2.4 per cent in 2013, do not fall further.

Ethical and environmental marketing objectives

In Chapter 6 we studied the different stakeholders in a business and their impact on business decisions. It is vital that the business satisfies the varying needs of its different stakeholders. Although this might create conflict between marketing objectives, businesses will tend to have a variety of marketing objectives that aim to fulfil their corporate social responsibilities. There is growing pressure on firms from the public, government and consumers to organise their activities in a way that protects the environment for both current and future generations. Consequently firms will tend to have marketing objectives that reflect this concern, such as targets for recycling and energy efficient products. Ethical behaviour is also a requirement of a growing number of stakeholders. The expansion of fair trade products is an objective for many businesses. For organisations such as supermarkets this has become a big influence on both their objectives and their decisions, particularly in respect to choice of suppliers.

Meeting the needs of customers *and* the organisation is not an easy task and the wide range of marketing objectives described in this chapter illustrate how difficult it can be to balance these purposes. This process is further complicated by the existence of competitors, whose own marketing goals will aim to prevent rivals from achieving their marketing objectives. The benefits and problems of setting marketing objectives are described below.

Value of setting marketing objectives

Why do businesses set marketing objectives? The reasons for setting any objectives are the same, regardless of the functional area being considered. These reasons are:

- to act as a focus for decision making and effort
- to provide a yardstick against which success or failure can be measured
- to improve co-ordination, by giving teams and departments a common purpose

Author advice

A business will have a limited range of marketing objectives so that it can focus on its priorities. A typical business will select only a few of the range of objectives considered in this chapter. Security/survival objectives are only likely to be set by a business that is trying to rectify a problem, so they are unnecessary for most firms.

- to improve efficiency, by examining the reasons for success and failure in different areas
- to motivate staff and improve their performance by setting challenging, but realistic, targets
- to establish priorities, so that staff understand the relative importance of different objectives.

Benefits of setting marketing objectives

- Marketing objectives should be SMART (specific, measurable, agreed, realistic and time-based). Setting clear objectives helps to ensure that decisions by different staff are consistent, because they are all designed to reach the same goal. For example, a target to increase market share will encourage staff to focus on decisions and actions that improve the firm's ability to out-perform its competitors.
- Specific objectives, such as achieving sales of 500 items of clothing, provide clarity for employees and enable both the marketing department and individual employees to see whether they have succeeded or failed to meet expectations.
- If members of a department or team all have a common purpose (to achieve a particular marketing objective) then they are more likely to adopt a team approach, enabling managers to provide a more united and co-ordinated approach to problem solving.
- Measurable and timed objectives allow managers and individuals to improve efficiency, by examining the reasons for success and failure in different areas. Practices that have worked effectively in certain areas can be adapted more widely and staff can learn from their failures, reducing the possibility of unsuccessful actions in the future
- If marketing objectives are achievable, but only through significant effort by employees, then individuals and teams are likely to be motivated to succeed and improve their performance
- There are many possible marketing objectives, as indicated above. If the marketing department gives a clear indication of the relative importance of each objective, it should enable employees to recognise their own priorities, so that their actions and decisions are consistent with the needs of the business as a whole.

Problems of setting marketing objectives

- External changes are not always easy to predict and so marketing objectives may be based on incorrect assumptions. The impact of the most recent recession in the UK continued for much longer than most analysts expected and so many firms' marketing objectives were too ambitious. The entry of a new competitor, a sudden rise in interest rates and higher unemployment may also have the same effect. In contrast, the reverse of any of these changes, such as a competitor going out of business, can lead to marketing objectives becoming unrealistic because they are too easy to achieve.
- Internal changes should be foreseeable and so they are less likely to create problems. However, over time factors such as a higher turnover of labour, cuts in the training budget and operational problems in the factory may all impact on the usefulness of marketing objectives. An objective to improve brand loyalty can be severely hampered by a reputation for unreliability or cuts in advertising or marketing promotions.

- As we have seen, there are many potential marketing objectives and in some cases, these objectives may conflict. For example, increasing market share (measured by volume) can be achieved by cutting prices, but this may hinder the achievement of a target to increase sales revenue. Similarly, a focus on new product development and innovation may help a business to develop new products in the long term, but may divert resources away from activities such as advertising, which can boost sales in the short term.
- There may be unclear priorities, with employees taking decisions to suit their own needs rather than meeting the objectives of the business. For example, sales staff are often paid on commission and so may be very aggressive in persuading customers to buy products, an approach that may alienate customers in the long run. Many financial organisations have been forced to compensate customers as a result of sales staff 'mis-selling' payment protection insurance.
- The business may not have sufficient resources or a marketing budget that is too small to enable the marketing department to achieve its objectives.
- If objectives are imposed, rather than agreed, employees may not feel 'ownership' of the objectives of the department. Consequently, they may not put in the effort to achieve the goals that have been set. Imposed objectives may also be unrealistic, as the manager imposing them may lack the detailed understanding possessed by the employees who have to deliver those targets.
- There may be a reluctance to set realistic objectives in times of difficulty. If sales are expected to fall it is psychologically difficult for people to set a target such as a 5 per cent fall in sales revenue. Consequently, the objectives may lack usefulness as they are not achievable.
- People like to set ambitious targets, as it shows a willingness to succeed, but this often means that marketing objectives lose their value because they are too ambitious.

Practice exercise 1

Total: 50 marks

Read the information in Table 7.2 and, using your knowledge of business, answer the questions that follow.

▼ **Table 7.2** Analysis of the UK market for new cars, 2012–2013

Manufacturer	Cars sold 2012	Cars sold 2013	% change	Market share 2012 (%)	Market share 2013 (%)
1 Ford	281,917	310,865	+10.3	13.8	13.7
2 Vauxhall	232,255	259,444	+11.4	11.5	11.4
3 Volkswagen	183,098	194,085	+6.0	9.0	8.6
4 Audi	123,622	142,040	+14.9	6.0	6.3
5 BMW	127,530	135,583	+8.6	6.2	6.0
6 Nissan	105,835	117,967	+11.5	5.2	5.2
7 Mercedes-Benz	91,855	109,456	+19.2	4.5	4.8
8 Peugeot	99,486	105,435	+6.0	4.9	4.7
9 Toyota	84,563	88,648	+4.8	4.1	3.9
10 Citroen	73,656	78,358	+6.4	3.6	3.5
Other makes	640,792	722,856	+12.8	31.2	31.9
Total market	**2,044,609**	**2,264,737**	**+10.8**	**100.0**	**100.0**

Source: The Society of Motor Manufacturers and Traders (SMMT), January 2014

1 How large was the market for new cars in the UK in 2013? *(1 mark)*

2 What was the percentage change in market growth between 2012 and in 2013? *(2 marks)*

3 Which company was the market leader? *(1 mark)*

4 Between 2012 and 2013, Ford had the largest increase in the number (volume) of cars sold. Calculate their increase in sales volume. *(2 marks)*

5 Between 2012 and 2013, which firm had the largest percentage increase in its sale of cars? *(1 mark)*

6 Hyundai fell from tenth to eleventh place in the UK market in 2013, despite recording a sales increase of 3.5% between 2012 and 2013. If Hyundai sold 76,918 cars in 2013, how many cars did it sell in 2012? *(3 marks)*

7 Why might the use of volume (the number of cars sold) give a misleading impression of the market share of a car manufacturer? *(4 marks)*

8 How was it possible for Ford to have the largest increase in sales volume and yet experience a decrease in its market share? *(7 marks)*

9 Volkswagen occupies third place in terms of UK market share. However, Volkswagen is part of a business that also owns Audi, Skoda and Seat (fourth, thirteenth and nineteenth in the market). Explain why a firm might make a decision to use different brand names for different cars in this way. *(8 marks)*

10 Analyse *three* factors that might influence the market size of the new car market in the UK. *(9 marks)*

11 Evaluate the usefulness of the information in Table 7.2 to a Chinese car manufacturer that wishes to establish itself in the UK market for new cars. *(12 marks)*

External influences on marketing objectives and decisions

External influences are those outside the business, such as the state of the economy and the actions of competitors.

Market factors

The growth or decline of a market will have a major impact on a business's marketing objectives. Organisations such as Apple can set ambitious growth targets as mobile communication is becoming increasingly popular, so the market is growing. However, DVD manufacturers, which were once in a growth market, are now likely to be setting survival targets rather than ones based on high growth and profits.

A change in market factors is likely to affect the decisions of staff in the marketing department. If market factors are hindering growth, additional money may need to be spent on marketing activities such as promotions and advertising. In certain cases it may require a change to the marketing objective, if the original objective is now proving to be unrealistic.

Competitors' actions and performance

If the market is highly competitive, such as dairy farming, it is difficult for an individual farmer to achieve a high market share. For this reason, many farmers are now starting to target niche markets, such as sales through farmers' markets, in which there is less direct competition. Such decisions will have an impact on marketing objectives such as market positioning and targeted market share. Ideally, a business will have anticipated the strategies of its competitors and have incorporated these ideas into its marketing objectives and decisions. However, competitors may well introduce new strategies and so these objectives and decisions may need to be modified so that the actions of competitors do not have a negative effect on the business's performance.

Technological change

Technology is a major cause of rapid change in consumer tastes and markets and this can make it more challenging for a business to set realistic marketing objectives. Businesses that can use technology effectively in their marketing, as Amazon and eBay have, will benefit from increased growth and an ability to set and reach ambitious marketing objectives. The pace of technological change requires businesses to constantly adapt their decision making to take into consideration new opportunities and threats offered by changes in technology. Technology has developed most businesses' understanding of their markets, through mechanisms such as loyalty cards and electronic point-of-sale (EPOS). This enables businesses to focus their marketing activities, enabling them to set more ambitious objectives and rely on promotions geared towards the needs and preferences of individual customers, rather than relying on broad advertising aimed at the market as a whole.

Economic factors

This is a very important influence on marketing objectives for most businesses. Some economic factors are outlined in Chapter 3, with more detailed coverage of economic factors being provided in your Year 2 textbook.

Growth or recession in the economy

If the economy is growing rapidly, customers will be purchasing more products, and therefore higher targets for sales and prices can be included in the business's marketing objectives. In the recessions of 2008–2009 and 2011–2012, GDP fell and consumers tended to cut back on purchases. These periods of recession had a major impact on many business's marketing decisions. In recent years the long-established supermarkets have needed to react to the emergence of low-cost retailers such as Lidl and Aldi. In the clothing market, companies such as Primark have enjoyed significant growth.

Interest rates

If interest rates are high it becomes more expensive for consumers to borrow money in order to purchase goods and services. As a consequence, demand for many products will usually fall. Higher interest rates tend to have a greater impact on products that are normally bought on credit, such as houses, cars and household durables. High interest rates may also encourage people to save rather than spend money and so demand will fall further. In recent years the UK has enjoyed record low levels of interest rates. This has helped boost sales of many businesses, particularly those involved in the housing market.

Suppliers

It is vital that a firm's marketing objectives take into consideration the capability of its suppliers to provide whatever the business believes can be sold. For this reason, many businesses deliberately source supplies of vital materials from a variety of different businesses, rather than relying on one major supplier.

The efficiency, cost effectiveness, quality, reliability and flexibility of suppliers will all influence the ability of businesses to meet the needs of their customers. A supplier that provides cost-effective products of high quality will help a business to achieve higher sales and higher prices. Suppliers can be a major constraint for marketing departments, particularly if the department wants to make claims about the qualities of its product. Sainsbury's target to obtain all of its fish from sustainable sources is timed for 2020, as its existing suppliers cannot meet that target at present.

Ethical and environmental factors

Environmental considerations are of growing importance and most businesses have adapted their marketing objectives so that they can demonstrate to consumers that they produce environmentally friendly products in an efficient manner.

Many consumers feel strongly about the potentially negative impact that business activities can have on our planet's resources. This has led to significant increases in demand for environmentally friendly products and manufacturing processes.

In order to prevent the possibility of damage to its brand image and the consequent decline in sales of its products, businesses must ensure that they respond to this desire for environmentally friendly decisions and actions. There has also been considerable growth in the number of consumers who consider themselves to be ethical (doing the 'right' thing).

Governments may also introduce legislation to ensure that businesses behave ethically – examples being legislation concerning child labour and working conditions. Behaving ethically can also open up market niches, with premium prices being charged for products such as fair trade tea and fair trade coffee. These higher prices often reflect the willingness of consumers to pay more for ethical products. They may also reflect higher costs as businesses make more generous payments to suppliers and their workers.

Other external factors

Some of the other external factors that influence the ability of a business to sell its products, and therefore its marketing objectives, are noted below.

Political factors

Government policies and pressures on issues such as child welfare and obesity have led to the advertising industry introducing voluntary restrictions on advertising during children's television programmes. This has impacted negatively on the sales of some products and led to changes in both advertising and the products themselves. Businesses involved in international marketing, in particular, need to be aware of any political developments that might influence their target markets, so that marketing decisions can be amended, if necessary.

Legal factors

Legal requirements can act as a constraint, as in the case of the ban on cigarette advertising on television. They can also act as an opportunity: for example, the need for greater safety has led to the growth of businesses providing safety equipment and training. Legislation also limits the claims that marketing departments can make about their products.

Author advice

The factors considered here are a summary of the external influences on a business's marketing and therefore on its marketing objectives and decisions. However, their precise impact will vary considerably between firms, according to the products they make and the markets within which they compete.

Internal influences on marketing objectives and decisions

Internal influences are those factors within a business, such as its workforce, resources and financial position.

Business/corporate objectives

The overall aims of the organisation are a key influence on functional objectives. The marketing department must therefore ensure that its objectives are consistent with the corporate objectives of the business. For example, Harrods has always tried to maintain a reputation for quality as a corporate objective. Consequently, the marketing department must make sure that its marketing objectives are based on quality. For this reason, brand image and loyalty are important objectives and influence decisions about the items that the business sells.

▲ Harrods' marketing objectives are based on quality

Finance

A business with a healthy financial situation can afford to put more resources into its marketing and therefore can set more challenging objectives. The marketing department will have limited funds available – the marketing budget. This is the amount of money that a firm allocates to spend on marketing activities. This money may be used for activities such as market research, advertising and sales promotions. Firms will often allocate a relatively large part of the marketing budget to any new product in order to allow it to become established in the marketplace. However, usually the marketing budget will depend on the level of sales of the product and the intensity of competition within its market. In the UK, on average, firms spend less than 2 per cent of their sales income on advertising and promotion, but in some industries, such as soap powders, this figure is much higher. Many firms have reduced their marketing budget in recent years and focused more on social media and internet-based promotions. Ultimately, the marketing department must compete with other functional areas, such as human resources, for the finances available within a business. Larger budgets should be allocated to the departments that will use the money most effectively in order to achieve the business's overall objectives.

Human resources (HR)

Marketing objectives must take into account the size and capabilities of the workforce. A motivated, efficient and productive workforce will affect marketing. Marketing objectives such as higher market share and improved reputation depend on the quality of the human resources within the business. Consequently, changes of staff and their training and skills may impact on the objectives and decisions taken by the marketing department.

Operational issues

The operations management of the business is critical if it is seeking to provide products at low cost or of high quality. For example, supermarkets rely heavily on the operations department to ensure that high quality, fresh products are available within stores. Furthermore, the operations department is also critical in ensuring that 'click and collect' services and

125

online customers get their products promptly and in good condition. The marketing objectives must be consistent with the operations department's approach. If the marketing plan is aiming to create an upmarket, quality image, it is vital that the operations department can manufacture products of a high enough quality to meet this requirement. High quality after-sales service will also be necessary if this target is to be achieved, especially if the marketing department has emphasised this as a key element of its plan.

Resources available

In the long term, resource availability is closely related to the financial circumstances of the business. A business in a strong financial situation can purchase whatever resources are required to achieve ambitious marketing objectives.

Nature of the product

This factor acts as both an opportunity and a constraint on marketing objectives. The popularity of the product is a key factor. Organisations such as Sony have earned a reputation for high-quality products in areas such as audio systems and games consoles. This leads to considerable word-of-mouth advertising and makes it difficult for competition to enter the market. Consequently, Sony is normally able to target high market share as one of its marketing objectives. However, the fact that the value of the Sony brand has fallen in recent years has led to a 30 per cent increase in its marketing budget in order to restore its brand image and improve brand loyalty.

Practice exercise 2
Total: 60 marks

1 Which of the following is an **internal** factor that might influence a firm's marketing objectives?
   a) Changes in suppliers
   b) Growth of the economy
   c) Level of skills of its employees
   d) New legislation
   (1 mark)

2 What does the formula below measure?

$$\frac{\text{Market size in Year} - \text{Market size in previous year}}{\text{Market size in previous year}} \times 100$$

   a) Market size
   b) Market growth
   c) Market share
   (1 mark)

3 Analyse two advantages that a restaurant might gain from setting marketing objectives. *(9 marks)*

4 Analyse two possible problems involved in using marketing objectives to assess the performance of the marketing department. *(9 marks)*

5 Explain one advantage and one disadvantage of using market share as a marketing objective. *(8 marks)*

6 In Chapter 1 the concept of SMART objectives was introduced. Give four examples of SMART marketing objectives. *(4 marks)*

7 What problem might arise if a firm's marketing department ignored its corporate objectives? *(4 marks)*

8 Analyse two reasons why a printing company would set marketing objectives. *(6 marks)*

9 Identify and explain two internal factors that might influence a fashion retailer's marketing objectives. *(9 marks)*

10 Identify and explain two external factors that might influence a fashion retailer's marketing objectives. *(9 marks)*

Case study: Vodafone's marketing objectives

Among its key performance indicators, Vodafone Group plc has five targets that are the prime responsibility of the marketing function:

1 To maximise growth in sales revenue from its services. This objective is a key element of Vodafone's marketing, and the company aims to achieve it by increasing both its customer numbers and increasing average revenue from each customer.

2 To increase significantly the percentage of consumer mobile phone contracts that integrate voice, text and data, rather than focusing on one of these services. Integrated contracts are seen by mobile phone providers to be the best way of attracting customers and also ensuring that an individual buys all of these services from the same company.

3 To increase Vodafone's sales of smartphones as a percentage of handsets bought by customers in Europe. Originally this objective was that 35 per cent of Vodafone customers would have smartphones by March 2013. This objective has now been updated to the achievement of 50 per cent having smartphones by March 2015.

4 To gain or maintain market share (measured by value rather than volume) in most of the company's markets.

5 To increase or maintain the number of markets where Vodafone is ranked number one for brand loyalty, using consumer net promoter score (NPS).

▼ **Table 7.3** Vodafone's review of its marketing objectives, 2011–2013

Marketing objective	2011	2012	2013	Comment
Sales revenue growth	+2.1 %	+1.5%	−1.9%	'More work to do'. Target missed in 2013 because of economic difficulties and cuts to meet new regulations in some countries
Integrated contracts	27%	44%	67%	Objective 'achieved'
% of customers using smartphones	19%	27%	36%	Objective 'achieved' in 2013 and 'on-track' for 2015
Market share gained or held	9/17 markets	11/17 markets	9/17 markets	Objective 'achieved' from 2011 to 2013 and 'on-track' for future years
To increase the number of markets in which Vodafone has highest brand loyalty (NPS)	8/20 markets	11/21 markets	8/21 markets	Generally high achievement but 'more work to do' to meet the objective set.

Vodafone's review of the mobile phone market from 2013

As a company, Vodafone has established high levels of brand loyalty and a well-developed infrastructure to support mobile networks around the world. It is one of the market leaders in a wide range of large countries.

Recent developments within the company have enabled it to target rapid growth in 3G and 4G mobile services. In recent years, Vodafone's growth in both Europe and North America has been disappointing, largely due to economic difficulties in those areas. However, this has been offset by Vodafone's continued growth in emerging markets, such as India. Vodafone's large scale enables it to be cost competitive in its markets and thus able to offer competitive prices. The company has identified future cost reductions that will save £300 million in Europe alone.

In 2002, the number of mobile phones was equivalent to 18 per cent of the world's population. By 2012 this had increased to 93 per cent, although this figure is influenced by some individuals possessing more than one mobile phone. Most of this recent growth has come from emerging markets, in which 90 per cent of the population now possess mobile phones. This growth has been aided by the lack of land lines in some countries. Future growth in mobile phones is also expected to come from emerging markets.

The industry is dominated by large firms that compete fiercely for market share. The market is also very heavily regulated by national governments and mobile phone providers must comply with licensing arrangements and restrictive legislation. 75 per cent of revenue comes from traditional phone calls, but internet browsing and email are growing rapidly and are expected to represent the majority of the future growth opportunities in the market. Advances in technology are a feature of this industry, with unified communications services and faster mobile networks being particular features of recent and future changes. External factors will continue to exert a considerable influence on Vodafone's marketing objectives and its marketing decisions.

Source: adapted from Chief Executive's Review and Industry Trends, from Vodafone plc Annual Report 2013

Questions

Total: 60 marks

1 Based on its marketing objectives and achievements between 2011 and 2013, some analysts believe that Vodafone's marketing decision making was at its best in 2012. Do you agree? Justify your view. *(20 marks)*

2 To what extent do you think that the achievements of Vodafone's marketing department indicate that the company's marketing objectives have been chosen well? *(20 marks)*

3 Do you believe that external factors are more likely to influence Vodafone's marketing objectives than internal factors? Justify your view. *(20 marks)*

8

Understanding markets and customers

Businesses need to understand their market. The value of market research is introduced in this chapter, and comparisons are made between primary and secondary market research and between qualitative and quantitative research data. Market mapping and the value of sampling in market research are also considered. The chapter then examines how marketing data is interpreted, looking at confidence intervals and considering the use of both correlation and extrapolation in the analysis of marketing data. A brief overview of the value of technology in gathering and analysing data for marketing decision making is provided. Detailed explanations of the concepts of price elasticity of demand and income elasticity of demand are given and their value to businesses explained. The chapter concludes with a summary of the use of data in marketing decision making.

Value of primary and secondary marketing research

Market research is undertaken for descriptive, explanatory, predictive and exploratory reasons.

> **Key term**
>
> **Market research** The systematic and objective collection, analysis and evaluation of information that is intended to assist the marketing process.

Descriptive reasons

The collection and analysis of data allows organisations to identify a number of important pieces of information:

- **Achieving objectives**: has the firm achieved its target sales figure or its desired percentage market share?
- **Identifying trends**: are sales rising or falling? Is the trend stable or unpredictable?
- **Comparisons**: how are the firm's sales performing relative to a competitor? Is its advertising expenditure matching its rivals? Is it appealing to the same market segments?

Explanatory reasons

Market research can help an organisation to investigate *why* certain things occur.

Predictive reasons

Information can be used to predict trends and find links between sets of data. This will help the business to predict what may happen in the future.

Exploratory reasons

On occasions, such as when a new product is introduced, there will be no existing information to guide an organisation. In this situation, a business may conduct research into the probable consumer reaction to a product or its marketing.

Types of market research

Market research is classified in two ways, according to:

- how the data are collected (**primary** or **secondary market research**)
- the content of the data (quantitative or qualitative).

> **Key terms**
>
> **Primary market research** Collection or commissioning of information, gathered first-hand, for the specific purpose of the initial user.
>
> **Secondary market research** Information that has already been collected for a different purpose.

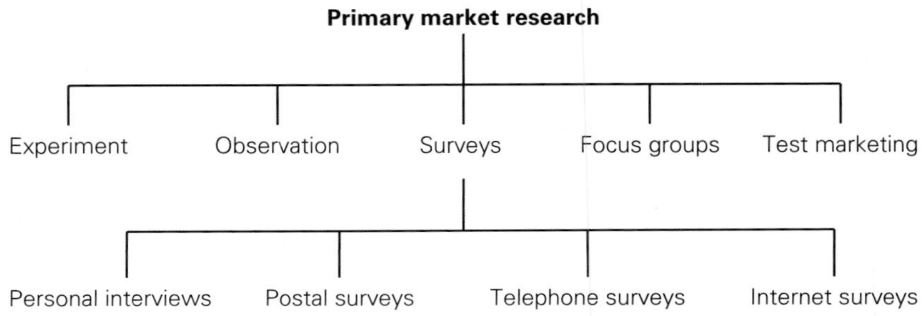

▲ **Figure 8.1** Types of primary market research

Primary market research

Although called 'primary', primary research actually comes second – it should only be used to complete the gaps that cannot be filled by secondary data. Because researchers often need to go out (into the field) to collect primary data, it is frequently called field research.

There are several methods of conducting primary research, each with its own benefits and drawbacks. Organisations will select the types of primary market research that meet their particular needs. The overall value of primary market research can be assessed by the benefits and drawbacks of the individual methods.

Experiment

An organisation experiments with a particular approach in certain areas or for a certain time. If successful, it then uses this approach nationally or on a more long-term basis. For example, Coca-Cola introduced Vanilla flavour as a Limited Edition experimental drink in 2013, but it was so popular that it has become a permanent flavour. Similarly, experiments by Greggs led to its decision to not offer Stotties (a flat round loaf that originated in the North East) in its southern stores.

The benefits of experiment are:

● It is a relatively cheap way of finding out customer preferences.
● It considers actual customer behaviour rather than opinions given in a questionnaire.

The drawbacks of experiment are:

● Consumer behaviour may not be the same throughout the country.
● It may delay the introduction of a potentially successful strategy.

Observation

Stores watch customers while they are shopping and gather information on customer reactions and thought processes. This enables the stores to gain useful data, such as the displays or offers that seem to attract the most interest. Psychologists are employed to offer opinions on customer reactions.

The benefits of observation are:

● The layout of displays can be modified if observation reveals any problems. For example, supermarkets used to place small packages of products on the top shelves, as they yielded lower profits, until observations showed that many of these products were required by elderly customers who were unable to reach them.
● Observation examines actual customer behaviour in detail and can sometimes show what customers are thinking.

The drawbacks of observation are:

● It is expensive to employ specialist psychologists to observe relatively limited behaviour.
● It shows what is happening rather than why it is taking place.

Focus groups

A group of consumers is encouraged to discuss their feelings about a product or market. Typically, focus groups meet at times convenient to their members, such as weekends and evenings.

The benefits of focus groups are:

● They enable a firm to gather detailed information on why consumers react in the way that they do, and can help a business to modify products according to these comments or to identify gaps in the marketplace.
● They can help to uncover new ideas on how to market products or services.

The drawbacks of focus groups are:

● There is sometimes an element of bias in focus groups, as the groups consist of people who have a particular interest in the product and may also want to please the company. Consequently, their views may be less critical than those of the average consumer.
● They are expensive to operate. A single focus group can often cost between £500 and £4,000.

Surveys

Consumers are questioned about a product or service. Surveys can take a number of forms, but usually involve the completion of a questionnaire that is designed to collate the characteristics and views of a cross-section of consumers. The main types of survey are listed below.

Personal interviews

These are conducted face-to-face, with the interviewer filling in the answers given by the interviewee.

The benefits of interviews are:

- A wide range of information can be obtained because questions can be closed (where a limited choice of answers is allowed) or open (where the interviewee chooses what to say). Closed questions are easy to collate and compare; open questions are better if *qualitative* information is needed.
- The interviewer can explain any uncertainties in the wording of the question to the interviewee, thus avoiding the possibility of answers that are misleading because of misinterpretation.

The drawbacks of interviews are:

- Personal interviews can be time-consuming, particularly as members of the public may be reluctant to answer questions.
- The person responding may give false answers to please the interviewer.
- The interviewer may not select an unbiased cross-section of the public.

Postal surveys

Surveys are posted to the addresses of potential customers, who are then expected to complete them at home and return them, usually in a prepaid envelope.

The benefits of postal surveys are:

- They are cheap, especially if the surveys are posted by hand rather than through the mail.
- It allows specific targeting of geographical areas.
- It may avoid the possible bias of a personal interview survey.
- Respondents have longer to answer the questions, so more detailed answers may be given.

The drawbacks of postal surveys are:

- Response rates are usually low (often less than 2 per cent are returned if no incentive is given).
- There is no guarantee that the responses are representative, as people completing them may have a strong opinion (or a great deal of spare time).
- Businesses often offer gifts or competition entries to encourage more replies, adding to their expense.

Telephone interviews

A market researcher telephones members of the public, seeking their answers to particular questions. Telephone interviews are particularly popular with businesses that are trying to get an opinion and often involve questions related to the recent purchase of a consumer durable such as a car or white goods (e.g. a refrigerator or washing machine).

The benefits of telephone interviews are:

● Telephone calls are cheap to make.
● They can be targeted directly at known customers.

The drawbacks of telephone interviews are:

● Detailed questions are difficult, as most interviewees are reluctant to spend too much time on the telephone.
● The increased use of unpopular telesales (often initially disguised as a survey) has led to customer resentment and a reluctance to engage in this type of research.

Internet surveys

Questionnaires on internet sites enable customers to express their views about a product, service or company, giving valuable information to the business whose website is visited.

The benefits of internet surveys are:

● It is relatively inexpensive to place a questionnaire on a website.
● Responders are most likely to be interested in buying the product, as they have made a conscious decision to visit the website. Therefore, response rates are much higher than for postal surveys.
● The surveys can be updated frequently, generating excellent topical data for the firm.
● It may be possible to use a detailed questionnaire, particularly if the respondent has an incentive to complete it.

The drawbacks of internet surveys are:

● The sample will tend to be biased towards people with a particular interest in the product or service.
● They will be less relevant for organisations whose target market does not use the internet.

Author advice

Make sure that you do not confuse 'telephone interviews', which are a method of gaining market research data, with 'telesales', which are a form of direct selling. These two concepts are easily confused because telesales are invariably introduced to the customer as market research, but the telephone caller then attempts to persuade the customer to buy a product or service.

Fact file

Market research and marketing

Market research is also used to adjust marketing strategies or to see if marketing has been successful.

● Costa regularly tests new marketing approaches to see if they will aid growth. At the time of writing (October 2014) it is offering a 25 per cent discount on drinks between 3 p.m. and 5 p.m. in 20 of its stores.

● Independent taste tests confirmed that Carlsberg should introduce a sweeter tasting lager – Carlsberg Citrus, with 70 per cent of the target market preferring it to competitors' products.

● Following a 15 per cent fall in sales of Special K breakfast cereal, market research led to the first change in the recipe for 30 years, with wholegrain being used and barley added to the wheat and rice recipe.

Secondary market research

Secondary information is found by examining published documents (also known as desk research). Firms may be able to save a great deal of money by using data that have already been compiled. As market research is never going to be 100 per cent reliable, it is often more cost effective to accept cheap, reasonably accurate and fairly relevant secondary research than to spend money on primary research. Primary research can then be used to fill any gaps.

Secondary research data can take many forms. Firms will select data that suit their particular purposes. Some key sources are described below.

- **Government publications**: the Office for National Statistics (ONS) provides information on economic and social trends that firms can use to investigate the implications for their business. Detailed surveys on individual industries are also prepared. The Census of Population provides a detailed survey once every ten years.
- **Newspapers**: broadsheet newspapers such as *The Times* and *Guardian* contain articles on specific industries and more general features.
- **Magazines**: publications such as *The Economist*, *Media Week* and *Grocer Today* can provide helpful data in the form of articles and surveys.
- **Company records**: the company's own records, sales figures, accounts and previous surveys are an easily accessible source and have no cost attached (they are secondary sources because they are not going to be used for their original purpose).
- **Competitors**: brochures, promotional materials, company reports and investor information can help a firm to study its rivals' actions.
- **Market research organisations**: in addition to conducting primary research, organisations such as Mintel and Dun & Bradstreet produce detailed secondary surveys, the results of which can be purchased by firms.
- **Loyalty cards**: cards such as Nectar allow a range of businesses to identify the spending patterns of consumers and target them with relevant promotions.
- **Internet**: this is a major source of secondary data, but it should be treated with caution as it may lack the reliability of the other sources listed.

Benefits of secondary market research

The benefits of secondary market research to a business vary according to the relevance and detail of the data, and whether it is reliable and up to date. Beyond these factors, the main benefits are as follows:

- The information is already available, so quick decisions can be taken based upon it.
- It is cheaper than primary research; for some government research and the business's own information, it will be free. Market research organisations usually charge for their general research, but the expenses are shared between different organisations, making the cost cheaper.
- Secondary surveys are often conducted regularly, so the information obtained is particularly helpful in identifying trends over time.

▲ Loyalty cards are a valuable source of customer information

Drawbacks of secondary market research

- The information may be dated and therefore could be misleading.
- Since the information is available to other organisations, it is unlikely to give the business any advantages over its competitors.
- There may be no relevant secondary data to meet the specific needs of the business.
- As the data are collected by other organisations for their own use, the secondary user may not know the level of accuracy and reliability of the data. Consequently, there is a danger that over-reliance on the data could lead to poor marketing decisions.

Qualitative market research

Market research may be classified in terms of its content into qualitative or quantitative research.

Qualitative market research deals with issues such as 'why?' or 'how?' With this information, ITV might be able to see why people watch *Emmerdale*: is it the quality of the acting, the stunning scenery or the brilliance of the story lines? An organisation can use the information gained from qualitative research to plan appropriate strategies. For example, Sky has been able to attract more advertisers to its football programmes as a result of market research showing that football matches are watched by larger groups of people than other programmes. The normal measure of demand (the number of television sets being used) therefore underestimated the number of people actually watching the programme.

Benefits of qualitative market research

- By examining why consumers behave in a certain way, the business can gain a greater insight into what it needs to do to appeal to its consumers. Qualitative market research can be used to gain an insight into why customers buy its products, meaning products can be modified to increase their appeal to new and potential customers, leading to increased sales.
- Qualitative research can highlight issues that the business was not aware of, enabling it to take action to overcome problems or seize opportunities that might not have been considered before.
- Qualitative research can give detailed insights into customers' thinking processes when they buy products. This can enable a business to modify its marketing strategies and methods in order to persuade customers to buy more.

> **Did you know?**
>
> In a survey, 'closed' questions
> (those with a restricted number
> of answers) tend to be used
> to gather quantitative data.
> Qualitative data, in contrast,
> are often gathered by 'open'
> questions (where the respondent
> can record his or her own
> answer), as this gives greater
> accuracy. However, some
> qualitative data are gathered by
> closed questions because where
> there are too many possible
> answers to open questions
> responses are difficult to collate.

> **Key term**
>
> **Market mapping** A technique
> that analyses markets by looking
> at the features that distinguish
> different products or firms.

Drawbacks of qualitative market research

- It is expensive to gather qualitative information, as it usually requires skilled personnel to interpret it. Consequently, most qualitative research is conducted on a small scale. This can lead to bias or unrepresentative opinions.
- It is difficult to tabulate the data and compare it with other data, as opinions are often unstructured. However, if research is too structured, it may inhibit the independence and accuracy of the opinions being expressed.

Quantitative market research

Quantitative market research can answer the following questions: 'how many?', 'who?' and 'how often?' For example, to help sell advertising space or sponsorship during *Emmerdale*, ITV finds it useful to be able to show that the programme is watched by about 5.5 million viewers, averaging 30 per cent of the viewing public. Nearly half of viewers are from social classes D and E, more than any other soap, and about two-thirds of its viewers watch every episode.

Benefits of quantitative market research

- It summarises data in a concise and meaningful way: for example, 8 out of 10 cat owners prefer Whiskas; Nissan has a 5 per cent market share in the UK.
- The use of numerical data makes it easier to compare results with those of other organisations, such as competitors, or other divisions of the same organisation.
- Numerical data can be used to identify trends and project future trends.

Drawbacks of quantitative market research

- It only shows 'what', rather than explaining 'why'. Therefore, the data produced are less useful than the qualitative data in helping an organisation to understand the reasons behind trends.
- It can lack reliability and validity if the sample is biased or too small.

Market mapping

A variety of features may be used in **market mapping**, varying according to the industry/product. In the case of the holiday market, people may buy holidays because they are:

- geared towards providing entertainment for certain demographic groups (e.g. facilities are specifically for families with children or aimed to appeal only to single people)
- cheap and easy to budget (e.g. an all-in-one package tour to a cheap resort)
- scenic, such as beautiful beaches or views
- of historical interest
- warm and sunny
- environmentally friendly (e.g. holidays that appeal to eco-tourists who want to visit relatively undisturbed sites without causing a negative impact).

Interestingly, in relation to the last point some people would argue that eco-tourists may be causing the damage that they wish to prevent, globally. To set against this factor, many eco-tourists try to raise funds to support communities or the environment they are visiting.

Features such as those listed above can be 'mapped' in order to identify the extent to which an individual holiday possesses them. Figure 8.2 shows an example of the market for female clothing. A computer-based model or map can examine any number of factors at the same time, but for convenience it is normal to show the two most important factors in a market map. For the female clothing market, these could be price and fashion. A firm or product at the centre of the map would not be seen to possess either feature significantly. In this market, Karen Millen represents a brand that offers fashionable products and is considered to be set at a premium price (often a measure of quality).

Market maps are useful to businesses because they show the position of each product in relation to the market being studied. In some market maps, circles of varying sizes are used to represent the size or market share of each firm in the map.

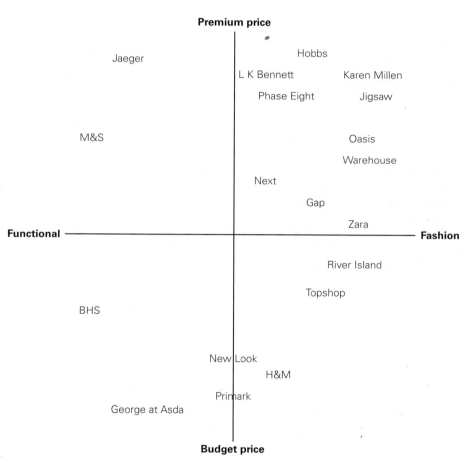

▲ **Figure 8.2** Example of market mapping
Source: adapted from J. Nowacki (2002) *Marketing*, Philip Allan Updates.

Benefits of market mapping

● Helps to identify a firm's closest rivals, in order to plan suitable competitive strategies.
● Helps to identify gaps or niches in the market that a firm could fill by introducing a new product or image.
● If carried out through market research, it can help a firm to understand the public's perception of an organisation as a business or brand.

- It may help a firm that needs to reposition itself in a market.
- Shows the overall level of competition in a market.
- Can be used to assess the relative popularity of the features being considered. For example, market mapping could show recent changes in the popularity of low-price goods as a feature of supermarkets.

Drawbacks of market mapping

- Can be an oversimplification of a product or business's position. For example, a business might be categorised as 'low-price' but have some expensive products within its range of products.
- They are very subjective and thus potentially inaccurate or biased, being based on the opinions of the person who drew up the market map.
- Apparent gaps in a market may exist because consumers are not interested in a certain combination of features. For example, market maps based on quality and price (two very common features of a product) tend to show gaps in the segment showing high price and low quality, because rational customers will not want this combination of features. Similarly, the low price and high quality segment will have gaps because businesses are unlikely to be able to make profit if they offer high quality products at low prices.

Practice exercise 1

Total: 50 marks

1 What is the difference between market research that has been collected for 'explanatory' reasons and market research that has been gathered for 'predictive' reasons? *(6 marks)*

2 Distinguish between primary market research and secondary market research. *(4 marks)*

3 Why might secondary market research be carried out before primary market research? *(4 marks)*

4 A music shop analyses the sales figures of a competitor to improve its understanding of its market. This is an example of:
   a) qualitative primary market research
   b) quantitative primary market research
   c) qualitative secondary market research
   d) quantitative secondary market research. *(1 mark)*

5 Explain one benefit of using personal interviews. *(4 marks)*

6 Explain one problem of using postal surveys. *(4 marks)*

7 State three different sources of secondary market research. *(3 marks)*

8 What is the difference between 'quantitative' and 'qualitative' market research? *(4 marks)*

9 A business operates in a market which includes many well-established competitors that regularly introduce new, innovative products. The business has suffered a significant decline in its sales levels. The Marketing Director believes that the business should focus on gathering secondary market research in order to improve its understanding of this situation. Do you agree? Justify your view. *(20 marks)*

Practice exercise 2

Total: 35 marks

1 What is meant by the term 'market mapping'? *(2 marks)*

2 Figure 8.2 (page 137) shows a market map that uses 'price' and 'fashion' to map different firms in the female clothing market.
   a) Suggest two different ways in which the car market could be mapped. *(2 marks)*
   b) Justify your choices. *(6 marks)*

3 Analyse the possible reasons why there is a cluster of firms in a similar place in the top right-hand quadrant of Figure 8.2. *(9 marks)*

4 Information in Figure 8.2 suggests a gap in the market for functional clothing that is in the middle range of the price levels. Evaluate the advantages and disadvantages of setting up a business that fills this gap. *(16 marks)*

Value of sampling

Sampling methods

There are a variety of methods that businesses can use when **sampling**. The most well-known method is random sampling. This occurs when each member of the target population has an equal chance of being chosen. Other methods include quota sampling and stratified sampling. These methods are usually based on obtaining a sample that reflects the types of consumers from whom the business wishes to gain information. For example, a business may focus its sampling on a certain gender or age to reflect its customers or potential customers.

Sample accuracy

Primary market research is undertaken by sampling the views of a limited selection of consumers. Sample size measures the number of people or items in the sample. When conducting primary research, a firm needs to balance the need for accuracy against the cost of the survey. Large samples increase reliability but cost more. Small samples decrease costs but are less reliable.

The degree to which the statistics are a reliable predictor of actual events is known as the confidence level. For example, a 95 per cent confidence level means that the prediction will be correct 19 times out of 20 (95 per cent of the time).

Opinion polling organisations estimate that they need to survey 2,000 (carefully selected) voters in order to be able to predict, with a 2 per cent margin of error, the voting intentions of the approximately 46 million voters in the UK. However, such organisations normally want a higher confidence level than a business conducting market research because their results will be closely scrutinised by the public.

Most businesses will have much smaller target markets than 46 million people and will not require such a high level of accuracy. A sample size that is large enough to give 95 per cent confidence in the results is usually acceptable. This may not involve huge surveys – often fewer than 1 per cent

> **Key term**
>
> **Sampling** Gathering data from a group of respondents whose views or behaviour should be representative of the target market as a whole.

of the target market. In some cases, however, such as research into the side-effects of prescription drugs, much higher levels of certainty are needed.

Benefits of sampling

- Asking a small group of customers or potential customers can provide a good indication of the likely behaviour of the whole market.
- Using sampling before making marketing decisions, such as the launch of a new product, can avoid expensive marketing errors.
- Sampling can be used flexibly. It can allow the business to focus its information gathering on a small market segment, possibly a new target market, or focus on the whole market. Similarly, sampling can be adapted to different needs. Small samples can be used if complex information is required; larger samples if only brief responses are required.
- Reliable information can be gathered from a fairly small cross-section of people. For a product that sells to the whole country, such as bread, reliable results can be gained from a sample of 2,000 people. Most businesses will use much smaller samples than this.
- It enables a business to learn about its market more quickly than if it tries to obtain a wide range of opinions. This means that the business can act quickly and gain an advantage over its competitors.

Drawbacks of sampling

- Samples may be unrepresentative (e.g. they may target the wrong people).
- There may be bias in questions or in the answers that they encourage (e.g. questions such as 'Do you clean your teeth every day?')
- It may be difficult to locate suitable respondents (e.g. people who listen to a particular radio programme).
- For reliable results, sampling should be based on an accurate profile of consumers of a particular product. However, the business may not have an accurate profile of its consumers. In fact, discovering the profile of its consumers might be the aim of the market research it is undertaking!
- In markets in which tastes are constantly changing, such as the music industry, the time taken to carry out and process the data from a sample may mean that the opinions registered are out of date.

Overall, sampling is most valuable if accurate results are obtained in a cost-effective manner.

Interpretation of marketing data

This section examines some of the statistical techniques used in the interpretation of marketing data:

- confidence intervals
- correlation
- extrapolation.

All three techniques are used for forecasting, particularly the prediction of future levels of sales.

Understanding the concept of confidence intervals

Confidence intervals are used to assess the reliability of sampled data when trying to forecast figures such as sales levels.

Market research results tend to be quoted as ranges. For example, company 'X' expects to sell between 38 and 42 products or have a market share of 38–42 per cent. This is because samples can only give an estimate of the exact figure.

Although a sample may conclude that 36 per cent of people asked will buy a product, there is a chance that the cross-section (sample) of people asked is not an accurate reflection of the whole population, especially if the sample is small. Therefore, the result shown may have a confidence interval of + or −4, meaning the survey shows that there is a high chance that 36 per cent of the whole population (+ or −4%) will buy the product. The conclusion drawn is that between 32 per cent and 40 per cent of the whole population will buy the product.

The degree to which statistics are a reliable predictor of actual events is known as the **confidence level**. For example, a 95 per cent confidence level means that the prediction will be correct 19 times out of 20 (95 per cent of the time). Many businesses use 95 per cent as their choice of confidence level.

Combining the confidence interval and the confidence level allows a qualified conclusion to be drawn from the sampling. So in the example above, a 95 per cent confidence level means that 95 per cent of the time the number of buyers will fall between 32 per cent and 40 per cent of the whole target market.

Factors influencing the confidence interval

A business will try to work within a fairly low margin of error (low confidence interval) so that it can be more confident of its conclusions. There are three main factors that influence the size of the confidence interval for a given confidence level:

1 **Sample size**: the larger the sample size, the more sure a business can be that the answer provided by a sample is a true reflection of the opinion of the total population. As the sample size increases the confidence interval falls, but the relationship is not proportional as a significant increase in sample size may only lead to a small fall in the confidence interval.

2 **Population size**: this represents the target population for the product/ service being surveyed. Population size has only a minor impact on the confidence interval. A given sample size can be almost as accurate in predicting the behaviour of 50,000 people as it is for predicting the

> **Key term**
>
> **Confidence interval** (or **margin of error**) The plus or minus figure used to show the accuracy of statistical results arising from sampling.

behaviour of 50 million people. Large increases in population size only cause a small increase in the confidence interval/margin of error.

3 **Percentage of sample choosing a particular answer**: if very high or very low percentages of a sample express a particular opinion, there is less margin of error and so the confidence interval will be low. For example, if 98 per cent of a sample of 500 people say they will buy a product, it is likely to be highly accurate, even if the total population is 20 million people. However, if a more central figure results, such as 49 per cent, then there is likely to be a much larger margin of error/ confidence interval.

Confidence intervals are useful for a business when it tries to understand the results of its surveys. They can be used to find the likelihood of achieving a certain sales target or ascertaining whether a new product is likely to be preferred to an existing one.

Positive and negative correlation and an understanding of the strength of the relationship

Businesses will attempt to forecast sales by examining measurable factors, such as price, advertising budgets and consumers' incomes, all of which are expected to have an influence on sales levels. The relationship between such data and the business's sales levels is known as **correlation**.

Correlation is a useful technique for sales forecasting, as it can show (statistically or graphically) the degree to which factors such as price, the advertising budget or even external factors, such as the proximity of competitors, are linked to sales of a product.

Graphically, the correlation between two sets of data is shown in a scatter diagram or scatter graph. The independent variable (the one causing the other to change) is plotted on the horizontal, x-axis. The dependent variable (the one being influenced) is plotted on the vertical, y-axis. So if we are trying to look at different factors that influence sales of a product, we plot sales on the y-axis and the other factor on the x-axis.

Once the points have been plotted, a line of best fit (or regression line) is added. The line can be drawn graphically 'by eye' but is more accurate if calculated mathematically. (An Excel spreadsheet will construct a scatter graph and will then calculate and add the line of best fit (regression line) to any pairs of data that need to be compared.)

The line of best fit (regression line) is used to forecast. For any value of x, a line is drawn vertically until it meets the regression line. From this point, a line is then drawn horizontally to the y-axis in order to read the forecast value of the dependent variable. For example, in Figure 8.3(a) if $x = 20$, we would forecast $y = 4$. In Figure 8.3(b) if $x = 20$, our forecast for y would be 12.

Figure 8.3 shows seven different examples of correlation.

Figures 8.3(a), (b) and (c) show **positive correlation**. This means that as x increases in value, the value of y also increases.

Figures 8.3(d), (e) and (f) show **negative correlation**. This means that as x increases in value, the value of y decreases.

Key term

Correlation A statistical technique used to establish the strength of the relationship between two sets of values.

Figures 8.3(a) and (d) show **perfect correlation**. All of the points plotted lie on the line of best fit. This means that we would expect 100 per cent accuracy in our predictions. In the business world, it is unlikely that any sets of data would ever be linked as closely as this.

Figures 8.3(b) and (e) show **strong** or **high correlation**. The line of best fit is fairly close to the points plotted on the graph, so we could be confident that our forecasts were fairly reliable.

Figure 8.3(c) and (f) show **weak** or **low correlation**. The line of best fit is not close to all of the points, although there is some link between the sets of data. If we were to use the line of best fit to make forecasts, these forecasts would not be reliable.

Figure 8.3(g) shows **no apparent correlation** between the two sets of data. Forecasts should not be made because there is no detectable link between the two variables.

Causal links in correlation

A quote attributed to Mark Twain is: 'There are three kinds of lies – lies, damn lies and statistics.' He was probably thinking about correlation when considering the third type of lie!

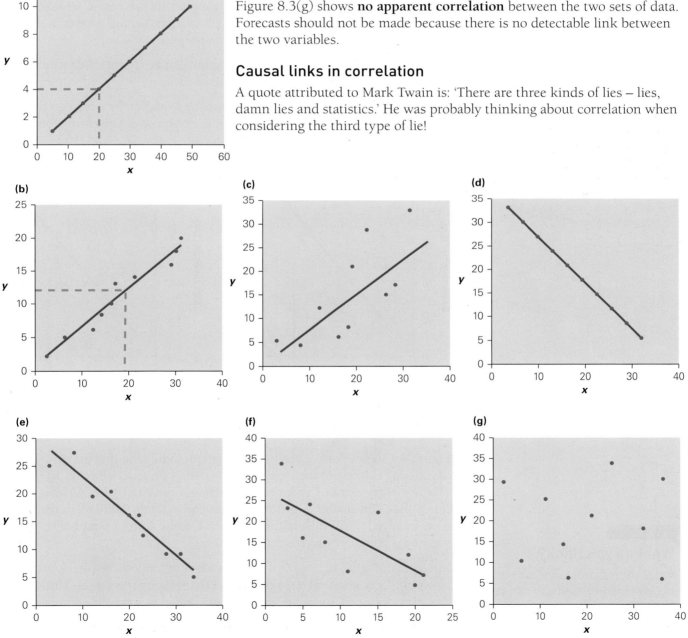

▲ **Figure 8.3 a)** Perfect positive correlation, **b)** Strong/high positive correlation, **c)** Weak/low positive correlation, **d)** Perfect negative correlation, **e)** Strong/high negative correlation, **f)** Weak/low negative correlation, **g)** No apparent correlation

It is highly probable that one set of statistics will correlate with another. After all, over time a set of numbers can go up, go down or stay the same. This limited set of alternatives means that it is possible to find apparently close connections between sets of data purely by coincidence. The rise in obesity in the UK correlates very strongly with the increase in medals for the UK at the 2012 Olympics. However, it is unlikely that the two could be connected!

Before drawing any conclusions that there is a link between two sets of information, it is essential that a **causal link** is discovered. It is logical to expect that more hours of sunshine will cause people to consume more ice cream because of the desire to eat something cool. However, if it was found that more people bought overcoats in the summer, there would be no logic in suggesting that the temperature rise caused this behaviour. Instead we would need to look for other factors (such as shops selling overcoats cheaply at this time of year to get rid of old stock/inventory).

Once a causal link is discovered, correlation can be useful to identify the extent of the link between the two series of data.

There is a tendency to assume that a company would prefer a high correlation to a low correlation. This may be true for the purpose of forecasting, but accurate forecasts are not everything. Compare Figures 8.4 and 8.5.

▲ Is there a causal link between warm weather and ice-cream consumption?

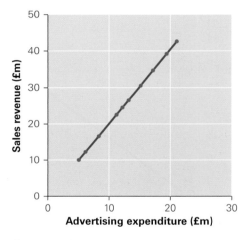

▲ **Figure 8.4** Impact of advertising expenditure on sales revenue

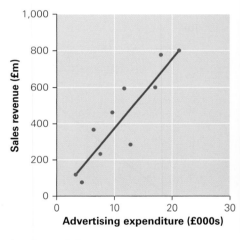

▲ **Figure 8.5** Impact of advertising expenditure on sales revenue

Figure 8.4 shows perfect positive correlation, indicating that extra advertising is likely to increase sales revenue by an exact amount. In this case, for every extra £1 spent on advertising, sales rise by £2. Although this is high correlation, it is not successful advertising. With all of the other costs involved, it is unlikely that a firm can make a profit if half of the sales revenue is going on advertising.

In contrast, Figure 8.5 shows a much lower level of positive correlation. However, look at the regression line and the scale on the y-axis. This shows that every extra £1 spent on advertising is linked to a possible increase in sales revenue of £40. Although the forecast is much less certain, it shows that advertising is probably much more effective in creating extra sales than in the situation described in Figure 8.4.

Key term

Causal link A link between two sets of information or types of behaviour.

What do you think?

Apply your understanding to the business world. Can you suggest any real-life examples of scatter diagrams that might resemble Figures 8.4 and 8.5?

Unit 3 Decision making to improve marketing performance

144

Understanding extrapolation

A trend is the underlying pattern of change indicated within a set of numerical data.

A seasonal variation occurs when there are peaks or troughs at particular, regular times, such as annual peaks in greetings card sales at Christmas and weekly falls in rail travel on Saturdays.

Trend analysis examines the pattern of historic data and assumes that this pattern will continue in the future. If sales of a product have increased at 5 per cent per annum in the recent past, the process of **extrapolation** will forecast that sales will continue to rise by 5 per cent a year. Future sales can therefore be predicted using extrapolation.

Extrapolation can be carried out visually or by calculation, although the latter method is recommended for greater accuracy.

Table 8.1 shows the increase in global sales of smartphones between 2008 and 2013. A smartphone manufacturer such as Samsung might wish to forecast future levels of global sales, in order to estimate its own future sales levels.

▼ **Table 8.1** Global sales of smartphones 2008–2013

Year	Global sales (millions of handsets)
2008	132
2009	168
2010	286
2011	440
2012	710
2013	812

To extrapolate/forecast sales for 2014 onwards we need to calculate the trend (the average increase per annum). Between 2008 and 2013 (5 years), sales rose from 132 million to 812 million, an increase of 680 million. The average annual increase is therefore 680 million divided by 5 = 136 million per annum.

Projecting the trend therefore gives us the forecasts for the next four years shown in Table 8.2.

▼ **Table 8.2** Sales forecast for smartphones, 2014–2018

Year	Global sales (millions of smartphones)
2013	812 (actual sales)
2014	812 + 136 = 948
2015	948 + 136 = 1,084
2016	1,084 + 136 = 1,220
2017	1,220 + 136 = 1,356
2018	1,356 + 136 = 1,492

Of course, this is only an estimate. Using quantitative analysis, it could be argued that the rate of growth is varying (+36 million in 2009, peaking at +270 in 2012 and then only +102 million in 2013). Our method uses the annual average of these different increases, so it does not take into account the fact that the rate of growth has generally increased but then fallen slightly.

145

Key term

Extrapolation Using previous patterns of numerical data in order to predict values in the future.

Did you know?

When choosing the time over which a trend can be found, you should eliminate possible seasonal variations. For this reason, many trends are based on a series of annual figures.

Qualitatively, it could be argued that the global smartphone market is in its growth stage, but might reach maturity soon. This information would lead us to predict further growth in the short term but then a significant slowing down of the rate of growth in a few years' time.

For these reasons, the actual forecast may be based on a combination of methods, such as extrapolation and correlation. Forecasts may also be based on personal opinion (qualitative forecasting).

Figure 8.6 shows the data in Tables 8.1 and 8.2 as a graph. Visually, it is easy to see how the level of sales of smartphones is expected to increase in the future. The line shows that total sales in 2013 were 812 million.

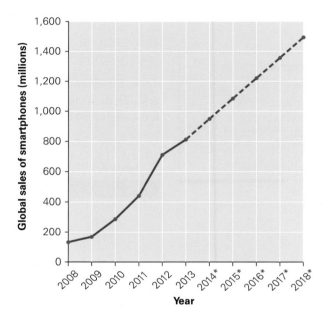

▲ **Figure 8.6** Global sales of smartphones, 2008–2018*
(*Actual = 2008–2013; Forecast = 2014–2018)

Where there is a pattern of change (as in Figure 8.6), it is easy to calculate the trend by calculating the average change for a period of time and extrapolating data into the future, on the assumption that this trend will continue. Global sales have been increasing at a rate of 136 million smartphones per annum in recent years. Based on the 2013 level of 812 million and adding 136 million each year, we can predict global sales in the future.

In Figure 8.6, the dashed (extrapolated) line shows that global sales in the future are forecast to be as follows:

2014: 948 million

2015: 1,084 million

2016: 1,220 million

2017: 1,356 million

Author advice

Always try to use a specific method of forecasting, where possible. You should always look critically at the reliability of the data. In the example above, we are predicting increases of 136 million for every year, but it is clear from the data that the increases have varied considerably from year to year.

Author advice

In many sets of data there are seasonal variations, such as peaks of sales at Christmas or in the summer. For items such as soft drinks, there may be an overall trend showing a fall or rise, but this trend is interspersed with seasonal fluctuations. To predict sales in these cases, the trend must be separated from the fluctuations.

Sales may be increasing at an average rate of 5 per cent per annum, but sales predictions need to be above this trend when the seasonal variation is in favour of the product, or below this trend when the seasonal variation is unfavourable.

Strengths of extrapolation

- It is quite common for past trends to continue into the future.
- Some consumers adopt new ideas more quickly than others and so products experiencing sales growth steadily build up a larger base of customers. A similar process is experienced during a product's decline.
- Businesses will often target a rate of steady growth and so their efforts are focused on future figures that are based on past trends. This may help to ensure that steady growth, based on extrapolating earlier figures, becomes the norm.

Weaknesses of extrapolation

- It is less reliable if there are fluctuations. Seasonal and cyclical changes are rarely repeated exactly and random fluctuations are very unpredictable. Many seasonal factors relate to the weather, which is notoriously unpredictable.
- It assumes that past changes will continue into the future and so does not take into account changes in the business environment that will influence sales, including changes within the business itself.
- It ignores qualitative factors, such as changes in tastes and fashion.
- It ignores the product life cycle, which suggests that most products will experience growth but ultimately decline in sales.

Value of technology in gathering data for marketing decision making

Technology has had dramatic effects on information gathering for marketing purposes. Traditionally, businesses gathered data from their own sales records, from market research surveys and from their sales forces. While these sources are still important, technology now allows businesses to access data in many other ways.

- **Information from business links**: over time, information systems of suppliers, manufacturers and retailers have become more detailed and inter-linked. This means that manufacturers have greater access to more information from retailers concerning the popularity of products and

▲ Social media is being used increasingly in marketing

trends in consumer tastes. They may also get information from suppliers concerning new materials. These data enable them to modify their products or marketing strategies.

- **Internet**: the internet provides a wealth of information, although sources should be scrutinised to ensure that they are reliable.
- **Loyalty cards**: these can create consumer loyalty, but arguably their most important function is to enable a business to gather data on the lifestyles and tastes of its customers. Retailers such as Tesco use this information to target offers specifically to customers that have an interest in a particular product range, increasing their marketing effectiveness.
- **Competitors' websites and data**: technology means that more information is in the public domain, so businesses are able to gain a greater understanding of their markets by accessing information about competitors.
- **Social media**: websites can also enable businesses to target promotional offers. More significantly, social media is being used to enable businesses to gather profiles of the likes and dislikes of their target markets and public opinion on strategies that they adopt.

Value of information technology in analysing data for marketing decision making

Technology is of particular significance in market analysis because it allows businesses to analyse and distribute a wealth of data, often quickly and cost effectively. Some examples of the ways in which technology can assist market analysis are described below.

- Computer software can complete quantitative forecasting calculations almost instantaneously, saving time and money for a business.
- The time saved by technology allows a business to compare a number of different strategies, enabling it to improve its planning.
- Organisations are able to link their sales records to other databases so that every time an item is sold it is registered immediately. This means that any sudden changes in trends or patterns of sales can be detected quickly and the necessary action taken.
- Organisations can use loyalty card data to tailor services or products to individual customer needs.
- The internet or company intranet allows more data to be stored cheaply and accessed more quickly by a wide range of individuals. Sophisticated programs enable businesses to draw up correlations between data and extrapolate changes. However, the vast growth in data means that businesses must be selective in their use of data, as they can be overwhelmed by the variety of analyses possible.
- New analytical software allows businesses to analyse their own sales figures, linking them to promotional campaigns, special offers and even factors such as the weather.

Practice exercise 3

Total: 65 marks

Read the following data on tourism in the UK and answer the questions that follow.

Domestic tourism in the UK: UK tourists visiting UK sites

▼ **Table 8.3** Visitors to coffee shops: main factors influencing choice of coffee shop, based on 95 per cent confidence levels

Factor	% of respondents	Confidence interval (25,000 people surveyed)	Confidence interval if 2,500 people surveyed
Location	45	± 0.62	± 1.95
Quality	31	± 0.57	± 1.81
Atmosphere	21	± 0.50	± 1.67
Price / loyalty card	3	± 0.21	± 0.67

▼ **Table 8.4** Data on UK tourism visits by UK residents, 2006–2013

Column 1: Year	Column 2: GDP (Index number)	Column 3: Domestic holiday visits (millions)
2006	228.0	40.4
2007	244.4	41.3
2008	281.0	39.8
2009	265.7	47.0
2010	217.3	43.5
2011	226.0	46.2
2012	243.2	46.0
2013	244.0	44.9

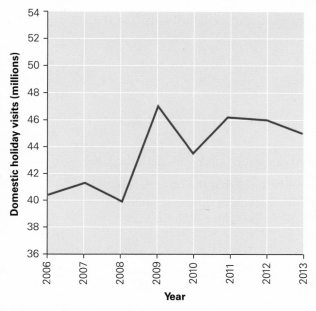

▲ **Figure 8.7** UK tourism visits, 2006–2013

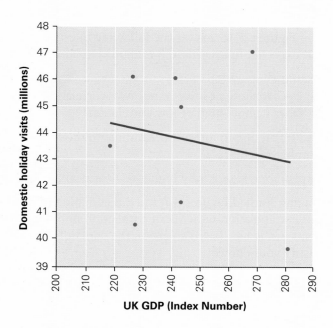

▲ **Figure 8.8** Scatter graph showing GDP level & UK tourism visits, 2006–2013

1 State three possible sources for the data in Table 8.4. *(3 marks)*

2 Explain one way in which technology might be used to analyse the data in Table 8.3. *(5 marks)*

3 Based on Table 8.3, are the following statements **true** or **false**:

   a) We can be 95 per cent certain that between 30.43 per cent and 31.57 per cent of customers rate quality as the most important factor. *(1 mark)*

   b) We can be 95 per cent certain that location is the most important factor influencing choice of coffee shop. *(1 mark)*

   c) We can be 95 per cent certain that fewer than 21 per cent of coffee shop users value the atmosphere most when choosing a coffee shop. *(1 mark)*

   d) If these figures had been acquired from a survey of 2,500 people, we could be 95 per cent certain that more than 30 per cent of coffee shop users believe that quality is the most important factor. *(1 mark)*

4 Explain how a coffee shop might use the data in Table 8.3 to increase its market share. *(6 marks)*

5 Identify two factors that would reduce the confidence interval (margin of error) of a survey. *(2 marks)*

6 Select one of the factors you have chosen in question 5 and explain why that factor would reduce the confidence interval. *(4 marks)*

7 Study Table 8.4. Based on the data in columns 1 and 3, use extrapolation to calculate the annual increase in domestic holiday visits in the UK. Show your working. *(3 marks)*

8 Use your answer in question 7 to forecast the level of domestic holiday visits in the UK for:

   a) 2014 *(2 marks)*

   b) 2017 *(2 marks)*

9 Use your answer in question 7 to answer the following question: In which year are domestic holiday visits in the UK expected to exceed 49.0 million? Show your working. *(4 marks)*

10 Using Figure 8.7, use extrapolation to forecast the level of domestic holiday visits in the UK for:

   a) 2014 *(1 mark)*

   b) 2017 *(1 mark)*

11 Use Figure 8.7 to answer the following question: In which year are domestic holiday visits in the UK expected to exceed 50.0 million? Explain your answer. *(3 marks)*

12 Examine Figure 8.8.

   a) Does it show positive or negative correlation? *(1 mark)*

   b) Does it show high or low correlation? *(1 mark)*

13 Use Figure 8.8 to forecast the number of domestic holiday visits in the UK, if the GDP index number reaches 250. *(1 mark)*

14 Explain one reason why higher GDP appears to lead to a fall in domestic holiday visits in the UK. *(6 marks)*

15 Having studied Figures 8.7 and 8.8, a market research manager believes that the business should use extrapolation rather than correlation in order to forecast future levels of domestic holiday visits in the UK. Based solely on the data in Figures 8.7 and 8.8, do you agree with his view? Justify your choice. *(16 marks)*

Interpretation of price and income elasticity of demand data

Types of elasticity

Elasticity of demand measures the degree to which the demand for a good or service is affected by the value of another variable. There are two main elasticities of demand: **price elasticity of demand** and **income elasticity of demand**.

The formulae for calculating these elasticities are:

$$\text{price elasticity of demand} = \frac{\text{\% change in quantity demanded}}{\text{\% change in price}}$$

$$\text{income elasticity of demand} = \frac{\text{\% change in quantity demanded}}{\text{\% change in income}}$$

Price elasticity of demand

Price elasticity of demand can be elastic, inelastic or unitary:

- **Elastic demand**: if the change in price leads to a greater percentage change in the quantity demanded than the percentage change in price (ignoring the minus sign), the calculation will yield an answer greater than 1. This indicates that demand is relatively responsive to a change in price.
- **Inelastic demand**: if the change in price leads to a smaller percentage change in the quantity demanded than the percentage change in price, the calculation will yield an answer less than 1 (ignoring the minus sign). This indicates that demand is relatively unresponsive to a change in price. When price elasticity demand is 0 (zero) there is no change in quantity demanded when price changes. This is known as perfectly inelastic demand. If price increases by 10 per cent then sales revenue will increase by 10 per cent.
- **Unit (or unitary) elasticity**: this name is given to the situation where both percentage changes are the same, giving an answer of (–)1. In theory, the price change is exactly cancelled out by the change in quantity demanded, so sales revenue stays the same.

Example calculations

Calculation 1: Price falls from 25p to 20p, leading to an increase in quantity demanded from 200 to 220 units.

$$\text{\% change in quantity demanded} = \frac{\text{change in quantity demanded}}{\text{original quantity demanded}} \times 100$$

$$= \frac{(220 - 200)}{200} \times 100 = \frac{+20}{200} \times 100 = +10\%$$

$$\text{\% change in price} = \frac{\text{change in price}}{\text{original price}} \times 100$$

$$= \frac{(20 - 25)}{25} \times 100 = \frac{-5}{25} \times 100 = -20\%$$

$$\text{price elasticity of demand} = \frac{+10}{-20} = (-)0.5$$

An elasticity of −0.5 means that demand is *inelastic, so the demand is not affected very much by the change in price.*

Calculation 2: Price rises from £11 to £13, leading to a decrease in quantity demanded from 76 units to 52 units.

$$\% \text{ change in quantity demanded} = \frac{\text{change in quantity demanded}}{\text{original quantity demanded}} \times 100$$

$$= \frac{52 - 76}{76} \times 100 = \frac{-24}{76} \times 100 = -31.6\%$$

$$\% \text{ change in price} = \frac{\text{change in price}}{\text{original price}} \times 100$$

$$= \frac{(13 - 11)}{11} \times 100 = \frac{+2}{11} \times 100 = +18.2\%$$

$$\text{price elasticity of demand} = \frac{-31.6}{+18.2} = (-)1.7$$

An elasticity of 1.7 means that demand is *elastic, so the price change leads to a significant change in quantity demanded.*

Effect of price elasticity of demand on sales revenue and profit

The effect of price elasticity of demand on sales revenue and profit depends on whether demand is elastic, inelastic or unitary.

Inelastic demand

If demand for a good is inelastic, when its price rises the quantity demanded falls by a smaller percentage. This means that the impact of the price increase will outweigh the relatively small percentage change in demand, so sales revenue will increase. For example, a 50 per cent rise in price from £1 to £1.50 leads to a smaller (20 per cent) fall in sales from 100 to 80 units. Price elasticity is therefore −0.4.

Sales revenue increases from £100 (£1 × 100) to £120 (£1.50 × 80). Does this mean extra profit? The answer is *yes*. The total costs of producing 80 units will be lower than those of producing 100 units, so costs will fall at the same time as revenue increases. Thus, *a price rise will always increase sales revenue and profit if price elasticity of demand is inelastic.* Similarly, *a price fall will lead to lower sales revenue and profit if price elasticity of demand is inelastic.*

Elastic demand

If demand for a good is elastic, when its price rises the quantity demanded falls by a larger percentage. This means that the impact of the price increase will be outweighed by the relatively large percentage change in demand, so sales revenue will decrease. For example, a 20 per cent rise in price from £1 to £1.20 leads to a larger (50 per cent) fall in sales from 100 to 50 units. Price elasticity is therefore −2.5.

Sales revenue decreases from £100 (£1 × 100) to £60 (£1.20 × 50). Does this mean a decrease in profit? The answer is *not necessarily*. It will be cheaper to produce 50 units than 100, so costs will fall as well as income. If costs fall by more than income, profit will still be improved. But if costs fall by a smaller amount, profit will fall. Thus, *a price rise will always decrease sales revenue if price elasticity of demand is elastic, but the effect on profit will depend on cost savings.* The chances of more profit are higher if there is a high profit margin on the good.

In the case of a price fall, the sales revenue of a good with a price elastic demand will always increase. However, the quantity demanded rises and so production costs will rise. Consequently, it is impossible to predict the effect on profits without knowing about the costs of production.

Unitary elasticity

If demand for a good is unitary, sales revenue will be the same whether price rises or falls. A price rise would then be advisable if the business is aiming to increase profit, because this means a lower volume of sales would be required, which would enable production costs to fall. However, the business may not increase price if it has other aims, such as increasing its market share.

The impact of price changes on sales revenue is summarised in Table 8.5.

▼ **Table 8.5** Effect of price changes on sales revenue

Price elasticity of demand (PED)		
Price change	PED → 1 (elastic)	PED = 1 (unitary)	PED ← 1 (inelastic)
Price increases	Sales revenue falls	Sales revenue unchanged	Sales revenue rises
Price decreases	Sales revenue rises	Sales revenue unchanged	Sales revenue falls

Factors influencing the price elasticity of demand

A number of factors influence the price elasticity of demand and these are described below.

Necessity

If a product is essential, such as bread and milk, consumers will still buy similar quantities even if the price is very high. However, a reduction in price will not tend to encourage buyers to purchase much more, as they will have already satisfied their need at the higher price. The more necessary a product, the more *inelastic* is the demand.

Habit

Some products are habit forming. Typical examples are cigarettes, chocolate, alcohol and watching television. In effect, a habit means that the product or service becomes a necessity to that individual. This means that cigarette manufacturers can increase the price of their product and demand will stay roughly the same. The stronger the habit, the more *inelastic* is the demand for the product.

Availability of substitutes

If there are no alternatives to a product, a consumer is likely to buy a similar quantity if the price changes. However, if there are many alternatives, customers will switch to a close alternative. The impact will also depend on consumer tastes: for example, how close the alternative is seen to be. Some buyers may see beef as a close alternative to pork, but other customers will not see them as substitutes.

Did you know?

A major reason for the high prices of some habit-forming products (notably alcohol and cigarettes) is the excise tax charged by the government. The government places heavy taxes on these (inelastic) goods, knowing that people will continue to buy them (and so pay taxes). If the government taxed goods with elastic demand, it would not raise as much money, because many consumers would stop buying the goods.

The greater the availability of close substitutes, the more *elastic* is the demand, as small price rises will encourage consumers to buy alternatives. This can be seen in the market for petrol. In remote rural areas or at motorway service stations, prices tend to be higher than they are in big cities, where it is easier to find an alternative supplier. Demand at any particular garage is more elastic in cities than it is in the countryside.

In the long term, demand becomes more elastic as consumers search out and switch to alternative products.

Brand loyalty

Firms will attempt to create brand loyalty by various means, such as the quality of the product, advertising and other forms of promotion. In addition to increasing sales volume, the creation of loyal customers will also influence people's reactions to price changes. A consumer who insists on wearing Armani clothing will not be put off by a higher price. The greater the level of brand loyalty, the more *inelastic* is the demand.

Proportion of income spent on a product

Consumers will be less concerned about price rises if a product takes up only a small percentage of their income. For example, a 20 per cent increase in the price of a box of matches will only be 2p or 3p, so the consumer is unlikely to change the number of boxes bought (demand is inelastic). On the other hand, buying a car will use up a lot of income, so consumers will be affected by small percentage changes in price. This factor will make the demand for cars more elastic.

Consumer income

Wealthier people are less worried about price rises than poorer individuals, and, as individuals, will have more inelastic demand for the products they buy. David Beckham will pay hundreds of pounds for a haircut, but most consumers would try to find a cheaper alternative if this was the price advertised by their local barber or hairdresser. For this reason, businesses will often target rich consumers. The prices of brands bought predominantly by wealthy consumers can be increased without affecting sales very much, so their demand is *inelastic*. Shops in exclusive areas can often set higher prices because their customers are less conscious of price.

Time

If prices change, consumers will often look around for alternatives before deciding to switch to another product. This process may take some time and so price changes tend to have less impact in the short term. Price elasticity of demand therefore tends to be more inelastic in the short term but more elastic in the long term.

Overall, the elasticity of demand of a product will be determined by a combination of the above factors.

Income elasticity of demand

Income elasticity of demand indicates how demand will be affected by changes in income. A 10 per cent increase in income will enable consumers to spend approximately 10 per cent more in total on products, but the change in spending will vary considerably between individual products.

What do you think?

Firms prefer their products to have price-inelastic demand. A business will not just accept that its products are price elastic or inelastic, but may take steps to change customers' views. How can a firm make its products more inelastic? How easy is it to change the price elasticity of demand of a product?

- For **luxury products** the income elasticity of demand will be greater than 1. Expenditure on holidays, for example, tends to increase by a larger percentage than the change in income as an economy grows richer, so holidays in general are *income elastic*.
- For **necessities** there is likely to be a rise in demand that is smaller than the rise in income. This will give an elasticity that is greater than zero, but less than 1. These products are *income inelastic*. When income elasticity of demand is 0 (zero) a change in income will have no effect on the quantity demanded or the sales revenue of the business.
- For some products, such as cheap cuts of meat, demand falls as people experience increases in income and can afford better alternatives. These products have *negative income elasticity* and are known as **inferior goods**.

Calculating income elasticity of demand

$$\text{Income elasticity of demand} = \frac{\text{\% change in quantity demanded}}{\text{\% change in income}}$$

Example 1: Income rises by 10 per cent, leading to an increase in the quantity demanded from 250 to 300 units.

$$\text{\% change in quantity demanded} = \frac{\text{change in quantity demanded}}{\text{original quantity demanded}}$$

$$\frac{(300 - 250)}{250} \times 100 = \frac{50}{250} \times 100 = +20 \text{ percent}$$

% change in income = +10 per cent (given in question)

$$\text{Income elasticity of demand} = \frac{+20 \text{ per cent}}{+10 \text{ per cent}} = +2$$

An elasticity of +2 means that demand is income elastic.

Firms cannot control the levels of income in a market, so the main use of income elasticity is to forecast demand.

Example 2: Firm X produces three products, as shown in Table 8.6.

▼ **Table 8.6** Income elasticity of demand

Product	Income elasticity of demand	Current sales (units per annum)
A: luxury	+3.00	1,000
B: necessity	+0.25	4,000
C: inferior good	−0.50	500

Next year consumer incomes in the UK are expected to grow by 4 per cent. What sales levels can be expected for this company's three products?

Product A:

$$\frac{\text{\% change in quantity demanded}}{\text{\% change in income } (+4\%)} = \text{income elasticity of demand } (+3)$$

% change in quantity demanded = +4% × +3 = +12%

+12% of 1,000 units = +120 units.

Therefore sales are forecast to increase from 1,000 to 1,120 units.

Product B:

$$\frac{\text{\% change in quantity demanded}}{\text{\% change in income } (+4\%)} = \text{income elasticity of demand } (+0.25)$$

% change in quantity demanded = +4% × +0.25 = +1%

+1% of 4,000 units = +40 units.

Therefore sales are forecast to increase from 4,000 to 4,040 units.

Product C:

$$\frac{\text{\% change in quantity demanded}}{\text{\% change in income } (+4\%)} = \text{income elasticity of demand } (-0.5)$$

% change in quantity demanded = +4% × −0.5 = −2%

−2% of 500 units = −10 units.

Therefore sales are forecast to decrease from 500 to 490 units.

The inferior good seems to be doomed to failure. Can you think of three reasons why a firm would continue producing an inferior good? (Answers on page 539.)

Value of the concepts of price and income elasticity of demand to marketing decision makers

Elasticity of demand is useful to marketers because it can be used to interpret the market, as the following example shows.

Market analysis using price and income elasticity of demand

▼ **Table 8.7** Elasticity of demand data

	Product X	Product Y
Price elasticity of demand	−4.0	−0.3
Income elasticity of demand	−0.6	+2.5

The following conclusions about products X and Y might be inferred from the data in Table 8.7.

Conclusions for product X

- Price elasticity of demand is −4.0 (very elastic). A change in price leads to a proportionally larger change in quantity demanded. This product is not a necessity and is likely to have many close substitutes.
- Income elasticity of demand is −0.6 (negative). As incomes increase, this product will lose sales. It is an inferior good.
- Product X is probably a cheap, low-quality alternative to other products in a very competitive market and is likely to be purchased by consumers who cannot afford a better alternative.

Conclusions for product Y

- Price elasticity of demand is −0.3 (inelastic). The product is a necessity or has few close substitutes.
- Income elasticity of demand is +2.5 (high). This product is a luxury, showing a large percentage increase in sales as income rises.
- Product Y probably has few close substitutes and may be habit-forming or appeals to consumers who can afford higher prices.

Marketing strategies for product X

In the short term:

- Charge a lower price to increase sales revenue, but not if the company is operating on low profit margins.
- Change the product's image because, as the economy grows, the sales of this product will continue to decline and so market share will be lost. However, during a recession the sales would grow.

In the long term:

- Reposition the product in order to appeal to higher income sectors.
- Alternatively, if profit margins are reasonable, the company may keep the product unchanged. It may act as a **cash cow** and in periods of fierce competition price cuts should enable the company to generate high sales volumes (see Chapter 10 for more on 'cash cows').

Marketing strategies for product Y

In the short term:

- Increase price as there will be a relatively small fall in demand, creating a rise in sales revenue from a lower level of output.
- Aim for high profit margins on product Y.

In the long term:

- This product appears to be a cash cow and should be 'milked'.
- Keep the price high.
- Safeguard the product's exclusive image.

> ### Author advice
>
> Be careful when analysing changes in price and income. For example, an elastic demand for a product means that a price *cut* leads to an increase in sales revenue (but a price *increase* has the opposite effect).

Limitations of price and income elasticity of demand

Elasticity of demand can be very unreliable because of the difficulties involved in calculating it. Elasticity of demand calculations assume that 'other things remain equal' while price or income changes. In practice, this does not happen. However, computer software now enables businesses to make more accurate predictions of elasticity of demand by using multivariate regression, which isolates the impact on demand of individual factors such as price and income.

Difficulties in calculating (and using) elasticity of demand

- There may have been significant changes in the market, affecting the level of demand independently of price or income. For example:
  - consumer tastes may have changed
  - new competitors may have entered the market or previous competitors may have left the market
  - technological change may have influenced the market
  - the image of the product may have changed.

- Changes in price may provoke a reaction from rival firms who may try to match the change or modify their marketing in response to the change. This reaction may not always be the same. For example, in some markets competitors are more likely to match a rival's cut in price than they are to match a rival's increase in price.
- Consumers may react differently to increases in price or income than decreases. For example, a decrease in price might not encourage consumers to buy more, but an increase may tempt them to buy from competitors.
- It may be difficult to use secondary market research to calculate elasticity, as the planned change in price (or expected change in income) may be different from anything experienced in the past.
- Consumers may be unable to predict how their spending will be affected by price or income changes, and so primary surveys may be unreliable.

Even the company's own actions may reduce the reliability of any calculations. Firms will often promote their price reductions and so brand awareness (and thus the quantity demanded) may increase for this reason rather than because of the price cut.

Practice exercise 4

Total: 50 marks

1 An inferior good has a:
  a) negative price elasticity of demand
  b) positive price elasticity of demand
  c) negative income elasticity of demand
  d) positive income elasticity of demand.
(1 mark)

2 Which of these changes would lead to an increase in sales revenue for a product?
  a) An increase in price for a good that has price elastic demand.
  b) A decrease in price for a good that has price inelastic demand
  c) An increase in consumer incomes for a product with negative income elasticity of demand.
  d) An increase in price for a good that has price inelastic demand.
(1 mark)

3 In which two situations below will sales revenue stay the same (you must choose two of the seven options):
  a) Price rises by 10 per cent; price elasticity of demand is −10.
  b) Price rises by 2.5 per cent; price elasticity of demand is −1.0
  c) Price rises by 5 per cent; price elasticity of demand is −0.5
  d) Price rises by 7.5 per cent; price elasticity of demand is 0
  e) Incomes rise by 10 per cent; income elasticity of demand is −1.0
  f) Incomes rise by 5 per cent; income elasticity of demand is +0.5
  g) Incomes rise by 2.5 per cent; income elasticity of demand is 0
(2 marks)

4 What is meant by the term 'price elasticity of demand'?
(2 marks)

5 State whether each of the following factors will make demand price elastic or price inelastic:
  a) It is habit forming.
  b) There are many substitutes.
  c) It is aimed at a wealthy market segment.
  d) Advertising has created brand loyalty.
  e) The product is a necessity.
  f) It takes up a very small percentage of consumers' incomes.
(6 marks)

6 Average incomes rise from £20,000 to £21,000 per annum. Sales of playing cards fall from 4 million to 3.9 million per annum. Calculate the income elasticity of demand. *(3 marks)*

7 Complete the sentence which follows. If demand changes by a greater percentage than the percentage change in price, the price elasticity of demand is said to be ……………… *(1 mark)*

8 How should a business market a product that has price-inelastic demand and a high income elasticity of demand? *(9 marks)*

9 Analyse how a firm might increase the income elasticity of demand of one of its products. *(9 marks)*

10 Discuss the reasons why it would be more difficult for a computer manufacturer to use elasticity of demand than it would for a company marketing pencils. *(16 marks)*

Use of data in marketing decision making and planning

Data analysis is a growing feature of marketing in the twenty-first century, with different aspects of data use helping the marketing department in different ways.

- Market research enables businesses to gain a better understanding of their customers and the marketplace.
- Market mapping shows the business their place in, and potential opportunities within, the market.
- Sampling ensures that sufficient data is gathered in a cost-effective manner.
- Statistical techniques enable the business to analyse its market, particularly with a view to forecasting sales. These techniques can also enable the business to assess the likely accuracy of its forecasts.
- Technology allows businesses to gather a much broader range of data and conduct more sophisticated analysis to support its marketing decision making.
- Data on price elasticity of demand and income elasticity of demand assist marketing decisions by giving businesses further insights into two critical factors that affect the demand for their products.

However, despite the usefulness of data, its use must also be treated with caution. Businesses will usually support their marketing data with more qualitative judgements, such as the personal opinions of experienced marketing staff. These 'qualitative' judgements are most likely to be included in marketing decisions in the following situations:

- When the product or business is new, so there is no previous information on which to base predictions. In these circumstances, people's opinions are the most reliable predictor of the future.
- When there is no clear statistical indication of future sales. It is possible that quantitative methods are unable to produce a reliable forecast.
- When trends have changed, so that it would be unwise to predict on the basis of past statistics.
- When the factors influencing sales are not easy to quantify (measure in terms of numbers). Fashion items and the entertainment industry are often difficult to predict, and an experienced manager may be able to deliver a more accurate forecast than any attempt based on statistical data.

- When the character of the individuals is important. For example, if a particular manager is responsible for the forecast, he or she will probably want to make the final decision.

Businesses rely on accurate data and forecasting in their business planning.

If sales are overestimated, there is likely to be a waste of resources as the firm will produce too much. The cost to the firm will depend on whether the products are perishable and how expensive they are to store.

Underestimation also causes problems. The opportunity cost of lost sales is high, especially if customer goodwill is undermined.

In general, it is easier for marketing managers to justify decisions if they are based on appropriate data rather than personal opinion. As analytical techniques continue to develop, the use of data in marketing is likely to grow further.

Case study: Non-store retailing

Non-store retailers are those that do not operate from a physical store. Traditionally, this sector has consisted of mail order companies, sales through catalogues and telephone sales. However, in recent years, internet sales have grown to dominate this sector. Figure 8.9 shows monthly figures for 'non-store' (mainly online) sales from January 2009 to May 2014. The blue dots in Figure 8.9 show the actual sales figures and the black line shows the linear trend for non-store sales.

A number of factors influence consumers' decisions to shop online. The links between online sales and two particular factors – the weather and unemployment levels – are shown in the two scatter graphs in Figures 8.10(a) and 8.10(b).

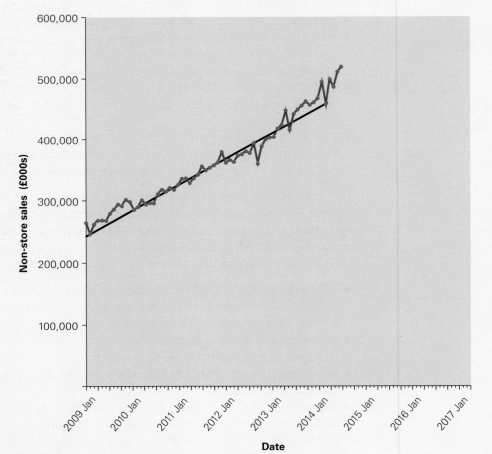

▲ **Figure 8.9** Non-store sales (monthly), January 2009 to May 2014

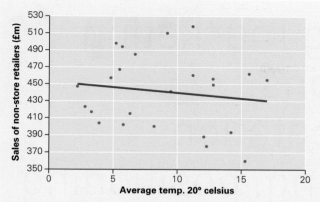

Figure 8.10a Scatter graph showing temperature (degrees Celsius) and non-store sales

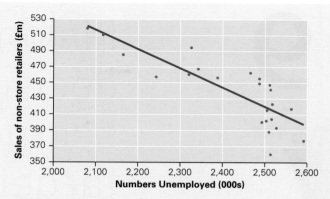

Figure 8.10b Scatter graph showing level of unemployment and non-store sales

The ability to easily compare prices online has had a fundamental impact on the ways in which companies compete. Analysts believe that non-store sales have led to products having more price elastic demand.

However, the income elasticity of demand for goods traded online is more variable, with non-store retailers offering both income elastic and income inelastic products.

Questions

Total: 65 marks

1 Using Figure 8.9, forecast the level of non-store sales for the following months:

a) May 2015 *(1 mark)*

b) January 2017 *(1 mark)*

2 Explain why your forecasts in question 1 may be unreliable. *(5 marks)*

3 Use Figure 8.10(a) to forecast the likely level of sales if the average monthly temperature is:

a) 10 degrees Celsius. *(1 mark)*

b) 20 degrees Celsius. *(1 mark)*

4 Is your prediction in question 3(a) likely to be more or less reliable than your prediction in question 3(b)? Justify your answer. *(4 marks)*

5 Use Figure 8.10(b) to forecast the likely level of sales if the average monthly level of unemployment is 2 million. *(1 mark)*

6 Correlation is used to try to confirm causal links between two variables. Explain:

a) how and why the monthly temperature might affect non-store sales levels *(5 marks)*

b) how and why the level of unemployment might affect non-store sales levels. *(5 marks)*

7 Based on Figures 8.10(a) and 8.10(b) **and** your answers to questions 6(a) and 6(b), do you believe that the weather has a greater impact on non-store sales than the level of unemployment? Justify your view. *(16 marks)*

8 Analyse why online selling is likely to lead to products becoming more price elastic in demand. *(9 marks)*

9 Why are both income inelastic and income elastic products likely to be purchased online? Justify your view. *(16 marks)*

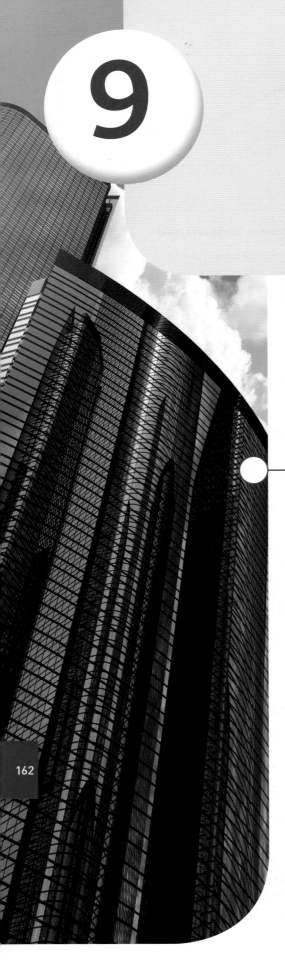

Making marketing decisions: segmentation, targeting, positioning

With a few exceptions, most businesses cannot target the complete range of potential customers. This chapter looks at the process of segmentation, targeting and positioning by which a business decides on which customers it will prioritise. Methods of segmentation considered include demographic, geographic, income and behavioural. The value of the stages in this process will be assessed. It also considers the various influences on choosing a target market and market positioning, including a discussion of niche and mass marketing.

Process and value of segmentation, targeting and positioning

Market segmentation

> **Key term**
>
> **Market segmentation** The classification of customers or potential customers into groups or sub-groups (market segments), each of which responds differently to different products or marketing approaches.

Types of market segmentation

A number of different ways of segmenting a market can be identified. The AQA A-level Business specification classifies **market segments** into four categories:

1 **Demographic segments**: examples include classifying consumers according to age, gender, marital status, family size and family life cycle.
2 **Geographic segments**: examples include classifying consumers according to region, country, urban/rural and ACORN (**A** **Cl**assification **O**f **R**esidential **N**eighbourhoods).
3 **Income segments***: examples include classifying consumers according to family income, occupation and social class.

Stage 1: Market segmentation

Step 1: Identify bases for segmenting market

Step 2: Gather profile of consumers in each of these market segments

↓

Stage 2: Market targeting

Step 3: Assess the nature of each market segment and identify those that provide the best match to the business's existing capabilities

Step 4: Select the market segment or segments on which the business will focus its efforts

↓

Stage 3: Market positioning

Step 5: Decide on the important characteristics of the product/ business that will be used to appeal to the targeted market segment(s)

Step 6: Develop a marketing mix for each market segment (the focus of Chapter 10)

▲ **Figure 9.1** Steps in segmentation, targeting and positioning

4 **Behavioural segments**: these are often based on consumers' attitudes to a particular product. Examples include heavy/light user, degree of brand loyalty, early/late adopter, like/dislike, nature of benefits sought from the product. Behavioural segments may also be based on the character of the consumer, such as lifestyle, interests and opinions.

* The types of segmentation in this category are often classified as examples of demographic segmentation.

Demographic segmentation

The main forms of demographic segmentation are age and gender.

- **Age**. For many products and services, age is a crucial influence on demand, so firms will segment on this basis. Holidays are a classic example: Club 18–30 targets its holidays at a specific age range, while Saga holidays are aimed at people aged over 50 years. Large firms try to provide a range of products that will reach all ages. A magazine publisher will produce different magazines for teenagers, 20- and 30-somethings, the middle-aged and the elderly.

- **Gender (sex)**. Some products are targeted specifically at males or females. The market for perfume is dominated by females, while attendance at sporting events has been dominated by male customers. However, in both these cases, firms have recognised the potential for growth by targeting the other gender.

▲ Older people will want different sorts of holidays to younger people and families

163

▲ Surfing is an activity that's influenced by geographical location

> **Author advice**
>
> Remember that market segmentation is based on **customers** rather than markets or products. It is a method of putting different customers into categories, to help a firm market its products.

Geographic segmentation

Although regional variations in taste are becoming less significant, there are still major differences in tastes and purchasing behaviour based on geographical features. Rambling, surfing, theatre visits and night-clubbing are all activities that are influenced by the place where someone lives. Geographic variations may be linked to regions (e.g. differences in tastes between the north and south), to the differences in spending patterns in urban as opposed to rural areas, and to geographical features such as the terrain and climate.

One of the main geographic methods is ACORN. This approach segments the market according to types of housing. Over 30 different categories of housing are identified by this technique. Families in suburban detached houses are expected to have very different tastes from those living in terraced houses in rural areas. Postcodes can be used to identify these segments, helping firms to target their marketing.

Income segmentation

Income is an important influence on consumer spending. Sophisticated databases enable businesses to have a greater understanding of the level of income of individuals and families, so that products and marketing messages can be targeted at people whose incomes make them more likely to buy a certain product or brand. Although it is not a totally reliable relationship, occupations can provide a guide to incomes and tastes. In the UK social class is a basis for market segmentation.

Social class

This method classifies families according to occupation:

I/A   Professional

II/B   Managerial and technical

IIIN/C1   Skilled: non-manual

IIIM/C2   Skilled: manual

IV/D   Partly skilled

V/E   Unskilled

In general, social class influences purchasing habits because class A receives more income than class B and so on. However, there are some activities that may appeal to particular social classes regardless of income: for example, golfers are more likely than football supporters to be from the middle classes, A, B and C1.

Behavioural segmentation

Two examples of behavioural segmentation are outlined below:

● **Lifestyle**. This type of segmentation is becoming more popular as businesses can use credit card and loyalty card records to identify the pattern of individuals' expenditure. Family food purchases are classified into categories according to the tendency to buy takeaways, organic food, economy brands, health foods, etc. Leisure pursuits are also used to segment customers for marketing purposes.

● **Usage/frequency of purchase.** Some customers, known as 'early adopters', like to be the first to try new products; in contrast, 'followers' are more cautious. Awareness of these customer types allows a firm to target the right people. Similarly, consumers can be classified according to how often they purchase products. A frequent purchaser will have a different view of a product from an occasional, casual user.

What type of segmentation?

The exact type of segmentation used depends on the business or the product. For example, in the case of clothing, gender is important and so is age, especially for children's clothing. Not every type of segmentation is used by every business. In general, organisations identify the market segment or segments that are relevant to their products and services. Products, services and the organisation's approach to marketing are then geared to the targeted segments. Most market segmentation combines different features, such as active men living in urban areas or young women with families who are frequent purchasers of a particular product.

Fact file

Advertising on ITV

Advertisers want to know who their adverts are reaching, so that they can target customers effectively. Research by BARB (Broadcasters' Audience Research Board) showed the popularity of different ITV programmes throughout 2013. However, it also showed major differences in the age profiles of viewers.

▼ **Table 9.1** Ranking of viewer numbers for the most popular ITV programmes in 2013

Programme	Age 16+ Ranking	Age 16–24 Ranking	Age 25–44 Ranking	Age 45–64 Ranking	Age 65+ Ranking
I'm a Celebrity …	1st	1st	1st	2nd	
Downton Abbey	2nd			1st	1st
Britain's Got Talent	3rd	3rd	3rd	5th	
Coronation Street	4th	4th		4th	7th
The X Factor	5th	2nd	2nd	6th	
Broadchurch	6th			3rd	6th
Doc Martin	7th			7th	3rd

To reach customers over the age of 16, advertising during 'I'm a Celebrity …' would have reached the largest audience. However, viewers over the age of 65 showed little interest in this programme, which was not ranked in the top seven ITV programmes for that age group.

In contrast, Downton Abbey had the second most popular appeal overall, but was not popular with viewers aged below 45. To reach viewers aged 16–44, advertising during Champions League programmes would have been more effective, as this programme was in the top seven programmes for viewers aged 16–24 and for those aged 25–44 (although not shown in the table above). Given the fact that this programme appeals more to males than females, it is an ideal programme for targeting males aged 16–44. In terms of channels, the Sky Sports channels are the most male-biased channels on TV.

Data such as these enable firms to use market segmentation to reach their target market and achieve their market positioning.

Source: Ofcom; Based on research by BARB, http://stakeholders.ofcom.org.uk

▲ Mobiles were initially targeted at business users

Benefits and drawbacks of market segmentation

The benefits and drawbacks of market segmentation apply to all the types of segmentation. However, the extent to which a particular organisation might benefit from segmentation depends on the degree to which:

- a particular segment can be easily identified
- consumer behaviour varies according to market segmentation
- the firm is able to reach that segment directly in its marketing and market research
- the firm is able to generate profit from that market segment.

Benefits of market segmentation

- **To increase market share**. An organisation can identify market segments that have not been reached and adapt its products and marketing to reach those segments. For example, Sky channels have a bias towards male viewing and so Sky Living was introduced. It is the TV channel with the highest percentage of female viewers.
- **To assist new product development**. Gaps in market segments can be used to indicate the scope for introducing new products. The Nintendo Wii has attracted casual games users and is much more popular with girls and young children than other games consoles.
- **To extend products into new markets**. Mobile phones were initially targeted at business users before being extended to teenagers and then whole families.
- **To identify ways of marketing a product**. A company that recognises its customers' characteristics can target its advertising to media used by that market segment. For example, someone in social class A is more likely to read *The Times*, whereas someone in social class E has a greater tendency to read the *Daily Star*. Similarly, promotional methods and messages can be modified to suit specific segments – for instance, young people prefer different images to older consumers.

Drawbacks of market segmentation

- **Difficulty in identifying the most important segments for a product**. Successful segmentation requires market segments to be identifiable, reachable and distinct. In practice, a business may be unable to categorise its customers. Some segments, such as gender, are easy to identify, but it is more difficult to put consumers of bread, household cleaners and pillows into categories.
- **Reaching the chosen segment with marketing**. Lifestyle categories in particular are difficult to identify or locate. Which media would you use to attract primary school parents on a national scale? In general, socio-economic class tends to be the most difficult of the demographic segments to target.
- **Recognising changes in the segments interested in the product**. Markets are dynamic and businesses cannot assume that an existing segment will always stay loyal to their product, so they must constantly research their market segments.
- **Meeting the needs of customers not included in the chosen segment**. Emphasis on market segmentation may lead to a business ignoring other potential customers. This may prevent a business from attracting the mass market.

Fact file

Experian

Experian plc is a global information services company which undertakes market research and market analysis. For the fashion industry Experian uses 35 segments to classify consumers. These segments are based on demographic factors (gender and age) and behavioural characteristics (clothing interests).

Each segment is identified by a person's name, such as Sara, Clive and Virginia. Of the 35 segments 20 are female and 15 are male. For the 18–25 age group, there are five female segments and three male segments. A brief summary of the characteristics of the male segments is shown in Table 9.2 below.

▼ **Table 9.2** Experian Male Fashion Segments: Categories for those aged 18–25

Male Type 3: Lee	**Functional Fashion Seekers**: 'Fashion-conscious young men who search out style at a reasonable price'	• Lives with parents or sharing • Fashion-conscious; spends time on clothing but limited budget • Favourite shops: JD Sports, Sports Direct, Burton
Male Type 11: Luke	**Brand Boy**: 'Young men for whom brand and image are everything'	• Lives with parents • Brand and styling important; above average spending and enjoys shopping • Favourite shops: Next, House of Fraser, Debenhams and Gap
Male Type 12: Dominic	**Dressed in the Best**: 'Young men with a taste for expensive clothes'	• Living at home or sharing • High spending on relatively few, high quality/expensive items • Favourite shops: independent clothes stores, John Lewis, Hennes (H&M)

Source: www.experian.co.uk

What do you think?

How useful would the market segmentation shown in Table 9.2 be for a fashion retailer? Reflect on the benefits and drawbacks of this classification of male consumers. Why might there be gaps in these profiles?

Visit the website www.experian.co.uk for more details on male fashion segmentation and to find out whether your dad is a 'Philip – Youthful aspirations' or a 'Malcolm – Any shirt will do.'

Females aged 18–25 can find out whether they are an Ana, Katie, Natasha, Tammy or Annabel.

Key term

Market targeting Deciding on the consumers/market segment(s) to whom you intend to sell your products or brands.

Influences on choosing a target market

The first step in **market targeting** is to assess the nature of each market segment and identify those that provide the best match to the business's existing capabilities. This will then allow the business to focus on the next step which is to *either* select a specific market segment or segments on which the business will focus its efforts (niche marketing) *or* aim to appeal across all market segments (mass marketing).

167

These approaches are described below.

● Concentrated marketing – instead of targeting a small share of a large market, the company goes after a large share of one or a few sub-markets (market segments). This is particularly beneficial if the business has limited resources.

● Differentiated marketing – the company targets several market segments and designs separate offers for each segment. This involves product variations and differences in marketing approach, based on the character of each.

● Undifferentiated marketing – in this approach, the company aims to appeal to the whole market with one product. Marketing concentrates on emphasising what is common in the needs of consumers rather than on differing needs.

Niche and mass marketing

A critical decision for many businesses is whether to aim for a narrow range of customers or a broad range. Both niche and mass marketing strategies can meet most of a business's marketing objectives.

Niche marketing

One example of a business aiming its product at a particular market segment is Build-A-Bear Workshop, a shop that offers custom-made, personalised teddy bears, complete with birth certificates, personal recorded messages and customised clothing.

Niche marketing is an attractive proposition for small firms, as there may be little competition in their segment. However, many firms involved in niche marketing are owned by, or are divisions of, larger organisations. IPC, one of the UK's largest magazine publishers, is a mass market publisher but its products appeal to niche markets. Even its top sellers, such as *Woman's Own, NME* and *Amateur Gardening* are aimed at specific segments. Niche markets are served more obviously by *Mountain Bike Rider* and *Cage and Aviary Birds*.

Some niche markets are based on exclusive or high-quality products (e.g. Ferrari) or are located in remote areas, where higher prices can be charged because of the inconvenience for consumers of finding a substitute. But many niche markets focus on lower-priced goods, appealing to customers who want simple pricing, (e.g. Poundland), possibly because larger firms are put off by the low profit margins.

Advantages of niche marketing

● **Less competition**. There may be fewer competitors, as large companies are not attracted to a relatively small market. For example, there is only one magazine about orienteering, a minority sport, because the potential readership is too low to interest large businesses with high overheads. The lack of competition enables firms to gain enough customers to earn a decent profit. In some niche markets, the lack of competition may help firms to charge a much higher price for their products. Selling relatively few products at high profit margins may enable these firms to achieve good profits.

Key term

Niche marketing Targeting a product or service at a small segment of a larger market.

- **Costs**. The lack of scope for cost reduction by producing on a large scale may mean that small firms can compete more effectively in a niche market. Usually, large, mass market firms can produce goods at low unit cost because they can afford more efficient machinery or can buy in bulk at a discount. In a niche market, there may be too few customers for a large business to gain these advantages. Therefore, a small firm may be able to match the costs of larger rivals in a niche market.
- **Small-scale production**. The limited demand may suit a small business that would lack the resources to produce on a large scale. A sole trader, for example, would only be able to produce enough products for a small market niche.
- **Tailor-made products**. A business can adapt its product to meet the specific needs of a niche market, rather than compromise between the needs of many different groups of consumers. Tailor-made products, designed to meet the specific needs of a customer, are quite common in niche markets. This makes the product much more attractive to the customer and not only increases demand but also allows the firm to charge a higher price. The product will have a **unique selling point/ proposition** (USP). (A unique selling point is a feature that makes a product different to its competitors. Businesses use USPs to increase demand and/or price.)
- **Targeting customers**. It can be easier for businesses to target customers and promote their products effectively when they are only selling to a certain type of customer. The content of advertisements can be designed to appeal to the specific market segment being targeted. Furthermore, the media used can be selected according to the market segment. For example, children's toys are advertised during children's television programmes, using messages and images that attract children's interest.

Disadvantages of niche marketing

- **Lower profits**. The small scale of the market limits the chances of making a high profit. Even if a high price can be charged, the lack of customers will reduce the total profit made. In addition, unit costs tend to be higher relative to larger competitors, again reducing the potential for high profit margins. If a niche is large enough for a small business to make a reasonable profit, it is likely to attract competition from other businesses. If a number of businesses are sharing relatively few customers between them, they may find it difficult to survive, particularly if these firms compete fiercely for their customers.
- **Changes in demand**. Small businesses in niche markets can be vulnerable to changes in demand. Niche markets are specialised, so firms operating in them are not able to spread their risks. For this reason, a decline in interest among consumers may threaten the firm's existence, as it has no other products to fall back on. Larger, mass market firms are able to avoid this risk by producing a wide range of goods and services.
- **Market entry**. An increase in interest among consumers may be enough to attract larger firms into the market. Holland and Barrett identified health foods as a market niche many years ago, but the company has not grown quickly. This is because, as the demand for health foods increased, the large supermarkets decided to offer many more health foods. In rapidly changing times, it is likely that firms in niche markets will make high profits only in the short term, unless they can continue to react quickly to changes.

Mass marketing

Examples of mass market goods are petrol and baked beans. Within a mass market there is only limited scope for targeting. For instance, there is little scope to modify petrol to appeal to a niche market, although cars can be modified to run on environmentally friendlier fuel. There are more variations to baked beans, aimed mainly at children, but most baked beans are sold in the mass market.

Advantages of mass marketing

- **Large-scale production**. With **mass marketing**, production on a large scale is possible, which will help to lower costs per unit as a result of factors such as bulk buying. This should improve profit margins, particularly as many businesses will not be large enough to compete in the mass market.
- **High revenues**. The sheer volume of customers enables companies to earn huge revenues. The chemicals industry in the UK is worth over £57 billion per annum. There are over 400 UK chemical firms with sales turnover in excess of £10 million per year.
- **Barriers to entry**. Mass marketing allows businesses to use the most expensive marketing because there is greater opportunity for large increases in revenue that will more than pay for the marketing. Not only does this help to eliminate smaller rivals, but it can also act as a barrier to entry for new firms. For 60 years, the soap powder industry has been dominated by two large companies (Unilever and Procter & Gamble) both of which have huge marketing budgets. This has limited the opportunities for new firms to break into the market, as they cannot afford the advertising budgets required.
- **Research and development**. In industries such as pharmaceuticals, it is necessary to appeal to large, profitable mass markets in order to be able to fund the research and development costs needed to introduce new products. It is estimated that discovering a major new pharmaceutical product and bringing it to the market costs a business about £400 million.
- **Brand awareness**. Mass marketing increases brand awareness. This not only assists sales of the branded product but can also help to break down consumer resistance to new products. Firms such as Cadbury's and Coca-Cola can use their high level of brand awareness to encourage customers to try new products that they might have been reluctant to try if they did not recognise the brand name.

Disadvantages of mass marketing

- **Fixed capital**. High fixed capital costs are incurred, such as the purchase of large factories, extensive and expensive machinery and other assets such as delivery lorries. This will prevent many businesses from operating in the mass market.
- **Changes in demand**. Businesses in mass markets are vulnerable to changes in demand. A fall in demand will lead to unused spare capacity, increasing unit costs. As the pace of change accelerates, this is becoming a much greater problem because customers want the latest products. Small, niche market firms will be less affected as they will not have spent so much on their factories.

> ### Key term
>
> **Mass marketing** Aiming a product at all (or most) of the market.

▲ The UK chemicals industry is worth over £57 billion per year

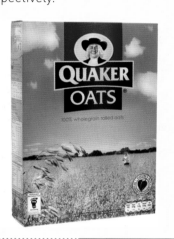
- **Effects of standardisation**. It can be difficult to appeal directly to individual customers because mass market products must be designed to suit all customers. As a result, prices tend to be lower, reducing the opportunities for high profits.
- **Competition**. Mass market organisations are much more vulnerable to low-cost competition from abroad, as the UK cannot match the low wage levels and other low costs in these countries.
- **Adding value**. In mass markets there is less scope for adding value. As customers' incomes increase, there is a growing tendency for them to want high-priced, unique products. This trend is helping niche marketing but making it harder for businesses that concentrate on the mass market.

Through careful market research, businesses in mass markets can reduce these risks, but there is always a danger that demand for their products will fall. Consequently, such firms must regularly examine their products in order to ensure that their goods continue to suit the market.

Product differentiation in the mass market

In order to compete in a mass market, a business needs to make sure that its product is different from competitors' products. If consumers value this difference, it will benefit the firm in two ways:

1 increased sales volume

2 greater scope for charging a higher price.

In a mass market, product differentiation will usually be achieved by employing elements of the marketing mix (see Chapter 10). Examples include:

- design, branding and packaging to improve the attractiveness of a product
- clever promotional and advertising campaigns to boost image and sales. Are Nike sportswear and trainers of better quality than their competitors' products, or are they just marketed more effectively?
- different distribution methods. Avon cosmetics differentiated itself by selling cosmetics directly to the customer; Amazon differentiated itself through internet selling, without the use of a traditional shop outlet.

Many mass market firms achieve product differentiation through **product proliferation**. This occurs when a variety of products are produced to serve different tastes. In some cases, this can mean significantly different products, such as IPC magazines producing *Woman's Own*, *Loaded*, *Ideal Home*, *Uncut* and *NME*. However, the need for mass production in order to cut costs will limit the number of different products that can be offered.

171

Influences on choosing market positioning

Key term

Market positioning Where your product or brand stands in relation to the products or brands of other businesses.

Key term

Competitive advantage A benefit that allows a business to gain and retain more customers than its competitors.

Fact file

Market positioning at Paddy Power

Paddy Power tries to maintain a market position as a 'quirky' business. During the 2014 World Cup in Brazil the company released images of a message of support for the England football team that appeared to be formed by the cutting down of trees in the Amazon rain forest. During the 2012 Olympics it suggested that it was the main sponsor of the biggest athletic event ever held in London. This was revealed to be sponsorship of an egg and spoon race in London – a small village in Burgundy, France.

Market positioning attempts to influence the consumer's view of a product or brand. It aims to achieve a unique and beneficial perception of a product or brand in the consumer's mind, possibly enabling it to achieve a USP (unique selling point). Good market positioning means that consumers believe that they will receive benefits from buying the product; this makes it easier for the business to charge higher prices and introduce new variations.

Process of market positioning

Having conducted market research and identified its target market segments, the business will be in a position to decide how to position its product. This background enables the business to find out the product characteristics that its targeted market segments value most. The business can then draw up a market map (see Figure 8.2, page 137). In practice, because the market map is likely to feature more than two factors, it would be generated by a computer program. The business can then decide where it wants to place its product within the market map. Consumers will choose products that give them the greatest value. To attract and keep customers businesses must understand their needs and buying processes better than competitors. A business can position itself as providing superior value to its target markets, either by offering lower prices than competitors or by providing more benefits, in the minds of its customers, to justify higher prices. Such a business will gain **competitive advantage**.

Market positioning may be decided on the basis of a number of factors:

- **Attributes and benefits of the product.** Does the product have a unique selling point? What product qualities will help the business to differentiate itself from other products?
- **Competition.** Does the business want to occupy a part of the market that is different to that of any other business? This will probably require low marketing expenditure but is likely to mean a small market segment. Alternatively, if the business is confident that its product is superior to its competition, then it may deliberately position itself against a rival product in order to capture its market share.
- **Product user.** The business's market research and market segmentation may have given it an excellent understanding of a particular market segment. In this case the product and its marketing may be adapted to suit the needs of the product users, rather than trying to persuade consumers to buy a given product.
- **Pricing.** Differentiated marketing is often linked to high pricing as targeting a small niche requires greater added value from each product. However, a business may want to make competitive pricing its USP, in which case market positioning will focus on the lower price area of the market.
- **Product use or application.** In markets such as the car market, the use of the product provides a key basis for positioning. Cars are often designed to meet needs such as family use, off-road purposes or vehicles suited for urban driving.

The value of market positioning is that it:

- allows a business to maximise sales revenue, by increasing sales volume
- can often give the business scope for high prices, as a result of establishing a unique selling point
- reduces costs by gaining an excellent understanding of the media to use for its marketing
- enables the marketing department to save money by focusing its marketing budget on those customers who are going to react favourably to its products
- increases marketing efficiency because its understanding of consumer needs means that it can use marketing communications and offers that appeal to its target market.

Practice exercise 1

Total: 60 marks

1 Which one of the following approaches to market segmentation is demographic?
   a) Regular users
   b) Social class
   c) Urban users
   d) Gender *(1 mark)*

2 A business decides to focus its marketing on a certain group of consumers. This is known as:
   a) market positioning
   b) market segmentation
   c) market targeting. *(1 mark)*

3 Market positioning, market segmentation, and market targeting are three activities undertaken in marketing planning. In which order would a business organise these three elements of its marketing decision making? *(2 marks)*

4 Explain the meaning of 'product differentiation'. *(3 marks)*

5 Explain one reason why social class is a useful approach to market segmentation. *(6 marks)*

6 Analyse why 'behavioural segmentation' is growing in popularity. *(9 marks)*

7 State two examples of niche markets. *(2 marks)*

8 Why might a magazine publisher target a niche market? *(5 marks)*

9 Explain two benefits of mass marketing. *(6 marks)*

10 Explain three factors that might form the basis of market positioning. *(9 marks)*

11 Is it inevitable that businesses in a niche market will be unable to break into a mass market? Justify your view. *(16 marks)*

Case study: Lush Cosmetics

Lush Cosmetics was originally set up in 1978, supplying cosmetics to The Body Shop. However, an ill-fated venture into mail order led to its collapse.

Lush recommenced trading in 1994, producing soaps, shampoos, cosmetics and related products. This time it decided to open its own retail outlets. It has been so successful that, in addition to manufacturing all of its own products, it has set up 106 stores in the UK alone. Overseas, there are over 400 franchises in 51 different countries. In 2013 its worldwide profit for the year, before tax, was £21.9 million.

Lush focuses on its range of products. Each bar of soap, shampoo, etc., contains fresh (not synthetic) ingredients, ranging from the predictable (aloe vera, lemon and tea tree oil) to the peculiar (Belgian chocolate and almond shells). In this way, Lush sees itself as operating in a niche market of people who want unusual and a varied selection of cosmetics, rather than in a mass market. Its products have never been tested on animals. For its overseas franchises, the products are manufactured locally to guarantee freshness.

Marketing is mostly by word of mouth and through an in-house magazine, which has also been used to re-establish a mail-order service. The nature of the ingredients means that the location of a Lush shop can usually be detected by smell from a considerable distance (depending on the wind direction). This can also help to encourage consumers to visit the shops.

Over 200 products are made, with the range changing constantly according to demand. Unsuccessful products are quickly eliminated and there is constant research aimed at producing new products. The product range is updated every three months. Its most recent new product development is in the field of cosmetics. This new range of products spent two years in development and was created to match the needs of its target market. Consumers and press reports are used to provide marketing slogans, such as 'Lush is like the AA, pretty vital in a crisis' and 'It's better to bathe in sweets than to eat them'. Interest is also aroused through unusual product names such as 'Honey I Washed the Kids' and 'Sex Bomb'. Staff are encouraged to spot celebrities, and a list of famous names, and their Lush purchases, is regularly updated on the company website.

With typical product prices at about £3.10 for a 100 g bar of soap, Lush achieves high profit margins. The ingredients of a bar of soap can cost as little as 70p.

In 2013, a *Which?* magazine survey of nearly 12,000 consumers placed Lush as the number one cosmetics business in the UK. Lush came in first place in 14 different factors including price, service, store environment, product quality, product range and after-sales service. Paul Wheatley, director of Lush retail, was pleased with the result: 'We focus on the freshest products, innovation and excellent customer service. Shoppers tell us they like to visit shops where they can see and touch the products available. Lush sells distinctive products that are hard to get elsewhere at lower prices and presents them attractively in store in unique ways.' Although Lush sells its products online it focuses much more on sales from shops.

Lush operates in a niche market and targets a variety of market segments. It is based mainly in urban shopping centres and targets females aged 18 to 45 years. Its consumers are generally well educated and in social classes A, B and C1. Lush positions its products to appeal to consumers who are concerned about environmental and sustainability issues and who want fresh products. Customers are mostly regular users who place a high value on fresh products. These customers want value for money but are prepared to pay high prices if the individual and unique products meet their functional and emotional needs.

Sources: www.lush.co.uk and www.cosmeticsdesign-europe.com

Questions

Total: 65 marks

1 What is meant by the term 'target market'? *(2 marks)*

2 State two examples of behavioural segmentation indicated in the article. *(2 marks)*

3 Analyse two reasons why Lush introduces new products every three months. *(9 marks)*

4 Analyse two reasons why Lush might have decided to open its own shops when it re-launched the business in 1994. *(9 marks)*

5 Analyse how Lush's market positioning allows it to achieve differentiation from its competitors. *(9 marks)*

6 Analyse the possible difficulties faced by Lush as a result of its decision to produce a range of 200 different products. *(9 marks)*

7 Analyse the benefits for Lush from operating in a niche market. *(9 marks)*

8 Lush uses market segmentation in its planning. Evaluate the usefulness of market segmentation in enabling Lush to make large profits. *(16 marks)*

10

Making marketing decisions: using the marketing mix

This chapter introduces the concept of the marketing mix (the 7 Ps) – product, price, promotion, place (distribution), people, process and physical environment (physical evidence) – and considers the factors that influence a firm's marketing mix. The seven elements of the marketing mix are examined in turn, through a study of the key decisions made in relation to each of the 7 Ps and the effects of those decisions. The chapter then examines the importance of, and influences on, an integrated marketing mix. It concludes with a study of the value of digital marketing and e-commerce.

Traditionally the **marketing mix** consisted of four elements, known as the 4 Ps: product, price, place and promotion, but as service industries grew and customer service became more important a fifth P (people) was added. The increased focus on service industries has been instrumental in the addition of two more Ps: process and physical environment.

Key term

Marketing mix Those elements of a business's approach to marketing that enable it to satisfy and delight its customers.

Elements of the marketing mix (7 Ps)

Key terms

Product The good or service provided by the business for its customers.

Price The sum of money paid by the customer for a unit of a product.

Promotion In the context of marketing, promotion is the process of communicating with customers or potential customers. Promotion can also describe communication with other interested groups, such as shareholders and suppliers.

Place The location at which the purchase of a product is made and the means of distributing the product to the consumer.

People In the context of the marketing mix this is anyone who represents the firm and comes into contact with the firm's customers.

Process The system involved in ensuring that an efficient service is provided to prospective and actual customers.

Physical environment The nature and appeal of the physical evidence a customer will observe during a transaction, such as the company stationery and brochures, delivery lorries and staff uniforms.

Influences on the elements of the marketing mix

Finance

A business's decision in any functional area will be influenced by its financial position. As marketing involves significant expenditure before any results are achieved, and will always include an element of risk, the finances of a firm are critical. The following examples illustrate this:

Cash flow

If a business is suffering from cash-flow problems, it may need to reduce spending on items such as promotion, as this can lead to significant expenditure before any revenue is received. Similarly, difficulties with cash flow may encourage a business to cut its prices dramatically, in order to bring in much-needed cash in the short term.

Discounts

Is the organisation large enough to acquire raw materials at a low price? In the UK, the large supermarkets can obtain products such as milk at a much lower price than small grocers and they can pass on these lower prices to consumers.

Marketing budget and cost of promotions

Businesses generally base promotional decisions on cost effectiveness. This is often measured by the **cost per thousand** (CPT). Thus a promotional campaign costing £60,000 and reaching 600,000 people would have a CPT of 10p per consumer.

Technology

Technology affects the marketing mix in several ways.

Technologically advanced products

In most cases, if a product is technologically advanced, it will be more popular with customers. There is an obvious connection between advanced technology and the price that is set. Furthermore, technologically advanced products such as the iPhone require much less effort in terms of promotion, as the products themselves and word-of-mouth advertising help to sell them.

Sophistication of the organisation's database

If a business has acquired information on specific customers, it is more likely to use direct mail or internet contact to attract them. Organisations such as Sainsbury's (through its loyalty card) and Expedia and Trainline (through previous bookings) gain an understanding of consumers' tastes and are able to target them with specific promotions and special offers.

Lower costs

Advances in technology enable firms to produce high-quality products at relatively low costs (and therefore relatively low prices). Consequently, the marketing mix can focus more on promotion and place in order to differentiate a product from those of the firm's competitors.

Online selling

Technology in the form of the internet is having a significant impact on place, with companies such as Amazon not requiring a traditional shop from which to sell their products. The internet also offers an ideal opportunity to promote products and target customers by placing adverts on popular web pages.

Social media

More and more businesses are using social media directly to promote their products. By encouraging people to register their likes and opinions it can also encourage viral marketing where promotions are passed from one social media user to other users.

Market research

Market research provides information to a business, which helps it to adapt its marketing mix in order to gain an advantage. The following examples illustrate this.

Level of competition

If market research reveals the existence of a great deal of competition, a business needs to differentiate its product from those of its competitors. This is achieved through branding, patenting original ideas and constantly developing new products to replace those in decline. In some industries, such as telecommunications, barriers to entry can limit the level of competition, as new firms cannot afford the huge capital costs involved.

Availability of substitutes

Market research may reveal the existence of substitutes for the business's product. Businesses must look beyond their own market and appreciate that other industries can have an impact on their success. For example, bus companies are in competition with trains and the car industry. In some areas, companies such as Stagecoach have used the results of market research to take over both bus and train routes, thus overcoming the risk of competition. This lack of competition enables them to charge higher prices and can mean that they need to spend less money on promotions.

Consumer opinions

Ultimately, this is the most important factor. A business's products must satisfy the needs of customers, so continuous market research is required to determine what these are. With greater scope for targeting particular market segments, there is now a tendency for businesses to aim towards more variety in the product range, with each variation targeted at a different market segment.

Niche or mass marketing

Market research will guide a business towards either differentiated or undifferentiated marketing. If the product is aimed at a niche market, promotions will be placed in media that are used by the consumers within that niche. If the mass market is targeted, media with a broad coverage, such as national newspapers and television, will be used. Again, market research will be used to discover the best form of media to attract particular customers.

Market segment

Some target markets may be easier to reach through certain media. Specialist magazines are used to promote products such as cosmetics and computer games because the profile of the magazine's readership matches the market segment that the business is trying to attract. Similarly, the targeted market segment can influence price – if a product is targeted at a wealthy market segment, a high price can be charged.

Other factors

Several other factors influence the marketing mix.

Relative power of buyers and suppliers

If a firm is in a strong position to dictate terms to its suppliers, it is more likely to be able to acquire cheap supplies. In the UK, banana supplies are in the hands of a few suppliers that can dictate the price to small grocers, meaning that small grocers cannot compete on price. However, the large supermarkets can bargain for a much lower price than small grocers and emphasise low prices in their marketing mix. This, in turn, allows them to focus more on price in the marketing mix. If a product has only a limited number of buyers, this may weaken the seller's position, as the fact file on the power of buyers in the milk industry shows.

Quality of the promotion

There is an element of chance in any promotional campaign. Some campaigns have failed because they were not cost-effective – both Hoover and McDonald's ran campaigns that were stopped because of the financial difficulties they caused. (Hoover offered expensive flights to people purchasing a product and McDonald's offered 'two meals for the price of one'.) Other campaigns have captivated consumers and been successful in generating extra sales, for example Topshop and the Kate Moss range, and Marks and Spencer's use of iconic figures such as Twiggy in its advertising.

Elasticity of demand

If a high price does not stop customers buying a product, an even higher price can be charged. However, for some products a high price will lead to a large fall in demand, so only a low price can be set in these cases.

Reputation of the business

Some businesses deliberately avoid price cuts because they may adversely affect their upmarket image; others, with a reputation for providing value for money, will deliberately emphasise lower prices.

Convenience of location

In many industries, customers want easy access to the place where the product is being sold. 'Place' is considered to be the most important element in the marketing mix for supermarkets and a vital element in the clothing and confectionery industries.

Effects of changes in the elements of the marketing mix

These effects will be dealt with in detail as each of the seven elements of the marketing mix is examined throughout this chapter. A brief summary of what each of the 7 Ps tries to achieve is outlined below.

- **Product**: a product should possess the features that appeal to its target market and which are consistent with its market position.
- **Price**: in general a low price will attract a greater volume of customers. However, high prices may prove to be more profitable as they can generate greater income and have wider profit margins.
- **Promotion**: large expenditure on promotional activities should enable the business to increase its sales. However, each element of the promotional mix must be examined in terms of its cost effectiveness in generating extra revenue.
- **Place**: in general a business will want its products to be available for purchase in as many places as possible. However, if it is trying to project a certain image for its products then it will only be trying to make the product available in places that match the image of the product or service.
- **People**: to maximise sales of both goods and services, it is important to ensure that any people who are in direct or indirect contact with customers are knowledgeable, enthusiastic and well trained.
- **Process**: to consumers, their time is a valuable commodity. The process involved in buying a product, such as the initial enquiry and the placing of an order, must be conducted with speed and efficiency by the business, so that the customer gets the product that they want at the time and place that they desire.
- **Physical environment**: in any situation where the customer comes into contact with the business, such as the buildings, website and any methods of communication used by the business, a favourable impression must be given. This will encourage the customer to purchase goods and services from that business.

A key aim of many marketing mixes is the creation of a **unique selling point** or unique selling proposition (USP). The USP is what differentiates a product from its competitors. The USP might be a feature of the product, such as the hole in a Polo mint, or the image created by its promotions, such as having a good time when drinking Coca-Cola. Often, each element of the marketing mix contributes towards the USP, as variations to each of the 7 Ps can lead to a product that is not matched by any competitor.

Product decisions

The first product decision is the choice of target market – will the business focus on the industrial market or the consumer market?

There is a tendency to regard marketing as an interaction between a business and individual consumers. However, if we take the product back one stage, we can see that this is not the only type of marketing. Manufacturers of consumer goods, such as soft drinks, must use marketing techniques to persuade retailers to stock their products. Suppliers of components, such as producers of tyres, must market their products to the companies, such as car manufacturers, who will want those components or raw materials.

Goods involved in **business-to-business** transactions of this type require very different marketing approaches.

Industrial marketing

The main features of **industrial marketing** are as follows:

- **Larger transactions**: millions of pounds worth of products may be bought and sold in one transaction.
- **Specialist buyers and sellers**: buyers and sellers will be specialist employees of organisations and will therefore have much greater knowledge and understanding of the products being exchanged.
- **Quality**: the buyer's reputation will often depend on the quality of the product being sold by the seller, so there is much greater emphasis on quality and related factors, such as after-sales servicing and maintenance.
- **Informative advertising**: promotions and advertisements tend to be informative rather than persuasive, as buyers will base their decisions on factual information.
- **Pricing**: the importance of pricing depends very much on the nature of the market. If there is a wide choice of suppliers, low prices may be critical in securing the deal. However, if there is only one supplier, the seller can set a much higher price.
- **Buyer–seller relationship**: this is much more critical and in some cases, an organisation's systems will depend on replacements and additions being compatible with earlier purchases, such as in a computer or security system. There is often a delicate balance between the need for profit and the need to maintain goodwill and good relationships with a customer. News of poor customer service will tend to be publicised and become well known more quickly in business-to-business transactions than in **consumer marketing**.

Consumer marketing

Features of **convenience products**:

- consumed and purchased regularly
- consumers purchase them by habit
- purchased by a very large proportion of the population
- tend to be low-price items and so businesses need to sell them in large volume to make profit
- consumers do not tend to shop around as there is limited scope for saving money by switching brands
- impulse buys, placed near the tills in shops, are often examples of convenience products.

Examples of convenience products are bottled water and crisps.

Features of **shopping products**:

- consumed and purchased quite often, but less regularly than convenience products as a rule
- because consumers plan their purchase they do not need to be displayed so prominently in stores and are likely to be available in fewer stores

---

Author advice

The term 'product' is often used to describe both goods and services.

If a business sells products in a consumer market, its marketing will be affected by the types of consumer product it sells. The marketing mix should be adapted according to the classification of its products. **Consumer products** are classified according to consumers' shopping habits and can be **convenience products**, **shopping products** or **speciality products**. Speciality products can also be described as specialty products.

Key terms

Consumer marketing Where a firm targets individual consumers with its product.

Consumer products Products that are purchased in order to directly satisfy the needs and wants of consumers.

Convenience products Products that are purchased frequently and with minimum thought and effort by consumers.

Shopping products Products that consumers want to be readily accessible, but which involve thought and planning before purchase.

Speciality products Products whose purchase is planned by consumers, who will seek out these products for purchase.

▲ Cruises are a specialty product

- consumers may purchase them because of augmented qualities, beyond the basic use of the product (such as a feeling of prestige from buying a fashionable brand), so there is often brand loyalty
- for sellers there is more scope for higher prices and greater added value than for convenience products.

Examples of shopping products include furniture, household durables and hairdressing.

Features of **speciality products**:

- these products will often have unique characteristics
- consumers are much more selective and there is greater emphasis on image and brand when making purchasing decisions
- people may travel some distance to purchase speciality products
- price is not a key consideration in the decision to purchase and so high profit margins can be gained.

Examples of speciality products include designer clothes, wigs and luxury cruises.

Product features and design

Product design means deciding on the make-up of a product so that it works well, has an attractive design and can be produced economically. Products should satisfy customer wants. They should be developed as a result of market research into those wants and an understanding of the requirements of the firm's target market. Products can be tangible (goods) or intangible (services). In practice, most goods include aspects of service, such as the quality of customer service and after-sales service. Similarly, many services feature products too, such as the food when purchasing a restaurant meal.

The main elements of a successful product are its features and design. To appeal to consumers a product must possess certain characteristics. The characteristics of a good product will vary according to the consumer and the product. The key features influencing tablet computer purchases provide a useful illustration:

- **Reliability**. Manufacturers such as Samsung, Sony and Apple have a reputation for reliability that appeals to tablet computer buyers.
- **Functions and compatibility with other devices**. Buyers of tablets desire a flexible product which can be used for a wide range of activities and which can transfer data and activities to and from other products, such as computers and mobile phones.
- **Size and weight**. In general, customers prefer mobile devices that are light. Small size will thus appeal to customers who prioritise weight, but other users prefer a larger screen. Currently, Sony provides the largest screen option while Apple's iPad has become thinner, to reduce weight.
- **Convenience of use**. Tablet providers make sure that their controls are designed for ease of use, with all of the key controls within easy reach. Because of their use on the move the design is intended to aid use with one hand.
- **Fashion**. Tablet designs and covers are made to appeal to fashion-conscious consumers as they have become an accessory to many people.

- **Aesthetic qualities.** Apple and Sony products are renowned for their appearance and design and so competitors in this industry must try to match their reputation.
- **Durability.** Given their usage this is an important feature and so organisations such as Samsung place a high priority on durability.
- **Value for money.** In the UK Tesco's Hudl provides a tablet that gives similar output at a lower price than competitors.

The above features are those that satisfy the needs of the computer tablet-buying consumer. Similar features, but with variances in importance, will be relevant to other products. In addition, other elements of product design are important to a business, for example:

- its financial viability
- legal requirements, such as designs to ensure safe use
- its effect on the organisation's reputation
- whether the business can produce it without difficulty.

Fact file

Glastonbury Festival

The Glastonbury Festival is a good example of a 'service' whose main marketing attempts are focused on its qualities as a 'product'. Whereas other festivals are advertised heavily through the media and promotions, Glastonbury relies on a number of unique attractions:

- its image as a 'lifestyle' event rather than a 'big gig'
- its relative lack of corporate sponsorship
- the views and leadership of its organiser, Michael Eavis
- its financial support for charities such as WaterAid and Greenpeace
- its tradition and reputation as an institution
- the range of music in its typical line-ups: in 2014 performers on the Pyramid Stage ranged from Dolly Parton to Ed Sheeran, Metallica and the English National Ballet

- its ability to attract acts without incurring the huge fees charged to other organisations.

Source: www.glastonburyfestivals.co.uk

Key terms

Boston Matrix A tool of product portfolio analysis that classifies products according to the market share of the product and the rate of growth of the market in which the product is sold.

Product portfolio The range of products or brands provided by a business.

Value of product portfolio analysis and the Boston Matrix

Most large businesses provide a variety of products. Therefore, a key product decision for such businesses is to decide on its product portfolio, i.e. the range of products it will produce. The **Boston Matrix** enables a business to analyse its **product portfolio**.

In a multi-product firm, the product portfolio covers a wide range of products. For example, at one time Heinz had 57 varieties of products. Most firms plan their marketing strategy in a way that spreads their risk. If one product has low sales, it may be supported by other, more successful products.

Businesses should carry out product portfolio analysis regularly. This is the study of the range of products with a view to deciding whether new products should be added to the portfolio and whether any existing products should no longer be provided.

A popular method of product portfolio analysis is the Boston matrix (sometimes referred to as the Boston box or Boston grid). This matrix, shown in Figure 10.1, helps a firm to assess the balance of its portfolio of products.

The Boston Matrix is used in general terms to help an organisation recognise the situation of its products in the market. A product with a high market share is clearly in a strong competitive situation, as it will probably have high levels of customer loyalty. The growth rate in the market is also important. A growing market opens up more opportunities for future expansion, which will enable the organisation to increase sales revenue. However, competitors are more likely to be interested in developing and supporting products in a growing market.

The Boston Matrix allocates products to one of four categories: stars, cash cows, problem children and dogs.

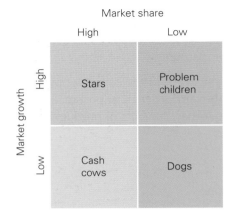

▲ **Figure 10.1** The Boston Matrix

Stars

These are products that have a high percentage market share in a high-growth market. They enjoy increasing sales revenue but, because the market is growing, competitors will be encouraged to focus on this market. As a result, stars need a great deal of promotional spending and may involve the business in capital expenditure (to increase capacity). Therefore, in the short term, they may cause outflows of cash to exceed inflows. However, they will usually generate profits that can be used to support other products.

Cash cows

These products have a high percentage market share in a low-growth market. Cash cows often exist in established markets that have reached maturity. The low rate of growth discourages new businesses from entering the market, so it is possible to spend less on advertising. The name arises from the fact that companies can 'milk' the cash cow in order to support other products. A high proportion of cash cows is ideal for companies seeking high profits, but firms with cash cows will want to develop new products in order to enter high-growth markets. AB Foods foresaw that its core business was growing slowly and used its cash cows, such as Twinings Tea, to finance the development of Primark and the purchase of Ryvita.

Problem children

This term applies to goods or services with a low percentage market share in a high-growth market. The name is given because they pose a difficult problem for a firm (they are also known as 'question marks' or 'wildcats').

By definition, problem children are competing in a competitive market, but as the market is growing, there is scope for future sales increases even if the product does not increase its market share. Many new products will be problem children when first released, so it is inevitable that a firm will possess some of these products. They tend to need a large amount of market research and promotion in order to succeed. If successful, however, they may become stars or cash cows.

Dogs

Dogs are goods with a low percentage market share in a low-growth market. Businesses need to think carefully about retaining such products, as they offer little scope for profit making. In a recession, these products are likely to be withdrawn if they become unprofitable. However, dogs should not be written off too lightly. Cadbury's Whole Nut chocolate bar, for example, could be seen as a dog as it has only a 1 per cent share of a low-growth market (confectionery). However, this 1 per cent market share represents over £45 million of sales per year.

▲ Cadbury's Whole Nut bar is a dog that generates a lot of revenue

On balance, a business would like to have a portfolio of cash cows and stars. However, before drawing firm conclusions from the Boston matrix, those factors that are *not* considered in the matrix should be examined:

Exact meanings of 'high' and 'low' market share

In markets such as vegetable supply, most businesses operate on a small scale and a 10 per cent market share would be considered high; for mobile telephone networks this same figure would be considered low. Ultimately, the number and size of competitors will have a large impact on the success of a product.

Exact meanings of 'high' and 'low' market growth

Similarly, with most economies growing at less than 3 per cent per annum, 'high' market growth may not be that much greater than 'low' market growth. It is also unlikely that high market growth will be sustained for a long period, as markets become saturated. In effect, the anticipated future market growth (which will be unknown) is likely to be just as relevant as the rate of growth already recorded.

Size of the market

A mass market with 'low' growth might offer far more opportunities to increase sales revenue and profit than a small, niche market with 'high' growth.

Definition of the market

This is also vital. Cadbury's bought Green and Black's so that it could enter a niche market for fair trade chocolate. Does Green and Black's have a large market share of a high-growth niche market (making it a star) or a small market share of the chocolate market overall, which is not experiencing high growth (making it a dog)?

How profitable is the product?

For many years, UK car producer Rover enjoyed a high market share in a low-growth market, but its cash cows lost money. The product range of LG, the South Korean electronics company, predominantly consists of cash cows and stars, but it lost almost $60 million in the final quarter of 2013. However, a profit is projected for 2014.

185

Consumer opinions and loyalty

Market share may be a reflection of how long a business has been in a market or the success of its recent marketing mix. If there is a high level of loyalty among customers for a particular business, this might enable it to overcome apparent weaknesses in terms of its products' positions in the Boston Matrix.

In conclusion, it is important to be careful when using the Boston Matrix to analyse a firm's product portfolio as it provides only a simple view of the position of products in relation to market share and market growth. For example, cash cows can lose money and dogs can be profitable in the right circumstances. Always use business theories critically when applying them to a particular situation; they are usually a guide to analysis rather than a scientifically proven fact.

Value of the product life cycle model and extension strategies

Figure 10.2 shows the stages of the **product life cycle**. These stages are:

1 development
2 introduction
3 growth
4 maturity
5 decline.

We will examine each of these stages in turn.

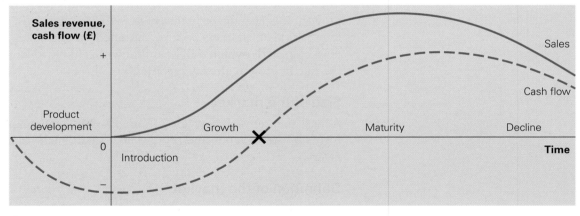

▲ **Figure 10.2** The product life cycle

Note that the examples that follow are based predominantly on goods. However, the product life cycle applies to both goods and services.

1 Development

During this stage, an organisation will undertake various activities to prepare for the launch of its product, including:

- generation of ideas
- analysis of ideas
- product development
- test marketing
- launch.

> **Key term**
>
> **Product life cycle** The stages that a product passes through during its lifetime – development, introduction, growth, maturity and decline.

As can be seen in Figure 10.2, there is no sales revenue during the development stage and a negative cash flow. Cash is required to fund the research and, if the product is going to be launched, there will be a period of high outflows of cash to purchase equipment, employ staff, conduct research and finance advertisements for the launch.

2 Introduction

This stage starts with the launch and continues during the period in which the product is new to the market. Usually, sales pick up slowly at first, as shops are not always keen to stock a new, unknown product and customers are reluctant to change from their existing brands. Intensive introductory marketing and special offers can lead to increased sales volume as customer awareness grows. However, cash flow continues to be negative during the introduction stage because of high marketing costs and low production levels, which mean high average costs of production. Furthermore, sales revenue might also be low if low prices are used to encourage sales (**penetration pricing**). If the product has a successful introduction, it will pass on to the next stage.

3 Growth

As the product becomes more popular, it enters the growth stage. Retailers are more likely to provide shelf space and brand recognition helps to increase sales. Profitability may be reached as the initial burst of marketing is no longer needed and it becomes cheaper to produce each product.

4 Maturity

During this stage, the firm will hope to make a profit and sales will tend to stabilise. However, they may increase steadily if the product is in an expanding market. For example, sales of garden plants have continued to grow, even though plants such as daffodils have been in the maturity stage for many years.

If the market stabilises and stops growing (sometimes an additional stage in the product life cycle, known as **saturation**, is used to describe this), then new competitors are unlikely to be attracted to the market. This may mean that the company does not need to spend so much money on marketing and, with low unit costs of production, it can reap high profits.

5 Decline

Eventually, sales of a product will fall. However, some products, such as Kellogg's Cornflakes, have existed for almost a century. Similarly, the major products of each of the three largest UK chocolate manufacturers were launched respectively, in 1905 (Cadbury's Dairy Milk), 1922 (the Mars Bar) and 1935 (Nestlé's KitKat). In more dynamic markets, such as computer games and the popular music industry, product life cycles are measured in weeks. Once a product is in decline, the firm may decide to remove it from its range to prevent financial losses.

Strategic use of the product life cycle

In theory, a business should aim to have as many products in 'maturity' as possible because these are the products that should generate most profit. However, to achieve this in the long run a firm needs to have a policy of **new product development**, so that it has products in the introduction and growth stages that will eventually enter maturity. Consequently, firms attempt to have a balance of products under development and in the introductory and growth stages, financed by the profits generated by their mature products.

The exact strategies used by a business depend on the stage of the product life cycle.

Introduction

Pricing strategy is a key element at the introduction stage. Very low prices are an excellent way to persuade consumers to try a product for the first time. However, it is usually advisable to make it clear that the low price is for a limited period, as all of the goodwill from customers could be lost if there is a sudden price rise later on. For more exclusive products, a high price may be set to show that the product is superior to its rivals. Whatever pricing strategy is employed, promotion and advertising are needed to help customers recognise the product and to increase their awareness of it. The business also needs to put considerable effort into encouraging retailers to provide shelf space for the product. Without this, its other strategies are doomed to failure.

Growth

During growth the business will adapt its strategies according to its market research results. Possible strategies include modifying the product, targeting new market segments through different promotions, widening the distribution and changing price.

Maturity

A firm will wish to keep its products in this stage for as long as possible and will try to do this by extending their life. It can do this by using **extension strategies**.

The main types of extension strategy are as follows:

- **Attracting new market segments**. Firms may target new groups of consumers or market niches in order to expand sales. Bannatyne Spas have extended their range of treatments to cater for males as well as their original target of female customers.
- **Increasing usage among existing customers**. Kellogg's is promoting its cereal products as items that can be eaten throughout the day, rather than just at breakfast time. This is particularly important as fewer people are eating breakfast.
- **Modifying the product**. Coca-Cola has introduced many variations to its basic product, such as Diet Coke, in order to appeal to different consumers.
- **Changing the image**. Lucozade was originally promoted as a drink to help overcome illness; it has been much more successful as an energy drink.
- **Targeting new geographical markets**. This can involve moving beyond the original region or country targeted by the product. Tobacco companies have been very successful in increasing sales in developing countries.
- **Promotions, advertising and price offers**. To maintain consumer interest, new advertisements, prizes, competitions and promotions such as 'buy one, get one free' can be introduced.

Key term

Extension strategies Methods used to lengthen the life cycle of a product by preventing or delaying it from reaching the decline stage of the product life cycle.

Decline

If the business sees a decline in sales for its product as temporary, it should continue to use extension strategies. Once decline is seen as inevitable, however, the firm can 'milk' the product. By cutting advertising expenditure, it may be able to achieve high profits for a period of time. Eventually, the firm should take the product off the market, but only if it has ceased to be profitable. The sales of most national newspapers are currently in decline but they can still generate a profit. If their rivals leave the market first, it is even possible that their sales will recover.

Problems of predicting the product life cycle

The product life cycle is of limited use in strategic planning because the exact life span of a product is never known. In industries that experience relatively few changes, the life cycle can be easier to predict, but it is more useful in explaining past events than future trends. The confectionery market is relatively stable, with some products having extremely long lifetimes. Recent sales figures suggest that Kellogg's Special K may have entered its decline phase, but this could just be a temporary fall – only time will tell.

Despite the problems of predicting the product life cycle, it is important for a business to consider it in order to assess whether a product launch is feasible. A business needs to know whether it can operate at a loss during the introduction and growth stages and must have a clear idea of when it can expect profit to be made. For example, a record label knows that a download will need to make a profit within months of its launch; a bus company can expect its bus services to take much longer to make a profit.

Fact file

Oxo cubes

Oxo cubes were introduced in 1910, but in the 1950s they went into an apparently terminal decline. Analysts suggested that the product was too old-fashioned to survive. Rather than accept this advice, Oxo repackaged the product and started to promote it heavily. Product variations and highly successful advertising campaigns have kept Oxo in maturity for a further 60 years. Ironically, one of the main reasons for the repackaging was to save costs – the expensive tin containers, which turned out to be the main cause of consumers' dislike of the product, were replaced by cheaper, paper packaging that presented a more modern image.

Financial implications of the product life cycle

There is a tendency to look at the product life cycle purely in terms of its implications for marketing. However, it is also important for the business to monitor a product's life cycle from a financial perspective.

Figure 10.2 (page 186) shows a typical product life cycle and the pattern of cash flow that arises. The dangers of releasing a new product are clear, as it will take some time for a product to generate positive cash flow. The problem is worsened by the fact that many products will incur the costs shown but never reach the introduction or growth stages.

During the development stage, research and development costs are incurred and some market research is necessary. If it is intended to launch the product, expenditure will be incurred in promoting it just prior to launch, and production costs will be high, especially if new equipment is needed to make the product. No cash inflows will be received at this point.

During the introduction stage, some cash will be received from sales, but promotion costs will be very high to make the public aware of the product. Price offers may reduce the inflows of cash. Production costs per unit may be high, as the scale of production will be low.

The growth stage is generally the first opportunity to make profit. It may become possible to cut back on promotion costs, and with growth, lower production costs per item can be achieved. The increased sales revenue should enable the business finally to achieve a positive cash flow situation (shown as point X in Figure 10.2).

In the maturity stage, the firm will receive the highest revenue from the product and unit costs of production should be at their lowest. Consequently, this is the stage where the majority of the profit is made (most cash cows tend to be in the maturity stage of the product life cycle).

Finally, in the early stages of decline, a firm may save money by cutting back on advertising. However, if sales volume falls below a certain level, cash flow may become negative again, particularly because products that are declining in popularity may need price cuts to encourage consumers to buy them. A business may be able to anticipate these problems and withdraw a product before this situation arises.

In conclusion, the product life cycle can be very useful in determining the marketing strategies that a business should use for its individual products. It can also help make decisions about whether to remove a product from sale. However, because product life cycles in general are shortening, this is reducing the value of product life cycle as an aid to marketing decision making.

Influences on, and the value of, new product development

Stages of development of new goods and services

Every new product or service will pass through certain stages before it is launched. Each stage is designed to reduce the level of risk, but even after these stages have been completed, it is still the case that most new products will not survive. The stages of new **product development** are described here.

1 **Generation of ideas**. For some products, ideas are likely to come from within the company. This might take the form of research and development, leading to the introduction of a new product (a common approach in the pharmaceutical industry). Alternatively, in industries such as broadcasting, ideas are likely to be generated through meetings

> **Key term**
>
> **Product development** When a firm creates a new or improved good or service, for release into an existing market.

190

or suggestions by staff. For other products, ideas will normally come from external market research that will identify the types of new product that customers wish to buy. (Convenience foods are often developed from researching consumer buying habits.)

2 **Analysis of ideas**. The next step is to look at the feasibility of the idea, to consider whether it meets the firm's objectives and fits in with its image.

3 **Product development**. The working of the product may be tested through a prototype or by simulation on a computer.

4 **Test marketing**. The use of test marketing (a small-scale release of the product, usually in a limited area) is helpful as it can avoid heavy financial losses if a product proves to be unpopular.

5 **Launch**. The launch will take place after the business has made modifications suggested by the previous activities. Evidence suggests over 70 per cent of new products that are launched will fail within three years, so firms will want to look closely at the likely future success of any product before its launch. The vast majority of ideas for new products will never reach the launch stage.

Example of product development: PG Tips

The following example shows how these stages were applied to the development of PG Tips Pyramid tea bags.

1 **Generation of ideas**. Unilever (the owners of PG Tips) wanted to increase the appeal of tea to younger consumers. The need for the 'ultimate tea bag' design was identified as the key feature.

2 **Analysis of ideas**. Consumer research was conducted, and the product and its packaging were modified as a result. This led to the setting of objectives. The aim of the new product was to achieve consumption levels of 35 million cups a day, with a higher percentage market share of consumers in their twenties. At this point, different advertising agencies submitted ideas and one was commissioned to develop a campaign of advertising and promotion. Unilever sales forces were then used to demonstrate the product and its support package (the advertising and promotions) to retailers and wholesalers, to evaluate their views and to try to persuade them of the benefits of stocking the new tea bags.

3 **Product development**. The specialist machinery needed to make the new style of tea bags was tested and the production line established. Working prototypes were made to support the visit of the sales force to retailers. It was decided not to use test marketing, as the gradual launch described below allowed Unilever to learn from its early experiences in certain regions of the country.

4 **Launch**. The product was launched region by region in a rolling programme, to make sure that the firm had the resources to support the new product (and to minimise wastage of the old square bags).

The product launch took four years in total, during which constant research led to numerous changes. Market research continues to identify consumer reactions and to inform future strategies and tactics.

Source: www.unilever.co.uk

Did you know?

Tetley's Tea, the market leader for round tea bags, challenged PG's advertisements which claimed that pyramid tea bags enabled the tea to flow more freely and release more taste. In July 2014, the ASA (Advertising Standards Authority) accepted scientific evidence that PG's pyramid tea bags are more efficient in releasing the taste than round tea bags.

Influences on new product development

Ideas for new products come from a variety of sources.

Technology

- New technology can allow new products to be developed that are considered superior to existing products. The success of Dyson 'cyclonic' cleaners is based on the fact that the technology is superior to 'vacuum' cleaners, which previously dominated the market.
- Technology can lead to the development of totally new products that meet a consumer need that was previously unfilled. Mobile telephones are an example of such a device.
- Improvements in technology can bring products into a wider market. As technology has improved, household items such as computers have moved from niche, business-based markets to mass consumer markets.
- Production and process technology has advanced considerably, enabling organisations to produce goods and services that are more advanced and can be made more cost-effectively.
- Information and Communication Technology (ICT), in particular, has enabled businesses to produce goods and services that are tailored to the individual specifications of the consumer. Organisations such as insurance companies can provide a much quicker quotation for a customer and can show the effects of any modifications to the type of insurance cover provided through a laptop linked to a database.
- Technology now allows companies to be aware of any changes in consumer wishes. Much of this is achieved through loyalty cards and monitoring of sales records. A more unusual example of the use of technology is Cadbury's Wispa bar. Production ceased in 2003 but an internet campaign and petition by fans led to its relaunch in 2007. Other products that have been reintroduced as a result of internet campaigns are Walker's Worcester Sauce crisps and Golden Wonder cheese and onion Ringos.

▲ A campaign by fans caused Cadbury's to bring back the Wispa bar

Competitors' actions

- The introduction of a new product by a competitor may take away the business's market share. In response, the business will try to introduce its own new product (known as a 'me-too' product) in order to match its competitor.
- New products from competitors can give a business ideas for a new product. For example, Apple's iPhone has led to the introduction of similar products by its competitors.
- Changes in consumer tastes may be detected through the actions of a competitor. This may lead to an organisation introducing new products or services to fulfil consumers' wishes. High street stores often produce new ranges of clothing by copying styles that have worked well for competitors.

Entrepreneurial skills of managers and owners

- If an entrepreneur can be the first person to identify a gap in a market or a potentially successful idea, his or her business can gain 'first mover' advantage. This is the benefit of being the first business to develop a certain product or concept. Bill Gates and Paul Allen, the founders of

Microsoft, were among the first people to recognise the importance of operating systems and software in the computing industry. Previously, most computing companies focused on hardware. The success of Microsoft has enabled Bill Gates to be recognised as the world's richest man in 15 of the last 20 years, with a net worth of $76 billion in 2014.

- Many organisations try to encourage and reward managers who come up with innovative ideas. Organisations use suggestion boxes, kaizen groups or consultation in order to create a culture in which staff are encouraged to think creatively. This approach means that new ideas, such as suggestions for new products and services, are more likely to occur. Virgin is an example of an organisation that encourages this approach.
- Some new products arise from research and development. Many organisations devote considerable resources to the investigation of new products, especially in industries such as pharmaceuticals, engineering and motor vehicle manufacture. Although results are not guaranteed, these organisations are more likely to develop new products as a result of their initiative than organisations that do not devote resources to such activities.

Fact file

Tea 42

In November 2013, William Hannah and Jason Abbott launched Tea 42 in Manchester. Tea 42 is a tea room/restaurant offering gluten-free food. According to Hannah, 'A tenth of people in the UK have a gluten-intolerance, whether diagnosed or undiagnosed. And there's a growing trend of healthy eaters who are trying to cut down on gluten.' The priority has been to produce high quality food. The quality can be witnessed by the fact that 70 per cent of customers are not gluten-intolerant. The tea room/restaurant is on course for annual sales of £800,000 in its first year and is planning to roll out 20 outlets across the UK, with three opening within the next six months. According to Hannah, 'It is about being able to capitalise on what people want and when they want it. A first-mover advantage is central to building a national gluten-free dining brand. The big chains are always improving their gluten-free offering, so we keep an eye on that, but there's no direct competitors yet.'

Source: 'Tea 42 makes dough out of gluten-free dining', by Rebecca Burn-Callander, *Daily Telegraph*, 1 July 2014

Other factors

Several other factors are important in the development of new products.

- **Market research**. This enables organisations to identify potential new products or services that can meet consumer needs.
- **Ideas from other countries**. Many businesses observe the success of products or services in other countries. Karaoke, for example, originated in Japan but has been adapted in other countries.
- **Personal experience**. Some products arise from individual experiences. Tony and Maureen Wheeler founded Lonely Planet as a result of their back-packing experiences; Levi Roots introduced Reggae Reggae Sauce based on family recipes developed by his mother and grandmother.

- **Personal need and inventiveness**. Heather Gorringe, founder of Wiggly Wigglers, was faced with a problem when her father gave her responsibility for a herd of sheep. Faced with large piles of manure, her response was to use worms to create compost from the sheep's waste. Since 1990 the business that developed from this idea has grown into one with sales in excess of £3 million per annum.
- **Environmental awareness**. This factor is leading to a number of new products and adaptations to existing ranges. In an attempt to reduce landfill and save energy, Waitrose is cutting its level of packaging and using lighter and more biodegradable materials. Researchers are developing new varieties of grass and clover that will reduce emissions of methane gas from cows. Currently, cows account for between 20 and 25 per cent of methane gas emissions that arise as a result of human activity. Methane gas has a warming effect over 20 times greater than that of carbon dioxide.

Value of new product development

New product development may enable a business to achieve a unique selling point/proposition – this is a feature of a product or service that allows it to be differentiated from products offered by its competitors.

If a business can improve customer awareness and goodwill by making new products that are different from rival products, it can increase both its sales volume and its price. Loyal customers are also less likely to stop buying the firm's products. Note that the value of an item is the price that people are prepared to pay – branding can improve people's desire for a product and thus add value. Coffee is a classic example of a product that has achieved higher added value through marketing. People will pay much more for coffee than the cost of its original ingredients for several reasons:

- Brand names have persuaded customers that certain coffees are superior to others.
- Images created by advertising (e.g. for Gold Blend) attract people who wish to relate to that image.
- Modifications to the blend (decaffeinated, Colombian, etc.) can attract specific segments of the market.
- Packaging may enhance the perceived quality of the product.
- The service provided by coffee shops has created a cultural change. Shoppers are prepared to pay much more for a coffee because of the attractive environment in which they consume it.
- Greater individuality of blends, as provided by companies such as Costa, has aroused a higher level of interest and has persuaded customers to purchase more coffee at a higher price.

Partly as a result of this marketing activity, coffee is now the UK's second largest commodity market (after oil).

In order to maximise the value of new product development, businesses must ensure that they have an appropriate range of products. Views on product strategy vary between companies and over time. Some businesses are noted for their focus on core products or services, providing a relatively narrow range of products. Coca-Cola and McDonald's are good examples. Other businesses develop a diverse range of goods and services (known as product proliferation) – notable examples being Unilever and Virgin. Table 10.1 summarises the key reasons for each approach.

What do you think?

Select any two companies not previously mentioned in this chapter and explain how they achieve product differentiation. Explain the reasons for any differences and similarities between the methods that they use.

In the 1960s and 1970s, business strategies often concentrated on the need for expansion and diversification, mainly so that UK firms could compete with manufacturers from larger markets, such as the USA. However, since the 1980s business thinking has tended to support smaller, more flexible business structures that are able to respond more quickly to consumer tastes. This has led to firms moving from wide product ranges towards more limited, focused product ranges.

▼ **Table 10.1** Benefits of different product strategies

Focus on core	Product proliferation
• Concentration on areas of expertise will lead to greater efficiency, as the firm will benefit from specialisation.	• Increasing the number of products will spread risks and this may help to secure the firm's future.
• The firm is more likely to understand the nature of its core business and so is more likely to recognise the needs of the market.	• Different products or variations of a product can appeal to different market segments, so this approach will allow a firm to increase sales.
• Each product is likely to be produced on a much larger scale, so the firm will benefit from internal economies of scale.	• Market saturation may mean that a firm can grow only if it diversifies into different areas of activity.
• Consumers will trust a firm's ability to deliver quality if it concentrates on a few carefully selected areas of activity.	• Customer tastes may be changing and widening as people want more variety.
• Directors will be more capable of controlling an organisation with a narrow focus than one that covers many different activities.	• There may be greater scope for expansion in other product areas.

Firms that desire product proliferation are more likely to focus on new product development. However, it is essential that companies that focus on their core ensure that their core products are modified or new products introduced in order to meet changes to customer needs.

Fact file

Focus on core business at Ford

Ford Motors is an example of a company that is returning to a focus on core products. Having diversified into luxury car brands such as Aston Martin, Volvo and Jaguar, Ford then decided to sell those businesses in order to concentrate on its core range of family cars.

Fact file

Product proliferation at Fat Face

Fat Face started as a business in 1988, providing printed T-shirts for skiers and snowboarders. Joint owners, Jules Leaver and Tim Slade, realised that in order to sustain turnover throughout the year they would need to produce other products. To satisfy demand in the summer months, they produced T-shirts and fleeces that appealed to sailing and windsurfing enthusiasts. In 2014, sales turnover had grown to £200 million per annum.

Source: www.fatface.co.uk.

The state of the economy also influences the choice between core business and product proliferation. In boom times, businesses are anxious to attract as many customers as possible and will therefore broaden their product range. In times of recession, businesses seek to cut costs. A reduction in the number of products can be a cost-effective way of achieving this, especially as one product may be 'cannibalising' (taking away) sales from another of the firm's own products.

Practice exercise 1

Total: 60 marks

1 Goods that are purchased and consumed regularly by a lot of customers and tend to be sold at low prices are:
   a) convenience goods
   b) industrial goods
   c) shopping goods
   d) speciality goods   *(1 mark)*

2 Designer clothing is most likely to be a:
   a) convenience good
   b) industrial good
   c) shopping good
   d) speciality good   *(1 mark)*

3 Analyse possible reasons why 70 per cent of all new products fail within three years.   *(9 marks)*

4 In the Boston Matrix, what is the difference between a 'star' and a 'dog'?   *(4 marks)*

5 Why are some products in the Boston Matrix called 'cash cows'?   *(3 marks)*

6 State one example of a product's USP.   *(1 mark)*

7 Explain how a firm's marketing mix might have helped to create this USP.   *(6 marks)*

8 Explain two advantages for a firm that decides to focus on its core business.   *(6 marks)*

9 Explain one benefit of product proliferation.   *(4 marks)*

10 Identify the four stages of the product life cycle that follow the launch date of a new product.   *(4 marks)*

11 Identify the most profitable stage of the product life cycle.   *(1 mark)*

12 Why might a business not want all of its products at this stage of the product life cycle?   *(5 marks)*

13 Identify three extension strategies and give a real-life example of each one.   *(6 marks)*

14 Analyse two factors that might influence a product's marketing mix.   *(9 marks)*

Pricing decisions

There are many approaches that a business can use to decide on its prices. This chapter will focus primarily on **penetration pricing** and **price skimming**.

Penetration pricing

In penetration pricing, low prices are set to break into a market or to achieve a rapid growth in market share. Many firms use this strategy when a product is first released or to entice new customers. For example, credit card companies often make introductory offers in order to gain new customers. In this way, they increase their market share and possibly increase brand awareness.

Although penetration pricing is often associated with new products, it is also used for established products. In this instance it is an example of an extension strategy. Over time, some consumers tend to slowly reduce their consumption of a product, unless they are reminded of its benefits through promotions or other elements of the marketing mix. A significant cut in price can be a very effective way of encouraging consumers to return to this product and remember the reasons why they have bought it regularly in the past. However, firms using penetration pricing in this way have to be cautious. Consumers often see the lower price as the standard price for this product and this can have a detrimental effect on consumption once the price returns to its previous higher level. For this reason, penetration pricing is often clearly promoted as a special offer, such as '10% off' or 'three for the price of two'.

Penetration pricing can also be used to attract a new market segment, particularly one that is more price-conscious. However, this is often linked to a slight modification in the product so that existing customers can continue to buy the original product at a higher price.

Price skimming

In effect, this is the opposite of penetration pricing. This method of pricing is often used during the introduction of a product, particularly in the case of technology or fashion products. These products, when first released, appeal to **early adopters** – people who want to be among the first to purchase a new product. Such consumers will pay for the status of being an early adopter.

In the long term, firms use this strategy for products that they hope will 'skim the market'. This means appealing to a more exclusive, upmarket type of customer. Apple, Chanel, Harrods and Bang & Olufsen are brands that employ this pricing strategy. The objectives in these cases are to maximise value added or profit margins and to establish a prestigious brand name.

In competitive markets, it can be very difficult to follow a policy of price skimming, as customers will find it easy to find alternative product. Therefore price skimming is normally linked very closely to other elements of the marketing mix. If a firm can provide a unique product with features

What do you think?

Look for a recently introduced product. How much lower is the introductory price than those of its competitors? Have you purchased any new products because the price seemed to be so low?

▲ Chanel employs a price skimming strategy

that differentiate it from other alternatives, or if the process of buying can be made so much easier and user-friendly than that of its competitors, then people are more likely to be prepared to pay a high price for the product. A similar result can be achieved through the other Ps of the marketing mix. In this way the marketing mix enables the business to use price skimming and therefore achieve higher profit margins.

Other approaches to pricing

Price leadership and price taking

In price leadership a large company (the price leader) sets a market price that smaller firms (price takers) tend to follow. Large retailers such as Currys and manufacturers such as Ford influence prices for electrical goods and cars in this way. In some industries, such as petrol, price leadership may be shared among a few major firms. Small firms will usually follow the price leader's price because a lower price could trigger a **price war**, while a higher price might mean that they lose customers. By becoming the established brand leader, a firm can ensure that prices are set at a level that suits it and discourages price competition.

Predator (or destroyer) pricing

In this strategy, a firm sets very low prices in order to drive other firms out of the market. For example, cut-price airline fares have led to some small airlines closing or being taken over by competitors.

Loss leaders

Some firms, such as supermarkets, set low prices for certain products in order to encourage consumers to buy other, fully priced products. Cheap bread and milk (at the back of the supermarket) will lead customers through the store, during which time they may buy many other products from which a greater profit is made. (In practice, 'loss leaders' are often sold at reduced profit margins rather than at a loss.) Manufacturers use loss leaders too – the main product may be a loss leader, but the accessories can create the profit.

Psychological pricing

Psychological pricing is intended to give an impression of value (e.g. £3.99 instead of £4, or £99 rather than £100). Although a few retailers, such as Marks and Spencer, do not use this approach any more, the frequency of its use suggests that firms believe that it does attract extra customers.

Paintballing is an industry that uses this technique in a slightly different way. The full-day fee at the local paintball venue may be £30. This price encourages customers and provides them with everything that they need to 'destroy' their enemies, including 100 paintballs. However, the average 'paintballer' uses 500 paintballs a day and additional paintballs can add between £30 and £80 to the price.

Influences on the pricing decision

The two main influences on the pricing decision are:

● the costs of production
● the price elasticity of demand.

Costs of production

All the pricing decisions described above rely on setting a price that customers find acceptable. However, a business also needs to ensure that it makes a profit, so the price of a product must be high enough to cover costs (unless a loss leader or predator pricing approach is being used). To make sure that the price suits both the customer and the business, businesses often use cost-plus pricing.

In cost-plus pricing the price set is the average cost of a product plus a sum to ensure a profit. For example, a clothes retailer typically adds 100 per cent to the wholesale cost of purchasing a dress, while a pet food manufacturer adds 30 per cent to the manufacturing costs when selling to a supermarket chain. Thus a dress purchased wholesale by a retailer for £50 is sold to the customer for £100; a tin of cat food that costs 30p to make is sold to the retailer for 39p, and the retailer then adds on a profit margin before selling to the customer. The percentage added on to the average cost is known as the mark-up.

In determining what percentage mark-up to add to its costs, a business must remember that it needs to make profits and appeal to the market. If the percentage added on is too low, it may mean a lost opportunity to make profit; if it is too high, it will reduce sales. The percentage added on depends on:

● the level of competition
● the price that customers are prepared to pay
● the firm's objectives, for example, whether it is aiming to break even, to maximise profit or to gain a high market share.

Price elasticity of demand

This topic was examined in Chapter 8. To recap briefly, if a product has high (elastic) price elasticity of demand, then a price decrease by a certain percentage will lead to a larger percentage increase in demand and so lead to an increase in total sales revenue. In contrast, a price increase will lead to a larger percentage decrease in the number of customers buying the product and so sales revenue will decrease.

For a good with a low (inelastic) price elasticity of demand (between 0 and −1), a price decrease by a certain percentage will lead to a smaller percentage increase in demand. Therefore, a price decrease will lead to a fall in total sales revenue, while a price increase will lead to a rise in total sales revenue.

Practice exercise 2
Total: 35 marks

1 What is meant by the term 'psychological pricing'? *(3 marks)*

2 The following costs apply to a product: wages 50p, raw materials 60p, other costs 70p.
   a) What price would be set if cost-plus pricing were used and a mark-up of 100 per cent were chosen by the business to set the price? *(3 marks)*
   b) Wages rise by 10 per cent and the mark-up is reduced to 80 per cent. Calculate the new price. *(4 marks)*

3 Explain two reasons why a company might use price skimming and state two real-life examples of this strategy. *(8 marks)*

4 Explain two reasons for penetration pricing by a business. *(8 marks)*

5 What is the difference between a 'price leader' and a 'price taker'? State one example of each. *(6 marks)*

6 What is meant by a 'loss leader'? *(3 marks)*

Case study: Shakeaway

Shakeaway is a retailer specialising in unusual flavours of milkshake. The business opened in Bournemouth in 1999 and now operates 35 outlets, mostly in the south of England, focusing mainly on tourist resorts and upmarket towns.

The stores offer over 180 different milkshakes, with flavours such as apricot, Bakewell tart, Bourbon biscuit, Parma violets, Toblerone and Trebor spearmint softmints. These are blended with ice cream and milk to create the finished product. This culinary experience can be improved further by adding products such as bran, wheatgerm, chocolate flake and marshmallows. Jelly Tot fans can choose a Jelly Tots milkshake topped with Jelly Tots. Although the product range has expanded steadily, some products are taken off the market as their popularity declines.

At present this is a niche market, as most other providers of flavoured milkshakes have not ventured far beyond strawberry and chocolate. However, competition is entering the market in the form of businesses such as 'Shakeaholic', although this is based in the North East.

In response, the business has diversified slightly into yoghurts, hot drinks (including hot milkshakes) and confectionery, but the vast majority of its sales come from milkshakes.

Shakeaway stores tend to adopt a standardised layout, designed to attract its target market of teenagers and families. Milkshakes are prepared fresh, to order, by trained 'shakettes'. However, there is a conflict between the need to make the product to order and the waiting time, as the milk shakes are often bought by shoppers with limited time.

Shakeaway currently uses psychological pricing, with its standard milkshakes priced at £2.99 (regular) or £3.99 (large). However, customers can pay £1 more for 'luxury milkshakes' and can pay 49p or 98p for extra ingredients. Shakeaway decided on a price-skimming policy when it opened its shops. Price-skimming policies are popular for new products. Shakeaway was able to maintain this pricing strategy for the first five or six years of its existence, with profit margins increasing each year. However, during and since the recession price rises have not kept pace with the increases in its costs. There are worries that its existing psychological pricing approach may reduce profits in the future.

The cost of ingredients for a typical, regular milkshake is estimated at £1.10. Labour and other costs are estimated at £380 per day, during which an average of 500 milkshakes would be sold.

Sources: various, including www.shakeaway.com

Questions

Total: 65 marks

1 As a brand, Shakeaway has a large market share in a fast-growing niche market. In terms of the Boston Matrix, the Shakeaway brand is a:

a) Cash cow

b) Dog

c) Problem child/question mark

d) Star *(1 mark)*

2 Explain two important features of the Shakeaway product that have helped the business to succeed. *(6 marks)*

3 Are Shakeaway milkshakes a convenience good, a shopping good or a speciality good? Justify your view. *(8 marks)*

4 Explain two benefits of product proliferation for Shakeaway. *(6 marks)*

5 Explain one way in which knowledge of the product life cycles of its products might benefit Shakeaway. *(4 marks)*

6 What is meant by the term 'price skimming'? *(3 marks)*

7 Look at the figures in the case study.

a) Calculate the average cost of production of a regular milkshake. *(5 marks)*

b) Shakeaway uses a cost-plus pricing method. Use your answer to part (a) to calculate the percentage that Shakeaway adds on to the average cost in order to set its price for a regular milkshake. *(4 marks)*

8 Analyse why Shakeaway originally used price skimming. *(8 marks)*

9 Shakeaway believes that demand for its milkshakes is price inelastic. Analyse two reasons why this might be true. *(8 marks)*

10 Evaluate the main factors that may lead to Shakeaway being forced to change its current strategy of psychological pricing. *(12 marks)*

Decisions about the promotional mix

Value of branding

Building a brand is a time-consuming matter. Consumer loyalty to a brand usually arises from constant exposure to the firm's products, its promotions and advertising. This can be very expensive, but many firms believe that the benefits of **branding** more than outweigh the expenses involved in building a brand.

Benefits of branding

- **Increased demand**: a popular brand will attract more consumers and therefore increase the volume of sales. If the volume increases this will offer opportunities for the business to produce on a large scale and so reduce unit costs, allowing the business to enjoy a higher profit margin on the branded product.
- **Increased price**: one of the key benefits of branding occurs when its popularity makes it more valuable to customers. If the business can convince customers that there is no close alternative (because the product is so well differentiated from its competitors) then it will enable the business to increase price without losing many customers. In effect, branding is a factor that can lead to price inelastic demand. A business with products that have price inelastic demand can increase sales revenue by increasing the price of these products. Not only will the price increase lead to higher sales revenue, but also it will cut costs because the higher price will have reduced sales volume slightly, meaning fewer products need to be produced. Therefore this is a guaranteed way of increasing profits.
- **Reduced competition**: it is very difficult to compete against popular brands, such as Coca-Cola and Facebook. These large brands can become so popular that they eliminate or take over competitors. They can also create barriers that prevent or discourage small competitors from entering the market, as it will be very difficult for such firms to get a foothold in the market. If there is no competition in the market then this will enable the business to both increase its sales volume and price as customers will find there are few alternative products available.
- **Protection against downturns**: popular brands tend to survive recessions and economic difficulties more than other products, as in these situations customers usually avoid the risks of buying a product that may be unreliable or unknown.
- Popular brands can help a business in other aspects of its operations. The human resource function will find it easier to recruit staff as people will want to work for a well-known company or brand. Suppliers and retailers will also be more anxious to build up links with the business, as their association with a strong brand will help them to succeed too. This puts the brand owner in a strong position when negotiating contracts and agreements.

Finally brands have a value in their own right as they are an intangible asset (something that has value but cannot be seen). The 'Did you know?' feature on the left and 'What do you think?' feature that follows provide some illustrations of this value.

What do you think?

A number of organisations publish league tables of company brands and their values. In 2014 *Forbes* list of brand values rated Apple as the world's most valuable brand.

▼ **Table 10.2** Value of selected business brand names

Rank	Brand	Country	Value ($ millions)
1st	Apple	USA	104,680
2nd	Samsung	South Korea	78,752
3rd	Google	USA	68,260
4th	Microsoft	USA	62,783
5th	Verizon	USA	53,466
Selected others:			
16th	Vodafone	UK	29,612
18th	Shell	UK/Holland	28,575
20th	HSBC	UK	26,870

Source: www.forbes.com

How can brands be valued in this way? Do you think these measures are reliable? What do you think?

Key terms

Advertising The process of communicating with customers or potential customers through specific media (e.g. television and newspapers).

Promotion In the context of marketing, the process of communicating with customers or potential customers. Promotion can also describe communication with other interested groups, such as shareholders and suppliers.

Author advice

Do not confuse advertising and promotion. Advertising is just one element of promotion, although it is often the key element in the promotional mix of a product. The distinction between the two will become clearer as this chapter describes the other elements of the promotional mix that can be used alongside or instead of advertising.

Promotion

Promotion and **advertising** can be informative or persuasive. Informative promotion is intended to increase consumer awareness of the product and its features. Persuasive promotion is intended to encourage consumers to purchase the product, usually through messages that emphasise its desirability.

Promotion is often categorised as:

● above-the-line promotions – advertising through media (newspapers, television, radio, the cinema and posters)
● below-the-line promotion – all other promotions, such as public relations, merchandising, sponsorship, direct marketing, personal selling and competitions.

Promotion has many different aims. A popular model that is used to demonstrate the different aims of promotion is **AIDA**. This is a mnemonic that stands for Attention, Interest, Desire, Action, and describes the process of a successful marketing campaign.

● **Attention**. The first step in a promotional strategy is to get the attention of the consumer. Attention-raising is mainly an attempt to improve awareness of the name and product among the target audience. Typically, advertising at this stage is used to make people aware of the product, but it does not aim to provide them with detailed information.
● **Interest**. Promotional campaigns are usually drip-fed over a period of time, using various forms of media, in order to gain the interest of consumers. After hearing a brand name repeatedly, consumers are more likely to trust it. The intention is to make consumers want to find out more about the product. The choice of media, messages and images will be based on the interests of the target market.

● **Desire**. Having gained the consumer's interest, promotions may change in nature to provide the consumer with more specific reasons for purchasing the product. This often involves informative advertising, such as giving the technical specifications of a piece of equipment. However, in some markets, desire is fuelled by imagery. In such cases, promotions will be persuasive rather than informative.

● **Action**. The final and crucial step is converting desire on the part of the consumer into the action of purchasing the product. Point-of-sale displays, special offers and competition entries are popular methods of achieving this aim. In the case of goods that are 'impulse buys', promotions in the shop itself are much more likely to be successful.

AIDA should be seen as an integrated whole. A brilliant shop display is unlikely to be successful if earlier stages have been missed and the consumer fails to recognise the item being displayed. Similarly, attention, desire and interest may not convert into action if the product cannot be located in a store.

Fact file

How important is media advertising?

Media advertising is popularly seen as the most significant form of promotion, but the AIDA model puts it into perspective. It is unlikely that a consumer's decision to purchase something will be based on advertising alone, especially if it is not a printed form of advert. Television, radio and cinema campaigns are usually meant to bring people's *attention* to a product, raising their *interest*. As a general rule, it is the more detailed informative promotions that create *desire*, and brochures and merchandising activities that trigger *action*. However, as with so many business issues, there will be plenty of exceptions to this rule.

Did you know?

A classic example of a successful 'attention' campaign was the Amy campaign in 1984. A poster of a young girl appeared on bus shelters across the country accompanied by the sentence 'I'm Amy and I like slugs and snails.' After a time without any further information, the national media picked up on the story, and they tried to discover who Amy was and what she was meant to be promoting. Eventually, market research revealed that 75 per cent of the UK population had heard of Amy. At this point it was revealed that Amy was promoting the idea of using bus shelters for poster advertising. With 75 per cent awareness achieved, advertising agencies began to recognise the effectiveness of this (previously unpopular) method of advertising. This style of attention or awareness raising is known as a 'teaser campaign' and has been used successfully by organisations as diverse as the government and Orange.

Author advice

Be careful not to confuse the marketing mix and the promotional mix. The marketing mix covers ALL techniques designed to sell a product; the promotional mix only examines promotions that are designed to sell a product.

Elements of the promotional mix

The promotional mix is the co-ordination of the various methods of promotion in order to achieve overall marketing targets.

Public relations (PR)

PR involves gaining favourable publicity through the media.

The public will recognise that an advert is designed to sell a product and will therefore be wary of the messages being sent. However, an article in a newspaper that praises a product can raise awareness in a cost-effective way. If Jeremy Clarkson can be persuaded to test drive the new Porsche on television, it can help Porsche to sell more cars. Newspapers may publish a 'press release' from a business if the story is considered newsworthy, so firms will often try to find a human interest story connected to their product. Successful PR relies on the reaction of the media to the story being put forward by the firm. As a result, it is more unreliable than most other forms of promotion, but it is extremely cost-effective when it works.

Merchandising

Merchandising attempts to persuade consumers to take actions (usually buying the product) at the point of sale (PoS) – also known as the point-of-purchase (PoP). Kellogg's tries to persuade retailers to offer more shelf space (e.g. by producing variations of basic cereals); Procter & Gamble has a special team that advises small retailers on the most attractive way to display its products; Tic Tac produces displays that persuade consumers to buy at the point of sale.

Both manufacturers and retailers try to maximise sales by using psychological research. To improve the shopping environment in supermarkets, pleasant smells (e.g. fresh bread) are pumped around the building and colourful displays of fresh produce are placed near the entrance. Merchandising is well suited to 'impulse buys' of convenience goods, but because merchandising works at the point of sale, it is effective only if other methods are successful in enticing customers to the point of sale.

Sales promotions

Sales promotions are short-term incentives used to persuade consumers to buy a particular product.

Popular sales promotion methods include competitions, free offers, coupons, 'three for the price of two' or BOGOF (buy one, get one free) offers, introductory offers, product placement (featuring a product in a film), credit terms (allowing customers to delay payment) and endorsements by famous personalities.

In the case of business-to-business promotions, approaches such as offering credit terms or providing 'hospitality' (invitations to attend an event or a meal) are often used as sales promotions. Sales promotions are an excellent way of providing a boost to sales, especially when a product is new to the market or would not have been purchased otherwise. If the consumer enjoys the product, it can mean that a new loyal customer has been gained.

Short-term price cuts are often used to persuade consumers to try a product for a short time, in the hope that they will then become loyal customers. However, the cost-effectiveness of promotions needs to be assessed carefully. They often provide only a short-term boost and in many cases they allow customers to purchase more cheaply a product that they would have bought anyway.

Direct selling

Direct selling is the process of communicating directly to the individual consumer through an appropriate form of communication (e.g. by email or telephone) and there are four main forms.

- **Direct mail**: this describes promotions that are sent directly to the customer and is growing rapidly as a form of promotion. Databases are becoming more detailed, so businesses are able to discover an increasing amount about their customers. Businesses such as supermarkets, in particular, use loyalty cards to obtain information on buying habits. This enables them to target direct mail offers for certain items to specific consumers. ('Junk mail' now contains less junk because the offers are more likely to interest the person who has been targeted.)
- **Telephone**: as many households block or throw away 'junk mail', many companies have resorted to making telephone contact, often initially disguised as market research but then transforming into attempts to achieve a sale. Although these tactics are often resented by customers and can be blocked, companies have found them to be quite successful because many people are reluctant to be rude to a telephone caller. However, they can create a negative image of a company.
- **Door-to-door drops**: these are promotions that are delivered directly to houses. They are often delivered with the local free newspaper and can be highly cost-effective and targeted. IKEA, for example, delivers its catalogues in August and September, the beginning of the run-up to Christmas. Postcodes that provide the highest sales are identified through sales records and houses in these postcode areas are targeted to receive the catalogue.

- **Personal selling**: this is considered to be a crucial element in the final action to buy by consumers. In general, high labour costs have led to a decline in door-to-door selling, but for durable items such as housing, cars and household goods, the role of the individual salesperson is crucial. In these cases, customers may value the expertise or details provided by the salesperson. Personal selling is particularly important in commercial marketing, where a company's sales force contacts other firms that are seen as potential customers.

In general, direct selling – particularly telephone contact – is often seen by consumers as an invasion of privacy, so businesses must use it with caution.

Advertising

Advertising is the process of communicating with customers or potential customers through specific media (e.g. television and magazines).

The main media chosen for advertising are outlined below, with a brief comment on their use.

Fact file

Television advertising

Although television advertising has experienced some decline, it still remains an effective medium. Slogans such as 'Beanz meanz Heinz' and 'A Mars a day helps you work, rest and play' are remembered long after the firm stops using them.

Did you know?

Programmes such as *Coronation Street* and *Emmerdale* gained the nickname of 'soaps' because traditionally they were watched by housewives who decided which soap powder the family should use. As a result, the advertising slots during these programmes became the most popular times for companies that wanted to advertise their soap.

Television

Television has the advantage of being memorable, as it can present both moving images and sound. It is ideal for mass market, fast-moving consumer goods. Although the cost of television advertising is relatively high when considered against the number of viewers reached, the cost per thousand (CPT) can be quite low. The CPT is an indicator that is used commonly in the advertising industry to assess and compare the expense of different forms of promotion.

With the increase in the number of television channels and more specialisation of programmes, often with a narrow focus in terms of audience make-up, television advertising is also becoming more suited to niche market products.

Radio

Radio advertising has increased in popularity, because it is flexible enough to target a small local area as well as national markets. Radio advertising tends to be cheaper than many other media, so it is ideally suited to job advertisements in the local area and local events, such as fairs. Mass market companies also use radio advertising, because the low cost per advert means that a wide spread of local radio stations can be used to achieve national coverage at a reasonable overall cost.

Cinema

Cinema advertising can be targeted to specific audiences. For example, the advertisements placed during a Disney film will be different from those featured during a horror film. Cinema advertising can also be used to promote complementary activities such as a restaurant or nightclub to be visited after watching the film. Between 2011 and 2013 the significant decline in viewing by the 15–24 age group was attributed to the release of films whose target audience was the 45+ age group. Viewing by this age group predictably increased from 22 per cent to 36 per cent in this period. This had implications for business which use cinema advertising, because it is traditionally targeted at younger people.

Source: British Film Institute (www.BFI.org.uk)

National newspapers

Although sales of national newspapers have declined, the most popular newspapers, such as *The Sun*, are still read by millions of people every day. Consequently, national newspapers remain a popular medium. Advertisements can be placed on pages that relate closely to the interests of the readership, increasing the effectiveness of the advertisement. This aspect of newspaper advertising is particularly prevalent in weekend newspapers, where magazine supplements featuring interests such as fashion, travel and personal finance contain advertisements related to those features.

Posters

Posters are a highly flexible medium and can be used for mass market products or geared towards certain market segments. In places where customers are likely to be waiting for a period of time, such as the London

Underground, detailed informative advertising can be provided. In general, however, posters are a persuasive form of media, usually geared towards trying to gain initial attention or interest in the product or service.

Magazines

Most magazines in the UK tend to be specifically targeted at a focused audience. This means they are ideal media for promoting niche market products, although magazines are also used by mass market companies trying to boost sales in a particular market segment. The use of colour in magazines and the high quality of print enhances their effectiveness as an advertising medium. In some cases, there is an additional benefit for magazines, such as *Reader's Digest*, that remain in circulation long after their date of release, because they are often found in doctors' and dentists' surgeries as reading material for patients who are waiting for appointments.

Internet

Although internet users may not always be aware of it, they are constantly exposed to promotions while surfing the net. Furthermore, the advertisements on internet pages are invariably specific to the material on that page, so internet advertising can be a cost-effective way of reaching target audiences at a time when they are expressing an interest in a particular topic or product.

Local and regional newspapers

Local or regional newspapers tend to be significantly different from national newspapers in terms of advertising. Advertisements tend to concentrate on goods and services that are sold on a local basis, rather than nationally. Particular products that lend themselves well to local and regional newspaper advertising include new and second-hand cars, property, local entertainment and job opportunities.

Sponsorship

Sponsorship means giving financial assistance to an individual, event or organisation. For example, sponsorship of popular football teams can generate a great deal of publicity for companies. Sponsorship can also be targeted towards a particular audience, as with O2's sponsoring of the O2 Arena in London, a venue that often hosts events that are geared towards O2's target market. Sponsorship can enable organisations that face advertising restrictions to reach customers, and it often improves goodwill when it is seen to be supporting a good cause (e.g. sponsorship of litter bins). It can also give a company access to attractive events such as Wimbledon, performances at the Royal Albert Hall and Grand Prix races. The company can then pass on invitations to customers or suppliers and build goodwill and closer links. However, sponsorship can be unpredictable. An unexpectedly good cup run for a rugby team or a scandal involving the person sponsored can affect results.

Trade fairs and exhibitions

Although some exhibitions are popular with the general public, most exhibitions and trade fairs are used to target other businesses. They can be used to 'network' (get to know people in other businesses), but more importantly they are used to demonstrate products to potential customers and to provide detailed information and brochures. At exhibitions, customers can test and order products, so they can be vital to the success of some firms, especially in industries where new products are constantly being developed.

Influences on the choice of promotional mix

When deciding what form of promotion to use, a business will consider the following factors.

Campaign objectives

If the firm is trying to introduce a new product, it will focus on using media that raise awareness, such as television. If it is aiming to provide information, the internet or newspapers will be more relevant.

Costs and budgets

Small businesses cannot justify the use of a television campaign because of the expense involved. For these businesses, local radio or newspapers are a better choice. Media companies calculate the cost per thousand (CPT) to show how much it costs to get a message to 1,000 consumers. National companies find it much more cost effective to use national newspapers and television, as one advert can reach a large number of people. The marketing budget allocated to the manager will influence the media that can be used. Ryanair is a large firm, but its relatively low marketing budget prevents it from using television advertising in the way that its rivals do.

Target market

Lord Leverhulme, formerly of Unilever plc, is famously quoted as saying: 'Half of what I spend on promotion is wasted. The trouble is I don't know which half.' Firms will spend more eagerly on a medium that reaches their target market. Channel 4 advertisements have a higher CPT because many of the channel's programmes are targeted towards specific groups of people. For the same reason, magazines and local media can be more effective than national media.

Balance of promotions in a campaign

Advertising must be planned along with other promotions to maximise effectiveness. As seen in the AIDA model, advertising usually introduces a campaign, while more specific methods of promotion, particularly merchandising, complete the process. However, the effectiveness of sponsorship can be enhanced by having advertisements running at the same time, such as Barclays plc advertisements during a Barclays Premiership football match.

Legal factors

Restrictions on the use of media, such as limits on alcohol advertising on television, may encourage firms to use different media. Businesses that cannot use television and newspaper advertisements use the internet for word-of-mouth advertising to bypass these restrictions.

External factors

Changes in the overall wealth of a country and the social and political environment can all influence promotions. Customers will usually be more receptive to promotions if they are experiencing higher living standards. The style of the promotions and the images and messages used must also fit in with society's views. For example, more restrictions are now being placed on advertisements targeting children because of changing views about what is acceptable in this area.

What do you think?

Targeting children

Food manufacturers have been criticised for targeting their advertising at children through the cinema, the internet and social networking websites such as Bebo. Examples such as the 'Kids Zone' on McDonald's website and Coco Pops adverts before the most recent Harry Potter film on television have been cited as evidence of this trend. Ofcom has banned television adverts that promote sugary, salty or fatty foods during programmes targeted at children under the age of 16.

Should there be more restrictions on promotions targeted at children?

Practice exercise 3

Total: 70 marks

1 What is the difference between 'promotion' and 'advertising'? *(6 marks)*

2 What does the mnemonic AIDA stand for? *(4 marks)*

3 What is an 'impulse buy'? *(2 marks)*

4 Which media would you select in order to advertise the following? In each case justify your choice.
   a) A job vacancy for a checkout assistant in Asda. *(3 marks)*
   b) A new model of a car. *(3 marks)*

5 Explain one benefit and one problem of direct selling. *(8 marks)*

6 Explain one benefit and one problem of merchandising. *(8 marks)*

7 Explain the difference between sponsorship and public relations. *(4 marks)*

8 Identify two products that might use exhibitions or trade fairs as a form of promotion. *(2 marks)*

9 Identify three examples of sales promotion. *(3 marks)*

10 Briefly explain one advantage and one disadvantage of using the following media for advertising:
   a) television *(6 marks)*
   b) cinema *(6 marks)*
   c) internet *(6 marks)*

11 Analyse factors that an organisation should consider when planning its promotional mix. *(9 marks)*

Distribution (place) decisions

Importance of location

There is a saying in business that the three factors most critical to a firm's success are 'location, location, location'. An important part of decisions about 'place' is making sure a business operates in the right location. This involves the following elements.

- **Convenience**: for major purchases, such as cars, people may be prepared to put time and effort into researching the best deal and locating their ideal product. However, for most products, convenience is crucial. An individual will not want to spend much time trying to find the cheapest litre of milk. Furthermore, for a minor purchase such as a bottle of milk, the time involved and cost of travelling to purchase it from a cheaper source may outweigh the advantage of buying from the local convenience store, where the milk costs more but time taken and travel costs are much lower. Even supermarkets have discovered that convenience is vital. Despite their different reputations, product ranges, pricing policies and promotional techniques, supermarkets' own research has found that the convenience of their location to customers is the most important factor.
- **Accessibility**: the place of purchase must be easy to reach by usual forms of transport. Usually, the further the store is from the town centre, the less likely it is that consumers will find time to visit. However, in some areas, town centre shops may not have an advantage over remoter locations if it is difficult to park and traffic jams are a regular occurrence.
- **Cost of access**: out-of-town shopping centres that provide free car parking have an advantage over town centre shops in some cases. Some councils are now restricting the building of out-of-town shopping centres because their low access cost for shoppers using cars has led to a decline in town centres, damaging the attractiveness of the town centre. Businesses such as Currys are tending to close town centre locations in favour of out-of-town shopping centres and supermarket expansion is largely taking place outside town centres.
- **Reputation**: this is vital for certain goods and services. Private doctors in Harley Street and fashion houses in Knightsbridge benefit from the prestige attached to such addresses. This is reflected in both their volume of sales and in the prices they are able to charge. In many communities there are shopping areas geared towards upmarket shops.
- **Localisation**: some retailers tend to locate close together for consumer convenience. In such cases, any new retailer in that line of business would be strongly advised to choose the same location. Electrical retailers often locate close to each other, despite the fact that it might seem wiser to be in a unique location. This is because customers like to compare prices for major purchases such as washing machines. If two or three electrical retailers are located close together, this will enable the customer to compare products and prices quickly and efficiently. The customer is then unlikely to travel to other locations to examine isolated retailers. Localisation is also common in the case of estate agents, clothing and shoe shops, and solicitors.

Fact file

The Midlands Riviera?

Access to a local beach was never available to the residents of Nottingham before. However, following successful projects in Paris, London and Birmingham, Nottingham has created its own city centre beach. Since 2009, Old Market Square has been turned into a beach from July to September, with 250 tonnes of golden sand. Beach-style entertainment, such as a paddling pool, rides and games are also included. The plan has been so successful that neighbouring Derby has responded with two summer beaches of its own. The beaches have been funded by local councils who recognise that an attractive 'place' encourages consumers to shop in a particular area.

It also encourages some local residents to stay in Nottingham during the summer.

Fact file

Store design

Store design and layout are also vital for success. In April 2014, Marks and Spencer opened its latest 'green' store in York. The new store designs use less energy and have cut carbon emissions by 90 per cent compared with its earlier stores. Marks and Spencer first introduced 'eco' stores in 2007. In 2012, it announced that it had become the first major retailer in the UK to become carbon neutral.

House of Fraser has been changing strategy in a different way. Its most recent stores have been much smaller than its older stores, focusing primarily on fashion items. In April 2014, House of Fraser was taken over by a Chinese company – Sanpower. Sanpower has announced that it intends to open up 50 House of Fraser stores in China, while also establishing a presence in Russia and Abu Dhabi.

Fact file

Jeeves of Belgravia

Jeeves of Belgravia is an upmarket dry cleaners, based in the West End of London. It is able to use its name and reputation, partly arising from the area of London it trades in, to charge higher prices than branches of the business in other areas. The other branches trade under the name of Johnson Service, the owners of Jeeves of Belgravia.

Placement in the point of sale

Market research into groceries indicates that 70 per cent of buying decisions are made in store and that a shopper is exposed to 1.6 pieces of in-store marketing every second.

It is evident that sales can be increased by the careful placing of products in the point-of-sale outlet. Some examples of this practice, based on supermarket placements, are as follows:

- similar products, such as biscuits, being placed together, so that shoppers can make comparisons and more easily tick off their purchases if they are using a shopping list
- supermarkets and greengrocers arranging brightly coloured, attractive fruit and vegetable displays so that they are visible from outside the store
- impulse buys, such as sweets, being placed by the checkouts to catch people's attention while queuing
- popular products, such as Kellogg's Corn Flakes, being given greater shelf space so that they are more likely to be seen and so that the store is unlikely to run out of stock
- loss leaders being scattered around the store, with some placed well away from the entrance, in order to encourage shoppers to walk around the whole store
- standard, everyday purchases, such as bread, being placed at eye level, so that shoppers will find them easily
- complementary products being placed in close proximity, such as cooking sauces being located close to pasta and rice.

Supermarkets sometimes rearrange their store layout. Although this can upset customers in the short run, it is often done to force them to look around the whole store. This can draw their attention to new goods that they may not previously have been aware of, or interested in.

Placement also applies to direct selling. Catalogue shops, such as Argos, and internet sites, such as Amazon, put considerable effort into how products are arranged in their catalogue or website, to make it easy and attractive for shoppers to use.

Number of outlets

Persuading retailers to stock products is often crucial to success. The more outlets that stock the product, the more sales a business can generate. For impulse buys, in particular, the number of outlets is vital. Almost 40 per cent of mint eaters drive while eating mints. Given the limited space in most garage shops, mint producers see place as important. If only one type of mint is stocked, that will be the one purchased, unless the consumer has a very high level of brand loyalty. Therefore, persuading the garage to stock your product in preference to a rival's can be vital.

Businesses can take a variety of measures to increase the number of outlets stocking their products, as described below.

Promotional campaigns

Retailers may be persuaded to stock a product by advertisements in trade magazines. Promotions aimed at consumers may increase demand and so persuade a shopkeeper that he or she needs to stock that product, rather than lose customers. For this reason, manufacturers always keep retailers informed of any future marketing campaigns.

Providing extra facilities or attractive displays

For example, in the frozen food market, manufacturers provide free freezers in return for agreements to stock the firm's frozen foods. In small stores, the lack of space means that this arrangement can also help to exclude rival frozen food manufacturers. Häagen-Dazs achieved large increases in sales by supplying upright freezers. These saved floor space compared with the usual chest freezers and were seen as more attractive by customers. For these reasons they were preferred by both retailers and customers.

Offering high profit margins to retailers

Retailers want to use their space as effectively as possible. Supermarkets have been persuaded to devote more space to non-food items because they can make higher profit margins. Sainsbury's target is for its 'non-food' sales to reach 45 per cent of its total annual sales by 2020.

Paying generous commission to sales staff

This gives the sales force the incentive to persuade retailers that they should stock the products. Sales staff are often paid low basic hourly rates with high commission rates. Commission is a percentage of the order that they secure from the retailer.

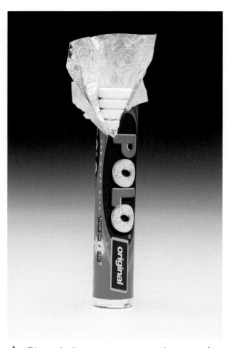

▲ Place is important to producers of mints

Increasing brand variety

Firms such as Heinz and Birds Eye may gain extra shelf or freezer space (at the expense of competitors) if they bring out new ranges of products. With their wide ranges, Heinz and Birds Eye are able to secure more space for their products in the shop. However, if sales of a product are too low, retailers may decide not to stock it. Heinz Salad Cream found itself in this situation when sales became too low and some supermarkets decided not to stock the product; this was partly caused by customers preferring Heinz Mayonnaise.

Getting sole brand deals

In some trades, notably pubs and clubs, producers try to secure a deal to sell only their version of a product. By giving large discounts for bulk buying, companies such as Pepsi-Cola may persuade a pub to make Pepsi the only 'cola' drink served. This approach tends to occur where there is a captive audience. Supermarkets are unlikely to agree to this because customers might choose to go elsewhere if their favourite brands are not stocked.

Investigating alternative outlets

Increased sales may be achieved by discovering new retailers or ways of selling. Some coffee shops have located in larger stores such as Homebase or bookshops such as Borders, while vending machines have become more popular in recent years.

Integrating place with other elements of the marketing mix

No aspect of the marketing mix can work in isolation from the other six Ps and place is no exception. The following example illustrates the importance of integrating the marketing mix – in this case, focusing on place and product.

Example of integrating place and product – the case of the didgeridoo

Where on earth would you buy a didgeridoo? Australia would be a good place to start, but where would you find one in the UK?

The didgeridoo is a product that is growing in popularity, but retailers need to identify the key features of the didgeridoo that make it an essential item for certain individuals. Recognising the key features that appeal to different consumers helps a business to maximise sales. So what is a didgeridoo to its potential customers, and where would you buy one?

- To some, the didgeridoo is a musical instrument. Musicians will pay in excess of £200 for a didgeridoo that has been correctly crafted from a termite-infested eucalyptus tree – but it will need to pass the 'boing' test to be suitable as a musical instrument. These consumers will naturally seek out a didgeridoo in a music shop, but the limited demand may make it difficult for manufacturers to persuade shops to stock them.
- Other customers see the didgeridoo as a spiritual object or a lifestyle statement, as evidenced by the number of sellers at certain festivals. Ideally, potential sellers should reserve a pitch at festivals such as WOMAD.

Fact file

Vending machines

For impulse buys, place is particularly important. The decline of small convenience stores has threatened sales of impulse purchases. Companies such as Mars have responded by placing vending machines in public places to increase the chances of impulse buying. In the UK, Mars has lost market share to Cadbury and Nestlé. However, through owning Klix and Flavia drinks machines, Mars has obtained more knowledge of the vending market and has used this to its advantage.

In the UK there are over 1 million vending machines, generating sales in excess of £3.5 billion per annum. The top three chocolate brands sold through vending machines belong to Mars – the Mars Bar, Twix and Snickers. However, vending machines are even more important for sugar-based sweets, with Fruit Pastilles and Starburst leading the way. At a time when confectionery sales generally are slowing down, vending machine sales are growing by 10 per cent per annum.

- For some buyers, the didgeridoo is an item of ornate decoration, to be artistically placed against a wall. For these customers, craft shops are the best location.
- More socially responsible consumers see the didgeridoo as a way of supporting aboriginal craftsmen and their traditional way of life. These customers are usually targeted by direct mail or internet suppliers.

Place is critical to the marketing of didgeridoos, because there is limited scope for promotion. A magazine, *Didgeridoo*, which was published four times a year, has now ceased trading and so most promotion takes place at the point of sale (often websites).

Did you know?

In 2011, D.C. Thomson, publishers of the *Beano* and *Dandy*, converted their comic strips, such as 'Dennis the Menace', into digital slideshows that can be sent, using paid-for apps, to the growing number of children owning tablets and mobile phones who are making fewer visits to newsagents. There is also a Beano website which includes a retro area for older viewers.

Not only has this increased sales revenue but it has also increased revenue from advertisers. In 2014, Beano had a weekly readership of 528,000, 86 per cent of whom were aged 7 to 10. Advertisers are keen to use a form of media with so many regular users in this age bracket.

Types of distribution channel

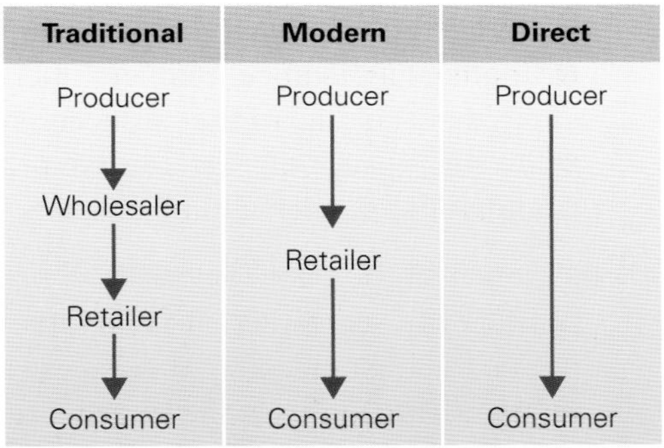

Traditional	Modern	Direct
Producer	Producer	Producer
↓	↓	↓
Wholesaler		
↓	Retailer	
Retailer	↓	
↓		
Consumer	Consumer	Consumer

▲ **Figure 10.3** Channels of distribution

> **Key term**
>
> **Distribution channels** Channels or routes through which a product passes in moving from the manufacturer (producer) to the consumer.

Movement of a product from the manufacturer to the consumer in international trade may involve additional agents, but most domestic distribution involves one of three methods, as shown in Figure 10.3.

A summary of the role of each organisation in the **distribution channel** is presented below.

Producers

The job of producers (or manufacturers) is to make the product.

Wholesalers

The main task of wholesalers is to buy in bulk from the manufacturer (producer) and sell in smaller quantities to the retailer. The existence of wholesalers can benefit both manufacturers and retailers.

- Wholesalers help producers by purchasing their stock of finished goods as soon as it is produced and storing it until consumers want it. This means that producers save on storage costs. By paying immediately, wholesalers can also help the cash flow of producers. This reduces producers' risks – if a product does not sell, it is the wholesaler's problem. Delivery costs are also reduced, as each producer can send a range of products to the wholesaler in one delivery.
- Retailers can also benefit from lower delivery costs, as the wholesaler stocks products from many different manufacturers and will usually deliver the order. This allows the retailer to compare products and prices in order to get the best deals. Retailers may also gain from credit terms being offered by the wholesaler.

Despite these benefits, the role of wholesalers has declined. Wholesalers charge for their services, usually by 'marking up' the price they charge to retailers in order to cover their costs and make a profit. Large supermarkets tend to buy in bulk directly from producers and receive deliveries either straight from the producer or via their own warehouses. Wholesalers have tried to prevent their decline by supporting the small retailers that still use them. Organisations such as the Society for the Protection of the Average Retailer (SPAR) have helped retailers to get together to share orders, in order to keep prices competitive.

Retailers

The main role of the retailer is to hold stocks (inventories) of goods for sale. This serves the needs of the customers wanting those goods by providing:

- convenience: a 'place' that is easily accessible to consumers
- advice: knowledge to help consumers reach the right buying decision
- financial assistance: retailers often provide credit terms or accept payment in a form that suits consumers' needs
- after-sales support: for durable products, the quality of the guarantee or after-sales service can be crucial.

Where a shop is not necessary to perform these roles, it is possible for a producer to sell directly to consumers. Catalogues can provide convenience, financial assistance and after-sales support, eliminating the need for the retailer. Amazon uses the internet directly in order to sell and deliver directly to customers. In the holiday trade, where travel agents add 15 per cent to the costs, direct selling from holiday providers has grown considerably.

Consumers

Consumers are the individuals (or businesses) that purchase the finished product for their own use. The distribution channel used must meet their needs and lifestyles. With more consumers experiencing less leisure time, convenience has become more important. Furthermore, as digital communication has improved, sellers and consumers are able to make direct contact.

Fact file

Tilda and Patak's

Two UK companies founded by Asian immigrants, Tilda and Patak's are now selling rice and curry in India. As the Indian economy has developed, an increasing number of Indians have more money to spend but less time to shop. As a consequence, many middle-class Indians are buying branded, pre-packaged rice from supermarkets rather than visiting traditional markets. This has opened up an opportunity for brands such as Tilda and Patak's to extend their distribution to include India, especially as Western brands are viewed as high quality and prestigious.

Multi-channel distribution

Multi-channel distribution is not new. Companies such as Mars are major users of vending machines, allowing them to sell directly to consumers. However, in order to supply the needs of consumers who buy chocolate from the local corner shop, Mars supplies its chocolates to wholesalers from whom the small retailers buy their stock (inventory). Finally, Mars supplies chocolates directly to major retailers, such as the supermarkets. Referring to Figure 10.3, Mars uses all three channels of distribution.

Screwfix is another business to use multi-channel distribution. For customers who do not want to scrutinise the product in detail before purchasing it, customers can buy directly through the internet. For customers who want to see the product, retail outlets with catalogues are used.

Although multi-channel distribution has existed for a long time, its nature has changed dramatically in recent years. Mars' use of multi-channel, indicated above, was designed to attract different target markets and so there was no integration between different channels. In fact, it was important to keep the customer groups apart, as the prices from each channel tended to vary significantly.

Multi-channel distribution can also provide flexibility for customers. If a customer requests a good from a store that has no inventory of that good, the employees of the store can use the company's IT system to arrange for it to be delivered directly to the customer from another store or warehouse.

More significantly, different methods can work together to meet consumers' needs. For example, a consumer might respond to a promotion by visiting a website. A link on the website can lead to a customer adviser, who can discuss the product with the consumer, perhaps providing more detailed information through a text message or email sent to the customer's mobile phone. The customer can then click-and-collect, ordering online (paying directly from their credit card whose details may already be held by the business) and choosing a place from which the consumer can collect their purchase.

Factors influencing the method of distribution

The final choice of distribution channel depends on a number of factors.

- **Size of the retailer**: in general, large retailers will want to bypass the wholesaler, for reasons already given.
- **Type of product**: for a perishable product being sent to a limited number of retailers, it may be desirable to bypass the wholesaler, but for items such as newspapers there is more need for a wholesaler. Figure 10.4 shows an example where three manufacturers each supply ten local shops through a wholesaler. This involves a total of 13 journeys: three from the manufacturers to the wholesaler, and ten from the wholesaler to the retailers. If each manufacturer had to supply each retailer directly, this would require a total of 30 (3×10) journeys. Similarly, delivering 12 different newspapers to each of 100 newsagents would involve $12 \times 100 = 1,200$ journeys. With a wholesaler, only $12 + 100 = 112$ journeys are needed.

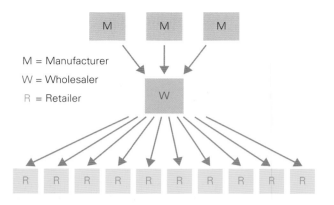

M = Manufacturer
W = Wholesaler
R = Retailer

▲ **Figure 10.4** Distribution through a wholesaler

- **Technology**: with significant advances in technology, more and more products are being sold through the internet, effectively bypassing the wholesaler and retailer. The music industry has already become dominated by internet sales. In 2014, Tesco reported a 14 per cent rise in online sales over the previous year, with online sales of non-food items increasing by 25 per cent. A third of online orders were placed by customers using smartphones or tablet computers, including Tesco's Hudl device, which was one of Tesco's best-selling devices.
- **Geography of the market**: in a remote rural area, it is less likely to be cost-effective for a manufacturer (producer) to deliver directly.
- **Complexity of the product**: if a product is highly complex, direct contact with the producer or an expert retailer may be important.
- **Degree of control desired by the manufacturer (producer)**: in order to control quality and protect their reputation, some firms deliver directly to selected retailers only. For example, Nike and Levi's have prevented retailers such as Tesco from selling their goods.

Fact file
Zara

Place is an important weapon in the armoury of Zara, the Spanish clothing retailer. Zara controls both the production and retailing of its clothes. In this way it can provide much more flexibility. Half of Zara's clothes are produced within 15 days of design, so Zara's fashion experts can copy a fashion idea and produce it within a short time.

Store managers are allowed to make their own decisions on stock, so individual shops can meet local needs. A few copies of each item are distributed directly to each shop and additional orders of those that sell well can be delivered quickly. This has kept Zara at the forefront of fashion retailing. In Spain, customers queue up outside stores when a delivery is expected – a phenomenon dubbed as 'Zaramania' by the Spanish press.

Another advantage for Zara is the impact that its policy has had on customers. The whole stock of a shop is likely to be turned over in a few weeks, so customers know that they must quickly purchase an item that they admire because it is unlikely to be there for long. It also means that customers visit the shop more regularly, as completely new styles of clothes arrive constantly.

Practice exercise 4

Total: 50 marks

1 What is meant by the term 'place' in the context of the marketing mix? *(4 marks)*

2 Explain two reasons why the location of a store is important. *(6 marks)*

3 Why do manufacturers of convenience goods see place as an important factor in the marketing mix? *(6 marks)*

4 Explain two ways in which a company such as Birds Eye can increase the amount of space that retailers provide for its products. *(6 marks)*

5 Describe two services that a retailer provides for its customers. *(6 marks)*

6 Explain two factors that influence the method of distribution chosen for a product. *(6 marks)*

7 To what extent do you believe that the use of multichannel distribution will continue to increase in the future? Justify your view. *(16 marks)*

Case study: Levi Strauss

Formed in the 1850s, Levi Strauss' worldwide sales of Levi clothing and other Levi products peaked at $8 billion in the 1990s, but by 2012 had fallen to less than $4 billion. Research by Levi Strauss revealed that the main reasons for the loss of sales were as follows:

- Denim is no longer seen to be a fashionable material and the Levi Strauss brand is so closely linked to denim.
- Consumers want lower prices; Levi Strauss uses price skimming for the brand.
- The brand has lost its USP as the company's promotions focus on images and messages that are no longer considered to be relevant and attractive. Brands such as 'Diesel' are now considered to be more valuable by Levi's target market.
- Levi Strauss's distribution outlets are less attractive to consumers. Shoppers are moving to fast fashion outlets, such as Zara and H&M, which focus on new fashion rather than tried and tested products.
- Fashion changes have also affected demand. At work there is greater formality in men's clothing while women are buying more 'athleisure' products – clothing suitable for the gym but which can be worn outside too.

According to Ashma Kunde of Euromonitor International, 'the Levi brand is trapped in its denim heritage'.

Levi Strauss considered two alternative marketing strategies:

1 Move production back to the USA and focus on using promotions to emphasise Levi Strauss's unique American heritage. This strategy was rejected, because focusing on moving upmarket would leave the middle ground free for its main competitor – Wrangler.

2 Shift the brand away from its association with working-class men (its 'rugged edginess') in order to achieve a more middle of the market image. A broad promotional mix was used to attempt this change in consumers' perceptions, but the campaign failed to change people's views of the Levi Strauss brand.

Having failed to achieve its aims through promotion, Levi Strauss moved its attention to place. A quarter of its sales were from its own outlets. These outlets sold less than one top (such as a shirt or blouse) for every pair of jeans. However, other retailers it supplied sold more than two tops for each pair of jeans. Levi Strauss decided to focus on selling more complementary products, such as shirts, to its customers with retailers being encouraged to display shirts and jeans together and encourage customers to purchase complementary clothing together.

Other changes to its marketing mix included:

- Broadening its product range by moving into 'athleisure', focusing promotions on cycle tops and gym wear. Levi also signed contracts with leading sports teams, such as the San Francisco 49ers, to sell branded men's shirts.
- Targeting new markets in both India and China. These are the two countries with the largest populations in the world and both of these countries have large areas in which denim products are not sold or available. Levi would withdraw its cheaper brand (called Denizen) from these markets and focus only on selling higher-priced products, under the brand name of Levi Strauss.

Questions

Total: 50 marks

1 Analyse the possible reasons why a new promotional mix failed to change customers' views of the Levi Strauss brand. *(9 marks)*

2 Analyse two ways in which the marketing mix could be employed in order to encourage customers to buy complementary clothing. *(9 marks)*

3 Do you think that Levi Strauss are right to target the Indian and Chinese markets, in order to increase their global sales levels? Justify your view. *(16 marks)*

4 Levi Strauss has largely focused on promotion and place in order to improve its profitability. Do you think it has focused on the right elements (Ps) in the changes to its marketing mix? Justify your view. *(16 marks)*

Decisions relating to other elements of the marketing mix: people, process and physical environment

As the importance of service industries has grown, three additional Ps – people, process and physical environment (physical evidence) – have been added to the original four Ps of product, price, promotion and place.

People

This element of the 7 Ps focuses on the **people** within a business who come into contact with customers. For a physical good, these are likely to be the people involved in the initial selling process and those who are instrumental in providing any after-sales service. However, for a service the people element is of more critical importance as it will be people who provide the service itself. These 'contact' employees are critical because they can have a significant effect, both positive and negative, on customer satisfaction.

To ensure that the people element of the marketing mix is operating effectively a business must:

● recruit workers with a supportive attitude towards customer service
● use motivational techniques to ensure that employees behave in a positive manner while working with customers
● provide training to ensure that customers are provided with a high quality service
● emphasise the importance to employees of the crucial role of after-sales service in creating goodwill and helping to increase repeat purchases.

For services, customers may find it impossible to distinguish between the quality of the service and the quality of the product itself. People may enjoy a restaurant meal because of the prompt and friendly attitude of the staff. In the case of after-sales service for a car, the customer's immediate view of the quality of the service is more likely to be based on the people the customer is in contact with, rather than the technical quality of the work done on the car itself. Many customers cannot separate the product or service from the person who provides it, which is why consumers of services such as hairdressers will often insist on choosing the individual who will provide the service. From a business perspective, managers will try to ensure that the quality of service provided by staff is of the same high quality, regardless of the individual employee providing it.

Process

Consumers want businesses to be 'easy to do business with'. In places, the quality of the **process** is inseparable from the people involved in providing the process.

The nature of service industries is that there is often a requirement for queueing or waiting to be served, and potentially the need for scheduling of the service.

Most services are perishable. For example, if a hairdresser has no appointment available at 11 a.m. then the opportunity to provide that service is permanently lost; similarly the revenue lost from a hotel room that is empty on a certain night can never be regained. Service businesses must ensure that their processes maximise the sales revenue available from time slots, but without inconveniencing the customer. If the customer is constantly faced with a situation in which a hotel's rooms are fully booked, that customer is likely to stop enquiring about rooms in that hotel.

Key elements of process include:

● ensuring that customer enquiries are dealt with promptly
● training and empowering contact staff so that they can answer customer enquiries directly. This means that customers are not passed between different contacts and the length of the process taken for their query to be resolved is shortened
● managing the process to try to reduce the possibility of queueing, by matching supply to demand wherever possible
● enhancing the experience of queueing where necessary. For example theme parks may provide entertainment for people who are queueing for a specific ride
● communicating effectively, so that customers know how promptly they will be dealt with.

Physical environment (physical evidence)

Although the service itself may be intangible, the process of communication between business and customer may involve a number of tangible elements.

Examples of these elements of the **physical environment** include:

● the business's reception area
● company brochures
● letterheads
● the company website
● signage
● equipment
● staff uniforms or the appearance of staff with whom the customer has contact
● physical layout of the environment.

The physical environment may provide the only tangible evidence that a customer possesses before deciding to use the services of a business. If the physical environment/evidence gives a positive message about the business then the customer is more likely to use their services. An unattractive reception area, low quality brochure and non-user-friendly website are likely to dissuade customers.

> **Key term**
>
> **Physical environment** Often known as 'physical evidence', this refers to the tangible features of the service that can enhance customers' experience.

Importance of and influences on an integrated marketing mix

Importance of an integrated marketing mix

A good marketing mix needs to be co-ordinated so that each element supports, and is consistent with, the other parts of the mix. Some examples of the importance of an integrated marketing mix are described below.

- If the main selling point of a product is its excellence, then the quality and design of that product must match consumers' expectations. Wealthy consumers would expect to see a high price and an upmarket place where they can buy the product.
- A supermarket will want its low-price, economy range of products to be packaged simply so that consumers can see that money is not wasted on packaging. Consumers will also not expect to see expensive advertising campaigns for such products, as they might then question whether the business is really making a serious effort to keep costs low.
- What is the purpose of promotion? Invariably, it is needed to draw the attention of consumers to features of the product that will make them want to purchase it. Promotion may be used to emphasise desirable features of the product, especially where informative advertising is used. The promotions may also emphasise the price being charged. A firm using price cuts is unlikely to succeed if no one is aware of the price cuts.
- Efficient distribution (place) may enable a firm to keep costs and prices low. The point of sale can be used to show the product and to promote it through posters. These posters, if appropriate, may promote price cuts or special offers.
- People are an essential element of any service. Hotels can differentiate themselves through product – the quality of accommodation and facilities – but invariably customers will expect the facilities to match the price paid. However, the quality of the services provided by reception, catering and cleaning staff are likely to have a major influence on whether the customer's expectations have been surpassed or remain unfulfilled.
- Process is particularly important where people want their purchase to operate smoothly. A well-planned promotional mix and competitive price may attract the customer, but their custom will be lost if the purchasing process itself is unwieldy.
- Physical environment/evidence must also be consistent with other elements of the 7 Ps. A trip promoted as a luxury cruise is more likely to be bought if there is evidence provided to the potential customer before purchasing. It is critical that this representation is accurate, so that the experience matches the customer's expectations.

In most cases, all elements of the marketing mix are important, but it is generally believed that the *product itself* is the key to a successful marketing mix. Promotions may encourage consumers to buy a product; the price may attract interest and lead to a purchase; and consumers will only buy the product if it is available in a place where they are looking. However, if the product fails to satisfy consumers, the marketing mix is unlikely to succeed.

Although product is invariably key, there will be instances when other elements of the marketing mix dominate. At a festival, only one type of bottled water might be available, so the decision on which brand to buy is dictated by 'place'. Consumers with limited money might choose the item with the lowest price because they have insufficient resources to purchase other products. A persuasive promotion might encourage a purchase,

Author advice

Do not assume that an organisation will always want to use the media that reaches most consumers, notably television. The cost per thousand for television advertisements may be high when measured in relation to targeted customers. Specialist magazines or local media can be much more cost effective.

particularly if the product is an impulse buy. Customers may only have purchased their tickets because the process was reasonably easy.

Co-ordinating the marketing mix with other business functions

We saw earlier that the 7 Ps must be co-ordinated for marketing to succeed. The success of the marketing mix also depends on other functional areas of the business, such as operations, finance and human resources. Any business must ensure that each of its functional areas works co-operatively with other areas. The points below show some examples of how the marketing department must co-ordinate with the other business functions.

- The marketing department's aims must be consistent with the operations/production department's approach. If the marketing mix is aiming to create an upmarket, quality image, it is vital that the products being manufactured meet this requirement.
- Similar co-operation is needed between the finance and marketing departments. If the marketing mix is ambitious, it may be necessary to curtail certain marketing activities if there is insufficient funding. However, if the marketing department can justify the expenditure, the finance department will investigate alternative sources of funding. The finance department must also allocate sufficient money to each department that is supporting the marketing effort. Ultimately, the marketing budget and all other budgets must be agreed with the finance department.
- A successful marketing mix needs people to deliver it. Consequently, the human resource and marketing departments need to co-ordinate their activities. Staff in the marketing department must be recruited effectively and each department must have the right number of suitably qualified staff with the required skills. Changes in the marketing mix may well require changes in staffing and/or training. Customer service training is a specific example of human resource/personnel activities that affect the marketing function.

Fact file

Integrated marketing at The Co-operative

The Co-operative is an example of a business that has developed an integrated marketing mix in order to target a large niche market – the UK's 2 million blind and partially sighted people. The Co-operative pioneered the use of Braille on packaging for certain medicines in 2001 and uses Braille labelling on its 300 own-brand products.

The Co-operative has signed up to the Guide Dogs for the Blind Association's High Street Charter and is relying on word-of-mouth advertising – a strategy based on the close-knit network of blind people. The Co-operative is guaranteeing that prices for Braille-labelled products will be the same as its usual own-brand range, in keeping with its stance on ethical and socially responsible behaviour.

The other main focus is on 'place'. To assist blind and partially sighted people, the supermarket is training its staff on the new labelling and on the Charter. The Charter advises shops on ways to help blind people, such as offering explanations of store layout, providing store guides and helping them to pack their shopping.

In May 2013, the Co-operative Bank launched 'talking' ATMs (cash dispensers) specifically for its blind customers, with a target to convert the vast majority of its ATMs by the end of 2014.

Influences on an integrated marketing mix

There are many factors that influence the need for integration of a company's marketing mix. Key influences on an integrated marketing mix are discussed below.

Position in the product life cycle

During the introduction stage focus should be on developing the product, with promotion being introduced just prior to launch. Launch often features pricing strategies such as penetration pricing, with widespread promotion to raise customer awareness.

During growth the focus on promotion will continue, with 'place' becoming more important as distribution widens and more channels are needed. It is also vital that customer expectations are met through well-trained 'people' and an efficient 'process' for purchasers.

To maintain sales through maturity, promotions and possible special offers may be used, with product modifications where appropriate. For services, maintaining high sales will require an attractive physical environment, in keeping with customer expectations of a popular product. The marketing mix changes during decline; it is likely to feature price cuts to regain sales and cutbacks in promotion as sales decline, if the business feels that decline is inevitable. Fewer retailers may offer shelf space to a product in decline.

Boston Matrix

Cash cows require promotion, so that customers are regularly reminded of their existence and strengths. Where appropriate, the purchasing process and people involved in transactions must be professional in their approach. As the product is popular, it should require little or no modification, although product proliferation may enable it to appeal to a wider audience. Price cuts should be avoided, as these will merely lower the profit margin.

Stars will require heavy promotion and possibly penetration pricing in order for them to increase their market share of the expanding market. In the short run, the marketing expenditure may appear to be very high in comparison to the sales generated, but if this strategy succeeds then the star will provide high profits in the future.

Problem children/question marks provide challenge. If the business believes that they will succeed then it should focus heavily on promotion and/or training for people who have direct contact with customers. However, the business may decide to put little effort into the marketing mix if it believes the problem child will eventually become a dog.

Dogs may make profit if they are small parts of a large market and so the complete range of marketing mix activities should be integrated. However, if there is no profit to be made then marketing activity may be withdrawn.

Type of product

Products with inelastic demand should command a high price. The remainder of the marketing mix will need to be consistent with the image required to fetch a high price, so for example, promotion will need to emphasise the luxury features of the product. The place and the physical environment must also give an appearance of being upmarket. The product must be of high quality, and people and process must also give an appearance of quality and efficiency.

Products with an elastic demand will need a lower price and therefore customer expectations of quality might be lower. However, in order to achieve high profit, such products must be available in a wide range of places and feature frequent promotions, unless they are being sold on low price alone.

Marketing objectives

Marketing objectives can vary considerably and so the marketing mix must be adapted to the particular marketing objectives for a product. If sales growth is required it is essential that the product has features that appeal to many customers. The marketing mix is likely to feature high levels of promotion combined with low prices. The process of buying must be easy and the product made widely available.

Target market

Target markets will vary considerably and so the marketing mix must reflect the desires and interests of that group. For example, a local nightclub will need to focus on local media for its promotions, offer reasonable prices and an attractive physical environment. The use of social media is likely to be an important part of the promotional mix too.

Competition

High levels of competition are likely to mean that price is more significant as an element of the marketing mix. However, even though this will usually mean lower prices, in order to differentiate itself in the marketplace a business may use a high price, although this means the business needs to ensure that product quality matches the price. The quality of the product can be an important aspect of the marketing mix in a competitive market and promotions will be needed to create an augmented product that differentiates itself from competitors' products.

Positioning

If a business decides to place its product or service in a certain position in the market, then it is important that the marketing mix is consistent with that position. For example, Harrods is recognised as a business with high prices and high quality products and services. Therefore, it is essential that its products are of high quality and the people assisting the consumers and the physical environment both support the high price/high quality characteristic in order to appeal to consumers.

Understanding the value of digital marketing and e-commerce

Key term

Digital marketing The anticipating and satisfying of consumer wants through the use of different forms of technology. Digital marketing includes social media marketing, the use of search engine marketing, digital displays and marketing through other forms of digital media.

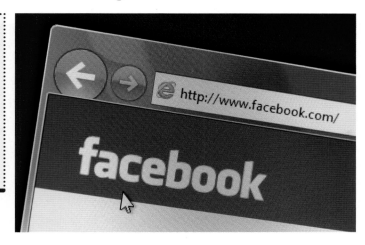

Benefits of digital marketing to businesses

- **Reduced costs**: the use of its own website can incur no significant cost to a business and so prospective customers can be reached at little or no cost. Advertising on search engines and digital displays does incur costs, but these tend to be considerably lower than traditional forms of marketing because digital imagery is much cheaper than printed materials.
- **More personalised and targeted marketing**: technology allows businesses to build a much more detailed profile of individual customers. Loyalty cards provide background on spending patterns, while sources such as social media can provide details of lifestyles and other factors that might influence consumer tastes.
- **Marketing can be related to consumers' interests**: digital marketing enables firms to reach consumers who have a particular interest by placing advertisements on websites that reflect those interests. For example, customers with interest in sport can be reached through websites that feature particular sports.
- **More immediate impact**: print and broadcast media usually require some time for preparation and organisation, particularly the latter. Digital technology is much more flexible and promotions can be geared to events as they are happening. Not only does this make the advertising more effective, but it is much easier to measure the level of benefit gained from the promotion as increases in sales are more immediate. In many cases the increases in sales may also be online and therefore can be attributed more directly to the promotion that created the sale.
- **Easy to evaluate success or failure**: because of the immediacy of any change in sales it becomes much easier for businesses to ascertain whether a particular campaign was effective. This means that unsuccessful ideas are less likely to be repeated.
- **Viral marketing**: digital technology enables people to communicate and send images and messages to each other very rapidly. If a digital marketing campaign captures public interest, people will send it to their friends – this is known as 'going viral'. The more a campaign goes viral, the greater its probable success, as it will reach a much larger audience.

- **Greater exposure to international markets**: digital marketing has the potential to reach a much wider cross-section of people as it is not limited to one country or region.

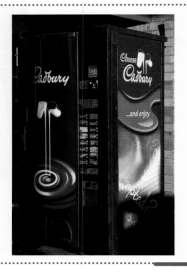

What do you think?

The Cadbury's Joy Generator

In June 2014, Cadbury's launched a new vending machine, the 'Joy Generator', in Australia. At the vending machine the customer logs into Facebook and, using the person's Facebook profile, the Joy Generator dispenses the bar of chocolate that matches the customer's personality and interests.

What do you think? Would you let a machine choose your bar of chocolate for you? Can businesses identify customers' tastes from digital data?

Benefits of e-commerce to businesses

- **Saves costs**: orders can be processed much more cheaply as there is no need for paperwork and records can be kept digitally.
- **Saves time**: it is much quicker to process orders digitally because of a lack of paperwork and postage required. Furthermore, for regular customers the database will already hold the necessary details and so orders can be processed much more quickly. Therefore fewer administrative staff will be needed.
- **Facilitates customisation of products**: because of improved communication between suppliers and customers, customer orders can be met more quickly. With reduced lead times, customers can specify their exact requirements (tailor-making the product) and the product can be made to match their needs.
- **Inventory (stock) levels can be reduced**: traditional methods require sellers to hold inventory in order to satisfy customer needs. With greater mass customisation and the ability to tailor-make specific products, sellers do not need to hold such high levels of inventory. Instead the details are sent immediately to the supplier who makes the product to meet the specific requirements of the customer.
- **E-commerce improves cash flow**: by reducing the need to hold inventory businesses do not need to pay large sums of money to buy inventory and do not require such large storage areas in which to hold inventories.

In general, **e-commerce** has enabled specialist businesses to survive and thrive by extending the marketplace. With more goods being transported to individual customers, small firms can now target national and overseas markets and compete with large-scale multinationals that may have a broader range of products, but that also have a higher cost base.

Key term

E-commerce The buying and selling of goods and services through the use of electronic media.

Issues involving digital technology and e-commerce

Although both digital technology and e-commerce provide many benefits, as shown above, they tend to share certain issues that may reduce the overall value of new technology to businesses.

- **Security**: it is difficult to guarantee the security of personal details held through digital technology and expensive to install suitable security systems. This may lead to many customers being reluctant to use technology, as they believe that their personal details are insecure.
- **Initial costs**: although technology can greatly reduce the operating costs of marketing and other aspects of business activity, it can be very expensive to install the initial systems required to operate e-commerce and related systems. These high initial costs will provide a significant deterrent to smaller businesses, as they are likely to be concerned that they will not make enough money to repay these costs.
- **Integration problems**: a fully operational system should enable the business to integrate all of its functional areas so that, for example, the marketing department can co-ordinate customer orders with departments such as finance and operations. This can be quite challenging for businesses, especially as many departments work on slightly different systems. As a consequence, customer goodwill can be lost as promises made by the marketing department are not fulfilled by the other departments involved in the transaction.
- **User resistance**: some customers, particularly those in older age groups, may be resistant to the use of technology in their buying habits. Similarly, young children may be keen to use the technology but have limited access. It is important that businesses assess such factors before deciding to use digital technology and e-commerce.
- **Lack of direct contact with the product**: for some products, such as fashion items, customers usually like to experience the product before making the final decision to purchase. As a consequence, the scope for digital marketing and e-commerce may be restricted. However, digital marketing can also overcome this issue to a certain extent (see 'What do you think?' on Google Glass below).

What do you think?

Google Glass and Nike

Google Glass is wearable technology, with the appearance of spectacles but providing a display screen. Wearers communicate with the internet through voice-activated software. It features a camera and a fashion app (Glashion) which allows users to take a picture of clothes worn by passers-by. This image can be sent to a shop for comparison to similar items. The customer can then arrange for the closest match to be sent.

Nike produces trainers that can track the running mileage of the user. The trainers then inform the user when it is time to buy a new pair.

Do you think these ideas will catch on more widely?

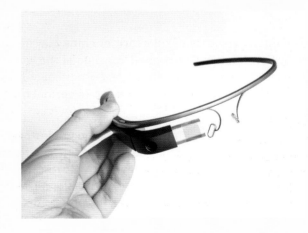

Practice exercise 5

Total: 60 marks

1 What is meant by the term 'integrated marketing mix'? *(6 marks)*

2 Explain two ways in which the product life cycle might influence the marketing mix. *(6 marks)*

3 Explain two ways in which marketing objectives might influence the marketing mix. *(6 marks)*

4 Explain two factors that might reduce the effectiveness of 'process' in the marketing mix of a service. *(6 marks)*

5 Analyse how 'physical evidence' can lead to a more successful marketing mix for a service. *(8 marks)*

6 What is the difference between 'digital marketing' and 'e-commerce'? *(4 marks)*

7 Explain one advantage of digital marketing for a business. *(4 marks)*

8 Explain one possible problem that might arise when a business introduces e-commerce. *(4 marks)*

9 'People' is only an important element of the marketing mix for services. It has no relevance for goods. Do you agree? Justify your view. *(16 marks)*

Case study: The Eden Project

According to Karen Robinson of the *Sunday Times*:

'Eden does a superb job of combining a 'visitor attraction' – with an excellent restaurant serving organic local produce and shops that sell garden plants and local crafts – with serious but easily accessible information about its real purpose: to raise environmental awareness about the quality of life at all levels.'

The Eden Project website declares: 'The Eden Trust didn't build this place to be a theme park. It must entertain but also encourage action and provide the means for them [people with an interest in the environment] to take action.' In its first year of opening (2001), it attracted 2 million visitors, far exceeding the target of 750,000 visitors. As expected, numbers have since stabilised at a lower level. In 2013, numbers fell to 858,000 but 2014 attendances show a 2 per cent increase to date, despite transport issues in the West Country with the closure of the only rail link at Dawlish. Financial cutbacks and lower visitor numbers have meant that the plans for a fourth biome have been postponed. Instead, efforts have been put into activities that have lower costs and more immediate revenue streams. Special events have been organised onsite to raise money and to

The Eden Project is set in a former china clay quarry near St Austell in Cornwall. It consists of the world's two largest biomes (dome-shaped greenhouses), which are big enough to contain the Tower of London.

These amazing structures house two distinct sets of plants. The 'warm temperate' biome contains plants from the Mediterranean, South Africa and California, while the larger 'humid tropics' biome features lush vegetation from areas such as rainforests and a waterfall that cascades from the top of the 55-metre high structure. There is also an open biome featuring plants suited to the local climate.

encourage repeat visits. In 2014 the Eden Project opened *Skywire,* the longest (600 metres) and fastest (up to 60 mph) zip wire in Britain. There has also been a greater focus on selling items such as souvenirs to visitors. Spending per person increased in 2014.

For many local people, the project is seen as a way of regenerating the local economy. Eden has created over 1,700 full-time equivalent jobs in the West Country (600 employed directly by the project) and many locals who visit the site view it as a community project. It has also helped to attract more tourists to the area, providing benefits to other businesses, and some of the £100 million-plus funding already spent has been provided by local councils and the European Union.

The standard entrance fee is £23.50 per day. Because of the project's educational focus, children aged 5–16 pay £13.50. Family tickets are £68 and discounts are available for advanced bookings, eco-friendly travellers and group visits – the latter make up a significant percentage of visitors. Discounts are available for regular visitors.

Souvenirs, natural and organic products and the restaurant are important revenue earners, with a **price skimming** policy being adopted for most products offered for sale.

Direct mail has been used in the local area and the Eden Project website is visited by many potential customers. However, the unique nature of the project means that it has interested the media as a story in its own right.

For this reason, **public relations** (PR) has been used heavily as a cost-effective way of promoting the project. Many national papers featured the project during its development and since its opening, and Eden has relied a lot on word-of-mouth advertising as a way of increasing awareness.

Journey times from the UK's main population centres mean that the Eden Project is not in the most convenient location. However, this is set against Cornwall's reputation as a family holiday destination, which means that the project is well placed for people taking holidays in the West Country.

There is little competition in the area to draw visitors away, especially on less sunny days. There are rival attractions, such as the Lost Gardens of Heligan (again featured on television and other national media), which may compete with the Eden Project. However, activities such as this also encourage visitors to the area and so may help the Eden Project to get more customers.

A disused quarry is not generally seen as an ideal location, but the spectacle of the buildings themselves overcomes this obstacle.

Source: www.edenproject.com

Questions

Total: 70 marks

1 What is meant by the term 'price skimming'? *(3 marks)*

2 What is meant by the term 'public relations'? *(3 marks)*

3 What is 'word-of-mouth' advertising? *(2 marks)*

4 Explain two possible reasons why Cornwall is a good place to locate the Eden Project. *(6 marks)*

5 Explain two reasons why the entrance ticket for a child is approximately half the price charged to an adult visitor. *(6 marks)*

6 To what extent was it wise for the Eden Project to have spent only a limited sum on promotions and advertising? *(14 marks)*

7 Would the price elasticity of demand for a visit to the Eden Project be elastic or inelastic? Justify your view. *(16 marks)*

8 To what extent are product and the physical environment the most important elements of the marketing mix for the Eden Project? Justify your view. *(20 marks)*

Case study: The marketing mix at Ryanair

Ryanair is a classic example of a business that uses price as the key element of its marketing mix – a 'traditional' marketing mix. However, price cannot work in isolation from the other six Ps. In order to maintain its policy of long-term low prices, Ryanair has needed to look closely at all elements of its marketing mix.

Ryanair based itself on the highly successful model established in the USA by Southwest Airlines, a company that had been operating low-cost flights in the USA since the 1960s. Ryanair's chief executive, Michael O'Leary, attempted to create a low-cost airline by examining every element of Ryanair's activities, in order to cut costs in the way that Southwest Airlines had.

Process

O'Leary started by eliminating 'frills' and 'unnecessary' expenditure.
- Travel agents were eliminated, based on the idea that Ryanair's customers would not then be paying towards the costs of their city-centre premises and trained staff.
- Internet bookings were introduced, saving approximately 15 per cent per booking.
- Bookings only require limited paperwork at the airport; customers just needed to provide a boarding pass and their passport.

Product

- Seats are not usually allocated to passengers; they are taken as passengers board the plane.
- These factors reduce administration costs further, but the main bonus is time savings. The turnaround time on Ryanair planes is 25 minutes on average – half that of British Airways (BA). This means that the planes are more productive and can make more journeys per day.

Physical environment

- Free meals are not provided – customers must pay for any food they require. Not only does this save costs (especially on staffing and cleaning because passengers eat and drink less), but it also provides an additional source of profit that can be used to keep prices low.
- Facilities at airports are kept to a minimum.

- Staff numbers are minimised to save costs. Although this may cause queues, the lack of seat bookings reduces the problems associated with having so few staff. However, it does lead to pressure on customers to get to the front of any queues.

People

Some examples of Ryanair's cost savings have been less well received by customers. Its customer care department employs six staff (one-tenth of BA's equivalent staff, based on staff per customer) and Ryanair does not offer some facilities, such as food, that are provided free by some airlines. However, these pared-down features reinforce the company's USP.

Place

Ryanair's cost-cutting approach does restrict expansion plans. O'Leary has decided against expansion into the USA because long flight times would make it impossible to replicate many of the company's cost-saving measures, such as quick turnaround of planes and avoiding overnight hotel bills for pilots and aircrew.

A key element of Ryanair's strategy is that it only flies to popular destinations, giving it more security of custom. This policy meant that when Ryanair took over Buzz, many of Buzz's flights were removed, where Ryanair considered the destinations to lack popularity. Ryanair tried to take over Aer Lingus in order to eliminate competition on some routes, but the competition authorities prevented any takeover.

A major cost saving for Ryanair has arisen from the locations that it has chosen. By using Stansted airport, Ryanair estimates that it saves £3 per customer in comparison with Heathrow. Some of this saving arises from the relatively strong bargaining position of Ryanair. It is vital to Stansted's success as an airport and can therefore negotiate lower charges.

Ryanair also saves money by using secondary rather than 'main' airports in other countries. This means lower costs for Ryanair that can be passed on to customers, softening the blow that the airport is further from the customer's intended destination than they had hoped. In some cases, airports have been so keen to attract Ryanair that they have paid the company to choose that airport. The airport's revenues will increase from retailing activities in the airport as passenger numbers rise.

Promotion

Traditionally, Ryanair keeps advertising to a minimum, relying on newspaper advertisements and posters rather than more expensive television adverts. Simple messages reinforce the philosophy of low cost, low price. As an economy measure, advertising agencies have not been used. As a result, there have been some controversial promotions attacking competitors or presenting issues insensitively.

Recognising the benefit of joint activities, Ryanair takes a percentage of any bookings made through its website (typically car hire and hotel bookings). It has also allowed its planes to be used as flying billboards, advertising products such as Kilkenny beer. These ancillary revenues help to boost the firm's profits.

Price

Given the vital role of safety in the airline industry, Ryanair has not economised on aircraft – it only uses Boeing 737s. However, shrewd timing of aircraft purchases to coincide with excess supply (just after the Gulf War and again during and after the Iraq War) brought Ryanair some bargains. Estimates suggest that the most recent order for 175 Boeing 737s, in 2013, cost the company less than half the normal £56

million price tag. This order coincided with Boeing's loss of a key order from Indonesia.

Ryanair has adopted the following pricing policies:
- Its normal pricing is based on penetration pricing, in order to secure enough bookings to make the flight financially viable. Typically, the first 70 per cent of seats are sold on this basis. Special offers are often one-way – an example of psychological pricing, as customers believe that they will pay less than they actually do. This psychology also applies to baggage – Ryanair is much more likely to charge its customers for the baggage they carry, which can often increase the price of a flight quite substantially.
- Unlike traditional airlines, which sell any remaining empty seats at a low price (enough to cover variable costs), Ryanair uses price discrimination. The airline's view is that anyone seeking to book a flight at the last minute is probably in desperate need and therefore likely to be willing to pay a higher price. Thus the final 30 per cent of the seats are sold at higher prices.
- At times, short-term, very low promotional prices are charged. These could be seen as penetration pricing (to increase market share), but some analysts see them as predator prices, used to drive away competition. In practice, many of these promotional flights are one-way only and so the savings for customers are less significant than they originally seem (unless the passenger does not want to return).

Ryanair's marketing has been highly successful. In terms of passenger numbers, it is Europe's second largest airline (after Lufthansa) and the market leader among budget airlines. However, Ryanair has been widely criticised for its poor customer service and policy of charging customers for 'extras', such as baggage.

Following concerns among shareholders and a loss being recorded in the third quarter of 2013, Ryanair decided to change its marketing approach.

Ryanair's 'new' marketing mix

From 2014, seats can be reserved in advance (at a cost of €5). More significantly, Ryanair tripled its advertising budget to £30 million, changing its marketing mix to focus more on the product and brand than price. The main changes to the marketing mix are cutting fees, introducing allocated seating and allowing customers to alter their bookings. Ryanair appointed the first marketing director in its history. Chief Executive Michael O'Leary, argues that Ryanair has already satisfied the 81 million customers it carries every year, who purchase on the basis of low price. The company is now trying to target 20 million customers who are not price conscious, such as business travellers, who have been put off by Ryanair's poor reputation and 'less than optimal' website. O'Leary says, 'Just like IKEA, Aldi and Lidl, who came in on the back of price and are now advertising quality, we're doing the same thing. We want people to like flying with us, not just for the savings but because they like us.'

This new marketing mix requires heavy investment in information technology and digital marketing to improve the website and make it easier for customers. New marketing director, Kenny Jacobs, is excited by the prospects. 'This is a brand that has a poor website, doesn't really do email marketing or digital marketing, doesn't really capture or use data, doesn't advertise and yet still has a strong brand. Imagine how it could perform with marketing techniques applied.' In keeping with the new brand image, Ryanair launched a brand-new app on 14 July 2014 in both iPhone and Android formats. This will allow customers to search Ryanair's routes, make faster flight bookings, book allocated seats, hotels and car hire and monitor live flights.

Sources: *The Money Programme*, BBC2, 4 June 2003; articles in *Marketing Week*, 3 February 2014, 27 March 2014 and 10 April 2014; article by Gwyn Topham in *The Guardian*, 17 April 2014

Questions

Total: 90 marks

1 In the context of the marketing mix, what is meant by the term 'process'? *(2 marks)*

2 Explain why the physical environment might be a weakness in Ryanair's traditional marketing mix. *(6 marks)*

3 What is meant by digital marketing? *(3 marks)*

4 Explain how Ryanair uses 'penetration pricing'. *(5 marks)*

5 Explain how Ryanair uses 'price skimming' *(5 marks)*

6 Explain the possible reasons why Southwest Airlines did not attempt to bring its low-cost approach to Europe before Ryanair used the idea. *(6 marks)*

7 Explain why 'people' will become a more important element of the marketing mix in Ryanair's new marketing mix. *(6 marks)*

8 Ryanair charges low prices to early customers and higher prices to people who book flights later, because it believes that demand for early flights is price elastic whereas demand for late flights is price inelastic. Analyse the reasons for this difference in price elasticity of demand over time. *(9 marks)*

9 Analyse the benefits to Ryanair from its decision to make greater use of technology in its marketing mix. *(12 marks)*

10 Evaluate the potential difficulties faced by Ryanair in trying to change its marketing mix in order to widen its appeal. *(16 marks)*

11 Some analysts believe that it is inevitable that low-price providers, such as Ryanair, Ikea and Aldi, must move into target markets that involve higher prices. Do you agree? Justify your view. *(20 marks)*

11

Setting operational objectives

This chapter introduces operations management and examines the value of operational objectives and decisions. Examples of types of operational objectives are provided and the internal and external factors that influence them are studied. This chapter provides the foundation for subsequent chapters that study operations management decisions.

Key term

Operations management The process that uses the resources of an organisation to provide the right goods or services for the customer.

Providing the 'right' goods or services means providing 'what the customer wants'. This may vary between customers – for example, it may mean quality and price to one customer, but convenience and flexibility to another.

Identifying operations management issues

When purchasing products, customers have many requirements and so operational management considers a variety of issues that ensure the business produces the 'right' goods or services for its customers. The following aspects of **operations management** will be covered.

- Encouraging efficient methods of production and effective use of the workforce in order to reduce the costs of goods or services.
- Ensuring that waste is minimised during the production process.
- Choosing the mix of resources to use in production.
- Managing capacity utilisation.
- Using technology to improve business operations.
- Ensuring high quality goods and services are produced.
- Providing flexibility, speed of response and dependability.
- Organising inventory control to meet the needs of customers quickly and cheaply.
- Working closely with suppliers in order to improve efficiency.

Did you know?

Although operations management originated in the production of goods, over two-thirds of UK spending is on services, so operations management has been widened to apply to both goods and services.

Value of setting operational objectives and decisions

Why does a business set objectives for its operations management function? The reasons for setting objectives are the same, regardless of the functional area being considered. These reasons are:

● to act as a focus for decision making and effort
● to provide a yardstick against which success or failure can be measured
● to improve co-ordination, by giving teams and departments a common purpose
● to improve efficiency, by examining the reasons for success and failure in different areas.

As operations management is concerned with getting the right goods or services to the customer, **operational objectives** can be used to measure the efficiency with which this overall aim is achieved. As indicated above, operations management covers a wide range of activities. Consequently, a range of operational objectives are set to assess whether operational activities have been performed satisfactorily. In this chapter we will look at some operational objectives that are used to assess operational performance in relation to:

● costs
● quality
● speed of response
● flexibility
● dependability
● environmental objectives
● added value.

Costs

In order to be competitive in the marketplace, a business will try to reduce the cost of each unit that it produces. Lowering costs enables a business to lower its price and therefore increase sales. Alternatively, a business may decide to keep price high and benefit from the higher profit margin that occurs when costs are low and selling price is high.

▲ Lidl is a discount supermarket that concentrates on keeping costs low

Commonly used cost targets for businesses include the following:

- **Reducing unit costs**: this is likely to be the primary aim of most businesses in terms of cost targets. Low unit costs enable a business either to keep prices low or to enjoy a higher profit margin by keeping prices at their same level. In late 2013, the four largest supermarkets all recorded a loss in market share, the first time this has happened. The primary reason was the growth in market share of discount retailers Aldi and Lidl. By focusing on lowering costs these discounters have been able to gain customers from the more recognised supermarkets. Lower unit costs can be achieved in two ways:
  - **reducing fixed costs**: although most cost targets are expressed in terms of unit costs, a business might focus on cutting fixed costs. This allows a more specific focus and is often a more manageable target than a broader, unit cost reduction. Reducing fixed costs is a common aim for businesses that have recently merged or been taken over. Mobile network EE was formed by the UK merger of T-Mobile and Orange, in 2010. EE stated that once the business had cut branches and unnecessary radio masts the newly merged business's target would be to save costs of over £445 million each year, from 2014 onwards.
  - **reducing variable costs per unit**: manufacturers and retailers constantly strive to find cheaper sources of supply or cheaper ways of manufacturing. By cutting labour and raw material costs, a business can reduce its variable costs per unit. This target can also be achieved by improving labour productivity because this means that employees' wages are spread over a higher level of output.

Quality

A business which satisfies and delights its customers with the **quality** of its goods and services will have a competitive edge over businesses with lower quality. Not only will this lead to greater sales volume it can also enable a firm to charge much higher prices without losing many customers. High quality is also likely to lead to repeat purchases and high brand loyalty amongst customers.

Quality objectives

There is no single, agreed measure of 'quality'; it depends on people's opinions, so there will be different views about what it means. Below are some examples of measures of quality and a brief comment on the logic behind their use. Note that this is just a sample of quality measures – a good quality measure will be geared towards the specific needs of the individual firm.

- **Customer satisfaction ratings**. A survey of customers can reveal customer opinions on a numerical scale (e.g. 1 to 10) or using qualitative measures (e.g. excellent – very good – good, etc.). As the purpose of a product is to satisfy the needs of the customer, this is an excellent way of measuring whether quality has been achieved.
- **Customer complaints**. This calculates the number of customers who complain (it is sometimes measured as a percentage of the total number of customers). Although it might seem to take a negative view, it is a good way of measuring whether a company has problems that it needs to rectify. It is said that one unhappy customer can damage a company's reputation far more than a large number of satisfied customers can boost it, so companies need to concentrate on preventing customer complaints.

> **Key term**
>
> **Quality** Those features of a product or service that allow it to satisfy (or delight) customers.

- **Level of product returns**. If customers return a high percentage of goods that they have purchased, it is a sign of dissatisfaction with that good. This category of quality objective can set a target based on previous levels of returns, average rates from other products made by the company or return rates for competitors' products.
- **Scrap rate**. This calculates the number of items rejected during the production process as a percentage of the number of units produced. It shows the business whether its production methods are working effectively, guiding it towards areas that might need improvement. Rejected products will also lead to higher costs.
- **Punctuality**. This calculates the degree to which a business delivers its products (or provides its services) on time. It is often measured as a percentage:

$$\text{punctuality } (\%) = \frac{\text{deliveries on time}}{\text{total deliveries}} \times 100$$

This measure is used as a measure of quality by many businesses, especially those involved in transporting goods (e.g. haulage firms) or customers (e.g. rail franchises).

Author advice

Punctuality is included here as a measure of quality. However, it can also be classified as an aspect of 'speed of response' (see below).

What do you think?

Transport punctuality

An example of a punctuality objective is Network Rail, whose objective is to ensure that 91 per cent of all train journeys arrive on time. 'Punctual' is defined as arrival within five minutes of schedule for commuter journeys and ten minutes for longer journeys. Network Rail oversees all the different train companies that operate passenger services. In the year to 19 July 2014, the national rate of punctuality was 89.7 per cent.

At this time, Grand Central was the train operator that had the least punctual train service. Only 82.0 per cent of its trains arrived on time during the 12 months

reviewed. The most punctual train operator was c2c Rail with 96.6 per cent punctuality.

These figures seem to compare favourably with aircraft punctuality. In the first quarter of 2014, only 84 per cent of flights arriving at UK airports were punctual (arriving within 15 minutes of schedule). However, this was an 8 per cent increase on the first quarter of 2013 and the highest punctuality since records began in 1992. London City Airport recorded the highest punctuality (90 per cent), while Heathrow was the lowest with 82 per cent.

Are comparisons between different rail service providers and different airports a fair comparison of operational performance? Can rail transport be compared to air transport? What do you think?

Speed of response

Speed of response is usually measured by the difference in time between a customer requesting a good or service and the time at which they receive that good or service. However, it can also be used to measure more specific activities such as the time taken to reply to an email or written communication, the time taken to answer the telephone or the time taken to fulfil the needs of a telephone caller.

Key term

Speed of response The time taken for a customer requirement to be fulfilled.

A quick response will lead to customer satisfaction and can help build customer loyalty. In some cases it can also enable the business to charge a higher price. For example, Royal Mail charges a much higher price for first class post than second-class post. Speed of response may reduce costs, as a quick response might mean that fewer hours of work have been put in by the labour force. It can also mean savings in costs associated with storage space, if inventory is moved in and out of the premises more quickly. Monitoring the achievement of speed of response objectives can also enable a business to modify its approach to improve customer service. (See fact file on PlusNet.)

Office environments such as call centres often have targets for speed of response. Three examples of such objectives are the time taken to answer the telephone (e.g. within 15 seconds or by the fifth ring), the number of calls answered per hour (e.g. 15 calls per hour) and the percentage of problems solved at the first call (e.g. 80 per cent of calls).

Fact file

Royal Mail

The table below shows Royal Mail's operational objectives and achievements for 'speed of response'.

▼ **Table 11.1** Royal Mail's operational objectives and achievements for 'speed of response', second quarter of financial year, 2013–14

	Operational objective	Actual achievement
1st class mail: delivery by next day	93.0%	93.2%
2nd class mail: delivery within three days	98.5%	98.8%

Source: www.royalmailgroup.com

Fact file

PlusNet

PlusNet is a broadband and phone service provider. It monitors the time taken to answer calls. By monitoring peak times on a continual basis it is able to ensure that it has sufficient staff to answer customer queries. Once a query is raised, PlusNet has two 'speed of response' targets:

1. queries raised through a telephone conversation must be dealt with or passed to the appropriate person within 24 hours

2. connection faults must be dealt with within seven working days.

Key term

Flexibility The ability of an organisation to change its operations in some way.

Flexibility

Flexibility can take many different forms:

- product flexibility – being able to switch production from one product to another
- volume flexibility – being able to change the level of output of a product in accordance with changes in customer demand
- mix flexibility – being able to provide a wide range of alternative versions of a particular good or service
- delivery flexibility – being able to adapt quickly to changes in the timing and volume of deliveries to customers.

Each of these different types of flexibility enables a business to adapt to changes in customer requirements. As with other operational objectives, this should increase the volume of sales and also lead to a decrease in costs. However, flexibility can add to costs, because product and mix flexibility both require more sophisticated machinery on the production line and, where workers are involved, more highly skilled workers who can adapt to changes in products. Changes in volume can only be achieved if there is spare capacity, which means that efficiency cannot be at its highest possible level. Delivery flexibility means that scheduling is more difficult and therefore additional costs are likely to be incurred if changes are made at short notice.

Did you know?

In 2014, Royal Mail introduced Sunday deliveries for parcels. This service is designed to offer improved flexibility and delivery choice for online shoppers who buy goods from retailers. Fortnum & Mason was the first company to offer customers Sunday deliveries. Ewan Venters, CEO of Fortnum & Mason, said: 'Our customers are busier than ever and as such they need their shopping when it suits them.'

Dependability

Key term

Dependability Measures whether a business is 'on time' in providing for its customers' needs.

As with quality and flexibility, **dependability** can have different meanings:

- for services, dependability may be applied to the consistency of quality or the punctuality of delivery
- for products, dependability can be measured in terms of whether the product is durable, long-lasting and unlikely to break down.

If a business does not provide its service on time it is likely to lose customers and obtain a reputation for being unreliable. Customers may no longer use a delivery service or form of transport that is not dependable. Being late can also add to costs. For example, for a train company it may mean that other journeys must be cancelled and it can mean that drivers and other staff are not in the right place at the right time to carry on with their work.

As indicated, the meaning of dependability can vary according to the product and market. For supermarkets, customers' views of dependability may be linked to the freshness of produce, keeping the number of goods out of stock to a minimum and low queueing times.

Fact file

Online sales – the importance of operational factors

Rakuten is a large Japanese online retail business. A global survey by Rakuten, in 2013, indicated that reliability was the second most important factor for online consumers when deciding on which company to use. Of those surveyed, 61 per cent of customers believed that low price was important, while 49 per cent chose reliability/dependability and 40 per cent chose mix flexibility. However, price and flexibility were both more important to UK consumers than those in other countries, with 67 per cent valuing low price and 44 per cent valuing flexibility.

Environmental objectives

Key term

Environmental objectives The aims set by a business that indicate its commitment to helping those aspects of the environment where it has an impact.

Environmental objectives are becoming a much more important aspect of operations management for several reasons:

- Many businesses recognise that they have a duty of care for the environment.
- Their stakeholders, such as shareholders and the local community, want businesses to protect the future by taking more care of the environment.
- A business can attract more customers and workers if it can demonstrate a positive attitude towards improving the environment.
- Many environmental objectives, such as recycling, will allow the business to save costs.

Typical environmental objectives include:

- reducing water pollution by a certain level or percentage
- reducing the business's carbon footprint or reducing carbon dioxide emissions
- reducing noise levels
- reducing the use of energy
- minimising waste products or materials
- increasing levels of recycling
- making products that can be easily and largely recycled

- achieving self-sufficiency in energy use
- reducing the use of non-renewable inputs
- replacing resources that have been extracted or used.

Fact file

BP and the environment

BP has a range of environmental objectives. In the examples below its objective is to reduce the level of these performance indicators. These include:

- number of oil spills (exceeding a 159-litre barrel of oil)
- carbon dioxide emissions (millions of tonnes)
- methane emissions (millions of tonnes)
- environmental and safety fines ($ millions).

Table 11.2 below shows BP's environmental performance from 2009 to 2013 in relation to these four objectives. The final row shows BP's replacement ratio (new oil and gas reserves discovered as a percentage of existing reserves consumed). A figure exceeding 100 per cent means that the business discovered more new reserves than it consumed in that year and so this figure has environmental implications. If years such as 2012 (when the reserves replacement ratio was 77 per cent) continue, then shortages of oil and gas may occur in the future.

▼ **Table 11.2** Environmental performance at BP

	2009	2010	2011	2012	2013	% change 2009–2013
Number of oil spills (→1 barrel)	122	142	102	102	74	− 39.3%
Carbon dioxide emissions (millions of tonnes)	60.4	60.2	57.7	56.4	46.0	− 23.8%
Methane emissions (millions of tonnes)	0.22	0.22	0.20	0.17	0.15	− 31.8%
Environmental/safety fines ($m)	66.6	52.5	77.4	22.4	2.5	− 96.2%
Reserves replacement ratio (%)	129	106	103	77	129	–

Key terms

Adding value The process of increasing the worth of resources by modifying them.

Added value (value added) Sales revenue minus the cost of bought-in materials, components and services.

Added value

Adding value is the process of increasing the worth of resources by modifying them. The production process is seen to be a major factor in adding value. For example, the transformation of various components into a television set adds value, as people place a higher value on the television set than on the parts used to make it. Similarly, distribution and retailing add value, by bringing the product within easier reach of the customer. Other services, such as marketing, also add value by:

- creating a unique selling point/proposition (USP) – this may be real, such as a different design or different components, or it may be based on image and branding
- identifying an attractive mix of design, function, image and service.

If a business can improve customer awareness and goodwill by using operations management to make its product different from rival products, it may be able to increase both its sales volume and its price. It may also acquire loyal customers who are less likely to stop buying the business's products.

In order to make a profit, businesses need to add value to the resources that they possess. This can be achieved in different ways. For example, a restaurant such as McDonald's might aim to minimise costs by using low-cost inputs and/or transforming them in a cost-effective way. This

Author advice

Be cautious when using 'added value' and 'profit margin'. On a single product, added value is the selling price minus the cost of goods and services. The profit margin is the selling price minus all costs that are linked to that product, including a proportion of fixed costs. Value added is not profit as it does not allow for costs such as fixed costs and marketing.

allows McDonald's to make high profits and **added value** by lowering unit costs but keeping the price unchanged. In contrast, the Ritz Hotel can sell afternoon tea at a high price (and high added value) by concentrating on the quality of its service and products.

Calculating added value

Retailers often add value by giving consumers easier access to products. Buying fruit and vegetables from a supermarket is more convenient than trying to purchase them from a farm and so retailers can add a 'mark-up' to the price they pay to the farmers or suppliers. In this case the 'cost of bought-in materials and services' is the price paid to the farmer.

Additional value can be added by processing products. Value can be added to fish by adding breadcrumbs or batter or by undertaking the cooking process. Popular brands also attract higher added value as consumers pay more for products with trusted brand names.

What do you think?

Table 11.3 shows estimates* of added value on certain fruits and vegetables sold in Tesco in June and July 2014.

▼ **Table 11.3** Estimates of added value on fruit and vegetables

Fruit/vegetable	Selling price (pence per kg)	*Cost of bought-in good (pence per kg)	Added value (pence per kg)
Cherries	749	351	398
Plums	499	117	382
Onions	79	37	42
Cabbage	60	29	31
Carrots	75	31	44
Mushrooms	268	181	87

Sources: Tesco (www.tesco.com) and DEFRA (www.gov.uk)

* Cost is based on wholesale prices in June and July 2014; these may not match the prices paid by Tesco.

Why does fruit attract larger added value than vegetables? Why are mushrooms able to achieve higher value added than other vegetables?

What do you think?

Value added

A wholesaler will provide 330 ml bottles of water for 20 pence. A TravelSupermarket survey in 2013 revealed that you would be charged £1.80 for this product on a Jet2 flight. Ryanair charged £1.74 for a 150 ml can of 7Up (wholesale price: 30p). A Twix, costing £1.20 on an easyJet flight, had a wholesale price of 32p.

Higher added value is also a feature of motorway service stations. WhatCar? researchers found that petrol prices were 5.2 per cent more expensive at motorway services than other garages, and that food prices were significantly higher than many non-motorway retailers.

Visitors to the 2012 London Olympics also experienced high prices. Heineken, the only lager available, was sold for £4.20 for a 330 ml bottle – equivalent to £7.23 a pint. The average UK price was £3.17 for a pint. Other Olympic Park prices included £8 for Fish & Chips; £2.30 for a 500 ml bottle of Coca-Cola and £2 for a cup of tea.

Can these high levels of added value be justified? What do you think?

Internal and external influences on operations objectives

Assessing internal influences on operational objectives

Internal factors affecting operational objectives are those within the business, such as its workforce, resources and financial position.

Corporate objectives

The operations department must ensure that its objectives are consistent with the corporate objectives of the business. For example, Beaverbrooks has always tried to maintain a reputation for quality as a corporate objective, so it limits its jewellery to more expensive items. In contrast, one of FW Hinds' corporate objectives is to provide affordable jewellery, and therefore its operations function must ensure a wider range of cheaper jewellery for its customers.

Finance

Operations management objectives rely on considerable expenditure on capital equipment or research and development. Therefore, a healthy financial situation is necessary.

Human resources (HR)

The skills, training and motivation of a business's human resources will have a major impact on operational objectives. If there are weaknesses in human resources, less ambitious objectives will need to be set.

Resources available

If the business is well resourced with state-of-the-art machinery and equipment, well-known brands and a good reputation for quality and customer service, then it is much easier for it to produce high-quality products cost effectively.

Nature of the product

Some products are well suited to mass production, while others are more appropriate for individual methods of production. The type of product can also influence the ease with which high quality and good customer service can be achieved. The impact of the product and its manufacturing process on the environment will also vary according to the nature of the product. All of these factors need to be taken into account when the business is setting its operational objectives.

Assessing external influences on operational objectives

External factors are those outside the business, such as the state of the economy and the actions of competitors. A brief summary of their impact on operations management is provided below.

Market factors

The growth or decline of a market will have a major impact on a business's operations management objectives. If demand changes, the business may need to modify its production levels. If sales are declining, it may need to introduce new products to replace those in decline.

Competitors' actions and performance

Competitors' actions may influence a business by encouraging it to introduce new products that are proving successful for the competitor. Alternatively, it may confirm that a type of product is in decline throughout the market.

Technological change

Technology has a major impact on a business's costs, the level of quality of its products, the ways in which waste can be reduced and levels of productivity within the business. These four factors are key performance targets for the operations management function of most businesses and therefore technological change is, arguably, the most important factor for many businesses when it comes to deciding on its operational objectives.

Economic factors

Interest rates are one economic factor that has a major impact on operations management targets. The effectiveness of operations management is heavily dependent on capital investment, and if interest rates increase, this can have a negative effect on the success of the operations management function in two different ways:

1 It can increase costs by increasing the rate of interest that has to be paid on any loans, therefore reducing the profitability of the investments. As a result, certain projects such as the introduction of new machinery may be delayed, thus reducing the efficiency of production.
2 It may reduce sales levels as people cannot afford the repayments on loans and so cut back on their purchases. This will mean lower levels of output are required and so some targets, such as low unit costs, will be harder to achieve because bulk-buying opportunities have been reduced.

Political factors

Operations management departments are often responsible for targets related to minimising production costs. This can bring them into conflict with politicians, who may disagree with the methods used to reduce costs, especially if this involves potential exploitation of workers or unsafe working conditions in factories.

Legal factors

Because of the potential for health and safety risks, the operations management function is heavily controlled by legislation.

Environmental factors

As a result of environmental legislation and pressures, firms are now much more closely controlled in terms of the products that they can produce, the ingredients and raw materials that they use, and the manufacturing processes that take place in their factories.

Suppliers

Most businesses work closely with suppliers to ensure flexibility, high quality and relatively low-cost materials. A supplier that delivers these three factors can help a business to achieve its operations management targets and help it to compete effectively with rivals.

Practice exercise 1

Total: 30 marks

1 What is the formula for calculating unit costs? *(2 marks)*

2 Which one of the following objectives is not an operational objective?
   a) Improving quality
   b) Lowering energy costs
   c) Identifying new markets
   d) Improving speed of response *(1 mark)*

3 'Those features of the product that allow it to satisfy and delight customers.' This is a definition of:
   a) dependability
   b) flexibility
   c) quality
   d) unique selling point *(1 mark)*

3 In order to cope with an increase in customer demand for a product, a business should ideally have:
   a) delivery flexibility
   b) mix flexibility
   c) product flexibility
   d) volume flexibility *(1 mark)*

4 The business aims to reduce the time taken to deliver a product. This is an example of:
   a) an added value objective
   b) a dependability objective
   c) an environmental objective
   d) a speed of response objective *(1 mark)*

5 The business aims to increase the difference between price and cost of materials. This is an example of:
   a) an added value objective
   b) a dependability objective
   c) an environmental objective
   d) a speed of response objective *(1 mark)*

6 Explain two benefits of setting operational objectives. *(6 marks)*

7 A business is scheduled to deliver 50 items to its customers. Eight items are not delivered. The remaining items are all delivered, but six of them arrive late. What is the punctuality percentage for these deliveries? *(2 marks)*

8 Explain two ways in which quality can be measured. *(8 marks)*

9 Explain why improved flexibility might increase the costs of a business providing office supplies. *(7 marks)*

Practice exercise 2 Data response

Total: 35 marks

Table 11.4 shows data on the performance of the operations management function of Fine Furniture plc.

▼ **Table 11.4** Operations management performance of Fine Furniture plc, 2015

Measure of performance	Data for Fine Furniture plc	Performance of closest competitor
Customer satisfaction rating (max. = 10)	8.4	6.9
Customer complaints	1.2%	5.9%
Wastage/scrap rate	5.6%	2.8%
Punctuality of orders	95%	90%
Weekly output (items)	180	280
Number of workers	30	40
Weekly production costs	£32,400	£42,000

Fine Furniture plc's operational objectives for 2015 were as follows:

- unit costs = £175 per item
- labour productivity = 6.5 items per worker per week
- customer satisfaction rating = 7.5
- customer complaints = 2%
- punctuality of orders = 92%

Based on the data in the table and the operational objectives listed above, answer questions 1 to 3.

1 Calculate Fine Furniture's unit costs for 2015. Did the company achieve its unit costs objective for 2015? *(3 marks)*

2 To what extent might Fine Furniture plc's senior management be satisfied that it has achieved its operational objectives? *(16 marks)*

3 Fine Furniture plc is looking for advice on the operational objectives that it should set for 2016. In the light of your answer to question 1 and the performance of Fine Furniture's main competitor, answer the following question: To what extent does Fine Furniture need to change its operational objectives for 2016. Justify your view. *(16 marks)*

Case study: Operations at Toyota

In the UK, Toyota manufactures cars in Burnaston, Derbyshire and engines in Flintshire, North Wales. The vast majority of these cars and engines are exported from the UK. Both of these factories opened in 1992.

As with any manufacturer, operations management plays a key role in Toyota's overall performance. Toyota has a wide range of operational objectives. Three categories are considered in this case study:
- productive efficiency
- quality
- environmental objectives.

Productive efficiency and suppliers

- Toyota aims for its production to be localised (sited close to the customers). Efficiency is gained through its key production principles of standardisation, just-in-time and kaizen (continuous improvement).
- Toyota has targeted cost savings of over £1 billion from its purchasing of materials.

- Suppliers are selected on the basis of fair competition and local sourcing.
- Toyota's overall aim is to provide customers with the highest-quality vehicles at the lowest possible cost, in a timely manner and with the shortest possible lead times.

Quality

- Toyota is introducing hybrid cars that are more energy efficient.
- Toyota uses a system of total quality management (TQM), where each member of the production line is responsible for the quality of their work. Each member (worker) has an objective: never to pass on poor quality to the next member. Each member can stop the production process if anything unusual is seen.

Environmental objectives

Toyota's philosophy is to minimise the environmental impact of its vehicles and their manufacturing process. The company's broad aims are based on the five Rs:

- **Refine** – no CFCs and use water-based paints where possible.
- **Reduce** – use of natural resources (i.e. water, gas and electricity).
- **Reuse** – 99.9 per cent of packaging should be reused.
- **Recycle** – as much material as possible.
- **Retrieve energy** – for example, exhaust gases are used to reheat other production processes.

Toyota's operational objectives are to continually reduce its environmental impact. The UK plant is targeted for innovation, in order to achieve 'sustainable plant' activities and minimise its environmental impact. Its achievements since the plant opened in 1992 are to reduce its environmental impact as follows:

- energy use per vehicle – over 70 per cent
- water use per vehicle – over 75 per cent
- volatile organic compound emissions – 70 per cent plus
- waste generated per vehicle – 60 per cent plus.

Toyota achieved its objectives and gained 'Big Tick awards' from 'Business in the Community' for its environmental leadership and for achieving each of the four targets identified above. It has achieved a target of zero waste to landfill sites, the first UK car manufacturer to achieve this environmental target.

Toyota's objective of being environmentally friendly also includes a tree planting programme which has led to 350,000 trees on its site.

In order to further improve its operational efficiency, Toyota's continual improvement (kaizen) programme has modified the Flexible Body Line (FBL) system that helped it to achieve its high standards. The FBL system is being replaced by Global Body Line (GBL). The operational objectives for GBL are to achieve:

- 30 per cent reduction of the time a vehicle spends in the body shop
- 70 per cent reduction in time required to complete a major model change
- 50 per cent cut in the cost to add or switch models
- 50 per cent reduction in initial investment
- 50 per cent reduction in assembly line footprint
- 50 per cent reduction in carbon dioxide emissions due to lower energy usage
- 50 per cent cut in maintenance costs.

Questions

Total: 55 marks

1 Analyse how Toyota's new GBL system will help to improve its flexibility and dependability. *(9 marks)*

2 Analyse how Toyota's new GBL system will help to lower its unit costs. *(9 marks)*

3 Explain one reason why the achievement of quality is a key objective for Toyota. *(5 marks)*

4 Toyota's operational objectives place a very high priority on the achievement of its environmental

objectives. To what extent do you believe that this emphasis on environmental objectives will improve Toyota's competitiveness as a car manufacturer? *(16 marks)*

5 Toyota's operational objectives are influenced by both internal and external factors. Do you consider internal or external factors to be the more important influence on Toyota's operational objectives? Justify your view. *(16 marks)*

Analysing operational performance

Ideally, operational objectives should be measurable. In this chapter we will consider some specific aspects of operational performance that lend themselves to measurable objectives. For each measure, we will show how performance can be calculated and how the results of these calculations can be interpreted.

Calculation and interpretation of operations data

As operations management is concerned with getting the right goods or services to the customer, operational targets measure the efficiency with which this overall aim has been achieved.

The following measures of operational performance will be explained, their calculations demonstrated and the results of calculations interpreted:

- labour productivity
- unit costs (average costs)
- capacity
- capacity utilisation.

Labour productivity

Both the operations management and human resource management functions of the business will endeavour to find ways to improve the efficiency of the workforce by increasing output per worker.

> **Key term**
>
> **Labour productivity** A measure of the output per worker in a given time period.

Labour productivity is calculated as follows:

$$\text{Labour productivity} = \frac{\text{Output per period}}{\text{Number of employees per period}}$$

If 25 workers produce 600 units of output in a week, then labour productivity per week is 24 units (600/25).

Increases in labour productivity can benefit a business by enabling it to:

- increase output without affecting costs. Using the example above, if labour productivity per week increased from 24 units per worker to 30 units per worker, then the 25 workers could increase total production from 600 units per week to 750 units (25 × 30) per week
- reduce costs without affecting output. Based on the above increase in labour productivity, the company could cut its workforce and still be able to produce 600 units per week. With labour productivity of 30 units per week, only 20 workers will be needed to achieve 600 (30 × 20) units of output.

The increase in labour productivity would mean it is possible for the business to increase output and cut costs at the same time. Cutting the number of workers to 22 would cut costs but still increase output to 660 units (22 × 30).

Increases in labour productivity may be achieved in a variety of ways, not all of them as a result of operational decisions. Some examples are:

- introducing new technology that speeds up the production process
- modifying the production system so that it operates more efficiently
- recruiting new workers with better qualifications and skills
- implementing new approaches to improve the workforce's motivation
- providing better training for the workforce
- improving the flexibility of operations so that less time is wasted.

Although improvements to labour productivity are desirable, a business may need to be cautious because of two possible issues:

- **Cost of improving labour productivity**: each of the methods above involves additional expenditure and so the business should only implement them if the improved labour productivity generates enough additional revenue to pay for the changes.
- **Improving labour productivity may conflict with other objectives**: if workers are focused on producing higher levels of output they may lose sight of other operational issues, such as flexibility, dependability and quality. If, say, quality is of vital importance to customers, then the productivity gains may lead to more problems than benefits.

Unit costs (average costs)

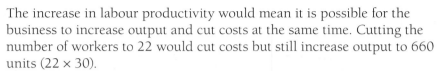

$$\text{unit cost} = \frac{\text{total cost}}{\text{units of output}}$$

The unit cost is also known as the average cost (AC) or average total cost (ATC). For example, if a business produces 100 units of output at a total cost of £5,000, the average (or unit) cost is £50 (£5,000/100).

Remember that total costs = fixed costs + variable costs.

In Chapter 1 we saw how total costs increased as output increased. However, we can now look at the impact on average or unit costs. Table 12.1 is the same as Table 1.2 from Chapter 1, but with a fifth column added that shows the unit cost (or average cost).

▼ **Table 12.1** Monthly costs and output for a magazine producer

Units of output (000s)	Fixed costs (£000s)	Total variable costs (£000s)	Total costs (£000s)	Unit cost (average cost per unit)
0	50	0	50	–
20	50	20	70	3.50
40	50	40	90	2.25
60	50	60	110	1.83
80	50	80	130	1.63
100	50	100	150	1.50
120*	50	120	170	1.42

*Assume that 120,000 units is the capacity – the maximum possible output.

In this example, the most efficient level of output is 120,000 because this is the output at which the unit cost is at its lowest (£1.42 per unit).

Comparing operational efficiency with competitors

In an industry in which competition is based on prices, it is vital for a business to achieve the lowest unit costs. Look at Table 12.2.

▼ **Table 12.2** Unit costs of four different companies

	Units of output	Fixed costs (£)	Total variable costs (£)	Total costs (£)	Unit costs (£)
Company A	40	200	160	360	9.00
Company B	80	300	300	600	7.50
Company C	100	500	600	1,100	11.00
Company D	150	600	675	1,275	8.50

The most efficient company is B, where unit costs are £7.50 per unit. The least efficient company is C, where unit costs are £11.00 per unit.

Unit costs and labour productivity

Labour productivity has a significant impact on unit costs, particularly in businesses that use a great deal of labour as a factor of production.

Table 12.3 shows the link between labour productivity and unit costs in four different firms.

▼ **Table 12.3** Labour productivity and unit costs in four different firms

A	B Units of output (per week)	C Number of employees	D Labour productivity (column B/column C)	E Wage costs* (£) (column C × £400)	F Wage costs per unit (£) (column E/column B)
Firm W	400	2	200	800	2.00
Firm X	660	4	165	1,600	2.42
Firm Y	750	5	150	2,000	2.67
Firm Z	1,080	6	180	2,400	2.22

* Column E assumes that each firm pays its employees £400 per week.

The higher the labour productivity, the lower the wage cost per unit (assuming each firm pays the same wage level). Firm W has the highest labour productivity and the lowest wage costs per unit. Similarly, firm Y

What do you think?

From Table 12.3 it might seem obvious that a firm will try to reduce wages in order to lower its labour costs (and thus its unit costs). Why might this not be the best approach to adopt?

Key term

Capacity The maximum total level of output or production that a business can produce in a given time period. A company producing at this level is said to be producing at full capacity.

Key term

Capacity utilisation The percentage of a firm's total possible production level that is being reached. If a company is large enough to produce 100 units a week, but is actually producing 92 units, its capacity utilisation is 92 per cent.

has the lowest labour productivity but the highest wage costs per unit. Although there are other costs to include, it will be difficult for firm Y to match the overall unit costs of firm W when there is such a big difference in wage costs per unit.

Capacity

The ideal **capacity** will depend on a number of factors:

- level of demand for a product
- flexibility of production lines
- seasonality of output
- seasonality of demand
- implications of failure to meet demand
- opportunities for sub-contracted or outsourced production.

These factors will be discussed in more detail in Chapter 13.

Ideally, the level of capacity should be sufficient to meet the maximum anticipated demand, but only if it is cost effective to do so. The operational objective will be to have a certain maximum capacity. For example, a newspaper publisher might want the capacity to print 1 million newspapers each day; a restaurant owner might want the capacity to serve 40 restaurant customers per hour.

Capacity utilisation

Capacity utilisation measures the extent to which the company's maximum possible output is being reached. It can be calculated using the following formula:

$$\text{capacity utilisation} = \frac{\text{actual output per annum (month)}}{\text{maximum possible output per annum (month)}} \times 100$$

A company capable of producing 3,500 units but actually producing 2,800 units is working at 80 per cent capacity:

$$\frac{2,800}{3,500} \times 100 = 80 \text{ per cent}$$

It could increase production by 700 units or 20 per cent. This is known as its spare capacity.

Capacity utilisation can be measured over any chosen time period. For some organisations it may be most appropriate to calculate it on a daily basis, but weekly or monthly calculations may be more relevant to other firms.

There is no one ideal target percentage. At 100 per cent there is no scope for maintenance and repair, because all resources, including manpower and machinery, are being fully used to produce at maximum capacity. For the same reason, the business is also unable to respond to sudden orders or to deal with emergency situations that may occur. However, every percentage point below 100 represents 'unused' resources and higher fixed costs per unit produced.

Link between capacity utilisation and other operational targets

Although capacity utilisation is a target in its own right, it is also important because of its impact on the other operational targets:

- **Capacity utilisation and labour productivity**. A business's capacity is often, but not always, determined by the level of machinery or equipment in the factory or office. If there is low capacity utilisation a lot of the machinery will be standing idle and therefore not being used productively. This may well lead to a situation where there is less work completed by individual workers, because the amount being produced is much lower than the firm's capacity to produce. In this case, output per worker will fall and so labour productivity will fall. The situation is more likely to arise if full-time, permanent employees are used. For more flexible workforces, it may be possible to reduce the number of workers if there is a plan to cut production levels.

- **Capacity utilisation and unit costs**. The higher the level of capacity utilisation, the more efficiently a business is using its resources. If a business has a factory, it will incur fixed costs, such as rent, regardless of its level of output. Let us assume that the factory has fixed costs of £120,000 per annum and can produce 10,000 items at full capacity. Table 12.4 shows the link between capacity utilisation and the fixed costs per unit. It can be seen that high capacity utilisation means much lower fixed costs per unit. At 50 per cent capacity utilisation, the fixed costs per unit are twice as high as the figure when capacity utilisation is 100 per cent. Below 50 per cent the fixed costs per unit increase dramatically, as capacity utilisation falls.

▼ **Table 12.4** Fixed costs per unit at different levels of capacity utilisation

Level of output (units)	Capacity utilisation (%)	Fixed costs (£)	Fixed costs per unit (£)
10,000	100	120,000	12.00
9,000	90	120,000	13.33
8,000	80	120,000	15.00
7,000	70	120,000	17.14
6,000	60	120,000	20.00
5,000	50	120,000	24.00
4,000	40	120,000	30.00
3,000	30	120,000	40.00
2,000	20	120,000	60.00
1,000	10	120,000	120.00

Taking these two other measures of operational performance into consideration, and the need for some flexibility, many businesses recognise that a level of 90 per cent capacity utilisation is an ideal balance.

Practice exercise 1 Data response

Total: 30 marks

Brilliant plc has four factories – J, K, L and M. Each factory has been given the same operational objectives:

- to exceed 80 per cent capacity utilisation
- to achieve weekly labour productivity of more than 200 units per worker
- to achieve unit costs of less than £4.80 per unit.

Factory M is the newest and largest factory and so more production is allocated to it. The Operations Management Director has decided to close one of the four factories in order to improve capacity utilisation. Her decision was based on the data in Table 12.5. Her assistant used the data in Table 12.5 to calculate the operational performance of each factory. These calculations are shown in Table 12.6.

A	B	C	D	F	G	H
Factory	Capacity units of output (per week)	Actual units of output (per week)	No. of workers	Wage costs (£ per week)	Other costs (£ per week)	Total costs (£ per week)
J	1,600	1,000	5	1,900	2,700	4,600
K	1,550	1,120	6	2,220	3,200	5,420
L	1,900	1,330	7	2,625	3,975	6,600
M	3,000	2,650	10	3,600	5,400	9,000
TOTAL	**8,050**	**6,100**	**28**	**10,345**	**15,275**	**25,620**

▼ **Table 12.6** Brilliant products plc: Operations performance data for 2014, based on data in Table 12.5

A	B	C	D
Factory	Capacity utilisation (%)	Labour productivity (units per worker)	Unit costs (£)
J	63	200	?
K	?	187	4.84
L	70	?	4.96
M	88	265	3.40
OVERALL	**76**	**218**	**4.20**

1 Calculate the capacity utilisation of Factory K. (2 marks)

2 Calculate the labour productivity of Factory L. (2 marks)

3 Calculate the unit costs of Factory J. (2 marks)

4 Based on the data in Tables 12.5 and 12.6, analyse two possible reasons why the unit costs of Factory M are lower than the unit costs of the other factories. (8 marks)

5 Weekly demand for the company's products is fairly consistent, averaging 6,100 units per week. The Operations Director decides to close Factory L. Do you agree with this decision? Justify your view. (16 marks)

13

Making operational decisions to improve performance: increasing efficiency and productivity

This chapter begins by investigating labour productivity and efficiency – how they can be increased and the difficulties involved in doing so. You will also look at how an optimal mix of resources can improve labour productivity and efficiency. The importance of capacity and the efficient utilisation of capacity are considered. The chapter then considers the benefits and difficulties of lean production, before concluding with an examination of how technology can improve operational efficiency.

Importance of labour productivity and efficiency

In Chapter 12 we saw that labour productivity measures output per worker in a given time period (output ÷ number of workers).

Labour productivity measures the efficiency of labour, whereas **efficiency** takes into consideration all factor inputs – labour, capital, land and natural resources and enterprise. These inputs are often known as the factors of production. (see Did you know? on page 256)

> **Key term**
>
> **Efficiency** Output (production) is maximised from a given level of inputs.

Benefits of high labour productivity and efficiency

- Efficient use of inputs allows businesses to maximise production and therefore satisfy the needs of more consumers.
- Efficient use of inputs means that fewer inputs are needed to produce a given level of output. This reduces unit costs for the business.
- Lower unit costs enable a business to gain a competitive advantage because a business can lower its prices and yet still maintain the same profit margin on its products.
- Where consumers desire high quality, the cost savings from greater efficiency can be used to improve the quality of the product.

Did you know?

Resources used for production are often classified into four categories, known as the factors of production.

1 **Labour**: the physical and mental effort of people involved in production of goods and services.

2 **Land**: all natural resources, such as land itself, but also natural and mineral resources such as plants, livestock, fish, coal, oil and gravel.

3 **Capital**: goods that are made in order to produce other goods, such as machinery, shelving, lorries, factories, shops and offices.

4 **Enterprise**: the act of bringing together all of the factors of production in order to create goods and services. This is carried out by entrepreneurs whose reward is the profit made from these activities.

Businesses and economies have limited resources (inputs) available to them and so it is vital that these inputs are used efficiently.

● By comparing its labour productivity with its level of efficiency, a business can recognise whether it should modify the balance of its inputs in order to improve overall efficiency. For example, if the business has high labour productivity and low efficiency, this suggests that it can improve its efficiency by increasing its labour force and reducing the use of other inputs, such as capital. Similarly, if there is low labour productivity and high efficiency, this suggests that labour should be replaced by other inputs in order to improve overall efficiency.

● High labour productivity and efficiency can also enable the business to increase its appeal to its stakeholders. Greater efficiency may allow the business to:
  ● pay higher wages to its workers
  ● offer lower prices or improve quality for consumers
  ● spend more money on the local environment
  ● increase overall profits for its shareholders.

How to increase efficiency and labour productivity

There are a number of ways in which the efficiency of the factors of production (inputs) can be improved, in order to create greater output.

● **Improving the fertility of land**. Modern agricultural techniques enable farmers to achieve greater output per acre. Similarly, factory farming can enable a farmer to generate greater productivity from livestock farming.

● **Using renewable or recyclable resources**. Many factories are now designed to minimise waste and improve energy efficiency so that resources are used more effectively.

● **Greater education and training of the workforce**. This can lead to much greater output from labour, which is particularly important in the UK as the skills of the labour force are an essential element in allowing UK businesses to compete with countries that have lower wage levels.

● **Increasing the level of investment in capital equipment**. High-quality capital goods, such as modern machinery, can greatly enhance the efficiency of a labour force. Businesses that are able to continually update their machinery and technology will be able to operate much more efficiently and provide goods and services that meet the ever-changing requirements of customers.

- **Improvements in management skills and a willingness to take risks by businesses**. These may greatly improve efficiency because factors of production will be converted into goods and services that meet customer needs.
- **Combining the factors of production in a balanced way**. This can help a business to avoid problems, such as the reduced efficiency that may arise if one factor of production is overused in comparison with the other factors.
- **Extending the overall scale of production**. As a business grows larger it tends to improve both labour productivity and efficiency. The benefits that lead to these improvements are known as **economies of scale**.

What do you think?

Labour productivity and efficiency in the car industry

In 2013, the UK built more cars than France; the first time this has happened since 1966. UK production is predicted to reach 2 million cars per annum for the first time ever in 2018. Analysts believe that high labour productivity, modern factories with capital intensive methods, skilled labour, good employer–employee relationships and favourable external factors such as economic and business conditions have all contributed towards this achievement. The Nissan plant in Sunderland is often cited as the car factory with the highest labour productivity in Europe, with annual productivity in excess of 90 cars per employee.

A 2013 international survey by Deloitte ranked the world's most competitive countries. Rankings at the top of the list were closely correlated to car manufacturing output. In order, the world's five most competitive countries are China, Germany, USA, India and South Korea. The world's largest car manufacturers are China, USA, Japan, Germany, South Korea and India (Japan is the tenth most competitive country). The UK was ranked as the fifteenth most competitive country in the world, with France in twenty-fifth place. In terms of car production the UK is in thirteenth place and France is in fourteenth place, but French car production fell by 11.6 per cent in 2013 while UK sales grew by 1.6 per cent.

Can the UK stay ahead of France in the production of cars in the future? What do you think?

Economies of scale

Fixed costs, such as the depreciation of machinery and administrative expenses, must be paid, regardless of the number of units that an organisation produces and sells. This enables large firms that utilise their equipment effectively to produce at much lower costs per unit.

Internal economies of scale (often abbreviated to **economies of scale**) can be classified under a number of headings. Examples of economies are outlined below.

Technical economies

- Modern equipment that will improve efficiency can be installed. This should lower unit costs and improve the quality and reliability of the product or service.
- Mass production (flow) techniques can be employed to improve productivity.
- Highly trained technicians can be employed to improve the reliability of the production process.

- Large-scale transportation can reduce distribution costs per unit.
- The purchase of computer systems can improve efficiency in both production and administration.
- Improvements in communication systems using new technology can enhance customer service and the working environment, improving the company's operations and its reputation.

Specialisation economies

Large firms can afford to employ specialists with particular skills. In smaller organisations, staff tend to take on a wider variety of tasks, and specialist skills, when needed, are bought from outside at a relatively high price.

Production techniques can be adapted to encourage division of labour (specialisation) in large firms.

A small firm is unlikely to be able to pay a high enough salary to attract the best staff, so larger firms should be more efficient. Training to improve specialist skills is also easier in large firms.

If staff are able to specialise, they are likely to become even more skilled in their role, again increasing the efficiency of the firm.

Did you know?

Technical economies of scale are particularly important in mass production industries such as textiles and cars. Small firms in these markets need to compete on factors other than price because they cannot match the low costs obtained by the largest firms.

Fact file

Tesco plc

Tesco removed control of distribution (transportation) from many of its suppliers and took control itself. Tesco used to pay suppliers a price that included delivery to its stores or warehouses, but the transport costs of its small suppliers were high because they were too small to benefit from economies of scale. Tesco now uses its specialisation in transportation to save money. It buys the supplies at a lower price than before, but picks up supplies from the suppliers' factories and delivers the goods itself. Over two-thirds of Tesco's supplies are now purchased in this way, with mainly the very large suppliers delivering directly to Tesco. Tesco's huge buying power also means that it can buy additional transport cheaply at short notice, giving it a competitive and flexible system. However, in recent years Tesco has changed its focus from low price to differentiation and is holding more specialist stock that sells more slowly. This has led to more direct deliveries from specialist suppliers, as the order sizes limit the scope for economies of scale.

Purchasing economies

- Large firms can buy in bulk. This reduces costs because suppliers can produce in large quantities and thus lower their own costs.
- Suppliers may give greater discounts in order to guarantee or keep a contract with a large customer, as the latter has a stronger bargaining power. In March 2014, Tesco announced a price cut for milk. Other major supermarkets followed suit, leading to a price war. The supermarkets and milk wholesalers used their bargaining power to push down the price paid to farmers. This price had peaked at 34.6p a litre but had fallen to 32p a litre by June 2014.

Marketing economies

- Large firms can use more expensive media that reach more customers in a more persuasive way. This can both increase the effectiveness of the advertising and reduce unit costs.
- Large firms can also do more market research, so that they understand markets more fully than smaller competitors.

Financial economies

- Because they are considered to be safer, large companies should be able to get loans more easily and at lower rates of interest.
- They will find it easier to access funds through other sources, such as retained profits and shareholders.

Research and development economies

- Large companies can afford to devote more money to innovation and research and development. This expenditure should enable a business to discover new products or to find easier ways to produce goods.

Social and welfare economies

- Larger companies are able to provide social facilities such as sports clubs, canteens and relaxation areas. Welfare facilities such as medical care, health insurance and pension funds may also improve conditions for staff.
- Such benefits will make it easier to recruit workers and should improve morale among existing staff, leading to a more highly motivated workforce with lower levels of absenteeism and a lower rate of labour turnover.

Managerial and administrative economies

- Large companies can employ the best managers and adopt more cost-effective administration procedures. These economies should reduce the overheads of the business and thus improve its competitiveness.

Difficulties increasing labour productivity and efficiency

In the previous section we examined the ways in which the efficiency of the factors of production (inputs) could be improved, in order to create greater output. However, for each of these approaches there are difficulties that might limit or prevent improvements in labour productivity and efficiency.

- It is unlikely that the fertility of land can be increased indefinitely. In some places modern agricultural techniques have been blamed for destroying fertility rather than increasing it. There are also conflicts with environmental objectives, particularly in the case of factory farming.
- Many resources are not renewable and as world demand increases we are likely to face future shortages of essential resources.
- Education and training can improve productivity but they also consume resources too, particularly time. The opportunity cost of education and training must be considered when assessing the benefits gained.
- Increasing the level of investment in capital equipment means that resources must be diverted from consumer goods (which usually give immediate satisfaction to consumers) to capital goods, which create future wealth. Too much emphasis on capital goods can mean that consumers have fewer products available to them in the short term, because the business sector is using more of the economy's resources to produce machines rather than products that give immediate satisfaction to consumers, such as furniture and cars.

Key term

Diseconomies of scale (also known as **internal diseconomies of scale**) The disadvantages that an organisation experiences due to an increase in size. These cause a decrease in efficiency and/or an increase in unit costs of production.

● In the previous section we saw that extending the overall scale of production can improve both labour productivity and efficiency through economies of scale. However, there are also problems that arise from extending scale. These problems are known as diseconomies of scale.

Diseconomies of scale

As organisations grow, they may suffer disadvantages that lead to a lowering of efficiency and higher unit costs of production. These are known as **diseconomies of scale** or **internal diseconomies of scale**. Some examples are given below.

Co-ordination diseconomies

● There may be a loss of control by management as an organisation becomes more complex, particularly if the organisation becomes more geographically spread or management experiences an increasing workload.
● Individuals are less likely to follow organisational policies if the level of control is reduced. This happens in larger organisations because managers have larger spans of control and there are more levels of hierarchy.
● Large firms often have more rigid and inflexible policies. These are imposed to limit the loss of control described above but reduce the ability to respond quickly to changing customer needs.

Communication diseconomies

● Too many levels of hierarchy in a business can reduce the effectiveness of communication. Messages can be distorted (as in Chinese whispers) and it is possible that communications do not reach everyone.
● Difficulties also occur as spans of control widen. It becomes much more difficult for managers to meet with subordinates.
● In large firms, inappropriate methods of communication are likely to be used, as standardised, large-scale approaches are more common.
● Employees who do not receive, or are not involved in, communications may feel unvalued and demotivated.

Motivation diseconomies

● It is more difficult to assess the needs of many individuals. Even if motivational methods are used, it is less likely that the managers will know the best approach for each subordinate.
● In large firms there may be less time for recognition and reward.
● Large hierarchies create feelings of distance between decision makers and employees.
● Large firms often have the financial wealth to introduce schemes to motivate employees, but they can lack the management time to provide recognition.
● These problems occur in firms of all sizes. They are only diseconomies of scale if they have been caused by the large size of the organisation rather than by other factors, such as poor management.

Other diseconomies of scale

Other diseconomies of scale include the following:

- **Technical diseconomies**: production on a very large scale can become difficult to organise.
- **Excessive bureaucracy**: as organisations grow, the number of levels of management increases and this may slow down decision making.
- **Staff problems**: industrial relations problems and higher staff turnover and absences may result from the factors described above.
- **Less flexibility**: as firms grow and the above factors emerge, firms may fail to meet the changing needs of their customers.

Economies and diseconomies of scale and unit costs

Table 13.1 provides an example of the effect of both economies of scale and diseconomies of scale. It shows how, initially, the unit (average) costs of production fall as the company increases its output. This occurs for three main reasons:

1 The fixed costs stay the same (and so fixed costs per unit fall) as output rises.
2 Variable costs increase at a slower rate because large-scale production enables the organisation to combine its factors of production more efficiently.
3 The firm can benefit from the economies of scale described earlier.

▼ **Table 13.1** Economies and diseconomies of scale

Units of output	Fixed costs (£)	Total variable costs (£)	Total costs (£)	Unit (average) costs (£)
0	240	0	240	–
1	240	200	440	440
2	240	340	580	290
3	240	420	660	220
4	240	476	716	179
5	240	520	760	152
6	240	570	810	135
7	240	642	882	126
8	240	736	976	122
9	240	849	1,089	121
10	240	1,000	1,240	124
11	240	1,201	1,441	131
12	240	1,476	1,716	143

However, once the output rises beyond nine units, diseconomies of scale outweigh economies of scale. Although economies such as bulk buying may be helping to lower unit costs, problems such as co-ordination are having a larger impact and so, overall, the unit costs are beginning to rise.

Firms use information on economies and diseconomies of scale in order to plan their most efficient size, but exact guidelines cannot be established and opinions change over time. Thirty years ago, the emphasis was on large-scale operations to achieve the benefits of economies of scale. Since that time, however, greater flexibility has been demanded and as a result many firms have demerged or split themselves into smaller operations to avoid diseconomies of scale. For example, Racal, the company that created Vodafone, viewed any operation with more than 800 staff as too large and had a policy of splitting any division that exceeded this size. This led to Vodafone being split away from Racal Tacticom, the division that dealt with mobile communications for military purposes.

How to choose the optimal mix of resources

As we saw at the beginning of this chapter, the resources or inputs that firms use are often known as the factors of production:

- enterprise
- labour
- land
- capital.

Enterprise and land tend to be unique. However, labour and capital are resources that can often be used interchangeably in the production process, so a business must decide whether its production methods will be predominantly based on the use of capital or the use of labour.

Factors influencing the choice between capital-intensive and labour-intensive production

A business will weigh up a number of factors before deciding whether to use capital- or **labour-intensive production**. The most significant factors are described below.

Method of production

In general, mass production on a large scale, such as at a car plant, requires capital equipment. Machinery can produce more quickly and consistently than a human being. Consequently, large-scale production usually means that a firm will choose **capital-intensive production** methods.

In contrast, if products are specifically designed for the consumer, then labour-intensive methods are more likely. The success of the business will depend more on the workers than on machinery.

Skills and efficiency of the factors of production

A business that depends on the skills of its workers (such as a hair salon or a theatre company) will use labour-intensive methods. However, if machinery or other forms of capital can greatly lower unit costs or produce a more consistent, high-quality product, then capital-intensive methods will be employed.

Key terms

Capital-intensive production
Methods of production that use a high level of capital equipment in comparison to other inputs, such as labour. A fully automated factory (e.g. a Fiat car plant) and a nuclear power station are examples of capital-intensive production.

Labour-intensive production
Methods of production that use high levels of labour in comparison to capital equipment. Many service industries, such as retailing, restaurants and call centres, use a large number of people in comparison to equipment.

▲ Hairdressing is labour intensive

Relative costs of labour and capital

Labour is relatively expensive in Western Europe compared to some other parts of the world. As a result, firms that operate in this area will benefit from replacing labour with capital equipment. Ever fewer people in Western Europe are now employed on production lines, as firms have automated production (i.e. replaced workers with machinery). In some other parts of the world, such as India and China, labour is much cheaper to use and so production lines are more labour intensive. This situation has led to multinational corporations moving production from Western Europe to other parts of the world.

Another consideration is the reliability of labour and capital. Industrial relations problems in industries such as car manufacturing led firms to decide that capital-intensive production methods were more cost effective because disruptions to production were very expensive. Conversely, unreliable equipment may encourage firms to choose labour-intensive production.

Size and financial position of a business

Capital equipment is expensive to buy. It may not be possible for small businesses or firms with cash flow difficulties to purchase the equipment needed for capital-intensive methods. As a consequence, these firms will choose labour-intensive production.

Product or service

The more standardised a product, the greater the advantages of capital-intensive production because machinery can produce vast quantities at low unit costs.

Customers

If customers want personal contact, this may limit the scope for capital intensity. The banking industry has lowered its costs by automating many of its processes, but many of its customers prefer the more sociable nature of a branch to the automated cashpoint. NatWest has used its 'labour intensity' as a selling point in its marketing campaigns.

▲ Many banking processes are now automated

Did you know?

Portakabin Ltd

Portakabin Ltd provides temporary or quickly erected buildings. It uses a mixture of capital- and labour-intensive methods. Capital intensive methods are used to provide the basic structure and standard fittings for a building and are also used to lay the foundations for the new building at the customer's site. The items are then delivered to the site, where more labour-intensive methods are used to add the special internal features required by the customer.

Fact file

Computer games – from labour intensive to capital intensive to virtual

Ian Higgins, former chief executive of Empire Interactive, a games publisher and developer, says that when the company was founded in 1987 its first game cost £4,000 to produce. By 2008 new generation games titles were costing between £4 million and £6 million to develop. Production had changed from being labour intensive to capital intensive. Initially, two people could produce a game. Twenty years later it needed a team of 20 to 40, including programmers, artists, sound engineers, producers and so on. However, it was the need for more sophisticated capital in the form of new technology that has been the main feature of the changes in the industry. Although a new game requires 10 to 20 times as many people, the overall costs had risen by a multiple of 1,000 to 1,500. These vast changes reflected the much greater emphasis on state-of-the-art capital equipment.

Large firms gained from technological economies of scale and also had stronger bargaining power when dealing with retailers.

In 2000, there were over 300 computer games publishers in the UK, but the need for high technology and cost effectiveness means that individuals with bright ideas were excluded from the market, unless they could get employment with a publisher.

The research organisation Screen Digest compared the market share needed by a single game to reach breakeven between 1993 and 2008. Table 13.2 shows the results of this research.

▼ **Table 13.2** Analysis of required breakeven market share of worldwide computer games market

Year	1993	1998	2003	2008
Size of market ($m)	9,108	14,997	18,471	23,901
Wholesale market ($m)	4,910	8,085	9,959	12,886
Development spend ($m)	982	1,617	1,992	2,577
Typical development budget per game ($m)	1.125	2.25	5.0	8.0
Breakeven market share	0.11%	0.14%	0.25%	0.31%

The need to typically spend $8 million to develop a game led to the removal of small firms from this market and even some large businesses were reluctant to commit $8 million to an investment that had an increasingly high risk of failure.

More recently, the growth in sales of smartphones and tablets has transformed this industry. The traditional computer games market appeals to committed 'gamers' and is dominated by Sony, Nintendo and Microsoft. However, smartphones (and the Nintendo Wii, to a lesser extent) have led to growth in 'casual gamers'. In 2008 this market did not exist; according to *Juniper Research*, by 2013–2014 annual revenue from games for mobiles was $20,900 million and is expected to reach $28,900 million by 2016. Within six years, the traditional, console games market has changed from labour-intensive small providers to large-scale developers such as EA. However, small businesses can still compete with larger businesses in the mobile gaming market, because there are fewer economies of scale and casual users are less likely to require high quality graphics and sound.

Sources: Empire Interactive; IHS Screen Digest

Practice exercise 1

Column 1	Column 2	Column 3	Column 4
Units of output	People employed	Profit	Level of factor inputs

1 Using the information in the table, labour productivity would be measured by:
   a) Column 1 divided by Column 2
   b) Column 1 divided by Column 4
   c) Column 3 divided by Column 2
   d) Column 3 divided by Column 4 *(1 mark)*

2 Using the information in the table, efficiency would be assessed by comparing:
   a) Column 1 with Column 2
   b) Column 1 with Column 4
   c) Column 3 with Column 2
   d) Column 3 with Column 4 *(1 mark)*

3 In Table 13.1 (page 261), the firm is at maximum productive efficiency when output is:
   a) 1 unit
   b) 8 units
   c) 9 units
   d) 12 units *(1 mark)*

4 Using Table 13.1, the fixed costs per unit at 4 units of output are:
   a) £60
   b) £119
   c) £179
   d) £240 *(1 mark)*

5 Analyse two possible economies of scale that might occur in a national newspaper publisher, or another firm of which you have knowledge. *(9 marks)*

6 Analyse two possible diseconomies of scale that might occur in a national newspaper publisher, or the firm that you chose in question 5. *(9 marks)*

7 Distinguish between labour-intensive production and capital-intensive production. *(4 marks)*

8 Analyse two factors that would influence a farmer when deciding whether to use labour-intensive production or capital-intensive production. *(9 marks)*

9 Read the fact file on computer games. To what extent was it inevitable that firms providing games for consoles, such as the Xbox or PlayStation, would change from being labour intensive to capital intensive? *(16 marks)*

10 Read the fact file on computer games. Analyse two reasons why it will be easier for small businesses to compete with larger firms in the market for games played on smartphones and tablets. *(9 marks)*

Case study: Productivity and efficiency in dairy farming

Since 1995, dairy farming has become more capital intensive and is based on fewer, but larger-scale farms. Supermarkets have used their bargaining power to reduce prices and farmers have also been hit by a steady decline in consumption of milk and dairy products by UK consumers. Low milk prices have made it difficult for dairy farmers to make a profit. Consequently, the number of dairy farmers has fallen from 30,000 in 1995 to 12,000 in 2014.

Low profits for dairy farmers have meant little scope for modernising and so efficiency remains low.

Table 13.3 shows data on output and the number of cows. While milk output has remained fairly static, falling by less than 5 per cent between 1995 and 2011, the number of cows has fallen by almost a third. Output per cow has increased by 41 per cent. In 2011, labour productivity was 311,661 litres per person.

▼ **Table 13.3** Data on productivity of dairy farming, 1995–2011

Year	Number of dairy cows (millions)	Milk output (millions of litres)	Average yield (litres per cow)	Labour* force	Average size of dairy herd
1995	2.35	12,502	5320	75,200	77
2003	1.89	12,470	6598	51,030	101
2011	1.59	11,893	7480	38,160	127

* Full-time equivalent employees and owners working in dairy production

Source: DEFRA (www.gov.uk)

As dairy farming is often a family business, the 60 per cent fall in dairy farmers since 1995 has been the main factor causing the large fall in the labour force in dairy farming. With output only falling slightly, this has led to a significant increase in labour productivity. However, despite this improvement in productivity, overall efficiency remains low. Table 13.4 shows that, on average, farms with herds of fewer than 150 cows have low levels of efficiency, because the value of their output is less than their inputs.

▼ **Table 13.4** Efficiency of dairy farms, by size of herd

Size of herd (number of cows)	Value of output per £100 of input (£)
0–50	75
51–75	89
76–100	91
101–150	99
151–200	109
201–300	105
301+	111

Source: DEFRA (www.gov.uk)

On average, only farms with herd sizes in excess of 150 cows are creating an output with a value that exceeds the value of inputs. The table indicates that there are probably economies of scale occurring. Due to price pressure from supermarkets it is unlikely that larger farms are able to negotiate higher prices for their milk. Consequently, these greater outputs per input are likely to come from lower unit costs

rather than higher prices. Nevertheless, the scope for economies of scale appears to be limited, because the efficiency of the very largest dairy farms (over 300 cows) is not very much greater than that of farms with herds of 151–200 cows. Furthermore, the value of output per input of farms of between 201 and 300 cows actually drops.

The increase in the average size of dairy herds suggests that there are some benefits from larger scale. Larger farms can afford to invest in machinery to improve efficiency and also have herd sizes that will utilise this machinery more effectively.

Agriculture is unusual in that external factors, such as the weather, can have a major impact on efficiency. In 2001, foot and mouth disease hit the UK and led to many dairy farmers leaving the industry. However, major occurrences such as this are rare. In 2011–12 dairy farming net income (profit excluding payments to the farmer) increased by 31 per cent, mainly because of increases in the price of milk. In 2012–13, net incomes fell by 40 per cent, largely because poor weather caused shortages of cattle fodder which led to very high feeding costs for cows. Net incomes are expected to fall again in 2013–14, because of lower prices paid to farmers for milk.

Efficiency has been driven by internal changes too. The increasing scale of operations, investment in capital equipment and improved understanding of how to maximise the average yield per cow have all contributed to greater productivity and greater efficiency. A key cause of improved efficiency has been the huge fall in the number of dairy farmers. Many of the least efficient dairy farms have been forced to leave the industry, with only the most efficient remaining.

Cutting unit costs in dairy farming has been the driving force behind efficiency gains, but many believe that there is limited scope for further improvement. Improved efficiency in the future may come from higher prices for dairy products, rather than lower costs. Three factors suggest this may happen:

- The reduction in potential supply because so many farmers have left dairy farming

- Increased competition between milk wholesalers such as Arla, Wiseman and Dairy Crest. These three businesses dominate milk wholesaling and all three have recently increased their processing capacity and may be prepared to offer higher prices to farmers. These businesses will want to work close to full capacity and so reduce their unit costs.
- The growth of direct selling through farm shops and farmers' markets and the scope to gain higher profit margins by processing milk to produce specialist cheeses and other dairy products.

Sources: DEFRA and Report in 2013 by DairyCo on 'The structure of the GB Dairy Farming industry – what drives change?'

Questions

Total: 50 marks

1 Based on the information in Table 13.4, what size of dairy herd is most efficient? *(1 mark)*

2 Based on the information in Table 13.3, calculate labour productivity in 1995. *(2 marks)*

3 Based on data in the article and your answer to question 2, has productivity per cow improved more than labour productivity? Show your working. *(5 marks)*

4 What evidence is there to suggest that dairy farming is NOT an efficient industry? *(6 marks)*

5 Choose one of the bullet points in the final paragraph of the case study. Explain how the factor described might lead to an increase in efficiency in dairy farming. *(5 marks)*

6 Explain two reasons why dairy farming is becoming more capital intensive. *(6 marks)*

7 Analyse the possible impact of the current low profits in dairy farming on the future efficiency of dairy farming. *(9 marks)*

8 To what extent is the efficiency of a dairy farm outside the control of the dairy farmer? Justify your view. *(16 marks)*

The importance of capacity

Key term

Capacity The maximum total output or production that a business can produce in a given time period.

Capacity is the maximum total level of output or production that a business can produce in a given time period. Capacity is important because it enables a business to meet the demands of its customers. However, increasing capacity usually requires an increase in capital equipment, land and other resources and so it is important to avoid excess capacity which will merely add to a firm's costs.

Capacity is important to a business for the following reasons.

- It can enable it to meet the level of demand for a product. If demand is high, a large capacity will mean that a business can still meet consumer demand. Insufficient capacity will not only mean the loss of a customer in the short term, but possibly the loss of goodwill in the long term, if customers are frustrated by the business's inability to supply.

267

- Efficient capacity management can ensure that a firm is not spending excessive amounts on capital equipment and other resources and therefore is able to control its unit costs. Low unit costs help the firm to achieve higher profit margins.
- Ideally, a firm's capacity should allow some flexibility between different production lines, so that supply can meet demand if one particular product experiences a sudden increase in popularity. In this situation, capacity for that particular product can be increased by shifting resources from the production of another, less popular product.
- Some industries, such as farming, have seasonal production. Such industries need to ensure that they have the capacity to cope with the peak production period.
- Some industries, such as tourism, have seasonal demand. These industries need to plan capacity to cope with the periods when demand peaks.
- The importance of capacity can depend on other factors too. If a firm has no close competition, a lack of capacity may be less of an issue, because customers will not be able to find alternative supplies. In very competitive industries, a lack of capacity could have more serious repercussions. Many firms use outsourcing or sub-contracted production to cope with sudden increases in demand. Outsourcing or sub-contracting production means that a firm does not need to spend money on expanding capacity, but it is likely to be more expensive because the company actually producing the product will be charging a price that includes their profit margin.

In order to achieve the optimum level of capacity — one that allows it to meet customer demand but avoid excessive costs — a business may need to increase or decrease its capacity. These methods will be discussed in the next section.

How to utilise capacity efficiently

In terms of capacity utilisation, there are two types of situation that a firm needs to manage:

- under-utilisation of capacity (also known as **excess capacity** or **spare capacity**)
- capacity shortage.

These two situations must be managed in radically different ways. As spare capacity is the more normal situation, this will be looked at first, starting with the possible reasons why it occurs.

Spare capacity

There are several reasons why a firm may be operating below its maximum possible output.

- **New competitors or new products entering the market**. For example, it has become increasingly popular to open pizza restaurants in recent years, in response to increased demand. However, the growth of competition has been so high that in some places there is now excess capacity in the market, so the average turnover for each outlet has begun to fall.

▲ Seasonal demand

- **Fall in demand for the product due to changes in taste or fashion.** McDonald's has been forced to close some of its restaurants because of a fall in demand caused by many consumers wanting more varied and healthy food.
- **Unsuccessful marketing.** Benetton grew rapidly in the UK, partly as a result of brand awareness created by its advertising. Its decline coincided with negative publicity related to some of the controversial images that it used in its posters.
- **Seasonal demand.** The tourist industry must build facilities to accommodate visitors at peak times of the season. Attractions such as Alton Towers therefore have excess capacity during the winter months. During the working day, organisations such as cafés and fitness clubs also have varying levels of spare capacity.
- **Over-investment in fixed assets.** Littlewoods was originally established as a mail-order business in 1932, promoting its clothes through catalogues. In the 1950s it opened high street shops and expanded quickly. By 2004, internet shopping was booming for the company but its high street stores were struggling, with low levels of capacity utilisation. In 2005, its owner, the Shop Direct Group, closed all 126 of its high street stores so that it could focus on internet shopping.
- **A merger or takeover leading to duplication of many resources and sites.** The takeover of Derbyshire Building Society by the Nationwide meant that some towns had two building societies providing the same service and so were unlikely to be reaching full capacity. As a result a number of Derbyshire sites were sold off to overcome this problem.

Impact of spare capacity

Under-utilisation of capacity helps a firm to cope with unexpected problems or increases in demand, but it can increase costs.

Disadvantages of spare capacity

Spare capacity has several disadvantages:

- Firms have a higher proportion of fixed costs per unit. If utilisation falls, the fixed costs must be spread over fewer units of output. This leads to higher unit costs.
- These higher unit costs will lead to either lower profit levels or the need to increase price to maintain the same profit levels, and therefore to lower sales volume.
- Spare capacity can portray a negative image of a firm, suggesting that it is unsuccessful. For an organisation such as a fitness club or retailer, where the low utilisation can be physically seen, this may put customers off and lead to lower sales.
- With less work to do, employees may become bored and demoralised, lowering their motivation and efficiency. If the problem appears to be permanent, it may even lead to workers worrying about losing their jobs.

Fact file

Capacity utilisation at Marks and Spencer (M&S)

M&S is a business that usually operates with high levels of spare capacity. However, the period leading up to Christmas Day accounts for a large percentage of the group's sales and without making changes it would suffer from a capacity shortage during this time, mainly because of a lack of staff. In 2012 it recruited 20,000 extra staff and installed additional tills to ensure that it could cope with the increased demand at Christmas time. In the week prior to Christmas over 35 million customers visited its stores.

What do you think?

The Channel Tunnel

Under-utilisation of capital is a greater problem for organisations such as Eurotunnel (the owner of the Channel Tunnel), with high fixed costs. The Channel Tunnel opened in 1994 with a capacity to take freight trains and 14 million passengers annually. Eurotunnel's original five-year plan predicted that it would have 13 million customers by 1999. For 2013 the estimated figure stood at 9.9 million, giving a capacity utilisation for passenger trains of 71 per cent. More significantly, only six freight trains use the tunnel each day and so the overall capacity utilisation for all trains is only 57 per cent. Eurotunnel charges freight services €3,645 per train and these costs have led to a decline in freight services. Passenger trains are charged €4,320 + €16.60 per passenger. The European Commission has taken legal action to bring these charges down so that capacity utilisation is increased. Eurotunnel is reluctant to take this action as a previous attempt to increase the number of passengers through price offers and promotions cut the average price by 20 per cent, but led to only a 4 per cent increase in passengers.

Should Eurotunnel be forced to find ways to increase capacity utilisation? What do you think?

▲ Spare capacity allows a business to respond to an increase in trade, for example, at Christmas

270

Advantages of spare capacity

- There is more time for maintenance and repair of machinery, for training and for improving existing systems. During a period of spare capacity, a business may spend the available time improving its set-up and skills, making it better prepared for an increase in trade.
- There may be less pressure and stress for employees, who may become overworked at full capacity.
- Under-utilisation allows a company to cope with a sudden increase in demand. Businesses in expanding markets will increase their capacity beforehand, so that their sales are not limited by the size of the factory or shop.
- A firm may use calculations of spare capacity to see the maximum possible sales that it could achieve before it needs to expand its capacity. For example, if a business earns sales revenue of £12 million and operates at 80 per cent capacity level, it can calculate that its maximum possible sales revenue is £15 million, without increasing its capacity.

$$\frac{\text{maximum capacity}}{\text{current capacity level}} = \frac{\text{maximum sales revenue}}{\text{current sales revenue}}$$

$$\frac{100\%}{80\%} = \frac{£x}{£12\text{m}}$$

If 80% = £12m, then 100% = 100/80 × £12m = £15 million

If a business has spare capacity, it might decide to follow a policy of **rationalisation** in order to reduce its capacity and save unnecessary expenditure. Rationalisation leads to a cut in the capacity of a firm and thus to a reduction in its maximum output. If a firm is capable of producing 200 units but actually produces only 96 units, its capacity utilisation is only 48 per cent If it rationalises and halves its capacity to 100 units, it will have a much more efficient level of capacity utilisation (96 per cent).

Ways of reducing capacity

- **Selling off all or a part of its production area.** This will cut fixed costs and is likely to be used if a company believes that its spare capacity problem is long term. For example, both Ford and Vauxhall have shut car production plants in the UK because they have too many factories worldwide. However, selling off production facilities will not be the best strategy if the under-utilisation is a short-term problem. It will be difficult to increase production again if the factory has been sold.

- **Changing to a shorter working week or shorter day**. This will save costs and cut production, but it may lead to lower motivation and a higher turnover of staff.
- **Laying off workers**. This will save more money and reduce costs, but fixed costs will remain high if this is the only action taken. If demand then rises, there will be problems relating to the recruitment of new staff – these people are likely to have less understanding of the job and lower skill levels.

Capacity shortage

The main cause of capacity shortage is an increase in demand, outpacing the firm's ability to increase its production levels. It is possible that capacity shortage might occur through the expiry of a lease on property, but firms can usually renew leases.

In order to overcome a capacity shortage a business needs to increase its capacity.

Ways of increasing capacity

For some firms, it is their shortage of capacity that causes them difficulties. This problem can be overcome in a number of ways:

- **Building or extending factories/plants**. For example, for the Last Night of the Proms, a video link to Regent's Park is used to offer the concert to additional customers. Successful retailers such as Aldi and Primark have extended the number and size of their branches.
- **Asking staff to work overtime or longer hours**. Many firms offer overtime pay at higher rates or give contracts to staff that allow them to request longer hours during times of peak demand.
- **Hiring new staff**. Recruiting full-time staff is appropriate if there is a long-term need for higher output. However, for a non-standard order or a seasonal or temporary increase in demand, temporary or part-time staff will be hired.
- **A flexible workforce**. Some firms overcome capacity problems by creating a flexible workforce. Core workers are employed to meet regular demand; fluctuations in demand can be met by introducing staff on flexible, short-term contracts or by varying the hours of part-time workers.
- **Outsourcing or subcontracting**. A business can increase its production by agreeing a contract with an external organisation to supply materials or finished products. This approach has grown considerably in recent decades. Outsourcing will be dealt with in more detail in Chapter 15.
- **Transferring resources from another area**. If spare capacity exists elsewhere in an organisation, resources can be shifted from one area to another. Retailers will often move staff temporarily from less busy stores to new ones to help cope with the high demand in the opening weeks.

Overall, it is often felt that 90 per cent capacity is ideal, as this gives the firm an opportunity to repair and maintain equipment and respond to changes in demand. However, for seasonal businesses or those expecting rapid growth, a lower percentage would be sensible.

Practice exercise 2

1 Which of the following factors is most likely to increase the level of spare capacity in a firm?
   a) The firm's product becoming more fashionable
   b) Closure of a factory
   c) New competitors entering the market
   d) An unsuccessful marketing campaign *(1 mark)*

2 A business that produces 600 units has a spare capacity of 25 per cent. Its output falls to 480 units. Calculate its new level of capacity utilisation. *(4 marks)*

3 Explain how a more flexible workforce might help a business to overcome a capacity shortage. *(4 marks)*

4 Explain two ways in which a firm can reduce its capacity. *(6 marks)*

Case study: Center Parcs builds a new resort to solve capacity problem

In 2004 Center Parcs decided to add a fifth UK site. The company was running at almost 100 per cent occupancy and was frequently criticised for its high prices and charges. To avoid further criticism it decided not to increase prices further in order take advantage of the high demand for its limited resources. Instead it opted to increase capacity by opening a fifth site. On 6 June 2014, Center Parcs opened its resort in Woburn Forest, Bedfordshire, seven years after receiving planning permission.

The new venue in Bedfordshire cost approximately £250 million to build. Difficulties in getting planning permission for such large-scale operations in the countryside mean that it is unlikely Center Parcs will ever open a sixth site. Any further increases in demand will need more inventive solutions.

Chief Executive Martin Dalby recognises that the product needs to evolve: 'We've done it four times now and we know exactly how it works. The core ingredients of Center Parcs will be exactly the same, but we will modify the style of the restaurants and the shops so they will be more contemporary. It is in our leisure activities where the innovations will come. For example, squash courts – which were popular when the first Center Parcs opened – are less in demand these days. Attractions such as spas are far more popular now.' Accommodation has been upgraded too, with the four-bedroom executive lodge featuring hot tubs and six televisions. Center Parcs' target

mix is predominantly middle-class families who are prepared to pay well but who want to participate in energetic family activities in a safe, attractive environment.

Center Parcs knows its market well. Sales were £304 million in 2013 and based on capacity of 3,416 units of accommodation, capacity utilisation was 97.2 per cent – as good as it gets in the holiday industry. That was not a freak occurrence either; the business has been achieving a figure of more than 95 per cent for many years.

Despite its popularity, Center Parcs regularly attracts criticism that its prices are too high and that it exploits parents by ramping up fees in the school holidays. At Woburn Forest a four-night midweek stay in two-bedroom accommodation in August 2014 cost £1,199; a four-bedroom cost £2,499. The equivalent break in mid-November 2014 cost £399 and £799 respectively. However, guest satisfaction ratings show that 96 per cent of visitors rank their holiday as excellent or good and over 60 per cent of sales turnover comes from repeat business. Center Parcs places a great deal of emphasis on the quality of its provision and has a capital budget of about £40 million a year to spend on improving the accommodation and facilities in its existing parks.

The quality of the facilities means that unit costs are high, but these costs can be passed on to the consumer in the form of higher prices and payments for activities. Once again, Center Parcs uses pricing to achieve high capacity utilisation. Although the main pools are free, popular activities, such as laser combat, cost £22. Bowling costs £18 an hour and table tennis is £5 an hour.

Source: www.centerparcs.co.uk

Questions

Total: 45 marks

1 What is meant by the term 'capacity'? *(2 marks)*

2 Analyse two benefits for Center Parcs of having high capacity utilisation. *(9 marks)*

3 Analyse two possible problems for Center Parcs if its capacity utilisation fell dramatically. *(9 marks)*

4 Center Parcs achieved annual sales of £304 million a year with capacity utilisation of 97.2 per cent. Assuming that the remaining 2.8 per cent of holidays could be sold for the same price, what would Center Parcs' annual sales revenue have

been if it had operated at 100 per cent capacity utilisation? *(4 marks)*

5 Center Parcs could increase its capacity by increasing the amount of accommodation provided at its existing sites. Why might it be reluctant to take this approach? *(5 marks)*

6 To what extent do you believe that Center Parcs' pricing policy is the most important factor in achieving high capacity utilisation at Center Parcs? *(16 marks)*

The benefits and difficulties of lean production

Lean production features a number of time-saving and waste-saving techniques:

- Just-in-time management
- Quality circles
- Total quality management (TQM)
- Kaizen (continuous improvement), and
- Cell production.

Some of these topics, such as Kaizen and total quality management (TQM), will be dealt with elsewhere in the A-level. This section will focus on **just-in-time**.

Key terms

Lean production Production based on the range of time-saving and waste-saving measures inspired by Japanese manufacturing companies.

Time-based management An approach that recognises the importance of time and seeks to reduce the level of 'unproductive' time within an organisation. This leads to quicker response times, faster new product development and reductions in waste, culminating in greater efficiency.

Key term

Just-in-time A Japanese philosophy that organises operations so that items of stock (inventory) arrive just at the time they are needed for production or sale. The ultimate aim is to eliminate the need for stock, although in practice this is not always ideal.

273

Key term

Reduced lead times Reducing the time taken between an order being received and the final product being delivered to, or provided for, the customer.

Did you know?

The move to flexible production is being driven by consumers. Companies such as Dell, a computer provider, have led the way in providing fast, customised products for consumers. In the travel industry, the fastest-growing sector is the provision of tailor-made holidays built around the requirements of the individual customer.

In some organisations, time is used as a selling point – the ability of the firm to respond to a customer request can give firms a competitive advantage. The AA, RAC and other motoring organisations see quick response times as a means of improving customer loyalty. They pay particular attention to the needs of female motorists and families, who might be considered to be in need of a more rapid response.

More specific applications of time-based management can be seen in the form of **reduced lead times** or shorter product development times.

Shorter product development times

Constant changes in customer demands and the high failure rate of new products mean that companies which can produce new products quickly are able to stay competitive. Flexible production methods can also allow firms to modify their products quickly in response to the market. Information technology has helped businesses to modify and adapt their processes very quickly.

The end result of these two methods is that the new product is brought to the market or the customer's order is met more quickly. The firm can therefore beat its competitors in the race to provide the newest version of a product or the fastest delivery of a product or service.

Just-in-time

The main aim of just-in-time is to reduce waste by eliminating the need for high levels of inventory. This can enable a business to reduce costs by cutting warehouse space and staffing costs linked to the warehouse. Lower inventory levels also reduce the losses to a firm caused by pilferage (theft), damage during storage or products perishing or becoming obsolete (out-of-date).

Just-in-time techniques also save time, as stock can be delivered straight to the production line or shelves, ready for use, saving on the time spent moving them from the 'goods in' area to the warehouse and then on to the production line or shelf. The space saved makes the production line more compact, reducing distances between different stages of production and avoiding some of the problems of stock cluttering up the factory (commonplace in factories that do not use just-in-time methods).

Just-in-time also aims to provide flexibility for customers. Companies with zero inventory levels are more willing to respond to changes in customer tastes, as they will not suffer from unsold stock if there is a sudden shift to the production of new goods.

A central business aim is to 'add value'. Inventory in a warehouse is not adding value to the business; it only adds value when it forms part of the finished product. Just-in-time places inventory straight on to the production line, where it immediately adds value.

Features of just-in-time operations

Just-in-time methods are often described as a system based on 'pull' rather than 'push'. Traditionally, businesses made products which were 'pushed' through the production process in the hope that they would then sell in the marketplace. The driving force behind the decision to manufacture was the firm's desire to sell a product. Just-in-time is linked to customers' needs instead. Customers place an order, which leads to the product being made. The product is 'pulled' through the production process by the desire of the customer to have a particular design on a particular date. The push system led to stocks of finished products waiting to be sold. The pull system means that there is a customer waiting for the finished product, eliminating the need for high inventory levels.

Just-in-time links closely to people management. Greater responsibility is placed on individual employees. Many factories give authority to production line workers to stop the production line if they detect that a delivery of new stock is substandard and likely to endanger the quality of the finished product.

Flexibility and multi-skilling are also key features of just-in-time. Workers in the factories of suppliers must be prepared to complete a job at short notice, if an organisation wants an immediate delivery. Similarly, workers at the organisation must react quickly to sudden changes in the requirements of their customers. Multi-skilling and job enrichment have become essential features of organisations, so that the workforce has the ability and authority to meet urgent requests from customers without having to consult with and involve other staff or managers. It is also possible that well-trained, highly skilled staff will be able to anticipate changes in the market and prepare the business in a proactive manner, rather than constantly reacting to changes after they have happened.

Benefits of just-in-time as a method of lean production

Lean production has been widely adopted because it creates a variety of advantages for firms. These include:

- increased productivity because better methods are identified by staff and greater flexibility prevents bottlenecks and idle time on the production line. These methods increase labour productivity and efficiency
- a more motivated workforce as a result of their greater skills and more interesting jobs, with greater chances of recognition and responsibility. This will reduce labour turnover and should increase workers' output
- increased worker participation in decision making leading to better, more informed ideas and methods, because more people are contributing ideas to the decision-making process
- reduced waste and inventory holding costs, because there is little or no inventory in the factory before production takes place. This improves the firms' cash flow position
- higher quality and a greater variety of goods and services that are continuously improved for the customers' benefit.

Difficulties of using just-in-time as a method of lean production

Firms implementing and operating a lean production system can face difficulties. These include:

- fewer opportunities for bulk buying, as supplies arrive more frequently but in smaller quantities; this can increase costs
- halting of production. If a supplier fails to deliver one component it can be impossible for production to go ahead because there is no inventory

to fall back on. Just-in-time requires very reliable suppliers or the use of a variety of suppliers. In the latter case, there is less risk if one supplier fails to deliver. However, the fact that there will be smaller orders to each of a number of different suppliers means that bulk-buying opportunities are lost

● undetected product faults. By trusting suppliers to provide high quality components or raw materials, a business is vulnerable if a component is faulty because there is no time for the manufacturer to test it beforehand. There have been a number of product recalls in recent years, following the discovery of faults by customers.

To be successful, lean production has certain requirements that must be met. If any of these requirements are not met fully then a lean production system will encounter difficulties.

● Excellent communications and high levels of co-operation and flexibility from suppliers. Ironically, to guarantee just-in-time deliveries to their customers, some suppliers need to keep high levels of stock in case of problems. If suppliers cannot provide this flexibility then lean production will not work effectively.

● Reliable and flexible employees who are prepared to modify their workloads to cope with sudden increases in activity. Many organisations may need to agree new contracts and working conditions with their employees, because rigid job descriptions prevent the success of just-in-time methods. Workforces may also need to change to include more short-term or part-time workers, who can help a business to cope with sudden changes in workload. These types of employment contracts may not be viewed favourably by workers.

● A flexible approach to managing workers, so that employees see tangible benefits (such as financial rewards or time off) from their own greater flexibility. In this way the workforce will be more supportive of changes made to improve flexibility. A benefit that has suited both employees and employers has been increased training to allow workers to become multi-skilled (able to do a wide range of jobs). This has increased job opportunities for workers and flexibility for the organisation. Management must show that workers can benefit from lean production.

● Suitable equipment so that machinery can be adapted quickly to changing needs. Many production lines can be changed in this way. For example, to change their production, cinemas only need to insert a different film, so they can plan their schedules on a short-term basis according to customer demand. Car manufacturers can modify the fittings, colours and components of a particular model of car so that six different versions of a model are completed in sequence. These are then driven straight on to the transporter, for delivery to the garage whose customers ordered those styles of car. Without this equipment, lean production will not be more effective than traditional methods.

Fact file

The Japanese tsunami

On 11 March 2011 the fifth largest earthquake since records began in 1900 occurred off the eastern coast of Japan. The resulting tsunami led to an estimated 16,000 deaths and damage to over 1 million buildings, many of which were totally destroyed.

For Japanese firms relying on just-in-time methods, this meant that they were unable to produce any products. The area affected by the earthquake was largely agricultural but did possess many businesses that supplied components to other businesses. Initially, Japan lost 31 per cent of its capacity to supply refined oil as a result of the tsunami, leaving many businesses short of essential fuel. Two plants that accounted for 25 per cent of the world's supply of silicon wafers for computer chips were also closed, as a result of the tsunami. Various electronics manufacturers were affected, both in Japan and worldwide, because of damage to factories and local infrastructure. NEC and Sony were among the companies affected. Power supplies were affected too, because a Hitachi factory providing vital equipment was affected. The supply of Fujitsu computers was also hit, affecting both consumers and businesses. The highly integrated nature of production using just-in-time methods compounded the problems. For example, the lack of silicon wafers meant that some businesses were unable to complete the manufacture of computer chips which then impacted on manufacturers of computers.

Japan managed to resolve many of these issues within weeks, rather than months, but some businesses were still experiencing shortages of supplies six months after the tsunami. Lean production can be high risk.

Table 13.5 summarises the main features of lean production, contrasting it with the features of more traditional (mass production) methods.

▼ **Table 13.5** Features of lean production compared to traditional (mass) production

Lean production	Mass production
Short lead times	Longer lead times
Minimal stock levels	High stock levels
'Right first time' quality	Quality inspection of finished product
Elimination of unnecessary processes	No close scrutiny of unnecessary processes
High levels of worker responsibility	Low levels of worker responsibility
Multi-skilled workers	Specialist or unskilled workers
Excellent two-way communications	One-way communications
Frequent, small deliveries from suppliers	Fewer, large-scale deliveries from suppliers

Author advice

The topics of human resource management and operations management are closely linked. The whole process of lean production is focused on giving employees more autonomy and responsibility, particularly for product quality and control over their own work situation. Rotation of job roles provides variety and less likelihood of boredom or monotony. Project teams lead to improved communications, which can lead to improvements in motivation. These factors are linked to Herzberg's motivators and the higher-level needs in Maslow's hierarchy (see Chapter 23).

Fact file

Lean production at easyCar – the car rental firm

An example of a business that employs lean production techniques is easyCar. When it was established its goal was to simplify the product that it offers and pass the benefits on to customers in the form of lower prices.

- Customers were expected to return the car in a clean condition (or pay a charge for cleaning set by easyCar).
- An empty-to-empty fuel policy was used, to save on staff costs for refuelling.
- A target of 90 per cent utilisation of cars was set.
- Only one type of car was stocked at each branch.
- Customers had to make their own way to and from the easyCar base – no delivery or collection was arranged.

easyCar has evolved since those initial techniques were established. Currently easyCar acts, in effect, as a booking agent. Customers hiring cars from easyCar are actually using a car from an established car rental company, such as Hertz and Europcar, with easyCar earning a commission.

In February 2014, easyCar launched easyCar Club, a peer-to-peer hire system. People can register their cars for hire on the easyCar Club website, indicating the days on which they are available for hire and the location from which they can be collected. Customers wishing to hire a car can book any cars that are listed as available. Prices are set by the car owner, with easyCar taking commission for organising the transaction, arranging insurance and organising key collection through secure boxes.

Source: easyCar website (www.easycar.com) and other sources.

Practice exercise 3

Total: 20 marks

1 What is meant by the term 'lean production'? *(2 marks)*

2 What is meant by the term 'just-in-time production'? *(2 marks)*

3 Study the fact file on easyCar and analyse the characteristic of lean production that the company uses most often. Justify your choice. *(7 marks)*

4 Analyse how just-in-time methods can improve the efficiency of a manufacturer of packaging materials, such as cardboard boxes. *(9 marks)*

Case study: Comparison between Marks and Spencer and Zara

Marks and Spencer represents the traditional, large-scale approach to fashion retailing. Zara, a Spanish company, is an example of lean production in this trade.

Marks and Spencer buys in large quantities and enjoys the benefits of economies of scale. However, because it is 'pushing' garments into the stores, it is taking a risk that its idea of this year's fashion may differ from its customers' views. For this reason, Marks and Spencer has been most successful in providing high-quality items where fashion has been less important (such as socks and underwear). If fashion changes quickly, Marks

>>> >

and Spencer struggles because its high-quality, high-price strategy becomes irrelevant. Marks and Spencer tried to change into a more fashion-focused store, but has met resistance from both existing and potential customers. Its strategy of targeting the teenage fashion market was withdrawn within six months.

In contrast, Zara's approach is based on speed and economy. Zara's designers are crucial to the company's success. They must decide on the stock to be produced, although this is mainly choosing which items to copy from the popular designer items in fashion shows and celebrity events, and then simplifying them so that they can be made quickly and cheaply. This is a demanding role, as designers need to combine a sense of fashion with considerable understanding of the manufacturing process. Design time is minimised and production and distribution take about five days. Zara manufactures 76 per cent of its clothes in Europe, which ensures fast delivery to its European shops. A few copies of each item, in a limited range of sizes and colours, are delivered to each store. The decisions on whether to order further stock are made by shop managers, who can identify which items are selling well. Thus there is less risk of unsold stock – a major problem for Marks and Spencer.

For Zara, quality is not the main priority, but with new stocks in the shops every two to three weeks it is unlikely that the garments will be worn long enough for quality to become a problem. Zara has also found that customers visit its stores more frequently, because they know that a completely new batch of stock will have arrived. In addition to empowering the designers and shop managers, Zara has given more independence to its workshops, which deliver directly to the shops in most cases. The differences in approach between Zara and Marks and Spencer are summarised in Figure 13.1.

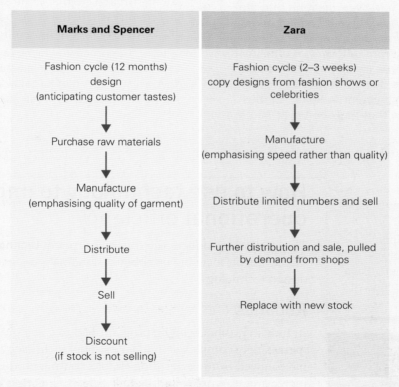

▲ **Figure 13.1** The fashion cycles at Marks and Spencer and Zara

Zara has been flattered by the number of businesses seeking to copy its approach. Visits from senior managers of businesses such as Marks and Spencer are a testament to the success of Zara's approach to fashion retailing. From its formation in La Coruña in Spain in 1975, Zara has grown to become the world's biggest fashion retailer, with over 6,390 stores in 88 different countries, including 67 Zara fashion stores in the UK.

Sources: various, including www.inditex.com and www.marksandspencer.com.

Questions

1 Explain two benefits to Marks and Spencer arising from its approach to large-scale retailing. *(8 marks)*

2 Explain why Marks and Spencer's approach is more suited to socks and underwear than to fashion items. *(6 marks)*

3 Zara's production and supply of clothing operates on a just-in-time basis. Analyse two factors that might lead to problems in using this approach. *(9 marks)*

4 To what extent is the success of Zara's operations management dependent on its strategy of empowering some of its key employees? *(16 marks)*

5 Evaluate the advantages and disadvantages to Zara of its shorter product development times. *(16 marks)*

What do you think?

Zara's lean production approach is focused on time management. However, its parent company, Inditex, has also attempted to reduce waste by setting up a business to sell the 'left-over' designs that did not sell out in Zara shops. Unsold fashion items from the previous year are sold through a business called Lefties (derived from leftovers). Lefties sells online and has 102 stores in Spain and Portugal where the products are sold at reduced prices. With high youth unemployment in Spain, Lefties has expanded at a time that has seen over 40 Zara shops closed.

Carlos Hernandez, of retail consultancy Planet Retail, believes that Inditex are preparing Lefties for expansion: 'I think they could export the brand to other countries where Inditex has a large presence like the UK and Germany,' he said. 'Spain is not the only country where the crisis has taken its toll.' In the UK, Lefties would compete with H&M and Primark.

Following a successful online launch, Inditex is opening its first Stradivarius store in Stratford, London, in late 2014. This retail outlet targets 20–35-year-olds, but its pricing fills the gap between Zara and Lefties.

Do you think there is a space in the UK market for Stradivarius or Lefties?

Key term

Technology In the business world, the application of practical, mechanical, electrical and related sciences to industry and commerce.

How to use technology to improve operational efficiency

This section introduces the different types of **technology** used in operations management, focusing on robotics, automation, communications and design technology.

Robotics

In industry, robots can be programmed to carry out both routine and increasingly complex activities. As robot technology has improved, robots have moved from performing simple, routine production tasks to an increasingly complex and flexible array of business activities. Some of the main applications of robotics are described here.

- **Handling operations**. On a production line, robots can be used to manipulate materials and components into position, in order for other production activities such as welding to take place.
- **Welding**. Robots can be programmed to join together materials (e.g. sheets of metal) during the production process, in order to build up and shape the final product.

- **Other production applications**. Activities such as dispensing liquid, painting and coating materials, sealing components and gluing different materials together can all be completed more quickly using pre-programmed robots or robotic systems. Other applications that can be carried out by robots include cutting, grinding and polishing.
- **Assembling**. The actual construction of the finished product from a range of materials or components can be completed with much greater speed and accuracy. This has become even more significant with improvements in micro-technology, as this requires a high level of accuracy in working with components that are too small for the human eye to handle accurately.
- **Packaging and palletising**. To improve the efficiency of production, many products are now automatically packaged by robots. They are then placed on to pallets and loaded on to lorries or other forms of transportation, for immediate delivery to the customer.
- **Measurement, inspection and testing**. Robots are able to scrutinise both finished products and partially completed products on an assembly line with great accuracy. This means that they are ideally suited to checking the accuracy of sizes and quality of products.
- **Hazardous applications**. There are instances when carrying out a particular process is dangerous to human life. In such cases, specially constructed robots can be made to withstand hazardous environments.

Automation

Automation is the use of machinery to replace human resources.

Computer-aided manufacturing (or manufacture), known as CAM, uses computers to undertake activities such as planning, operating and controlling production.

Planning

Production planning is an area of operations management that benefits from the use of technology. Networks are constructed and manipulated on computer and 'what if?' analysis is applied to examine the implications of any modifications to the network. By using this approach for all of its activities, a business can plan the use of resources more effectively. Once the production line is up and running, any variations to the planned schedule can also be monitored by computer and, if necessary, remedial action taken to modify the approach used.

Operating process

Technology can also be useful in the manufacturing process. In CAM, the use of robots and fully automated production lines, controlled by computers, has increased productivity and reduced the problems arising from human error. With greater use of miniaturisation in production, many components are now too small for human beings to manipulate. Flexible programming also allows a fully automated line to produce different varieties of a product.

Controlling

Once the manufacturing process begins, it is vital that the quality of the product and the efficiency of the process are scrutinised constantly. Maintaining control of the process through computer-based quality assurance systems can overcome the possibility of human error and also provide more rigorous scrutiny of quality.

Stock control

One area of operations management that uses technology to improve efficiency is stock control. This is aided by technology in the following ways:

- Computer programs linked to statistics on patterns of consumer purchases allow firms to anticipate changes in stock levels more accurately. This reduces the possibility that a business will run out of stock or build up unnecessarily high levels. Firms are now able to operate with lower levels of stock and so reduce their costs.
- Computerised systems allow organisations to access instantly their current stock levels, reducing the need for time-consuming manual checks (although these will still be needed on occasions to check for problems such as pilferage).
- Retailers are able to link their tills to stock control through **EPOS (electronic point of sale)** systems. Every time an item is sold, the EPOS system adjusts the stock level. These systems can also order new stock from suppliers automatically when a particular item has fallen to a certain level (known as the **reorder level**).
- Organisations with many branches can use technology to establish the locations where stock is being held, so that in an emergency stock can be moved between branches.

Communications

Another area of business in which technology has led to major changes is information collection, storage and communication. This area is known as information technology (IT) or information and communication technology (ICT).

ICT is the acquisition, processing, storage and dissemination of vocal, pictorial, textual and numerical information by a microelectronics-based combination of computing and telecommunications.

The role of ICT in the business world has increased dramatically in recent decades. The use of business software packages, the internet, automatic money transfers, bar codes and email has transformed business activities. There is almost no part of a business that has not been affected by ICT. It has replaced manual systems in activities such as planning distribution and office work has changed because ICT can undertake routine activities far more effectively and flexibly than people can. The way marketing is undertaken has been changed through improvements in the data held on customers, obtained via EPOS technology and loyalty cards.

ICT assists communications in the following ways:

- It allows a business to improve both internal and external communications, improving efficiency and the business's understanding of its market.
- Internal information can be processed and amended more quickly. By keeping employees up to date and facilitating two-way communication, ICT improves the efficiency and motivation of staff.
- Company intranets enable employees and, where necessary, suppliers and customers to access company information at any time. Individuals are not always aware in advance of their information requirements, so a system that provides data at the press of a button saves a considerable amount of time.
- Technology increases the speed of communication and the scope for greater responsibility. As such, it allows organisations to de-layer and operate wider spans of control.
- The growing use of loyalty cards allows firms to accumulate information on the buying habits of their customers. Firms can use these data to tailor goods or services to customer needs. Relationship marketing arises from this process, whereby marketing techniques are based on the firm's understanding of its individual consumers.
- The internet has been the most significant ICT development in recent years. It has led to the creation of a whole new category of business (e-commerce or dot.com companies) and brings a number of specific advantages. First, the internet can eliminate the need for expensive high-street premises. Operations can be moved to places where costs such as rent and wages are considerably lower. Second, it can reduce the need to employ staff. Organisations such as banks have closed many of their branches as people have moved to internet banking. Third, it adds flexibility to business operations, which no longer have to fit in with traditional business structures. For example, 24-hour opening is possible and decisions such as credit card approval can be made on the basis of information that is accessible via computer. Finally, data can be stored more cheaply and accessed at greater speed if an individual needs to refer back to a previous communication.

What do you think?

Mothercare offers customers who purchase instore the option of having their receipt emailed. This makes it easier for customers to store receipts electronically. It also allows Mothercare to monitor the purchases made by individual customers and gives the company an email address through which they can directly contact customers.

What do you think?

Will m-retailing (mobile retailing) replace e-retailing?

Online sales reached £91 billion in 2013, an average annual rise of 25 per cent since 2005. In 1997 online sales totalled only £100 million. IMRG CapGemini, a market research company, estimates that online sales will continue to grow at about 18 per cent per annum. It is now estimated that e-retail accounts for 21 per cent of the total retail market.

Much of the unexpectedly high growth in 2013 can be attributed to the growing influence of m-retail in 2013, with sales via mobile devices (smartphones and tablets) increasing 138 per cent on 2012. As with the wider e-retail sector, a strong year for m-retail was topped by a very strong performance during December, with 27 per cent of all online sales coming from a mobile device, equating to £3 billion. This is twice as much as that spent during the same time the year before. According to the IMRG CapGemini Index, 82 per cent of mobile sales came from tablet devices. However, sales using smartphones increased by 186 per cent in 2013, compared to an impressive 131 per cent via tablet devices.

Will m-retailing eventually overtake e-retailing?

Source: www.imrg.org

What do you think?

Online gambling

One industry whose operations have been transformed by the internet is gambling. Two major beneficiaries are, coincidentally, based in the same office block in Gibraltar. 888 Holdings plc was launched in 1996 and in 2013 it achieved sales revenue of £294 million; all of it online. In 2014 its market capitalisation was £427million. Its rival, bwin. party, has also been successful. Launched in 1997, its www.partypoker.com and related websites helped it to achieve sales revenue of £562 million in 2013 and achieve market capitalisation of £684 million by 2014. When the two companies floated on the London Stock Exchange, they both immediately entered the FTSE 100 as two of the Stock Exchange's top 100 most valued companies.

Online gambling has made it easier for people to gamble. Some countries, such as the USA, have placed restrictions on online gambling. Do you think there should be more controls to limit gambling or should people be free to make their own choices?

Source: www.888.com, www.partypoker.com, www.bwin.party.com

Design

Technology assists design in two principal ways:

- **Comparison and testing of new ideas**. Different ideas can be introduced and compared much more quickly in a computer-aided design (CAD) system than in a manual one. For many products, two-dimensional drawings can be transformed into three-dimensional images and rotated in order to demonstrate the whole range of possible views. Where appropriate, the CAD system can also include programs to simulate testing (e.g. wind tunnel simulations). This can save considerable

sums of money by eliminating the production and testing of expensive prototypes.

- **Creation of new products**. Traditional leisure pursuits, such as playing cards, have been hit by computer-based alternatives, such as computer games. Among the new products created using new technology is Robosapien, a programmable toy robot designed by a former NASA scientist. The design of Robosapien has led to similar products being produced, such as Roboraptor and Roboreptile.

Computer-aided design (CAD) is the use of computers to improve the design of products. CADCAM is an approach that combines computer-aided design and computer-aided manufacture, using IT to assist both the design and the manufacture of an item.

Technology and employment

Employment has been affected in several ways by the introduction of technology:

- **New skills and jobs**: traditional workforce skills, such as newspaper printing, have been replaced by tasks requiring computer operators and a number of new jobs requiring data handling have been introduced. The 'communication age' has increased the demand for data and has been instrumental in shifting the balance of employment in the UK from manufacturing to services. Even in manufacturing companies themselves, there has been a shift towards more service jobs, as computers have led to automated production lines that require fewer manual employees. At the same time, this shift has created more jobs in administration and planning.
- **Multi-skilling**: technology is allowing companies to benefit from the multi-skilling of staff, creating jobs that are less rigidly defined and more adaptable to changes in the workplace. It has also been a key factor in the development of many small businesses operating from home or small premises.
- **Changes in working practices**: ICT offers greater flexibility in terms of the place of employment. It is encouraging teleworking (i.e. people working from home and other locations and keeping in contact through ICT). Occupations such as market research, design and software development can all be based away from the office. This can motivate staff by giving them more independence and responsibility, while reducing Herzberg 'hygiene' factors such as travel time and expense (see Chapter 23). However, projections that the typical office will cease to exist are probably unrealistic, as many teleworkers find that they miss the social aspects of working alongside colleagues. Moreover, some teleworkers find it difficult to separate work from leisure and find it hard to switch off from work – a major cause of stress.

Benefits of using technology in operations

The use of technology has grown because it offers many advantages to businesses. Some of the main benefits are summarised under the headings below.

Reducing costs

- The use of technology to replace manual systems in areas such as planning, office work, manufacturing and stock holding has greatly reduced labour costs. In some particular jobs, it has eliminated the need for workers altogether.
- ICT can be used in production planning in order to devise the most cost-effective way of manufacturing a product.
- Reductions in waste allow a business to reduce unnecessary costs, thereby improving its competitiveness.
- Use of the internet enables businesses to locate away from expensive sites. In the financial services industry, for example, transactions are invariably conducted remotely by internet, by telephone or through an automated teller machine (ATM). Banks and insurance companies have been able to cut back on both staff and expensive high-street premises.

Improving quality

- Computer-based quality assurance systems can overcome the possibility of human error and also provide more rigorous scrutiny of quality. This benefit applies particularly in situations where people are unable to monitor quality because of a hazardous environment or because the level of precision needed cannot be achieved by human beings.
- ICT enables business to understand customers' requirements more fully. As a result, businesses can adapt their products to include those features that customers perceive to be important.

Reducing waste

- Stock control systems ensure that orders are placed at the most appropriate time so that excessive stock levels do not build up. This means that there is less chance of stock becoming out of date, getting damaged or being pilfered, so stock wastage is reduced.
- Integrated systems of stock control can identify branches holding stock that is needed by other branches. Transferring one branch's excess stock to a branch in need of that item can be effective in reducing the possibility that stock will not be sold.
- Arguably, the most significant waste reduction provided by technology is that of time. Many business activities can be carried out much more quickly with the appropriate technology, which therefore greatly improves the efficiency of the business.

Increasing productivity

- Machines can work at a much faster and more consistent speed than a workforce without the benefit of such technology. As a result, output per head is considerably increased by technology.
- Computerised systems allow organisations to keep much closer control over their stock levels, reducing the need for time-consuming manual checks and therefore reducing wage bills.
- ICT may be used to plan the most efficient approach to production. This enables the business to use its resources most effectively and reduce costs.

Fact file

Royal Mail

In August 2014, Royal Mail announced plans to expand their offer of 'click and collect' services to include 20,000 small- and medium-sized businesses (SMEs) as well as larger businesses to which it had been available beforehand. Time-poor customers of SMEs can now elect to pick up parcels ordered online from their local post office. It is estimated that 82 million deliveries will be made in 2014 through 'click and collect', a 17 per cent increase on 2013. This market is expected to double in size by 2018. The move by Royal Mail is also a response to Amazon's recent decision to set up its own delivery fleet. Currently, 6 per cent of Royal Mail's parcel deliveries are for Amazon.

Other benefits

- **Flexibility**. Technology enables businesses to provide an immediate response to consumers' demands. Production lines can be adjusted to change the product being produced; salespeople, while in a face-to-face meeting with a customer, can make immediate contact with the company's headquarters to adjust plans to suit that customer.
- **Financial monitoring**. ICT greatly improves the budgeting process. The speed of processing data and the ability to access information directly enable businesses to plan their budgets more rigorously. Alternatives can be scrutinised to make sure that budgets are allocated efficiently. Perhaps the greatest benefit to the budgeting process is in budgetary control. With every item of expenditure being recorded on an integrated ICT system, it is possible to monitor actual expenditure against the budget in order to identify areas of inefficiency. This helps businesses to take prompt action to resolve any problems.
- **New and better goods and services**. New goods/services can be made available and higher-quality goods/services can be produced through new technology. Businesses will thus benefit by improving customer satisfaction levels.
- **Better working conditions**. Technology can lead to improvements in the working environment, through factors such as reductions in the level of noise and greater control over temperatures in the work area.

Issues in introducing and updating technology

The use of new technology can also cause problems. An organisation will need to weigh up the pros and cons before deciding on whether it should introduce or update its technology.

- **Resistance to change**. People are often concerned by change. ICT can lead to job losses for workers in traditional skilled crafts. This causes stress for existing workers, as they will fear for their future. Consequently, productivity may fall.
- **Lower morale**. ICT can undermine group morale by breaking up teams. If job losses are involved, morale may fall because workers are concerned for colleagues who have been made redundant. Again, productivity may fall as a result.
- **Cost**. For many businesses, the most significant problem is the cost of new technology. Not only is it expensive to introduce, but it also needs regular updating and servicing. In some situations, it may be more cost effective to employ less advanced techniques to avoid constant expenditure on updating technology. For some businesses, the cost of technology can make them uncompetitive and so threaten their survival.
- **Keeping up with change**. Technology changes constantly, so hardware and software need to be updated regularly. Staff will also have to undergo frequent training, again adding to costs and threatening efficiency if a business is unable to keep up with the pace of change.
- **Lower barriers to entry**. ICT helps international communication, so businesses can gain from the opportunities offered by the opening up of world markets. However, ICT poses a threat to some businesses, because it reduces some of the barriers to entry in certain industries. Consumers can use the internet to compare prices, so ICT has the potential to force prices and profits down, especially in high-wage economies such as the UK.

287

Did you know?

Microsoft changes focus

In July 2014, Microsoft announced that it was going to cut 18,000 jobs worldwide – representing job losses for one in seven of its workforce. The company is shifting emphasis from orthodox software and mobile phones (Nokia is a subsidiary) to cloud services and apps for mobiles. These new technologies require fewer inputs and so less capital and fewer workers are required.

Author advice

Remember that technology affects all businesses, even those that do not use it directly. Businesses may lose their competitive advantage if their competitors are using technology efficiently. However, the high cost of new technology can lead to problems for businesses that adopt it in their operations.

Practice exercise 4

Total: 35 marks

1 What is meant by the term 'technology'? *(2 marks)*

2 What do the initials EPOS stand for? *(2 marks)*

3 Distinguish between CAD and CAM. *(4 marks)*

4 State two ways in which robots can be used in a business. *(2 marks)*

5 Analyse two advantages to a retailer of using technology in its inventory control. *(8 marks)*

6 Analyse two benefits of technology to a car manufacturer. *(8 marks)*

7 Explain three ways in which the use of information technology might create difficulties for a firm. *(9 marks)*

Case study: Automation for dishwashers

Dishwashers are not only replacing people in the kitchen, they are also replacing them on the production line.

Bosch Siemens is a business that manufactures high-quality dishwashers, aiming its products at customers who value quality, reliability and durability above price competitiveness. One of its unique selling points is that it offers guarantees for ten or more years on some of its dishwashers.

The company relies increasingly on automation for the manufacture of its dishwashers. It faced a particular problem of trying to install pads to deaden the sound of the dishwasher. The solution involved four robots working together as two pairs. One pair of robots picks up the dishwasher unit while the second pair of robots applies the pad to the rear panel. Unlike previous systems, each robot can work with 100 per cent precision, if necessary adjusting the position of its gripper before attaching the pad to the dishwasher.

The production process requires the robots to bend at an angle of 90°, a movement that caused great discomfort to production line workers before the robots were introduced. Further discomfort to production line workers had been caused by the high temperatures involved in the process.

The robots are also programmed to pick up any defects in materials or in the dishwasher, ensuring a high-quality finished product.

Bosch Siemens has reaped a number of benefits from the introduction of the robots:

- gentler handling of the components, which eliminates waste
- greater reliability in the accuracy of the process
- improved quality in the final product
- greater productivity, achieved most significantly by the 100 per cent availability of the robots – this contrasts sharply with the limited hours of availability of the workforce
- improved working conditions for employees – in addition to coping with the high temperatures, an individual employee previously had to lift materials with a cumulative weight of 7 tonnes per shift, without any mechanical aids.

It was necessary for employees working with the robots to undergo suitable training. However, Bosch Siemens calculated that the high cost of introducing the new technology would be recovered, as a result of greater profitability, within two years.

Source: www.bara.org.uk.

Questions

1 Explain one reason why employees may oppose the introduction of robots on Bosch Siemens' dishwasher production line. *(5 marks)*

2 Analyse two reasons why employees may support the introduction of the robots. *(9 marks)*

3 Bosch Siemens identified a number of benefits to the business arising from the introduction of the robots. Evaluate the major advantages to Bosch Siemens of introducing these robots. *(16 marks)*

Making operational decisions to improve performance: improving quality

This chapter examines the importance of quality to a business and considers methods of improving quality, such as quality assurance. The benefits and difficulties of improving quality are analysed and the chapter concludes by assessing the consequences of poor quality.

Importance of quality

In Chapter 11 we saw that quality is those features of a product or service that allow it to satisfy (or delight) customers.

Quality is subjective – a matter of personal opinion – and views about it will vary from individual to individual. In most cases, quality is a tangible factor, such as speed or durability, but some customers place emphasis on intangible factors, such as the assurance provided by a firm's name.

Tangible measures of quality include the following:

- **Appearance**. For fashion clothing, this is the all-important measure.
- **Reliability**. Machinery will be in constant use, so reliability is needed.
- **Durability**. A firm hiring lorries would expect strength and a long-lasting vehicle.
- **Functions** (added extras). Smartphones are made more attractive by the range of additional functions and apps available.
- **After-sales service (cost, promptness and effectiveness)**. High-quality after-sales service is needed for a firm's IT network, because breakdowns will be costly.
- **Repair and maintenance needs**. A car that requires less servicing and few repairs would be considered to be of high quality.

There are several intangible measures of quality:

- **Brand image**. Cadbury is seen as a good brand, even though it has diversified well beyond its original products. Diversification can be a problem if customers believe that a business has moved away from its core competencies. The Cadbury brand's reputation for quality has been reduced by concerns about health in recent times.
- **Reputation**. An organisation such as *The Times* newspaper has developed a reputation for quality.

▲ Brand image is important to Cadbury

- **Exclusiveness**. Brands such as Chanel are assumed to have superior qualities because of a certain mystique or limited availability. Such businesses are able to use their name to introduce new products and charge high prices, even though the product itself is not known to customers, because customers assume that they must be of high quality.

Intangible measures of quality may also relate to other values, such as a firm's treatment of its staff or the environment or ethical issues. For example, Nestlé's image has suffered because of its marketing of powdered baby milk in less developed countries. This caused health problems for the babies because the powdered milk had to be mixed with water and the local water supply contained impurities. The end product was considered to be less healthy than breast milk.

What do you think?

Motorway services

A recent survey by *Which?* magazine rated the quality of the UK's main service stations. The key measures, according to those surveyed, were clean toilets, fast service, reasonable food and dedicated children's facilities, such as nappy changing rooms and children's menus. These facilities are rated on a numerical scale and converted to a percentage. A rating of 100 per cent represents the highest possible performance in every category tested.

Tebay services, a family-run service station on the M6, was the only one to achieve the *Which?* 5-star award, receiving a top score of 90 per cent in the survey. Other high-ranked services were Wetherby on the A1, with 69 per cent and Cobham on the M25, with 67 per cent. Which? members also ranked the well-known motorway service chains. The best performers were Extra (60 per cent) and Roadchef (50 per cent). The survey focused on the most visited service stations. In general, smaller service stations were regarded as having higher quality than the larger ones.

Is it more difficult for large chains to match the quality of smaller businesses? What do you think?

Source: www.which.co.uk

Customers' views of quality will depend on what they expect from the product. In Chapter 11 we considered five possible quality objectives, each based on different views of quality. These measures were:

- customer satisfaction ratings (in Chapter 7 we also examined Net Promoter Score (NPS), which is a popular measure of customer satisfaction)
- customer complaints
- level of product returns
- scrap rate
- punctuality.

Importance of quality to a business

In deciding whether to introduce quality systems into its operations, a firm must weigh up the benefits of quality against the costs and issues involved in introducing and managing a quality system. These are described below.

Gaining a competitive advantage

Business may gain a competitive advantage by offering lower prices, derived from its ability to keep costs low. However, more and more businesses are aiming to achieve *differentiation*. This occurs when the business produces products with unique qualities that cannot easily be replicated by competitors. A unique product or process can be patented to prevent other businesses from copying it for about 20 years. This means that the business is likely to be able to use quality to make much larger profits, because it can maintain its competitive advantage.

Impact on sales volume

If a product or service meets the needs of the firm's customers, then demand for the product will increase, thus enabling the business to increase its profit level. As people become richer, their desire for high-quality products increases rapidly because they are less constrained by their level of income. The John Lewis Partnership (John Lewis and Waitrose) has experienced annual growth in sales of 8 per cent per annum from 2009 to 2014, because many consumers in their market prefer quality rather than competitive pricing.

Creating a unique selling point

High quality is not achievable for all businesses, especially those that are trying to keep their costs low. Consequently, businesses can use the quality of their products as a unique selling point (USP) in order to increase demand. For example, there is often an eight-week waiting list for weekend bookings for afternoon tea at the Ritz Hotel in London. This is because potential customers see this service as unique: it is a classic example of a mix of tangible quality (the high quality of the goods and services provided) and intangible quality (the image linked to the name of the hotel). The uniqueness of the service increases customers' desire to enjoy it, ensuring regular and high demand.

Impact on selling price

Having a unique selling point created by quality has a further benefit – it encourages consumers to pay a higher price for the product or service. For example, food prices at Waitrose and Marks and Spencer are generally higher than those in other supermarkets, because customers are willing to pay a higher price for better quality. Higher prices help these two supermarkets to increase their profit margins, although it should be noted that better quality materials and production methods are usually needed to achieve high-quality products, and so costs of production will be higher too. Using quality as a USP is particularly common in niche markets, as evidenced by companies such as Harrods and Hotel Chocolat. The greater the perception of quality, the higher the selling price a firm can charge. For example, afternoon tea at the Ritz costs £47 per person.

Pricing flexibility

A reputation for quality also gives a business the ability to be more flexible in its pricing. Airlines such as British Airways and Virgin Atlantic are able to charge high prices to customers who value the quality of the service provided on their flights. These airlines then have the flexibility to offer discounted prices in order to fill their planes on occasions when this might be necessary – the higher prices paid by earlier customers will have already guaranteed the firm a profit.

Cost reductions

While it can be costly to implement a quality system, in many cases such a system can reduce a business's costs. If a business makes a product that is faulty or fails to satisfy the customer, it will lead to the scrapping of the product and possibly the recall of many other products that have already been sold. This is an expensive process that could have been avoided if a quality system had been there to prevent the product leaving the business. There are also costs involved in either reworking products that have been made in a faulty manner or the waste of materials that have been put into a faulty product.

In extreme cases, good quality can protect a business from legal action by dissatisfied customers. This type of action can lead to high legal costs and, perhaps more damagingly, negative publicity.

Brand loyalty and a firm's reputation

High quality will encourage brand loyalty. This will mean a larger customer base and one that is less likely to shift to a competitor. Not having a quality system can be costly in terms of the business's reputation. The damage to a firm's reputation can be severe as customers tend to remember negative publicity. An effective **quality system** can prevent problems and help a business to avoid any damage to its reputation.

Assessing the benefits and problems of improving quality will allow a business to decide whether a quality system should be introduced. However, consideration also needs to be given to the particular quality system to use because each has its own benefits and problems. The remainder of this chapter examines the various methods by which organisations can seek to provide quality, focusing particularly on the distinction between **quality control** and **quality assurance**.

Methods of improving quality

Quality control

Traditionally, quality inspectors were employed by organisations to check the accuracy of completed work and also the quality of goods received from suppliers. This approach was taken because it was believed that:

- many workers would not take responsibility for quality and needed close supervision
- specialist staff were needed to recognise the suitability of a product for consumers or the production line.

Benefits of inspection

- Inspection at the end of the process can prevent a defective product reaching the customer, thus eliminating a problem with a whole batch of products.
- It is a more secure system than one that trusts every individual to do his or her job properly.
- Inspectors may detect common problems throughout an organisation, so mistakes can be put right more efficiently. It is possible that an incorrectly trained group of workers will not realise that their work does not reach the right level of quality.

Drawbacks of inspection

The idea that an inspector (rather than a worker directly involved in production) should be 'responsible' for quality has lost favour, for three main reasons:

1 By placing responsibility for quality failures on the inspector, it does little to encourage individuals to improve the quality of their output.
2 Employing an inspection team is an expense that could be viewed as unnecessary if products are produced 'right first time'.
3 Giving workers responsibility for their own work helps to increase the interest, variety and responsibility within a job, and so helps to motivate workers.

Quality assurance

For the reasons given above, many companies have moved from quality control to **quality assurance**, and from checking by inspectors to **self-checking**.

While quality control is based on the end product or service, quality assurance concentrates on the *process* of production. The idea of self-checking is crucial to quality assurance.

Benefits of quality assurance

- A sense of ownership of the product rests with the workers rather than with an independent inspector, giving workers greater responsibility. Theorists such as Herzberg argue that there are positive effects on motivation because of this sense of ownership and recognition of workers' responsibility.
- Costs are reduced because there is less waste and less need for reworking of faulty products. Under inspection, it is possible for a fault to occur at the first stage of production and yet for many more components to be added before the product is inspected and judged to be unsuitable.
- With all staff responsible for quality, there should be a higher and more consistent level of quality, which can lead to marketing advantages for the firm.
- Because quality assurance processes make individual workers responsible for their job, they should also allow workers to reject any partially completed item that they receive from the person before them in the supply chain, if it is below standard. An individual will not want to be blamed for a faulty product if the fault lies with the previous person on the production line or in the office. This system effectively means that inspection now takes place at the beginning and end of every part of the production process, greatly reducing the possibility of a faulty end product.

Key term

Quality assurance A system that aims to achieve or improve quality by organising every process to get the product 'right first time' and prevent mistakes ever happening.

Author advice

Make sure that you are aware of the difference between quality control and quality assurance. These two approaches are very different and offer many opportunities to tie in your understanding of operations with that of people management. Quality control is generally seen as a traditional approach where workers are not trusted. Quality assurance is based on trusting workers to guarantee the quality of their own work. It is an area that gives great scope for evaluation. However, be cautious – many systems of quality combine the two together. Even Toyota, who are regarded as a significant influence on the development of quality assurance systems, use checking and inspection as a part of their quality procedures.

Systems of quality assurance

Many firms create their own approaches to quality assurance, to make sure that it meets the specific needs of the organisation. However, others adapt common approaches to quality assurance. The most widely recognised quality assurance system is total quality management, often known as TQM.

Total quality management

TQM is a culture of quality that involves all employees of a firm. Under TQM, businesses consist of **quality chains** in which people treat the receivers of their work as if they were external customers and adopt a target of 'right first time'. In this way, every department of a business contributes to the quality of its products.

Kaizen

The Japanese philosophy of **kaizen** has given rise to quality systems based on 'continuous improvement'. The incremental changes are invariably suggested by employees and emanate from a corporate culture that encourages employees to identify possible ways of improving the operation of the business.

In the words of the late Sir John Harvey Jones, the former head of ICI, 'If you are not making progress all the time, you are slipping backwards.' In a dynamic business environment, quality improvement must be a constant challenge, as any business that believes it has produced the highest-quality product will soon be overtaken by its rivals.

> **Key term**
>
> **Kaizen** A policy of implementing small, incremental changes in order to achieve better quality and/or greater efficiency.

▲ Sir John Harvey Jones, former head of ICI

> **Did you know?**
>
> Six Sigma is a very popular, statistically based method to improve quality by monitoring processes and outcomes. It was first used by Motorola in the USA. Workers with the necessary skills to deliver six sigma improvements are described as 'black belts' and 'green belts' and work in teams to deliver better quality.

Benefits and difficulties of improving quality

Benefits of improving quality

The benefits of having high quality products were covered earlier in this chapter. Any improvements in quality can enable a business to more fully reap the following benefits:

- gaining a competitive advantage
- increasing sales volume
- creating a unique selling point
- more scope to increase selling price
- greater opportunities for pricing flexibility
- cost reductions
- greater brand loyalty and enhancement of a firm's reputation.

(For a detailed analysis of these factors please see pages 291–293.)

Fact file

The Rug Company

The Rug Company is a London based firm, set up by Christopher and Suzanne Sharp, in 1997. The firm's handmade designer rugs can cost between £2,000 and £8,000 for a standard 9ft by 6ft rug and into tens of thousands of pounds for larger rugs. Their high profile customers include Bill Gates, the Kardashians, Cameron Diaz, George Osborne and Sir Alex Ferguson.

In 2013–14 the business achieved sales of £22.4 million and a profit of £4.3 million. The business operates 22 shops globally, including the rug department at Harrods. Mr Sharp believes the firm's success can be credited to their collaborations with well-known designers, including Paul Smith, Vivienne Westwood, Diane von Furstenberg and the late Alexander McQueen, whose designs account for half of its sales. 'Because we work with all these designers it's always new. No one else does modern rugs the same way in the UK,' he claims.

Woven in Nepal, where the firm employs 2,000 staff, each rug takes an average of four months and 20 people to craft. Mr Sharp believes this makes the rugs 'good value' despite their high price.

The combination of low manufacturing costs and high price reveals clearly how quality can help to develop a reputation and increase profits.

Source: Adapted from various news sources

Difficulties of improving quality

A business trying to improve quality can face a number of obstacles and difficulties.

- It may be difficult to convince people that there is a problem.
- If there is agreement on the nature of the problem, there may be difficulties in agreeing the best solution, particularly if it requires restructuring of employees' roles.
- Many quality systems give greater responsibility to staff. This may require changes in how people are managed and their whole approach to work. Such changes may not be received well by all workers.
- Resistance to change may be an element of the company's culture; overcoming this may be difficult.
- Introducing new methods and retraining staff so that the new approach can operate efficiently may be time consuming.
- Keeping pace with changing customer views on quality may be difficult.

Improving quality can be very expensive. Some of the main costs are:

- the cost of running new training for staff, so they can operate the new quality procedures. There may also be a need to train staff to think differently, for example, if quality assurance is replacing quality control
- developing quality systems and methods; this can involve a heavy administrative burden
- introducing or updating information systems so that quality can be achieved and monitored more effectively
- organising testing of the quality of inputs/resources before they reach the production line
- employing more inspection staff or allocating more time to workers who have greater responsibility for quality
- installing equipment for quality testing.

Ultimately, a business must decide whether the benefits of improving quality outweigh the costs. However, some of these benefits and costs (such as impact on reputation) are intangible.

Consequences of poor quality

Reputation

Poor quality can damage a business's reputation. This can be very harmful as customers remember adverse publicity far more than positive news. A business that has little or no competition may not suffer drastically, because consumers will have no alternatives. This is one of the main reasons why levels of competition are monitored and can be controlled by government. In a very competitive environment, poor quality products are likely to be very damaging, especially if a firm's reputation is built on quality. For products such as pharmaceuticals and baby foods, poor quality can damage a reputation so severely that the business is unable to recover. In 1985, a baby milk called Ostermilk was linked with salmonella. The product was withdrawn and the company's reputation damaged.

Lower sales volume

If a product or service fails to meet the standards expected by customers, then demand for the product will decrease. As society becomes more affluent, quality generally becomes a much more important factor in people's purchasing decisions. Consequently, poor quality is likely to have a more damaging effect on sales in the future.

Lower price

Low quality products will only be purchased if they offer value for money. If a product is viewed as low quality by customers, the producer will be forced to lower the price just to maintain sales volume. As a result, the profit margin will fall.

Lower profits

The consequence of the factors above will lead to lower profits. This can cause a vicious circle, as lower profits will mean a business has less profit to reinvest in the business to finance improvements (such as improvements in quality). Consequently, one of the main consequences of poor quality is the fact that the quality of a business's products in the future may deteriorate.

Waste/less productive use of assets

Poor quality represents waste because materials are likely to be discarded if the poor quality is detected late. It can also involve a waste of resources that are not involved directly in producing goods and services, but are merely being used to check on the effectiveness of other resources. Similarly, low quality materials may mean that processes break down or operate slowly, reducing the efficiency of production.

Increased costs

Some costs can be linked directly to poor quality:

- Scrappage: this is money wasted on materials that must be thrown away because they form part of a product that was rejected during the production process or returned by the customer because of its lack of quality.
- Cost of replacement materials, where more expensive materials are required to overcome situations that led to scrappage.

- Wages paid to staff who need to rework a product that was faulty or start afresh on making a replacement.
- Cost of time spent on transporting and checking recalled products and the administrative time involved in dealing with complaints.
- Loss of reputation and goodwill, which may mean a loss of revenue or expenditure that is designed to restore the firm's reputation.

Fact file

Armand Feigenbaum

Armand Feigenbaum is acknowledged to be the first person to separately classify the costs involved in achieving quality. His classification is set out in Table 14.1 below.

▼ Table 14.1 Feigenbaum's classification of quality costs

Cost area	Examples
Costs of control: prevention costs *These costs result from activities to prevent defects occurring*	Quality training for staff Developing quality systems/methods Information systems to monitor quality
Costs of control: appraisal costs *These costs result from detecting defects through inspection or testing*	Testing quality of inputs Inspection staff Equipment for testing
Costs of failure of control: internal failure *These costs result from discarding or repairing defective items*	Scrap Purchasing replacement materials Wages paid to rework defective items
Costs of failure of control: external failure *These costs result from defective items that reach customers*	Product replacement and recall Time spent dealing with complaints Loss of reputation and goodwill

The first two areas of Feigenbaum's classification (costs of control) relate to the difficulties of improving quality and emphasise that ensuring quality is a costly process. The other two areas (costs of failure of control) relate to the consequences of poor quality. Saving small sums of money, by economising too much on processes in the first two categories, can lead to very high costs in the third and fourth categories.

Practice exercise 1

Total: 30 marks

1 Which of these factors is a *tangible* feature of quality?
   a) Durability
   b) Exclusiveness
   c) Image
   d) Reputation
   (1 mark)

2 Which of these factors is an *intangible* feature of quality?
   a) Additional features
   b) After-sales service
   c) Brand
   d) Reliability
   (1 mark)

3 'Right first time' is a feature of:
   a) inspection
   b) kaizen
   c) quality assurance
   d) quality control
   (1 mark)

4 Which one of these costs would not be a direct consequence of a failure to control quality?
   a) Prevention costs
   b) Product recall costs
   c) Reworking costs
   d) Scrappage costs
   (1 mark)

5 What is meant by the term 'quality'?
   (2 marks)

➤➤➤

6 Explain why firms have tended to move from quality control to quality assurance. *(6 marks)*

7 Analyse two difficulties a business might face when trying to improve the quality of its products. *(9 marks)*

8 Analyse two possible benefits to a business that result from the high quality of its products. *(9 marks)*

Case study: Constance Products

Jake Turner was determined to succeed. Since his appointment as operations director at Constance Products, he had vowed that he would restore the company's tarnished image.

Jake's first action had been to dismantle the firm's quality control inspection at the end of production. With the backing of the managing director, Sarah Hall, Jake had presented his ideas to the workforce. Each worker would become responsible for the quality of their own work and any worker could stop the production line if he or she felt that there was a problem. The workers were particularly pleased to hear that the production line would be closed down for two weeks to enable it to be redesigned and that they would be given training in the new quality assurance procedures.

The first few weeks were a disaster. Everyone produced slowly to avoid mistakes, but gradually productivity improved. For Jake, the subsequent improvement in quality was the most pleasing result. The workers saw it differently. After nine months they were finding that greater responsibility meant a more interesting job. Sam Bulmer, the human resources manager, was overjoyed at the increased morale of the workforce and the fall in staff turnover. Everyone was looking forward to the productivity bonuses that were being anticipated in three months' time.

Sarah wanted to be certain that the new quality assurance system was improving quality. She asked Jake to provide data on the main quality measures used by the company, to show levels of performance before, during and after the introduction of the new quality system. The results are summarised in Table 14.2.

▼ **Table 14.2** Measures of quality at Constance Products plc

	Before change	Early stages of implementation	After change
Delivery time (days)	1.4	3.0	0.7
Deliveries on time (%)	93	93	99
Scrap rate (%)	1	5	3
Customer satisfaction rating (%)	88	68	96
Customer complaints (%)	2	7	3
Employee satisfaction rating (%)	63	51	92

Questions

Total: 50 marks

1 Analyse the reasons why a shift to quality assurance led to 'increased morale of the workforce'. *(9 marks)*

2 Identify one measure of quality that could still be improved and analyse two ways in which Constance Products might improve that aspect of its operations. *(9 marks)*

3 To what extent did quality suffer during the early stages of the change from quality control to quality assurance? *(16 marks)*

4 Evaluate the overall success of the new system once it had been fully established. *(16 marks)*

Case study: Quality of the visitor experience: Alice Holt 2013

In England, around 40 million visits are made to Forestry Commission areas each year, including 3 million to sites with visitor centres.

These areas meet certain aims of the Forestry Commission because they provide:
● outdoor recreational facilities for people to enjoy
● activities that can improve fitness and encourage a healthy lifestyle
● experiences that can help people deal with stress.

In some of its forests, the Forestry Commission tries to achieve these aims through:
● ensuring that the woodlands encourage people to access them
● providing facilities that give a quality visitor experience
● maintaining areas so that they are safe and welcoming.

In 2013, Beaufort Research conducted research for the Forestry Commission into the quality of visitor experience at some of its woods and forests. One of the woods involved was Alice Holt in Hampshire.

Customer views of Alice Holt as a place to visit were extremely positive: 56 per cent rated the site and its facilities as 'excellent' and 41 per cent said it was 'very good'.

Ratings on how safe and welcoming it was were also favourable, with 54 per cent saying 'excellent' and 44 per cent saying 'very good'.

Only a very small proportion of visitors gave a 'good' rating and none gave a rating lower than 'good'.

The survey asked whether visitors would be likely to recommend Alice Holt as a place to visit to a friend or relative. Using a score of 0–10, where zero equalled 'Not at all likely' and 10 equalled 'Extremely likely', the average score for Alice Holt

in 2013 was 9.4/10, an increase of 0.2 since the previous survey in 2010–11.

The Net Promoter Score (NPS) divides customers into three types:
● 86 per cent were Promoters (loyal enthusiasts) – score of 9–10.
● 11 per cent were Passives (satisfied but unenthusiastic) – score of 7–8.
● 3 per cent were Detractors (somewhat less satisfied) – score of 0–6.

The Net Promoter Score (NPS) subtracts 'detractors' from 'promoters'. For Alice Holt the NPS was 83 (86 – 3), 7 points higher than the 2010–11 survey score.

Visitors to Alice Holt were asked what they liked most about the site. The aspect of the site liked by the highest proportion of visitors was the activities available for children (63 per cent); much higher than in 2010–11 (48 per cent) and significantly higher than the average of 22 per cent for woods with visitor centres in England. The walks, paths and trails (45 per cent) were also popular, a 7 per cent increase on 2010–11.

The quality of the facilities was also surveyed. Figure 14.1 shows the results.

The Go Ape facility, which allows visitors to climb and experience a 126-metre zip wire, is aimed at the more adventurous, and its popularity has more than doubled since 2011. This experience costs £24 or £32. However, only a minority use the Go Ape facility and for most visitors, costs are low. On average, visitors spent £4.07, much less than the average of £6.13 spent by visitors to Forestry Commission sites as a whole.

Source: Data based on 241 visitor interviews conducted between 1 August 2013 and 30 October 2013; Research Report – Quality of the Visitor Experience: Alice Holt 2013, by Beaufort Research for the Forestry Commission

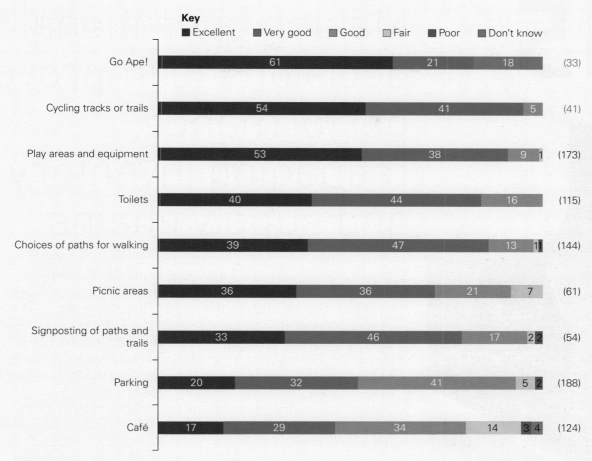

Key
■ Excellent ■ Very good ■ Good □ Fair ■ Poor ■ Don't know

Facility	Excellent	Very good	Good	Fair	Poor	Don't know	(n)
Go Ape!	61	21	18				(33)
Cycling tracks or trails	54	41	5				(41)
Play areas and equipment	53	38	9	1			(173)
Toilets	40	44	16				(115)
Choices of paths for walking	39	47	13	1 1			(144)
Picnic areas	36	36	21	7			(61)
Signposting of paths and trails	33	46	17	2 2			(54)
Parking	20	32	41	5	2		(188)
Café	17	29	34	14	3	4	(124)

▲ **Figure 14.1** Rating of Alice Holt site facilities (where used) 2013

Questions

Total: 34 marks

1 A Net Promoter Score (NPS) greater than 80 is considered to be exceptionally high. Analyse two possible reasons why a visitor attraction, such as Alice Holt, is able to achieve such a high score. *(9 marks)*

2 Analyse two ways in which Alice Holt might improve its attractiveness to visitors. *(9 marks)*

3 Evaluate the key factors that led to Alice Holt achieving a high rating for quality from its customers. Justify your view. *(16 marks)*

15 Making operational decisions to improve performance: managing inventory and supply chains

In this chapter we examine ways of improving flexibility (focusing on mass customisation), speed of response and dependability and assess the value of improvements in these aspects of operations management. The chapter then considers the management of supply in order to match demand and the value of doing this. It focuses in particular on the value of outsourcing and then goes on to examine the factors that influence the amount of inventory held by a business. The chapter concludes by looking at influences on the choice of suppliers and the value of effective and efficient management of the supply chain.

Ways and value of improving flexibility, speed of response and dependability

In Chapter 11 we saw that businesses set operational objectives for flexibility, speed of response and dependability. The ways of improving performance in these aspects of operations management, and the value of doing so, will each be examined in turn.

Improving flexibility

Flexibility is the ability of an organisation to change its operations in some way. The main types of flexibility are product flexibility (switching production from one product to another); volume flexibility (changing the level of output to match changes in consumer demand); delivery flexibility (changing the timing and volume of customers' deliveries); and mix flexibility (providing a wide range of alternative versions of the same basic product).

Product flexibility can be achieved by designing production lines that can be quickly altered to change the end product. With the growth of just-in-time supply of materials, greater automation of production lines and more adaptable machinery, it becomes easier to switch production between different products.

Volume flexibility can be achieved by maintaining high levels of spare capacity but this is expensive as it represents unused resources. Many businesses have used outsourcing production so that other businesses provide the manufacturing of products. In this way, businesses can increase volume without having high spare capacity.

Delivery flexibility relies on having a flexible workforce, particularly in terms of working hours, a sophisticated database to manage deliveries in a flexible way and access to delivery vehicles (usually through subcontracting or outsourcing).

Mix flexibility requires a combination of the factors outlined above. To provide different customers with different variations of the same product requires:

- a production line that can be altered or adapted quickly
- a sophisticated database to match customer requirements with the version of the product being made for that particular customer
- a flexible workforce with sufficient skills to adapt to making significant variations of the same products.

Growing demand for mix flexibility by customers has led to the growth of mass customisation.

Mass customisation

The mass production view of production is exemplified by the quote concerning the Model T Ford, attributed to Henry Ford: 'Any customer can have a car painted any colour he likes, so long as it is black.' Mass production uses 'push' methods of production, geared towards providing products at the lowest possible unit cost. Specialising in a limited range of choices enables businesses to produce on a large scale in order to lower costs. The products are then 'pushed' to the customers in the hope that they will be attracted by the competitive pricing offered.

In contrast, **mass customisation** focuses on products designed for the individual, albeit produced using large-scale methods. Mass customisation is based on 'pull' methods: a customer chooses a particular version of a product, which then leads to the manufacture of that product meeting the specific needs of that customer.

Customisation has existed for many years, but not on a large scale. For example, tailor-made suits have always been made according to the exact specifications of the customer, in terms of fabric, colour and size. In most industries, conditions were not suitable for the introduction of mass customisation on a wide scale until recently and even now there are many industries where its use is limited or non-existent.

In his 1993 book *Mass Customisation: The New Frontier in Business Competition*, Joseph Pine II identified four types of mass customisation:

1 **Collaborative customisation**. This is where businesses work closely with individual customers to develop a product that suits the individual customer's precise needs. An example is Dell computers, a company that makes computers in accordance with the stated preferences of its customers.

303

2 **Adaptive customisation**. In this case the business produces a standardised product which can then be customised or adjusted by the consumer. An example would be some audio tours of museums whereby the customer can alter the order of each audio clip to suit the order in which they wish to visit each exhibit.

3 **Transparent customisation**. This type of customisation occurs when unique products are provided to each customer but these are not specifically identified as customised products. For example, Ritz-Carlton hotels keep a database, often compiled from employees' observations of its customers, to provide a personalised service for its regular customers. For example, the hotel may provide a particular newspaper and toiletries, based on this knowledge.

4 **Cosmetic customisation**. Where standardised products are produced but marketed to different customers in different ways. For example, Planters Peanuts packages its products using different designs, specifications and sizes, to meet the varying needs of different retailers.

Factors required for mass customisation

Mass customisation has become more prevalent in recent years because of changes in business activity. In order for mass customisation to take place certain requirements are necessary.

- **A market in which customers value variety and individuality**. If customers are not prepared to pay a premium price for individuality then there will be no incentive for businesses to introduce mass customisation. Products such as matches and light bulbs are examples of products that continue to be made using mass production methods.
- **Quick responsiveness to market changes**. Businesses must be able to detect market changes so that products can be adjusted to the changing requirements of customers. The wealth of data held by businesses and other organisations now enables businesses to have a much better understanding of consumer desires and any changes in patterns of demand. This data helps businesses to understand the types of customisation required.
- **Ability to provide customisation (a wide variety of alternative versions of the same product)**. Capital equipment and software now make it possible to program adjustments to individual products on a production line. For example, car production lines can now be adjusted to provide a wide variety of versions of a certain model; two successive cars on a production line may have different engine sizes, colours and other technical specifications.
- **Scope for mass efficiency/economies of scale**. In the past, customisation tended to be a very specialist activity, such as tailor-made suits. This meant that customisation was a very expensive process and the price of the end product reflected this. Simple adjustments to a production line now mean that goods produced through mass customisation can be comparable in price to those made using mass production methods.

Fact file

Levi Strauss – mass customisation

Levi Strauss, the manufacturer of Levi jeans, introduced mass customisation in 1994. The company gave customers options such as colour and design and measured them in store. These measurements were then sent electronically to the factory which produced the customised jeans and sent them directly to the customer. Currently, 20 per cent of Levi's sales of jeans for females are produced through mass customisation.

Benefits of mass customisation for businesses

- **Cost reductions**. The use of the pull methodology means there is less waste because businesses do not need to keep stocks of products. Instead the products are manufactured and then provided directly to the customer.
- **Higher revenue**. Customisation meets consumer needs more closely and therefore should lead to greater demand for products overall. Furthermore, because the exact requirements of the customer are being met the customer is likely to be prepared to pay a higher price.
- **Greater customer loyalty**. If customers are highly satisfied, they tend to be more loyal and provide the business with repeat orders.
- **Competitive advantage**. Customisation provides a unique selling point and therefore gives a business a competitive advantage.
- **Improved understanding of customers' wants**. Although mass customisation relies on a good understanding of customer wants, it also improves a business's understanding of those wants. This is because transactions between a customer and the business will provide a record of the customer's wants and preferences and any developments in their feelings towards the business's products.
- **Greater protection from market changes**. Mass production means that businesses are vulnerable to sudden changes in tastes because their production methods are geared towards production of a limited range of products. The flexibility offered by mass customisation production means that it is probable that existing methods of production can be adapted to meet any changes in the market.
- **Improved workforce motivation**. Customisation provides variety for workers and should lead to a more contented and motivated workforce.
- **Higher profits**. Increased profit margins arise from the combination of significant increases in price and slight increases in unit costs. However, profit may also rise because mass customisation often allows the producer to deal directly with the end-user and so the profit of the middleman (usually a retailer) is now taken by the producer.

Difficulties of mass customisation for businesses

- **Requirement for sophisticated and expensive management and information systems**. Because the management systems required to record and analyse data are more complex, mass customisation is likely to require a large capital input in the first instance. This can make the business more vulnerable if mass customisation does not succeed.
- **Greater expense in terms of IT, capital equipment and staff training**. These expenses are likely to be higher and although they can be covered by higher prices for customers, the end result may be no change in profit margins.
- **Problems with rejected products**. If the customer rejects a customised product as unsuitable, it will be more difficult for the business to then sell it to another customer. This is because the product has been devised to meet the very specific needs of one customer. This can lead to high wastage costs.
- **Unsuitable supply chains**. Mass customisation requires high levels of flexibility from suppliers. This can be a major obstacle as this flexibility will be expensive for the supplier, who may prefer to sell standard items in bulk. At the very least, the producer will need to pay higher prices for raw materials and components.

Value of improving flexibility

Although improving flexibility, as outlined above, has both advantages and disadvantages, the growing demand for individuality suggests that the benefits outweigh the problems. However, the value will vary between industries and over time. For example, using mass customisation, Dell broke into the top three for worldwide sales of personal computers (PCs) in 1997 and has remained in the top three ever since. It was the market leader for five years between 2001 and 2006. Improving flexibility is less attractive to businesses producing low-cost, low-price products where the lack of scope for high profit margins means that producers find it difficult to make sufficient profit.

In general, flexibility is most advantageous for products that meet two key criteria:

- Production can be modified cost effectively, so that customised products are more expensive, but not always significantly more so than mass-produced alternatives.
- Customers are prepared to pay a higher price for the flexibility offered, whether it is in the form of a customised product, changes in volume or delivery flexibility.

Improving speed of response and dependability

In Chapter 11 we saw that **speed of response** is the time taken for a customer choice to be fulfilled. **Dependability** has a number of alternative meanings, such as whether a product is durable, reliable and long-lasting, but in this context it is a measure of whether a business is 'on time' when providing a good or service. Both 'speed of response' and 'dependability' can be achieved by having:

- an effective and up-to-date information technology system, so that customer requirements can be recognised and dealt with quickly
- a flexible workforce that is prepared to focus on priority tasks even where this involves changing their expected pattern of work
- targets for meeting customer requirements that are challenging but achievable
- integrated systems that enable staff involved in a customer order to draw on information from all areas of the business
- close relationships with suppliers, distributors and other organisations involved in the provision and delivery of the product.

Value of improving speed of response and dependability

Speed of response and dependability can provide a business with a competitive advantage if they are provided at a higher level than rivals. This is critical if these particular aspects of operational performance are important to customers. Businesses using just-in-time methods will often place a high value on speed of response and dependability when choosing suppliers. Customers who are cash-rich but time-poor will also tend to value these qualities. Overall, good performance in these operational activities will be of value to a business because it will:

- increase customer satisfaction and therefore lead to higher levels of customer loyalty and more repeat business in the future

- lead to higher prices, if customers recognise this as something that adds value to the product. For example, in many cases customers are prepared to pay more for quick delivery.
- reduce costs, because more efficient delivery will probably mean fewer labour hours for delivery staff. Storage costs will be cut too, because inventories of finished products and raw materials will tend to be reduced by faster delivery.

How to manage supply to match demand and the value of doing so

In order to maximise its efficiency a business will try to achieve full capacity utilisation. This can be done by balancing demand and supply of products. If there is spare capacity it can try to increase demand in order to match its capacity to supply.

Managing demand

A business can attempt to improve its marketing mix in order to increase demand. McDonald's has widened its product range in order to overcome its problem of spare capacity. Hotels regularly offer off-peak special deals to increase capacity utilisation at these times. The marketing mix is used to increase demand; details of how a business might increase demand for its products are provided in Chapter 10.

On rare occasions, a firm may suffer from the opposite problem – a capacity shortage. There is always a high demand for tickets for the Last Night of the Proms at the Royal Albert Hall. The organisers therefore charge a higher price than usual in order to reduce the demand to a reasonable level and to maximise sales revenue. Theatres and concert halls regularly try to anticipate the level of demand for tickets at different prices. With this knowledge they can set higher prices for popular events and lower prices for less popular events, so that the demand for tickets matches the number of seats available. In this way, they achieve full capacity and high sales revenue.

Managing supply

If there is a mismatch between supply and demand, the focus will be on trying to manage supply in order to match demand. Methods of increasing or decreasing capacity (in order to match demand) are outlined in Chapter 13. In general, a business will aim to make as much profit as possible and so it will attempt to increase demand as much as possible. Therefore the focus will usually be on increasing supply to match the increased demand.

In Chapter 13 we saw that increasing capacity required significant expenditure on items such as machinery and vehicles for delivery. When demand is low, these items can prove to be an unnecessary expense. As a result, many businesses use a flexible approach to production. Often this involves the establishment of a core capacity to produce a given level of production, supported by a flexible structure that enables the business to react quickly to changes in demand. The main approaches are:

- producing to order
- use of temporary and part-time employees
- outsourcing.

307

Did you know?

Burger King first used 'producing to order' as a marketing campaign strategy in 1974, using the slogan 'Have it your way' to demonstrate to customers that they could customise their burgers to a certain extent. This approach helped Burger King to become the second largest burger chain in the world. In 1998, market research showed that customisation and producing to order were becoming more fashionable and so Burger King introduced a new campaign, using the slogan 'When you have it your way, it just tastes better.' The campaign targeted Burger King's main rival, McDonalds, whose focus was on large scale and low cost production of a limited choice of products. Since this campaign McDonalds has taken steps to provide a more customised range of food.

Producing to order

Producing to order uses 'pull' methods of production, as the product made corresponds to the wishes of the customer. As such, it is similar to mass customisation and contrasts with the typical mass production 'push' approach, often known as build to stock (BTS).

Producing to order tends to cover a broader range of businesses than mass customisation, because it includes small-scale, tailor-made products (such as made-to-measure suits) and large-scale, one-off planes whereby the basic model is predetermined but the layout and fittings are modified according to the wishes of the customer.

Build-to-order products often adopt a modular approach to manufacturing. This means that there is a basic element of the product which is fixed, alongside elements of the product that can be customised. For example, a car may have certain set features such as the body shape, but can be customised by changing elements such as the engine size and internal specifications.

Advantages of producing to order

- **Ability to supply a product that meets a customer's exact specification**. This will increase customer satisfaction and brand loyalty and may give the business a USP.
- **Reduced costs of holding inventory**. If every unit of output is planned for a particular customer then there will be no need to hold any inventory of finished goods. This will save considerably on costs such as rental payments and potential losses through pilferage and damage.
- **Potential for higher prices**. Customers will expect to pay higher prices for a product that is exactly suited to their needs. If the production method enables producing to order to be comparable in cost to mass production methods, then the business should be able to improve its profit margin.
- **Production planning is easier**. The business does not need to employ staff to forecast demand, in order to plan production schedules. There is also less need for sales staff whose job is to persuade people to buy products that have already been made. In rapidly changing markets, there is less risk of losing a lot of money by having unwanted inventory or goods that need to be discounted in order to sell.
- **Targeting markets**. Build to order allows a business to modify basic products in ways that allow the business to target a mass market with the basic product and also niche markets through modifications that appeal to those niches.

Disadvantages of producing to order

- **Considerable fluctuations in production levels over time**. This can prove to be more inefficient than a production schedule that spreads output more evenly throughout the year, because the latter will tend to use capital equipment and permanent labour much more cost effectively.
- **Higher costs**. Inefficient capacity utilisation will result from fluctuations arising from build to order; this will lead to higher fixed costs per unit.
- **Inability to take advantage of sudden interest in a product**. Producing to order means that there is no inventory held. If a customer has an unexpected demand for the product then it will be impossible to meet

increase supply to match demand without the need to increase its own factory size. Similarly, it can reduce supply to match a fall in demand by reducing the amount of work that it outsources or subcontracts, without making any changes to its own factory size. Many council services, such as waste management, are subcontracted to private firms such as Veolia and Biffa. Private firms subcontract specialist services, such as information services, to other organisations.

Value of outsourcing

Advantages of outsourcing

- Businesses are able to react to changes in demand more quickly if they have access to a number of other firms' production plants.
- Outsourcing providers may be more specialised and therefore more efficient in a particular line of activity. A car manufacturer buys tyres from a specialist firm such as Michelin, rather than making its own, because its own tyres are likely to be inferior to those produced by the specialist.
- Outsourcing lets a firm focus on its core business and helps it to avoid becoming involved in activities at which it is less competent.
- A non-standard order can be given to an outsource provider so that the business benefits from the order but suffers no disruption to its normal production.

Disadvantages of outsourcing

- Firms must recognise that the quality of their service is no longer directly under their own control. An unreliable outsourcing provider may influence the reputation of a business. Customers will blame a supermarket if its own-label cornflakes are of poor quality, even though the supermarket did not produce them.
- Excessive outsourcing erodes a company's operations base and its ability to initiate research and make changes.
- The cost of outsourcing should be evaluated. The outsourced producer also wants to make a profit, so it is possible that it will be more expensive to subcontract or outsource production rather than produce in-house.
- Outsourcing may require a firm to give confidential information to a supplier, such as details of its methods and patents. This may mean the firm loses its competitive advantage if the supplier steals its ideas.

Overall, the value of outsourcing will depend on the balance of advantages and disadvantages for a particular business and its circumstances. Circumstances that might affect any decision to outsource are described below.

Factors influencing decisions to outsource

- **Available capacity**. If a business has high levels of spare capacity it will be more inclined to produce in-house rather than outsource or subcontract. However, if there is a shortage of capacity then outsourcing becomes a much more financially viable solution.
- **Expertise**. If a business has considerable expertise in the production of an item then it may be reluctant to outsource as it will not be playing to its strengths. However, in many cases the company to which the work is being outsourced possesses better production (or other appropriate) skills, in which case outsourcing will lead to more efficient production.
- **Quality considerations**. If a business sells its product on the basis of quality, outsourcing can be risky because it is more difficult for the business to control and therefore maintain the quality of the products that it sells. A number of UK business activities, notably those involving call centres, are being re-shored (returned to the UK) because of concerns relating to the quality of the service being provided by offshore providers (**offshoring**).
- **Nature of demand**. In many instances outsourcing arises because of the business's need to protect itself from sudden fluctuations in demand. If, however, demand is stable or consistent over a period of time, then a business may be more inclined to produce in-house rather than use outsourcing.
- **Cost**. If production is not one of the core competencies of a business, it will make good sense for it to be outsourced. This is particularly evident in the case of products that are offshored in countries overseas that benefit from low costs, such as low wage levels and reduced rental payments for property.
- **Level of risk**. Outsourcing can increase risk, because of a loss of control over operations and a possible loss of know-how. Toyota have experienced quality and safety issues with accelerators in their cars, arising from a decision to outsource production of this component. Boeing have outsourced approximately 70 per cent of the production of the 'Dreamliner' aircraft – the highest level of outsourcing of any of their aircraft – and have experienced quality problems as a result.
- **Impact on profit**. Companies will expect to make a profit from any work they undertake. Therefore, a decision to outsource or subcontract may result in lower profits because another business is making profit from that particular element of production. Businesses should examine the financial implications of any decision to outsource, to ensure that it is not damaging the overall profitability of the business.

Key term

Offshoring Used to describe outsourcing/subcontracting when the activity being transferred takes place in a different country to the contracting company.

▲ Boeing outsource 70% of the production of the Dreamliner

Fact file

IT outsourcing in the UK

Research by Arvato showed that outsourcing of IT and business processing activities by UK firms increased by 132 per cent between the first six months of 2013 and the first six months of 2014. Other research shows that information technology and administration are the two major business activities that are outsourced.

Source: www.arvato.co.uk

Practice exercise 1

Total: 65 marks

1 A business is scheduled to deliver 1,000 items of a product to a customer on 21 July. On 20 July the customer requests a modification to the order so that the delivery on the next day will be of a different version of the product. This is an example of:
   a) delivery flexibility
   b) mix flexibility
   c) product flexibility
   d) volume flexibility
   (1 mark)

2 Mass customisation is:
   a) an approach to production that uses 'push' methods
   b) based on companies keeping high levels of inventory so that customers have a wide choice of products
   c) offering individually tailored products to customers on a large scale
   d) a production system that customises goods but not services
   (1 mark)

3 Customisation where the consumer is unaware of the customisation is:
   a) adaptive customisation
   b) collaborative customisation
   c) cosmetic customisation
   d) transparent customisation
   (1 mark)

4 Which one of the following is most likely to be based on mass production methods?
   a) Producing to order
   b) Mass customisation
   c) Built to stock
   d) Tailor-made production
   (1 mark)

5 Explain one problem facing a business that uses mass customisation. *(4 marks)*

6 Explain two factors that are necessary for mass customisation to take place. *(6 marks)*

7 Analyse how a hotel might use temporary or part-time staff in order to improve flexibility. *(9 marks)*

8 Explain two factors a business might consider when deciding on whether to outsource its production. *(6 marks)*

9 Explain two benefits to a clothing manufacturer as a result of improvements in its flexibility. *(6 marks)*

10 Explain how a business might improve its speed of response. *(5 marks)*

11 Analyse two reasons why aeroplanes are built to order. *(9 marks)*

12 Evaluate the pros and cons of mass customisation for a fast-food provider, such as Burger King. *(16 marks)*

Case study: Dell (Part 1)

In 1984, Michael Dell founded PCs Limited with $1,000, selling and installing kits to upgrade computers for university students. A year later the company built its first complete computer.

Dell came up with a completely new idea – mass customisation of computers (PCs). He decided that he would sell directly to customers, designing the computers to the exact specifications of their order. The key factor influencing this decision was Dell's lack of money – he could not afford to build a PC unless he had a guarantee that it would sell. He also employed just-in-time manufacturing methods, because this

allowed him to keep his inventories low. Although Dell initially produced on a small scale, this approach enabled him to compete with much larger PC providers that relied on mass-production, BTS (build to stock) methods, because the larger providers had such high inventory costs. Within four years, Dell's annual sales revenue rose from $80,000 to $73 million.

By 1992, Dell was one of the USA's 500 largest companies and became the world's largest computer provider in 2001.

As Dell grew quickly, it faced problems trying to match its capacity to supply to the ever-increasing levels of demand for its PCs. Dell assembled the final products in the USA, but the basic units were supplied from Taiwan and so this meant that Dell had to choose between holding increasing levels of inventories of base units or demanding greater flexibility from its suppliers. As worldwide sales grew, new assembly factories were built in Ireland, Malaysia, China and Brazil. These locations allowed Dell to cut both production and delivery costs.

Dell's view was that its core capability was in customising basic units, to suit customer needs. However, other businesses were learning from Dell and introducing similar methods. In order to reduce costs further, Dell decided to outsource more production, representing 25 per cent of its manufacturing. In time, this led to problems for Dell. Asus, one of its component suppliers, offered to produce motherboards (containing the main electrical components of a computer) more cheaply and so Dell outsourced this

activity to Asus. Later, Asus moved on to assembling the computers for Dell. As a result, Dell lost some of its core skills. This problem was highlighted in 2005, when Asus set up as a competitor in the PC market.

Dell also outsourced customer support by moving its call centres to India in 2001. However, its rating as the computer provider with the best customer service was hit by issues with the new call centres and by 2004 some of its call centres were moved back to the USA. In 2009, the Irish factory was closed and replaced by a factory in Poland, to reduce costs.

Dell's mass customisation enabled it to achieve a worldwide market share of 16.8 per cent of the PC market in 2005. Between 1999 and 2008, Dell and HP/Compaq were the two dominant companies, but companies such as Acer and Lenovo were catching up. Dell decided to change its strategy. (Continued in Dell (Part 2) on page 328.)

Questions

Total: 30 marks

1 Explain how mass customisation reduces inventory costs for a company such as Dell. *(5 marks)*

2 Analyse two reasons why Dell experienced problems when trying to match supply to demand. *(9 marks)*

3 To what extent was 'outsourcing' beneficial to Dell's aim to achieve sales growth? *(16 marks)*

Key terms

Inventories Items that firms need to produce for, or supply to, customers.

Inventory control Management of levels of raw materials, work-in-progress and finished goods in order to reduce storage costs while still meeting the customer's demands.

Influences on the amount of inventory held

Inventories can take three different forms:

- **Raw materials**: components or ingredients that will be used in the making of the good.
- **Work-in-progress**: part-finished products. For a business using mass production, it is common for some goods to be moving through the production process at any given point of time.
- **Finished goods**: completed products that are owned by the firm until a sale has been agreed.

Inventory control is another method that can be used to ensure that production matches demand. By holding high inventory levels, a business is able to release additional products onto the market when demand increases. During periods of low demand, the level of inventory can be replenished by producing more than is being demanded. However, it is not easy for a business to be certain of its optimum level of inventory. There are advantages to holding high inventory levels and also advantages to having low inventory levels, as shown in Table 15.1. Businesses must weigh these up before deciding on inventory levels.

The ideal level of inventory therefore depends on circumstances.

- Low inventory levels are sensible if a company is located in an area in which rents are high (meaning space to store inventories is costly); or if it has a perishable product and suffers from cash flow problems and so needs to ensure its inventories are sold and turned into cash quickly.
- High inventory levels would suit a business that gains large cost savings by bulk buying a product that has unpredictable peaks in demand.

▼ **Table 15.1** Advantages of high and low inventory levels

Advantages of high inventory levels	Advantages of low inventory levels
• Customers' demands are met promptly.	• Reduced warehousing costs are possible.
• There is no loss of goodwill caused by running out of inventory.	• Opportunity cost is low.
• Sudden increases in demand can be dealt with efficiently.	• Security and pilferage costs are lower.
• Production lines are not halted because of shortages of raw materials.	• Perishable products are less likely to deteriorate and problems of obsolescence (a product becoming outdated) are minimised.
• Companies can benefit from bulk buying and from longer production runs.	• Cash flow problems due to cash being tied up in inventory are less probable.

Controlling inventory levels

An **inventory control chart** is a diagram that is used to register levels of stock/ inventory over a period of time. An example is shown in Figure 15.1. The ideas below are essential in order to understand how an inventory control chart works.

Buffer level of inventory

As firms try to save costs by minimising storage costs, it is becoming common for suppliers to make smaller but more regular deliveries of inventory, so **buffer inventory levels** are falling. However, high inventory levels are still maintained in some organisations. For example, when certain health dangers are prevalent hospitals will tend to hold high levels of vaccine, in case of an emergency. There has also been concern about low inventories of blood in hospitals.

Re-order level

Both the **re-order level** and the **re-order quantity** will depend on three factors:

1 **The supplier's lead time**: how long the supplier takes to deliver once an order has been placed. A high **lead time** means that more inventory will be used up while awaiting delivery. Therefore, a higher re-order level is needed to avoid the possibility of running out of inventory. Similarly, a larger re-order quantity will be needed as more items need to be replenished.

2 **Demand for the product**: the higher the demand, the higher the re-order level must be, as inventory levels will fall more quickly if demand is high.

3 **Consequences of running out of inventory**: if customers can easily switch to a competitor then it is vital to keep high levels of inventory, by having a high re-order level and high re-order quantities.

A lot of inventory control is automated. In many shops, each time an article is sold the computer will register the fact that the inventory level has fallen by one unit. When the number of items sold reduces the inventory level to the re-order level, the computer (which will be linked to the supplier's computer) will automatically place an order for new inventory.

Firms will usually have a **maximum inventory level.** This is the highest amount of inventory that the company is able to store.

Table 15.1 shows the advantages of holding high and low inventory levels: these are the factors that influence a firm's decision about the amount of storage space it requires.

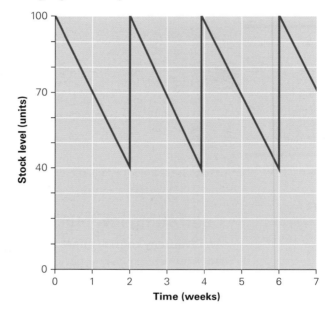

▲ **Figure 15.1** Inventory control chart

Figure 15.1 shows an inventory control chart where everything operates in a predictable manner. The company starts with an inventory level of 100 (its maximum inventory level). Inventory is used up at a rate of 30 units per week. After one week the re-order level (70 units) is reached and 60 units are ordered. The lead time is one week, so the 60 units are delivered at the end of the second week. At this point the inventory has reached the buffer inventory level of 40 units, so the inventory level jumps to 100 units (40 in inventory + 60 just delivered). This process then repeats itself every two weeks.

Inventory wastage

There are a number of causes of **inventory wastage**:

- raw materials being wasted during storage and production
- defects in production
- pilferage or theft
- damage to inventories during storage and production
- obsolescence (products becoming outmoded or being kept beyond their sell-by date).

Inventory rotation

Under **inventory rotation**, warehouses are designed to make sure that new inventory is not placed in a position where it blocks access to older inventory. In shops, shelves are stacked so that the new inventory is placed behind the old inventory, to avoid the chances of products perishing.

Improving the efficiency of inventory control

Many firms now realise how vital inventory management is in their operations. Traditionally, businesses kept high inventory levels 'just in case' they were needed. However, this led to the need to sell off unwanted inventory in 'sales' at the end of the year. Japanese firms led the way in challenging this idea, arguing that it was a waste of space and inventory, costing the company money. This led to the introduction of **just-in-time** measures.

Just-in-time inventory control

Just-in-time is a Japanese philosophy that organises operations so that items of inventory arrive just at the time they are needed for production or sale. The ultimate aim is to eliminate the need for inventory, although in practice this is not always ideal.

This form of inventory control has a number of implications:

- Costs of raw materials are likely to be higher, as smaller but more frequent orders are placed. This means that there are fewer economies of scale for the purchaser.
- Problems may be experienced in getting raw materials on time. Any delays can halt the production line or mean disappointed customers. For this reason, firms prefer to deal with suppliers located nearby. For example, when Honda, which uses just-in-time, decided to locate in Swindon, there were no significant suppliers of car components there. Since then, many suppliers have moved there in order to be close to Honda and supply its just-in-time requirements.
- Costs of storage and insurance fall as inventories are delivered directly to the production line or placed immediately on to the shelves. Similarly, inventories of finished goods are sent out of the factory immediately, reducing the need for large areas of storage. This frees up space for more productive use. Typically, supermarkets used to devote two-thirds of

their space to storage. Just-in-time deliveries have led to much of this space being changed to selling space, allowing a supermarket to serve far more customers from the same-sized building.

- There is less likelihood of inventory perishing or becoming obsolete because goods spend little or no time in the warehouse.
- Production areas are less cluttered with work-in-progress and working environments may become safer.

Practice exercise 2

Total: 40 marks

1 Identify the three different forms of inventory. *(3 marks)*

2 Explain two advantages of holding high levels of inventory. *(6 marks)*

3 Explain two problems of holding high levels of inventory. *(6 marks)*

4 Explain two factors that will influence the re-order level of a product. *(6 marks)*

5 State three possible reasons for inventory wastage. *(3 marks)*

6 What is meant by just-in-time inventory control? *(2 marks)*

7 Analyse two benefits of just-in-time inventory control for an electrical goods manufacturer. *(9 marks)*

8 Why might suppliers dislike supplying to a company that operates on a just-in-time basis? *(5 marks)*

Case study: Inventory out of control

Mich Magni looked at the inventory control chart and wept. He couldn't understand where it had all gone so horribly wrong. For 20 years his company had successfully survived in the competitive world of pizzas. At first it had been easy. The local demand in his home town of Bedford had given him a firm base on which to expand, and the excellent transport links had encouraged him to extend his target market into London and the Midlands.

Magni Pizzas produced a range of frozen pizzas, but its main business was in supplying freshly made pizzas to supermarkets. Magni purchased ready-made pizza bases from a local supplier, Bedford International Pizza Bases (BIPB) plc, and transformed them into completed pizzas by adding a variety of different toppings. There had been difficulties in facing up to competition from larger food manufacturers, but in recent years the market for more expensive, individually made pizzas had grown, and Mich's business had secured valuable contracts with two of the UK's largest supermarkets. This had

persuaded him to set up the new factory, which was fully automated. The ingredients were delivered regularly, in small batches, and fed straight into the production line. Each day's production schedule was based on weekly orders from the supermarkets, so that Mich's firm had sufficient time to buy in the inventory needed.

The new factory opened in October and operated smoothly for the first two months. After 20 years in the business and the successful expansion of his firm, Mich decided to take a long holiday in Naples, visiting relatives and friends whom he had not seen for many years. Mich's brother Hugo was placed in temporary charge.

Mich returned to Bedford in late January. Hugo had been very evasive on the telephone and Mich sensed that something might be wrong. The plane touched down at 6 p.m. on Sunday evening; by 8 p.m. Mich was in the factory trying to find some clues to Hugo's behaviour. Mich was disturbed when the first two letters that he opened were from his new supermarket customers, threatening to end the contracts 'unless immediate action is taken to improve the reliability of deliveries'. Unfortunately, the only other item that he could find was an inventory control chart, showing the inventory levels of pizza bases delivered by BIPB (Figure 15.2).

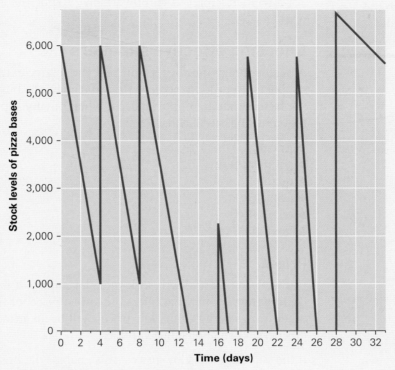

▲ **Figure 15.2** Inventory levels of pizza bases

Mich studied the chart, trying to piece together the events of the past month or so.

Questions

Total: 55 marks

1 In the first eight days, inventory control operated smoothly. Use this information and Figure 15.2 to work out the value of:

   a) the maximum inventory level   (1 mark)

   b) the buffer inventory level   (1 mark)

   c) the re-order level, assuming a lead
   time of 2 days.   (3 marks)

2 Briefly explain two factors that might have caused the company to run out of inventory on day 13.   (6 marks)

3 Explain why the zero levels of inventory during the period between days 17 and 28 were caused by different factors from those that led to the zero level of inventory on day 13.   (8 marks)

4 Explain one possible reason for the change in the chart after day 28.   (4 marks)

5 Evaluate the implications of the situation shown in the chart for Mich's business.   (16 marks)

6 To what extent could the problems shown have been prevented? Justify your view.   (16 marks)

Influences on the choice of suppliers

For a manufacturer, **suppliers** will mainly provide the raw materials and components needed to produce the finished goods.

For a retailer, suppliers will invariably provide the finished goods that the retailer sells.

Choosing effective suppliers

A business may improve its efficiency to a large extent by choosing effective suppliers. In order to achieve this efficiency, the business needs to identify the factors that are important to it when buying supplies. The main factors that a business will consider are:

- prices
- payment terms
- quality
- capacity
- reliability
- flexibility.

Prices

Primarily, a business will seek value for money. It is not simply a matter of finding the supplier that offers the lowest price for the materials, although other things being equal, low prices will be an attractive proposition to the business when choosing a supplier.

If the supplier offers low prices, this enables the business to benefit in two different ways:

- It can reduce the final selling price of its own product and therefore gain a competitive advantage.
- It can keep its final selling price the same but enjoy the benefit of higher added value. Remember, added value is the difference between the selling price of a good and the cost of the bought-in goods and services required to make it. With the exception of labour costs, the cost of raw materials is the major cost to UK businesses. Consequently, any reduction in the cost of (price paid for) raw material supplies will boost the profit margin of the business.

A business must be cautious when considering the prices that it pays to its suppliers. The prices charged by the supplier may be low because of deficiencies in the other factors relevant to the choice of supplier. It is possible that the prices offered are low because the quality of the raw materials from that particular supplier is inferior to the quality offered by other suppliers. In addition, the cheap supplier may be unreliable in terms of meeting delivery dates or it may lack the flexibility to deal with a problem when there is a sudden emergency.

The importance of the price charged by suppliers also depends on the type of market the business that is buying the supplies operates in. If its customers are prepared to pay high prices for the final product, it is unlikely to be at a disadvantage if it is paying a high price for its raw materials or components. Therefore, price will be a less important factor when deciding on the supplier. On the other hand, if the business is operating in a very competitive market, where low prices may lead to large rises in demand, it will want to undercut the prices of its competitors. In this situation, it is vital that the business finds a supplier that charges low prices for the relevant components and raw materials.

Another factor to consider is the financial position of the supplier. The reliability of the supplier is a crucial factor, because the business will need regular deliveries of materials so that it can continue to produce or sell. Therefore, the business will want to ensure that its suppliers do not have any cash flow problems and are making enough profit to continue supplying in the future. For some small suppliers, a large business customer may account for most of the supplier's revenue. In such cases, the price offered by the large organisation can greatly influence the profitability and cash flow of the supplier. Large businesses such as supermarkets must be careful that they do not use their size to bargain suppliers into offering such low prices that the suppliers go into liquidation. For a small business buying from suppliers, however, it is unlikely that this will be a vital factor, as it will almost certainly be one of a number of businesses buying from that supplier.

Did you know?

Organisations such as supermarkets insist on looking at the financial position of a supplier before agreeing a contract, to make sure that the supplier will be able to continue supplying in the future.

Fact file

Starbucks in China

In 2013, Chinese government agencies criticised Starbucks because of its abuse of its control of the supply of its materials. Starbucks often buys its supplies through its own subsidiaries and this can lead to higher charges for supplies, leading to higher prices for customers. A medium-sized latte cost $4.40 in China, compared with $3.20 in Chicago. One of the products sold at higher prices was a Starbucks coffee mug. These are sold in the USA for prices between $10 and $14, but are sold for $18 in China. Ironically, these mugs are manufactured in China.

Payment terms

Payment terms are the arrangements made about the timing of payment and any other conditions agreed between buyer and seller.

It is normal practice in the business world for **credit** to be offered to the buyer of supplies of materials. This means that when the purchase is made, the actual payment for the goods and services that have been supplied is delayed, often by 28 or 30 days. There are two major reasons for this type of agreement:

● First, buyers prefer this type of agreement because of the cash flow cycle. Typically, a business will purchase its materials on a particular date. It will then either transform these materials in some way to create a final product, or sell them directly if it is a retailer. Therefore, whether the buyer is a manufacturer or retailer, there will be a delay between the purchase of the materials and the receipt of revenue from selling the final

product. This delay can cause cash flow problems for the buyer, although they may be overcome or at least eased by a delay in payment for the materials.

A typical example of this process occurs with clothing. A clothes shop will buy and hold stocks of clothing for some time before they are sold. If the clothes shop is carrying high levels of stock, it will become short of cash. However, if the supplier provides payment terms of credit for 30 days, this will take away some of the cash flow pressure from the clothes shop. If the shop can sell the clothes within 30 days, it will have sufficient money from the sales revenue to pay the supplier. If the supplier provides payment terms in this way, it is particularly useful to a small business that may not have easy access to supplies of cash.

- Second, suppliers may be encouraged to offer payment terms in order to obtain business. A supplier may not have cash flow difficulties and therefore may be able to wait for payment without suffering from a shortage of cash. If this is the case, offering payment terms to its buyers will make it a much more attractive proposition and should boost sales, as it will be preferred to suppliers that do not offer credit.

Sometimes, the agreement will suit both supplier and buyer. Payment terms often allow the supplier to charge interest on payments. Therefore, if a buyer delays payment, the supplier receives a higher sum of money. This may suit the supplier, but it may also suit the buyer because it could be preferable to pay an additional sum of money in order to avoid a cash flow crisis.

The importance of payment terms depends on the situations of both buyer and supplier. If the supplier is manufacturing a component that takes a long time to produce, it is likely to need cash immediately because it will have paid costs such as wages over a prolonged period of time, without receiving any revenue. Therefore, it will not want to offer payment terms. However, if it is an organisation such as a wholesaler that has been given credit by the manufacturers supplying it, it will not be under pressure to get cash quickly. Therefore, it can offer credit terms to its buyers.

In summary, credit is most likely to be offered when buyers might face cash flow difficulties because the end product takes a long time to sell. Payment terms are less likely to be needed if the final product brings in sales revenue quickly.

Quality

As society becomes more affluent, consumers become much more selective. In many industries, price competitiveness is being superseded by quality considerations. Therefore, quality is a critical factor to consider when choosing and working with a supplier. The benefits of quality are explained in Chapter 14.

In order to reap these benefits, a business needs to work closely with its suppliers, both to maintain the quality expected by customers and to achieve consistency of quality.

In the case of a retailer, the quality of the products on sale is directly related to the quality of the materials provided by the supplier. For example, if the apples supplied by a greengrocer are of high quality, this will reflect positively on the reputation of the greengrocer. However, if fault is found with these apples, customers will not blame the farmer because they will be unaware of the origin of the apples. Instead, customers will blame the person who sold them the apples – the greengrocer.

In some cases, blame may be apportioned to both the retailer and the manufacturer. For example, a fault with a branded electrical product may be seen to be the responsibility of both the manufacturer that made it and the retailer that sold it.

Fact file

Quality and 'own-brand' labels

The growing use of 'own-brand' labels by supermarkets and other retailers is leading to a situation in which faulty supplies often damage the reputation of the retailer far more than the manufacturer, as the name of the manufacturer may not be known to customers. This places even more importance on 'quality' when dealing with suppliers, as mistakes by suppliers may damage the reputation of the retailer.

For manufacturers, it is arguably even more important to ensure that the supplier is providing high-quality components and materials. A substandard product on a supermarket shelf can be easily removed. However, a substandard component in a finished product can cause untold damage as the whole of the product may need to be scrapped or recalled. In recent years, there have been a number of occasions where whole batches of motor vehicles have been recalled because of a fault in one component. This issue not only costs money in recalling the cars, but can also cause a great deal of damage to a manufacturer's reputation.

To summarise, the significance of quality depends on the product in question. For an economy brand that is sold on the basis of its low price, quality will be relatively unimportant. However, if the retailer or manufacturer is promoting the product on the basis of its quality, then the product itself and its components must meet high standards.

The onus is on the supplier to provide proof that it can maintain high quality standards. Usually, buyers will visit suppliers in order to assess whether their quality control or quality assurance procedures are satisfactory. The achievement of a recognised quality standard such as ISO 9001 or BS 5750 is the most important factor here. A supplier that provides proof of a British or International Standard is more likely to be given contracts. Quality standards that have been authenticated by an independent body, such as the British Standards Institution (BSI), will almost certainly be accepted as proof of quality by potential buyers. A supplier that has acquired a quality standard must regularly provide proof that it is maintaining its level of quality. Quality standards therefore provide reassurance to a buyer that a supplier will continue to maintain consistently high quality.

Capacity

Capacity is the maximum possible output of an organisation. An organisation needs to be reassured that a supplier can provide the quantity of materials that it requires, and so this is another factor to consider when deciding whether a particular supplier should be used.

Capacity will be critical if the supplier is providing a unique component or material that cannot be obtained from other sources. If the supplier does not have sufficient capacity to supply, the buyer's business will suffer as a result of its inability to meet its customers' requirements. This might seriously damage the reputation of the buyer. Buyers need to reassure themselves that the supplier can meet the quantity that the business requires, both now and in the foreseeable future.

Many large organisations prefer to buy in bulk from one or two suppliers, so that they can benefit from bulk-buying discounts. This requires high capacity in order to meet the needs of the buyer.

However, if the supplier provides a component or material that can be sourced from other suppliers, its capacity may be less critical. There is a growing tendency for large organisations to spread their risks by getting supplies from many sources. For example, supermarkets are beginning to promote the fact that they buy locally made products in different areas of the country. Consequently, capacity may be less of an issue, although there will still be an expectation that the supplier has enough capacity to meet the needs of all of the stores in a certain area.

If an organisation is concerned about a supplier's inability to supply enough products because of its lack of capacity, it may encourage the supplier to increase the scale of its operations. Sometimes, the organisation may provide financial assistance to help the business extend its factory, but in many cases a contract with a major buyer is enough to help a supplier persuade a bank to lend it the money needed to increase its capacity.

Reliability

In this context, reliability is the extent to which the supplier meets the requirements of the buyer. Typically, it can be measured by the percentage of deliveries made on time or the degree to which a supplier meets the terms of the contract to supply. Organisations give a high priority to the reliability of their suppliers, so reliability will be a vital factor in almost every situation.

If the buyer is a manufacturer, an unreliable supplier can lead to the whole production line coming to a halt if a crucial material or component is not available. If the buyer is a retailer, a lack of produce can affect its reputation. Customers will blame the retailer if they are unable to buy a product they expect to be able to purchase in the shop.

When negotiating terms with a potential supplier, a business should always examine the supplier's track record for reliability before agreeing a contract. The contract between the business and its supplier will contain clauses emphasising the importance of prompt delivery and outlining any compensation payable to the business if the supplier proves to be unreliable (e.g. failing to deliver on time).

There has been a growing movement towards just-in-time methods in recent decades. The ultimate aim of just-in-time is to reduce or eliminate the need for businesses to hold large amounts of stock and this has had significant implications for the relationship between organisations and their suppliers. Previously, businesses held high levels of stock and therefore an unreliable supplier might have had relatively little impact – supplies could be taken out of the stock being held. With just-in-time methods, little or no stock is held, so the reliability of the supplier is a critical factor.

Just-in-time also has implications for quality. There will not be enough time to check the quality of a product when it is delivered, so it is vital that the supplier provides a product that meets the needs of the consumer.

The Co-operative Group became the first UK business to manufacture its own prescription drugs in China. A spokesman indicated that this was to improve reliability and flexibility, by allowing it 'to have greater control over its supplies'. Many organisations like to guarantee their supplies by owning suppliers. For example, the Co-operative Group is the UK's biggest farmer, and this enables it to supply its own stores.

Flexibility

There may be situations when an organisation needs to make radical changes to its orders from suppliers. Examples include:

- sudden changes in demand for a product
- the liquidation of a rival supplier, leaving buyers short of a product or component
- negative publicity concerning the ingredients or components of a product, or the way in which the product is manufactured
- transport difficulties preventing the delivery of supplies from other sources.

In these circumstances, an organisation will want its suppliers to be flexible enough to adapt to the changing circumstances. For example, a supplier that regularly provides 10,000 components a week may be asked to provide 20,000 components if a crisis has occurred. Although this may not always be possible or expected, any supplier that is flexible enough to cope with such a change will be able to build a good relationship with its buyers. The goodwill earned by the supplier may then enable it to negotiate more favourable terms and/or higher prices in the future.

Organisations like to have **contingency plans** – plans that are used in an emergency. A supplier that can help the business with its contingency plan will be very valuable to the organisation and is more likely to be rewarded with a regular contract.

The need for flexibility is one of the main reasons why many large organisations do not buy all of their materials from one single source, even where one supplier could easily do this. In emergencies, the organisation can then turn to a number of suppliers with which it already has a relationship. This gives the organisation greater flexibility when it finds itself in difficulties.

Conclusion

Different suppliers may provide different benefits to a business. A business buying supplies must weigh up the relative importance of the six factors outlined above, taking into consideration the needs of its customers and the nature of the market for its products, when deciding on its choice of suppliers.

How to manage the supply chain effectively and efficiently and the value of this

Effective management of the **supply chain** enables customers to receive greater satisfaction and businesses to achieve their corporate aims, such as making profit. The effectiveness and efficiency of a supply chain can be measured by its contribution towards the achievement of the firm's operational objectives:

- low costs
- high quality
- speed of response
- flexibility
- dependability
- environmental objectives
- added value.

Traditional approach to supply chain management

'Viking' ('volume is king') is a term used to describe the traditional approach to buying supplies. It is based on the policy of buying huge quantities in order to get the lowest possible price. Typically, businesses defined their role as the provision of one stage of production, such as manufacturing or retailing. The business would try to ensure that supplies were sourced as cheaply as possible and have sufficient quality, but few attempts were made to intervene in the management of the other businesses in the supply chain. However, some businesses did try to manage the whole chain by buying up other businesses within the supply chain. Examples included breweries, which bought hop farms and public houses, and oil companies, which drilled for oil, transported it, refined it and sold the product to end customers.

Modern approach to supply chain management

Many organisations have moved away from this traditional approach, in favour of buying smaller quantities from a number of different suppliers. This alternative approach provides more flexibility and may create competition between suppliers, resulting in improvements in quality. These changes have been a response to shifts in consumers' priorities, from price to quality and flexibility.

Many organisations also require their suppliers to meet environmental standards or social targets. For example, the insurance company Friends Life 'seeks to work with suppliers to improve its environmental and social

Key terms

Supply chain A network of sellers of raw materials, manufacturers that transform those materials into products, and wholesalers and retailers who get those products to customers.

Supply chain management The organisation of these activities to create value for the customer and profit for the businesses involved in supplying the products.

performance'. In this context, social performance is concerned with factors such as how the supplier treats its workers and suppliers.

Fewer businesses are now involved in takeovers of businesses within their supply chain. The tendency now is for businesses to define their core competencies and focus on those aspects of the supply chain, enabling other businesses to focus on other elements according to their core competencies. This approach leads to more efficient supply as every business is specialising in its area of expertise.

Fact file

Food transportation

Professors Jules Pretty and Tim Lang, from City University, London, have published a report which suggests that people should shop for their food locally, from within a 12-mile radius. In the study, the authors calculated that buying all foods locally, within this radius, would result in environmental and congestion costs falling by more than 90 per cent because of the reduction in transportation used.

The UK's big four supermarket chains responded by saying that they were committed to sourcing foods locally and to minimising the environmental impact of food transportation. In a statement, a spokesman for ASDA said: 'Across the UK we have 200 local suppliers, many of which are very small indeed, employing less than 20 people. It is ASDA policy for all its stores to sell more products from the local area – for example, our Cornish stores sell more Cornish products and our Welsh stores stock more Welsh products.'

Source: Adapted from various news sources

Porter's value chain and suppliers

According to Michael Porter in his book *Competitive Advantage* (Free Press, 1985), a business can gain a competitive advantage in one of two ways:

- cost advantage
- differentiation.

Working with suppliers, a business can achieve both of these benefits. It can gain a cost advantage if it is able to find a supplier offering the lowest possible prices. If a supplier is able to provide a unique product or material, then differentiation can also be achieved by the business if its competitors do not have access to that product or material. This differentiation may also be achieved through the supply chain helping to support other key operational objectives. A supply chain based on just-in-time methods can provide speed of response, flexibility and dependability, while a well-managed supply chain can prioritise quality at every stage, if this is the main requirement of the customer.

Practice exercise 3

Total: 35 marks

1 What is meant by the term 'supply chain'? *(2 marks)*

2 What impact does 'sale or return' have on the level of risk for the supplier and the buyer? *(5 marks)*

3 Identify and analyse three ways in which a supplier might help to improve the operational performance of a business that it supplies. *(12 marks)*

4 Evaluate possible reasons why oil companies have tended to keep to a more traditional approach to supply chain management, whereas car manufacturers have adopted the modern approach to supply chain management. *(16 marks)*

Case study: Dell (Part 2)

Although Dell introduced mass customisation to the PC market, in 2007 doubts about its effectiveness were beginning to emerge. The PC market in Europe and North America was beginning to decline. Dell found growth in Asia harder to achieve, because many customers were seeking to buy their first computer. However, Dell's approach to selling relied on the internet, which meant that customers already needed to have a PC to buy a Dell computer.

The competitive nature of the PC market meant that, in 2012–13, the major companies – Dell, HP, Acer and Lenovo – collectively made less profit than one firm – Apple, with its distinctive, high added value approach.

Dell offered many variations of its PCs in order to attract customers. However, this had implications for costs, as each modification added to unit costs. Furthermore, it meant that Dell had a complex supply chain because different items were sourced from different suppliers. Not only did this make it more difficult to manage its suppliers, but it also meant that individual orders were smaller and so Dell was less likely to benefit from economies of scale. Dell's own data told it that only a small percentage of possible PC configurations were wanted by its customers. Dell had always sold its computers based on competitive pricing and customisation and yet both of these elements were becoming more problematic. Furthermore, the company had no real history of innovation and research and development.

Three operational decisions were made by the company:

1 Streamline the degree of customisation offered, in order to reduce costs (this approach had already been taken by many of its competitors). Focus on a strategy of cost leadership through sourcing materials globally and achieving the lowest possible unit costs in the industry.

2 Focus its marketing strategy on selling more goods through normal distribution channels, such as supermarkets and electrical retailers.

3 Shift its focus to delivering specialist services to customers in the IT industry. To achieve this, Dell took over some other companies to acquire cloud computing and software service capabilities and skills.

One area of expertise that Dell has acquired through takeovers is in the field of travel and transportation. Dell's new focus on services has led to a contract with German airline, Lufthansa. Dell will provide maintenance and IT support for Lufthansa's booking systems for the next five years, enabling Lufthansa to focus on its core business.

Dell has turned full circle. From being a business that outsourced assembly and production (which it still does) it has become a business that provides outsourcing services to other firms, such as Lufthansa.

Questions

Total: 40 marks

1 Explain why Dell wanted to simplify its supply chain. *(6 marks)*

2 Analyse the implications for Dell's inventory control as a result of its decision to sell more goods through normal distribution channels, such as supermarkets and electrical retailers. *(9 marks)*

3 Analyse two benefits to Dell from providing outsourcing services to companies such as Lufthansa. *(9 marks)*

4 Was Dell right to choose to focus on a strategy of cost leadership in the PC industry? Justify your view. *(16 marks)*

16 Setting financial objectives

This chapter introduces the financial function of the business. It begins by outlining the value of financial objectives. The objectives and concepts of return on investment and proportion of long-term funding that is debt are explained. The distinction between cash flow and profit and between gross profit, operating profit and profit for year are explained, followed by a discussion of revenue, costs and profit objectives and cash flow objectives. Objectives for investment (capital expenditure) levels and capital structure objectives are then discussed. The chapter concludes with a consideration of the external and internal influences on financial objectives and decisions.

Value of setting financial objectives

Financial objectives must be consistent with a business's corporate objectives and should be constantly reviewed to ensure that the business is financially viable. Constant review will enable the business to ascertain whether the business's financial strategy is working effectively. It might also indicate whether its financial objectives are realistic.

> **Key term**
>
> **Financial objectives** The specific, focused aims or goals of the finance and accounting function or department within an organisation.

Types of financial objective

Managing a business's finances is a complex and varied task. Consequently there are many different types of financial objectives. It may be necessary to balance the conflicting needs of these different objectives, in order to achieve a sound financial performance overall. For example, businesses need to maintain reasonable levels of cash to make regular payments, such as wages to their workers. At times, this may mean that certain activities that are potentially profitable, but also risky, may need to be constrained.

The list below summarises the main types of financial objectives of a business:

1 Revenue objectives
2 Cost objectives
3 Profit objectives
4 Cash flow objectives
5 Objectives for investment (capital expenditure) levels
6 Capital structure objectives
7 Return on investment objectives
8 Objectives relating to debts as a proportion of long-term funding

Objectives 1 to 6 form the basis of this chapter and will be covered in the sections that follow this introduction. Objectives 7 and 8 are more specific and will be covered in this introductory section.

Benefits of setting financial objectives

The benefits of setting financial objectives vary according to the specific objective being considered and a firm's situation. Some major benefits are to:

- act as a focus for decision making and effort
- provide a yardstick against which success or failure can be measured
- improve co-ordination, by giving teams and departments a common purpose
- improve efficiency, by examining the reasons for success and failure in different areas
- allow shareholders to assess whether the business is going to provide a worthwhile investment
- enable outside organisations, such as suppliers and customers, to confirm the financial viability of a business.

However, there are difficulties involved in using financial objectives in these ways.

- It can be difficult to set realistic objectives, particularly for new activities.
- External changes, such as increased competition, may be beyond the control of a business, but may affect its ability to achieve its financial objectives.
- Certain objectives may be difficult to measure accurately.
- Reasons for success or failure may be impossible to determine.
- Responsibility for achievement of objectives may rest with the finance department, but the actual performance will be dependent on the performance of all departments.
- Some financial objectives may conflict with other objectives, both financial and non-financial.

Return on investment

The **return on investment** can be calculated by the following formula:

$$\text{Return on investment (\%)} = \frac{\text{Return on investment*}}{\text{Cost of the investment}} \times 100$$

* Return on investment = Financial gains from the investment − Costs of the investment.

An objective will be set for the return on investment (%) of a particular project, or for the investment to exceed a certain target %, or for it to be higher than the return on investment (%) of an alternative investment.

Key terms

Investment In the context of a business, investment describes items that are purchased by firms because they help them to produce goods and services. These items are often described as capital goods and include items such as machinery, delivery vehicles, factories and offices.

Return on investment A measure of the efficiency of an investment in financial terms, used to compare the financial returns of alternative investments.

The concept of return on investment can be applied to any major expenditure. For example, a business may be planning a new advertising campaign and wants to know if this is a better use of money than the purchase of some delivery vehicles.

● The advertising campaign costs £400,000 and, based on the revenue and costs that it generates, it provides an additional return of £32,000. Its return on investment = £32,000 ÷ £400,000 × 100 = 8%.

● The new delivery vehicles cost £350,000 and generate additional revenue of £700,000. However, costs increase by £670,000, including the £350,000 initial cost. The return on investment of the new delivery vehicles is therefore:

$$\frac{£700,000 - £670,000}{£350,000} \times 100 = \frac{£30,000}{£350,000} \times 100 = 8.6\%$$

Assuming the costs and revenues from these two projects cover the same length of time, and based purely on the return on investment, the purchase of the delivery vehicles is a more efficient use of the business's finance than the advertising campaign. However, the difference is very small and so non-financial factors should be considered when deciding on the choice of investment. If the business is borrowing money at 5 per cent interest, then both of these investments provide a greater return than the cost of borrowing the money. Therefore, it could be argued that both projects should be undertaken because the return on investment exceeds the cost of the investment.

Interpret returns on investment with caution. A closer look at the nature of the two projects is likely to reveal that the new vehicles will pay for themselves over a much longer period of time. If the figures used just cover one year, the new vehicles are more likely to keep generating long-term revenue than the advertising campaign. However, if the figures take into account the full lifetime of each project, then the new vehicles may require higher interest payments, because a longer-term loan will be required to fund this project.

Return on investment is a useful tool for calculating whether investments are profitable. However, in practice it can be difficult to calculate. For example, if sales increased after the advertising campaign, was this solely due to the influence of the advertising campaign? There are so many factors that influence profit, both internal and external, that it is likely that the exact impact of the advertising campaign will only ever be an estimate.

Despite these limitations return on investment should enable a business to recognise:

● the relative financial returns on different investments being undertaken by the business
● trends in financial performances, such as steady increases in returns on its investments
● changing levels of return for certain activities, so that the business can put more money into types of investments that are showing increasing returns
● the total level of investment that it should undertake. This figure could be deduced by undertaking all of the investments that exceed the cost of borrowing money and rejecting those where returns do not cover the cost of borrowing funds. However, because investments involve risk, the business might reject those investments where the expected returns are only slightly higher than the cost of borrowing. There may also be non-financial reasons for or against supporting a project, regardless of its financial return.

Did you know?

Individuals often use the word 'investment' to describe a situation in which they are using their savings to generate money, such as putting them into a bank in order to earn interest, or buying assets and hoping to sell them at a higher price. The financial return on these 'investments' is also described as the 'return on investment'.

What do you think?

Capsule hotels – a great way to get a high return on investment?

Capsule hotels, which offer bedrooms (pods) barely large enough for the bed, date back to 1979 in Osaka, Japan. In Asia, they have become popular in places where space is expensive, such as Tokyo, Seoul and Hong Kong. *Nine Hours*, a Japanese hotel chain, has just opened a 129-pod capsule hotel at Narita Airport in Tokyo. The pods contain a bed, but not much more, although customers can use shower facilities, Wi-Fi, storage lockers and a lounge area.

Capsule hotels are ideal for airport passengers as they can be hired by the hour. Rates at Narita are about £9 for the first hour plus £3 for each subsequent hour. For a whole night the price is £23. The efficient use of space gives a high return on investment. Capsule hotels:

- maximise room availability – instead of one 30 m² room, a capsule hotel can have fourteen 1.6 m² pods (two rows and two layers of 1.8m × 0.9m) capsules with a 1 m aisle.
- maximise revenue – generating twice or three times the revenue per square metre in comparison to a normal hotel room.
- minimise costs – few amenities, low staffing levels and low utility bills.

Businesses such as *Nine Hours* are looking to expand.

Do you think capsule hotels have a possible future in UK airports or places like London?

Debt as a proportion of long-term funding

Long-term funds include share capital (also known as equity), which businesses are not required to repay, as long as they are still operating. It also includes loans, such as bank loans for the purchase of buildings and equipment, which are often repayable after three or more years.

A formula to show this relationship is shown below.

$$\text{Debts as a proportion of long term funding} = \frac{\text{Debts}}{\text{Long term funding}} \times 100$$

If a business's only debt is a five-year bank loan of £4 million and its shareholders' funds are £16 million, then its debts as a proportion of long-term funding is:

$$\frac{\text{£4 million}}{\text{£4 million} + \text{£16 million}} \times 100 = \frac{\text{£4 million}}{\text{£20 million}} \times 100 = 20\%$$

A business must balance its long-term funds between funds provided by shareholders and **debts** arising from loans. Shareholders' funds will, initially, be the money paid to the business when the company's shares were first issued. However, once a business is operating, shareholders will often allow a significant percentage of the profit for year to be retained by the business, for purchasing items such as capital equipment. This will enable the business to expand and become more profitable, and so the shareholders should reap the benefits of this policy in future years because profits will be increasing. Furthermore this policy tends to lead to an increase in the share price as the value of assets within the business increases. Technically, however, the funds provided are the shareholders' funds, as they could have taken them as dividend payments.

Key terms

Debts Money owed by an individual or organisation to another individual or organisation. For example, money borrowed by a business from a bank is a debt, which will need to be paid back to the bank, usually by an agreed date.

Long-term funding Money provided to a business which does not require repayment within a year.

Debts, such as bank loans, present businesses with two potential problems:

- Interest payments on the debts must be paid regularly, in accordance with the schedule agreed with the bank (or organisation providing the money).
- The full amount of the loan must be repaid by an agreed date.

For a three-year bank loan, repayments of the loan and the interest payments are usually scheduled on a monthly basis. Thus, for a 36-month loan, one-thirty-sixth of the total loan and interest payments must be paid, each and every month, for three years. This can create cash flow problems for a business.

In contrast, share capital requires no repayment. Shareholders will expect a dividend (a share of the profit), which is usually paid every six months. However, if a business is in financial difficulty, the dividend can be cancelled or reduced. Of course, if the business is very profitable, then shareholders will expect a dividend that is much higher than the rate of interest charged by a bank. In these circumstances, the business is likely to be able to afford these high dividend payments.

The debt to long-term funding ratio can show the financial health of a company. If the ratio is high or increasing it shows that more of the financing is coming from external providers (known as creditors) than from the company's own resources. On average, in countries such as the UK the expected debt to long-term funding percentage is about 60 per cent. Lenders will be reluctant to lend to a business with very high debt ratios because there is a high risk of default on loans. In recent years, debt ratios have tended to rise because interest rates have been very low and so companies have wanted to borrow more money to take advantage of low repayment costs, but small businesses have found banks reluctant to lend money.

Fact file

BP and Shell

Table 16.1 shows the debt to long-term funding percentages of two of the UK's longest established companies: BP and Shell.

▼ **Table 16.1** Debt to long-term funding (%) for BP and Shell 2009–13

	2009	2010	2011	2012	2013
BP					
Debts ($m)	74,535	92,492	96,328	103,539	102,471
Long-term funding ($m)	176,648	188,383	208,913	223,291	232,878
Debt to LTF (%)	42.2	49.1*	46.1	46.4	44.0
Shell					
Debts ($m)	69,257	72,228	74,849	77,133	83,106
Long-term funding ($m)	207,392	222,008	234,815	253,315	264,254
Debt to LTF (%)	33.4	32.5	31.9	30.4	31.4

* In 2010 BP experienced a major oil leak in the Gulf of Mexico which led to increased debts.

Financial objectives tend to take one of three forms:

- comparison to a standard. For example, BP trying to keep its debt to long-term funding percentage below the standard level of 60 per cent.
- comparison to a competitor. For example, Shell aiming to achieve a percentage that is lower than its main competitor, BP.
- comparison to previous years. Having experienced a sharp increase from 42.2 per cent to 49.1 per cent between 2009 and 2010 it is probable that BP's objective was to reduce their debt percentage over the next few years.

Distinction between cash flow and profit

Cash inflows are the receipts of cash, typically arising from sales of products, payments by debtors (receivables), loans received, rent charged, sale of assets and interest received. **Cash outflows** are payments of cash, typically arising from the purchase of products, payments to creditors (payables), loans repaid or given, rental payments, purchase of assets and interest payments made. **Net cash flow** is the sum of cash inflows to an organisation *minus* the sum of cash outflows, over a period of time.

Profit is calculated by subtracting expenditure from revenue. It is easy to assume that a profitable firm will be cash rich, but this is not necessarily true. Profitable firms may be short of cash for the following reasons:

- If the firm has built up its inventory levels, its wealth will lie in assets rather than cash. These inventories may not be saleable in the short term.
- If the firm's sales are on credit, its wealth will be in debtors (receivables) rather than cash. The firm may have agreed with its debtors that they need not pay for a given time period. Although this helps marketing, it may damage **cash flow**.
- If the firm has used its profit to pay dividends to shareholders or repay long-term loans, it may be short of cash.
- If the company has purchased fixed (non-current) assets, such as a factory or a new IT system, this will have involved a large outflow of cash, but in the accounts the 'cost' of these fixed assets is spread over a number of years. Thus, in the year in which the fixed assets are purchased, the recorded 'costs' will be much lower than the actual loss of cash, leading to a potential crisis. (In practice, major purchases of fixed assets are often supported by loans that are repaid in future years.)

In the long term, a business must make profit in order to survive. A firm that continually records losses will find it difficult to acquire cash, as sales revenue will be lower than expenditure, and creditors and investors will be reluctant to give the firm credit or loans, or buy shares. This could lead to **liquidation**, which means the firm will be forced to close because it must sell its assets in order to make these cash payments. Liquidity is the ability to convert an asset into cash without loss or delay. Firms will want a reasonable level of liquidity, even if this means that they may have to delay profitable projects.

Author advice

Financial objectives come in many forms, so it is not advisable to memorise a specific list. When trying to analyse a business's financial situation, try to work out the financial objectives of the actual business you are studying. This will allow you to focus on the financial objectives most relevant to the particular situation or business concerned.

Key terms

Profit The difference between the total revenue of a business and its total costs. Profit = total revenue minus total costs

Cash flow The amount of money flowing into and out of the business over a period of time.

▲ Major purchases of fixed assets, such as a factory, involve a large outflow of cash

Distinction between gross profit, operating profit and profit for year

Gross profit

Gross profit is revenue minus the cost of sales. The **cost of sales** consists of items of expenditure directly related to the provision of the business's products, such as wages to shop floor workers, raw materials and inventory. The gross profit shows how efficiently a business is converting raw materials into finished products. To some extent, it indicates how well a business is adding value to its raw materials. However, as overheads (administrative expenditure) are excluded from the calculation, it is of limited use as a measure of performance.

Operating profit

Operating profit is profit made from trading (i.e. the main activities of the business). It is gross profit minus administrative expenses. Many analysts regard operating profit as the best measure of a company's performance, because it focuses on the profit (or loss) made from trading and ignores exceptional items that might distort the figures. For example, Table 16.2 below shows that Tesco achieved a sound operating profit in 2013–14, but a relatively weak profit for year. This is because Tesco lost money by selling off some overseas stores for a sum that was below their estimated worth. Selling property at a loss is a one-off item that does not reflect on Tesco's main trading activity as a supermarket.

Profit for year

This is the profit available to the owners (shareholders in a limited company). Profit for year includes all revenue, including 'non-trading' revenue, such as sales of assets, and all expenditure, including finance costs (such as interest payments on loans) and taxation. Occasionally, this can be misleading because a business may make a lot of money by selling an asset that it owns or lose money from selling a loss-making division. The latter decision is likely to improve operating profits in the future, but is shown as a loss in the year in which it happens. Because the figure is shown after tax it is not comparable to the other two measures of profit.

Profit for year is a useful measure for shareholders, because it shows how much they benefit from their ownership of the business. It will help existing and potential shareholders to judge whether the company is a good place to put their money.

Calculating measures of profit

Table 16.2 below shows how these measures of profit are calculated. In Chapter 19 we will examine ways in which profits can be increased.

▼ **Table 16.2** Financial data for selected supermarkets for the financial year ending in 2014

	Extracts from company income statements	Tesco plc Year ending: 22 Mar 2014	J Sainsbury plc Year ending: 15 Mar 2014	W M Morrison plc Year ending: 2 Feb 2014
1	Revenue (£m)	63,557	23,949	17,680
2	Cost of sales (£m)	(59,547)	(22,562)	(16,606)
3	Gross profit (£m)	4,010	1,387	1,074
4	Administrative expenses (£m)	(1,379)	(378)	(1,169)
5	Operating profit (£m)	2,631	1,009	(95)
6	Net finance and one-off items (£m)	(1,314)	(111)	(81)
7	Taxation (£m)	(347)	(182)	(62)
8	Profit for year (£m)	970	716	(238)

Notes

Figures in brackets show deductions or costs.

Gross profit (Row 3) = Revenue (Row 1) *minus* Cost of sales (Row 2)

Operating profit (Row 5) = Gross profit (Row 3) *minus* Administrative expenses (Row 4)

OR Operating profit = Revenue *minus* Cost of sales *minus* Administrative expenses

Profit for year (Row 8) = Operating profit (Row 5) *minus* Net finance and one-off costs (Row 6) *minus* Taxation (Row 7)

OR Profit for year = Revenue *minus* All expenditure *minus* Taxation.

One-off items can be a positive figure if a business has gained revenue from selling off assets.

Table 16.2 shows that Tesco made the highest levels of gross profit, operating profit and profit for year, mainly as a result of its much larger sales revenue. Not only is Tesco the largest supermarket in the UK, but it also has more overseas operations too. However, the figures show that Sainsbury's seems to have much better control of its administrative expenses and so its operating profit was 73 per cent of its gross profit, higher than Tesco (at 66 per cent).

The clearest conclusion was that 2013–14 was a bad year for Morrison's, because it experienced an operating loss (negative profit) of £95 million and its loss for the year was £238 million.

Revenue, costs and profit objectives

Revenue objectives

These tend to take three major forms:

- **Sales maximisation**: maximising sales volume or sales value (revenue).
- **Targeting a specific increase in sales revenue**: for example, setting an objective of 5 per cent growth in sales revenue or reaching sales of £2 million per annum.

- **Exceeding the sales of a competitor**: for example, Sainsbury's and Asda tend to compete to achieve the second highest level of supermarket sales in the UK; EE, which comprises Orange and T-Mobile, competes with O$_2$ and Vodafone to have the highest mobile phone network sales in the UK.

To achieve these objectives businesses will mainly rely on their marketing mix. For example:

- Lowering prices will invariably lead to an increase in the quantity demanded and so sales volume will rise. Use of the other elements of the marketing mix, such as new promotions or improvements in process, can also help to achieve this objective.
- If a business is aware of the price elasticity of demand for its products it might be able to increase sales revenue (by lowering the price if demand is price elastic or by increasing the price if demand is price inelastic). This increase in sales revenue might enable the business to reach its specific revenue objective.

Cost objectives

Cost minimisation means achieving the lowest possible unit costs. A business that reduces its unit costs can benefit in two ways:

- it can keep its price the same and benefit from a higher profit margin
- it can use its cost reduction to reduce the selling price of its finished product and so attract more customers.

Examples of cost minimisation objectives:

- **Achieving a certain cost reduction in the purchase of raw materials**. A business might try to lower raw material purchase costs by 10 per cent, for example, by locating cheaper suppliers overseas, such as in China.
- **Reducing wage costs per unit**. This may be done by improving the productivity of labour or reducing the level of overtime payments.
- **Lowering levels of wastage**. This saves costs by reducing the usage of raw materials or the number of items of finished products that are discarded.
- **Relocating a business to the 'least-cost site'**. Unit costs should be reduced if a business relocates to a place where wages and rents are lower; however, this is not a guarantee as productivity may be lower in low-cost locations.
- **Reducing the cost per thousand customers (CPT) of a business's promotion and advertising**. The internet and electronic communications are more popular than traditional forms of media, such as newspapers and television, because they are targeted more effectively and are a more cost-effective way of promoting products.
- **Improving the efficiency of production by reducing variable costs per unit**. This might be achieved through introducing new technology and just-in-time methods of production.

Targets based on cost minimisation must be used with caution. Cheaper raw materials may be of inferior quality and this in turn can reduce the quality of the finished products. Lower quality may be acceptable for customers seeking the lowest possible price, but for many customers lower quality would be unacceptable. If cost minimisation has adverse side-effects, it may not be an appropriate objective.

Fact file

Porter's generic strategies

According to Michael Porter, firms must try to achieve a 'sustainable competitive advantage'. This is an advantage that can be maintained in the face of sustained competition. Porter's theory suggests that there are two main approaches that can achieve this advantage:

- cost leadership
- differentiation or value leadership.

The first of these two approaches can be achieved by a business keeping its costs below those of its rivals, producing standard mass-produced products of an acceptable standard at a much lower cost than its competitors. In the UK, Poundstretcher, Asda and Lidl are examples of businesses using this strategy.

To adopt this strategy it is vital that costs are minimised. Asda has been helped in this strategy by its parent company, Wal-Mart, which is the world's largest supermarket. Wal-Mart has tremendous buying power and is able to keep its costs to a minimum, which helps Asda's competitiveness.

Profit objectives

The importance of profit was analysed in Chapter 1. Ultimately, objectives to increase revenue and reduce costs are set because they help to improve a business's level of profit.

Objectives for profit will apply to gross profit, operating profit and profit for year. As outlined earlier, each measure of profit shows the success (or failure) of a business's financial performance or aspects of that performance.

Profit targets usually take a similar form to revenue targets:

- **Profit maximisation**: maximising gross profit, operating profit and profit for year.
- **Targeting a specific increase in profit**: for example, setting an objective of a 10 per cent growth in profit or reaching a profit of £1 million per annum.
- **Exceeding the profit of close competitors**: for example, in the UK, Vauxhall might aim to make more profit than Ford and Volkswagen.

Fact file

Profit versus profitability

Comparing levels of profit with competitors can be unrealistic because there may be no business of comparable size in its market. For example, Vauxhall is in second place in the UK market for sales of cars. However, in 2013, Ford (in first place) sold 51,000 more cars than Vauxhall, while Vauxhall sold 65,000 more cars than Volkswagen, which was in third place. To allow for these discrepancies in size, business often set **'profitability'** objectives, rather than profit objectives. Profitability is an approach that examines the size of a company's profit in comparison to the size of the company. Profitability will be studied in Chapter 17.

In practice, profit maximisation is a difficult target to set, because it is hard to know if it has been achieved. Furthermore, it can conflict with other corporate objectives, such as fair treatment of workers and suppliers. The fact file on profit versus profitability illustrates that for some firms aiming for a larger profit than competitors may not be an ideal profit objective. Consequently, many firms focus on an objective to increase profit in comparison to previous years. Table 16.3 shows the profit levels of selected supermarkets in the financial years 2012–13 and 2013–14.

Measure of profit	Tesco plc		J Sainsbury plc		W M Morrison plc	
Year	2012–13	2013–14	2012–13	2013–14	2012–13	2013–14
Gross profit (£m)	4,154	4,010	1,277	1,387	1,206	1,074
Operating profit (£m)	2,382	2,631	882	1,009	949	(95)
Profit for year (£m)	24	970	602	716	647	(238)

If all three supermarkets were aiming for an increase in all three measures of profit between 2012–13 and 2013–14, then only Sainsbury's achieved its objectives, with all three profit measures increasing by more than £100 million. Tesco may want to examine why its gross profit margin fell, but its operating profit showed a steady increase, and there was a major improvement in profit for year, which would have pleased its shareholders. It does appear that this may be more a reflection of a poor performance in 2012–13, rather than a very good performance in 2013–14. The gross profit figure is consistent with a business using price cuts to get more customers, thus increasing profit through higher volume.

Morrison's figures are a cause for concern, especially the fall in operating profit in comparison to gross profit. This suggests poor control of overheads. Morrison's reacted to this loss by cutting prices, disposing of its loss-making Kiddicare subsidiary and going into an online venture with Ocado, because it had not matched its competitors in selling groceries online.

Cash flow objectives

Many businesses get into financial difficulties because of a lack of cash flow rather than a lack of overall profitability. Consequently, it is vital that businesses set themselves cash flow objectives to ensure that they are able to keep operating.

Examples of cash flow objectives:

- **Maintaining a minimum closing monthly cash balance**. For example, a minimum cash balance of £10,000 would be a sensible objective for a small newsagent.
- **Reducing the bank overdraft by a certain sum by the end of the year**. For a new start-up it is likely that an overdraft will be needed to support everyday expenses, which can be quite high in the opening few months of the business. However, it is not advisable to maintain a permanent bank overdraft, so reducing the overdraft would be an appropriate objective for such a business. The business might set an objective of paying off the bank overdraft by a certain date.
- **Creating a more even spread of sales revenue**. To avoid cash flow problems a business may set an objective to create a more even spread of sales revenue throughout the year. For example, one reason why Mars Ltd introduced the Mars Ice Cream was because sales of chocolate fall in the summer months. This strategy means that it is less likely that Mars Ltd will become short of cash in the summer months.
- **Spreading costs more evenly**. A business may pay its utility bills, such as gas and electricity, on a monthly basis rather than quarterly or once every six months.

Author advice

More detailed analysis of cash flow and methods of improving cash flow are provided in Chapters 17 and 19 of this textbook.

Key terms

Depreciation The fall in value of an asset over time, reflecting the wear and tear of the asset as it becomes older, the reduction in its economic use or its obsolescence.

Obsolescence When an asset is still functioning but is no longer considered useful because it is out of date.

Fact File

BP

In 2013, BP spent $24,520 million on capital expenditure. During that year, the value of its fixed (non-current) assets increased from $176,469 million to $195,310 million. This represented an increase of $18,841 million in its capital stock and $5,679 million required for replacement capital.

In 2012, BP spent $23,222 on capital expenditure. However, because of factors such as depreciation, its overall capital stock fell from $181,742 million to $176,469 million. Investment expenditure does not guarantee an increase in capacity for a business because fixed (non-current) assets wear out or lose their worth.

- **Achieving a certain level of liquid, non-cash items**. Many businesses set an objective of holding certain assets, such as short-term investments or stock. If the business does run low on cash, it can turn these assets into cash quickly.
- **Raising certain levels of cash at a particular point in time**. If the business knows through its cash flow forecasts that it needs to acquire a higher level of cash at a certain time (for example, a retailer building up stock levels for Christmas), it may set an objective of raising a particular level of cash.
- **Setting contingency fund levels**. Most businesses set an objective for a contingency fund, which is an emergency source of finance that can be used if unexpected difficulties occur.

Objectives for investment (capital expenditure) levels

In the section on 'Return on investment' (pages 331–333) we saw that business investment is expenditure on capital goods, i.e. items such as machinery that allow the business to increase its future production.

Two types of investment can be recognised:

- Replacement capital/investment – this investment is intended to replace assets that have depreciated (worn out). Replacement capital is not, therefore, adding to the stock of capital goods.
- New investment – this is expenditure on new capital goods that enables a business to increase its capacity to produce.

Overall, a business's objective for capital expenditure (investment) will be determined by these two factors. In general, a business will need to replace any capital that has depreciated. The business must then decide on how much new investment it requires.

For example, if a business has £100 million worth of capital and its annual depreciation is 10 per cent of this figure its replacement investment will be £10 million (10 per cent of £100 million). If it is planning production growth of 5 per cent then it will need £5 million of new capital equipment (5 per cent of £100 million). Thus its objective for total investment will be £10m + £5m = £15 million.

In practice, a business's total investment will consist of lots of individual items of capital expenditure. Businesses will only decide on individual investments which help the businesses to achieve their other objectives, such as increasing operating profit. Therefore investment objectives will depend on the likelihood of making good returns on investment. (In Year 2, we look at 'investment appraisal', which examines this topic in detail.) There are a number of factors that will influence these investment decisions.

Factors influencing investment decisions and objectives

- **Expected return on investment**. As we saw earlier, businesses will only invest in projects if expected returns are satisfactory.
- **Interest rates**. Rises in interest rates increase the cost of borrowing money and therefore may lead to businesses deciding that certain investment projects are not financially worthwhile.

- **Expected demand**. If a business expects demand for its products to be high in the future, then it is more likely to undertake capital expenditure because this will enable it to increase its capacity to produce.
- **Levels of technological change**. New technology can lead to obsolescence, or machinery becoming out of date more quickly. Therefore, replacement investment will need to increase so that new machinery is introduced on to the production line.
- **Availability of finance**. If a business is unable to get access to sufficient finance to fund new equipment, then it will need to cut back on its capital expenditure.
- **Business confidence**. Levels of spending on capital equipment depend on what businesses expect to happen in the future. If business decision makers are confident that growth will occur, then investment in capital expenditure will increase.
- **Attitude to risk**. Because the benefits of capital expenditure depend on future events, investment tends to involve potentially high risk. People who are prepared to take risks are more likely to decide on high levels of capital expenditure.
- **Level of spare capacity**. If a business has high levels of spare capacity, it will not need to spend on investment in new equipment. However, a business with a shortage of capacity is likely to need to spend on investment in new equipment so that it can match supply to demand.
- **Nature of production**. If production is capital intensive the new equipment will be needed to cope with increases in demand. If production is labour-intensive then new capital equipment will not be so necessary, instead the business will need to focus on recruiting more workers. However, in this case, it might be necessary to invest in new training programmes for the workforce.
- **Competitors' actions**. The benefits of new investment will be affected by competitors' strategies. Therefore, decisions on whether to purchase new items of capital expenditure will need to take into consideration the expected actions of rival companies.

Did you know?

Chapter 2 discussed the nature of limited liability for the shareholders of public and private limited companies. Limited liability not only limits the risk shareholders bear but also encourages limited companies to take risks – risks that help innovation and growth and which thus help the economy to grow.

Capital structure objectives

Businesses are funded by a combination of debt capital and equity capital.

Debt capital consists of borrowed funds. Primarily, these funds are likely to be bank loans, although they may be in the form of debentures. **Debentures** are used when external sources provide funding to a business in return for regular fixed interest payments and an agreed repayment date. Usually debentures are for a long period of time, such as ten years or longer. In return for the loan the debenture holder gets a certificate which can be sold on to another person or organisation. The owner of the debenture certificate receives the repayment at the agreed time.

Equity capital is provided by shareholders. Shareholders receive a dividend (their share of the profit) every six months. Usually shareholders will agree that some of the profit should be retained by the business. This is likely to increase the value of the business and therefore shareholders should gain because the price of their shares will rise.

A business will take into consideration two major factors when deciding on its ideal capital structure and consequently its capital structure objective.

- Businesses should match their capital structure to the timings of outflows and inflows of cash brought about by their investment plans. For example, a business seeking to finance the takeover of another business will experience a significant outflow of cash in the short term and then steady inflows, from the profits made, over a very long period. This will require the use of capital that will not be repaid for a long time – probably equity capital, but possibly a long-term debenture. On the other hand, the purchase of assets that will pay for themselves within two years is best financed by a bank loan repayable over the next two years.
- Businesses should balance the cost of their financing with the level of risk involved. Debt capital has potential risks, because it has to be repaid, but generally interest rates will be lower than dividend payments. Equity capital is less risky but can lead to higher payments if shareholders vote for high dividends. Also, selling extra shares spreads ownership and can increase the risk of take-over. Existing shareholders may not favour the issue of new shares, because any profits made will be shared amongst more shareholders.

Conclusion

A common capital structure objective is to set a target for the **debt to equity ratio**. This is a 'ratio' that is expressed as a ratio. For example, a business has share capital of £50 million. If it sets an objective of a 1.2 : 1 debt to equity ratio then it should have £1.20 of debt for every £1 of equity (share capital). This means it should aim to have debt capital of £60 million.

The calculation:

Debt : Equity gives an answer of £60m : £50m

This can be simplified by dividing both sides of the equation by £50m, giving a debt to equity ratio of 60/50 : 1 or **1.2 : 1**.

External and internal influences on financial objectives and decisions

Financial objectives should take into consideration external factors (such as the economy) and internal factors (such as a business's resources).

External influences on financial objectives

Chapter 3 discussed the external environment and its effect on costs and demand and included reference to PESTLE, a mnemonic used to classify the various external factors that can influence a business.

For each of the PESTLE factors *one* example of its influence on financial objectives is provided below.

Examples of external factors influencing financial objectives

Political factors

Financial objectives are often guided towards the wishes of the shareholders. However, greater openness has also led to expectations on businesses to serve the needs of other stakeholder groups, including the workforce, customers, the local community and the environment.

Economic factors

The state of the economy is a major influence on the financial performance of businesses. For example, if an economy is in recession, customers will purchase fewer products and so lower sales and profit targets will be set. For businesses dealing in luxury products, it is likely that these targets will be significantly lower. For some businesses, such as those selling staple foods, there will be only a limited effect.

Social factors

Society is constantly changing and businesses must adjust to suit society. People now expect access to businesses 24/7 if possible. This change in expectations can make it difficult for businesses to set targets that involve lower costs, but at the same time it opens up opportunities for targeting greater revenue and creating new ways of generating income.

Technological change

Technological change can lead to improvements in communication. A particular benefit is that financial targets can be monitored more regularly and more closely, and objectives or strategies modified in the light of changing circumstances.

Legal factors

In some industries, legal requirements have a big impact on the objectives of a business and changes in these requirements will lead to modified financial objectives. For example, in the motor industry, frequent updates in environmental legislation, covering both the manufacturing process and the end product, have increased the costs of manufacturing a car.

▲ Legislation is an important consideration in the motor industry

Environmental factors

Growing environmental awareness among consumers and actions by pressure groups have financial implications for businesses. Acquiring supplies and raw materials from environmentally friendly sources is now an aim for many businesses as they try to minimise their carbon footprint.

Other external factors that can influence financial objectives relate to the actions of other businesses, which are not part of the PESTLE model, are described below.

Market factors

The demand for certain types of product goes through cycles of expansion and decline, closely related to the life cycle for that type of product. When a product reaches maturity, high levels of profit will become the main financial objective for that specific product.

Competitors' actions and performance

Level of competition is also an influence on a firm's financial objectives. In recent years, the prices of utilities, such as gas and electricity, have increased substantially, because suppliers have been able to take advantage of the relatively limited levels of competition in those markets. Consequently, utility suppliers have been able to target and achieve very high levels of profit.

Suppliers

Suppliers can have a major impact on a business's financial objectives. The Co-operative Society (Co-op) is one of the UK's major farmers and supplies its shops with food products, particularly from its dairy farms. However, although this has provided the Co-op with a regular supply of food, this food is not among the cheapest in the UK and is more expensive than farm produce from some other countries. As a consequence, this has had an adverse effect on the Co-op's ability to set and achieve high profit targets.

Internal influences on financial objectives

Internal factors that affect financial objectives are those within the business, such as its workforce, resources and financial position.

Business objectives

The overall aims of an organisation are a key influence on the objectives of a functional area, such as the finance department. The finance department must ensure that its objectives are consistent with the corporate objectives of the business. For example, Aldi is aiming to increase customer numbers and trying to get customers to spend more on each visit to the store. This required the finance department, in co-ordination with the other functional areas, to set objectives focused on higher profit margins and a wider range of products.

Finance

There is a saying that 'money makes money'. A business in a healthy financial situation is in a much better position to achieve high levels of profits and cash flow. It can fund investment into items such as research and development, new technology and marketing campaigns that may help it to improve its overall financial performance.

Consequently, such a business can set more challenging objectives. For example, the high levels of profit achieved by Microsoft have enabled it to spend considerable sums of money on researching and developing new software so that it can stay ahead of competition. These high profits also enabled Microsoft to diversify into other areas of potential, such as computer consoles.

Human resources (HR)

Achieving financial objectives depends on the efforts and skills of the workforce. Effective planning of the workforce and a good recruitment and training policy can enable a business to increase its profitability, by increasing the efficiency of the workforce.

However, there can be conflict between the needs of the workforce and the business's financial objectives. Cost minimisation is a particular case in point. Workers may resist measures that might endanger their own jobs, such as the introduction of a new IT system or objectives that require unit costs to be cut by making workers extend their hours without additional pay.

Operational factors

The finance department relies on each of the other functional areas in order to reach its objectives. If the operations management function of the business is operating efficiently, the firm will be able to produce goods

of high quality and low cost. This combination will lead to good sales revenue and high profit margins and enable the business to achieve quite challenging financial objectives.

Available resources

A business which, over time, has built up a strong resource base will be able to target and achieve a strong financial performance. These resources might be in the form of premises, well-known brand names or the quality of its workforce.

Nature of the product

The success of a business is heavily influenced by its products and services. In many cases, successful businesses happened to be in the right place at the right time. Some of the most successful companies in the UK in recent years have been the mobile phone networks. However, as the market has reached maturity, companies such as EE and Vodafone have needed to devise innovation or extension strategies to reach their financial objectives. With continued rapid changes in mobile communications technology, it is by no means certain that the mobile phone, in its current form, will retain its popularity. However, with the increasing demand for mobile communication it may evolve into something even more desirable.

Practice exercise 1

Total: 55 marks

1 Which one of the following is not a type of financial objective?
   a) Capital expenditure objectives
   b) Cost objectives
   c) Productivity objectives
   d) Revenue objectives   *(1 mark)*

2 A business spends £50,000 on a project that increases its total profit from £10,000 to £15,000. The rate of interest is 2%. What is the return on investment (%)?
   a) 8%   **b)** 10%   **c)** 28%   **d)** 30%   *(1 mark)*

3 Explain two reasons for setting financial objectives.   *(6 marks)*

4 Explain one possible difficulty of setting financial objectives.   *(4 marks)*

5 Analyse possible reasons why a profitable firm might suffer from cash flow problems.   *(9 marks)*

6 Explain two possible disadvantages of prioritising cost minimisation as a major financial objective.   *(6 marks)*

7 Explain why it is important to have cash flow objectives.   *(5 marks)*

8 Why is investment in capital goods important for a business?   *(4 marks)*

9 Explain why spare capacity might influence a company's capital expenditure objective.   *(4 marks)*

10 State three **external** factors that might influence financial objectives.   *(3 marks)*

11 State three **internal** factors that might influence financial objectives.   *(3 marks)*

12 Analyse two reasons why shareholders might prefer a capital structure objective that increases debt rather than increases equity capital.   *(9 marks)*

Case study: Google and Apple

▼ Table 16.4 Data on capital structures of Google and Apple

	2012	2013
Google		
Debt capital ($m)	7,746	7,803
Equity capital ($m)	93,798	110,920
Long-term funding ($m)	101,544	118,723
Apple		
Debt capitial ($m)	19,312	39,793
Equity capital ($m)	137,522	163, 350
Long-term funding ($m)	156,834	203,143

▼ Table 16.5 Extract From Apple Financial Statements – 2014 (1st quarter only)

Financial objective	Targeted achievement	Actual achievement
Total revenue ($m)	$55 billion	$57.6 billion
Gross profit	$20 billion	?
Gross profit (%)	?	37.9%

▼ Table 16.6 Financial performance of Google (2011–13)

	2011 ($ million)	2012 ($ million)	2013 ($ million)
Revenue	37,905	50,175	59,825
Cost of sales	(13,188)	(20,505)	(25,824)
Gross profit	24,717	29,670	34,001
Administrative expenses	(13,085)	(16,910)	(a)
Operating profit	11,632	12,760	(b)
Net costs of finance, one-off costs and tax	(1,895)	(1,972)	(1,752)
Profit for year	9,737	10,788	12,214

Source: Apple Annual Report 2014 (http://investor.apple.com/financials.cfm); Google Annual Reports, 2011, 2012 and 2013 (http://investor.google.com)

Questions

Total: 45 marks

1 Use Table 16.6 to answer the following question: In 2011 how much profit was available to Google's shareholders?

   a) $37,905 million

   b) $24,717 million

   c) $11,632 million

   d) $9,737 million   *(1 mark)*

2 Using Table 16.4, calculate the debt to equity ratio of Apple in 2013.   *(2 marks)*

3 Using Table 16.4, calculate the debt to long-term funding (%) of Google in 2013.   *(3 marks)*

4 Explain one possible reason for the significant increase in Google's 'cost of sales' between 2011 and 2013.   *(4 marks)*

5 Explain one possible reason why Apple's debts have risen so dramatically between 2012 and 2013.   *(4 marks)*

6 Analyse two possible reasons why the debt to long-term funding ratios are so low for these two businesses.   *(9 marks)*

7 Based on the data in Table 16.5, calculate Apple's targeted gross profit (%) for the 1st quarter of 2014.   *(3 marks)*

8 Based on the data in Table 16.5, calculate Apple's actual gross profit in $billions for the 1st quarter of 2014. *(3 marks)*

9 Use Table 16.6 to calculate Google's operating profit for 2013. *(2 marks)*

10 Use your answer to question 9 and Table 16.6 to calculate Google's administrative expenses for 2013. *(2 marks)*

11 Assume that Google had targeted 15 per cent increases in its revenue and profit levels between 2012 and 2013. To what extent was Google's financial performance a success in 2013? Justify your view. *(12 marks)*

17

Analysing financial performance

This chapter begins by examining budgets: how to construct budgets, how to analyse budgets and the value of budgeting. It then focuses on cash flow forecasts: how to construct cash flow forecasts, the value of cash flow forecasting, and how to analyse the timings of cash inflows and outflows. The concept of break-even is then studied, looking at the key aspects of break-even, how it is calculated and how break-even charts are constructed and interpreted. This section concludes by examining how to calculate and illustrate on a break-even chart the effects of changes to price, output and cost, and assessing the value of break-even analysis as a technique. The chapter then introduces the concept of profitability and how to analyse it using ratio analysis. The concluding section of this chapter outlines the use of data for financial decision making and planning.

How to construct budgets

> **Key terms**
>
> **Budget** An agreed plan establishing, in numerical or financial terms, the policy to be pursued and the anticipated outcomes of that policy.
>
> **Budgeting** The process involved in setting a budget.

Types of budget

- **Income budget**: shows the agreed, planned income of a business (or division of a business) over a period of time. It may also be described as a revenue **budget** or sales budget.
- **Expenditure budget**: shows the agreed, planned expenditure of a business (or division of a business) over a period of time.
- **Profit budget**: shows the agreed, planned profit of a business (or division of a business) over a period of time.

Income budgets

The income budget should be linked closely to the marketing targets of a business. It is important to split this up into its component parts so that a detailed analysis of the sources of income can be seen. In a business providing a range of goods and services, it is feasible for sales of one product to be predicted to grow rapidly, while sales of another product are predicted to fall. By considering sales of each item individually, the business is more able to forecast expenditure accurately too.

The income budget should also include other sources of income, such as any rent received.

Expenditure budgets

Expenditure budgets are usually more complex than income budgets because many different items of expenditure are needed to produce a good or service. Costs that may be found in an expenditure budget include:

● raw materials/components
● labour costs
● marketing expenditure
● administration costs
● rent
● capital costs.

For a new business or project it is often useful to create a separate expenditure budget, known as a **capital budget**. This shows the items that must be budgeted for in these circumstances. These items of expenditure include:

● construction costs
● premises
● furniture and office equipment
● vehicles
● insurance
● legal costs.

This kind of expenditure budget is useful because it helps to estimate the level of risk involved in a new venture.

Profit budgets

Profit budgets are the result of income and expenditure budgets. They must be scrutinised carefully to ensure that a business is planning activities that are financially viable. Ideally, all budgets should be planned over a minimum period of 12 months. For profit budgets this is especially important because most businesses have periods of high and low sales and expenditure during the year. It is therefore best to make an overall assessment of profit after a completed year. However, constant review is always required to ensure that problems are not emerging.

Constructing budgets

Budgets are usually stated in terms of financial targets, i.e. relating to money allocated to support the organisation of a particular function. However, they also include targets for income, output, sales volume and profit. Budget holders will try to exceed targets for income and profit budgets, but to stay below the planned target for an expenditure budget. For large-scale construction projects, such as building a new factory, a capital budget will be allocated. This will exist only for the period it takes to complete the project.

Budgets should incorporate an element of flexibility. If changes in circumstances indicate that a sales budget is over-optimistic, adjustments can be made to reduce the related expenditure budget. If the newly

▲ Large–scale construction projects will have a capital budget

calculated budget target for profit is acceptable to managers of the business, the plans can still be implemented.

The stages of constructing a budget are shown in Figure 17.1. It should be noted that constructing a budget is not a one-way process – results from one stage may lead a business to reconsider or recalculate an earlier stage. Furthermore, the process may need to be repeated every time the budgeting process is reviewed. This may be annually, quarterly, monthly, weekly or even daily.

▲ **Figure 17.1** Stages of constructing a budget

In stage 1, it is vital to establish the business's targets before getting into detailed examination of any budgets. Research into costs, in stage 3, requires scrutiny of wage levels and the cost of materials and any items of equipment that the business is planning to purchase. Although the government's predicted inflation rate can be useful in estimating future costs, it is not always reliable and does not help to predict individual cost changes (see 'Did you know?').

The greater the number of divisions/departments in a business, the greater the number of budgets required for stage 7. There will also be some budgets that operate centrally, such as capital budgets (to plan expenditure on major assets such as building and machinery or a project, as described earlier).

Did you know?

Government data on price rises is often used to forecast costs for budgets. However, it is not always reliable for predicting individual costs. In the eight years between January 2006 and January 2014, UK prices on average rose by 27 per cent. However, some prices/costs, such as fuel and energy, rose much more. In this period petrol prices rose by 48 per cent, electricity prices increased by 62 per cent and gas prices doubled (a 100 per cent rise).

Completing budgets

The following examples, which cover a period of only one month, are provided to illustrate the process of completing a budget.

Income budget

As a general rule, it is sensible for a business to start by completing an income budget because most items of expenditure will depend on the level of sales that are budgeted.

The data below show the budgeted sales for ABC Ltd for January 2017:

- Product A — sales of 100 units at a price of £32 each
- Product B — sales of 80 units at a price of £15 each
- Product C — sales of 30 units at a price of £60 each

Table 17.1 shows the budget arising from these targets.

▼ **Table 17.1** Income budget for ABC Ltd, January 2017

Source of income	Income (£)
Product A	3,200
Product B	1,200
Product C	1,800
Total income	**6,200**

Expenditure budget

The expenditure budget is based on these levels of sales. For example, if raw material costs are budgeted at one-quarter of the selling price of each product, we can estimate that raw materials will cost £1,550 (a quarter of £6,200). Similarly, if labour costs are £10 per unit, regardless of whether product A, B or C is being produced, then labour costs will be £2,100 (100 + 80 + 30) = 210 units × £10.

Table 17.2 shows estimates for expenditure, including these figures of £1,550 for raw materials and £2,100 for labour costs.

▼ **Table 17.2** Expenditure budget for ABC Ltd, January 2017

Item of expenditure	Expenditure (£)
Raw materials	1,550
Labour costs	2,100
Marketing expenditure	150
Administration	450
Rent	750
Capital costs	0
Total expenditure	**5,000**

Profit budget

profit = income − expenditure

Therefore, the profit budget is constructed by taking the income budget and subtracting the expenditure budget. Table 17.3 shows the result.

▼ Table 17.3 Profit budget for ABC Ltd, January 2017

Item of income/expenditure	£
Total income	6,200
Total expenditure	5,000
Budgeted profit	**1,200**

Amending budgets

What happens if the finances are budgeted to change? Consider the following scenario. ABC Ltd is planning a large marketing campaign in February 2017. This will lead to:

- a trebling of marketing expenditure
- a 50 per cent increase in sales of products A and C
- a 10 per cent increase in sales of product B and an increase in price of product B to £25.

The business also expects a fall in rent to £700 per month but no change in administration costs and capital costs.

Labour costs will still be £10 per product and raw material costs will still be a quarter of sales income.

Tables 17.4–17.6 show the resulting budgets for February 2017.

▼ Table 17.4 Income budget for ABC Ltd, February 2017

Source of income	Amendment	Income (£)
Product A	150 × £32	4,800
Product B	88 × £25	2,200
Product C	45 × £60	2,700
Total income		**9,700**

▼ Table 17.5 Expenditure budget for ABC Ltd, February 2017

Item of expenditure	Amendment	Expenditure (£)
Raw materials	25% of £9,700	2,425
Labour costs	283 × £10	2,830
Marketing expenditure	3 × £150	450
Administration	No change	450
Rent	Falls from 750	700
Capital costs	No change	0
Total expenditure		**6,855**

▼ Table 17.6 Profit budget for ABC Ltd, February 2017

Item of income/expenditure	£
Total income	9,700
Total expenditure	6,855
Budgeted profit	**2,845**

How to analyse budgets

Variance analysis

An important aspect of budgeting is monitoring and reviewing the actual outcomes in comparison with the budgeted figure (the target). Differences between budgeted and actual figures are known as **variances**. **Variance analysis** is an essential element of budgetary control.

Calculating variances

A variance is calculated by the following formula:

variance = budget figure − actual figure

Thus a **favourable variance** is shown when:

- actual revenue is greater than budgeted revenue
- actual costs are below the budgeted costs.

An **adverse** (or **unfavourable**) **variance** is shown when:

- actual revenue is less than budgeted revenue
- actual costs are above budgeted costs.

For variance analysis, it is best to use 'F' for favourable variances and 'A' for adverse variances, rather than positive or negative numbers.

Example calculations

1 An expenditure budget allocates £2,000 for stationery expenses, but the actual amount spent is £2,200.

   £2,000 − £2,200 = (£200) A

   This is an *adverse variance* because costs are £200 higher than the budget and so, other things being equal, the profit will be £200 less than budgeted.

2 An expenditure budget allocates £23,000 for wages, but the actual amount paid in wages is £22,200.

   £23,000 − £22,200 = £800 F

   This is a *favourable variance* because wages are £800 lower than the budget and so, other things being equal, the profit will be £800 more than budgeted.

3 An income budget targets sales income of £56,000, but the actual amount of income received is £55,000.

   £56,000 − £55,000 = £1,000 A

   This is an *adverse variance* because revenue is £1,000 lower than the budget and so, other things being equal, the profit will be £1,000 less than budgeted.

4 An income budget targets sales income of £73,000, but the actual amount of income received is £74,800.

   £73,000 − £74,800 = (£1,800) F

Key terms

Variance analysis The process by which the outcomes of budgets are examined and then compared with the budgeted figures. The reasons for any differences (variances) are then found.

Favourable variance When costs are lower than expected or revenue is higher than expected.

Adverse (unfavourable) variance When costs are higher than expected or revenue is lower than expected.

Author advice

The simplest way to remember the difference between a favourable and an adverse variance is as follows:

- A **favourable** variance will mean **more profit** than expected.
- An **adverse** variance will mean **less profit** than expected.

This is a *favourable variance* because revenue is £1,800 higher than the budget and so, other things being equal, the profit will be £1,800 more than budgeted.

5 A profit budget targets a profit of £15,000, but the actual profit is £14,100.

£15,000 − £14,100 = £900 A

This is an *adverse variance* because the profit is £900 less than budgeted.

6 A profit budget targets a profit of £34,000, but the actual profit is £37,000.

£34,000 − £37,000 = (£3,000) F

This is a *favourable variance* because the profit is £3,000 more than budgeted.

Did you know?

Alternative names for an income budget are revenue budget or sales budget. Similarly, an expenditure budget may be described as a cost budget.

Author advice

Use the terms 'favourable' (F) and 'adverse' (A) rather than plus or minus signs when calculating variances. The use of a plus or minus sign can be confusing because, if the actual revenue is higher than the budgeted revenue, this is good for the business. However, if the actual costs exceed the budgeted costs, it is bad for the business. As variance analysis ultimately attempts to look at the overall effect of variances on the budgeted profit, it is more logical to use F (favourable) for any variance that is likely to increase profit and A (adverse) for any variance that is likely to decrease profit in comparison with the budgeted figure. Overall, adding all the Fs and subtracting all the As will give the change in profit.

Using variance analysis to assess performance and inform decision making

Example

Table 17.7 shows the variances in the revenue and costs of a fictitious company, Sceptre Paints, a division of HBH Chemicals.

▼ **Table 17.7** Budget variances for Sceptre Paints

	Budgeted income/ costs (£m)	Actual income/ costs (£m)	Variance (£m)	
Sales of emulsion paint	480	495	15	(favourable)
Sales of gloss paint	220	206	14	(adverse)
Total sales	**700**	**701**	**1**	**(favourable)**
Raw material purchases	50	56	6	(adverse)
Tins and packaging	14	14	0	
Manufacturing costs	88	75	13	(favourable)
Wages and salaries	240	251	11	(adverse)
Administration	96	100	4	(adverse)
Marketing	42	33	9	(favourable)
Distribution and warehousing	31	26	5	(favourable)
Other costs	27	27	0	
Total costs	**588**	**582**	**6**	**(favourable)**
Profit/loss	**112**	**119**	**7**	**(favourable)**

After calculating variances a budget holder will need to interpret their meaning. Adverse variances may indicate *inefficiency* and areas where the business has made mistakes. They may also indicate that *external influences*, such as changes in the market, have made it more difficult for a business to meet its targets.

A similar logic applies to favourable variances. Favourable variances may show efficiency, indicating that the business has operated well. They may also show that external influences, such as the state of the economy, have made it easier for a firm to meet its targets.

According to Table 17.7, the income of Sceptre Paints shows a favourable variance of £1 million and the costs show a £6 million favourable variance, so overall there is a favourable variance on profit of £7 million. These variances can be interpreted as follows:

- Sales overall show little difference; it is cost savings that have caused most of the favourable variance. The biggest saving has been in manufacturing costs. The business might have automated its production line or improved efficiency in some way.
- Marketing has kept within budget. Although this is a favourable variance, it may have unfavourable results if it leads to low sales. However, the sales figures do not appear to indicate a problem, despite a fall in sales of gloss paint.
- Distribution and warehousing expenditure is below budget too. Has the firm delivered in larger batches? Are warehousing costs lower because of lower stock levels? The policies in this part of the business have made significant savings and are worth investigating to see if other divisions can benefit from using the same policies or approaches.
- Although the overall variance is positive, Sceptre Paints should look closely at raw material costs, wages and salaries, and administration, as these are over budget. There may be valid reasons, such as the use of better-quality materials, but the variances could indicate unnecessary spending in these areas.
- Finally, Sceptre should look at its sales revenue to see if the reasons for the good performance of emulsion paints can be applied to gloss paints.

The interpretations of the variances in the example of Sceptre Paints are merely suggestions. In practice, a budget holder should be aware of all possible variances and will then be in a reasonable position to explain why they have happened.

Value of budgeting

Reasons for setting budgets

Budgets serve a number of purposes:

- **To gain financial support**. A well-reasoned business plan, incorporating clear budgets that indicate a good chance of success, is vital in persuading potential backers to invest in a start-up business. The quality of a budget can therefore be critical because without it a new business may never get started. This is one of the reasons why detail is so important in a budget — the more detail it contains, the more reassurance there is for financial backers looking for a carefully planned business venture.

- **To ensure that a business does not overspend**. Careful control of budgets will ensure that a firm's finances do not worsen unexpectedly, as a result of a failure to limit spending to agreed levels.
- **To establish priorities**. A budget is a plan for the future. Allocating a large budget to an activity can indicate the level of importance attached to a particular policy or division, sending a clear message to stakeholders such as employees and customers.
- **To encourage delegation and responsibility and to motivate staff**. Budgets allow local or junior managers to become budget holders and make decisions on spending in areas of a business in which they are more knowledgeable than senior managers. This improves the quality of the decisions and acts as a motivator for the budget holder.
- **To assign responsibility**. The budget holder is the person who is directly responsible for any success or failure. This makes it much easier to trace mistakes or recognise to whom credit should be given. Budget control can be included in the appraisal of a manager's work.
- **To improve efficiency**. Businesses can monitor and review budgets and are able to establish standards and investigate the causes of any successes and failures. They can use this information to improve future decisions. The discipline of working to a limited budget encourages managers to seek more efficient methods.

Fact file

Cobra Beer

Karan Bilimoria, creator of Cobra Beer, believes that careful budgeting is essential and a potentially great motivator.

'I will always remember the time in Bangalore – where Cobra was first brewed – when I prepared a spreadsheet. It was a 5-year target detailing month by month the exports of containers. For any company it is always a question of not only looking 5 years ahead but also breaking those 5 years down into achievable bite-size chunks and targets you can go for. The [income budgets] were ambitious but we managed to beat them all in the end.'

Problems of setting budgets

Setting budgets involves a number of potential pitfalls.

- **Managers may not know enough about the division or department**. In this case they will find it difficult to plan a reasonable budget. This problem is particularly acute for new firms or new ventures.
- **Problems in gathering information**. For a start-up business, it can be very difficult to get financial information from other firms. As a consequence, initial budgets may contain large elements of guesswork and therefore lack accuracy.
- **Unforeseen changes**. Predicting the future is always difficult and unforeseen changes will undermine the budgeting process.

- **Level of inflation (price rises) is not easy to predict**. Businesses tend to use the average inflation rate, but some prices can change by much greater levels. Farmers have been hit by falling prices, but property prices have gone up by more than most other prices.
- **Budgets may be imposed**. A key principle of budgeting is that the budget holder should be involved in setting the budget level. Unfortunately, budgets are often set by senior managers who may misunderstand the needs of a certain area. The resulting budget may appear to be unfair, causing resentment and reducing morale. On the other hand, a budget determined solely by the manager responsible may ignore potential scope for efficiency gains and fail to take account of developments outside that area of the business. Ideally, both the senior manager and the budget holder should find the time to discuss the budget fully, but this does not always happen.

Features of good budgeting

- **Consistent with the aims of the business**. This ensures that managers cannot use the company's finances for projects to boost their own careers or interests, rather than meeting the needs of the company.
- **Based on the opinions of as many people as possible**. Setting and using a budget is not an exact science and different people will be able to provide different ideas and expertise. Asking as many people as possible should help the budget holder to come up with a realistic set of targets.
- **Challenging but realistic targets**. As with any SMART objective (see Chapter 1), the budget set must be achievable, but only if staff demonstrate a reasonable and expected level of effort and skill in order to reach the target.
- **Monitored at regular intervals, allowing for changes in the business and its environment**. Budgeting allows a business to improve by identifying situations in which targets are being missed or exceeded. In the former case, remedial action can be taken to improve performance. In the latter case, the reasons for beating a target should be looked at, so that other parts of the business can benefit from the good management or work that is taking place. The more often a budget is monitored, the more quickly these actions can take place.
- **Be flexible**. Although budgets should have a set target, it is crucial that the budgeting process allows for changing circumstances. If a budget allocation is clearly inadequate, because of unforeseen circumstances, it may be necessary to adjust it to a more realistic level.

Practice exercise 1

Total: 15 marks

1 What is meant by the term 'variance analysis'? (*2 marks*)

2 What is the difference between a favourable variance and an adverse variance? (*4 marks*)

3 Explain two reasons why an adverse variance might not be a sign of poor management by the budget holder. (*9 marks*)

Practice exercise 2

Total: 10 marks

Tables 17.8–17.10 show an example of a budget for a social event at a university.

▼ **Table 17.8** Income budget for social event

Income	Price (£)	Number	Total (£)
Dinner tickets	25.00	100	2,500.00
Entertainment tickets	10.00	45	450.00
Total			**2,950.00**

▼ **Table 17.9** Expenditure budget for social event

Expenditure (incl. VAT)	£
Publicity	75.75
Dinners	1150.00
Welcome drinks	165.00
PA and lighting	276.25
Band	880.00
Sub-total	2,547.00
+ Contingency 10% of subtotal	254.70
Total	**2801.70**

▼ **Table 17.10** Profit budget for social event

Income	£2,950.00
Expenditure	£2,801.70
Profit	£148.30

1 Rewrite the budget, taking into account the changes listed below:

● Ten students have asked to switch from 'entertainment tickets' to 'dinner tickets'.

● The expenditure budget changes to take into account the 10 extra dinner tickets sold and the 10 extra welcome drinks that are provided to dinner ticket holders.

● The band has negotiated a 5 per cent increase in its fee.

● Publicity costs have fallen to £55.55.

Case study: Frank Roseland, dairyman and newsagent

Frank had taken over the family milk delivery business from his father in 2014. Frank found it difficult to work out whether the business was operating successfully, as his father had not kept very good financial records.

Frank needed to set a budget to see whether to continue the business. He needed to make at least £35,000 annual profit to make it worthwhile. He sifted through the records that his father had kept and was surprised to find out how many newspapers and groceries his father had delivered alongside the milk.

Frank also asked for advice from one or two other dairymen. They said that although the milk delivery industry had declined steadily over the previous 35 years it was beginning to stabilise. They also explained that sales were fairly consistent throughout the year, but with some seasonal variations. They indicated that it was normal for milk to be sold at a price that was 60 per cent higher than the cost of

purchase (although this made the price much higher than supermarket milk), while newspapers were sold at a price that was 33 per cent higher than their cost. Some, but not all, groceries could be sold for double the cost paid, as anyone buying the products from Frank's business was saving the delivery charges imposed by supermarkets.

Frank's father's records indicated that, although total sales had grown recently, sales of milk and newspapers were falling each year. All of the growth was coming from groceries. Many of his customers were elderly people living in rural areas and they bought a lot of groceries from Frank.

Frank's original attempt at budgeting had not worked out too well. Fortunately, he had reviewed his income and expenditure budgets for the first few months. This had shown him that milk sales were falling slightly faster than he had expected, mainly because a new supermarket had opened on one of the estates to which he delivered. However, this bad news was offset by the results of conversations with customers, who said that they valued his deliveries highly and would be prepared to pay much higher prices.

Frank's milk supplier told him that a competitor, who had charged higher prices, had retired. By increasing his marketing in the area previously served by this competitor, Frank was able to boost milk sales considerably, more than offsetting the decline in customers caused by the opening of the supermarket. Frank also discovered he could sell milk at a price that was 67 per cent higher than the cost of purchase, rather than the 60 per cent he had originally budgeted. Newspaper sales were declining as more people now got news online.

Frank realised that the future of the business depended on more growth coming from groceries. Towards the end of the first year, he had contacted some local farm shops and offered a delivery service for their products. One farmer responded and, although the farmer charged high prices for

them, they proved to be very popular with Frank's customers. In the last two months of the year, grocery sales started to rise dramatically, mainly because of the fresh products from the farmer.

Frank had underestimated the workload involved in running the business. After only two months he decided to employ a part-timer who would collect the newspapers and groceries early in the morning and deliver them to customers. At first, Frank was worried about this decision because it meant that he had to buy another van. However, towards the end of the year, the dramatic increase in grocery sales meant that the second van was used a great deal, as the part-time employee was making far more deliveries.

Frank had been carrying out variance analyses at the end of each month. At the end of the year, Frank sat down and compared his first yearly budget (2015) with the actual outcomes. Frank also set an amended budget for 2016. The results are presented in Tables 17.11–17.13.

▼ **Table 17.11** Income budget and actual income for Frank Roseland

| Source of income | 2015 | | 2016 |
	Budgeted income (£000s)	Actual income (£000s)	Budgeted income (£000s)
Milk	192	225	240
Newspapers	20	15	14
Groceries	42	51	73
Total income	**254**	**291**	**327**

▼ **Table 17.12** Expenditure budget and actual expenditure for Frank Roseland

| Item of expenditure | 2015 | | 2016 |
	Budgeted expenditure (£000s)	Actual expenditure (£000s)	Budgeted expenditure (£000s)
Supplies of milk	120	135	144
Newspaper purchases	15	12	11
Grocery purchases	25	30	40
Wages	18	24	24
Refrigerator rental	3	3	3
Marketing expenditure	0	4	2
Motor expenses	16	20	24
Administration	10	11	10
Capital costs	0	6	6
Total expenditure	**207**	**245**	**264**

▼ **Table 17.13** Profit budget and actual budget for Frank Roseland

Item of income/expenditure	2015		2016
	Budgeted profit (£000s)	Actual profit (£000s)	Budgeted profit (£000s)
Total income	254	291	?
Total expenditure	207	245	?
Profit	**47**	**46**	**?**

Questions

Total: 40 marks

1 The budgeted profit for 2016 is:

   a) £19,000

   b) £36,000

   c) £45,000

   d) £63,000 *(1 mark)*

2 The variance for the 2015 expenditure budget is:

   a) £19,000 – favourable

   b) £19,000 – adverse

   c) £38,000 – favourable

   d) £38,000 – adverse *(1 mark)*

3 What is meant by the term 'profit budget'? *(2 marks)*

4 The actual outcomes in 2015 were very different from the budgets that Frank set. To what extent was this due to Frank's inexperience in setting budgets? Justify your view. *(16 marks)*

5 Evaluate the overall usefulness of budgeting and variance analysis in helping Frank to manage the finances of his business. *(20 marks)*

Case study: Budgeting the Eden Project

The Eden Project is an example of a large-scale capital project that managed to be completed without an excessive adverse variance from the projected

budget. Many large-scale building projects exceed their capital budgets by considerable sums. The Channel Tunnel and the Millennium Dome are both examples of projects that actually cost more than twice the sum originally estimated.

In contrast, operating budgets (estimates of sales revenue and plans for day-to-day spending on running the business) tend to be much more accurate. Firms find this type of budget much easier to estimate, although ironically the Eden Project's operating budget for its first year was less accurate than its capital budget. With visitor numbers much higher than expected, the actual sales revenue was 2.5 times the budgeted figure and the £9 million actual wage bill was more than double the £4 million budgeted figure.

Table 17.14 summarises the main budget headings for the construction of the Eden Project.

▼ **Table 17.14** Eden Project: budgeted and actual costs of construction

	Budgeted cost (£m)	Actual cost (£m)
Purchase of site and car parks	10.0	10.0
Reshaping the ground	5.0	8.0
Construction of greenhouses (biomes)	20.0	25.0
Soil and plants, including nursery	6.0	5.5
Buildings and exhibits	19.0	19.0
Services to keep it running	6.0	7.0
Design, engineering, legal advice etc.	6.0	9.0
Wages and training prior to opening	2.0	2.5
Total	**74.0**	**86.0**

Originally, the Eden Project was to be funded by grants from the Millennium Commission (50 per cent), the European Union and various regional organisations, and by loans. When it was realised that there would be an 'over-spend' on the original budget, the Millennium Commission agreed to increase its grant from £37 million to £43 million. The site was opened to visitors before its final completion and visitor numbers were so high (160 per cent higher than the 'best-case' prediction) that the Eden Project found it easy to raise the remaining £6 million needed to pay the actual costs.

Construction work began in October 1998, in a disused china clay quarry the size of 35 football pitches. However, there were unexpected problems, as nobody had ever undertaken such a project before. Matters were complicated by 43 million gallons of water raining into the quarry in the first three months, forcing the builders to halt construction for these three months. Fortunately, specialist help from consultants overcame these problems and the project was completed on schedule in March 2001.

Source: Eden Project website (www.edenproject.com)

Questions

Total: 35 marks

1 What is meant by the term 'budget'? *(2 marks)*

2 Identify one favourable variance from Table 17.14. *(1 mark)*

3 Calculate the variance between the total budget and the total actual costs as a percentage of the budgeted cost. *(3 marks)*

4 Explain one reason why firms find it easier to estimate revenue budgets than capital budgets. *(4 marks)*

5 Analyse two factors that caused the actual expenditure for setting up the Eden Project to exceed the budgeted figure. *(9 marks)*

6 To what extent did the Eden Project benefit from the time spent on its budgeting? *(16 marks)*

How to construct cash flow forecasts

Cash flow cycle

The **cash flow** cycle is the regular pattern of inflows and outflows of cash within a business.

The pattern of inflows and outflows of cash in a business is shown in Figure 17.2.

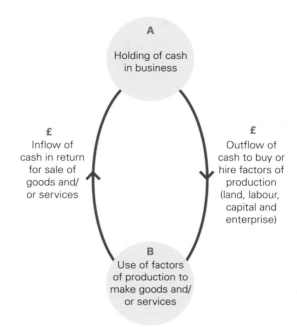

▲ **Figure 17.2** Cash flow cycle

It can be seen that cash leaves the business between A and B and then flows back into the business between B and A. There is, therefore, a delay between **outflows** of cash and **inflows** of cash. This means that it is in the nature of business activity that a typical business will suffer cash flow problems. The extent to which this is a problem will depend on a number of important factors:

- **Amount of cash held at the beginning of the cash flow cycle**. It is vital for a start-up to have an initial holding of cash from outside the business so that it can survive the difficulties presented by the cash flow cycle. This is the most critical stage for a business because there will be a delay before revenue is received from the sale of goods and yet considerable expenditure is needed to purchase the factors of production. This is particularly the case if fixed assets, such as buildings and equipment, are needed to get the business up and running. Even well-established businesses are subject to the difficulties presented by the cash flow cycle, because products must usually be made before revenue is received from selling them. Consequently, the issues presented by the cash flow cycle are continuous challenges facing any business.

- **Length of time required to convert inputs into outputs**. If a product or service can be produced quickly, the cash flow cycle may not create problems for a business. For example, a baker may buy the ingredients at the beginning of the day, bake the bread and sell it all within the same working day. However, this does not overcome the difficulties that the baker might have faced in purchasing the ovens and other equipment necessary for the business. Some products can take a long time to construct. House builders, for example, are vulnerable to cash flow difficulties because considerable expenditure must be incurred before it is possible to put the house on to the market and receive revenue.

- **Credit payments**. The analysis so far has assumed that all transactions use cash. In practice, a business may receive credit from its suppliers. In this case, payment for the factors of production may actually take place *after* cash has been received from a customer in return for finished goods or services. Therefore, the cash flow cycle does not cause problems for the business. However, cash flow may be worsened if the business needs to give credit terms to its customers in order to boost sales. This will lead to a further delay in the receipt of cash and therefore cause greater problems with the cash flow cycle.

Fact file

Cash flow and phone networks

It is not just small or new businesses that face cash flow difficulties. In 2000 the government earned £22.5 billion selling 3G licences to the mobile phone networks. The networks made this massive expenditure because each network was desperate to be the first one to offer 3G, which enabled phones to get internet connection. These high bids led to cash flow problems for all of the major mobile network providers. In 2013, bids for new 4G licences only raised £2.3 billion, because the networks had learned from their experience with 3G licences and put in much lower bids. Even so, the licence costs (Vodafone paid £791 million) and the high initial costs of upgrading networks have had a significant impact on their holdings of cash. Investing in technology can cause cash flow problems.

Key term

Cash flow forecasting The process of estimating the expected cash inflows and cash outflows over a period of time. Cash flow is often seasonal, so it is advisable to forecast for a period of one year.

Constructing a cash flow forecast

A cash flow forecast attempts to predict the future. As predicting the future is not an easy task, constructing an accurate cash flow forecast may be quite difficult.

In order to compile a **cash flow forecast**, a business uses a number of sources:

- previous cash flow forecasts
- cash flow statements – this is a description of how cash flowed into and out of a business during a recent particular period of time
- consumer research
- study of similar businesses, such as competitors
- banks
- consultants
- the cash flow forecast itself – it is important that early drafts of the cash flow forecast are used to build up the final forecast. If an early draft indicates a difficulty, such as a shortage of cash at a particular time, then the business can take steps to rectify this problem.

Structure of a cash flow forecast

The details of cash flow forecasts vary according to the type of business. However, the key items in constructing a cash flow forecast are described here:

- **Cash inflows**. This item usually contains details of income from sales. The timing of the entry depends on when the cash is received, so although cash sales are shown on the date that the sale is expected, goods that are expected to be sold on 60 days' credit terms in February will be shown as forecast cash receipts in April. Other cash inflows may be for items such as rent received, money borrowed in the form of loans and sales of assets.
- **Cash outflows**. Many items of expenditure could be included here. Raw materials, wages, rent and bills for utilities such as electricity will all need to be forecast. However, some of the difficulties involved in cash flow forecasting occur when a business fails to recognise the imminent need for major items or one-off payments, such as a new vehicle, extra machinery or a tax bill.
- **Net cash flow**. The formula for net cash flow is:

  net cash flow = cash inflows − cash outflows

  This shows the monthly situation and will help the business to foresee months when cash shortages may occur.

- **Opening balance and closing balance**. A company that starts a year with a cash surplus may be able to survive months with negative net cash flows. The final elements in constructing a cash flow forecast are to show the opening cash and closing cash balances. The formula for the closing balance is:

  closing cash balance = opening cash balance + net cash flow.

Note: In a cash flow forecast, the closing balance for one time period is the opening balance for the next time period.

A simplified cash flow forecast is set out in Table 17.15.

▼ **Table 17.15** Cash flow forecast (£) for Gideon Prewett's Pottery, January–June 2017

	Jan	Feb	Mar	Apr	May	Jun
Sales (Total inflows)	2,000	3,600	5,000	3,300	3,750	5,000
Materials	4,000	1,500	1,100	1,150	1,500	1,800
Wages and other costs	3,700	2,620	2,620	2,770	2,620	2,620
Total outflows	7,700	4,120	3,720	3,920	4,120	4,420
Net monthly balance	(5,700)	(520)	1,280	(620)	(370)	580
Opening balance	6,000	300	(220)	1,060	440	70
Closing balance	300	(220)	1,060	440	70	650

In order to construct a cash flow forecast, the business must gather data on all of the likely flows of cash into and out of the business over a period of time. A year is the most sensible choice, because for most businesses there will be some seasonal changes that can lead to significant changes in cash inflow (or cash outflow) at particular times of the year. For the sake of simplicity, we will construct a cash flow forecast that covers July, August and September 2017 for Gideon Prewett's Pottery.

Author advice

Organisations will often choose their own way of laying out a cash flow forecast. Table 17.15 is one example of a layout but you will certainly come across alternative ways of presenting such information. However, all cash flow forecasts must contain information on cash inflows and cash outflows and the opening balance of cash.

As long as you remember the formulae for net cash flow and closing cash balance, you will be able to understand any cash flow layout.

The data needed to forecast the business's cash flow for July to September 2017 are as follows:

- Sales income is expected to be £6,600 in July and £7,000 in August, but to fall to £6,000 in September.
- Materials will cost £2,000 per month in July and August, but only £1,600 in September.
- Wages and other costs will be £2,770 in July but £2,620 in August and September.

Putting these data into a cash flow forecast gives us the information shown in Table 17.16.

▼ **Table 17.16** Cash inflows and cash outflows for Gideon Prewett's Pottery, July–September 2017

	Jul	Aug	Sept
Sales (Total inflows)	6,600	7,000	6,000
Materials	2,000	2,000	1,600
Wages and other costs	2,770	2,620	2,620
Total outflows			
Net monthly balance			
Opening balance			
Closing balance			

Remember total outflows = materials + wages and other costs, so we can insert the total outflows figures for each month.

The 'opening balance' for July 2017 is the same as the closing balance for June 2017 (Table 17.15 shows this to be £650).

We can now complete the remaining gaps using the following formulae:

net monthly balance = total inflows − total outflows

closing balance = opening balance + net monthly balance

The completed cash flow is shown in Table 17.17.

▼ **Table 17.17** Completed cash flow forecast for Gideon Prewett's Pottery, July–September 2017

	Jul	Aug	Sept
Sales (Total inflows)	6,600	7,000	6,000
Materials	2,000	2,000	1,600
Wages and other costs	2,770	2,620	2,620
Total outflows	4,770	4,620	4,220
Net monthly balance	1,830	2,380	1,780
Opening balance	650	2,480	4,860
Closing balance	2,480	4,860	6,640

Value of cash flow forecasting

Why businesses forecast cash flow

Liquidity is the ability to convert an asset into cash without loss or delay. The most liquid asset that a business can possess is cash. All firms, however profitable, must manage their cash and their working capital (which includes those items that can be converted into cash most easily) to guarantee their survival. Thus, in the short term, a business must manage its cash flow in order to remain liquid.

Cash flow forecasts are important to a business because they enable it to foresee times in the future when the business will be short of liquidity. If shortages are anticipated far enough in advance, the business may be able to take measures to prevent the shortage from occurring.

The main benefits of forecasting cash flow are described below.

- **Identifying potential cash flow problems in advance.** The forecast can detect if current plans are going to lead the firm into a situation in which it cannot meet payments. This might involve a lack of funds at the end of the month to pay the wage bill or a shortage of cash when a tax bill is due.
- **Guiding the firm towards appropriate action.** Once a potential problem has been identified, action can be taken to overcome the difficulty. The problem may be solved by a change of plans, such as not extending the office accommodation, if this was one of the decisions that led to the predicted cash shortage.
- **Making sure there is sufficient cash available to pay suppliers and creditors and to make other payments.** By studying the cash flow forecast, the organisation can plan inflows of cash in time to make payments that might have been difficult to meet. Usually, this will mean arranging financial help such as a bank overdraft for a temporary cash shortage or a long-term loan for equipment purchase.
- **Providing evidence in support of a request for financial assistance (e.g. asking a bank for an overdraft).** The cash flow forecast should show the bank manager why help is needed, but it must also indicate how the overdraft can be repaid. An overdraft is intended to cover short-term problems, so the forecast must show that, eventually, the firm will be able to pay back the overdraft.
- **Avoiding the possibility of the company being forced out of business (into liquidation) because of a forthcoming shortage of money.** It is estimated that as many as 30 per cent of all companies that go into liquidation fail because they cannot get hold of cash, rather than because they are unprofitable. Profitable companies must check that they have cash, rather than having all their profit tied up in stock or buildings.
- **Identifying the possibility of holding too much cash.** This probably means that a firm has less machinery and stock than it could possess, which means it has less production and stock to sell, and so it makes less profit. Although this is perhaps less of a problem than a cash shortage, it is not wise for a firm to have too much cash.

Problems associated with cash flow forecasting

- **Changes in the economy.** Changes in economic growth or unemployment levels might mean that consumers have less (or more) spending power. If unemployment is higher than expected, sales of most goods will be lower than predicted. Changes in inflation may affect both costs and sales revenue.
- **Changes in consumer tastes.** In a dynamic environment, customers often change their opinions. This happens in all markets but is a major peril in fashion and technologically advanced markets.

▲ Changes in taste can make forecasting difficult in the fashion industry

Key terms

Receivables People who owe the business money, usually customers who have been given credit terms. Receivables are also known as **debtors**.

Payables People who are owed money by the business, usually these are suppliers awaiting payment, but they may be traders who have supplied services, such as gas, electricity and telephone systems. Payables are also known as **creditors**.

● **Inaccurate market research**. The research might target the wrong group of consumers, there might be interviewer bias in the questions or the sample might be too small. All these factors could lead to an incorrect sales forecast.

● **Competition**. New competitors may enter the market or a rival may be aiming to increase its market share. Competitors' actions cannot be predicted but will affect the business's level of success. (It is also possible that unsuccessful competitors will mean that the firm's predicted sales are lower than its eventual sales.)

● **Uncertainty**. Estimates of costs for new firms or major projects are often incorrect. Start-ups, in particular, often have problems forecasting cash flow because they lack experience of how the market works. Consequently, new businesses are much more likely to come across unexpected expenses than a well-established firm.

Overall, the value of the process of cash flow forecasting to a particular firm will be influenced by the balance of benefits and problems in the firm's particular circumstances. However, significant benefits are also gained from analysis of the timings of cash inflows and outflows. This is dealt with in the next section.

How to analyse timings of cash inflows and outflows

It is vital for a business to keep sufficient cash in order to pay its everyday expenses, such as utility bills, wages and materials. However, businesses will possess assets that can be turned into cash quickly, such as inventories of finished products, but also have situations which will lead to cash outflows in the near future, such as a bill that is almost due for payment. Consequently, management of cash flow also requires sound management of these types of items. These items determine a firm's **working capital**. Constant analysis of a business's working capital will enable it to improve its cash flow.

The working capital of a firm provides an indication of the firm's scope to pay its short-term debts. This is because it includes a firm's most liquid assets (the current assets), but excludes non-current assets, such as property, which may take a long time to sell.

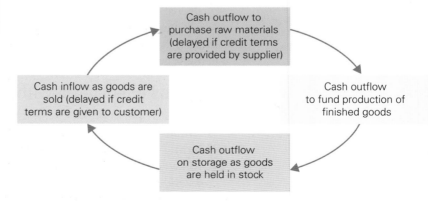

▲ **Figure 17.3** The working capital cycle

The length of the working capital cycle is calculated by studying the three main elements of working capital:

- inventories
- receivables
- **payables**.

The formula is:

length of working capital cycle = length of time that goods are held as inventories + time taken for **receivables** to be paid – period of credit received from suppliers (payables).

Here is an example of calculating the working capital cycle:

- Goods are held as inventory for an average of 14 days.
- Receivables are given 30 days to pay, on average.
- Suppliers (payables) give the firm 28 days to pay for the supplies that they purchase.
- The working capital cycle is: 14 + 30 – 28 = 16 days.

In effect, the company has to wait 16 days after it has paid for its supplies of materials to make its goods before it receives payment from the sale of its goods.

From a cash flow perspective, the ideal working capital situation for a business will be:

- holding low levels of inventory that sell very quickly
- receivables paying their debts to a business very quickly
- payables allowing a business a long period of time in which to pay for the items supplied.

However, a number of factors will influence these situations.

Factors influencing the length of the working capital cycle

Length of time that goods are held as inventories

A range of factors affect the number of days that inventories are held:

- **Nature of the product**. Items such as clothing that must be displayed in order to entice customers require higher inventory levels than those that do not need display.

- **Durability of the product**. Companies try to have lower levels of inventories of perishable items or finished products that may become unfashionable.
- **Efficiency of suppliers**. If suppliers can supply large quantities at short notice, a business will be able to hold lower inventory levels.
- **Lead time**. If it takes a long time to make a product, companies will be more likely to hold finished products as inventory.
- **Customer expectations**. If the customer is prepared to wait, it may be unnecessary to hold inventories; if the customer wants the item immediately, inventories should be held.
- **Competition**. A business needs to match its rivals, so inventory levels are influenced by the policies of competitors.

Fact file

How much working capital?

At certain times of the year, a business must possess a higher than usual level of working capital. This is because it must hold sufficient liquid assets to pay outstanding short-term liabilities, such as dividends to shareholders and corporation tax to the government.

▲ Clothing stores require higher inventory levels

369

Time taken for receivables to be paid

Factors that lead to delay in receiving payment will lead to cash flow problems.

- **Nature of the market**. Commercial products (sold to other businesses) are usually sold on credit, with 28 or 30 days being common credit periods.
- **Type of product**. Expensive, durable items such as vehicles, white goods and electrical products are often offered on credit. Smaller, everyday items are normally paid for immediately.
- **Bargaining power**. The offer of credit may depend on the relative bargaining power of the supplier and the buyer. A large supermarket may demand (and get) a credit period from a small supplier that is desperate for the contract. A small supermarket may be forced to pay immediately for supplies from a major supplier such as Coca-Cola. Tesco was successful in demanding two months' credit from its suppliers instead of the original one month credit.

Period of credit received from suppliers (payables)

The longer the period of credit offered to the business, the better it is for the business because it means payment can be delayed. The factors influencing the credit period are the same as those listed above. However, the impact on the business is exactly the opposite because in this case the firm is the receivable (debtor). Any factor that enables payments to suppliers to be delayed improves cash flow.

Conclusion

Analysis of a business's cash flow and its working capital should enable it to anticipate possible problems and thus take action to prevent cash flow shortages in both the short term and the medium term. If unexpected problems occur, analysis of the timings of cash inflows and outflows should enable the business to identify the cause and plan appropriate action to rectify the problem. Methods of improving cash flow are dealt with in Chapter 19.

Practice exercise 3

Total: 33 marks

1 Which of these formulae is correct? Net cash flow equals:
   a) Opening balance + Cash outflows
   b) Closing balance – Cash inflows
   c) Cash inflows – Cash outflows
   d) Opening balance – Closing balance

   (1 mark)

2 Which one of these items is a cash inflow to a business?
   a) Wages
   b) Capital costs
   c) Dividends received by shareholders
   d) Rent from property owned by the business

   (1 mark)

3 Draw a diagram to show the cash flow cycle.

   (4 marks)

4 Explain the meaning of the term 'cash flow forecast'. *(2 marks)*

5 Explain two problems that a firm might have when trying to predict its cash flow. *(8 marks)*

6 What is meant by the term 'liquidity'. *(2 marks)*

7 Calculate the working capital cycle based on the following information:
   a) Goods are held in stock for 23 days.
   b) Debtors are given 15 days to pay.
   c) Creditors give the firm 28 days to pay. *(3 marks)*

8 Analyse how control of receivables and payables might overcome a firm's cash flow problems. *(9 marks)*

9 Why is it sensible for a firm to make sure that its level of working capital is not too high? *(3 marks)*

Case study: Fun for Kids Ltd

Siu Wan decided to set up Fun for Kids because she had found it difficult to find a safe place for her young children to play. Although she had no business experience she believed that she understood what children wanted from a play centre. She discussed her plans with friends and asked them whether they would use the play centre that she planned. She used their replies to forecast likely sales. She has found ideal premises with an outdoor play area and knows the rent of the property. A meeting with her bank manager gave her some ideas on how much her other costs would be.

Fun for Kids was set up with enough capital to purchase the lease and convert the warehouse and grounds into an exciting and colourful play park, with rides and attractions ideally suited to young children. The business would commence trading on 3 May 2016.

Fun for Kids anticipates an opening balance of £16,500 in its bank account on 3 May. Siu has agreed an overdraft facility with the bank manager that will allow the business to overdraw its bank account up to a maximum of £11,600. The business will pay the annual rental in two instalments.

Siu is planning a major, £7,500 marketing campaign in the opening month (May). The main target market is local families. However, the business is located in a seaside resort and so Siu hopes to attract tourists in July and August. She is planning a further marketing campaign in June and July to attract tourists. Currently, all sales will be for immediate cash, but Siu is considering offering one month's credit to her customers. She thinks sales will increase by 10 per cent if she offers credit.

371

▼ **Table 17.18** Cash flow forecast for Fun for Kids' first year of trading.

	2016: Quarter 2 (£000s)	2016: Quarter 3 (£000s)	2016: Quarter 4 (£000s)	2017: Quarter 1 (£000s)
Total inflows (sales)	39.3	69.8	48.0	50.5
Wages	19.0	23.6	15.2	15.2
Rent	30.0	0	30.0	0
Marketing costs	9.7	4.9	0.9	0.9
Other costs	6.6	6.6	6.6	6.6
Total outflows	65.3	35.1	52.7	22.7
Net inflows/outflows	(26.0)	(a)	(4.7)	27.8
Opening balance	16.5	(9.5)	25.2	20.5
Closing balance	(9.5)	25.2	20.5	(b)

Questions

Total: 40 marks

1 Look at Table 17.18. What are the missing values in the cash flow forecast at (a) and (b)? *(2 marks)*

2 Explain two sources of information that would have helped Siu to construct this cash flow forecast. *(6 marks)*

3 Evaluate the main reasons why this cash flow forecast may be inaccurate. *(16 marks)*

4 Discuss the possible implications for Siu's business if she decides to offer credit terms to her customers. *(16 marks)*

Constructing and interpreting break-even charts

Contribution

Contribution is an important concept in business studies. It looks at whether an individual product (or activity) is helping the business to make a profit.

All firms need to pay their fixed costs in order to operate. These costs must be covered before a profit can be made.

Contribution ignores these fixed costs. Instead, it looks only at the variable costs of making the product. If the sales revenue from making the product is greater than the variable costs, the product is contributing towards either paying off the fixed costs or making a profit (if the fixed costs have already been covered).

For example, if the variable costs of making a pen are 7 pence and the pen sells for 18 pence, the **contribution per unit** is 11 pence (18 pence − 7 pence).

If the **total contribution** exceeds the fixed costs, the business is making a profit. If the fixed costs exceed the total contribution, the firm is making a loss. A firm will break even if the total contribution is equal to the fixed costs (or if total revenue equals total costs).

The total contribution of a product can be calculated in two ways:

1 contribution per unit × number of units sold

2 sales revenue − total variable costs.

> **Key terms**
>
> **Contribution per unit** Selling price per unit − variable cost per unit.
>
> **Total contribution** The difference between total revenue and total variable costs.
>
> Note that total contribution = contribution per unit × units of output.

Calculating contribution per unit and total contribution: an example

An entrepreneur is planning to set up a coffee shop. She predicts that her costs and revenue will be as follows:

- fixed costs (per week): £750
- variable costs: £0.90 per customer
- selling price (per customer): £2.75
- number of customers (per week): 700

The contribution per unit = £2.75 – £0.90 = £1.85.

Using the first of the two formulae above:

Total contribution = £1.85 × 700 = £1,295

The same figure for total contribution is obtained using the second formula:

(700 × £2.75) – (700 × £0.90) = £1,925 – £630 = £1,295

Weekly profit = total contribution – fixed costs = £1,295 – £750 = £545

What if variable costs increase to £1 per customer, the selling price increases to £2.80 and fixed costs increase to £800 per week?

The contribution per unit falls to £1.80 (£2.80 – £1), so the total contribution falls to £1,260 (£1.80 × 700).

Weekly profit becomes £1,260 – £800 = £460

Note that the change in fixed costs affects the weekly profit but has no impact on the contribution.

What do you think?

Tables 17.19a) and b) show the contributions made by four different 'water features' produced by a firm. The total of £971,000 is a contribution towards fixed costs and profit.

Look at the contributions made by each product.

Which product or products should be investigated to see if contribution can be improved?

(Answer on page 539.)

Table 17.19a) Contributions made by four different water features

Water feature	Price (£)	–	Variable costs (£)	=	Contribution per unit (£)	×	No. of units sold (000s)	=	Total contribution (£000s)
Cascade	30	–	25	=	5	×	40	=	200
Fountain	45	–	22	=	23	×	16	=	368
Stream	60	–	28	=	32	×	14	=	448
Waterfall	15	–	18	=	(3)	×	15	=	(45)

Table 17.19b) Contributions made by four different water features

	Sales (£000s)	–	Variable costs (£000s)	=	Contribution (£000s)
Cascade	(30 × 40) 1,200	–	(25 × 40) 1,000	=	(5 × 40) 200
Fountain	(45 × 16) 720	–	(22 × 16) 352	=	(23 × 16) 368
Stream	(60 × 14) 840	–	(28 × 14) 392	=	(32 × 14) 448
Waterfall	(15 × 15) 225	–	(18 × 15) 270	=	((3) × 15) (45)
Total contribution 971					

Key term

Break-even output The level of output at which total sales revenue is equal to total costs of production.

Break-even output

A business can use break-even analysis to discover its **break-even output** and the impact of changes in output on its profit levels. Break-even analysis is the study of the relationship between total costs and total revenue to identify the output at which a business breaks even (i.e. makes neither a profit nor a loss).

Assumptions of break-even analysis

A firm's costs and revenue must be investigated in order to discover the level of output needed to break even. As explained in Chapter 1, costs can be classified as either **fixed** or **variable**.

Fixed costs such as rent must be paid regardless of output. If a firm produces no units of output, it still has to pay its fixed costs. However, if output increases, it is assumed that these costs will not increase. For example, if fixed costs are £50,000, the firm must pay £50,000 whether it produces zero units, 1 unit, 10 units, 100 units or any other level of output.

Variable costs such as raw materials increase as output increases. It is usual to assume that variable costs stay at the same level per unit produced. Thus if 1 unit costs £5 in variable costs, then 2 units will cost £10, 10 units will cost £50 and so on.

Sales revenue follows a pattern similar to variable costs. If the price is £15, selling 1 unit earns £15, 2 units will earn £30, and 10 units will earn £150.

In practice, costs and revenue do not always behave in a set, predictable way. However, in order to study break-even, certain assumptions are made:

● The selling price remains the same, regardless of the number of units sold.
● Fixed costs remain the same, regardless of the number of units of output.
● Variable costs vary in direct proportion to output.
● Every unit of output that is produced is sold.

These assumptions mean that objective comparisons can be made between different products or firms.

Calculating break-even output

Break-even output can be calculated in three different ways:

1 using a table showing revenue and costs over a range of output levels
2 using a formula to calculate the break-even quantity
3 using a graph showing revenue and costs over a range of output levels

Using a table

In Table 17.20 it can be seen that the break-even output is 5,000 units. At this level of output, sales revenue is equal to total costs and profit is zero.

Below 5,000 units, the firm makes a loss. Above 5,000 units, the firm makes a profit.

▼ **Table 17.20** Deducing break-even output

Units of output (000s)	Sales revenue (£000s)	Fixed costs (£000s)	Variable costs (£000s)	Total costs (£000s)	Profit (£000s)
0	0	50	0	50	(50)
1	15	50	5	55	(40)
2	30	50	10	60	(30)
3	45	50	15	65	(20)
4	60	50	20	70	(10)
5	75	50	25	75	0
6	90	50	30	80	10
7	105	50	35	85	20
8	120	50	40	90	30
9	135	50	45	95	40
10	150	50	50	100	50
11	165	50	55	105	60
12	180	50	60	110	70

Author advice

Keep a close eye on the units of measurement being used, as it is easy to make a mistake if you are working quickly. A glance at Table 17.20 will tell you that the break-even output is '5'. However, the unit of measure is '000s' (thousands). Therefore '5' means 5,000 units. Similarly, the '70' in the bottom right-hand corner of the table means that when 12,000 units are produced, the firm earns a profit of £70,000.

Using a formula

For each additional (marginal) item that the company produces, its extra revenue will equal the price of the item, but it will incur more costs (the variable costs only, such as raw materials and wages of operatives).

Remember: contribution per unit = selling price per unit – variable cost per unit

This shows the amount of money that each unit provides (contributes) towards paying off the fixed costs (or creating a profit, once the fixed costs have been met). Thus a product with a selling price of £12 and variable costs per unit of £7 will contribute £5 per unit (£12 – £7), while a product with a price of £60 and variable costs per unit of £22 will contribute £38 per unit.

Total contribution = contribution per unit × number of units sold

In the latter example above, 100 units would provide a contribution of £3,800 (£38 × 100) towards fixed costs and profit.

If each unit contributes £38 towards fixed costs and fixed costs were only £38, then only 1 unit would need to be produced in order to break even. If fixed costs were £76, then 2 units would be needed to break even (2 × £38). From this we can see that the formula for calculating break-even output is as follows:

$$\text{break-even output} = \frac{\text{fixed costs } (£)}{\text{contribution per unit } (£)}$$

Using the data in Table 17.20, the price is £15 and variable costs are £5 per unit, giving a contribution of £10 for every unit sold. At £10 per unit, 5,000 units would need to be sold in order to pay the fixed costs of £50,000, so 5,000 units is the break-even output.

$$\text{break-even output} = \frac{£50,000}{£15 - 5} = 5,000 \text{ units}$$

Note how the £ signs at the top and bottom of the equation have cancelled each other out. The answer is 5,000 units, *not* £5,000.

Using a graph

Graphs used to work out break-even are known as break-even charts. This method is explained in the next section.

Constructing break-even charts

Sales revenue can be plotted against units of output. The gradient of the line will be steeper for a higher price than a lower price. Figure 17.4 shows the sales revenue at different levels of output for a product with a selling price of £15 per unit.

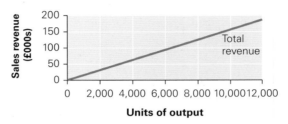

▲ **Figure 17.4** Sales revenue

In order to produce goods or services, a company must purchase fixed assets. The **fixed costs** incurred must be paid, regardless of the actual units of output produced. Fixed costs of £50,000 are shown in Figure 17.5.

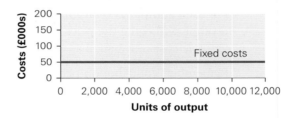

▲ **Figure 17.5** Fixed costs

Variable costs will vary directly with output. At zero output, no variable costs will be incurred. Each unit produced will require additional inputs of variable factors (primarily raw materials and direct labour). In this example, variable costs are £5 per unit. This would be plotted as shown in Figure 17.6.

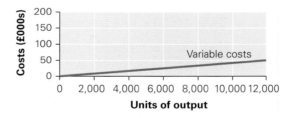

▲ **Figure 17.6** Variable costs

By adding fixed costs and variable costs, the **total costs** of production at different levels of output can be calculated. The total cost line is plotted in Figure 17.7.

It can be seen that costs are incurred even if no units are sold (because fixed costs are paid in anticipation that units will be sold). Therefore, low levels of sales are unlikely to produce a profit. As sales (and output) increase, the fixed costs become less of a burden as the fixed cost per unit (the average fixed cost) falls.

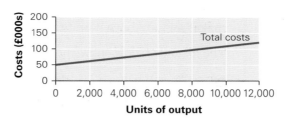

▲ **Figure 17.7** Total costs

Combining the sales revenue and cost lines enables the break-even point to be determined, marked with an arrow in Figure 17.8. The output required to break even is 5,000 units, at which level the sales revenue and costs are both equal to £75,000.

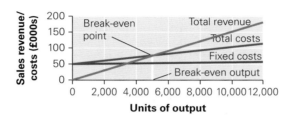

▲ **Figure 17.8** Break-even output

If actual output is 9,500 units, the **margin of safety** is 4,500 units (9,500 − 5,000). Table 17.20 (see page 375) shows potential output of 12,000 units. If this were the level of output, the margin of safety would be 7,000 units (12,000 − 5,000). A negative margin of safety means that a loss is being made.

Key term

Margin of safety The difference between the actual output and the break-even output. The formula for calculation is actual output *minus* break-even output.

Calculating and illustrating the effects of changes in price, cost and output on a break-even chart

What happens to break-even and profit when fixed costs, variable costs and selling prices change? These changes are examined below.

In the examples that follow, the original values are as follows:

- selling price = £16 per unit
- variable costs = £6 per unit
- fixed costs = £80

▼ **Table 17.21** Break-even data in tabular form

Units of output	Sales revenue	Fixed costs	Total variable costs	Total costs	Profit	Units of output	Sales revenue	Fixed costs	Total variable costs	Total costs	Profit
	(£)	(£)	(£)	(£)	(£)		(£)	(£)	(£)	(£)	(£)
0	0	80	0	80	(80)	7	112	80	42	122	(10)
1	16	80	6	86	(70)	8	128	80	48	128	0
2	32	80	12	92	(60)	9	144	80	54	134	10
3	48	80	18	98	(50)	10	160	80	60	140	20
4	64	80	24	104	(40)	11	176	80	66	146	30
5	80	80	30	110	(30)	12	192	80	72	152	40
6	96	80	36	116	(20)						

In Table 17.21, the break-even output is 8 units. Below 8 units the firm makes a loss. Above 8 units the firm makes a profit.

The formula below shows how to calculate the break-even output:

$$\text{Break-even output} = \frac{\text{fixed costs (£)}}{\text{contribution per unit (£)}}$$

In our example, the break-even output is:

$$\frac{£80}{£16 - £6} = \frac{£80}{£10} = 8 \text{ units}$$

In Figure 17.9 it can be seen from the gradient of the sales revenue line that the selling price per unit is £16. Similarly, the gradient of the variable costs line shows that variable costs per unit are £6. The fixed costs are £80 (at all levels of output).

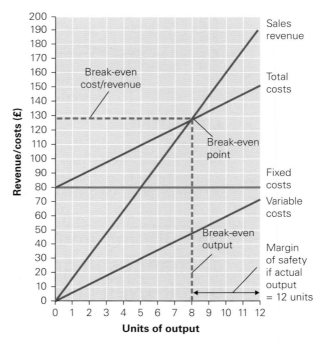

▲ **Figure 17.9** Break-even in the form of a graph

In the diagram, the break-even point is marked. The output required to break even is 8 units, at which level the sales (total) revenue and total costs are both equal to £128.

The margin of safety is the difference between the actual output and the break-even output. If actual output is 12 units, the margin of safety is 12 – 8 = 4 units.

Calculating profit on a break-even chart

Profit = Total Revenue (TR) – Total Cost (TC).

To calculate the profit you need to read off the TR and TC figures **for the actual level of output.**

In Figure 17.9, if actual output is 10 units then the TR line intersects 10 units at £160 and the TC line intersects 10 units at £140 units. Therefore, profit = £160 – £140 = £20.

If actual output is 5 units then TR = £80 and TC = £110. Therefore, profit = £80 – £110 = –£30 or (£30) – i.e. a loss of £30.

If actual output is 8 units then TR = £128 and TC = £128. Therefore, profit = zero. (This is the break-even output.)

Illustrating changes to price and cost on a break-even chart

There are six possible individual changes that can occur to a break-even chart. These are shown in Figure 17.10 (a–f).

The possible changes are:

- an increase in the selling price
- a decrease in the selling price
- an increase in the variable cost per unit
- a decrease in the variable cost per unit
- an increase in fixed costs
- a decrease in fixed costs.

In all parts of Figure 17.10, line A shows the original value and line B shows the new value, after the change.

How do the changes shown affect break-even output? Figure 17.11 shows the change in break-even output brought about by an increase in fixed costs, with no other changes.

Figure 17.12 shows the change in break-even output caused by a decrease in variable costs and an increase in the selling price, but with no change in fixed costs.

Break-even analysis allows a firm to use 'what if?' analysis to show the different break-even outputs and the changes in levels of profit that might arise from changes in its price, variable costs and fixed costs. This helps the firm to plan strategies for each of its products.

Businesses that foresee future changes (such as higher wage costs or lower prices) can examine the impact on individual products in their range. This can help them to identify products that may be successful now but vulnerable in the future (or vice versa).

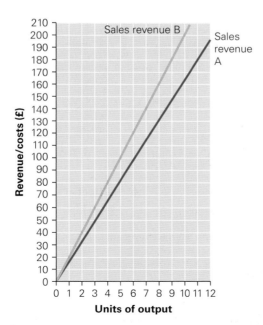

▲ **a) Effect** on sales revenue of an increase in selling price from £16 to £20 per unit

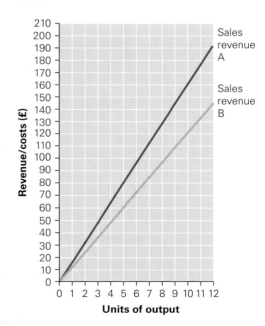

▲ **b) Effect** on sales revenue of a decrease in selling price from £16 to £12 per unit

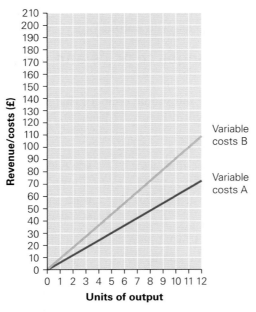

▲ **c) Effect** of an increase in variable costs from £6 per unit to £9 per unit

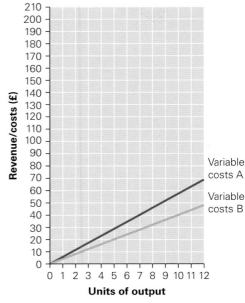

▲ **d) Effect** of a decrease in variable costs from £6 per unit to £4 per unit

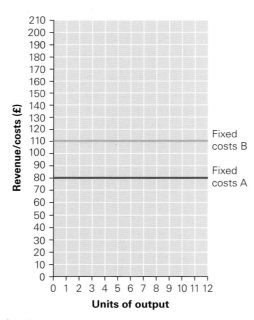

▲ **e) Effect** of an increase in fixed costs from £80 to £110

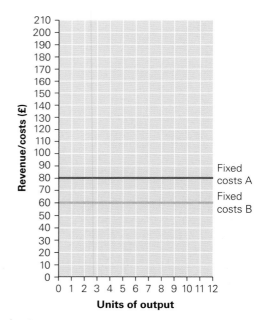

▲ **f) Effect** of a decrease in fixed costs from £80 to £60

▲ **Figure 17.10 (a–f)** Possible changes to the break-even chart

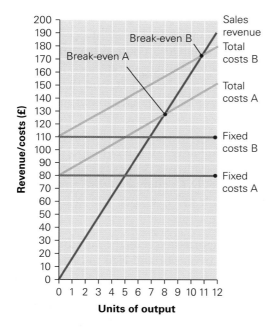

▲ **Figure 17.11** Change in break-even point resulting from an increase in fixed costs from £80 to £110

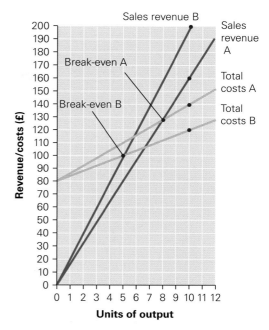

▲ **Figure 17.12** Change in break-even point resulting from a decrease in variable costs from £6 per unit to £4 per unit and an increase in the selling price from £16 per unit to £20 per unit

What do you think?

Figure 17.13 shows changes that lead to a change in the break-even output. Sales revenue A and total costs A show the original position. Sales revenue B and total costs B show the modified position after changes in selling price, variable costs per unit and fixed costs.

1 Based on Sales Revenue A and Total Costs A, identify the original:
   a) selling price
   b) variable costs per unit
   c) fixed costs

2 Based on Sales Revenue B and Total Costs B, identify the amended:
   a) selling price
   b) variable costs per unit
   c) fixed costs

3 Identify the original break-even output.

4 Identify the final break-even output.

(Answers on p. 539)

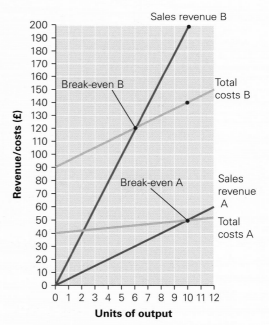

▲ **Figure 17.13** Changing price and costs

Changes to output on the break-even chart

Break-even output is determined by selling price, variable costs per unit and fixed costs. Changes in output have no impact on break-even output. However, assuming that output matches the number of units sold, changes in sales will affect TR and TC and therefore profit. The section on calculating profit shows how changes in output affect TR, TC and profit.

As output changes:

- total revenue (TR) changes in direct proportion (e.g. a 30 per cent increase in output leads to a 30 per cent increase in total revenue)
- total variable costs (TVC) change in direct proportion (a 6 per cent decrease in output leads to a 6 per cent decrease in total variable costs)
- fixed costs stay the same.

As long as the selling price exceeds the variable costs per unit, this will mean that increases in output will lead to increases in profit.

Value of break-even analysis

Strengths of break-even analysis

- Break-even analysis can be used to calculate how long it will take to reach the level of output needed to make a profit. This enables a business to assess whether or not a project or product is viable. Businesses often suffer from cash flow problems, so it is useful to know when to expect to reach a profit level. This information will help a business to get financial support, such as a bank overdraft.
- It is a simple, straightforward way of discovering whether a business plan is likely to succeed financially. Furthermore, it can show a business its margin of safety and so, if the sales forecast proves to be optimistic, the business can calculate by how much sales can fall before it drops below the quantity needed to break even.
- Break-even analysis is used to plan 'expected' results. It can also analyse the 'best-case' scenario and the 'worst-case' scenario. This allows the decision maker to see the maximum possible profit and minimum profit (possibly a loss). This information can indicate the level of risk involved.
- It allows a firm to use 'what if?' analysis to show the different break-even outputs and the changes in profit levels that might arise from changes in its price. If market research has been conducted that indicates the levels of demand at various prices, this information can be put into break-even charts to establish the break-even output. By studying the different break-even outputs and profit levels at various prices, the business can ascertain the most profitable price. It might even help the entrepreneur to ascertain whether the business itself is feasible. This type of analysis can be applied to individual products, enabling the start-up to see whether a particular product or service should be added to or removed from the business's range.

- 'What if?' analysis can also be applied to variable costs. A business start-up may want to consider purchasing high-quality, more expensive raw materials or employing more highly trained workers at a higher wage. It is likely that better materials and workers will lead to greater efficiency and possibly greater demand for the products or services being provided. This might offset the higher variable costs incurred. By putting this information into break-even charts, decisions can be made on the materials and workforce likely to lead to the highest levels of profit or the most achievable level of break-even output. This analysis will help the firm to plan strategies for each of its products.
- A break-even chart can show the different levels of profit arising from the various levels of output and sales that might be achieved. This means that a business can predict its profit levels if it knows the number of units that it is going to sell. Knowing its future profit levels can help a business to plan its future objectives and strategies.
- Many firms have a target to earn a certain level of profit. Break-even analysis can be adapted to discover the point at which a company might reach a particular profit level. This involves investigating the contribution needed to pay both the fixed costs and the target profit figure. For example, using the figures from the earlier section on 'Calculating break-even output' (see Table 17.20 on page 375), if the target profit were £30,000, the calculation would be the same as the break-even formula with £30,000 added to the fixed costs.

$$\text{target profit output} = \frac{\text{fixed costs } (£) + \text{target profit } (£)}{\text{contribution per unit } (£)}$$

$$= \frac{£50,000 + £30,000}{£10} = \frac{£80,000}{£10} = 8,000 \; units$$

Weaknesses of break-even analysis

Break-even analysis has the following problems:

- The information may be unreliable. Break-even charts are based on forecasts. It is difficult to predict the number of customers who will buy the firm's products, even with careful market research. Similarly, actual production costs can change, especially if there is a shortage of raw materials or a breakdown of equipment.
- Sales are unlikely to be exactly the same as output. Some output will probably remain unsold, particularly in the case of perishable goods. Furthermore, there is likely to be some wastage of raw materials.
- In practice, the selling price may change as more is purchased/sold. Demand theory indicates that, as price increases, the demand will decrease (significantly if demand is elastic). In this respect, break-even analysis is not particularly accurate, although many firms aim to set a fixed price for their products.
- Fixed costs, in practice, may not stay the same as output changes. For large increases in output, new machines and even new buildings may need to be purchased. This will lead to a sudden rise in fixed costs.
- The analysis assumes that variable costs per unit are always the same, ignoring factors such as buying in bulk. In practice, variable costs per unit will decline for larger firms, as they can get discounts per unit when buying raw materials in bulk. It is also possible that costs per unit will rise if communication problems cause inefficiency.

Author advice

Budgets, cash flow forecasting and break-even analysis are all aspects of management accounting, focusing on financial planning. All of these topics are therefore based on estimates for the future. When analysing this data you should look at the reliability of these predictions. A well-established business in a stable market is much more likely to be able to predict accurately than a new business in a changing market. The people making the prediction are also important. Are they experienced? Are they carrying out research or just estimating? Are they trying to prove a case (in which case there may be a bias)? Any conclusions you draw should consider these issues.

Practice exercise 4

Total: 25 marks

The following information applies to a product:

- units of output: 500
- fixed costs: £1,200
- total variable costs: £3,000
- selling price: £11 per item

1 What is meant by the term 'total variable costs'? *(2 marks)*

2 Calculate the contribution per unit. *(4 marks)*

3 Calculate the total contribution from 500 units. *(3 marks)*

4 Calculate the break-even quantity. *(5 marks)*

5 How much profit is made if all 500 units are sold? *(4 marks)*

6 What is the margin of safety if 500 units are sold? *(2 marks)*

7 Calculate the break-even quantity if the variable costs rise to £7 per unit and the fixed costs increase to £1,400. *(5 marks)*

Case study: Rocking horses

Chris Mass produces wooden rocking horses in a barn on his farm in Oxfordshire.

During the winter there is a quiet period on the farm and in the past Chris has always had to reduce his staff by two employees. He has overcome this by employing two of his workers (skilled wood craftsmen who had been made redundant by a local furniture company) to concentrate on making rocking horses for a national chain of toy shops.

On average the rocking horses sell for £600 each and Chris's workers can produce 26 horses between them during the three-month period. Chris's daughter then decorates and varnishes the horses to increase their individuality. Total labour costs are £360 per horse and raw material costs are £60 per horse. The fixed costs involved are £4,800. Figure 17.14 shows the break-even chart for this activity.

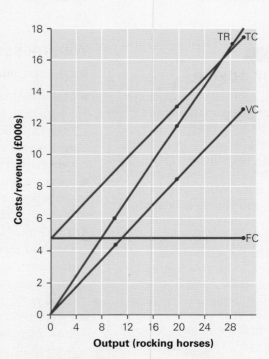

▲ **Figure 17.14** Break-even chart for rocking horses

Questions

1 On the break-even chart show the break-even point and the break-even output. *(2 marks)*

2 Raw material costs are expected to fall by £40 per horse.

a) Amend the total cost line to show this change and show the new break-even output. *(3 marks)*

b) Calculate the original break-even output using the formula. *(4 marks)*

c) Assuming that variable costs fall by £40 per horse, calculate the new break-even output using the formula. *(2 marks)*

3 Based on the original costs, calculate the *loss* that is made from selling 26 rocking horses. *(5 marks)*

4 Calculate the profit that would be made if variable costs fall by £40 per horse. *(3 marks)*

5 Discuss the possible ways in which Chris might be able to change this loss into a profit. *(16 marks)*

How to analyse profitability

Key term

Profitability The ability of a business to generate profit or the efficiency of a business in generating profit.

What is the distinction between profit and **profitability**? Profit is just a sum, for example a profit of £100,000. Profitability relates this sum to the size of the business. A large oil company such as Shell would be disappointed with a profit of £100,000, but for a small corner shop it would be a great achievement. Therefore, to put the £100,000 into a more meaningful form we need to compare it with the size of the business. There are two simple ways to measure the size of a business:

● sales revenue (adding up all the income it receives over a period of time)
● capital employed (adding up all the money that has been invested in the business by owners).

In Year 2 you will investigate **capital employed** and the **return on capital employed (ROCE%)** – which measure profitability based on capital employed. In this chapter we will study profitability based on the use of sales revenue as a measure of the size of the business.

Let us suppose that a business makes £100,000 profit in a year by selling £700,000 worth of goods and services over the 12 months. This means that for every £7 of revenue earned, £1 of profit was made.

Dividing the profit by the revenue gives: $\frac{1}{7}$

How does this compare with a smaller business that earns £16,000 profit from sales of £100,000? As a fraction this is: $\frac{4}{25}$

The easiest way to compare is to convert the fractions to percentages. In the first example:

$\frac{£100,000}{£700,000}$ or $\frac{1}{7}$ as a percentage is $\frac{1}{7} \times 100 = 14.3\%$

In the second example, the percentage is:

$\frac{4}{25} \times 100 = 16\%$ or $\frac{£16,000}{£100,00} \times 100 = 16\%$

Key terms

Gross profit margin or gross profit to sales (%) This measures gross profit as a percentage of sales (turnover). This ratio measures how efficiently the business is transforming raw materials into products.

Operating profit margin or profit from operations margin (%) This measures operating profit as a percentage of sales (turnover). This ratio measures how efficiently the business is making a profit from the resources that it is using for its trading activities.

Profit for the year margin or profit for the year as a percentage of sales This measures the profit that is available for shareholders, as a percentage of sales (turnover). This ratio measures how much the shareholders may benefit directly from the financial performance of the business.

By converting the fractions to percentages, it is much easier to see that the second business has a higher profitability than the first one, albeit only by a small percentage.

The three measures of profitability covered in this chapter relate profit to sales revenue. In all three measures, a high percentage represents a better performance than a low percentage, because we assume businesses want to earn high profits.

In Chapter 16 we investigated three measures of profit – gross profit, operating profit and profit for year. We now convert these measures of profit into the relevant profitability measures, which are:

● Gross profit margin OR Gross profit to sales (%).
● Operating profit margin OR Profit from operations margin (%).
● Profit for year margin OR Profit for year as a percentage of sales (%).

Calculating and understanding measures of profitability

The **gross profit margin** OR gross profit to sales (%) is calculated as follows:

$$\text{Gross profit margin } (\%) = \frac{\text{Gross profit}}{\text{Sales revenue (turnover)}} \times 100$$

The **operating profit margin** OR profit from operations margin (%) is calculated as follows:

$$\text{Operating profit margin } (\%) = \frac{\text{Operating profit}}{\text{Sales revenue (turnover)}} \times 100$$

The **profit for the year margin** (%) is calculated as follows:

$$\text{Profit for year margin } (\%) = \frac{\text{Profit for year}}{\text{Sales revenue (turnover)}} \times 100$$

Table 17.22 is an extract (rows 1, 3, 5 and 8) from Table 16.2 in the previous chapter (see page 337).

▼ **Table 17.22** Extracts of financial data for selected supermarkets for the financial year ending in 2014

	Extracts from company income statements	Tesco plc Year ending: 22 Mar 2014	J Sainsbury plc Year ending: 15 Mar 2014	W M Morrison plc Year ending: 2 Feb 2014
1	Revenue (£m)	63,557	23,949	17,680
3	Gross profit (£m)	4,010	1,387	1,074
5	Operating profit (£m)	2,631	1,009	(95)
8	Profit for year (£m)	970	716	(238)

Using the data in Table 17.22 we can calculate each ratio for Tesco plc for the financial year 2013–14.

$$\text{Gross profit margin } (\%) = \frac{£4,010m}{£63,557} \times 100 = 6.3\%$$

$$\text{Operating profit margin } (\%) = \frac{£2,631}{£63,557} \times 100 = 4.1\%$$

$$\text{Profit for year } (\%) = \frac{£970}{£63,557} \times 100 = 1.5\%$$

It is difficult to draw conclusions from single, isolated profitability measures. It is usual to make one or more comparisons:

- **Comparisons to competitors**. If a business's profit margin exceeds that of its closest competitors, then this would be deemed to be a favourable result.
- **Comparisons over time**. A good result would be an improvement in a profitability measure in comparison to the previous year or years.
- **Comparisons to a standard**. In some cases there is a standard level that represents an acceptable level of performance. For example, operating profit margins in the UK tend to average around 5 per cent, when the economy is not in recession.

Firms with high rates of inventory turnover tend to have lower profit margins, as their profit arises from the large number of products sold. Consequently, gross profit margins and operating profit margins may not be a reliable method of comparison between different industries. However, it is an excellent way of assessing the relative profitability of two firms competing with each other. As our data is based on three supermarkets, a comparison of profit margins between them would be appropriate. Businesses dealing with specialist, one-off products, such as tailor-made clothing, will have much higher profit margins, especially for gross profit. This is because specialist products sell in lower volumes but require greater skills to make, so profit is made from higher profit margins.

Table 17.23 incorporates the results of the calculations of Tesco's three profitability ratios (above). It contrasts these results with the profitability of Sainsbury's and Morrison's, based on the data in Table 17.22.

▼ **Table 17.23** Profitability ratios for selected supermarkets for the financial year ending in 2014

Profitability ratio	Tesco plc Year ending: 22 Mar 2014	J Sainsbury plc Year ending: 15 Mar 2014	W M Morrison plc Year ending: 2 Feb 2014
Gross profit margin (%)	6.3	5.8	6.1
Operating profit margin (%)	4.1	4.2	(0.5)*
Profit for year margin (%)	1.5	3.0	(1.3)*

* Figures in brackets represent negative numbers (a loss rather than a profit)

Analysis of Tesco's profitability ratios – comparison with competitors

Table 17.23 indicates that Tesco performed slightly better than its two competitors in terms of gross profit margin in 2013–14. This means that it is more effective at converting raw materials (the products it buys from its suppliers) into products that have achieved some added value.

Operating profit margin is considered to be the best measure of profit as it takes all costs involved in trading into account. This ratio indicates that Sainsbury's operated more profitably than Tesco during the year 2013–14. Although the differences are very slight, the comparison between the two ratios should be a cause for concern for Tesco. Its operating profit margin is 2.2 per cent lower than its gross profit margin, whereas for Sainsbury's this difference is only 1.6 per cent. This suggests that costs such as administrative expenses are inefficiently controlled by Tesco, in comparison to Sainsbury's.

Tesco's profit for year margin compares unfavourably to Sainsbury's. Sainsbury's profitability, using profit for year margin, shows that the profit available to a holder of a share in Sainsbury's is twice that available to a holder

Author advice

Studying measures of profitability can involve working with some large numbers. Do not worry too much about these numbers. As long as you know how to use the formula, your calculator will do the hard work. Once you have let it do the calculations, all you need to do is see which number is higher. In this example, the conclusion that Morrison's did less well than Sainsbury's can be made because its net profit margin is a lower number.

Fact file

Morrison's

In 2013–14, over 70 per cent of Morrison's administrative expenses were 'non-recurring' items. These consisted of costs amounting to £861 million to account for lower values of three assets: certain stores, losses in the value of land that Morrison's owned but was no longer going to use to build new stores, losses made in selling off its loss-making Kiddicare subsidiary for only £2 million.

These figures represent financial problems for Morrison's but are not likely to mean continued losses in the future. However, competition from discount supermarkets was taking away market share from Morrison's at this time and this was likely to be a long-term threat to its profitability.

Source: www.morrisons.com

of a Tesco's share. This indicates that items such as the cost of finance, one-off items and taxation have been a relatively much bigger drain on Tesco's finance.

The gross profitability ratio for Morrison's is on a par with the other two supermarkets, but its operating profit is very poor. The difference between its gross and operating margins (6.6 per cent) reveals Morrison's problem – it did not keep control of its administrative expenses.

Analysis of Tesco's profitability ratios – comparison over time

To investigate whether Tesco's profitability is improving we need to compare different years.

▼ **Table 17.24** Tesco's profitability ratios from 2009–10 to 2013–14

	2009–10	2010–11	2011–12	2012–13	2013–14
Gross profit margin (%)	8.1	8.3	8.4	6.3	6.3
Operating profit margin (%)	6.1	6.3	6.5	3.4	4.1
Profit for year margin (%)	4.1	4.4	4.4	0.2	1.5

Based solely on the profitability levels shown:

- Tesco's gross profitability rose slightly between 2009–10 and 2011–12, but fell sharply in 2012–13 and showed no signs of recovering in 2013–14.
- The operating profit (%) also grew slightly until 2012, but then fell (more sharply than the gross profit) before recovering slightly.
- Profit for year rose between 2009–10 and 2010–11 but then stayed constant for two years. The year 2012–13 showed a very poor return, with very little profit available for shareholders. The figure for 2013–14 was disappointing too, although it did indicate some improvement on the previous year.

What do you think?

The comments on Tesco's profitability are based purely on the data. To analyse Tesco's profitability more background information would be needed. The bullet points below show some significant developments during this five-year period.

- The UK experienced an 18-month recession in 2008 and 2009 and the economy also declined at the end of 2010. There was another recession from late-2011 to mid-2012.
- Customer views changed during this period, with many customers actively seeking lower prices.

However, there was also a movement by some groups of customers towards high-quality, higher-priced products.
- Aldi and Lidl undertook large expansion plans in this period.
- Online sales grew rapidly.
- Tesco's growth was focused more on convenience stores and overseas markets. Overseas markets accounted for over 30 per cent of Tesco's profit, despite losses in the USA.

In the light of these factors, to what extent do you believe that Tesco's performance worsened significantly during this period?

Analysis of Tesco's profitability ratios – comparison to a standard

For some financial data there are widely agreed levels that represent good performance. There is little guidance for gross profit, as it varies so much between different markets. Profit for year is also difficult to assess in this way, as it can be affected by factors such as taxation which are outside its control (see 'What do you think?' box on page 389.) Operating profit of 5 per cent has been considered to be a sign of solid, acceptable performance, but in the difficult trading circumstances of recent years, even this standard is becoming a matter of opinion.

On this measure, Tesco's performance was above standard from 2009–10 to 2011–12, but has fallen below this level since 2012.

Use of data for financial decision making and planning

Businesses collect data for many purposes. For example, the marketing department will collect data for forecasting and making decisions about the marketing mix; the operations department will collect data such as unit costs and capacity utilisation in order to measure the performance of the operations function and make decisions on how operations might be improved; and the human resources department will use data such as labour productivity and labour turnover to analyse the efficiency and motivation of the workforce.

The finance department uses data for two different purposes:

- **management accounting**
- **financial accounting.**

Note: In some cases data can serve both purposes. For example, data on profitability is published for external users (primarily shareholders) but as we saw earlier, it can also be analysed by managers (who are internal users) in order to improve the company's performance.

Management accounting data

The main examples of data for management accounting are outlined below.

- **Revenue, costs and profit objectives**. Data will be collected from all of the different departments so that the finance department can estimate likely revenue and costs and therefore set objectives for profit. This data will influence and be influenced by the income and expenditure budgets of the various departments.
- **Decision trees**. The finance department will liaise with departments using decision trees, in order to provide advice on likely revenue and costs, so that decisions are based on sound financial analysis.
- **Investment data**. In order to assess the viability of investment, data will be collected to estimate the likely financial returns of each major investment being undertaken. This will enable the business to calculate 'return on investment'. (In Year 2 you will look at investment appraisal techniques and the uses of this data in more detail.)
- **Capital structure data and sources of finance**. See section on financial accounting data below.
- **Cash flow forecasts and their outcomes**. Data will be collected to inform future predictions of inflows and outflows. Future cash flow forecasts will be influenced by the actual inflows and outflows that result.
- **Budgets and their outcomes**. Budgets are vital to a business's management accounting as they indicate where financial efficiency and inefficiency is occurring, mainly through the use of variance analysis.
- **Break-even charts**. Data used for break-even charts can enable a business to ensure that its plans will be financially viable. It also allows 'what if? analysis' to assess the likely risks of its plans.

Financial accounting data

The main examples of data for financial accounting are outlined below.

- **Cash flow statements**. Cash flow statements show the outcomes of cash flow forecasts and therefore it is useful for external users to assess whether the business has a healthy cash balance. This can influence the business's ability to attract investors.
- **Data on profitability**. Analysis of profitability is useful for external users when deciding on whether to invest in a business. However, it can also be used for management accounting purposes as it can reveal where problems are occurring.
- **Capital structure data and sources of finance**. Capital structure and details of sources of finance enable prospective investors to assess the level of risk of investment in a business. (Sources of finance are covered in Chapter 18.)
- **Income statements**. These data provide information on the breakdown of revenue costs and the different measures of profit. As such, they are mainly for external users, but can help internal users identify strengths and weaknesses.
- **Balance sheets**. These data show the value of a business, its capital structure and details of its assets (things that it owns) and liabilities (things that it owes). Again, they are mainly for external users, but can help managers (within the business) identify strengths and weaknesses.

Note: Income statements, balance sheets and data on profitability will be looked at in detail in Year 2.

Practice exercise 5

Total: 15 marks

1 Financial accounting is:
   a) used externally and focuses on past data
   b) used externally and plans for the future
   c) used internally and focuses on past data
   d) used internally and plans for the future   *(1 mark)*

2 Management accounting is:
   a) used externally and focuses on past data
   b) used externally and plans for the future
   c) used internally and focuses on past data
   d) used internally and plans for the future   *(1 mark)*

3 Which one of these items is the best example of financial accounting data?
   a) Budgets
   b) Cash flow forecasts
   c) Decision trees
   d) Income statements   *(1 mark)*

4 Which one of these items is the best example of management accounting data?
   a) Break-even charts
   b) Balance sheets
   c) Capital structure data
   d) Cash flow statements   *(1 mark)*

5 What is the formula for calculating gross profit margin?   *(2 marks)*

6 Analyse two internal factors that might influence a firm's operating profit margin.   *(9 marks)*

Case study: Google's financial performance

Table 17.25 below is a repeat of Table 16.6 from Chapter 16 (page 347).
Table 17.26 shows Google's profitability ratios for 2011 and 2012, but not 2013.

Read the data and answer the questions that follow.

▼ **Table 17.25** Financial performance of Google (2011–13)

	2011 ($ million)	2012 ($ million)	2013 ($ million)
Revenue	37,905	50,175	59,825
Cost of sales	(13,188)	(20,505)	(25,824)
Gross profit	24,717	29,670	34,001
Administrative expenses	(13,085)	(16,910)	(20,035)
Operating profit	11,632	12,760	13,966
Net costs of finance, one-off costs and tax	(1,895)	(1,972)	(1,752)
Profit for year	9,737	10,788	12,214

	2011	2012	2013
Gross profit margin (%)	65.2	59.1	?
Operating profit margin (%)	30.7	25.4	?
Profit for year margin (%)	25.7	21.5	?

Questions

Total: 50 marks

1 What is the difference between 'profit' and 'profitability'? *(4 marks)*

2 Explain one reason why it would be difficult to compare Google's profitability with a competitor. *(5 marks)*

3 Analyse two external factors that might have influenced Google's profitability. *(9 marks)*

4 Based purely on financial data, has Google improved its profitability between 2011 and 2013?

Use the data in Tables 17.25 and 17.26 and your own calculations to support your view. *(12 marks)*

5 'A company's profitability is the ideal way to measure its overall performance.' To what extent do you agree with this statement? Use examples from Google, or any other companies with which you are familiar, to support your arguments. *(20 marks)*

Making financial decisions: sources of finance

This chapter examines the different sources of finance available to businesses. The distinction between internal and external sources of finance are considered and short-term and long-term financing are then contrasted. In the context of these concepts, the chapter examines the various sources of finance, focusing on debt factoring, overdrafts, retained profits, share capital, loans and venture capital. Other possible sources of finance are also outlined. The chapter concludes with a brief summary of recent changes in business financing.

Internal and external sources of finance

Classifying sources of finance

Internal or external

There are two sources of finance: **internal** and **external**. Retained profit and debt factoring are ways of raising finance from *within* the business. Finance can also be raised using external sources of finance in the form of loans and overdrafts from *outside* the business.

> **Key terms**
>
> **Internal sources of finance** Ways of raising finance from within the business, such as retained profit or debt factoring.
>
> **External sources of finance** Ways of raising finance from outside the business, such as loans and overdrafts.

▼ **Table 18.1** Classification of sources of finance – internal and external sources

Internal sources	External sources
Debt factoring	Bank overdraft
Retained profit	Ordinary share capital
	Loans/bank loans
	Venture capital

Short term or long term

Short-term finance describes finance that is normally intended for repayment within 12 months. It is usually intended for revenue expenditure.

Long-term finance describes finance that is normally intended for capital expenditure and where repayment, if necessary, is due after three years or more.

Medium-term finance covers the period between short-term and long-term finance.

Capital expenditure and revenue expenditure

When considering sources of finance, the most critical factor is the length of time for which the finance is needed. Finance is used to fund the types of spending described below.

● **Capital expenditure.** This is spending on items that can be used time and time again (**fixed** or **non-current assets**), such as machinery. It may take a long time before these items generate enough revenue to pay for themselves, so a *long-term source of finance* is ideal. For items that pay for themselves more quickly, such as computer software, medium-term finance is most relevant. The long term is normally greater than three years, while the medium term is usually between one and three years.

● **Revenue expenditure.** This is spending on current, day-to-day costs such as the purchase of raw materials and payment of wages. Such expenditure provides a quick return, so the company should use a *short-term source of finance*, usually repayable within one year, but possibly two years.

Table 18.2 classifies the main sources of finance in terms of the usual time period for which the finance is needed.

▼ **Table 18.2** Classification of sources of finance by time period

Short term	Long term
Debt factoring	Retained profit
Bank overdraft	Ordinary share capital
	Loan capital/bank loan
	Venture capital

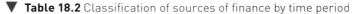

Advantages and disadvantages of different sources of finance for short- and long-term uses

Debt factoring (factoring)

Factoring is an **internal** source of **short-term** finance. The factoring company usually pays the firm about 75 per cent of its sales immediately and approximately 15–20 per cent on receipt of the debt. The firm therefore loses some revenue (about 5–10 per cent, depending on the length of time and current interest rates), which is the factoring company's charge for its service.

Key term

Factoring When a factoring company (usually a bank) buys the right to collect the money from the credit sales of a business (where customers of a business are allowed to delay payment to that business).

▲ Currys use debt factoring

Key term

Bank overdraft When a bank allows an individual or organisation to overspend its current account in the bank up to an agreed (overdraft) limit and for a stated time period.

Advantages of factoring

- **Improved cash flow in the short term**. This may save expenses such as overdraft interest charges and in extreme cases the immediate receipt of cash may keep the business alive by allowing it to pay its own debts on time. For businesses offering long credit periods to their customers as a way of boosting sales revenue, the immediate receipt of cash may be essential because it would be impossible for the business to wait a year for payment.
- **Lower administration costs**. Collecting and chasing up debts can be a costly and time-consuming process. The factoring company specialises in this and it is possible that it will be collecting more than one debt from the same firm.
- **Reduced risk of bad debts**. The factoring company takes this risk instead of the original business. However, it does reserve the right to refuse to factor a debt if it considers it to be risky. For this reason, firms such as SCS Furniture and Currys (which use factoring companies such as Barclays Partner Finance and GE Capital) will contact the factoring company before giving credit to a customer. The factoring companies will have lists of customers who may be a high risk.
- **Increased efficiency**. Factoring can encourage businesses to be more careful with their provision of credit. If a business gains a reputation for having no customers that turn out to be bad debts, then the factoring company will reduce the cost of factoring to that business. This will provide firms with an incentive to be much more efficient in their provision of credit.

Disadvantages of factoring

- **Loss of revenue**. The business using a factoring company loses between 5 and 10 per cent of its revenue. Ultimately, this reduces its profit, although it may be possible to increase the price charged to customers where credit terms are being offered.
- **High cost**. The business has to pay a factoring company more for its services than it would have to pay a bank for a loan, as there are administrative expenses involved in chasing up debts. This additional cost should be set against the administrative savings to the business from no longer having to chase up the debts itself.
- **Customer relations problems**. Customers may prefer to deal directly with the business that sold them the product. An aggressive factoring company may upset certain customers, who will blame their bad experience on the original seller of the product.

Although factoring involves costs, many large retailers take advantage of this service because large factoring companies can carry out the process of debt collection more cheaply, and pass on their cost savings to the retailer.

Overdrafts (bank overdrafts)

Bank overdrafts are an **external** source of **short-term** finance.

Overdrafts are widely used and flexible, and can overcome the cash flow problems suffered by businesses whose sales are seasonal or that need to buy materials in advance of a large order. The rate of interest is nearly always variable and only charged daily on the amount by which the account is overdrawn. As with a bank loan, the interest rate depends on the level

▲ Overdrafts are useful for seasonal businesses like farms

of risk posed by the account holder. Security is not usually required, so interest rates on overdrafts tend to be higher than those on bank loans.

Although the terms of most overdrafts allow banks to demand immediate repayment, this is rare. In practice, overdraft agreements are often renewed and are treated as a reliable source of finance. A bank manager will get to know the nature of a customer's finances and will be able to recognise times when an overdraft is required.

Bank overdrafts are mainly used to ease cash flow problems, sometimes being needed for just a few days to fund a major payment, so they are a *short-term source of finance*.

Advantages of bank overdrafts

- **Extremely flexible**. They can be used on a short-term basis (even just for a single day) if the business has a temporary cash flow problem.
- **Interest is only paid on the amount of the overdraft being used**. For loans, interest payments are based on the whole amount borrowed, because the loan is treated as a separate account by a bank. An overdraft allows a business's current account to be overdrawn ('go into the red') up to the agreed level of the overdraft. This means that every payment made into the current account, such as a payment from a customer, reduces the level of the actual overdraft being used. Because interest is based on the amount of the overdraft being used, any payment into the current account will mean a fall in interest payments.
- **Particularly useful to seasonal businesses**. Most businesses experience some degree of seasonal fluctuations in sales. During periods of low sales, businesses are likely to experience some cash flow problems. An overdraft is an ideal way to help a business during this period of the year.
- **Security is not usually required**. Consequently, non-repayment of an overdraft does not lead to the loss of assets, because none are being held as security.

Disadvantages of bank overdrafts

- **Level of interest rate charged**. There is less security for the bank and no guarantee that the full overdraft will be used. Consequently, banks usually charge a higher interest rate for an overdraft than for a loan.
- **Flexible interest rates**. Interest on an overdraft is charged at a flexible rate and so a business may find its payments going up (or down). This can make it difficult to budget because, unlike a bank loan, the payments are not fixed in advance.
- **Banks can demand immediate repayment**. An overdraft agreement usually allows the bank to demand immediate repayment. However, this is rarely used by banks.
- **Paperwork demands**. Cash flow forecasts and other evidence are usually needed to show the bank manager why an overdraft is needed. This can be time-consuming and distract managers from their core activities.

Retained profits

Retained profits are an **internal** source of **long-term** finance.

Retained profit is a good indicator of the success of a firm, but more importantly it allows a firm to use the surplus (profit) for future activities. The owners of a business (the shareholders in limited companies) expect a share of the profit as a dividend, but the remaining profit can be retained and used by the business. If this source of finance is used well, a company is likely to succeed and shareholders will gain because the share price is likely to rise.

Advantages of retained profits

- **Cheap source of finance**. As retained profits belong to the company, there is no need to pay interest on funds acquired in this way. The company can save on this expenditure by declaring a zero dividend, although this is likely to upset shareholders.
- **No security required**. When a company borrows funds from a bank, it has to provide some kind of security. In the case of large loans, it may have to mortgage its property or take the chance that the property will be sold by the lender if the debt is not repaid. However, for retained profit, security is unnecessary because the company is using its own funds.
- **Independence and confidentiality**. If a business uses other sources of finance, it loses its independence because it is obliged to provide documents and information so that people offering finance can assess whether it is a suitable risk for them. A company that uses retained profits does not need to reveal any business information that it might prefer to keep confidential.
- **Shareholder goodwill**. Retained profits, if used to improve the performance of a business, should lead to an increase in the share price, to the benefit of its shareholders.
- **Management of dividend payments**. During profitable periods, more profits can be retained to support capital investment. During difficult times the company can cut back on its capital investment. This allows the business to offer consistent dividends to shareholders, giving them a regular and predictable source of annual income. Some companies have even continued to pay dividends in years when losses were made, by accumulating funds from previous years.

Disadvantages of retained profit

- **Impact on dividends to shareholders**. By retaining profit within the business, the company is actually depriving its shareholders of money that is their right to receive.
- **Misuse of funds**. Retained profit may be misused by a company's managers who may not use the money judiciously or may even misappropriate it.
- **Possibility of overcapitalisation and ineffective use of funds**. Profit, when retained by a business over a period of time, may lead to overcapitalisation. This can occur if a business makes a lot of profit but is not in a position to use this profit to invest in profitable ventures. Any retained profit might just be used to improve cash levels, rather than being used to fund new capital equipment or research and development into potential or new products. In 2014, Apple was concerned about a relative lack of new innovations being developed within the business; this meant it was unable to identify enough profitable uses for its retained profit. As a result, Apple used $14 billion of its own funds to buy back its own shares. Reducing the available supply of shares in Apple meant that each existing share would get a larger percentage of any distributed profit in the future.

- **Opportunity cost**. Although retained profits do not incur an interest charge or dividend payment, there is an opportunity cost involved. For example, if £100 million profit was put into savings at 5 per cent interest, it would generate a return of £5 million a year. Therefore, profits should not be retained if the company cannot find a use for them that would yield a return of more than 5 per cent.

Share capital/ordinary share capital

Share capital is an **external*** source of **long-term** finance.

(* Although shareholders are owners of a business, when shares are first issued the company founders ask outside investors to buy shares. Thus, at the time of issue the finance is provided by people who are external.)

Ordinary share capital was introduced in Chapter 2. You may wish to revisit Chapter 2 for a more detailed background on the nature of ordinary share capital, the role of shareholders and influences on share prices.

Features of ordinary share capital

- Ordinary shares are known as **risk capital** or **equity capital**. Ordinary shareholders receive no promises from a company. If a company is successful, each shareholder receives a **dividend** (a share of the profits). A shareholder owning 1 per cent of a company's ordinary shares receives 1 per cent of the profit that is given to shareholders, and gets 1 per cent of the votes at the annual general meeting (AGM). The shareholders themselves decide at the AGM what dividend will be paid, but there is no guaranteed level of dividend. In profitable years, a high dividend may be paid, but creditors must be paid first. Sometimes the future of a company could depend on profits being retained in the business to finance capital expenditure. In these circumstances, no dividend may be paid at all.
- Ordinary share capital appeals to investors who are prepared to take a risk in return for (usually) higher rewards. If a business goes into liquidation and ceases to exist because it cannot pay its debts, money invested by shareholders will only be returned to them if there is anything left after every debt has been paid in full. On the other hand, because profitable businesses can borrow at low interest rates, they may rely mainly on loan capital as a source of finance. This will mean there are relatively few shareholders who are entitled to a share of the profits. These few shareholders will thus get high dividends when profits are high.
- In the case of liquidation, the shareholder is protected by the limited liability provided by limited companies. This means that shareholders can only lose the paid-up value of their shares and cannot be asked to pay any more money.
- Ordinary shares are often known as **permanent capital**, because a business will always have shareholders who own these shares and will never have to repay the value of these shares. (There are rules that allow a business to buy back some of its shares, but businesses can only do this in a limited way.) For this reason, ordinary share capital is used as a *long-term source of finance*, to set up the firm in the first place or for major expansion plans that cannot be financed from other sources.
- For expansion plans, companies will often use a **rights issue**, where the new shares are sold to existing shareholders. This reduces the

administrative costs of issuing ordinary share capital, because the new shares are often sold in proportion to the number of shares already held by existing shareholders (e.g. one share for every five already owned).

Advantages of ordinary share capital

- **Limited liability encourages shareholders to invest**. Consequently, businesses with ordinary shares (limited companies) find it easier to raise finance, because limited liability restricts the amount of money that shareholders can lose.
- **It is not necessary to pay a dividend**. If the business makes little or no profit (or a loss) it can decide not to pay a dividend to shareholders in that particular year. This contrasts sharply with loans – interest must be paid on these, regardless of the success or failure of the business.
- **Bringing new shareholders into a small business can add further expertise**. This usually applies when the additional share capital is being provided by a business angel or venture capitalist.
- **Increasing ordinary share capital can make it easier to borrow more funds from a bank**. Share capital can help to pay for assets that can be used as collateral (security) for a bank loan. Thus having more share capital may mean it is easier to get a bank loan, if required.
- **Ordinary share capital is permanent**. The company will never be required to gather together sufficient funds to repay its share capital; the money stays permanently in the business.

Disadvantages of ordinary share capital

- **Possible high dividend payments**. In profitable years, ordinary shareholders will expect good dividends and this is likely to be more expensive than the interest charged on a loan. This can limit the company's opportunities to use its profits for expansion.
- **Conflict of objectives**. The original objectives of a business may be lost as new shareholders may not have the same values as the original owners. For example, Cadbury's was a Quaker Company which placed a high value on religion and non-consumption of alcohol. After the take over of Cadbury's by Kraft, there were concerns in Bournville (where Cadbury's main factory is located) that these original objectives would be ignored.
- **Loss of control of original owners**. As a business grows, for example as a result of expansion financed by the issue of shares, it is probable that the percentage shareholdings of the original owner(s) will decline. This can ultimately lead to a smaller share of distributed profits for this group of shareholders and a loss of their control of the business.

What do you think?

Because the land owned in Bournville was provided through a trust set up by Quakers, it is not possible to get permission for alcohol to be served in this area. A recent attempt by a Tesco local store in Bournville to get a licence to sell alcohol was met by objections from Cadbury's. The licence request was turned down, so alcohol is still not available for purchase in Bournville.

Is it right for companies such as Cadbury's to exert this type of influence? What do you think?

Key term

Loan capital Money received by an organisation in return for the organisation's agreement to pay interest during the period of the loan and to repay the loan within an agreed time.

Did you know?

Lenders, such as banks, take security for loans that they provide for businesses. Usually, this is in the form of property (known as **collateral**), so that they can eliminate the risk of a loan not being repaid. If the loan is not repaid, they can sell the property and collect the sum that is owed to them.

Loans

A **bank loan** is a sum of money provided to a firm or an individual by a bank for a specific, agreed purpose. Banks are the main providers of loans to businesses in the UK.

Loans are an **external** source of **long-term** finance.

Providers of **loan capital** are known as **creditors**. They charge interest on the loan and must be paid before any dividends are received by shareholders. Similarly, if a business goes into liquidation (closes down), the money raised from the sale of its assets must be paid in full to creditors before any payment is made to the shareholders.

The terms of a loan usually specify the purpose, the interest rates and the repayment dates. The business receiving the loan is usually required to provide a form of security, such as the deeds to a property, and will repay the loan and interest on a regular basis over an agreed period of time. Bank loans tend to have fixed rates of interest, but this is not always the case and flexible rates are possible, particularly if the loan is for a long period of time. The Bank of England decides on a base rate of interest. Individual banks will charge interest rates a set percentage above this base rate, depending on how much risk they are taking. New and small firms usually pay higher rates of interest than larger firms.

Loans are useful because they can be set for any length of time, to suit the needs of the firm. They are normally used as a *long-term* or *medium-term source of finance*.

Advantages of loans

- **Easy for budgeting**. The interest rate and therefore the repayments are fixed in advance, making it easy to plan a schedule for repayments.
- **Lower interest rates**. Interest charges are normally lower than overdrafts because of the security provided. However, it is possible to get unsecured loans at a higher interest charge if the business cannot provide collateral.
- **Designed to meet the company's needs**. The size of the loan and the period of repayment can be organised to match the exact needs of a firm. As a rule, if a firm borrows money to finance a project or investment that is expected to take five years to pay for itself, then a five-year loan will be agreed.

Disadvantages of loans

- **Limitations on amount available**. The size of a loan may be limited by the amount of collateral that can be provided rather than by the amount of money needed by a business.
- **Inflexibility**. There is usually less flexibility with loans, especially bank loans, so a business will tend to pay interest for the agreed period, even if it gets into a position where it can pay off the loan early. It may be possible to repay the loan earlier, but often a fee must be paid for doing this.
- **Potential expense**. Loans can be more expensive than alternatives such as share capital. This is particularly true for start-up businesses, which are charged higher rates of interest because they are usually unable to provide the guarantees that a lender prefers.

Venture capital

Venture capital is an **external** source of **long-term** finance.

Venture capital commonly involves sums of between £50,000 and £150,000, which are provided by individuals (often known as **business angels**) or merchant banks. (Merchant banks are organisations, such as NM Rothschild, which specialise in providing finance to support businesses and trade.) It can take the form of loans or payment in return for share capital (or a mixture of the two). Although venture capitalists take a risk, small/medium high-risk companies can produce excellent returns.

Venture capital is used to fund expansion plans, so it is a *long-term source of finance*, although in rapidly changing industries it can be offered as a *medium-term loan*.

Advantages of venture capital

- **Suited to high-risk companies**. It is often provided to companies that are unable to get finance from other sources because of the risk involved.
- **Venture capitalists sometimes allow interest or dividends to be delayed**. This is because venture capitalists recognise the need for the start-up to become established before it pays out large rewards to its backers.
- **Source of advice and contacts**. Venture capitalists often provide advice to help a business (and their investment) succeed. Because of their business background, venture capitalists can often help a business to establish links with other people or businesses, such as suppliers, customers or people with appropriate skills, such as marketing and finance.

Key term

Venture capital Finance that is provided to small- or medium-sized firms that seek growth but which may be considered as risky by typical share buyers or other lenders.

Fact file

YUUworld

Gill Hayward and Kellie Forbes produced a range of ergonomically designed YUU and YUUtuu backpacks which were packed full of features for kids, such as a fold down desk and detachable pencil case. Each bag also included a free YUUfun pack, containing a magnetic snakes and ladders game, scribble sticks and pad and various other games.

To get expertise to help develop new products and secure the additional finance needed for expansion they appeared on the BBC's 'Dragon's Den'. They received offers from all of the dragons and agreed a £60,000 investment from dragons Deborah Meaden and Peter Jones in return for a 15 per cent stake for each dragon.

Source: www.Yuuworld.com; www.bbc.co.uk

Fact file

Levi Roots

Levi Roots is one of the biggest success stories from the BBC's 'Dragon's Den'. In 2007, his Reggae Reggae Sauce won support from two of the dragons – Peter Jones and Richard Farleigh. An exclusive deal for Sainsbury's to stock the sauce was agreed. Sainsbury's expected sales of 40,000 to 50,000 per annum, but the product achieved weekly sales of 50,000. The range of sauces has been extended and they are now available in a wide range of stores and restaurants and in a variety of different forms.

Source: www.leviroots.com; www.bbc.co.uk

Disadvantages of venture capital

- **Giving up some ownership of the business**. Venture capitalists often demand a significant share of the business in return for their investment. Levi Roots had initially been prepared to offer 20 per cent of his business in return for £50,000, but had to settle for giving up 40 per cent for the same investment.
- **Possible high finance costs**. In return for the high risks involved, venture capitalists often want high interest payments or dividends, potentially undermining the future growth prospects of the firm.
- **Excessive influence**. Venture capitalists may exert too much influence and so the original owner could lose his or her independence.

What do you think?

Professor John Mullins of the London Business School believes that raising money from venture capitalists too early on in the life of a company is a very bad idea.

Leaving it till later will enable owners to hold on to a larger equity stake in their business, he said: 'If you raise money early the investor is going to want a bigger stake in the business because it doesn't have value yet, whereas if you do it later the venture capitalist will be willing to take a smaller stake in the business because you have created more value.'

Do you agree or do high-risk businesses need help in the early years of the business?

Other sources of finance

There are many different sources of finance and businesses will choose the sources that most suit their particular circumstances. The list below shows some of the alternative sources of finance.

Short-term sources of finance

- **Sale and leaseback**: Immediate cash can be acquired by selling off a property the business owns and then renting (leasing) it back from the new owner. **Sale and leaseback** is an **internal** source of finance.

Long-term sources of finance

- **Debentures**. These are a long-term loan made to a business at an agreed fixed percentage rate of interest and repayable on a stated date. **Debentures** are an **external** source of finance. Traditionally, debentures were issued for 25 years, but the pace of change in the business world means that firms expect to be able to repay even very large loans much more quickly, so shorter periods are now more common. The current rate of interest is another factor. At the time of writing (summer 2014), interest rates are at their lowest level for half a century, so firms are finding long-term debentures very attractive because the interest rate is fixed.
- **Mortgages**. If business owner(s) already own a property, a second mortgage can be taken out to raise additional finance to establish the business. In effect, this method uses the property owned by the business as security for a loan. **Mortgages** are an **external** source of finance.

- **Sale of assets**. If a firm no longer needs an asset (it may be diversifying into other activities), it can sell this asset to fund the purchase of new assets in more profitable parts of the business. When used in this way, the sale of assets is NOT a short-term source of finance because it is being used to purchase an asset that will take a long time to pay for itself. **Sale of assets** is an **internal** source of finance.
- **Personal sources**. Small businesses are often established through funds provided by the owner or owners from their savings or personal assets. In this situation, **personal sources** of finance are an **internal** source of finance. In some cases, funds are borrowed from family and friends. In this case, **personal sources** are an **external** source of finance.
- **Peer-to-peer lending**. This is another form of loan capital and is usually carried out online. A website is used to match people who have savings to those businesses seeking to borrow money. The process is very quick, but guarantees are required from the business itself or its owners (such as some form of collateral security), so that the risk to the lender is reduced. **Peer-to-peer lending** is an **external** source of finance.
- **Crowdfunding**. This is another method of raising finance online. Businesses outline the details of their business and projects and invite people to help to provide funding. Prospective investors visit a crowdfunding website to get the details of these projects. They then decide whether or not to provide finance. For equity crowdfunding the finance provided by investors is in return for share capital. Investors can offer as little as £10, so the level of risk by investors can be limited. Crowdfunding can also be based on loans with an agreed interest rate, rather than share capital.

Choosing a source of finance

The relative importance of the different sources of finance may vary according to the specific context and circumstances facing a business. When deciding which source of finance to use, a business will weigh up the following factors.

- **Legal structure of the business**. Private limited companies and public limited companies sell shares; sole traders and partnerships rely on personal finance.
- **Use of the finance**. As indicated earlier, the purchase of fixed (non-current) assets must come from one of the sources of long-term finance, but if the business needs working capital, an overdraft or debt factoring is more appropriate. *The basic rule is that the length of time that it takes the business to earn the money to repay the source should match the length of time the business is given to repay the money.*
- **Amount required**. The larger the sum, the less likely it is that the owner(s) will be able to generate enough finance from internal sources. Larger sums therefore often mean that loans or share capital are needed. In practice, lenders want to see that the recipient of a loan is also taking a risk, so large loans may depend on a combination of internal and external finance.
- **Firm's profit levels**. A very profitable firm will have its own money and may not need external help, although banks and other lenders will be happy to lend it money. Ironically, unprofitable firms are those most likely to need a loan but least likely to be able to obtain one.

Each source of finance has its own benefits and problems, so analysing the reasons why a particular business chooses a particular source (or evaluating/judging the best source or sources) is a good test of your understanding of a business's finances. Your conclusion will depend very much on the particular circumstances of the business being studied. For example, the owners may want to keep control or may lack security for a loan, so certain sources may not be available.

- **Level of risk**. If an enterprise is viewed as risky, it will find it harder to attract loans, although venture capital may be a possibility. High-risk activities therefore tend to rely more on internal sources.
- **Views of the owners.** Shareholders or owners may be reluctant to lose control of a firm, so they may reject shares and venture capital for reasons of control rather than on financial grounds. Many small firms value their independence and will not want 'outsiders' to be a part of the decision-making process. Even if they are only providing a loan, some venture capitalists insist on having a say in how a firm is run. Some owners will value these opinions and want venture capital support, but others will take the opposite view.

Recent developments in business financing

Since the recession there have been significant developments in business financing. The banking crisis led to huge losses among Britain's main banks and as a consequence they have been more reluctant to lend money, especially to smaller firms that are considered a higher risk. Government schemes, such as Funding for Lending, appear to have had little or no impact on bank lending to businesses. The Funding for Lending scheme was launched in August 2012 and provides low-cost government loans to banks on the understanding that the banks use the money to provide loans to businesses. Figure 18.1 shows bank lending to businesses from 2007 to 2014.

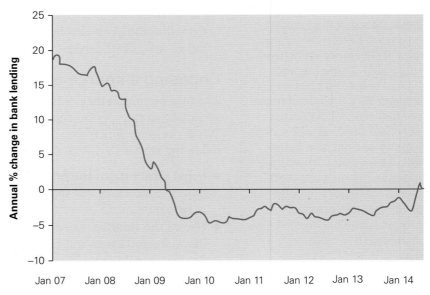

▲ **Figure 18.1** Bank lending to businesses, 2007–14 Source: TUC

This lack of support for businesses has led to calls for a state-owned bank to be set up to provide this finance. However, although the state-owned Business Bank was established in late 2014, its role is to advise businesses on where they can get finance, rather than providing finance directly.

The fall in bank lending has created a vacuum for others to enter the market. Challenger banks, such as Aldermore, have been established with a particular aim to provide funding for businesses, especially the small businesses that have found it difficult to get funds from traditional high street banks. More innovative sources of funding, such as crowdfunding and peer-to-peer lending, have also grown, but the scale of these activities is still small. For example, Aldermore increased lending to small and medium enterprises (SMEs) by £345 million in the nine months from April to December 2013. However, this was dwarfed by the cut in lending to SMEs of £2,217 million by Royal Bank of Scotland in the same period.

The belief that banks will be replaced by more innovative and responsive methods of raising finance, such as crowdfunding, is likely to be a bit premature.

Practice exercise 1

Total: 50 marks

1 Which of these sources of finance is an internal source?
 a) Debt factoring
 b) Loan capital
 c) Overdraft
 d) Venture capital *(1 mark)*

2 Which of these sources of finance is short-term?
 a) Loan
 b) Overdraft
 c) Retained profit
 d) Venture capital *(1 mark)*

3 Which one of these sources of finance is an external source?
 a) Crowdfunding
 b) Retained profit
 c) Sale and leaseback
 d) Sale of assets *(1 mark)*

4 What is the difference between 'short-term' and 'long-term' finance? *(3 marks)*

5 Explain the difference between internal finance and external finance. *(4 marks)*

6 Explain two benefits of using retained profit as a way of raising finance. *(6 marks)*

7 What is meant by 'ordinary share capital'? *(3 marks)*

8 Explain two reasons why a firm might decide to use internal rather than external finance. *(6 marks)*

9 Explain one reason why a firm might choose a short-term source of finance. *(4 marks)*

10 Describe the main differences between a bank loan and a bank overdraft. *(6 marks)*

11 Explain two possible disadvantages of using a bank overdraft. *(6 marks)*

12 Analyse two possible benefits of debt factoring for a business. *(9 marks)*

Practice exercise 2

Total: 50 marks

1 'The level of profit will always be the most important factor influencing the sources of finance that a business uses.' Do you agree? Justify your view. *(25 marks)*

2 From 2009 to 2014, bank lending to businesses has fallen. This decline in lending has been much greater for small businesses than large businesses. This trend is expected to continue. Evaluate the possible implications for the financing of small businesses if this trend continues. *(25 marks)*

Case study: CurriesOnline

CurriesOnline is a website-based business that allows people to identify alternative providers of Indian meals in a certain area and then choose a provider and either book a table or place an online order.

Director, Shamin Hoque, describes the difficulties the business faced in getting finance.

'When we set up CurriesOnline we looked at every available form of finance. I had an idea of how much I needed – about £100,000 – and at first I used my own savings. I couldn't secure a bank loan. CurriesOnline has three directors and we each put in some of our own money to get the business off the ground.'

Some friends offered support. Also, venture capitalists were interested in the business, but expected too large a shareholding in return.

Furthermore, the directors wanted to retain control of the business.

In the early months cash flow forecasting proved to be a problem. Development costs and website maintenance costs proved to be higher than anticipated and administration costs were underestimated.

According to Shamin, 'one of our biggest mistakes was not planning finances long-term'. However, after eight months of trading, the business's accountant helped the directors to develop a much better business plan and more rigorous cash flow forecasts. This enabled the business to get a bank loan.

Having established the business, the directors are now looking at various funding options to support expansion plans.

Source: www.startupdonut.co.uk

Questions

Total: 35 marks

1 What is meant by the term 'bank loan'? *(2 marks)*

2 Explain two possible benefits for CurriesOnline of agreeing to raise finance from venture capitalists. *(8 marks)*

3 Analyse reasons why the business was unable to secure a bank loan when it started. *(9 marks)*

4 How should CurriesOnline finance its expansion plans? Justify your view. *(16 marks)*

Case study: A golden opportunity

James Smith was the youngest of seven children. Initially, James worked in the family business as a goldsmith and became highly skilled in making gold jewellery and ornaments.

James intended to set up his own business using his savings and some **venture capital**, but could not raise enough money. When the family heard of his attempt, they offered their support. His father and uncle provided the ordinary share capital in return for 70 per cent of the shares, with James given 30 per cent as an incentive. A private limited company was set up with James as chief executive and his girlfriend, Katie Jones, as company secretary.

The business grew quickly and seven years later James was employing ten goldsmiths. James was based in Leeds but planned to expand into retailing elsewhere. The business had made high levels of profit, but these had been retained in the business and used to expand the premises in which the jewellery was made. There was also always a large amount of money tied up in stocks of finished jewellery and work in progress (partly finished pieces). This led to shortages of cash in the run-up to Christmas when inventory levels were high in readiness for the increased demand for jewellery. Over 50 per cent of the firm's sales were in the eight weeks leading up to Christmas.

James's goldsmiths had produced a number of unusual items of jewellery at the request of clients, and these speciality pieces were becoming a much larger part of the business. Some basic market research informed James that there was a gap in the retail market for unusual pieces of jewellery, but the main customer base was in London, and a store in Regent Street would be needed. According to James's research, a goldsmith with an unusual range of products would be likely to be successful there.

James and Katie estimated that they would need £2 million to establish the new store in London. Initially they planned to use a bank loan, but realised that this would involve possible problems. They believed that it would take three years before the London store made a profit, but after that time a profit in excess of £800,000 per annum could be made. However, as jewellery is a luxury, there was a risk that the venture might fail to make a profit if the economy did not grow. James wanted to raise the £2 million from a new issue of ordinary shares, but his father and uncle were reluctant to agree to this idea, because this would mean that the family was giving up exactly half of the business.

Questions

Total: 40 marks

1 Explain the meaning of the term 'venture capital' (page 406). *(2 marks)*

2 Explain two reasons why the business will need short-term finance and outline when this will be necessary. *(10 marks)*

3 Is the money needed to open the London store an example of capital expenditure or revenue expenditure? Briefly explain your reasoning. *(3 marks)*

4 James planned to raise £2 million to open the London store. Analyse two possible problems of using a bank loan to finance this plan. *(9 marks)*

5 Discuss the arguments for and against James using ordinary share capital in order to raise the £2 million finance needed to open the shop in London. *(16 marks)*

19

Making financial decisions: improving cash flow and profits

This chapter focuses on cash flow and profit. We examine the methods businesses might use to improve their cash flow and consider the difficulties involved in improving cash flow. We then look at the methods businesses might use to improve their profit or profitability and explain the possible difficulties involved in improving profit.

Methods of improving cash flow

In order to improve cash flow a business can use short-term sources of finance. Three short-term sources – overdrafts, debt factoring and sale and leaseback – were explained in Chapter 18, and so only a brief note is included here.

Bank overdraft

Basically a bank overdraft eases cash flow problems by allowing a business to overdraw its current account at the bank, so that a negative bank balance is held. An overdraft agreement indicates the maximum level of the overdraft (e.g. £10,000). In order to be agreed by a bank manager, a request for a bank overdraft should ideally be supported by a cash flow forecast (one indicating that the cash flow problem is not going to be permanent). This enables the bank manager to see both the need for the overdraft and the prospects of it being repaid. The business will need to pay interest on the amount overdrawn. The business will only need to pay interest on the amount of the overdraft that is actually used. Furthermore, it is only paid on a daily basis. For example, let us assume a business has an agreed overdraft limit of £10,000. It has £3,000 in its account but then withdraws £5,000. This means that it goes 'into the red' (needs to use its overdraft agreement), as it is overdrawn by £2,000. The business will only pay interest on the £2,000 and not on the £10,000 maximum that is allowed. Furthermore, this interest will cease on the day that the bank account returns 'into the black' (i.e. into credit). If £2,000 is paid into the account after three days, the interest payments will cease at this point. For a business that is constantly going into the red and then back into the black, a bank overdraft may prove to be quite a cheap way of solving cash flow problems. Technically, a bank overdraft does not *improve* the business's cash flow – as the business has a negative level of cash for a while – but it does mean that a business can survive during this period when it has no cash.

▲ By choosing to lease its assets such as vehicles, a business can overcome cash flow problems

Debt factoring

By converting the value of its receivables (debtors) into an immediate receipt of cash, a factoring company helps a business to improve its cash flow in the short-term. For businesses offering long credit periods to their customers as a way of boosting sales revenue, the immediate receipt of cash may be essential, because it would be impossible for the business to wait a year for payment. However, when the receivable (debtors) do pay the money, it goes straight to the factoring company, so it only helps in the short-term.

Sale and leaseback

Sale and leaseback of assets describes the process of selling assets that are owned by a firm in order to raise cash. The property is then rented back so that the firm can still use them for an agreed period of time.

Sale and leaseback helps to improve cash flow by providing an immediate inflow of cash – usually quite a significant amount, such as the £141 million received by Whitbread. It also means that a firm can be more flexible, because new and more efficient assets can be leased. This flexibility may also take the form of a greater willingness to relocate if the asset in question is a property. There is a tendency for businesses to be unwilling to relocate from sites that they own, but once a lease expires businesses can choose to relocate if they wish.

Leasing of non-current assets

Sale and leaseback relies on the business owning an asset so that it can sell it. The initial purchase of expensive assets, such as property, will lead to a major drain on a business's cash reserves, especially if the asset is being funded through retained profit. To overcome the possibility of cash flow problems caused by asset purchase, a business may choose to lease its assets. This is very popular with business vehicles. A regular lease (rental) payment for these assets helps to create evenly spaced outflows of cash, with the same sum being paid each month. Ownership of assets such as machinery, IT equipment and vehicles can also lead to a number of costs, such as maintenance. The owner of these assets – the leasing company – is therefore responsible for servicing and solving any problems. In this way, unexpected problems, such as a vehicle breakdown, will not cause sudden cash flow problems for a business. Owning an asset can distract a business from its core activity, because it has to get involved with additional activities such as property management or organising transport. There is a trend within business in the UK to lease rather than purchase assets, so that businesses can concentrate on their area of expertise.

Improved working capital control

Working capital is the day-to-day finance used in a business, consisting of current assets (e.g. cash, inventories and receivables) minus current liabilities (e.g. payables and overdrafts).

To stay solvent, a firm must manage its working capital. Working capital management involves careful management of a firm's main current assets (**cash**, **receivables** and **inventories**) to make sure that there is enough to pay payables and make other immediate payments.

The ways to manage the individual elements of working capital are outlined below:

Cash management

If a firm is short of cash, it has two main options:

- agree an overdraft with the bank (see Chapter 18)
- set aside a contingency fund to allow the company to meet unexpected payments or cope with lost income. In industries subject to more rapid change, a higher contingency fund should be kept.

Debt management (managing receivables)

Receivables (debtors) are customers who owe a business money. A business must decide whether customers should be given credit. If all sales are for cash, the company will have no debtors but more cash, and this should relieve any cash flow problems. However, there is a conflict between the desire for sales and profit and the desire for liquidity and cash. Giving customers credit facilities will encourage them to buy the products (hence helping profit in the long term), but will add to cash flow problems in the short term, because materials and wages have to be paid even though no cash has been received from sales.

A company must evaluate the benefits of an increase in sales and profit potential against the risks of late or non-payment. This judgement will depend on factors such as the policy of rival companies and customer expectations. For example, customers expect to be offered credit for purchases such as furniture and computers, but not for magazines and confectionery.

If it is decided that credit will be given to customers, the company must control its receivables to ensure prompt payment. The main methods are:

- obtaining a credit rating, which will testify to the customer's ability to pay and so minimise the risk of non-payment
- controlling product quality, as a satisfied customer is less likely to delay or dispute payment
- scrutinising the offer of credit, to ensure that its costs do not exceed the profits gained from offering it
- managing credit control, by monitoring and chasing customers to make sure they pay debts to the business as soon as they are due.

Inventory management

Traditionally, companies tended to keep high levels of inventory of both raw materials and finished goods, to guarantee continuation of production and immediate supply to customers. However, many firms now operate just-in-time systems that involve low inventory levels in order to minimise storage costs. Such systems rely on efficient suppliers and require them to suffer penalties if deliveries are late. Just-in-time companies can operate with lower levels of working capital than other organisations, thus improving their cash flow situation.

Different departments will view the ideal level of inventory from varying perspectives. From the finance department's perspective, inventory should be kept to a minimum because a higher inventory level means a lower holding of cash. However, the marketing department will want inventories of finished products to be readily available to meet customer demand. The operations department will need inventories of raw materials to make the products. Again, the company must weigh up the relative merits of these different views.

Management of payables

Businesses usually expect credit terms when buying raw materials or inventories from suppliers. The standard term is usually one month. However, by negotiating a longer credit period the business can delay its payments and therefore keep more cash, thus improving its cash flow.

What do you think?

Analysis by the *Daily Telegraph* in January 2014 showed that there are significant differences in the time taken for UK retailers to pay their suppliers. Whereas Mulberry and M&S paid their suppliers within 15 and 24 days respectively, Home Retail Group, which owns Argos and Homebase, and Debenhams both took 60 days to pay their suppliers.

The government has considered having a standard time for credit agreements, with a suggestion that businesses taking more than one month to pay their suppliers should be charged interest on the sum owed.

Do you think there should be a law to enforce interest payments where suppliers are not paid within a month?

Other methods

A business can also improve its cash flow by:

- diversifying its product portfolio to create a range that sells throughout the year. For example, Wall's sales of sausages in winter may be balanced by its ice-cream sales in the summer
- improved planning, monitoring and control, to help the business to anticipate when problems may arise
- holding a contingency fund that is set aside to allow the business to meet unexpected payments or cope with lost income.

▲ Walls sell more ice-cream in summer and sausages in winter

Fact file

Diversification at Sergio's Pools and Spas

Sergio's Pools and Spas had to find a way to boost business in the winter months, when pool construction and maintenance come to a halt. The answer was to set up First Response Construction, a business that repairs fire damage. 'Pools are obviously seasonal,' says owner Joe Sergio, 'and most of the house fires happen in winter.' Cash flow is now much more evenly spread throughout the year.

411

Difficulties improving cash flow

Seasonal demand

The demand for some products and services is seasonal, but companies typically incur costs in producing in advance of the peak season for sales. This causes a significant, but predictable, cash-flow problem for any seasonal business, especially for businesses in industries such as farming, where there is heavy expenditure just prior to the sale of the crop. At this point, it may be almost a year since the farmer received an income.

Although it is difficult to improve cash flow in certain seasons, the problem is predictable, so it is easy to persuade suppliers to provide credit or to negotiate a bank overdraft.

Overtrading

Firms may become too confident and expand rapidly without organising sufficient long-term funds and this puts a strain on their working capital. Businesses often give credit to their customers. Unfortunately, during rapid expansion this means that the business needs to buy more and more materials but lacks money because its customers are not paying it as soon as the goods are sold. This leaves the business short of cash. This difficulty can be reduced by growing in a slower, more managed way, but this will probably reduce the potential profit.

Over-investment in long-term assets

Firms may invest in long-term assets in order to grow, but leave themselves with inadequate cash for day-to-day payments. The more successful a small firm, the more eager the owners will be to purchase new shops or equipment. If such investments are not managed carefully, this can leave the business drained of finance and in danger of cash flow problems. Equipment and buildings cannot easily be turned back into cash, and in extreme situations the business might be unable to pay its debts, even though it has plenty of assets. Again, this difficulty can be reduced by growing more slowly, although leasing rather than buying is probably a better course of action.

Unforeseen changes

Cash flow difficulties might also arise from internal changes (e.g. machinery breakdown leading to lower receipts of cash for a period) or external factors (e.g. a change in government legislation that requires the business to spend money to comply with new regulations). These could be attributed to management errors or poor planning, but may just be bad luck.

Losses or low profits

Although cash flow and profits are different, the two are linked. A business whose sales revenue is less than its expenditure will usually (but not always) have less cash than one that is making a healthy profit. Furthermore, creditors and investors will be less likely to put money into a business that is not expected to make a profit in the future. Unless a loss-making business can show how it will become profitable in the future, it will find it difficult to overcome cash flow problems.

Improving cash flow may also be difficult because the methods of improving cash flow each have drawbacks:

- **Bank overdraft**. These require interest payments which are a further drain on a business's cash. In extreme circumstances a bank manager can demand immediate repayment, which may cause the business to liquidate.
- **Debt factoring**. The sum paid to a business by a factoring company will be less than the sum owed to the business and so the profit made from the transaction will be reduced. The factoring company may also refuse to factor a debt if it believes there is a possibility of a bad debt.

- **Sale of assets**. Assets such as buildings and machinery may be difficult to sell quickly. Usually, a business trying to make a quick sale has to accept a much lower price than the asset's true value.
- **Sale and leaseback**. Assuming that the business buying the asset expects to make a profit from the asset, in the long term it is likely that the business selling it will pay more in rent than it receives from its sale. Sale and leaseback reduces the value of a business's assets that can be used as security against future loans. This can make future borrowing more difficult and lead to higher interest charges. Also, a business may eventually lose the use of the asset when the lease ends, because a competitor may be prepared to pay a higher rental for the lease.
- **Leasing of non-current assets**: This leads to the same difficulties as sale and leaseback.
- **Cash management**. Keeping a large contingency fund reduces risk but limits the level of investment undertaken by a business. Therefore, it tends to reduce profit.
- **Chasing receivables for prompt payment**. Cash flow might be improved by this, but it may lead to a loss of goodwill. A business will not want to upset its customers, especially if its customers agreed to buy its products because of the opportunity to buy on credit.
- **Reducing inventory levels**. This can lead to higher cash levels but can reduce sales and profit because the products may not be available to prospective customers. This can be a major issue for 'impulse buys', which are often purchased because they are visible to the customer.
- **Delaying payments to payables**. This can also lead to a loss of goodwill and may even mean that suppliers refuse to supply products in the future.

Practice exercise 1

Total: 40 marks

1 The features of a bank overdraft usually include:
   a) a fixed interest rate
   b) repayments on a monthly basis
   c) the opening of a separate bank account – the overdraft account
   d) no need for collateral security *(1 mark)*

2 A system where the debts owed to a business are purchased by another business is known as:
   a) a loan
   b) factoring
   c) leasing
   d) sale and leaseback *(1 mark)*

3 Explain why delaying payments might not be a good solution to a cash flow problem. *(4 marks)*

4 Explain the differences between 'sale of assets', 'sale and leaseback' and 'leasing'. *(6 marks)*

5 Select two causes of cash flow problems. Analyse the best method of solving each of these two causes, justifying your choices. *(10 marks)*

6 Analyse how an electrical goods manufacturer might improve its cash flow by improving its working capital management. *(9 marks)*

7 Analyse two reasons why it might be difficult to improve a business's cash flow. *(9 marks)*

Case study: Khalid Ahmed's computer peripherals

Khalid Ahmed was worried. When he had opened up his store, he was the only specialist seller of computer peripherals in town. Now there were five other small shops selling ink cartridges, printers, keyboards, memory sticks, paper and other related items.

Khalid had not foreseen the dramatic increase in competition. Consequently, his move into a much larger store in 2012 was now proving to be a problem.

The new store had opened up the opportunity to extend his product range to include larger items, such as printers, tablets and computers themselves. This had helped Khalid to earn far more revenue, but it had also increased his costs dramatically. The profit margin on computers tended to be less than that on tablets, software and peripherals. Khalid also found that computer and tablet sales were seasonal and this led to cash flow problems at certain times of the year – particularly from September to November, when he had to buy a great deal of stock in the run-up to Christmas, but had not yet sold the computers and tablets.

Khalid had suffered further cash flow problems because he was forced to offer credit terms in order to generate customer interest. He cursed the big rivals such as PC World who had forced him into this position. The use of a factoring company had overcome this problem, although it had led to a reduction in his profits for a while.

Khalid was reluctant to borrow money but realised it would be necessary in order to survive. The lease on his shop, which cost him £30,000 a year, was about to expire and he had discovered that there was a well-located small shop for sale in an area where there was no direct competition. Khalid had considered adding mobile phones to his product range, but this was not his field of expertise and the shop had less selling space than his previous, larger store. Given the lack of competition in this new area, Khalid believed that his sales in 2016 would be 25 per cent higher than his 2015 levels. He also anticipated further growth in 2017. He visited his bank manager with a cash flow forecast (Table 19.1), based on the assumption that he would borrow the £200,000 necessary to buy the shop. He intended to repay the loan within five years.

▼ **Table 19.1** Cash flow forecast for Khalid Ahmed, 2016–17

	2016				2017			
	Qtr 1	**Qtr 2**	**Qtr 3**	**Qtr 4**	**Qtr 1**	**Qtr 2**	**Qtr 3**	**Qtr 4**
	(£000s)	(£000s)	(£000s)	(£000s)	(£000s)	(£000s)	(£000s)	(£000s)
Opening balance	2	(4)	(3)	(25)	9	8	17	3
Sales of hardware	20	30	25	75	22	40	35	95
Sales of software and peripherals	60	65	55	75	70	75	65	95
Total inflows	**80**	**95**	**80**	**150**	**92**	**115**	**100**	**190**
Hardware purchases	12	18	30	30	13	24	36	42
Software and peripherals purchases	24	26	22	30	28	30	26	38
Wages*	16	16	16	20	17	17	17	21
Repayment of loan	14	14	14	14	14	14	14	14
Other costs, including lease	20	20	20	22	21	21	21	23
Total outflows	**86**	**94**	**102**	**116**	**93**	**106**	**114**	**138**
Net cash flow	**(6)**	**1**	**(22)**	**34**	**(1)**	**9**	**(14)**	**52**
Closing balance	(4)	(3)	(25)	9	8	17	3	55

* Including annual wage of £28,000 (£7,000 per quarter) paid to Khalid himself.

Questions

1 How is the 'closing balance' calculated? *(4 marks)*

2 How did debt factoring help Khalid's cash flow? *(5 marks)*

3 The bank manager advised Khalid to take out an overdraft. Based on the data in Table 19.1, explain the reason for this advice. *(5 marks)*

4 Analyse two different factors that might be causing Khalid to experience cash flow problems. *(9 marks)*

5 Khalid decided to use a five-year bank loan to buy a shop rather than continuing his lease of the previous store. To what extent do you believe that this was a sensible decision? *(16 marks)*

6 Khalid has experienced cash flow problems in the early years of his business. Do you believe that these problems will occur after the end of 2016? Justify your view. *(16 marks)*

Methods of improving profits and profitability

Businesses have many objectives. John Lewis is a classic example – one of its objectives is to reward its employees as much as possible by paying them a bonus. In 2013–14 employees received a bonus that equalled 15 per cent of their pay. However, this bonus depends on the business making a good profit. All businesses aim to make a certain level of profit, in order to avoid making a loss, even if maximum profits are not their primary aim.

There are many ways of increasing profit. However, the three most basic methods are:

● changing the price
● decreasing costs
● increasing sales volume.

Changing the price

If a business increases the price of a product, it will widen the profit margin and therefore each product sold will generate more profit. This strategy will be particularly effective if the product is a necessity, has no close substitutes, or has price inelastic demand for other reasons, because customers will be willing to pay the higher price. However, the strategy of increasing the price must be treated with caution if there are many competitors for the product because the higher price may lead customers to switch to rival products or stop buying the product entirely. In this situation, it is possible that the price rise may cause a fall in demand that is so great that the higher profit margin will be offset by a dramatic fall in quantity.

For example, suppose that the profit margin is £10 per unit and 100 units are sold – the total profit in this case will be £1,000 (£10 × 100). An increase in price of £2 will mean that profit margin increases to £12. However, if only 80 units are then sold, the total profit will be £960 (£12 × 80), and so the price increase has actually led to a *fall* in profit.

In situations where there are many competitors, it may actually be more profitable to *cut* the price. Using the above example, if the firm decides to decrease the price by £2, the profit margin falls to £8 per unit. If this lower

price leads to an increase in the quantity demanded from 100 units to 140 units, the profit will increase from £1,000 to £1,120 (£8 × 140 units).

Fact file

Branding and profitability

How easy is it to increase price without losing customers? Research by the trade magazine, *The Grocer*, showed that 'branding' was a key to success. In the food industry, profitability was much higher for food producers such as Kellogg's and Jordans, which provide branded products. Those firms that produce own-label products for supermarkets have much lower profitability, although their profitability was slightly higher than those businesses that provided the basic food commodities before they are processed.

Overall, profit margins for own label products was 10 per cent higher than for basic commodities, but less than half the profitability of branded products.

Decreasing costs

If the business can cut its direct costs, such as wage levels or raw material costs, then the profit margin will increase. This means that each product will yield more profit and, assuming that there is no change in demand, this will increase the total profit. In most cases, changes in costs will probably not affect the level of demand, so this strategy will be successful in improving profits and profitability. However, if the change in costs leads to a decrease in quality or efficiency, demand for the product may fall. This could happen if costs are being cut because inferior raw materials are being used, or if the workers who accept a lower wage are less efficient than those being paid a higher wage.

Similar benefits can be obtained by reducing overheads, such as rent, office expenses and machinery costs. Once again, the business must be careful that cutting these costs does not damage sales. For example, a retail outlet may be reluctant to move to premises with a lower rent if the new location is less accessible to customers. In this case, the savings in costs may be much lower than the decline in sales revenue caused by the unfavourable location.

Author advice

The business concepts in this chapter are centred on **finance**. However, improving efficiency in order to increase profits is the role of most business activities. Most business topics relate to ways in which either:

● price can be changed, or
● costs can be decreased, or
● sales volume can be increased.
Try to link these aims to your study of the other functional areas:

● people
● operations management
● marketing.
This chapter can be used to bring together all the topics covered at AS level and many Year 2 topics too.

Increasing sales volume

If costs and price remain the same, it is still possible to increase profits by increasing the volume of products sold. This may occur simply because demand increases as the product becomes more established in the market. However, it may be due to the actions of the business, such as marketing or product development.

What do you think?

Bestway

Sir Anwar Pervez, the Chief Executive Officer of Bestway, is someone who focused on sales volume rather than profit margin. The former bus conductor started a convenience store in 1963 but moved into cash-and-carry wholesaling in 1976. At the time, wholesalers were making reasonable profit margins; Sir Anwar thought he could manage by having smaller profit margins. Within nine years he had six warehouses. His warehouses now achieve an operating profit margin of only 2.32 per cent, but with sales of £2.34 billion a year this means a £54.3 million profit. The profit margin was cut in 2013 to help Bestway's customers, who are mainly small retailers, compete with the supermarkets and larger grocery chains. This operating profit margin contrasts sharply with the Bestway Group's Cement Manufacturing division, which earned a profit of £57.9 million from sales of £177.7 million, an operating profit margin of 32.6 per cent.

Why is the profitability of cement manufacturing so much higher than cash-and-carry wholesaling?

Source: www.bestway.co.uk

Other methods of improving profit/profitability

Some other methods of improving profits are noted below, but this is not an exhaustive list:

- **Investment in fixed assets**. Purchasing new equipment, buildings or vehicles can enable a business to expand its scale of operation and possibly improve both the efficiency of production and the quality of the product. As a result, the business may be able to increase its profits by achieving higher sales volume, charging a higher price and cutting its costs.
- **Product development and innovation**. A business can introduce new, unique products in order to attract more customers. New products often carry higher prices because they are different from established brands, so the business can gain extra profits by selling more items and charging a higher price at the same time. In addition to introducing new products, innovation can lead to greater efficiency of production or other cost-saving measures.
- **Marketing.** Successful marketing strategies, such as a clever advertising campaign or sponsorship of a popular event, can encourage customers to buy more of the business's products. Furthermore, a great deal of marketing is intended to increase the value of the product to the customer, and so may encourage customers to pay a higher price. Although marketing adds to the costs of the business, these extra costs should be offset by the additional revenue generated, so profit should increase.
- **Human resource strategies.** The staff of an organisation are invariably its greatest asset. Careful selection, recruitment and training of staff, and strategies that motivate them, should lead to greater efficiency. This may lead to greater output, higher quality products and better customer service, all of which should contribute to higher profits.

Fact file

Does profitability depend on the industry in which a firm operates?

The evidence suggests not. Table 19.2 is based on *The Sunday Times* Profit Track 100 in 2014, which analyses the most successful **private limited companies** in the UK. It shows private limited companies, ranked in order of their percentage increases in profit growth over the last three years. The top ten private limited companies all trade in different markets.

▼ **Table 19.2** Private limited companies with the biggest profit margins

Rank	Private limited company	Activity	3-year average profit growth in (% p.a.)
1	The Hut Group	Online retailer	178 %
2	JCB	Construction equipment manufacturer	169 %
3	Acorn Stairlifts	Stairlifts manufacturer	142 %
4	Wetherby Building Systems	Insulation systems manufacturer	125 %
5	Thomsons Online Benefits	Employee benefits software developer	121 %
6	Dawson Construction	Civil engineering contractor	121 %
7	Centek	Oilfield equipment manufacturer	117 %
8	Express Engineering	Precision engineer	111 %
9	Immediate Media Co	Magazine publisher	107 %
10	Pret A Manger	Sandwich shop operator	105 %

Source: *The Sunday Times* Profit Track 100 in 2014

Difficulties improving profit

Internal factors

In order to increase profits a business can adopt three main approaches: changing the price, decreasing costs or increasing sales volume. Each of these approaches has its own difficulties.

Changing the price

We saw earlier (on page 415 of this chapter and in Chapter 8) that the impact of price changes on profit can be difficult to predict because the effect depends on the price elasticity of demand and the profit margin, both of which may be unknown when the decision is made.

Fact file

Tesco plc and pricing

During its period of growth, Tesco offered a varied range of commodities, appealing to a wide range of customers through its 'Finest' (most expensive) products, to its standard (mid-price) range and finally its 'Value' range, which sold some products at very low prices. Tesco also grew its sales volume on the basis of buying suitable sites, mainly building large-scale out-of-town stores. When Chief Executive Terry Leahy retired, his replacement, Philip Clarke, focused on a strategy of higher prices, hoping to benefit from Tesco's market dominance. This approach also led to the demise of some of Tesco's very cheap 'value' products. The strategy for higher profit was to upgrade the IT system, to improve its efficiency and to refit many stores to improve the attractiveness of the physical environment. After three profit warnings in 2014, a new CEO, Dave Lewis was appointed. His immediate response was to announce that Tesco would be cutting its prices and to ask employees to try to ensure high quality customer service.

Decreasing costs

A fall in unit costs will increase the profit margin and so it should lead to a rise in profit levels. However, there are difficulties involved in this approach, depending on the exact method employed. Some examples of these difficulties are outlined below.

● **Reducing wages**. Although this will cut labour costs it may have a negative impact on the morale of employees. This can be harmful to the company's profits in a number of ways:
  ● Lower labour productivity, because workers are demoralised or have higher rates of absence. This may cause unit costs to increase rather than fall.
  ● Higher staff turnover, which mean costs incurred replacing staff and possibly lost efficiency whilst new workers are trained.
● **Cutting raw material costs**. However, this may lead to lower quality and therefore a loss of sales volume and brand loyalty.
● **Cutting the marketing budget**. This will probably lead to lower sales, because promotions will be cut. Savings in market research may mean that the company has a poorer understanding of the wants of its potential customers.

These examples from the other three functional areas of the business (HR, operations and marketing) demonstrate the potential difficulties involved in trying to improve profitability by cutting costs.

Increasing sales volume

To increase sales requires effective marketing, good customer service and high quality production. It will require effective co-ordination between all of the different departments. Furthermore, all of these activities will add to the expenditure of the business and so there is a possibility that extra sales may not lead to increased profit.

External factors

In Chapter 3 we studied some of the external factors that affect businesses.

Business profits are influenced by these factors and if external conditions are not suited to the business it can lead to difficulties in increasing profit and profitability. Some examples are as described below.

● **Competition**. A price war between competitors will have an adverse effect on all businesses in a particular market. In some cases these price wars are an attempt by larger businesses to force smaller ones out of the market.
● **Market conditions**. In a market with restricted levels of competition, such as a monopoly and oligopoly, profits can be restricted by the actions of regulatory bodies, such as the Competition and Markets Authority (CMA) – formerly the Competition Commission.
● **Consumers' incomes**. If consumers' incomes fall, as many did in the recession, it will be more difficult for most businesses to increase their level of sales.
● **Interest rates**. High interest rates mean that it is more expensive for customers to borrow money for purchases. This tends to impact mostly on household durables, cars and houses – goods that are traditionally bought on credit. High interest rates also increase costs for businesses

419

What do you think?

Poundland and 99p store

For businesses producing 'inferior goods' (those that have a negative income elasticity of demand) it can be more difficult to increase profit in years when the economy is growing. During the recessions and difficult trading period that followed, discount stores experienced rapid growth, especially among social classes C2, D and E. Their growth is shown by the following data:

● Poundland grew from 80 stores in 2003 to over 500 in 2014.
● Poundworld started trading in 2004; by 2014 it had 225 stores.
● 99p Store started trading in 2001; by 2014 it had 250 stores.

These businesses have grown because consumer incomes were low. Are they doomed to failure when consumer incomes start to rise? What do you think?

that are borrowing money. With current (2015) interest rates at record low levels, this factor has **not** made it difficult to make a profit in recent years.

- **Demographic factors.** Changes in population can lead to changes in demand for certain products. The UK has an ageing population and so products appealing to older people, such as holiday cruises, may be experiencing a relative increase in sales and profit.
- **Environmental issues.** These can lead to greater costs, if businesses need to modify their processes to become more environmentally friendly. It can also lead to reduced sales from environmentally aware customers, if a business takes insufficient action to prevent environmental problems.

Practice exercise 2
Total: 30 marks

1 Which of the following situations would be certain to lead to an increase in profits?
   a) A price increase for a good with price elastic demand
   b) A price increase for a good with price inelastic demand
   c) A price decrease for a good with price elastic demand
   d) A price decrease for a good with price inelastic demand *(1 mark)*

2 Explain one way in which the operations management function might help to improve a business's profits. *(4 marks)*

3 Explain two problems that might arise if a business attempted to improve its profits by cutting costs. *(7 marks)*

4 Analyse two changes to external factors that might help a business to increase its profits. *(9 marks)*

5 Analyse two changes to external factors that might lead to a business experiencing a fall in its profits. *(9 marks)*

Case study: Improving profitability at Carphone Warehouse

Carphone Warehouse (CPW) has undertaken a number of measures to try to improve its profit and profitability.

2013

In 2013 its European division increased sales revenue by 11.5 per cent, with the UK division showing a particularly strong increase in its market share. A 10 per cent annual growth in the UK has been based on the quality of CPW's customer service and employee expertise, factors that have led to its status as a highly trusted brand. CPW's marketing mix has been instrumental in achieving this growth, with the main focus being on regularly updated 'Smart Deal' promotions and price offers on specific handsets. This approach has been supported by improvements in the physical environment of stores and investment in new online systems to speed up and improve the buying process for customers. Throughout Europe, and especially in Germany and the UK, CPW has benefited from getting an increasing number of its customers on to postpay contracts (pay monthly contracts) rather than prepay (pay-as-you-go contracts).

The UK mobile retail market is a mature one and therefore scope for growth is limited. In response to this limitation, CPW is moving into new markets in Europe, through joint ventures with established network providers. Countries targeted for expansion are the Netherlands, Germany and Spain.

Sales of property also brought in £51 million cash in the UK. This included CPW's headquarters in Acton, which was part of a sale and leaseback arrangement.

2014 and the future

Three major developments are likely to affect CPW's profit and profitability in 2014 and beyond.

1 4G mobile phone services

At the beginning of the twenty-first century there was rapid expansion in the popularity and use of mobile phones as 3G technology enabled mobile users to connect to the internet. 4G technology was launched in the UK towards the end of 2012 and by the end of June 2013 there were over 700,000 subscribers. Table 19.3 shows the number of subscribers to 4G and 3G phone services in selected countries. Based on the experience of 3G technology, the networks anticipate a surge in the number of subscribers using 4G phone services. The much faster connection speeds make it particularly attractive to tablet users. In 18 months, since its launch in South Korea in late 2011, nearly half the population of South Korea have subscribed to 4G networks. In May 2014, the UK's largest mobile phone network, EE, announced that it had achieved 3.6 million 4G subscribers and that new 4G subscribers to EE now exceeded new 3G subscribers. CPW believe that 4G will trigger a significant increase in overall demand for new mobiles and tablets.

▼ **Table 19.3** Top 3 countries using 4G and 3G phone services

Country	4G subscribers 2nd quarter 2013	4G penetration*	Country	3G subscribers 2nd quarter 2013	3G penetration*
Global	126m	1.77%	**Global**	1,750.3m	24.55%
USA	62.5m	19.61%	**China**	325.5m	24%
Japan	26.1m	20.67%	**USA**	225.0m	70.6%
South Korea	23.0 m	47.17%	**Japan**	111.5 m	88.3%

* Penetration is the percentage of a population using a product

Source: International Communications Union/Paul Lambert; mobiThinking (http://mobiforge.com)

In the UK, the number of 3G phones is 72.6 per cent of the UK population. The number of 4G phones is equal to 1.77 per cent of the UK's population.

2 EE threatens to leave Carphone Warehouse and Phones4U

In June 2014, EE announced a review of its sales through Carphone Warehouse and Phones4U, indicating that in future subscriptions to EE might only be available through its own stores.

Carphone Warehouse and Phones4U both rely on customers wanting a store where they can compare mobile deals between a number of different network operators. The network operators have focused more on direct sales to consumers in recent years. Three pulled out of Carphone and Phones4U in 2013 and Vodafone is spending £100 million on opening 150 new stores over the next year, to help it to achieve more direct sales.

In September 2014, EE announced the end of its agreement with Phones4U. If EE cease to use Carphone Warehouse, then Vodafone would be the only major network operator left using Carphone Warehouse.

3 Dixons–Carphone Warehouse merger

On 7 August 2014, Dixons Retail, which owns Currys and PC World, merged with Carphone Warehouse. The first seven combined shops opened in August 2014, with a further 23 planned before the end of the year. The company aims to guide consumers through the 'Internet of Things' (IoT) and advise on the best devices to connect their lives at home as well as on the move. The IoT refers to the trend of connecting everyday items such as phones, fridges and boilers to the internet so they can be 'smarter'. Tech group Cisco Systems thinks the IoT could be worth $14,400 billion by 2020 when 50 billion objects will be connected to the internet.

Fridges that write shopping lists, ovens that talk and Bluetooth-connected toothbrushes: all of these are forecasts for everyday life, where even the washing machine will be online. Mintel's senior trends analyst, Richard Cope, says that everyday objects will increasingly have 'digital identities'. 'Sensors are turning "dumb" everyday objects into perceptive machines.' The toothbrush for example sends a critique of your brushing style to your phone. 'They will become a portfolio of smart helpers with the potential to better serve our needs. Google's Android is no longer just a smartphone operating system; it's the backbone of a rising class of synched-up home appliances such as refrigerators, ovens and even watches.'

Analysts say this brave new world is within touching distance and its axis is the smartphone, which will become 'the remote control for your life'. The combination of an understanding of electrical devices and mobile phones is the reason behind the merger between Dixons and Carphone Warehouse; they believe their shared expertise will put them in a strong position to exploit the opportunities offered by these changes.

Source: Based on an article by Zoe Wood in *The Guardian*, 9 May 2014, and other sources

Questions

Total: 55 marks

1 Explain why postpay (pay monthly contracts) are more likely to achieve higher profits than prepay (pay-as-you-go contracts). *(5 marks)*

2 Explain why CPW's sale and leaseback of its headquarters would improve cash flow in the short term, but might worsen profit levels in the long term. *(6 marks)*

3 To what extent is the use of the marketing mix the most important method employed by CPW to improve its profit levels in 2013. *(20 marks)*

4 The case study features three major developments in 2014. Evaluate the likely overall impact of these three developments on Carphone's profitability in the future. *(24 marks)*

20 Setting HR objectives

This chapter introduces the human resource function of an organisation. It explains the terms human resources and human resource management and then goes on to consider human resource objectives and the value of setting such objectives. It considers human resource objectives related to employee engagement and involvement; talent development; training; diversity; alignment of values; number, skills and location of employees and a number of other areas. Internal and external influences on human resource objectives and decisions are discussed. In discussing internal influences, soft and hard human resource management approaches are examined.

Human resources (HR) and human resource management (HRM)

Human resource management (HRM) is the strategic process of making the most efficient use of an organisation's employees. People are a vital resource for businesses, and planning their use must be part of strategic management if a business is to compete effectively. HRM views activities relating to the workforce as integrated and vital in helping the organisation to achieve its corporate objectives. For example, HRM activities such as planning the workforce, recruitment and selection, training, appraisal, monitoring performance, and motivation and rewards are seen as being linked and integrated with all other areas and functions of the business and its development. In this sense, HRM is a proactive approach to managing an organisation's employees (or **human resources**).

Key terms

Human resources (HR) In its simplest form, this term is used to describe an organisation's employees; more usually it describes the department or function within an organisation that is focused on activities related to employees.

Human resource management (HRM) The management of people at work in order to assist the organisation in achieving its objectives. It includes conducting job analysis, recruiting the right people for the job, induction and training, managing wages and salaries, providing benefits and incentives, evaluating performance, resolving disputes and communicating with employees at all levels.

Human resource objectives

While the human resource (HR) objectives of any organisation will be determined by its overall corporate objectives, most organisations are likely to pursue HR objectives related to the following areas.

Employee engagement and involvement

Making full use of employees' potential by ensuring they are fully engaged, involved and motivated will improve their productivity, reduce labour turnover and absenteeism and, as a consequence, reduce labour costs per unit. Each of these measures is explained in Chapter 21. A range of financial and non-financial strategies are available to engage, involve and motivate employees, details of which are discussed in detail in Chapter 23.

Talent development

The Chartered Institute of Personnel and Development (CIPD) defines talent in an organisation as 'individuals who can make a difference to organisational performance either through their immediate contribution or, in the longer-term, by demonstrating the highest levels of potential'. It defines talent development or talent management as 'the systematic attraction, identification, development, engagement, retention and deployment of those individuals who are of particular value to an organisation, either in view of their "high potential" for the future or because they are fulfilling critical business roles'. These definitions underline the fact that it is not sufficient for an organisation to simply attract individuals with high potential. Developing, managing and retaining them as part of a planned strategy for talent is equally important, as well as adopting systems to measure the return on the investment an organisation makes in relation to these individuals. Many organisations are also now broadening these definitions and looking at the 'talents' of all their employees and working on ways to develop their strengths. At its broadest, the term 'talent development' may be used to encompass the entire workforce of an organisation. The case study on ARM Ltd and the fact file on the Added Value Group in Chapter 23 illustrate the importance of talent development to a business.

Training

Training is focused upon, and evaluated against, the job that an individual currently holds and is therefore different to talent development. Training and development programmes ensure that an organisation has the capabilities to achieve its objectives and to meet the changing skills needed to compete effectively. Training and development initiatives are also critical to building a pool of candidates with the requisite skills and experience for successively more responsible roles. An organisation needs to identify its training needs, set training objectives and decide the strategies to be adopted to achieve these objectives. The overall objective of any training programme is to fill the gap between the existing and the desired knowledge, skills and aptitudes of employees. Training objectives will usually include the following elements:

● Impart basic knowledge and skills to new entrants to enable them to contribute effectively and quickly to an organisation. This would usually be in the form of an induction programme. The fact file on the BBC, later in this chapter, mentions a course on understanding diversity as part of the induction training for new recruits to the BBC.
● Assist employees to function more effectively by exposing them to the latest concepts, information and techniques and to develop their skills in the fields in which they work.
● Develop different competencies to enable employees to progress to higher levels in the organisation. This might be specific training for aspiring and new team leaders or managers. The case study on Halfords at the end of this chapter, mentions the specific training it provides for assistant managers, store managers and area managers.

- Prepare employees to undertake different jobs in order to enable redeployment and maintain flexibility in the workforce so that changes in the external environment can be met.
- Encourage job satisfaction, by ensuring employees can use their skills, knowledge and ability to the fullest extent.
- Meet the objectives of the organisation by enabling employees to contribute to them as fully as possible.

Diversity

Diversity recognises that though people have things in common with each other they are also different in many ways. Everyone has a right to equal access to employment and when employed should have equal pay and equal access to training and development. Organisations must ensure all their employees are aware of the basic legal requirements regarding equalities and diversity (in terms of gender, age, race, religion, disability, ethnicity and sexual orientation) and have an understanding of the benefits of a diverse workforce, such as the wider range of skills and ideas they bring. (See the fact file on the BBC later in this chapter.)

Alignment of values

Alignment of values as an HR objective can be viewed from two perspectives, as described below.

Alignment of HR objectives with corporate objectives

Many businesses do not view HR functions as a strategic aspect of the business and, as a result, HR managers and directors sometimes play no part in overall business strategy. In such situations, the HR function has to react to strategies imposed upon them rather than working with strategies to which they have contributed. An important aspect of running a successful business and a successful HR department is to align corporate objectives and HR objectives. It involves recognising that all aspects of a business are working toward the same objectives. This requires that HR managers must assess every action in their departments in terms of how they contribute to business objectives and whether or not they add value. In this way, a business can ensure that HR objectives and business objectives are strategically aligned (i.e. in line and linked).

Research in 2013 by The Aberdeen Group found that firms with HR departments that are aligned with business goals and objectives are better able to plan for future workforce needs. However, aligning HR and business objectives can sometimes be difficult. HR managers and senior leaders of the organisation are likely to be looking at different measures of effectiveness. For example, HR managers are likely to look at measures such as labour turnover rates and rates of absenteeism, while CEOs are looking at share prices and other financial data. The key to aligning these measures is to find how they affect each other, for example how recruiting high quality employees positively affects the company's profitability. Sharing human capital management data (discussed in Chapter 21) with all stakeholders is an important strategy in aligning values. The Aberdeen Group reported that only 25 per cent of organisations made relevant human capital management data available to stakeholders and yet it could be argued that such data is as important as financial data.

Alignment of employee values with organisational values

Ensuring that the values of an organisation are communicated and understood by employees at all levels is essential to its success. It is equally important that the values employees, at all levels, demonstrate in their work, in dealing with colleagues, customers, suppliers or other stakeholders, are aligned with (or in line with) the values claimed by their organisation. If this is the case, it is likely to enhance the reputation and performance of an organisation. It is therefore important for the HR function to ensure that employees are fully engaged with, and motivated by, their jobs; that the methods of motivation and engagement are appropriate; and that employees see the connection between their work and the overall goals, objectives and mission of their organisation. For an example of where this was definitely not the case, see the fact file on Lloyds Banking Group in Chapter 23.

Number, skills and locations of employees

Matching the number, skills and location of employees to the requirements of the business is an important HR objective. Thus, if a new plant is to be opened or new technology is being introduced, the HR function will need to ensure that sufficient employees are recruited and/or trained to meet the business's needs. One SMART HR target in this case might be 'the new factory, which will be fully operational by 1 February 2015, is fully staffed by 2 January 2015 and staff at manager and supervisor level are in post by 1 November 2014'.

Maximising labour productivity and minimising labour costs

These two objectives are likely to be underlying HR objectives for most businesses in order to ensure they are operating efficiently. They will, however, be particularly important objectives when a business is suffering from financial problems. A SMART version of this objective might be 'to raise labour productivity by 5 per cent over the next two years and to reduce overall staffing costs or labour costs per unit by 10 per cent within the next two years'. This would then be translated into detailed strategies and more detailed short-term targets, for example: improving employees' skills and competencies; encouraging team work; introducing incentive schemes; cutting back on the recruitment of new staff; removing a layer of management and delegating their responsibilities to a lower level in the organisation's hierarchy; and limiting wage increases to below the rate of inflation.

Maintaining good employer/employee relations

Without good employer/employee relations, an organisation is unlikely to achieve maximum levels of productivity and is unlikely to have a committed, satisfied and motivated workforce. Effective employer/employee relations are considered in detail in Chapter 24.

Author advice

The HR objectives 'Maximising labour productivity and minimising labour costs' and 'Maintaining good employer/employee relations' are not included in the AQA specification but they are examples of objectives that would be generally relevant to HR functions in most organisations.

Author advice

Remember that, where possible, objectives should always be SMART, i.e. specific, measurable, agreed, realistic and time-bound. This concept was introduced in Chapter 1.

As mentioned in Chapter 1, corporate objectives at HP

What do you think?

Employee commitment and leadership capability at HP

As mentioned in Chapter 1, corporate objectives at HP (Hewlett-Packard) include 'employee commitment' and 'leadership capability'. These are described below.

Employee commitment: 'We demonstrate our commitment to employees by promoting and

rewarding based on performance and by creating a work environment that reflects our values.'

Leadership capability: 'We develop leaders at all levels who achieve business results, exemplify our values and lead us to grow and win.'

Try to develop SMART HR objectives that might assist HP in achieving the two corporate objectives listed above.

Source: www.hp.com

Fact file

Diversity at the BBC

An objective of the BBC's Diversity Strategy is to: 'advance equal opportunities to diversify and develop our workforce and our senior leaders so that they better reflect our audiences.' The Strategy suggests that the more diverse the BBC's workforce, the better able it is to respond to, and reflect, its audiences in all their diversity. It wants to attract the broadest range of talented people to be part of the BBC – whether that is to contribute to its programming or the wide range of non-production roles that it relies on to deliver its programming.

Relocating some of its programming activity to Salford gave it a unique opportunity to diversify the workforce based at that site. The BBC manages a number of initiatives to support its aspirations in relation to diversity, for example, 'Extend' is a paid work placement scheme for talented disabled people. Everyone at the BBC has a role in promoting diversity

on and off screen and air. An online diversity course has been developed for all new staff members, which is designed to raise awareness about diversity, why it matters to the BBC's programming and its work environment and what steps individuals can take to make a difference.

The BBC has clear diversity targets and monitors these to check achievement. It has done this for the following groups for some time: black and minority ethnic (BME) staff, BME senior managers, staff with disabilities, senior managers with disabilities. Following The Equality Act 2010, it reviewed its approach to monitoring in order to include sexual orientation and religion or belief. (The Equality Act 2010 increased the range of protected characteristics to nine – age, disability, gender reassignment, marriage and civil partnership, pregnancy and maternity, race, religion or belief, sex, sexual orientation.)

Source: www.bbc.co.uk

What do you think?

Review the fact file on the BBC's approach to diversity and in particular, those groups it targets and monitors.

Do you think it needs targets for other groups of individuals? If so, which groups and why?

Value of setting human resource objectives

As noted in Chapters 7, 11 and 16 on marketing, operations and finance objectives, respectively, the reasons for setting any objectives are the same, regardless of the functional area being considered. These reasons are to:

● act as a focus for decision making and effort
● provide a yardstick against which success or failure can be measured

- improve co-ordination, by giving teams and departments a common purpose
- improve efficiency, by examining the reasons for success and failure in different areas
- motivate staff and improve their performance by setting challenging, but realistic, targets
- establish priorities, so that staff understand the relative importance of different objectives.

The overall value of setting HR objectives will depend on whether the benefits of this process outweigh the problems. The main benefits each link to the reasons for objective setting, outlined above. The benefits and problems of setting HR objectives are the same as the benefits of setting objectives in the other functional areas of a business.

Benefits of setting HR objectives

- If HR objectives are SMART (specific, measurable, agreed, realistic and time-bound), this helps to ensure that decisions by different staff are consistent, because they are all designed to reach the same goal. For example, a target to encourage more females or black and minority ethnic (BME) staff to apply for promoted posts will ensure more thought is given to their training and development and to active support by their line managers.
- Specific objectives, such as ensuring everyone is retrained in the use of new IT software by a certain date, provides clarity for employees and enables both the HR department and individual employees to see whether they have succeeded or failed to meet expectations.
- If members of a department or team all have a common purpose to achieve a particular HR objective, they are more likely to adopt a team approach, enabling managers to provide a more united and co-ordinated approach to problem solving.
- Measurable and timed objectives allow managers and individuals to improve efficiency by examining the reasons for success and failure in different areas. Practices that have worked effectively in certain areas can be adapted more widely and staff can learn from their failures, thus reducing the possibility of unsuccessful actions in the future.
- If HR objectives are achievable, even though significant effort by employees may be required to achieve them, individuals and teams are more likely to be motivated to succeed and improve their performance than if objectives are completely unrealistic.
- As indicated earlier, there are many possible HR objectives. If the HR department gives a clear indication of the relative importance of each objective, it should enable employees to recognise their own priorities, so that their actions and decisions are consistent with the needs of the business as a whole.

What do you think?

HR objectives in a NHS Trust

Here are some human resource objectives in an NHS Trust:

By 2016, we will:

- be in the top 20 per cent of Trusts as measured by the NHS National Staff Survey
- have increased the capability of our organisation to help employees build their skills and deliver an improved service to our patients
- achieve sickness absence levels that are in the top 25 per cent of Trusts
- have increased staff engagement
- have increased the leadership and management capability of our organisation
- be in the top 20 per cent of Trusts for implementing and embedding diversity.

To what extent are the HR objectives of this NHS Trust SMART?

Fact file

'Matching' (or linking) human resource management (HRM) policies

Each individual policy adopted in the management of people, such as recruitment, training and payment systems, should fit with every other policy used. For example, an attempt to introduce flexible working needs to be considered in relation to the introduction of appropriate payment systems, training methods and appraisal systems.

Figure 20.1 illustrates how all of the policies adopted by HRM fit together. For example, individuals apply and are selected for their jobs, they perform their tasks and their performance is appraised. Appraisal results in decisions about reward and payment, which in turn has an effect on performance. Appraisal also leads to decisions about suitable training and development, which in turn affects performance and can lead to selection for a more senior position.

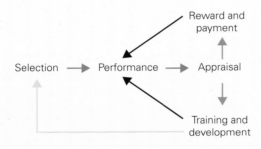

▲ **Figure 20.1** HRM policies and how they 'match' or link together
Source: adapted from C.J. Fombrun, N. M. Tichy and M. A. Devanna, *Strategic Human Resource Management*, John Wiley, 1984

HRM policies should fit with the overall strategic position of an organisation. This means that how people are managed is determined largely by the goals the company has set itself, and that employees are organised to ensure that these goals are met. This is achieved by another type of matching, this time between HRM policies and outcomes, and the corporate objectives and long-term direction of the company as a whole. A company that is attempting to expand significantly may consider moving towards a more decentralised structure (decentralisation is discussed in Chapter 22) and will need an HR strategy that takes account of this in relation to the staff it recruits and promotes, and in relation to training and payment systems.

Figure 20.2 illustrates this idea of matching HR policies with corporate objectives. It demonstrates how the approach of HRM is integrated into the long-term competitive position of the firm by linking the individual HRM policies and outcomes developed in Figure 20.1 with the goals of the organisation as a whole.

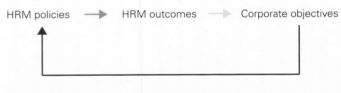

▲ **Figure 20.2** HRM policies and how they 'match' or link to corporate objectives

Problems of setting HR objectives

- External changes are not always easy to predict and so HR objectives may be based on incorrect assumptions. For example, the anticipated growth of a business and therefore the number of employees to recruit may not occur because of changes in the economy or because of competition in the market.
- Internal changes should be more certain and so are less likely to create problems. However, an objective to improve the recruitment of staff, especially highly skilled staff, might be severely hampered if, for example, a company's products develop a reputation for unreliability or the company is experiencing declining profits.
- The examination of HR objectives earlier in this chapter shows that there are many potential HR objectives. In some cases, these objectives may conflict. For example, providing appropriate training and development opportunities may, in the short term, conflict with the objective of maximising labour productivity. In the long term, however, labour productivity is likely to increase as a result of training and development.

- A business may not have sufficient resources or a large enough HR budget to enable the HR department to achieve its objectives.
- If objectives are imposed, rather than agreed, employees may not feel 'ownership' of the objectives of the department. Consequently, they may not put in the effort to achieve the goals that have been set. Imposed objectives may also be unrealistic because managers imposing them may lack the detailed understanding possessed by employees who have to meet them.
- There may be a reluctance to set realistic objectives in times of difficulty. If a business is doing badly, there may be a clear need to reduce staffing levels, but a reluctance to do this because of the impact on individuals.
- People like to set ambitious targets because it shows a willingness to succeed, but this often means that HR objectives lose their value because they are too ambitious

Fact file

Google and HR data

Google is one of the most valuable companies in the world. Its HR function is known as People Operations (POPS). POPS decisions rely on data. 'All people decisions at Google are based on data and analytics.' The goal of POPS is to 'bring the same level of rigour to people-decisions that we do to engineering decisions.'

Some examples of how Google is doing this are described below.

- **Retention**: selection and training incur significant costs for a company so retaining talented employees is not only important for success but also financially beneficial. Google analyses its data to identify which employees are likely to leave so they can take steps to prevent this. As a result, they have improved retention by more than 35 per cent.
- **Diversity**: Google analyses data to identify areas of opportunity to improve diversity in recruiting, retention and promotions. As a result, they have managed to increase the number of females working for the company and, in particular, the number of females remaining with the company following maternity leave and having children.

- **Selection**: how to identify the best candidates for a job is a difficult task, especially if the field of candidates is strong. Google established the optimal number of interviews to identify the most talented without making the selection process too onerous. It also has a system to review rejected CVs to find unusual candidates and put them back into the pool of candidates to be considered.
- **Workplace design**: Google has used its data to redesign the layout of offices and work spaces. It found that collaboration and having fun improved company performance. Individualised work areas and a communal café encourage networking as well as opportunities to learn and discover, and have increased productivity and helped with recruitment and retention.
- **Managing the managers**: managers are rated twice each year by employees. Analysis of this data enabled Google to identify the characteristics of its best leaders. The data also indicated that employees' retention and job satisfaction improved when they experienced one-to-one coaching and personalised feedback and interest from their managers.

Source: www.google.com

431

Internal and external influences on human resource objectives and decisions

Internal influences on HR objectives and decisions are those that arise from within a business, whereas external influences are those that arise outside the business.

Internal influences

- **Overall business aims**: the overall aims of the business are a key influence on functional objectives. The HR department must therefore ensure that its objectives are in line with the corporate objectives of the business.
- **Available finance and resources**: a business with a healthy financial situation can afford to put more resources into its HR activities. Equally, financial constraints may, for example, affect HR objectives relating to the provision of staff training and development. Some businesses allocate a relatively small budget to the HR department in comparison to other departments. Ultimately the HR department must compete with other functional areas, such as marketing and operations, for the finances available within a business. Larger budgets are likely to be allocated to the departments that will use the money most effectively to achieve the business's overall objectives.
- **Corporate culture**: the impact of financial constraints on HR objectives may not be as severe if the corporate culture is such that HRM has a high profile in the organisation and human resources (i.e. employees) are recognised as a valuable asset that needs to be trained and developed.
- **Organisational structure**: if the organisational structure becomes flatter (i.e. fewer layers of management) or if delayering (i.e. removing layers of management) takes place, this may influence HR objectives in relation to motivation and communication because there may be greater focus on providing employees with more autonomy and responsibility.
- **Trade unions and the relationship between employers and employees**: these may influence HR objectives concerned with the introduction of change, such as flexible working practices.
- **Overall business performance**: how the business develops or expands may influence HR objectives. For example, if unprofitable areas are closed down or the focus of the business changes, the number, skills and location of employees may need to change.

An additional internal influence on human resource objectives is whether an organisation decides to use hard or soft Human Resource Management (HRM) approaches. This influence and details about these different approaches are discussed at the end of this section.

External influences

- **Political factors**: for example, a change in government led to significant change in the attitude to trade unions and the amount of power they are able to wield in the workplace. The Conservative government in the 1980s, led by Prime Minister Margaret Thatcher, took a very firm stance with trade unions. As a result, and via legislation, many of the freedoms they had previously enjoyed in relation to strike action and picketing were curtailed. These changes had a major impact on HR objectives in relation to employer/employee relations at the time.

- **Economic factors**: for example, changes in the state of the economy may lead to changes in the demand for a firm's products and services, which are likely to cause changes in both the number and type of employees it requires.

- **Social factors**: for example, organisations have had to revise their HR objectives to take account of the increased emphasis on work–life balance

▲ Margaret Thatcher took a firm stance with the Trade Unions

and make moves towards more flexible working; customers increasingly expect access to business services 24/7, which can have an impact on work roles and hours of work; demographic changes and the presence of more elderly people in the workforce have implications for job roles, the nature of work and training provided.

- **Technological factors**: for example, HR objectives must encompass the need to ensure that relevant staff are well trained in the use of IT, but also that full account is taken of their health and safety if they are sitting at a computer for most of the day. New technology may influence HR objectives by affecting the amount and type of labour required, training requirements, communication and workers' motivation.
- **Legislation**: HR objectives will be influenced by the presence, or introduction, of a range of employment-related legislation, including equal opportunities legislation, conditions of employment and industrial relations legislation. This will apply, for example, to objectives related to the recruitment and selection of employees and to their training and promotion.
- **Actions of competitors and market factors**: these may influence HR objectives, for example, if there is a shortage of skills in a particular area, poaching of workers by competitors may occur and salaries may be forced up. If demand changes, the business may need to reduce or increase the size of its workforce and modify its organisational structure.

Hard and soft human resource management (HRM) approaches

There are two distinct approaches or strategies to achieve an organisation's HR objectives. These are known as hard and soft HRM strategies.

Hard HRM strategy

In this approach, the aim is to utilise employees as efficiently as possible by directing them. A **hard HRM strategy** treats employees simply as another resource, like raw materials or fixed capital. Just like any other resource, employees need to be monitored, used efficiently and have their costs controlled, in order to achieve the strategic objectives of the organisation. This approach sees HRM as essentially a control mechanism.

The style of management in organisations using a hard HRM strategy is likely to be authoritarian or autocratic, and because the approach requires that authority is kept in the hands of a few, it is likely to involve a centralised rather than a decentralised organisational structure. (Centralised and decentralised organisational structures are considered in Chapter 22.) This type of HRM strategy includes workforce planning, analysing the current and future demand for, and supply of, employees, and predicting labour turnover.

Soft HRM strategy

A **soft HRM strategy** focuses on motivational issues, organisational culture, leadership approaches and industrial relations. As it is essentially a strategy for the personal development of all staff, soft HRM is likely to be associated with a democratic management style. With this approach, managers will wish to pass authority throughout the organisation and are likely to favour delegation and decentralisation rather than centralisation. (Delegation, together with decentralisation and centralisation, is considered in Chapter 22.) Equally, because firms that embrace a soft HRM approach recognise that they will benefit from employees' ideas, they are likely to encourage high levels of employee participation. Issues relevant to a soft HRM strategy are closely linked to the ideas provided in the theories of motivation discussed in Chapter 23.

Strengths and weaknesses of hard and soft HRM strategies

Whether a company adopts a hard or soft HRM approach depends largely on the history and culture of the firm, the approach and attitudes of managers and their management style, their relationship with recognised trade unions, the skills and attitudes of staff, and the level of employee participation in decision making.

Today, employees are likely to react more favourably to the soft HRM approach than to the hard HRM approach. As employees become increasingly educated and skilled, they begin to expect greater involvement in business decision making. This is encouraged by trends in industrial relations in the workplace, such as the partnership approach adopted by some organisations and their recognised trade unions. The benefits of effective HRM strategies for a firm are huge, including more motivated and committed staff, who contribute more ideas and exhibit greater loyalty. These factors, in turn, are likely to lead to lower labour turnover, higher retention rates, less absenteeism, greater productivity and lower unit labour costs, all of which can be used as indicators of effective HRM within an organisation. (Labour turnover and retention rates, labour productivity and labour costs per unit and absenteeism are each explained in Chapter 21.)

Practice exercise 1

Total: 35 marks

1 Which of the following activities is not part of the HR function in an organisation?
   a) Recruitment and selection
   b) Appraisal
   c) Quality assurance
   d) Fringe benefits
   e) Training and development   *(1 mark)*

2 Explain why HR objectives should be related to corporate objectives.   *(5 marks)*

3 Identify two HR objectives and explain how they are likely to contribute to overall corporate objectives.   *(6 marks)*

4 Identify two internal factors and explain how they might influence the HR objectives of an organisation.   *(6 marks)*

5 Identify two external factors and explain how they might influence the HR objectives of an organisation.   *(6 marks)*

6 Distinguish between 'hard' and 'soft' HRM strategies.   *(6 marks)*

7 What are the relative strengths of the soft HRM strategy compared to the hard HRM strategy?   *(5 marks)*

Case study: The HR function in a business

Davinder works in HR in an insurance company and has a number of assistants. The aim of the insurance company is to provide its customers with quality advice and service at competitive prices. Davinder's boss is a director of the company and is mainly concerned with strategic issues and how the work of the HR function fits in with the broad corporate objectives. Davinder's department has its own set of objectives, which she and her boss identified together. These include reducing the levels of labour turnover and absenteeism for the company as a whole by 10 per cent within the next year. Because of the competitive nature of the industry, they are also looking at ways of restructuring how people work in order to improve efficiency. Davinder and her staff spend much of their time considering these issues, assessing current policies and practices, coming up with proposals and involving employees in designing and evaluating them.

Most of Davinder's time is spent with either her own staff or other departmental managers. She monitors absentee rates, labour turnover rates and a range of other personnel indicators on spreadsheets that are updated daily on her computer. Davinder's department provides advice to departmental managers, co-ordinates recruitment advertising and provides the associated paperwork and correspondence, but leaves responsibility for interviewing, appraising, disciplining and dismissing employees, etc., to departmental managers and their staff.

Questions

Total: 25 marks

1 Analyse how the HR objective related to labour turnover and absenteeism is likely to contribute to the achievement of overall company objectives.

(9 marks)

2 Based on the information provided, do you believe that the company uses a soft HRM strategy? Justify your response.

(16 marks)

Case study: Halfords Group plc

Halfords, which has been in operation for 110 years, is the UK's leading retailer of automotive and leisure products and leading independent operator in garage servicing and auto repair. Many of its brands and product categories hold number one sales positions.

Its vision is 'We help and inspire our customers with their life on the move'. Its operations have three elements:
- 'Supporting Drivers of Every Car'
- 'Inspiring Cyclists of Every Age'
- 'Equipping Families for their Leisure Time'

In order to deliver growth in each of these three elements, Halfords is pursuing 'Getting into Gear', a five-point programme designed to deliver a significantly improved customer experience. This programme involves:
- 'Service Revolution' – introducing improvements to customer service, for example, improving the expertise of employees.
- 'The H Factor' – reasserting its promise to support drivers of every car, inspire cyclists of every age and equip families for their leisure time, for example, by providing a strong brand, quality service and affordable prices.
- 'Stores Fit to Shop' – improving the quality of its stores.
- '21st Century Infrastructure' – ensuring systems and infrastructure support service and sales, for example opening autocentres on Sundays.
- 'Click with the Digital Future' – creating digital services, for example, online advice on car maintenance and online bookings for autocentres.

The aim of this programme is to help deliver sales in excess of £1 billion by the end of financial year 2016.

Some of Halfords' HR objectives relate to:
- ensuring employees have market-leading knowledge of a wide choice of products
- achieving a high level of safety training
- increasing the involvement of employees in the company

- practising ethical trading
- rewarding employees for their efforts.

Halfords also has HR objectives relating to diversity, labour turnover, employee engagement and training and development. Details of these are provided below.

Historically, more males than females have been attracted to work at Halfords. Through its recruitment, talent and development programmes it has tried to encourage more females in order to reflect the gender balance of its customers and the communities it serves. Its performance in relation to this is illustrated in the table below.

▼ **Table 20.1** Percentage of women working at Halfords 2012–14

	2012	2013	2014
Women in senior management	Not available	13%	22%
Women on the board	14%	25%	33%
Women in stores	29%	28%	29%
Women in distribution centres	13%	16%	19%
Women in autocentres	1%	1%	3%
Total women	26%	25%	24%

Halfords aims to reduce the percentage of staff leaving within three months of starting employment so that by 2015 it is fewer than 12.5 per cent and by 2016 it is fewer than 10 per cent.

Employer engagement is assessed by an annual survey of employers. In 2014, Halfords' measure of employer engagement stood at 80 per cent. It aims to increase this to greater than 85 per cent by 2015.

Halfords has introduced a new training programme involving three levels: Gear 1 is a three-month

induction programme for all new employees; Gear 2 develops expertise on the shop floor; Gear 3 involves high skill training for a limited group of employees to become technical experts in cycle and auto products. It aimed to ensure that all qualifying employees undertook Gear 1 in 2014 – and this was achieved. By 2015 it aims to get 50 per cent of employees through Gear 2 and 80 per cent through Gear 2 by 2016.

Halfords provides training and development programmes to support employees in leadership roles, with separate programmes for Assistant Managers, Store Manager and Area Managers.

In 2014, Halfords was included in the 2014 *Sunday Times* 25 Best Big Companies to Work For survey.

Some of the external influences affecting Halfords include the following:
- Changing consumer demand, for example the demand for children's cycles is declining as children and young people change their leisure pursuits in favour of more computer-based activities.
- A highly competitive market involving a wide variety of retailers, including supermarkets and car servicing providers, meaning that price, product range, quality, service and trustworthiness are vitally important.
- The economy and, for example, trends in employment and interest rates, have a major influence on consumers' discretionary income and therefore on their potential spending power.
- The weather has a significant impact on the take-up of leisure pursuits.

Source: adapted from information on Halfords' website, www.halfordscompany.com and from its Annual Report and Accounts 2014

Questions

Total: 60 marks

1 Identify and explain two areas, not mentioned in the case study, for which Halfords might set HR objectives. *(8 marks)*

2 Why might Halfords' HR objectives have been constrained by its financial objectives? *(5 marks)*

3 Select two areas for which Halfords has HR objectives and, on the basis of the information in the case study, and your imagination, produce a SMART objective for each. *(6 marks)*

4 Analyse why SMART objectives are more helpful to an organisation than objectives that are not SMART. *(9 marks)*

5 Discuss the reasons why Halfords and other companies will ensure that their HR objectives are linked to, and influenced by, their overall corporate objectives. *(16 marks)*

6 Discuss the extent to which internal and external factors are likely to influence Halfords' HR objectives and its ability to achieve these objectives. *(16 marks)*

21

Analysing HR performance

This chapter considers a range of human resource data, including labour turnover and retention rates, labour productivity and labour costs per unit, and employee costs as a percentage of turnover. In considering each of these examples of human resource data, the chapter explains how to calculate and interpret them and discusses the use of such data for human resource decision making and planning.

Labour turnover and retention rates

There are various types of human resource data that enable an organisation to measure the effectiveness of its workforce and to support its human resource decision making and planning. This chapter will consider the following data measures: labour turnover and retention rates; labour productivity and labour costs per unit; employee costs as a percentage of turnover.

Labour turnover and retention rates are linked. Labour turnover refers to the percentage of people who leave an organisation in a given time period and retention rates refer to the extent to which an organisation retains its employees.

Calculating and interpreting labour turnover and retention rates

> **Key term**
>
> **Labour turnover** The proportion of employees leaving a business over a period of time – usually a year.

The rate of **labour turnover** is calculated as follows:

$$\frac{\text{Number of employees leaving over a given period}}{\text{Average number employed over a given period}} \times 100$$

For example, if the average number of staff employed in a firm last year was 250 and the number of employees who left the firm last year was 10, the labour turnover would be 4 per cent [(10 ÷ 250) × 100].

Key term

Retention rate The proportion of employees with a specified length of service (normally one or more years) as a proportion of the total workforce.

If the number of employees leaving over a given period increases while the average number employed over a given period remains the same, the rate of labour turnover will increase. If the number of employees leaving over a given period falls while the average number employed over a given period remains the same, the rate of labour turnover will fall. If the number of employees leaving over a given period remains the same, but the number employed either rises or falls, the rate of labour turnover will decrease or increase respectively.

Retention rates are calculated as follows:

$$\frac{\text{Number of employees with one or more years' service}}{\text{Overall workforce numbers}} \times 100$$

For example, if the overall workforce comprised 250 workers and of these, 100 had worked for the firm for more than one year, the retention rate would be 40 per cent [(100 ÷ 250) × 100].

If the number of employees with one or more years' service rises while the overall workforce number remains the same, the retention rate will increase. If the number of employees with one or more years' service falls while the overall workforce number remains the same, the retention rate will fall. If the number of employees with one or more years' service remains the same, but the overall workforce numbers either rise or fall, the retention rate will fall or rise respectively.

Fact file

Stability index

It is important to recognise that although the labour turnover formula allows a business to keep track of the extent of its labour turnover and to benchmark (compare) its own rate with that of similar businesses, it is a rather crude measure. This is because the number of people leaving includes all leavers, even those who left involuntarily due to dismissal, redundancy or retirement. It also makes no distinction between labour turnover that might be beneficial for the firm, and that which definitely is not. Labour turnover that might be beneficial is where people leave who are not in tune with the culture of the organisation or whose skills are not as relevant as they might be. Once these people have left, new employees can then be recruited with more up-to-date or different skills, who can bring new ideas and new approaches into the business. Labour turnover that is definitely not beneficial might be losing employees with key skills and experience, whose absence is a definite loss to the company – especially if these individuals move to a competitor's employment. There is another formula that allows a firm to measure the labour turnover of its more experienced staff. This is called the stability index and is calculated as follows:

$$\frac{\text{Number of leavers with one or more years' service}}{\text{Total number of staff in post one year ago}} \times 100$$

For example, if the total number of staff in post one year ago was 250 and, of the 10 staff that left, 5 had been with the firm for one or more years, the stability index would be 2 per cent [(5 ÷ 250) × 100].

Fact file

Average labour turnover

According to the Chartered Institute of Personnel and Development (CIPD) 2013 survey, average labour turnover overall was approximately 13 per cent with average labour turnover rates being over 16 per cent in the private sector, 9 per cent in the public sector and over 15 per cent in the not-for profit sector. The average rate of labour turnover has fallen over the last decade, mainly due, in more recent years, to the challenging economic conditions. High levels of unemployment and few employment opportunities have meant employees have been reluctant to leave secure employment. Labour turnover is much higher among young people than older age groups and the ageing population means that overall labour turnover might remain at historically low levels for years to come.

Use of data on labour turnover and retention rates for human resource decision making and planning

Labour turnover and retention rates provide an organisation with data that can be used for human resource decision making and planning. If labour turnover is high and retention rates are low, this is likely to be reflected in problems elsewhere in the organisation. The types of problems created by high labour turnover and low retention rates are identified below.

Problems associated with high labour turnover and low retention rates

- High recruitment and selection costs to replace staff who leave. These include the administrative and management costs incurred in advertising positions, conducting interviews, etc. Such costs are likely to be higher for senior management and professional positions.
- High induction and training costs to ensure that new employees quickly become familiar with the practices of the business and learn the necessary skills to carry out their job effectively. This process can take a great deal of time, especially if the job requires specialised skills.
- A need to redesign jobs because in some industries where labour turnover is a particular problem, jobs have to be redesigned to keep them as simple as possible, so that it is easier to replace staff who leave.
- Reduced productivity due to the disruption caused by skilled staff leaving and new, usually untrained, staff joining the business. This could result in loss of production or sales, especially if a worker plays an important role in the company or has key knowledge or skills that the business will find difficult to replace.
- Low morale among existing workers as a result of the constant change of work colleagues and the unsettling feelings that this engenders.

If labour turnover is high and retention rates are low, an organisation needs to explore the possible causes of this. Typical causes of high labour turnover and low retention rates are identified below.

Typical causes of high labour turnover and low retention rates

In general, labour turnover and retention rates indicate how content the workforce in a firm is. If a company's labour turnover rate is increasing and its retention rate is declining, this could be a general sign of worker unrest or dissatisfaction. The specific causes of labour turnover can be internal or external.

Factors internal to the firm include:

- ineffective leadership and management techniques
- poor communications
- wages and salaries that are lower than those being paid by firms offering comparable jobs in the area
- poor selection procedures that tend to appoint the wrong people to the wrong jobs
- boring/unchallenging jobs that lack career and developmental opportunities
- poor working conditions and unpopular working practices
- low morale and motivation as a result of the above issues.

Factors external to the firm include:

- if the economy, or a particular sector of the economy, is improving, there will be more employment opportunities available, which will mean an increase in vacancies for more attractive jobs
- other jobs could be more attractive because they are more highly paid, offer better training and working conditions, are more interesting and challenging, or are closer to home or offer easier transport links.

Fact file

Variations in labour turnover

Labour turnover varies by occupation, industry and region. Successive CIPD surveys of labour turnover show that the highest levels are found in retailing, hotel, catering and leisure, call centres and among other lower-paid private sector services. In the case of hotel, catering and leisure, high turnover is likely to be related to the fact that this sector typically employs students and seasonal workers, whose turnover is naturally higher. Labour turnover is much higher in less skilled jobs, particularly among sales and customer service occupations. In contrast, managers and professional workers have lower levels of labour turnover. Labour turnover also varies by region. In areas with low levels of unemployment, labour turnover tends to be high because it is much easier for people to obtain more desirable alternative employment.

Once the human resource function of an organisation has identified labour turnover or retention rates as problematic and has explored the causes of it, managers can take steps to bring about improvements. There are a range of approaches that can be used to reduce rates of labour turnover and increase retention rates. Some of the key areas where improvements can be made are identified below.

Improving labour turnover and retention rates

- **Monitoring and benchmarking**. Many firms are either not proactive in dealing with labour turnover or unaware of its cost implications. A monitoring system that includes knowing how labour turnover in a firm compares with the industry average, tracking trends in employee turnover over time, and identifying areas, departments and roles in

a firm where labour turnover is particularly high or retention rates particularly low, might be useful.

- **Exit interviews**. These are useful to identify problem areas in an organisation and any characteristics that may be common to leavers who have not been with a firm for long. Issues to discuss include the job itself, supervision and management, pay and conditions of work, training and career prospects and equal opportunities.
- **Recruitment and selection**. The amount of money spent on ensuring that recruitment and selection procedures are effective will be more than recouped by the savings made from lower labour turnover later on.
- **Induction and training**. High-quality induction training to make new employees feel like part of a firm is as important as well-directed on-the-job training and supervision. It is important to ensure that new employees are kept sufficiently motivated and that their work is neither unchallenging nor too demanding.
- **Reducing turnover of long-term workers**. Employees who have been with a business for a long time accumulate a huge amount of firm-specific human capital, i.e. knowledge and skills that are of direct relevance to the business. If these employees leave, their knowledge and skills also disappear, so it is vital for the business to try to retain them. This may involve ensuring that some kind of career progression is available to them and examining their remuneration to ensure it is not out of line with that provided by other businesses offering similar jobs.

The consequences for a firm of having a high labour turnover and low retention rates are usually negative. The cost of recruiting and training new staff can lead to a weaker competitive position and a fall in efficiency. Evidence suggests that, in general, most firms are either unaware of the costs of high labour turnover or do not have systems in place to monitor or deal with the problem. Better human resource management (HRM) practices are therefore essential.

However, it is worth noting that there is likely to be a 'natural' level of labour turnover which is unavoidable and which will vary from firm to firm. Indeed, some labour turnover may be positive in bringing new ideas, skills, talents and enthusiasm to the labour force. Labour turnover can be healthy if it enables a firm to avoid complacency and an over-reliance on tried and tested ways of working, which may make it inflexible in response to changes in its environment. It can also allow a business to reduce its workforce slowly without having to resort to redundancies – this is often referred to as natural wastage.

There is a clear need for a balance to be struck in relation to labour turnover. Aiming for as low a rate of labour turnover and as high a retention rate as possible is not necessarily the best approach. Knowing how and why the rate of labour turnover or the retention rate is changing is probably as important as the figure itself.

Labour productivity and labour costs per unit

Labour productivity was explained in Chapter 12 in relation to the operations performance of a business. Labour productivity and labour costs per unit are linked. Both measure how efficient the employees of a business are. Labour productivity is a measure of how much, on average, an individual worker produces in a given period of time. Labour costs per unit are the average labour costs involved in producing one unit of output in a given period of time.

Calculating and interpreting labour productivity and labour costs per unit

Labour productivity is calculated as follows:

$$\frac{\text{Output per period}}{\text{Number of employees per period}}$$

Calculation 1: example of a labour productivity calculation

- Assume output in a given month is 18,000 units and 40 people are employed during that month to produce the goods.
- Labour productivity will be 450 units per worker [18,000 units ÷ 40 employees].

Labour costs per unit are calculated as follows:

$$\frac{\text{Total labour costs}}{\text{Total units of output}}$$

Calculation 2: example of labour costs per unit calculation

- Assume output in a given month is 18,000 units, 40 people are employed during that month to produce the goods and each employee is paid £1,000.
- Total labour costs will be £40,000 [£1000 × 40 employees] per month and labour costs per unit will be £2.22 [£40,000 labour costs ÷ 18,000 units].

Most organisations seek to increase their labour productivity because this means that more is produced by the same number of workers or the same amount is produced by fewer workers and so labour costs per unit are reduced.

Calculation 3: example demonstrating that an increase in labour productivity can result in an increase in output using the same number of employees

- Assume 40 people are employed, as in calculation 1, but new technology causes output to increase to 24,000 units.
- Labour productivity increases to 600 units per worker [24,000 units ÷ 40 employees].

Key term

Labour productivity A measure of the output per worker in a given time period.

Key term

Labour costs per unit A measure of the average labour costs involved in producing one unit of output in a given time period of time

Author advice

In general, productivity and labour productivity are terms that mean the same and are therefore used interchangeably.

Calculation 4: example demonstrating that an increase in labour productivity can mean the same amount of output can be produced using fewer employees

- Assume output remains at 18,000 units as in calculations 1 and 2 but productivity improves to 600 units per worker because of new technology, as illustrated in calculation 3.
- This means that only 30 workers need to be employed [18,000 units ÷ number of employees = 600 units per employee.]

Calculation 5: example demonstrating that an increase in labour productivity will lead to lower labour costs per unit

- Assume output increases to 24,000 units as a result of increased labour productivity as indicated in calculation 3, but labour costs per employee remain at £1,000 per employee per month.
- Labour costs per unit will fall to £1.67 [£40,000 labour costs ÷ 24,000 units].
- Assume output remains at the original level of 18,000 units, labour costs per employee remain at £1,000 per month and the number of employees falls to 30 because of increased labour productivity, as in calculation 4.
- This means that labour costs per unit will fall to £1.67 [£30,000 labour costs ÷ 18,000 units].

As demonstrated in the calculations above, an increase in labour productivity means that output will be increased using the same number of employees, or the same number of employees can produce greater levels of output. It also implies a lower labour cost per unit (assuming wages stay the same), which might enable a firm to charge a lower price and/or gain a higher profit margin.

Use of data on labour productivity and labour costs per unit for human resource decision making and planning

As mentioned earlier, most businesses want to improve their labour productivity and to reduce their labour costs per unit. When human resource data indicate that labour productivity is too low and labour costs per unit are too high, the causes need to be investigated. Typical causes of low labour productivity and high labour costs per unit are the same as the internal factors identified as causes of high labour turnover (see page 440 to review these factors.)

Having identified causes of low productivity and high labour costs per unit, appropriate human resource management (HRM) policies need to be implemented in order to bring about improvement.

Strategies to increase labour productivity and reduce labour costs per unit

- Recruitment and selection of suitably skilled and trained employees.
- Provision of training to enhance skills and attitudes of existing employees.
- Appropriate remuneration and non-financial benefits to improve motivation and effort.

Author advice

Note that although an increase in labour productivity might lead to an increase in output this is not always the case. Output per worker (i.e. labour productivity) may have increased, but a business may be producing the same level of output as before the increase in productivity and employing fewer workers. This is demonstrated in the calculations above. Make sure that you are very clear about the difference between the level of production (the total units of output) and the level of productivity (units of output per worker).

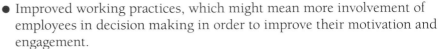

- Improved working practices, which might mean more involvement of employees in decision making in order to improve their motivation and engagement.
- Improved technology and capital equipment.

Specific ways to reduce labour costs per unit include:

- holding down wages. During the recent recession, a number of firms, rather than cut jobs, negotiated with trade unions to cut wages and maintain jobs. In this way, labour costs per unit were cut without necessarily reducing labour productivity. This was, however, a short-term strategy and it would be unlikely that workers would agree to this in the longer term.
- replacing workers with machines and technology. As technology improves, more and more tasks can be done more efficiently by machine than by a human. As a result, labour costs per unit will fall. This will usually be accompanied by improved productivity.
- outsource production to other firms. In this case, a business will no longer need its own employees for the particular tasks involved in the outsourced activity (see Chapter 15 for more on this concept).

A business's efforts to increase labour productivity and reduce labour costs per unit are likely to be more successful if it ensures that:

- employees recognise why the business needs to increase labour productivity, for example, because it needs to reduce costs in order to become more competitive and therefore safeguard jobs in the long term
- employees are involved in the changes
- jobs are not lost
- employees gain extra rewards as a result.

Where these conditions do not apply, employees may resist attempts to increase labour productivity. This is particularly the case if they know that the business does not want to increase the total level of output, but simply wishes to reduce labour costs per unit and maintain output at its original level. Redundancies are then likely because, given the increased productivity, the business will require fewer workers. Similarly, employees may feel that plans to increase productivity may involve a great deal of extra work on their part and may therefore demand higher rewards. This is why negotiations about both pay and productivity often take place at the same time.

In many ways, labour productivity is one of the most crucial measures of all. There is a direct connection between the productivity of a workforce and the competitiveness of a firm, mainly because labour costs are such a high proportion of total costs for most companies.

Employee costs as a percentage of turnover

Calculating and interpreting employee costs as a percentage of turnover

Employee costs as a percentage of turnover is calculated as follows:

$$\frac{\text{Employee costs*}}{\text{Sales turnover}} \times 100$$

For example, if sales turnover is £500,000 and employee costs* are £100,000, employee costs as a percentage of turnover are 20 per cent [(£100,000 employee costs ÷ £500,000 sales turnover) × 100].

* Employee costs include salaries, wages, payroll taxes and benefits, such as bonuses.

If employee costs increase while sales turnover remains the same, the percentage will increase. If employee costs fall while sales turnover remains the same, the percentage will fall. If employee costs remain the same, but sales turnover either increases or decreases, the percentage will fall or rise respectively.

Use of data on employee costs as a percentage of turnover for human resource decision making and planning

For business that are highly automated, labour costs are a relatively small percentage of the total cost of producing a product. For example, in highly automated oil refineries, it is less than 10 per cent. For labour intensive businesses, such as restaurants, labour costs are a much greater percentage of costs, averaging about 30 per cent.

Managing employee costs is one of the most difficult aspects of running a business. Employee costs as a percentage of turnover is one of the most common quantitative measures to determine if a business has the right number of employees. It is a valuable and frequently used method for analysing the most appropriate level of employee costs for a business and for keeping employee costs around a certain percentage of sales turnover – the ideal amount depending on the particular context of a business. Most industries have a benchmark (i.e. an average or ideal figure) with which an individual business can compare its own figures. By doing this a business can assess whether its own employee costs are too high or too low and take appropriate action.

When data suggests that employee costs as a percentage of turnover are too high, this is likely to be reflected in low profit margins or prices that are too high for the nature of the product offered and in relation to competitors. It may also be reflected in the fact that labour productivity might not be as high as it could be because too many staff have been taken on and not all are fully employed at all times. It could also be that employees are paid well above the industry average. None of these positions are sustainable in the long term. Action needs to be taken to reduce employee costs as a percentage of turnover to nearer the industry benchmark. This could mean reducing wages if they are too high, making some staff redundant or redesigning jobs to ensure each employee is working efficiently and at maximum productivity.

Fact file

Variations in absenteeism

The CIPD's 2013 survey indicates that the average level of absence is 7.6 days per employee per year. The highest levels are in the public sector (with 8.7 days per employee) and the lowest levels are in the manufacturing sector (with 6 days). Absence levels tend to increase with the size of the organisation regardless of the sector. The average level of absence in call centres is higher than all other sectors at 12.3 days per year. Over half of all organisations don't monitor the cost of their employees' absence. Monitoring is highest in firms with the largest number of employees.

Did you know?

The CIPD's most recent Annual Absence Survey suggests that the average cost of absence is £595 per employee per year. At the time of writing (spring 2015), the number of people in employment was almost 31 million, making the potential cost of absence across the entire workforce well over £18 billion per year.

When data suggests that employee costs as a percentage of turnover are too low, this might be reflected in poor service, incomplete work, delays and poor workmanship. This might be because insufficient staff are employed or staff are paid below the industry average and so the business cannot attract high quality workers. Labour turnover might increase if employees are unhappy about the pressure they may be experiencing and the level of demand and the competitiveness of the business are likely to suffer. Once such a situation is identified, actions need to be taken to improve the situation – for example, taking on more employees and ensuring they are paid an appropriate rate.

Absenteeism as an influence on labour productivity and labour costs

Absenteeism is the proportion of employees not at work on a given day.

For example, if 21 people out of a workforce of 300 are absent on a given day, the absentee rate is 7 per cent [(21 staff absent ÷ 300 staff in total) × 100]. Similarly, if a firm has an average daily absentee rate of 5 per cent and a workforce of 300, the typical number of people absent per day is 15 [(staff absent ÷ 300 staff in total) × 100 = 5 per cent absentee rate].

Absenteeism has a significant impact on labour productivity and labour costs. Cover for employees who are absent adds to labour costs. This will be the case especially if deadlines are looming and other employees need to be paid overtime to cover for absent colleagues, or if additional, temporary staff have to be recruited. Staff absences can also mean that important work is not completed, leading to possible delays in production. On the other hand, if new and less skilled staff have to be deployed, productivity and quality may be sacrificed. Eventually, such absences may lead to dissatisfied customers and adversely affect the profitability of the firm.

High rates of absenteeism tend to be an indicator of underlying problems either with the individuals involved or with the business itself. Some absences are unavoidable: for example, those resulting from an illness or a transport strike. However, there are other times when absenteeism may be a consequence of poor levels of motivation and commitment or ineffective management and communication in a business.

Fact file

What causes absenteeism?

In 2013 in the UK, 131 million days were lost due to sickness absence. This is a huge reduction on the equivalent figure of 178 million days in 1993. The most recent CIPD survey suggests that the top five causes of sickness absenteeism were as follows:

- minor illness (including colds, flu, headaches, stomach upsets)
- musculo-skeletal injuries (including neck strain, repetitive strain injuries)
- back pain
- stress
- recurring medical condition, such as asthma, angina, allergies.

The negative impact of absenteeism on productivity and labour costs means that a business needs to take appropriate action to minimise rates of absence. Some strategies are described below.

- Introducing more flexible working practices. This could involve flexibility in relation to annual leave, home working, part-time working and job sharing. It might also involve flexitime, where workers have some control over how they organise certain parts of their working day: for example, between 7 a.m. and 10 a.m. and between 3 p.m. and 6 p.m. An employee may wish to begin work at 7 a.m. and finish at 3 p.m. in order to pick a child up from school or attend a dental appointment.
- Ensuring that jobs are interesting and challenging, so that people enjoy work and want to turn up.
- Improving working conditions and thus reducing dissatisfaction.
- Improving relations between employers and employees, so that the latter feel valued and an essential part of the organisation.
- Introducing attendance bonuses to provide an incentive for workers to attend regularly. Some evidence suggests that, if these bonuses are set at attractive rates and if the scheme is carefully designed, attendance might improve. However, once people have taken one day off, they have lost the bonus and there is no incentive for them not to have more time off. In addition, if employees get used to a certain level of bonus, it ceases to have any impact.

Conclusion

Human resource data includes several measures of workforce (or personnel) effectiveness that provide a business with an indication of the quality of its human resource performance; that is, how well it is managing its most valuable resource – people. In general, any one of these measures taken in isolation is relatively meaningless. However, looked at over a period of time, and in the wider context of the business and its environment, together these measures provide a clear indication of what issues need to be addressed by the human resource function. This informs human resource decision making and planning so that a business can achieve its specific human resource objectives and its broader corporate objectives.

Practice exercise 1

1 Which of the following is not an example of human resource data?
   a) Labour productivity
   b) Employee costs as a percentage of turnover
   c) The rate of inflation
   d) Labour turnover
   e) Labour costs per unit
   f) Retention rates
   (1 mark)

2 Define the term 'labour turnover' and explain two problems that high rates of labour turnover might cause a firm. *(9 marks)*

3 Distinguish between labour turnover and retention rates. *(6 marks)*

4 In a firm, 190 workers were employed at the start of the year, 178 workers were employed at the end of the year, and during the year 24 workers left. Calculate the rate of labour turnover for the year. *(3 marks)*

5 A firm employs a total of 6,300 workers, 2,700 of who have been with the firm for more than one year. Calculate the retention rate. *(3 marks)*

6 Using worked examples, explain the terms 'labour productivity' and 'labour costs per unit'. *(8 marks)*

7 Outline two ways in which a firm might increase its labour productivity and reduce its labour costs per unit. *(6 marks)*

8 In a firm, output in a particular month is 60,000 units, 75 workers are employed and labour costs are £1,000 per worker per month. Calculate labour productivity and labour costs per unit. *(6 marks)*

9 Explain why employee costs as a percentage of turnover might be a valuable element of human resource data for a firm. *(5 marks)*

10 If sales turnover in a firm is £1,800,000 per annum and the firm employs 15 workers at a cost of £12,000 per worker per annum, what are employee costs as a percentage of turnover? *(3 marks)*

11 In a firm, the average daily absentee rate is 15 per cent and the total workforce is 300. What is the average number of workers who are absent on any one day? *(3 marks)*

12 Explain two consequences for a firm of a high rate of absenteeism. *(6 marks)*

13 Assess the extent to which labour productivity and labour costs per unit are more or less important to the success of a business than labour turnover and retention rates. *(16 marks)*

Practice exercise 2

1 Analyse why labour turnover in the hotel, catering and leisure sector tends to be higher than in most other sectors. *(9 marks)*

2 Discuss why a hotel or restaurant might want to reduce its labour turnover and increase its retention rates and how it might do this successfully. *(16 marks)*

Case study: Using human resource data

A small firm has the human resource data shown in Tables 21.1 and 21.2.

Over the last few years, there have been few changes in the operation of the business and the market for its product has been stable. Management has also been stable, although a new office manager was appointed to the administration section two years ago – a 53-year-old woman who is the sister of the managing director.

▼ **Table 21.1** Personnel data for a small firm, 2012–14

	2012	2013	2014
Total output (units)	67,000	68,000	69,000
Average number of employees	100	98	96
Number of employees employed for 1 year or more	50	40	40
Number of employees leaving	10	15	20
Number of working days	250	250	250
Total number of days lost due to absence	500	520	735
Total sales turnover (£)	6.7m	8.16m	8.66m

Average labour costs per employee remained at £15,000 per annum for each of the three years.

▼ **Table 21.2** Personnel data for a small firm, by department, 2012–14

	Marketing 2012	2013	2014	Production 2012	2013	2014	Administration 2012	2013	2014	Finance 2012	2013	2014
Employees	20	20	20	62	60	58	10	10	10	8	8	8
Leavers	1	1	2	8	6	8	0	8	9	1	0	1
Absenses	85	80	70	325	315	480	50	45	35	40	80	150
Age profile (2014)												
16–29			4			2			8			2
30–49			14			11			1			4
50+			2			45			1			2

Questions

Total: 50 marks

1 Using the data provided, calculate the following measures of workforce effectiveness *for each of the 3 years*:

   a) Labour turnover *(6 marks)*

   b) Retention rates *(6 marks)*

   c) Labour productivity *(6 marks)*

   d) Labour costs per unit *(6 marks)*

   e) Employee costs as a percentage of turnover *(6 marks)*

2 Using your calculations from question 1 and the data in Tables 21.1 and 21.2, discuss the issues, including causes and effects, which these human resource data indicators raise for the human resource management decision making and planning in this business. *(20 marks)*

22

Making HR decisions: improving organisational design and managing the human resource flow

The chapter begins with a consideration of job design and the influences on job design, including an explanation of the Hackman and Oldham model. Organisational design and influences on organisational design are then considered. A clear focus is given to authority, span, hierarchy, delegation, centralisation and decentralisation as being core to decisions about organisational design. Influences on delegation, centralisation and decentralisation are identified and the value of changing job and organisational design is analysed. The final section of the chapter considers how managing the human resource flow helps meet human resource objectives. In the context of human resource flow, human resource plan, recruitment, training, redeployment and redundancy are considered in turn.

Job design

Job design aims to improve motivation and job satisfaction and a sense of personal achievement by reducing repetitive and mechanistic aspects of work and increasing variety, challenge and responsibility in work. Through job design or redesign, an organisation aims to reduce labour costs (due to, for example, labour turnover and absenteeism) and improve labour productivity without offering additional monetary reward. Job enlargement, which includes job rotation and job enrichment, are techniques used in a job design exercise as ways of adding challenge to jobs. These are considered in Chapter 23 as non-financial methods of motivation.

Key term

Job design 'The process of deciding on the content of a job in terms of its duties and responsibilities, on the methods to be used in carrying out the job, in terms of techniques, systems and procedures, and on the relationships that should exist between the job holder and his superiors, subordinates and colleagues'.

Source: Chartered Institute of Personnel and Development (CIPD)

The origins of job design are linked to the rise of scientific management and work study, which sought to measure and sequence human inputs, alongside machinery, to achieve maximum efficiencies. (See Chapter 23 for more on the work of F.W. Taylor, founder of scientific management and work study.) Over time, theories of motivation were developed that recognised the importance of employees gaining job satisfaction in work, and research indicated the benefits of employees having autonomy and responsibility over how to perform at least some aspects of their jobs. (Again, see Chapter 23 for details of motivation theories, including those of Maslow, Herzberg and Mayo, and of other non-financial methods of motivation such as empowerment.) These developments led to changes in the approach to job design. Much of the work on job design is based on the work of Hackman and Oldham, which is considered below.

There are many influences on job design, some of which will be particular to certain forms of business activity or to particular organisational demands. The following are grouped into three sections: organisational influences, external influences and employee-related influences.

Organisational influences

These include the purpose and objectives of the organisation. Job design should support the purpose of the organisation, whether this is based on, for example, designing innovative products, providing hospitality and catering services or manufacturing standard kitchen utensils. Job design should also contribute to how well the organisation achieves its objectives, for example ensuring that, in the case of a business designing innovative products, employees have the flexibility and autonomy to be creative. In general, jobs should be designed to ensure the primary focus of the job holder is on things that matter to the organisation and add value to the organisation.

Other organisational influences:

- The nature, range and volume of tasks to be performed in a particular job and the sequence of relationships between those tasks in order to achieve a particular outcome.
- Ergonomics, that is, how well a job is designed to best fit the physical capabilities of employees doing the job, including any reasonable adjustments required to ensure a job can be carried out by someone with a disability. A simple example of the importance of ergonomics is the design of office desks and chairs to facilitate employees working at a computer, answering a telephone and making notes – sometimes at the same time.
- The way work is organised will have an effect on how tasks are designed and carried out. For example, some jobs may involve remote or home working, others may involve employees working in different types of teams, for example, in cross-functional teams that are focused on short-term projects.
- The quality standards in an organisation. Jobs should be designed to minimise the risk of errors and to include a degree of self-checking by employees to ensure the highest possible quality standards are met, whether in the provision of services or the production of goods.
- Speed required by the organisation's activities. Jobs should be designed to ensure the timeliness of task completion is appropriate to the job. For example, in certain jobs, such as accident and emergency services, the speed and appropriateness of the response is probably the most important feature of the job.

▲ The correct office furniture and arrangement can help staff perform their jobs

451

What do you think?

The CIPD states that job standardisation or repetitive work is inevitable in certain types of jobs, such as in manufacturing or in call centre operator roles. However, it suggests that the use of job design can ensure that the link between the job itself and the level of engagement of an employee is recognised and actions are taken to ensure that employees derive meaning and satisfaction from their jobs.

Do you think it is possible to make an essentially simple and repetitive job meaningful to an employee and so provide them with job satisfaction? Justify your view.

External environment influences

The external environment was discussed in Chapter 3 and, in terms of the human resource function, in Chapter 20. The design of jobs should be sustainable, in that they should be designed to ensure that an organisation can respond flexibly and quickly to changes in the external environment. Examples of changes in the external environment that influence job design include:

- technological developments that enable tasks to be performed in different ways, for example, where certain tasks are automated or, in the case of web-based customer services, where enquiries are dealt with via email rather than in person or via telephone
- general levels of education that influence the availability of certain skills, for example in computing, science, engineering and design
- social changes, for example the nature of customer demand and the expectation of 24/7 service.

Employee-related influences

These include considerations related to:

- employees' health, wellbeing and safety – ensuring jobs are designed that do not risk the wellbeing or safety of the job holder, their colleagues, customers or other individuals
- employees' need for fair reward and recognition – reflected in appropriately designed performance management processes
- employees' need for job satisfaction – reflected in designing jobs that provide meaningful, interesting and challenging work
- employees' need for a good work–life balance – which should incorporate sufficient flexibility, breadth and challenge to ensure employees are motivated, that stress is minimised and where possible that job security is assured
- employees' skills and capabilities – reflected in jobs designed to match and reflect the actual skills and capabilities of employees and potential employees; in addition, jobs should be able to accommodate developments in an individual's capabilities as they gain more experience.

Fact file

HSE management standards

The Health and Safety Executive's management standards cover six key areas of job design that, if not properly managed, are associated with poor health and wellbeing, lower productivity and increased sickness absence among employees. They are:

1 demands on employees – workload, work patterns and the work environment

2 control over work – how much say an employee has in the way they do their work

3 support for employees – the level of encouragement and resources provided by colleagues, managers and the organisation

4 relationships – the quality of interactions with others, including the likelihood of conflict and unacceptable behaviour

5 role of employees – the clarity of their role and their ability to fulfil it with the resources provided

6 change – the potential and actual impact of organisational change and how it is communicated to employees.

Source: www.hse.gov.uk

Hackman and Oldham job characteristics model

The job characteristics model, designed by Hackman and Oldham, indicates that employees will perform well when they are rewarded for the work they do and when that work provides them with satisfaction. It is based on the idea that the tasks involved in a job are the key to employee motivation. Essentially it indicates that a boring and monotonous job stifles the motivation to perform well, whereas a challenging job enhances motivation.

The model suggests that five core job characteristics can be combined to indicate how likely a job is to affect an employee's attitudes and behaviours. The five core job characteristics are: skill variety, task identity, task significance, autonomy and feedback.

The model goes on to propose that a high level of employee motivation is related to employees experiencing three psychological states while working. These states are: meaningfulness of work, responsibility for work outcomes and knowledge of work outcomes. Each psychological state is derived from certain characteristics of a job. These three critical psychological states and the related job characteristics are explained below:

Meaningfulness of work

This psychological state means that work should have meaning for an employee because it is something they can relate to, rather than just a set of movements to be repeated. This is fundamental to intrinsic motivation, i.e. that work is motivating in and of itself, rather than as a means to an end (such as money or status). In this sense, 'meaningful' means that an employee's contribution at work should significantly affect the overall effectiveness of the organisation. Meaningful work is based upon the following job characteristics:

- **Skill variety**: using an appropriate variety of skills and talents: too many might be overwhelming, too few, boring.
- **Task identity**: being able to identify with the work at hand as part of a whole, enabling more pride to be taken in the outcome of that work (e.g. instead of constantly repeating a single process on a production line making cars, working as part of a group that completes a whole car).
- **Task significance**: being able to identify the task as contributing significantly to other employees, a wider group of stakeholders, society at large and to the organisation's objectives (e.g. an office cleaner may not see their role as particularly significant, but the same job in a hospital may be seen as very significant in contributing to patients' health.)

Responsibility for work outcomes

This psychological state means that an individual is given the opportunity to be a success or a failure at their job because sufficient freedom of action has been given to them. Responsibility is derived from the autonomy (one of the five job characteristics identified in the model). Autonomy means a job provides an individual with substantial freedom, independence and discretion in organising their work and in determining the procedures to be used in carrying it out.

Did you know?

Maids International Inc., an American company that provides cleaning services to households and businesses, used job rotation to increase the skill variety of its workers. Maids cleaning the kitchen in one house, would clean the bedroom in another and the sitting room in another. Using this and other techniques, the company was able to reduce its labour turnover.

Knowledge of work outcomes

This psychological state comes from feedback, either from other people or from the job itself, about how effective an employee is in converting their effort in a job into measurable outcomes for the organisation. This could be, for example, in terms of production figures or customer satisfaction scores. Effective feedback then provides an individual with information that helps them to review how they have done and how they might do a job better in future.

According to the Hackman and Oldham model, by understanding these psychological states and job characteristics, an organisation should be able to design or redesign jobs so that they maximise opportunities for employees to feel motivated, engaged and involved and therefore maximise their contribution to helping an organisation achieve its objectives. Designing or redesigning jobs might involve:

● varying the pattern of work in order to broaden skill variety and make work more meaningful
● reorganising work so that groups of employees focus on the production of a whole product in order to improve task identity and make work more meaningful
● ensuring that employees understand the value of their work to other stakeholders, to society at large, and to the achievement of organisational objectives, therefore improving task significance
● delegating tasks to their lowest possible level in order to provide opportunities for greater autonomy and responsibility
● providing appropriate feedback to enable employees to improve their work and have more knowledge of their work outcomes.

Practice exercise 1 — *Total: 30 marks*

1 Explain the term 'job design'. *(4 marks)*

2 Explain one example of an organisational influence on job design. *(3 marks)*

3 Explain one example of an external influence on job design. *(3 marks)*

4 Explain one example of an influence on job design that is employee related. *(3 marks)*

5 Which one of the following is not one of the job characteristics in Hackman and Oldham's model?
   a) Skill variety
   b) Task identity
   c) Significance tests
   d) Autonomy
   e) Feedback *(1 mark)*

6 Give two examples of what might be involved in designing or redesigning jobs. *(4 marks)*

7 Explain the three psychological states that Hackman and Oldham suggest are important to achieve high levels of motivation and engagement. *(12 marks)*

Case study: Michelle's stressful job

Michelle is the receptionist in the head office of a large multinational company. She works on her own with no other support. She is based in the foyer of the building in central London.

Her role includes telephonist; dealing with, or passing on queries in person and by phone and email; directing visitors, accepting deliveries; welcoming job applicants.

A new CCTV camera has been installed in the foyer and she has been asked to monitor it and report anything untoward to security personnel.

Michelle is the only person with access to a locked cupboard that keeps a range of confidential forms and stationery (none of which are available online for security reasons). Throughout the day staff come down to request forms from Michelle – and they expect them to be provided immediately.

The lift in the foyer is activated by a code, which all employees have been given. Because visitors do not have access to the code, they cannot use the lift without being accompanied by a member of staff. The building is a large one with many floors and, rather than waste their time going all the way to the foyer to meet visitors and then take them back up to their offices, staff often ring down and ask Michelle to guide their visitors to the lift and input the code – the relevant member of staff will then meet their visitor at the lift when they arrive at the right floor.

At most points during most days, the foyer is full of waiting clients, couriers and other delivery people, office equipment servicing reps and job applicants and the phone never stops ringing.

Michelle is well groomed, articulate and competent. On one level she enjoys her job – meeting clients and the variety of tasks she does every day. She knows how important her job is because everyone tells her this, constantly. Despite this, she often feels stressed. People waiting in the foyer often get irritated because she cannot deal with them quickly enough or because she is interrupted while she is dealing with them – and this makes her more stressed. She sometimes takes a day off, ringing in to say she isn't feeling well, when really she's just dreading the day because she knows it will be really busy. She has started looking for a new job.

Questions

Total: 25 marks

1 Explain three influences on job design.

(9 marks)

2 Does Michelle's job indicate the features of good job design according to Hackman and Oldham's model? Justify your view. *(16 marks)*

Organisational design

Early approaches to **organisational design** focused on structures and tight managerial control and tended to ignore people and the job roles that are most likely to encourage them to work effectively. The previous section on job design mentioned F.W. Taylor, author of scientific management and work study. This type of approach was widely applied to assembly lines in the last century (most notably at the Ford Motor Company). Even today, businesses that are dependent on standardised, routine work tasks, such as call centres and certain manufacturing sectors, combine top-down control, efficiency measurements and formal, hierarchical structures. However, organisations have had to become more flexible in order to adapt to changes in the external environment. As a result, more attention has been given to the culture of organisations and to the people in them. This in turn has meant more attention has been given to which organisational design

▲ Businesses that employ skilled craftsmen are likely to have a narrow span of control

might be the most appropriate to promote employee job satisfaction and achieve business objectives.

Organisational design and organisational structure are two closely related, but different, concepts. Changes to one, often result in changes to the other.

- Organisational design is a strategy that defines how a company unifies its departments and individuals in order to achieve company objectives. It is a formal process of integrating people, information and technology together in the right mix to achieve those objectives. These are management choices that form an organisational culture.
- Organisational structure represents the formal lines of authority and power and the relationship between different people and functions in an organisation – both vertically, from shop-floor workers through supervisors and managers to directors, and horizontally between different functions and people at the same level. The structure is a statement of the current state of affairs, not the ideals or intentions of the organisation. Organisational structures are usually presented in the form of organisation charts, which are diagrams that show the lines of authority and layers of hierarchy in an organisation.

Decisions relating to organisational design include a need to consider span and hierarchy, authority and delegation, centralisation and decentralisation. Each of these is reviewed in turn.

Span (or span of control)

If a manager has many subordinates answerable to him or her, the **span of control** is said to be wide. If a manager has relatively few subordinates answerable to him or her, the span of control is said to be narrow. Normally, the greater the degree of similarity in what a group of workers does, the wider the span of control can be. This is because if people are doing more or less identical jobs, it is likely to be easier to manage them. The ideal span is influenced by the industry a particular firm is in, the firm itself and the nature of the work involved. For example, with craftsmen the number is likely to be quite small because each worker is carrying out different tasks and so the level of supervision required is high. With mass production, however, the span of control can be many times higher because each worker has a clearly defined task to perform, requiring little regular oversight. This explains why there is a narrow span of control at more senior levels of management, but shop-floor supervisors have wider spans of control. In Figure 22.1 the span of control for senior managers is narrower than for the shop-floor supervisors.

Spans of control can be deliberately enlarged by making workers more autonomous and more capable of managing themselves. This should mean fewer supervisors and so each individual supervisor has more subordinates (a wider span of control). They can also be enlarged by increasing the number of rules and limiting the freedom of junior employees to make mistakes, so little regular oversight is needed and each supervisor can manage more subordinates.

The emergence of virtual organisations made managers take a new look at the concept of span. In a virtual organisation people work as independent self-contained units, either individually or in small teams. They have access to (electronic) information that lays down the boundaries within which they can be autonomous. But at the same time they are allowed to be completely free within those boundaries. In such an environment, the ideal span of control can be very large. Indeed, sometimes it can hardly be called a span of control and is more like a span of loose links and alliances.

Fact file

Virtual organisations

Virtual organisations are groups of people or organisations who share resources, but without sharing the same physical space. Usually these shared facilities are IT based, with groups working together through email or groupware, which allows members of the virtual organisation to access the same information. Virtual organisations exist in many industries but often tend to be involved in research-based or new product development activities. Businesses such as Sun Microsystems, Siemens and Apple use this approach for certain projects.

Hierarchy

Key terms

Organisational hierarchy The vertical division of authority and accountability in an organisation.

Levels of hierarchy The number of different supervisory and management levels between the shop floor and the chief executive in an organisation.

The **organisational hierarchy** refers to the levels of authority and accountability in the organisation. Each line linking two different levels of the management hierarchy represents a relationship where instructions are passed downwards, and reports and feedback are passed upwards within the organisation. Because lines are used to show the link between an employee and his or her supervisor or manager, it is customary to describe the person immediately above someone in the organisation chart as his or her line manager. Thus in Figure 22.1, supervisor B's line manager is the production manager for product A. This reporting system from the top of the hierarchy down to the bottom is called the chain of command. A formal hierarchy, such as that illustrated in Figure 22.1, has a clear vertical chain of command.

Figure 22.1 is an example of a traditional structure that divides an organisation into functional areas, including marketing, production, human resource management and finance. Within each function there are a number of layers of hierarchy. For example, the marketing function has two **levels of hierarchy**, whereas the production function for product A has three levels.

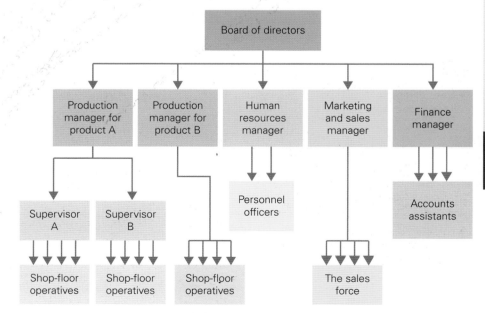

▲ **Figure 22.1** Traditional organisation chart

457

What do you think?

Some people dislike the idea of hierarchies and feel that people should be able to contribute equally to decision making without the need for a particular person or people in charge. The following is a quote from a blog about online gaming:

'I learned about leadership and hierarchy from gaming. In order to kill the biggest boss monster in the quickest way, you had to go as a group. However if no one researched the boss monster's weakness, planned a strategy, recruited the optimal group, set the schedule, and then explained it 30 times to each person that doesn't listen, the boss monster would be happy to kill every single person in 2 bites.'

Even if you don't take part in online gaming, this quote should make sense to you. To what extent does it suggest that a well-managed hierarchy is among the most effective weapons for getting rid of the type of friction, incompetence, and politics that plague badly managed organisations or groups of online gamers?

All organisations, even the smallest, have a certain amount of hierarchy. When an organisation grows, it needs to formalise that hierarchy. Some organisations choose to give employees a lot of autonomy within that hierarchy, while others don't. Whatever they do, though, they all have bosses, reporting lines, rules and procedures. Most evidence indicates that it is impossible to run a business successfully without them.

Relationship between span of control and levels of hierarchy

Traditionally, organisations have tended to have tall hierarchical structures, i.e. many layers of management, each with a narrow span of control. More recently, hierarchies have become flatter, meaning that the number of layers of management has been reduced and each manager has a wider span of control (see Figure 22.2). Table 22.1 contrasts the features of a flat organisational structure with wide spans of control with the features of a tall organisational structure with narrow spans of control.

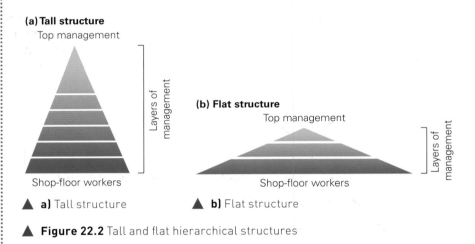

▲ a) Tall structure   ▲ b) Flat structure

▲ **Figure 22.2** Tall and flat hierarchical structures

▼ **Table 22.1** Tall versus flat organisational hierarchies and narrow versus wide spans of control

Features of tall structures with narrow spans of control	Features of flat structures with wide spans of control
• There may be more promotional opportunities because the career ladder has more rungs on it. However, more layers mean more staff, which in turn means higher company overheads.	• Individual managers may have less time for each subordinate and must therefore delegate effectively.
• Less delegation* might mean less stress, but it could lead to low morale and a lack of commitment.	• More delegation means that staff are given greater responsibility, which might mean more opportunity to use their ability. But staff may become overstretched, which may in turn cause stress.
• Narrow spans allow tight control to be kept of the organisation, which might be beneficial if factors such as quality, safety or security are crucial and where any mistake will have serious consequences.	• Fewer layers of hierarchy between the bottom and the top of the organisation may mean that vertical communication improves.
• Important detail or information may be lost in reporting up through the levels of the hierarchy and the chain of command. An undesirable gap may emerge between what management intended and what actually happens.	• Together with the reduction in overhead costs, improved communication should mean greater efficiency within the organisation.
• A longer chain of command means that it takes longer for decisions to be made and implemented.	• A shorter chain of command should mean decisions are made and implemented more quickly.

(* Delegation is discussed on pp. 461–463.)

What do you think?

On your own or in a group, try drawing the organisation chart for your school, college or workplace. Ask your tutor or supervisor for further information that you might need. Consider whether it has a tall or a flat structure and whether the span of control at different levels of the hierarchy is narrow or wide.

Think about the issues of span and hierarchy in relation to how your organisation is run and decide whether the current organisation chart is the most effective structure.

Practice exercise 2

Total: 40 marks

1 Explain the term organisational design. (4 marks)

2 How does organisational design differ from organisational structure? (5 marks)

3 What does an organisation chart illustrate? (3 marks)

4 What is meant by the chain of command? (4 marks)

5 Explain the terms 'hierarchy' and 'span' and the relationship between them. (6 marks)

6 Explain two implications for a business of having a flat organisational structure with a wide span of control. (6 marks)

7 Explain two implications for a business of having a tall organisational structure with a narrow span of control. (6 marks)

8 Explain two factors that might influence the structure of an organisation. (6 marks)

Case study: High Class Furnishings

High Class Furnishings makes furniture for two very different markets. Its original products, made in its Rugeley factory, are high-priced, handcrafted, traditional furniture, often individually designed to the customer's specifications. In its Uttoxeter factory, which opened three years ago, it makes flat-packed furniture for the lower-priced end of the market. Its head office is based at the Rugeley site. High Class Furnishing's organisation chart is shown in Figure 22.3.

At present, High Class Furnishings has a fairly traditional organisational structure, broadly based on functional divisions. Although both product ranges are successful, it has had some problems in co-ordinating the activities of all departments and is considering a change in structure, to one where its divisions are based on operational lines. One of the suggestions is that the two product ranges should form two separate divisions, with their own marketing, personnel and financial functions. However, the production director is worried that such a change will adversely affect the current clear lines of accountability and responsibility.

The directors are also concerned because there has been a lack of innovation (new products or methods) and development of the firm's products. Customers are becoming dissatisfied by the limited choice of furniture offered by the firm.

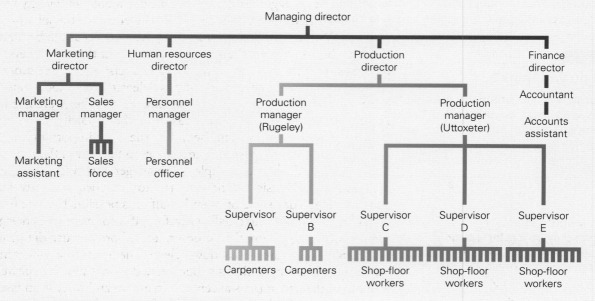

▲ **Figure 22.3** High Class Furnishings: organisation chart

Questions

Total: 40 marks

1 Explain the usefulness of an organisation chart to High Class Furnishings. *(6 marks)*

2 What are the spans of control of supervisor C in the Uttoxeter factory and of supervisor B in the Rugeley factory? *(2 marks)*

3 Is there an ideal span of control? Evaluate your answer in relation to the spans of control of the directors and of the production supervisors at High Class Furnishings. *(16 marks)*

4 Discuss the production director's view that a change in structure might 'adversely affect the current clear lines of accountability and responsibility'. *(16 marks)*

Authority and delegation

When **delegation** occurs, managers transfer their duties and responsibilities to subordinates and also give them the necessary authority for performing the responsibilities assigned. At the same time, managers remain accountable for the performance of their subordinates.

Responsibility, **authority** and **accountability** are important terms to understand in relation to delegation:

- **Authority**. A manager would not be able to function efficiently without proper authority. Authority is an essential element of the job of a manager. Without authority, in a sense, managers cease to be managers, because they cannot get their policies carried out through others. It indicates the right and the power to make decisions, to give orders to and instruct subordinates. Authority is delegated from above but must be accepted from below, i.e. by the subordinates. In other words, authority flows downwards. Subordinates must have the authority to undertake the various tasks delegated to them. It is therefore important that the manager has formally passed authority on to them, and that the authority is clear and explicit. For example, if a manager who was due to be away did not give their assistant the authority to sign cheques or invoices, or generally make decisions on their behalf, it is possible that the firm's activities would come to a halt. Therefore, if responsibility is delegated, it is important to ensure that appropriate authority is also delegated. It is equally important to lay down clearly the limits to a subordinate's authority: for example, that a subordinate does not have the power to hire and fire in their manager's absence. Passing on authority is an issue that many managers find difficult, but if sufficient authority is not transferred, delegation will be unsuccessful.

- **Responsibility**. A person who is responsible for the performance of a department, section or team will be required to explain and justify performance that falls short of expectations and to ensure that things are put right. For example, a production manager may be responsible for ensuring that products are produced in the right quantity, to the right specification and on time. A human resource manager may be responsible for ensuring that all employees receive appropriate training for their particular job. What the responsibilities are and to whom the subordinate is responsible are usually indicated in a job description.

- **Accountability**. Accountability means an individual is answerable for the performance of duties assigned to them. When a manager delegates authority to a subordinate, the subordinate is accountable to their manager for their performance in relation to the delegated duties. However, if the subordinate does a poor job, the superior cannot evade the responsibility by stating that poor performance is the fault of the subordinate. This is because someone in a superior position in an organisation is normally responsible for, and thus accountable for, all the actions of the groups of employees under their supervision, even if they are several layers down in the hierarchy. So, despite delegating responsibility and authority, the manager is still accountable, both in law and in fact. He or she has chosen to delegate tasks to a subordinate, has recruited and trained subordinates, and has made the decision that the subordinate is capable of exercising power efficiently. Accountability, however, remains firmly at the top of the organisation structure.

Key terms

Authority The right or power assigned to a particular role in an organisation in order to achieve organisational objectives; it is the right to give orders and the power to exact obedience.

Accountability The extent to which a named individual is held responsible for the success or failure of a particular policy, project or piece of work; the obligation of an individual to report formally about the work he or she has done to discharge their responsibility.

Delegation The process of passing authority down the hierarchy from a manager to a subordinate.

Responsibility The duty assigned to a particular position in an organisation; the obligation to perform the particular tasks assigned to individuals and identified in their job descriptions.

Did you know?

It is often said that delegation can be both the most important but also the hardest thing for a manager to do well. Ronald Reagan, the fortieth President of the Unites States of America, is quoted as saying, 'Surround yourself with the best people you can find, delegate authority, and don't interfere as long as the policy you decided upon is being carried out.'

Advantages of delegation

- **Frees up management time**. Delegation is necessary in all organisations because there is a limit to the amount of work managers can carry out themselves. Delegation reduces the stress and burdens of management and frees up time for managers to concentrate on more important strategic tasks.
- **Motivation**. Delegation empowers and motivates workers. It provides subordinates with greater job satisfaction by giving them a say in the decision making that affects their work and by demonstrating trust in their abilities.
- **Local knowledge**. Subordinates might have a better knowledge of local conditions affecting their area of work and therefore might be able to make better-informed decisions.
- **Flexibility**. Delegation may allow greater flexibility and a quicker response to changes because if problems do not have to be referred to senior managers, decision making should be quicker.
- **Staff development**. By giving subordinates the experience of decision making, delegation provides a means of grooming them for higher positions and is thus important for management development purposes.

▲ Delegation empowers and motivates staff

Limitations of delegation

- **Less common in small firms**. In some small firms, managers delegate little – often because they do not have the staff to delegate to or because they have set the business up on their own, are used to controlling all aspects of the operations and are therefore reluctant to relinquish control.
- **Customer expectations**. Often, customers want to see the manager in charge, regardless of the fact that responsibilities may have been delegated further down the hierarchy.
- **Attitudes and approach of management**. The leadership style in an organisation will largely dictate the extent to which responsibilities are delegated down the hierarchy.
- **Quality of staff**. The extent to which responsibilities can be delegated will be influenced by the quality and skills of the staff who are employed.
- **Crisis situations**. In emergency or crisis situations where decisions need to be made quickly, delegation is less likely and is often less effective.
- **Confidentiality**. Where there is a need for confidentiality or extreme security, less delegation is likely to take place.

Improving the effectiveness of delegation

- Delegation should be based on mutual trust between the manager and the subordinate.
- It is important to select the most suitable person to delegate to – someone who will be able to complete the task efficiently and effectively. The person should be appropriately skilled, trained and informed about the particular task for which he or she will be responsible.
- Interesting and challenging tasks should be delegated as well as the more routine ones. Managers should not delegate tasks simply because they dislike doing them (for example, because the tasks are dull or difficult) or because they are overburdened with work.
- The tasks and responsibilities to be delegated need to be explained clearly in order to avoid subordinates making mistakes or feeling unsure or insecure because of a lack of information. An effective support system

should be provided – one that allows the subordinate to question and discuss issues connected with the delegated tasks. This should improve understanding and ensure that subordinates have the skills necessary to carry out their tasks.

● When delegating responsibility for carrying out a certain task, managers must also delegate the authority to carry it out and communicate this to others in the business, in order to avoid difficulties such as someone else questioning the authority of the subordinate. The limitations of the subordinate's authority should be made clear too.

● It follows that managers should avoid interfering with delegated tasks unless it is evident that things are going seriously wrong. They must relinquish control in order to ensure that subordinates feel they are trusted and that the manager has confidence in them.

Practice exercise 3

Total: 30 marks

1 Explain the term 'delegation' and why it is important to the success of an organisation. *(5 marks)*

2 Distinguish between the terms 'responsibility', 'authority' and 'accountability'. *(9 marks)*

3 Explain one advantage and one limitation of delegating responsibility in a business. *(8 marks)*

4 Explain two factors that are likely to make delegation more effective. *(8 marks)*

Case study: Peter's problems
Tuesday

Peter Smith is the sales manager of a textile firm in Lancashire. He is currently working on the draft of a document that will detail the current performance of the firm's various products in each of its sales regions, together with forecasts, based on market research findings, for the next three years. So far he has drafted some rough notes, identified the information he needs, and asked his secretary to collect the information and have it ready for him first thing on Thursday morning, so that he can work on it on Thursday and Friday. The document will form the basis of a presentation he is due to make next Tuesday at the board meeting.

Peter's real passion is for selling, but since his promotion to sales manager, he finds that he does less and less of this and spends an increasing amount of time looking at figures, justifying performance and attending board meetings, none of which he particularly enjoys.

As well as a secretary, Peter has an assistant, Sam, who helps him in travelling around to meet the regional sales team and generally co-ordinating the regions. Sam is keen to take on more responsibility; she is good with figures and would like to be more involved in the planning and reviewing process, which is mainly Peter's responsibility. At present, Sam feels a little constrained by the fact that she spends most of her time on the road travelling.

463

Wednesday

At a local business forum meeting, Peter learns of a conference in Germany that will focus specifically on the long-term potential in Eastern Europe for the types of product his firm produces and sells. The three-day conference starts tomorrow. Peter feels that he needs to go, but he is aware of the important board meeting next Tuesday when he is due to present the document, which he has not yet really started producing. He decides that this is the right time for Sam to step up – Sam has always said that she wants Peter to delegate more tasks to her, so here is her chance.

Peter arrives back at the office at 3 p.m., with 20 minutes to spare before his next meeting, which will go on until late in the evening. He calls Sam in and tells her that he will be away for the next three days in Germany. He explains that he wants Sam to cancel all her commitments for Thursday and Friday, and to compile the document that Peter will need for the board meeting next Tuesday. Peter gives Sam his rough notes and explains the information that he has asked his secretary to get ready for early tomorrow morning. He tells Sam that he will check the document on Monday and will talk to her about it then. After this he dashes off to his meeting.

Sam is stunned. She has a number of appointments booked for the next two days, which are important and which she is reluctant to cancel. However, although producing the document is rather daunting, she is keen to have a go and therefore follows Peter's instructions, rescheduling her appointments.

Thursday

Sam arrives at the office early and goes to Peter's secretary for the information. The secretary has half of the information required, but says that the rest is with another manager who wants to speak to Peter before releasing it. Sam rings the manager to explain the task she has been set, but the manager refuses to provide her with the information, saying that it is confidential and that Sam needs Peter's authorisation before she can have access to it.

Friday

Sam does her best to produce the document. However, she is not particularly happy with it and knows there are significant gaps in it owing to the lack of information. She has tried on a number of occasions to contact Peter in Germany, but has been unable to get hold of him. She is also aware that her lack of experience and limited skills in terms of report writing mean that the document does not show the information in the best possible light.

Monday

Peter does not turn up until 2 p.m., having attended a meeting all morning. He finds Sam's report on his desk, together with a note. He ignores the note and scans the document. He then calls Sam into his office. 'This is awful – there are all sorts of gaps in the information and the format is wrong. I can't find the slides for the presentation either ...'

Questions

Total: 30 marks

1 Explain why Sam might want Peter to delegate more tasks to her. (5 marks)

2 Managers rely heavily on effective delegation. Analyse this statement in the context of the above case study. (9 marks)

3 To what extent was Peter's failure to delegate authority the main cause of the difficulties that Sam faced in completing the report? (16 marks)

Did you know?

Successful organisations develop and adapt their structures to the dynamic environment in which they operate. Supermarkets centralise decisions on shop layout (because the head office researches the best layouts), but decentralise recruitment of workers because local conditions in the labour market are different between areas. They also devolve decision making about products and promotions to local branch managers, which means that each branch provides slightly different stock and promotions in order to suit the local market

Centralisation and decentralisation

On the one hand, organisations desire stability, uniformity and centralised control. However, they also recognise the differences in regional characteristics, customers and products, the fact that individuals tend to identify more readily with smaller work groups than with the whole organisation, and that they desire more authority and involvement in decision making. How these considerations are balanced influences whether an organisation has a centralised or a decentralised structure.

Centralised structures

Organisations that keep their decision-making power firmly at the top of the hierarchy, rather than delegating decisions to local levels or lower down the hierarchy, have a centralised decision-making structure. Burger King and other fast food chains are examples of organisations with centralised structures. You can recognise this because the meal, service and décor are exactly the same regardless of which branch you enter.

Advantages of centralisation

● Consistent policies on marketing and production mean greater control and standardisation of procedures.
● Decisions can be made quickly without the need to consult with all branches or sections.
● Every branch of a retail business is identical, meaning that customers know exactly what to expect.
● Enables tight financial control, efficient use of resources and lower overheads.
● The corporate view can be clearly emphasised, because decisions are based on the views of the head office rather than the preferences of local managers.
● Strong centralised leadership is useful in times of crisis.

Disadvantages of centralisation

● The manager of a local branch may have far better knowledge about customers' needs, but has little input into the decision-making process.
● The lack of decision-making powers of managers in local branches may adversely affect their motivation.
● Can lead to inflexibility and inappropriate decisions at local level and may also lengthen the whole decision-making process.

Decentralised structures

A decentralised structure is where the power and authority to make decisions is delegated from head office to management in the local branches or lower down the hierarchy of a business. This delegation should be backed up by financial resources. Decentralisation involves less uniformity in how things are done, as decisions are likely to be made in relation to local circumstances and opportunities.

Advantages of decentralisation

● Can empower local managers, encouraging them to be more innovative, and so improving their job satisfaction.
● Their local knowledge may have beneficial effects on sales and promotions, which may be targeted more accurately.

- It reduces the volume of day-to-day communication between head office and local branches.
- Senior managers should have more time to consider long-term strategy rather than day-to-day issues.
- Flexibility should improve as an organisation becomes more responsive to changing customer demands.
- All these changes should enhance motivation and in turn improve performance and reduce labour turnover.

Disadvantages of decentralisation

- Customers may not like the reduction in uniformity of branches.
- By focusing on local issues, local managers may not see the big picture and hence may miss an opportunity or trend that would have been picked up more effectively in a centralised structure.

Organisational structures

Common types of organisational structures include:

- Functional organisational structures, i.e. the traditional organisation structure with departments organised according to the different functions present in a business, for example, marketing, operations, finance, HR (see Figure 22.4). More detail on this structure is provided below.
- Geographical organisational structures, i.e. organised according to the location of operations. These are usually a variant of the functional organisational structure and are often used by organisations that operate across national boundaries, such as multinational companies. They have the advantage of enabling more local decision making that can ensure products are tailored to meet the needs of local markets. However, if brand image is strong and consistency of offer important, this type of structure can be less effective (see Figure 22.5 (a)).
- Product-line based organisational structures, i.e. organised according to different products made by a business. These are usually variants of the functional organisational structure and are often used by large organisations that produce a few major product lines, for example a transport business focused on bus services and coach tours (see Figure 22.5 (b)).
- Customer/market-based organisational structures, i.e. organised according to the customers or markets they serve. This type of structure is often used where a business relies heavily on one or more large customers, each of which accounts for a large proportion of total sales. For example, car component manufacturers might separate plants for the production of components for Toyota and for BMW to ensure they focus fully on their major customers' needs.
- Matrix organisational structures, i.e. organised so that hierarchical and functional approaches are combined. This is a more flexible organisational structure in which tasks are managed in a way that cuts across traditional departmental boundaries, and is often used in organisations that are highly project based (see Tables 22.2 and 22.3). More detail on this structure is provided below.

Functional organisational structure

A traditional functional organisational structure is illustrated in Figure 22.4. This structure could be adapted and used for businesses that organise themselves according to geographical regions or product lines. Figure 22.5 shows some organisational charts based on product lines and regions.

Features of functional organisational structures:

- They are based on a hierarchy in which each department operates separately under the leadership of those above it.
- Co-ordination between the different functions must occur at the top, as each division in effect operates as a separate organisation. This is therefore a relatively inflexible type of structure and can result in a 'silo' mentality, i.e. a lack of lateral or cross-functional thinking.
- The size of the department varies according to the business needs. Manufacturing businesses often have production departments that are much larger than other functions.
- Employees with specialist skills are employed in the relevant departments.

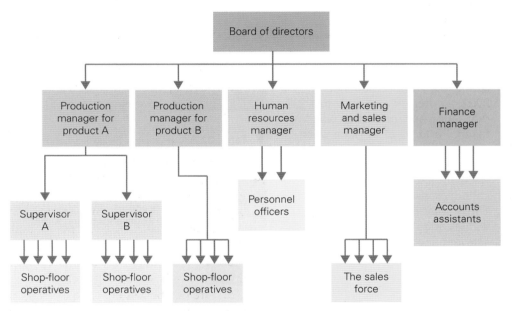

▲ **Figure 22.4** Traditional organisation chart

(a) Based on geographical region

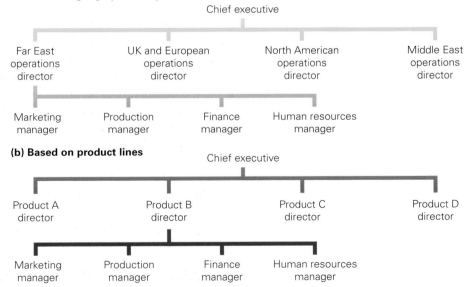

(b) Based on product lines

▲ **Figure 22.5** Functional organisation charts based on geographical region and product lines

Matrix organisational structure

A matrix organisational structure tends to be used alongside a functional organisational structure, not instead of it. Employees involved in a project team will report to the team leader on issues linked to the project, but will also be answerable to their departmental manager for their other roles. An example of matrix management is a new product development team that includes an engineer, a marketing manager, a designer and an accountant, as shown in Table 22.2. In universities, business schools are often organised on matrix management lines. For example, the staff who contribute to teaching on a BA in Business Management will be co-ordinated by a specific course tutor, but will also belong to their own specialist academic divisions, where they will have a line manager (see Table 22.3).

▼ **Table 22.2** New product development team: matrix management

	Engineering department	Marketing department	Design department	Finance department
New product team manager	The new product team manager takes staff from each of the above departments to form the new product development team			

▼ **Table 22.3** A university business school

	Academic divisions	Accounting and finance	Economics	HRM	Marketing	Operations management	Strategy
Course tutor for BA in Business Management	The course tutor takes staff from each of the divisions in column 1 to form the course lecturing team.						

Features of matrix organisational structures:

- They enable individual projects to be better co-ordinated and allow for the possibility of synergy, although lines of accountability can become unclear.
- They give people in different departments the opportunity to use their abilities and share their knowledge. This in turn prevents a single view – for example, about costs – dominating the decision-making process.
- They can lead to greater motivation for employees.
- Each team member can end up with two bosses – their departmental boss and the project leader, which can be problematic. Sometimes there is a lack of co-ordination between departmental heads and project leaders and, as a result, individuals may suffer if both bosses make heavy demands on them.

New forms of organisational structure

More recently new forms of organisation have been emerging. These have come about because of technological advances in virtual working, the rise in flexible contracts, an increase in self-employment and the idea of empowerment, or devolving decision making down the organisational hierarchy. These new approaches are very different to organisations with traditional hierarchical structures. They focus instead on collaboration, self-management and shared leadership. A prime example of a collaborative, non-hierarchical way of organising a business that most people will be aware of is Wikipedia. Another trend is working 'beyond the organisation' or collaboration between organisations for mutual benefits. For example, large-scale construction projects, such as Terminal 5 at London Heathrow Airport and the London Olympic Park, have been designed, developed and then made operational in partnership by several organisations working towards the same goal.

Influences on organisational design and structure, delegation, centralisation and decentralisation

Influences that determine the organisational design of a business will in turn influence all elements of that design, including the extent of, and how well, delegation is managed, and whether a centralised or decentralised approach is used.

Influences on organisational design and structure:

- **Business objectives**. Ensuring that the choice of organisational design is aligned appropriately with the business purpose is essential for the success of a business. Organisational structures should fit appropriately with the relevant business purpose, for example whether product-line based or customer/market based, whether centralised or decentralised. Importantly, the organisational design and structure may have to evolve as a business's purpose and objectives change over time.
- **Size of the organisation**. The larger the organisation, the more complex its structure and design is likely to be and the more layers of hierarchy, divisions or departments it is likely to have. A larger organisation also provides more opportunities for different organisational designs and structures, for example whether to make use of more decentralised approaches and greater levels of delegation.
- **Nature of the organisation**. A business's structure and design will depend on whether it is in the manufacturing or service sector, national or multinational, single product or multi-product, and whether it operates in an area where tight control, safety or security issues are paramount.
- **Culture and attitudes of senior management**. Organisational culture will be covered in your Year 2 textbook. Organisational design and culture is influenced by whether the management style is autocratic and controlling, or democratic and participative. The culture of an organisation will determine whether it is highly centralised and formal, with lots of procedures and rules, lots of levels of hierarchy and a top-down approach to communication, or whether it is decentralised, more flexible and informal, with quite a flat structure, very open forms of communication and lots of delegation. Innovative business entrepreneurs, such as those who founded Apple, Google and Twitter, have created organisational cultures that have had a significant impact on the design and structure of these organisations. The design and structure of multinational organisations are influenced by global cultural differences.

- **Skill and experience of workforce**. The nature of the workforce – whether the majority of workers do low-skilled, repetitive jobs or whether they are highly skilled, each doing very different jobs – will influence a firm's organisational design and structure and the extent to which delegation is used.
- **HR processes and systems**. The sophistication and effectiveness of existing HR processes and systems are important elements that influence organisational design and structure. For example, how well current processes and systems use technology effectively in recruitment, performance management and communicating will determine how well a business is likely to be able to move to more sophisticated network systems of organisational design. Similarly, the level of trust and respect between subordinates and managers will influence how effectively an organisation can move from a tall organisational structure with little delegation to a flatter organisational structure where more tasks are delegated. The choice of processes influences organisational design. For example, workers who are expected to focus on only one process repeatedly in the production of a finished product, in order to develop their expertise and skill, will require a different choice of organisational design than if employees are expected to work in groups to carry out all processes in the production of the finished product and take responsibility for the quality of the finished product. The level of autonomy and empowerment employees have to do their jobs, and the extent of delegation, will influence organisational design. For example, staff working at Burger King have virtually no discretion over the food they prepare and present to customers whereas an interior designer will have huge levels of discretion and autonomy when working with customers to meet their needs. Thus the nature of jobs and job design will be an important influence on, as well as being influenced by, organisational design.
- **External environment**. The external environment was discussed in Chapter 3 and, in relation to HR, in Chapter 20. Businesses need to be constantly aware of the opportunities and threats emerging in the external environment to ensure that their organisational design and structure are appropriate to meet the challenges. For example, the impact of technological change has had significant effects on how organisations are designed and how their structures are determined. The section on new organisational structures on page 468 provides examples of this. The increasing emphasis on work–life balance is leading to greater flexibility in how firms deploy their staff; a recession or credit crunch may mean a firm needs to reduce costs, perhaps by becoming more centralised, or by delayering its organisation (i.e. removing a layer of management); a successful takeover bid may lead to a complete restructuring of the organisation.
- **Stakeholders**. These were discussed in Chapter 6. Businesses need to check if stakeholder needs are being met and, if not, whether changes to the organisational structure might be needed. Stakeholders, such as important customers, can have a significant influence on the design and structure of organisations. For example, a small- or medium-sized business that has the government or a huge multinational organisation as its major customer, may find that the requirements of the contract with this large customer influence its organisational design and structure.

Just as there are a range of influences on organisational design, so organisational design influences other aspects of a business. In Chapter 23, we consider the influence of organisational design on the choice and assessment of reward systems.

Value of changing job design and organisational design

Previous discussions about job and organisational design have conveyed the value of each of these HR activities.

All organisations need to be responsive to changes taking place in both their external and internal environments. This includes ensuring that job and organisational design are appropriate for the circumstances.

When a business establishes its mission or purpose and its vision about how it will operate and how it will develop in the future, these ideas will be translated into key business objectives. To achieve its objectives, a business must develop appropriate business strategies. To implement business strategies will require organisation, people and other resources. Organisation, in this sense, includes having appropriate job and organisational design. For example, if a retail supermarket wishes to develop and sell a new product line – whether this be IT products or clothing – people and resources will need to be deployed and this will have an impact on job and organisational design – both of which will have to change in order to accommodate these new developments.

Once people, resources and organisation are in place, business strategies can be implemented. Evidence will then begin to emerge about whether strategies are working and whether job and organisational design are appropriate or not.

A process of review and evaluation will check how well the business is achieving what it set out to. It also allows it to check if its structures and systems are appropriate – in particular if its job and organisational design are the most appropriate given what it wants to achieve or whether they might need to be changed. The value of changing job and organisational design is exemplified in the fact file below on research by the Chartered Institute of Personnel and Development (CIPD).

Did you know?

One way of looking at the difference between mission, vision and strategy, is to think of mission as asking the question, 'What do we do?', vision as asking the question, ' Where do we want to get to in (say) the next five years?' and strategy as asking the question, 'How do we get there?'

Fact file

Research by CIPD into SME (small- and medium-size enterprises) growth shows why businesses need to constantly review their job and organisational design. The research suggests that many start-up businesses begin with a 'spider web' structure where a group of individuals work towards the vision of the founding entrepreneur or group of entrepreneurs. Over time, such businesses often develop unintendedly tall hierarchies that separate senior and junior members of staff. CIPD research also suggests that larger companies with established HR processes and a strategy for innovation are more likely to work towards removing levels of hierarchy in order to provide greater individual autonomy for employees and to speed up decision making.

Practice exercise 4

Total: 55 marks

1 Distinguish between centralised organisational structures and decentralised organisational structures. *(6 marks)*

2 Explain one advantage and one disadvantage of a centralised organisational structure. *(6 marks)*

3 Explain one advantage and one disadvantage of a decentralised organisational structure. *(6 marks)*

4 Which of the following is not a form of organisational structure?
   a) Matrix
   b) Functional
   e) Customer/market
   c) Fractional
   d) Product line
   (1 mark)

5 Distinguish between a functional management structure and a matrix management structure. *(6 marks)*

6 Explain three influences on organisational design and structure. *(9 marks)*

7 Identify and explain one influence on delegation in an organisation. *(4 marks)*

8 Identify and explain two influences that determine whether an organisation adopts a centralised or decentralised approach. *(8 marks)*

9 Analyse why job and organisational design might change and why such change might be of value to an organisation. *(9 marks)*

Case study: Ragbags

Ragbags is a producer of fine leather handbags. It has grown from a single small factory in Leeds to a much larger manufacturer, with six new production sites throughout the UK and its headquarters based at its original site in Leeds. It sells its products to upmarket department stores and leather retailers only.

Initially, the owner and managing director, Joe Watts, managed the small factory well. His approach was somewhat paternalistic, but he knew everyone and made a point of having an 'open door' policy as far as staff were concerned. All staff, regardless of their position, knew they could see him personally to raise issues and make suggestions about any aspect of their work.

As the company grew, the organisation adopted a more formal structure, with more layers between senior management and the workforce. The organisation chart for the growing company is shown in Figure 22.6.

The new structure, which simply evolved rather than being carefully designed to meet the needs of the growing business, meant that some directors were never seen at any one site for months at a time. In addition, issues that staff at one site might be concerned with, were never communicated to other sites, and there was a general feeling among staff of being left in the dark. Increasingly, staff spent tea breaks moaning to each other and talking about looking for new jobs. Despite this general feeling of unhappiness, so far there had been no adverse effects on productivity rates and production levels.

Robina Smith was appointed to the post of business manager – a new appointment with responsibility for administrative staff and procedures across all sites. Each of the six new sites had an administrative supervisor answerable to Robina. Robina saw her role as that of a strategic manager and did not feel that 'meeting the troops', as she put it, was an essential part of this – she thought that this element of the job could be done much better by the administrative supervisors. She did, however, believe in communicating with all her staff and she did this regularly – always by email. Every week, staff received endless emails from her about new policies and procedures she was introducing. People ignored many of these emails because they knew the policies and procedures would never work.

The administrative supervisors were a bit put out by Robina's approach. They could tell that she was highly efficient and keen to change and update their working practices, but they felt that they should be the ones who communicated changes to their staff. They felt as if the organisation had what they'd heard management specialists call a decentralised structure – but only on paper – and that in fact control was kept firmly in the centre – with Robina – so in fact it was more like a centralised structure. The six of them were required to travel to Leeds once a month for a meeting with Robina, but they had no other opportunity to meet each other or her. It was often difficult to raise issues of concern at these meetings because the agenda, set by Robina, was very tightly structured and the meetings always kept to time.

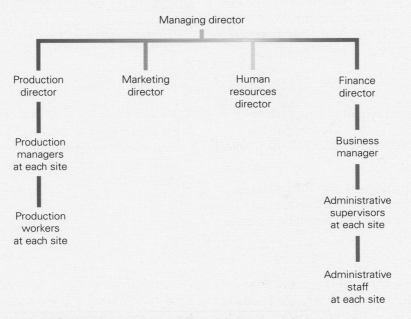

▲ **Figure 22.6** Ragbags organisation chart

Production staff at one of the sites were increasingly unhappy about the way their shift-working system was developing. It seemed as if their production manager had decided on a new system that meant more inconvenient working hours and fewer opportunities for overtime than at the other sites where there had been no change. The production director had told the six production managers that they could use their discretion to make changes to systems at their sites if the changes were likely to improve productivity and reduce costs. But he hadn't really given them any guidelines or limits about what was and wasn't allowed. The production managers did talk to each other a lot on the phone and corresponded by email, mostly complaining about the lack of involvement of senior management in the operations of the six sites, and the failure of anyone at senior management level to take their views and the views of their workers into account. Bill Sykes,

one of the production managers, felt the same but was also a bit concerned about the changes being made to the shift patterns at one of the sites and felt that the production manager there had overstepped the mark.

Joe Watts, the MD, had little idea of the discontent at the various sites. As far as he was concerned, the company was prospering, sales were high a nd growing, and profitability was excellent. He was currently setting up talks with a group of businesses in Japan to discuss the possibility of selling the company's products in Japanese department stores. The company had recently invested a significant amount of money in improving its ICT, including its communication systems, and all the directors had talked positively about the beneficial impact of this in terms of communication with the different sites.

It came as something of a surprise to Joe when he met Bill Sykes by chance at HQ. Bill had been with the company from the start, and Joe knew that he was a first-rate production manager who was loyal and hard working. Bill had come to HQ for one of his monthly production meetings. They started talking and Joe learned that Bill was leaving at the end of the month. Joe assumed that Bill had got a promotion and congratulated him on 'moving up the ladder'. Bill said that it was not a promotion, just a sideways move to another firm. Joe was worried. He reasoned that unless it is to do with personal circumstances, most people do not move sideways to another company unless they are unhappy with their present job. Bill said: 'Quite honestly Joe, I don't feel that the structure of the organisation is working well. We're supposed to be decentralised but most of the control comes from the centre. When we are given discretion over what we can do, no one tells us what the limits of our delegated responsibilities are. I could go on but instead I'm getting out.'

Joe decided that he needed to raise this at the next day's senior management meeting. As far as he knew, none of the directors were aware of any problems – which meant the situation was even more serious.

Questions

Total: 34 marks

1 Analyse why a more thoughtful approach to organisational design might have helped the organisation as it grew in size. *(9 marks)*

2 In moving from a single-site producer to a multi-site producer, analyse the issues the company should have been aware of in order to ensure that a more decentralised approach would be a success. *(9 marks)*

3 Discuss the influences that might impact on the organisational design of a company like Ragbags. In doing so, consider the influences on job design, delegation, centralisation and decentralisation. *(16 marks)*

How managing the human resource flow helps meet human resource objectives

The concept of a '**human resource flow**' was first used by Michael Beer in *Managing Human Assets* (1984). The flow through organisations can be split into inflow, internal flow and outflow.

- Managing the inflow involves decisions about recruitment, selection and induction of new employees.
- Managing the internal flow involves decisions about transfers, redeployment, promotions and demotions within an organisation and also about training, evaluating employees' performance and rewarding them. The internal flow must be managed so as to ensure employees' skills and competencies are developed to meet organisational needs, while at the same time satisfying employees' own career aspirations.
- Managing the outflow involves decisions about when and how employees leave an organisation, including retirement, redundancy and dismissal.

Key term

Human resource flow The flow of employees through an organisation, including the inflow – when they are recruited; the internal flow – what happens to them within the organisation; the outflow – when they eventually leave the organisation.

Figure 22.7 shows the human resource flow and three important influences on it.

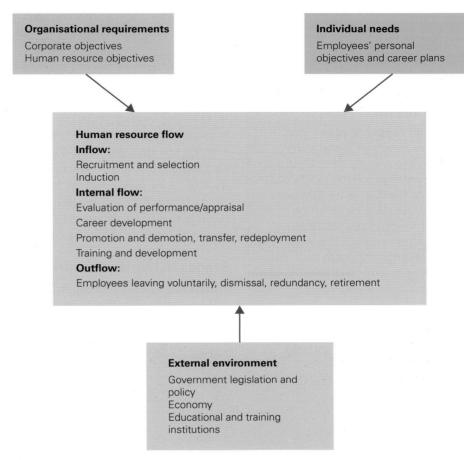

▲ **Figure 22.7** The human resource flow and influences on it

- **Organisational requirements**. The challenge for the human resource department is to ensure that the flow is managed so as to meet human resource objectives, which in turn should be designed to allow for the successful achievement of corporate objectives. For example, if a business is expanding and opening another plant, the focus is likely to be on recruitment to fill jobs at all levels of the organisation's hierarchy. On the other hand, a business may need to downsize because its market is shrinking. In this case, it is likely that recruitment will stop, voluntary redundancy or early retirement may be offered or employees may be offered opportunities to retrain in order to be redeployed elsewhere in the organisation. In the case of the latter situation, such actions allow for the corporate objective of (say) reducing costs by reducing productive capacity to be met as well as the human resource objectives of (say) cutting the workforce without reducing their morale.
- **Individual needs**. This involves taking account of employees' personal objectives and their career plans, so that the workforce is not only appropriately skilled but also well motivated.
- **External environment**. This includes the range of external influences that affect a business and therefore influence its human resource flow. For example, government legislation on equal opportunity and diversity will affect the nature of recruitment; government policy and the state of the economy will affect the number of potential employees required and

available; the skills and qualifications of school leavers and graduates will influence the quality of potential employees.

The human resource flow includes the **human resource plan**, recruitment, training, redeployment and redundancy. Each of these will be considered in turn.

Human resource plan

The three key elements of the human resource planning (often known as workforce planning) process are forecasting labour demand, analysing present labour supply and balancing projected labour demand and supply. Human resource planning consists of analysing and identifying the need for and availability of the human resources required by an organisation to meet its objectives. It is a process by which an organisation ensures that it has the right number and kinds of people, at the right place, at the right time, capable of effectively and efficiently completing those tasks that will help the organisation achieve its overall goals and objectives.

Stages in human resource planning

Human resource planning involves a number of stages to ensure that the right people are in the right place at the right time in order to meet the organisation's objectives. These stages are summarised in the resource planning cycle illustrated in Figure 22.8 and explained in more detail below:

▲ **Figure 22.8** Human resource planning cycle

- **Setting objectives**. This involves setting human resource objectives based on the corporate objectives of the organisation and converting these human resource objectives into human resource requirements.
- **Forecasting future demand for labour**. This should be done for the short term (e.g. to cover sick leave or maternity leave), medium term and long term (e.g. to meet future growth or expansion overseas). Forecasts should be constantly reviewed and updated. Forecasting should provide estimates of the size and nature of the workforce required, including how many workers are needed, what type of workers are needed, in which location they are needed and when they are needed.
- **Assessing the current workforce**. This involves identifying how many workers there are, what type (e.g. full time or part time), and their characteristics in relation to age, length of service, qualifications, staff

> **Key term**
>
> **Human resource plan** Often known as a workforce plan, this is the process that links the human resource needs of an organisation to its strategic plan to ensure that staffing is sufficient, qualified and competent enough to achieve the organisation's objectives.

turnover rates and reasons, promotion patterns and retirement rates. To do this effectively requires an organisation to keep detailed and up-to-date personnel records on an ongoing basis.

- **Identifying a shortfall or oversupply between the current workforce and that needed in the future**. The organisation needs to compare the future demand for skills and staff with the organisation's current workforce, and estimate the changes required in the existing supply of labour in the short, medium and long term, taking into account potential labour turnover and retirement. These changes need to be fully costed to determine whether the organisation can afford them.
- **Reviewing internal and external supply of labour in relation to future requirements**. This involves estimating the future state of the labour market and the availability of staff with the skills and attributes that a firm needs in the short, medium and long term.
- **Developing strategies to fill gaps or reduce oversupply of labour**. These will form the basis of human resource plans for the short, medium and long term.

Internal and external influences on human resource plans

Human resource plans require constant review and update to take account of both internal and external influences that may affect both the demand for and supply of labour.

Internal influences on an organisation's human resource plans:

- **An organisation's corporate or strategic plan, including its corporate objectives**. It is vital that human resource planning, which ensures that human resources are sufficient to facilitate the meeting of overall corporate objectives, is recognised as a part of the strategic planning process. Changes in corporate objectives, for example, as a result of a change in ownership, are likely to lead to changes in human resource plans.
- **An organisation's marketing and production plans**. This also includes its marketing and production objectives. For example, innovation and technological developments may require employees with different skills. Expansion abroad may require marketing staff with the ability to speak a number of different languages. Human resource planning needs to ensure that sufficient workers, in relation to skill and job level, are available to meet the requirements of the marketing and production departments.
- **The financial position of the organisation**. The budget available for recruitment and training will determine whether the organisation is able to fund the requirements of the human resource plan and thus enable it to meet its objectives.
- **The Internal labour supply**. This is influenced by internal promotional opportunities; training and development opportunities; changing employment conditions, such as flexible working or job rotation; retirement and staff turnover; and legal requirements that, for example, influence redundancy.
- **Other internal factors**. These include the organisation of work (whether cell production and teamwork or traditional production line work) and motivational and other issues that result in changes to labour turnover.

External influences on an organisation's human resource plans:

- **Market conditions**. These may cause demand for products to change. For example, an increase in competition may cause demand to fall, leaving the firm with too many employees. Unless demand is expected to pick up, the firm may have to consider issuing redundancy notices. Similarly, a firm may face a sudden huge increase in demand for its products because a competitor has gone out of business. In such a situation, it may be faced with a sudden shortage of staff.
- **Labour market and demographic trends**. These will influence the supply of labour from which an organisation can recruit its staff. For example, fewer young people may be available for full-time work if more decide to apply to university rather than apply for apprenticeships.

Fact file

Workforce planning for National Health Service dentists

Table 22.4 illustrates a stage in national workforce planning for dentistry in the NHS by identifying a range of factors and how they affect the supply of, and demand for, dental services in the future.

▼ **Table 22.4** Factors influencing the supply of, and demand for, dental services

Demand factors	Estimated effect on demand
Increasing proportion of elderly in the population	Increase in demand
Increasing number of individuals with own teeth	Increase in demand
Increasing number of more complex treatments available	Increase in demand
Increasing public expectations of dental treatments	Increase in demand
Increasing proportion of children with untreated decay	Increase in demand
Reduction in oral disease	Reduction in demand
Technological changes	Increase/reduction in demand
Supply factors	**Estimated effect on supply**
Predicted decline in number of registered dentists	Reduction in supply
Increased early retirement and part-time working	Reduction in supply
Increased availability of dentists from overseas	Increase in supply
Reduction in UK dental graduates	Reduction in supply
Loss of dental workforce to other countries	Reduction in supply
Increase in non-NHS working	Reduction in supply
Dissatisfaction with working conditions	Reduction in supply

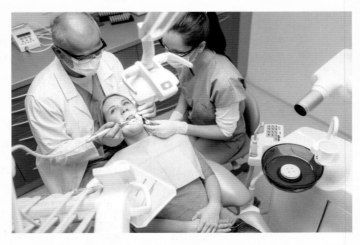

On the basis of the information in Table 22.4 and working in a group, identify possible strategies that the government might consider in order to ensure that sufficient dentists are available in the NHS in the future.

▲ Raising the retirement age means more older people in the work place

On the other hand, there may be more people aged over 60 available for work as a result of changes to pension and retirement ages. The migration of workers from other countries, such as Eastern Europe, may increase the supply of workers who are prepared to work for lower wages than British workers. Similarly, the concentration of particular skills may change; there may be insufficient people available with the skills required by a business, and the wages they demand may increase as a consequence. In such a situation, the business may decide that it is more efficient to train its own staff than to recruit trained staff from outside.

- **Economy and government policy**. These factors may affect the demand for products and services, the number of workers available and the level of wages and salaries that must be paid.
- **Legislation**. Human resource plans may be affected by changes in the law, for example, by legislation requiring an organisation to ensure that it meets stringent equal opportunities and health and safety requirements.
- **Local factors**. Travel to work patterns, the availability of housing and amenities, local unemployment rates and the cost of living all influence an organisation's ability to attract workers.

Issues in implementing a human resource plan

- **Employer/employee relations**. In order to maintain good employer/ employee relations, effective human resource planning involves consultation with employees and their trade union representatives so that the final plan is accepted throughout a business and can be implemented successfully.
- **Corporate image**. Successful implementation of a well-thought-out and widely accepted human resource plan will enhance the corporate image of the organisation. On the other hand, a plan that is imposed and that is not acceptable to employees or their representatives is likely to lead to industrial unrest and have a negative impact on an organisation's corporate image.
- **Cost**. Sufficient financial resources need to be guaranteed so that the human resource plan can be implemented fully.
- **Training**. Ensuring the successful implementation of a human resource plan usually requires extensive training and development activities, including the induction and training of new staff and the retraining or updating of current staff.

Value of using a human resource plan

The benefits of effective human resource planning are significant, in that it ensures that an organisation has a sufficient and appropriately skilled workforce to meet its objectives. On a practical level, it enables an organisation to avoid labour shortages and therefore ensures that production continues. This means that customer demand is met on time, with products in sufficient quantity and of the right quality. Human resource planning therefore allows an organisation to compete more effectively in the market.

Without effective human resource planning that takes into account appropriate forecasting of future trends, problems might occur. For example, there could be problems in recruiting and selecting appropriately skilled individuals, or staff could be inadequately trained for new processes that are introduced. Morale and motivation problems might occur if existing workers are expected to cover staff shortages. This in turn might lead to high levels of stress, more absenteeism and higher labour turnover, and increased costs for the business, which in the longer term may affect demand and competitiveness.

Without human resource planning, managers will simply react to events when they occur rather than being prepared for them, which may lead to hasty and poor-quality decision making when it comes to staffing. Firms undergoing continual change may find human resource planning more difficult. However, such firms still need to recruit the right number of employees and ensure that staff have the right skills and attitudes. Human resource planning is likely to be even more important for firms operating in markets that are constantly changing than in other markets, since few firms can afford either to have too many staff or to be short of staff at critical moments.

Practice exercise 5

Total: 50 marks

1 Explain the three elements of the human resource flow. *(6 marks)*

2 What is a human resource plan? *(3 marks)*

3 Identify four stages involved in human resource planning. *(4 marks)*

4 Explain two factors that might influence the internal supply of labour in a firm. *(6 marks)*

5 Explain one local factor that might influence the external supply of labour to a firm. *(3 marks)*

6 Explain two national factors that might influence the external supply of labour to a firm. *(6 marks)*

7 Explain two methods that a firm might use to overcome a potential shortage of labour. *(8 marks)*

8 Briefly explain two internal and two external influences on human resource plans. *(8 marks)*

9 Explain two possible long-term consequences for a firm that does not have a human resource plan. *(6 marks)*

Case study: Workforce planning in the mining industry

Recent years have been a challenging time for companies in the mining industry. They have had to call a halt to planned projects and reduce their capital spending. Some have been forced to cut their labour costs in order to streamline their operations and improve efficiency.

While the economic climate presents obvious challenges, the mining industry also faces challenges from other directions, including the difficulties of attracting, recruiting and retaining skilled workers.

According to data from a recent survey of mining employers, approximately 20 per cent of their workforce will become eligible to retire in the next three to five years. Furthermore, the mining industry will need to hire over 100,000 new workers by 2023, with over 60,000 of those workers filling vacancies caused by impending retirements.

In response to this industry-wide problem, companies are collaborating to find solutions about how to balance the outflow of skilled workers with active recruitment of new workers and the training and retention of existing workers. When financial resources are tight, new ways to solve such problems are necessary and the benefit of collaboration between businesses to provide new solutions becomes more important.

A key aim is to encourage mining businesses and their human resource experts to introduce strategies that enable them to be able to endure mining's cyclical peaks and troughs by developing a workforce able to withstand such cyclical fluctuations. For example, introducing strategies that allow a business to transfer and retain the knowledge of experienced employees who are about to retire or leave for other reasons. Without this transfer of knowledge, there are likely to be significantly negative effects on health, safety and productivity. Another example involves implementing strategies that allow a business to anticipate specific gaps in the workforce in order to help it deal with these gaps more effectively.

Questions

Total: 40 marks

1 Consider how a business in the mining industry might benefit from producing a human resource (or workforce) plan. *(6 marks)*

2 Explain how a company's corporate objectives are likely to influence its HR objectives and its human resource plans. *(8 marks)*

3 Identify two factors that are likely to influence the supply of labour to the mining industry. *(2 marks)*

4 Explain two ways in which businesses in the mining industry, or an industry you are familiar with, might fill the gaps between its demand for labour and the supply of labour. *(8 marks)*

5 Discuss the major internal and external influences that are likely to require a business in the mining industry, or a business of your choice, to review its human resource plans to ensure it can meet its objectives. *(16 marks)*

▲ **Figure 22.9** Summary of the recruitment and selection process

Recruitment

The **recruitment** and selection process is summarised in Figure 22.9. It involves the stages described below.

> **Key term**
>
> **Recruitment** Identifying the need for new employees, attracting the 'best' candidates for the job and then selecting the most suitable candidate in order to meet the staffing requirements of an organisation.

Human resource (or workforce) planning

The human resource requirements of the organisation need to be determined by the use of human resource planning techniques. Many organisations decide to fill vacancies that occur without really considering whether there are alternatives to recruitment and selection. Good human resource management will consider alternatives, including redeployment of existing staff, increased use of overtime, employment of temporary workers, introduction of new technology and outsourcing of certain functions.

Job descriptions

Once it is established that recruitment and selection need to take place, job analysis should be undertaken. This is where the tasks, skills, responsibilities, duties and performance level required are analysed and a job description is produced. The job description tells candidates what is expected in the job and helps the firm to identify the qualities needed in the individual to be selected for the job. It consists of the job title, the main purpose of the job, who the job holder is answerable to, the main duties and tasks contained in the job and any authority the job holder has.

Person (job) specifications

A person (or job) specification is then drawn up. This provides details of the ideal candidate by listing the essential and desirable characteristics of that person. It is used to identify the criteria that should be used in short-listing and then in selecting the best candidate from those who apply for the position. There are a number of different formats for a person specification. Such specifications are usually based on a set of competences identified as necessary for the performance of the job. In general, specifications should include details of:

- skills, aptitude, knowledge and experience
- qualifications (which should be only those necessary to do the job – unless candidates are recruited on the basis of future potential, e.g. graduates)
- personal qualities relevant to the job, such as ability to work as part of a team.

These factors are then ranked as either essential or desirable and applicants are judged against them at interview.

Deciding on internal or external recruitment

Once the job description and person specification have been drawn up, decisions must be made about whether to consider internal or external sources of candidates. Internal recruitment means filling a job vacancy by selecting a person who is already employed in the organisation. External recruitment means filling a job vacancy by advertising outside the firm.

Arguments in favour of recruiting internal candidates include the following:

- the employee's abilities are known already
- internal promotional opportunities are motivating for the workforce
- the recruitment and selection process is quicker
- a shorter induction period is required
- it is less expensive
- it reduces the risk of employing the wrong person.

Despite these advantages, internal promotion usually creates another vacancy further down the hierarchy that will need to be filled.

In contrast, external recruitment brings the following advantages:

- it often provides a larger choice of well-qualified applicants
- it brings in 'new blood' with new ways of thinking
- it overcomes jealousies that may occur if one member of a group is promoted above his or her colleagues
- it can help a firm to improve its understanding of how other firms operate.

Advertising media

Decisions must then be made about the most appropriate advertising media to use in order to attract the most suitable candidates.

Social Worker (
CMHT (Older Persons) Me
£29,728 - £33,291 per annu
Permanent contract, 37.5 hr
A vacancy has occurred with the
and we are looking to recruit an e
working and championing Older P
over the age of 65 years and at any
The team has a multidisciplinary app
offers a broad range of therapies, co
involve our day hospital colleagues ir
rvice and offer clients and ca
e office base is in Wel
eagues in Fr
all of

There are many different kinds of advertising media:

- National and local newspapers
- Trade or professional magazines
- Job centres, which help people to find jobs locally and can also direct individuals to government-funded training schemes for young people and the unemployed.
- Commercial employment agencies, which will provide shortlists of candidates for interview. Because the agencies do the advertising and initial shortlisting, this removes the administrative burden from the firm. However, agencies charge quite large fees and often deal only with temporary staff.
- Specialist careers centres such as the army
- University 'milk rounds', where companies visit universities to recruit students who are about to graduate.
- Local schools or colleges
- Local radio, the internet and social media sites
- Internal newsletters, notice boards and billboards
- Word of mouth
- Headhunting, where recruitment consultants seek the right person for a job. This tends to be used to recruit very senior managers and top-ranking professionals. The main advantage of headhunting is that headhunters may find someone who is ideal for the job, but who is not actually looking for work and would therefore not notice an advertisement. However, headhunting is expensive because it is labour-intensive.

Application forms and CVs

Candidates attracted by the vacancy will be asked to send in a completed application form and/or curriculum vitae (CV) and a letter of application. An application form provides information in a standard format. This allows a business to collect information from job applicants in a systematic way and assess objectively a candidate's suitability for a job, therefore making it easier to pre-select candidates. Although CVs include similar information (details of individuals, their qualifications, their experience and why they are suitable for the job), they can vary considerably and hence may be more difficult to compare. A CV is usually accompanied by a letter of application. Note that, increasingly, both application forms and CVs are completed and submitted on line.

Shortlisting

The best candidate for the job must then be selected. This is usually done by assessing candidates' application forms or CVs against the criteria set out in the person specification. The result will be a shortlist of a small number of applicants. References from previous employers or tutors are then requested in order to confirm information about candidates' abilities, skills and experience.

Interviews and other methods of assessment

Suitable candidates will then be called for interview and/or asked to take part in other methods of assessment. Research suggests that, although interviews are the traditional and still the most popular method of selection, they are not necessarily the most effective in indicating how well an individual will perform in a job. This is because interviewers tend to be swayed by appearance and personality and are often overly influenced by first impressions. For this reason, other selection techniques are often used in addition to interviews. These include:

- **Aptitude and attainment tests**: these measure how the applicant copes when presented with a particular business situation or how good the applicant is at a particular skill such as word processing, a foreign language or basic arithmetic.
- **Psychometric or personality tests**: these measure the personality, attitude and character of applicants, for example, whether they are team players or loners, whether they are passive or assertive, how good their problem-solving skills are, how good they are at dealing with the unknown, how creative they are. These tests are more common for graduate and management-level jobs. There are criticisms about the effectiveness of psychometric tests, such as whether it is wise to want all managers to have particular, and therefore similar, characteristics, and the extent to which people answer questions truthfully or simply give answers that they think will get them the job.
- **Assessment centres**: here a group of candidates are invited to a particular location for a day or a few days for an in-depth assessment. They are likely to be observed performing a range of tasks, including oral and written activities, role-play, teamwork, presentations, simulations and case studies that reveal their leadership, team-working and problem-solving skills. Research suggests that this method is the most effective one for predicting successful job performance. However, it is an expensive and time-consuming method and tends to be restricted to large firms and government departments and to the selection of those people who are likely to fill senior positions in the future – for example, those on high-flying graduate trainee programmes.

The interview or assessment method chosen should be the most appropriate one for ensuring that the most suitable candidate is selected. Whichever method is used, it is increasingly the case that the human resources department provides support to the functional departments, allowing departmental or line managers to be much more involved in recruitment and selection decisions.

Did you know?

One way of checking the effectiveness of recruitment is to keep records of the proportion of people who remain with the business for more than a set period of time.

Appointment

Once the best candidate has been selected and informed of the decision, he or she must confirm acceptance of the position. At this point it is good practice to debrief those shortlisted candidates who were not successful. Explaining why they were not successful can be extremely useful to them if it is done sensitively and constructively. In relation to the whole process of recruitment and selection, it is vitally important that firms take into account the legal implications of equal opportunities legislation, including sex discrimination, equal pay, race relations, disability discrimination and age discrimination. This not only avoids legal challenges to decisions, but also ensures that the best candidate is appointed to the job.

▲ Firms cannot discriminate on the grounds of disability, race, age or sex

Factors affecting methods of recruitment and selection

- Level of the job in the organisation – whether shop floor or senior management level.
- Size of the organisation – whether a large multinational or a small shop.
- Resources available to fund the recruitment and selection process.
- Cost of a particular method – recruitment and selection can be an expensive process and includes the cost of advertising, the cost of administering, perhaps, thousands of applications and the time spent shortlisting, interviewing and assessing.
- Supply of labour – whether there are plenty of potential applicants with relevant skills and experience or whether there are few.
- Culture of the organisation and the extent to which this dictates that internal recruitment and promotion are the norm.

What do you think?

Birmingham's John Lewis store

The upmarket department store, John Lewis, is to open a new £100 million store at Birmingham's New Street station in 2015. An estimated 650 jobs will be created at the store, which will form the centrepiece of the transformed station. The store will be one of the John Lewis Partnership group's largest sites outside London. Like all John Lewis department stores, the new store will feature more than 350,000 products including fashion, furniture, homeware, beauty and the latest technology.

Discuss the ways John Lewis might go about the recruitment of the 650 jobs it needs to fill in readiness for when it opens its store in Birmingham.

Importance of effective recruitment and selection

Ineffective selection can cause increased labour turnover, which in turn leads to additional costs in terms of further advertising, interviewing and training as well as its impact on productivity and employee motivation. Effective recruitment and selection could lead to lower labour turnover, lower costs, improved productivity and more highly motivated employees.

Practice exercise 6

Total: 35 marks

1 Identify the main stages in the recruitment and selection process. *(6 marks)*

2 Explain one advantage of recruiting an internal candidate for a job and one advantage of recruiting an external candidate for a job. *(6 marks)*

3 Distinguish between a job description and a person specification. *(6 marks)*

4 Identify and explain two methods of selecting the best individual for a job other than by interview. *(6 marks)*

5 Identify and explain two factors that will influence the method of recruitment and selection used. *(6 marks)*

6 Explain the importance of effective recruitment and selection to an organisation. *(5 marks)*

Case study: Ernst & Young and its use of social media in recruitment

Ernst & Young (EY) is one of the largest professional service firms in the world and one of the 'Big Four' accounting firms – others include Deloitte, KPMG and PriceWaterhouseCoopers.

EY is known to be very good at recruiting talent via social media and, in particular, via Facebook. Its career website is designed to help people find exactly what they're looking for. Rather than provide a single career page, potential applicants (whether students, recent graduates, experienced workers or executives), can communicate with EY via the website in order to get answers to their specific questions.

EY mainly focuses on Facebook to reach students and graduates because it believes this is the best place to target potential young professionals. Via the Facebook career page, EY aims to build a relationship early on with potential applicants, to get them to learn more about the company and its career opportunities. The page currently has over 85,000 'likes'. People can directly engage on the Facebook wall with the EY team, discovering the company's values through photos and videos.

Depending on whether the potential applicant is experienced or a student, the approach is to try to answer each individual's questions. So, for example, under the student tab, questions and answers aim to cover anything a student/graduate might raise, along with tests and videos. The page tries to provide good information about what it feels like to work at EY and therefore what the company is looking for in their candidates. It's both about attracting potential recruits and making sure the right people apply.

EY's aim is to be relevant to its audience. On Twitter, numerous accounts have been created depending on what content is shared. On the @EYnews Twitter account, general news is shared. People who are following @EY_CareersUK can stay connected to career opportunities. The Twitter link is a good way to generate interest and bring users straight to EY on Facebook, YouTube or their website and drive more potential applicants to consider the company.

Source: adapted from an article on linkhumans.com by Marion Muller, 5 October 2014

Questions

1 Analyse the benefits of Ernst and Young's social media approach to attracting and recruiting new staff compared to more traditional methods.
(9 marks)

2 Having attracted people to consider applying to the company, explain the additional processes that will be involved before the company will be able to select the right candidates. *(10 marks)*

3 Discuss the issues that Ernst and Young or other companies might face in deciding whether to recruit middle and senior managers from within the company or from outside. *(16 marks)*

Did you know?

It is useful to distinguish between training and development. Training is the process of instructing individuals about how to carry out tasks directly related to their current job. Development, on the other hand, involves helping individuals to realise their full potential. Development covers general growth and is not necessarily related specifically to employees' existing posts.

Fact file

Cost of replacing staff

A recent report by Oxford Economics suggests that it costs over £30,000 to replace a member of staff. There are two main factors that make up this cost: the cost of lost output while a replacement employee gets up to speed and the logistical cost of recruiting and inducting a new worker. The logistical cost of replacing an employee includes advertising costs, agency fees, the time involved in processing applications and interviewing and assessing prospective candidates and the cost of hiring temporary workers to cover the time between an employee leaving and a replacement starting.

The cost of lost output is the major part of the total cost. The report suggests that, on average, new workers in micro businesses (which employ between 1 and 9 workers) reach optimum productivity in 12 weeks, in small and medium enterprises (which employ between 10 and 250 workers), the time to reach optimum productivity is 24 weeks and in larger firms (employing over 250 workers) the time to reach optimum productivity is 28 weeks.

Source: 'The Cost of Brain Drain: Understanding the Financial Impact of Staff Turnover', Oxford Economics, February 2014

Key term

Training The provision of work-related education, either on-the-job or off-the-job, involving employees being taught new skills or improving skills they already have.

Training

Training needs

The need for **training** essentially arises when the knowledge and skills required by a firm exceed or differ from those that workers currently possess. Training is often a response to some sort of change, whether internal or external. Possible changes are:

● the development and introduction of new products and services
● restructuring of a firm
● the development and introduction of new technology
● changes to procedure, including improvements to customer service
● high labour turnover

- low morale
- changes in legislation.

Benefits of training

- Helps new employees reach the level of performance expected of experienced workers.
- Ensures that employees have the necessary skills, knowledge, attributes and qualifications for the job, both at present and in the future.
- Develops a knowledgeable and committed workforce, with increased motivation and job satisfaction.
- Increases efficiency and productivity, enabling a business to produce high-quality products and services, which may in turn lead to improved profits.
- Can identify employees' potential and thus increase employees' job prospects and chances of promotion, which may improve motivation.
- Reduces costs in the long term by, for example, reducing the number of accidents and injuries, reducing wastage and poor-quality work and increasing workers' productivity.
- Encourages employees to deal with change more effectively and to be more flexible, for example, about the introduction of new technology.
- Encourages employees to work towards an organisation's aims and objectives.
- Improves the image of a company. Customers will have more confidence in well-trained staff and a better image will attract more able recruits.

Induction training

The aim of induction training is to help new employees settle in quickly, in order to ensure that they reach the level of performance expected of experienced workers. It includes familiarising new recruits with the layout of an organisation, health and safety issues, security systems, key personnel, the hierarchical and departmental systems, the main policies of an organisation, job descriptions, the culture of an organisation, an organisation's history and development, terms of employment including disciplinary rules, employees' benefits and services, and physical facilities. In general, an effective induction programme is likely to:

- reduce labour turnover
- improve employees' understanding of both the corporate culture and the situation in which an organisation is placed
- enable employees to contribute to an organisation more quickly
- increase motivation.

External and internal training

External training, such as joining a college course on business management or supervisory training, is appropriate if there are only a few employees with a specific training need and if the training requirements are not specifically linked to the organisation. External training gives employees the opportunity to meet people from other organisations, allowing an interchange of ideas and a broadening of understanding. It can also make employees feel valued and increase motivation.

Internal training is appropriate if training needs are specific to the individual organisation – for example, if employees need to learn how to use a particular new computer system.

On-the-job and off-the-job training

On-the-job training is where an employee learns a job by seeing how it is carried out by an experienced employee (also known as 'sitting by Nellie').

On-the-job training is likely to be cheaper than off-the-job training, as existing employees and equipment can be used. Such training takes place in a realistic environment, therefore avoiding any problems in adjusting between, say, a college environment and a work situation, and there is also no loss of output. However, the quality of training depends on the ability and willingness of the instructor and the time available. The employee who is chosen to be an instructor might be unable to teach the proper skills, or might have developed bad habits or short-cuts that are passed on to the trainee. In addition, the work situation might be noisy and stressful and not conducive to effective learning.

Off-the-job training involves all forms of employee education apart from that at the immediate workplace. Off-the-job training may be conducted internally – for example, in a conference room – or externally, at a college. Either way, there is less immediate pressure from work. Employees might attend college during working hours through either day release or block release or in the evening or at weekends. Such training can also involve online learning. The training will be focused on skills, attitudes and theories that relate to work, and is likely to include generic skills and knowledge that are useful at work, rather than job-specific content. Off-the-job training often uses specially trained experts to do the teaching. This may result in training being more highly valued by employees, leading to increased motivation. If it is also external, off-the-job training will give employees an opportunity to meet staff from other organisations and to learn about their systems. In general, it is more straightforward to estimate the costs of such training and it is easier to monitor progress. However, it can be expensive and there is a question as to whether the skills learned can be transferred effectively to the actual work environment.

Evaluating the effectiveness of training

Evaluation of training is reasonably easy if the outcome can be observed by, for example, the effective use of an IT system or the production of a product, but it is more difficult in relation to management training courses. In such situations, questionnaires are needed to assess people's views and perceptions before and after a course, and perhaps at a later point. In relation to customer care courses, businesses can use mystery visitors, who act as members of the public to check how staff are responding to customers after their training. Training can also be evaluated by monitoring improvements in the quality of output, reductions in labour turnover, increases in candidates coming forward for internal promotion, and reductions in accidents, mistakes and wastage.

Do firms spend enough on training?

UK firms have been criticised for spending less on training than their competitors in Europe and the USA. This can arise from the working of competitive markets.

Poaching employees means attracting workers who have already been trained by another business. If company A wants workers with particular skills that can only be acquired with training, it might attempt to poach them from company B, which has already trained its workers in that particular skill. Poaching would mean attracting workers by offering higher salaries. This saves company A the cost of the training process, but means that company B has wasted its resources in training the workers who have now left. If done widely in an economy, poaching might lead employers to stop or reduce their training of employees. They will realise that it is pointless training employees who then leave the firm, and will consider it more cost effective to hire ready-trained staff. If those staff leave, the firm does not lose out as a result of having paid for their training.

In this way, the market leads to inefficiencies rather than efficiency, and it may be desirable for the government to intervene by providing tax incentives for organisations that train their own staff, for example.

In general, research suggests that firms in the UK fail to invest sufficiently in training and development, viewing training as a cost and failing to consider the long-term benefits to the organisation and to the individual. In addition, training programmes tend to be developed in response to current problems rather than in anticipation of future knowledge and skills requirements.

Practice exercise 7

Total: 20 marks

1 What is the difference between 'on-the-job training' and 'off-the-job training'? *(4 marks)*

2 Explain two advantages of internal training. *(8 marks)*

3 Explain two advantages of external training. *(8 marks)*

Case study: Recruitment and training at McDonald's

Recruitment

A two-step application process is used for potential crew members. First an online application is completed. If successful, the applicant is invited to a restaurant for an On the Job Evaluation (OJE) and interview. The OJE provides an opportunity for a manager to evaluate an applicant's customer service skills and allows the applicant to check if the environment suits them. The whole process lasts about 30 minutes.

If successful, recruits then attend a welcome meeting that involves watching a DVD about the company and discussions with the manager. An online health and safety and food safety test must be completed in their own time. The first shift begins with a tour of the store, highlighting health and safety and food safety issues. This induction process lasts about two hours.

For a trainee manager role, a four-step process is involved.

● An initial screening process to ensure candidates meet basic criteria.
● An online personality questionnaire to ensure candidates have the desired attributes and preferred style of working.
● A restaurant-based 'On the Job Evaluation' (OJE) involving doing the job for a day.
● An interview with a senior manager.

If successful, a trainee manager completes an intensive 18-week management development programme that provides training and development in all the skills needed to be an effective assistant manager.

▶▶▶

Training

McDonald's invests more than £36 million in training and development each year. McDonald's believes its success is built on the quality, service and cleanliness it provides for customers and that well-trained crew and managers are the first step to achieving this.

Crew member training

The first stage of training is provided at the welcome meeting where standards and expectations are explained. This is followed by a structured training programme that provides training in all areas of the business from front counter to grill area. Most of the training is on-the-job, learning from crew trainers and colleagues by working alongside them. The timescale for this training depends on whether employees are full time or part time. Employees must also complete workbooks and unit tests on quality, service and cleanliness. Following this initial training, all employees receive ongoing training in each work area. Skills are assessed by observation and the ratings go towards annual performance reviews.

Management training

Training begins within the restaurants. It includes a shift management development programme that involves developing the skills needed to manage a shift and restaurant leadership skills including team building, decision making and communication. Training also includes development days that cover areas such as customer care, first aid and restaurant safety. If the management entrance exam is completed successfully, employees attend a training course off-the-job before returning to the restaurant in a management capacity. Management training involves on-the-job training, open learning development modules and courses and seminars at the national and regional training centres. Managers are usually seconded to work, for a time, in a regional office in order to develop and learn new skills, see a new side of the business and become more aware of how each department's strategies have a role to play in achieving the company's goals.

McDonald's provides a company website with access to online courses leading to nationally recognised level 1 and level 2 skills qualifications. These allow learners to study whenever and wherever they feel comfortable and at their own pace. It also offers other nationally recognised qualifications, including apprenticeships and a Foundation Degree.

Source: McDonald's website (www.mcdonalds.co.uk), 5 October 2014

Questions

Total: 25 marks

1 Explain why McDonald's offers induction training to all its employees. *(5 marks)*

2 Do you believe that McDonald's training programme is suited to the needs of both the company and its employees? Justify your view. *(20 marks)*

Key term

Redeployment The process of moving existing employees to a different job, or different location within the same organisation.

Key term

Redundancy When an employer dismisses an employee because their job no longer exists. This might be because the business is changing what it does; doing things in a different way (e.g. becoming more automated); changing location or closing down. Redundancies can be compulsory or non-compulsory.

Redeployment

Redeployment may be offered because certain jobs are being made redundant and vacancies elsewhere in a business are available. For example, in a multi-product firm, the demand for one of its products may be declining but demand for another is increasing. So, while jobs are being made redundant in one area of the firm, vacancies may be available in another area. Similarly, organisational change may be taking place to improve efficiency, which may lead to changes in the nature of jobs or jobs disappearing because of the introduction of automated machines or new processes. This might mean that while certain jobs are redundant there are opportunities in other areas of the organisation.

Redeployment may also take place because of personal reasons associated with an individual employee. For example, it may occur as a result of a recommendation for medical reasons or as an outcome from an harassment and bullying complaint, or other reasons, as agreed with the HR department.

There are a number of advantages to redeployment for both employees and employers:

- maintaining job security for employees whose current jobs are at risk
- improving the morale of the workforce because of the actions of their employer in retaining employees whose original jobs have disappeared
- retaining valuable skills, knowledge and experience in an organisation
- reducing the cost and time associated with recruitment and selection and the time needed for induction and training of staff new to an organisation.

Redundancy

Organisations can try to avoid redundancies, particularly in the short term. Ways of doing this include:

- natural wastage and recruitment freezes – this means that when individual employees leave for whatever reason, they are not replaced
- stopping or reducing overtime
- asking people to volunteer for early retirement
- retraining or redeployment
- pay freezes
- short-time working (whereby workers have lower weekly hours)
- pay cuts in return for taking time off work
- 'alternatives to redundancy' (ATR) schemes in which employees do not work for their employer for a specified period and are free to seek new work while receiving an ATR allowance. During the recent recession many employers adopted a wide range of alternatives to **redundancy**.

Offering a voluntary redundancy package and then seeking willing redundancy volunteers may avoid compulsory redundancies altogether.

The process of making employees redundant usually involves extensive consultation with recognised trade unions or elected representatives and individual employees. Employees have the right not to be unfairly selected for redundancy. Employees selected for redundancy must be very carefully identified to avoid accusations of unfair dismissal. Where there is a choice between employees, selection must be based on objective criteria which may include:

- length of service (only as one of a number of criteria)
- attendance records
- disciplinary records
- skills, competencies and qualifications
- work experience
- performance records.

Did you know?

Care must be taken in choosing the criteria used to select for redundancy in order to avoid factors which may be discriminatory on any grounds. For example, selection of part-timers could be discriminatory if a high proportion of women or elderly people are affected. Similarly, as a result of age discrimination legislation, 'Last in, first out' (LIFO) might be a risky selection method, because those with less service are likely to be younger employees.

Fact file

Redundancy

It is unfair to automatically select employees for redundancy based on the following reasons: trade union membership (or non-membership); part-time status; pregnancy or maternity-related reasons. In addition, selection for redundancy because of an employee's age, sex, sexual orientation, marital status, disability, race or religion or any other protected characteristic will constitute a breach of the Equality Act 2010.

Depending on their length of service, employees may be entitled to redundancy pay if they are made redundant. All employees under notice of redundancy have the right to reasonable time off to look for a new job or arrange training. Employers must consider offering suitable alternative work (i.e. redeployment opportunities) to employees whose jobs are at risk of redundancy. Different factors that determine whether a job is deemed as 'suitable alternative employment' include:

- how similar the work is to the employee's current job
- the terms of the job being offered
- the employee's skills, abilities and circumstances.

An employee's entitlement to a statutory redundancy payment is removed if they unreasonably refuse a suitable alternative employment. An employee is entitled to a four-week trial period in a new role. If the employer and employee then agree that the role is not a suitable alternative, the employee reverts to being redundant.

Some organisations have well-designed redundancy programmes that provide opportunities for employees likely to be made redundant to refresh their interview skills, redraft CVs and reply effectively to job advertisements. These programmes are often known as outplacement services. They aim to maintain the morale of those employees at risk of being made redundant and help them find alternative employment.

Fact file

Malaysia Airlines to cut jobs

In August 2014, Malaysia Airlines announced plans to cut jobs as part of a major restructuring programme.

The announcement comes after the disappearance of one of its flights over the southern Indian Ocean in March 2014 and the shooting down of another of its flights over Ukraine in July 2014. The incident in March involved a flight from Kuala Lumpur to Beijing with 239 people aboard. The incident in July involved a flight from Amsterdam to Kuala Lumpur with 298 people on board.

Its struggle to overcome the impact on the business of the two disasters led to the decision to cut approximately 6,000 jobs, which is about a third of its total workforce. The job losses are part of a major restructuring of the airline with the aim of restoring its reputation, ability to compete and its profitability.

A new chief executive will be in place in 2015 and the business is being taken over by the Malaysian government.

Fact file

Job cuts at BlackBerry

By August 2014, BlackBerry had finished its long restructuring process and was even considering recruiting new employees for jobs in product development, sales and customer service. It started laying off employees in 2011 because it failed to compete successfully with other firms in the smartphone sector. It is reported to have made approximately 6,000 employees redundant in 2012 out of a total workforce of 16,500. The company aims to focus on a niche market of large corporation and government agencies that require highly secure mobile communications.

Redundancy is a traumatic event for the employees concerned. It can also have a very damaging effect on an organisation because it is likely to have an adverse impact on the morale, motivation and productivity of the remaining employees. A demoralised workforce, anxious about job security and critical of the handling of the redundancies of colleagues, is unlikely to remain committed to an organisation or work with enthusiasm and initiative. Depending on the publicity it receives locally or nationally, redundancy can also damage the reputation of a business. In addition, there are a number of costs to employers associated with redundancy. These include direct costs, such as redundancy pay, and costs associated with the indirect effects of making people redundant, including higher labour turnover and lost output as a result of the lower morale of the remaining workforce.

Practice exercise 8

Total: 30 marks

1 Explain the term redeployment.   *(3 marks)*

2 Explain two advantages to a business of providing redeployment opportunities for its staff.   *(6 marks)*

3 Explain the term redundancy.   *(3 marks)*

4 Identify two reasons why redundancy might occur.   *(6 marks)*

5 Identify three alternatives to making employees redundant.   *(3 marks)*

6 Which of the following is unlikely to be one of the criteria for choosing which employees will be made redundant?
   a) Length of service
   b) Attendance records
   c) How far away from the firm they live
   d) Disciplinary records
   e) Skills and qualifications   *(1 mark)*

7 Explain the negative effects the announcement of redundancies can have on a firm.   *(8 marks)*

Case study: Cadbury job cuts

In January 2014, the Birmingham-based chocolate maker, Cadbury, warned that jobs would be cut despite a £75 million investment in its Bournville plant. The investment is to be used to make the Bournville site a world-class manufacturer of chocolate by updating machinery and ensuring the site can operate efficiently and profitably. The business is hoping to increase its manufacturing volumes and its capability to introduce new products. The investment would include replacing out-of-date production lines and opening new ones. At the moment, production costs at the site are twice as high as many of its competitors. The Bournville plant also includes the company's chocolate research and development site, which works on the creation of new chocolate bars.

The Bournville factory, which opened in 1879, currently employs about 960 workers. It produces some of the firm's most popular chocolate bars, including Dairy Milk (which was first produced in Bournville in 1905), Creme Eggs and Wispas.

The Unite trade union said at the time that the investment was desperately needed because some of the plant and equipment was more than 30 years old. It also said that the company had been transparent about its plans, but that the union favoured voluntary redundancies and would oppose compulsory redundancies.

Both the unions and management say the £75 million investment may create more employment opportunities in the long term.

1 Explain two alternative actions Cadbury might have introduced rather than making a large number of its employees redundant. *(8 marks)*

2 Assess the potential negative effects on a business such as Cadbury of carrying out a programme of redundancies and how it might minimise these negative effects. *(16 marks)*

3 Evaluate why investment, such as that planned at Cadbury, might lead to redundancy in the short term but more employment in the long term. *(16 marks)*

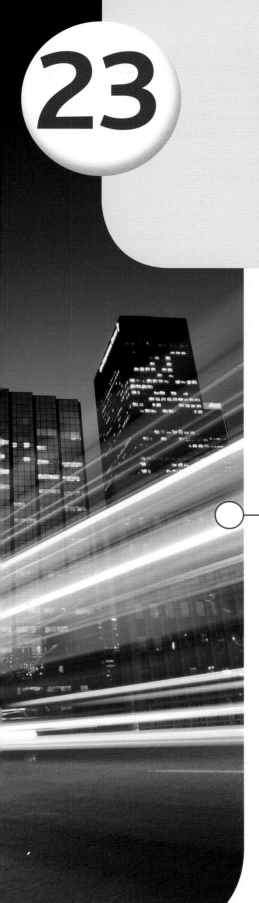

23 Making HR decisions: improving motivation and engagement

This chapter begins by identifying the benefits for an organisation of having motivated and engaged employees. In doing so, it considers a number of theories of motivation, including Taylor, Maslow and Herzberg and assesses the value of these theories. The chapter then discusses how to improve the motivation and engagement of employees. In relation to this, both financial and non-financial methods of motivation are considered. Financial methods include piece rate, commission, salary schemes and performance-related pay. The chapter concludes with a summary of influences on the choice and assessment of the effectiveness of financial and non-financial reward systems.

Benefits of motivated and engaged employees

Key term

Motivation The desire and energy to be continually interested and committed to a job, role or subject, or to make an effort to attain a particular goal.

A motivated workforce is a consequence of the interaction of a number of factors, including the intensity of a person's desire or need, the incentives available to achieve the particular goal, and the expectations of the individual and of his or her peers. In a work context, it is a study of factors that influence the behaviour of people at work. In studying for A-levels, your **motivation** to work very hard may be because you are very interested in the subjects you have selected, want to get a high grade in your exams in order to go to a good university and then onto a well-paid job and that you want your family to be proud of you.

▲ What's your motivation to work hard for your Business A-level?

Employee **engagement** is more than just job satisfaction and is about individuals' involvement with, and commitment to, their jobs. Evidence from the Chartered Institute of Personnel and Development (CIPD) suggests that, in general, women tend to be more engaged than men; younger workers are less engaged than older workers; those on flexible contracts are more engaged; managers are more engaged than non-managers.

The benefits to an organisation from having motivated and engaged employees can include any or all of the following:

- **Improved productivity**: it is generally accepted that happy workers tend to be productive ones. As employee engagement rises, so does company efficiency because increased engagement leads to less employee distraction, more eager volunteers for challenging tasks and the chance for better ideas and greater achievements for the organisation as a whole.
- **Reduced costs**: labour turnover is likely to fall because motivated and engaged employees enjoy their jobs, appreciate their work colleagues and are committed to the organisation's goals. If sickness and accident rates fall, the reduced absenteeism will improve productivity and reduce unit costs. Reduced quality assurance and quality control costs will occur because workers are more concerned to do their jobs well.
- **Improved reputation for the organisation**: in relation to customers, potential employees and suppliers. If employees are proud of their company, they tend to recommend it to others or talk positively about it and, as a result, the company becomes more attractive as a workplace. Customer service and the quality of products improve because when employees are motivated and engaged, they try harder.
- **Improved likelihood of meeting company objectives**: employees who are fully engaged tend to identify closely with their company's values and strive to achieve company objectives.
- **Improved work ethic**: surveys indicate that engaged employees are twice as likely to stay late at work and to recommend improvements, they are enthusiastic about the work they do and are often more creative and put forward more ideas. This is often infectious and the actions of engaged employees are more likely to encourage other employees to want to do great work.
- **Competitive advantage**: surveys indicate that on average, companies with highly motivated and engaged employees are rated higher by their customers; they are also more likely to achieve higher productivity and enjoy higher profitability.

A number of theories of motivation provide possible explanations for what motivates and engages employees and how to improve employee motivation and engagement. These theories are discussed in the next section.

Theories of motivation

F.W. Taylor and scientific management

F.W. Taylor (1856–1915) was a US engineer who invented work-study and founded the scientific approach to management. He considered money to be the main factor that motivated workers, so he emphasised the benefits of piecework, where workers are paid according to how much they produce. He argued that piecework provided high rewards for hard work, benefiting both the worker and the business.

The principles of scientific management were laid down in Taylor's book, *The Principles of Scientific Management*, originally published in 1911. Scientific management is the process of business decision making based on data that are researched and tested quantitatively in order to improve the efficiency of an organisation. In his book, Taylor stressed the duty of management to organise work, using the principles of specialisation and the division of labour, so as to maximise efficiency. According to Taylor, this was to be achieved by 'objective laws' based on 'science' that management and workers could agree upon. This in turn would reduce conflict between management and workers since, as he saw it, there could be no disagreement about laws based on science.

Taylor believed that the following three methods are the main ways of improving productivity and efficiency:

1 Extreme division of labour, where a job is broken down into small, repetitive tasks, each of which can be done at speed and with little training. By specialising in a particular task, individuals can quickly become expert at their job, leading to increased productivity.
2 Payment by piecework, which means payment by results (i.e. payment per item produced). It provides an incentive to work hard but can encourage staff to concentrate on quantity at the expense of quality.
3 Tight management control, which ensures that workers concentrate on their jobs and follow the correct processes.

Value of Taylor's theory of motivation

Taylor's methods had considerable influence on business, most famously on the mass production processes introduced at the Ford Motor Company. However, his influence on the workforce was less successful. Extreme division of labour meant that jobs became more boring and repetitive. The lack of skills needed by workers also led to a loss of power for individual workers. This led to low morale and poor industrial relations and had some influence on the growth of trade unions.

▲ Henry Ford employed Taylor's methods

Did you know?

Work-study is the measurement and timing of work processes in order to identify the best method and the most realistic output targets. First, a work-study consultant (or 'time and motion' person) would observe people at work and note down the different actions of which the job was made up, and the sequence of these actions. Then the consultant would assess this to determine whether it was the most efficient method. Each action would then be timed, and the motion and the effort used noted down. The presence of 'time and motion men' quickly became a cause of industrial relations disputes.

499

To an extent, Taylor saw human beings as machines with financial needs. No account was taken of individual differences or the fact that the approach determined by the time and motion study might not suit everyone.

Maslow's hierarchy of human needs

Abraham Maslow (1908–70) was a US psychologist whose work on human needs has had a major influence on management thinking. His hierarchy of needs suggests that people have similar types of need, which can be classified into a hierarchy. Needs range from lower level ones, such as the need for food, clothing and shelter, to higher level ones, such as the need for achievement and self-esteem.

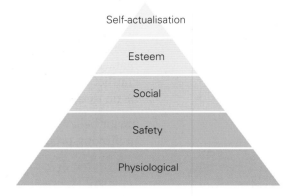

▲ **Figure 23.1** Maslow's hierarchy of needs

Maslow's five categories of need, as shown in Figure 23.1, are as follows:

1 **Physiological needs**: the requirements for food, clothes and shelter. In relation to work, this means the need to earn an income in order to acquire these things and have reasonable working conditions.

2 **Safety needs**: the need for security and freedom from danger and anxiety. In relation to work, this means the need to have a secure job, a safe working environment, adequate pension arrangements and clear lines of accountability in relation to responsibilities.

3 **Social needs**: the desire for friendship, love and a sense of belonging. In relation to work, this means being part of a team, getting along with workmates and being provided with social facilities such as staff rooms and canteens.

4 **Esteem needs**: the need to have self-respect and respect from others. In relation to work, this means the need to receive positive feedback, to gain recognition and status for achievement and to have opportunities for promotion.

5 **Self-actualisation**: the need to fulfil one's potential through actions and achievements. Maslow did not believe that this need could be satisfied fully and thought that people would always strive to develop further and achieve more.

Maslow believed that an unsatisfied need was a motivator of behaviour and that while it remained unsatisfied, higher-level needs were unimportant. He therefore believed that, starting from the bottom of the hierarchy, each level of need had to be fulfilled before the next level became important. However, once satisfied, a particular level ceased to be important and the next level of unsatisfied need became a motivator.

Value of Maslow's theory of motivation

Maslow's theory is intuitively appealing but it can be criticised. In relation to work, it is true that if people have insufficient income to enjoy adequate food, clothing and shelter, they are unlikely to be overly influenced by whether a job is permanent, whether it has good pension arrangements or whether their workmates make them feel welcome. Maslow's theory

▲ Facilities like canteens help fulfill social needs

▲ Pay was one of Herzberg's hygiene factors

makes broad assumptions about the fact that everyone has the same needs. However, once people satisfy their physiological and safety needs, it is questionable whether, for all individuals, social needs come before esteem needs. Many individuals are high achievers and are motivated by this need to achieve, sometimes to the exclusion of any desire to be part of a team or to get along with their colleagues. A further problem with Maslow's work is that it offered no empirical evidence for his theory because he had not tested his ideas out on large groups of workers to find out whether they did actually respond to different needs in the way he suggested.

Herzberg's two-factor theory

Frederick Herzberg (1923–2000) was a US psychologist whose research led him to develop the two-factor theory of job satisfaction and dissatisfaction. This theory suggests that some factors have the potential to provide positive job satisfaction, while others can only really reduce dissatisfaction.

Herzberg called the factors that motivate and give job satisfaction motivators. They include:

- a sense of achievement
- recognition for effort and achievement
- the nature of the work itself – that it is meaningful and interesting
- responsibility
- promotion and improvement opportunities.

All of these concern the job itself rather than issues such as pay. They are all likely to motivate workers and so may improve productivity.

Factors that can reduce job dissatisfaction are called hygiene or maintenance factors. They include:

- company policy and administration, which includes paperwork, rules, red tape, etc.
- supervision, especially if workers feel that they are over-supervised
- pay
- interpersonal relations, especially with supervisors and peers
- working conditions.

All of these factors 'surround' the job; they do not concern the job itself. Ensuring that they are acceptable to the workforce prevents dissatisfaction rather than causing positive motivation. For example, improved canteen or staffroom facilities and better pay are unlikely to motivate the workforce in the long term, but they will reduce the level of dissatisfaction. This is not to say that hygiene or maintenance factors are unimportant or less important than motivators. They are clearly vital and, if inappropriate, will cause dissatisfaction, with severe consequences for the organisation.

Herzberg also distinguished between 'movement' and motivation. He saw 'movement' as short-term or temporary motivation, for example, when someone does something for a specific purpose or because he or she has to. Motivation, on the other hand is when someone wants to do something for its own sake. If an individual works harder or puts in more hours because he or she is saving up for a holiday or a car, this is movement rather than motivation. Herzberg suggested that reward-based systems, such as bonuses, would provide only short-term motivation or 'movement'.

Value of Herzberg's theory of motivation

One of the main policy recommendations that stemmed from Herzberg's work is job enrichment – the attempt to motivate employees by giving them the opportunity to use their abilities and allowing them to exercise greater independence and authority over the planning, execution and control of their work. Job enrichment is considered in detail later in this chapter.

Criticism of Herzberg's theory is mainly based on the fact that he drew conclusions about workers as a whole from a limited sample of 200 accountants and engineers. It is also criticised for making too little of the role of groups and teams in the workplace and the motivational influences they have on individuals. Despite this, many of Herzberg's ideas have been borne out in practice. For example, wage increases and changes to conditions of work are rarely sufficient to produce a highly motivated workforce. Equally, what are perceived to be inadequate wage increases and changes to working conditions can create immense dissatisfaction, often with dire consequences.

Elton Mayo and the human relations school

Elton Mayo (1880–1949) was a follower of F.W. Taylor, but his experiments led him to conclude that scientific management could not explain important aspects of people's behaviour in the workplace. Many of his findings, including the 'Hawthorne effect', came from research he did at the Western Electric factory in Hawthorne, USA, and provided the foundations for the human relations school of management.

Mayo's early research involved trying to measure the impact on productivity of improving the lighting conditions in the Western Electric factory. He followed Taylor's scientific principles by testing the changes in lighting conditions for one group of workers against a control group of workers who worked in a section of the factory with unchanged lighting. Productivity rose in the area where the lighting was improved but, surprisingly, productivity also rose, and by a similar amount, in the area with unchanged lighting. Further experiments by Mayo revealed that it was the extra interest paid by managers to workers during the research that was crucial. This extra engagement with employees led to feelings of importance and self-worth among the employees and increased their motivation. These results brought into question Taylor's assumptions about the importance of money in motivating employees and instead emphasised the importance of human relations in the workplace.

Mayo's findings suggested the following:

- Recognition, belonging and security are more important in motivating employees than simply money and working conditions.
- Work is a group-based activity and employees should be seen as members of a group.
- Managers need to pay attention to individuals' social needs and the influence of the informal groups to which they belong, since these groups exert significant influence over an individual's attitudes.

Author advice

A study of Elton Mayo is not a specific requirement of the AQA specification. Details are included here because the authors feel that Mayo makes an important contribution to ideas about motivation, in particular in relation to the influence of human relations on motivation.

Did you know?

The 'Hawthorne effect' is the fact that workers' motivation and productivity are influenced by the degree of interest and recognition shown in them and the groups to which they belong, by their managers.

▲ Mayo's work saw the introduction of facilities like sports clubs in some work places

- Managers must communicate with informal groups, ensuring that their goals are in tune with those of the organisation. This could occur by, for example, allowing them to become part of the decision-making process, which would in turn improve worker commitment and loyalty.
- Increases in output are due to greater communication and improved relations in informal groups.

Value of Mayo's theory of motivation

Mayo's research is really about the result of group norms rather than individual motivation. Important developments resulted from Mayo and the human relations school. These included the introduction of social facilities at work, such as canteens and sports clubs, the appointment of personnel officers whose responsibility was the welfare of employees, and an increase in the quantity and quality of communication and consultation taking place between management and employees.

Links between the theories of motivation

- Mayo and Maslow: Maslow's social needs are very similar to the issues raised by Mayo's work about recognition and teamwork.
- Maslow and Herzberg: Intrinsic rewards come from the job itself, for example, because of the degree of authority given to an individual at work or the sense of achievement gained from completing a task well. Intrinsic rewards are linked to Herzberg's motivators and the higher-level needs in Maslow's hierarchy. Extrinsic rewards are not directly related to the work itself but are associated with doing the job, for example, financial incentives, fringe benefits, good working conditions and interaction with people at work. Extrinsic rewards are related to Maslow's lower-level needs and Herzberg's maintenance or hygiene factors.

Figure 23.2 demonstrates the link between these two theories.

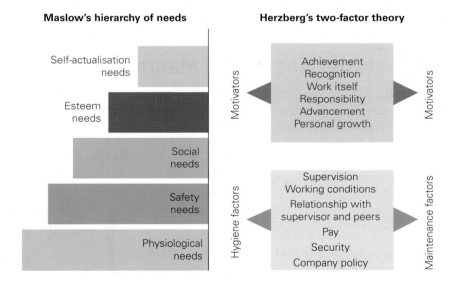

▲ **Figure 23.2** Links between Herzberg's and Maslow's theories of motivation

Practice exercise 1

Total: 70 marks

1 Explain the terms motivation and engagement. *(6 marks)*

2 Explain two benefits to an organisation of having motivated and engaged employees. *(8 marks)*

3 Briefly explain the views of F.W. Taylor and the scientific management school of thought. *(6 marks)*

4 Outline the main problems with these views in relation to motivating employees. *(6 marks)*

5 Briefly explain the views of Elton Mayo and the human relations school of management. *(4 marks)*

6 Identify and explain each of the levels of Maslow's hierarchy of human needs. *(10 marks)*

7 Explain the relevance of Maslow's hierarchy of human needs in a work context. *(6 marks)*

8 Which of the following is not one of Herzberg's motivators?
   a) Sense of achievement
   b) Responsibility
   c) Company policy
   d) Recognition for effort *(1 mark)*

9 Which of the following is not one of Herzberg's hygiene or maintenance factors?
   a) Pay
   b) Supervision
   c) Promotion opportunities
   d) Working conditions *(1 mark)*

10 Distinguish between the effect of Herzberg's motivators and that of his hygiene or maintenance factors on the motivation of employees. *(6 marks)*

11 Assess how valuable the various theories of motivation considered in this chapter are to organisations today. *(16 marks)*

Case study: Herzberg, Maslow and teachers

Despite the huge success of Herzberg's theory, there have been major criticisms of his research. These centre on the fact that the research took place in 1959 and covered a relatively small group of 200 accountants and engineers. A number of studies have tried to replicate the results, usually unsuccessfully.

One example concerned research with US teachers in primary and secondary schools. The findings from this research suggested that in relation to Herzberg's main motivators, achievement ranked as the most important. However, the overall conclusion drawn from the research was that salary was the single most important influence on motivation and satisfaction at work, and that the teachers in the study perceived the amount of salary increase they received to be tied to achievement and the other motivators.

▶▶▶

In relation to Maslow's hierarchy of needs, it appeared that the teachers in the study were less satisfied with their personal achievement of esteem (i.e. their self-respect and the respect they earned from others) than with their achievement of self-actualisation (i.e. fulfilling their potential). The research concluded that fulfilling one's potential (self-actualisation) might provide the basis for self-respect and gaining the respect of others.

The research went on to suggest that this might explain why good teachers were leaving education and moving to other, higher-paying occupations, but also suggested that managers in schools should focus more closely on the esteem needs of teachers.

Questions

Total: 25 marks

1 This passage shows how theories can always be challenged. Identify and explain other problems with the theories of Herzberg and Maslow, using examples from real organisations wherever possible. *(9 marks)*

2 Discuss how the 'esteem needs of teachers' in schools could be met more effectively by their senior managers. *(16 marks)*

Case study: ARM Ltd

ARM designs and licenses intellectual property in the field of semiconductor chips. Technology from ARM is used in 95 per cent of the world's mobile phones and in over a quarter of all electronic devices, including tablet computers, smartphones, digital cameras and digital televisions. ARM does not manufacture or sell the actual finished products but gains royalties from the licenses it sells to other firms. ARM was founded in 1990 and now has offices around the world.

ARM provides employees with opportunities to fulfil higher order needs through challenging and interesting work. Engaging employees in providing solutions to business problems and involving them in decisions about the future direction the business might take and the products it might focus on, challenges them to fulfil their potential and enables them to contribute to meeting business objectives.

ARM expects its employees to be stretched intellectually through challenging work. It believes that to stay ahead of the competition, employees need to learn and develop continuously. To support this, it provides a variety of training opportunities, aiming to promote and enable the development of everyone. Employees therefore take responsibility for their own jobs and are constantly involved in improvement and change.

Teamwork within ARM provides employees with opportunities to share knowledge and ideas and to contribute to innovation and to use their ideas to influence processes and products. Central to effective teamworking is the need for open and honest communication. ARM also uses a range of different methods of communication, including internal conferences, newsletters, question-and-answer sessions with directors and internet blogs. It has an 'open door' policy where employees can go to senior managers at any time with questions or issues.

Good working conditions, a safe and supportive working environment and competitive pay are features of ARM. It provides employees with a paid sabbatical of one month every four years, to use as they wish – a way of paying them back for the hard work they contribute to the organisation. ARM encourages its employees to work hard but also wants them to have fun, for example, arranging team events such as marathons or team bike rides.

ARM does not rely on pay as a motivator. Creating innovative products in teams needs people to genuinely want to do whatever it takes to make a product work. They believe a happy individual will be successful and motivated in the workplace.

ARM encourages employee engagement to motivate staff and to develop a genuine attachment to the teams in which they work. Regular reviews encourage individuals to reflect upon the contributions they make while providing feedback and support that enables them to develop their professional capability. Incentives are provided, including company shares, which ensure employees have a stake in the future of the company, and bonuses based on how well the business as a whole is doing. This encourages employees to identify with the company and its aims and to understand how they can contribute to these and to be able to see that their contribution is appreciated and recognised.

Source: adapted from *The Times* 100 case studies and www.arm.com

Questions

Total: 20 marks

1 Assess how well the ideas of each of the motivation theorists you have studied are being applied at ARM Ltd.

(20 marks)

Improving employee engagement and motivation

A range of strategies to improve engagement and motivation are available to leaders and managers in human resource departments. These include:

- A clearly defined vision that employees understand and can identify with, together with well-defined job descriptions so that employees understand their roles and feel a sense of purpose while at work. Employees need to understand how the job they do contributes to the overall goals of the organisation and where they fit into the bigger picture.
- Good quality environmental conditions, including temperature, lighting, décor and ergonomics, that promote efficiency and allow staff to both be comfortable and have the tools needed in order to do a good job.
- Appropriate training, development and support that meets employees' needs, helping them to develop their skills and extend their experiences.
- Good communication between employees and their managers and leaders so that employees know they are valued, understood and listened to.
- A supportive work environment based on respect and trust between employees and their managers and leaders.
- Involving employees in planning and decision making within the organisation so that they feel that they own projects they work on and have a vested interest in seeing a project succeed.
- Incentive programmes that reward strong performance and are linked to agreed targets. These can attract and retain high quality employees. Rewards and incentives can be extrinsic – such as additional pay, benefits or opportunities for promotion, or intrinsic – through gratitude, praise and recognition for a job well done. Employers need to gauge which type of reward is appropriate in each individual situation, based upon overall aims and the expectations of staff members. In a survey by McKinsey Consultants, praise from immediate supervisors and attention from company leaders were found to be just as important, or more important, than financial reward.

Fact file

Iceland Foods Ltd

Iceland Foods Ltd is ranked number 1 in *The Sunday Times* Best 25 Large Companies to Work for, 2014.

Staff say there's always something to look forward to, no matter what level you work at. The annual Christmas incentive, for example, saw people at 51 of its 800-plus stores win a week's wages while six store managers received trips to Ibiza with their partners. Then there's the annual managers' conference being held this year in Dubai (previous destinations have included Florida and Paris) or the retail conference/celebration party for team members and the annual charity week in which all stores participate.

Employee engagement is big at Iceland. 'We believe passionately that it is the prime factor in our success. We try to make it fun for all the staff. It is not just about pay, it is about behaviour. Everyone wants the company to succeed, and people are motivated and encouraged,' says chief executive and founder, Malcolm Walker, who set up the Deeside-based multi-billion pound business 44 years ago with £30 and two freezers. 'We say happy staff make happy customers and happy customers put cash in the till.'

One employee says, 'I have been in jobs where you go to work to pay the bills. This is out of this world. Retail is difficult but we have fun along the way. I love my job.' It's a feeling shared by employees around the country. Workers, who also can win prizes from iPods to paid days off and up to £500 for going the extra mile, don't feel under too much pressure and everyone is treated fairly.

Though the firm pays the second highest hourly rate on the high street at £7.05p an hour, 86 per cent of the almost 25,000 mostly part-time workers earn £7,500 or less. Yet, people are happy with their pay and benefits.

It certainly helps that managers are given the freedom to make flexible and common sense agreements on working hours with individual members of staff.

'We also believe in flexibility beyond the day-to-day schedule,' the company says. 'A colleague has recently had a nine-month sabbatical to allow her to care for her terminally ill husband. After he sadly passed away, she was welcomed back into her store team to resume her job in an environment in which she felt comfortable and valued. Iceland feels like family, and like a family, it understands that sometimes work has to fit round the important things in life.'

Managers ensure people have the resources they need to do their job including the basics such as comfortable chairs at the checkout. Issues such as this are raised by Talking Shop reps, who meet senior managers on a regular basis.

There are regular opportunities for those employees interested, and having the talent, to be considered for promotion to the next level and Iceland, which plans to open 50 new shops this year, recently promoted 12 store managers. While their job is good for their personal growth, work doesn't interfere with responsibilities at home. 'It is a fantastic company to work for', says an area manager who joined in 2000. 'I do not envisage ever leaving Iceland.'

Source: adapted from *The Sunday Times* 25 Best Largest Companies to Work For, 2014 and Iceland's website, www.iceland.co.uk

What do you think?

How do each of the strategies described in the Iceland fact file link to the ideas of the various motivational theorists discussed earlier in this chapter?

What do you think?

Joe is a very competent project manager at a software development company. He was recruited a few months ago but is already thinking of looking elsewhere. 'I get no feedback whatsoever from my manager,' he said. He has no sense of how his work fits into the company's overall goals or how well he is performing. As a result, he lacks motivation. 'The hours are much better at this company than my previous company', he admits, 'but I'm not as engaged in the work – I just don't care as much.'

What strategies might Joe's employer introduce to improve Joe's motivation and engagement?

On the whole, strategies to improve motivation can be categorised as financial or non-financial methods of motivation. Each category is discussed in detail in the following sections of this chapter.

Use of financial methods of motivation

A range of different financial methods can be used to motivate employees, including piece rate, commission, salary schemes and performance-related pay.

Piece rate

Paying workers a rate for each item produced is an attractive and simple way of providing them with an incentive to work hard and was favoured by Taylor as an important motivator. However, it can cause the following problems:

- It may encourage staff to concentrate on quantity at the expense of quality in order to boost their pay. To some extent, a **piece-rate system** can reduce the supervision needed to keep workers on task, but because staff are paid on the basis of the amount they produce, greater levels of scrap and reduced focus on quality are likely to occur. As a result, the savings on supervision costs may be cancelled out by increased costs of reworking and wastage.
- It may mean that the firm's output is heavily influenced by workers' needs rather than customer demand. For example, evidence suggests that piece-rate workers speed up in July and again in December in order to boost their earnings for the summer and Christmas holidays, even though this may not coincide with customer demand patterns.

Herzberg considered that this type of reward system would reinforce behaviour, with repetitive tasks being emphasised and linked to pay. In this way, piece-rate systems are likely to increase resistance to change because change will tend to slow production in the short term.

Herzberg also suggested that incentive systems such as piece rates and bonuses are the most ineffective way to reward staff, since such systems do not change an employee's commitment or attitude to work, but simply, and temporarily, change what the worker does, that is, they cause, what Herzberg called, 'movement', not motivation.

Commission

Commission may be paid in addition to a salary or instead of a salary. It is, therefore, a form of incentive pay. Like piece rates, it is a reward for the quantity or value of work achieved. Businesses that commonly use commission-based payments systems for their sales staff include estate agencies, car showrooms and insurance and financial services.

There are two basic ways to set commission. One is a flat rate commission. This is usually a percentage that is likely to depend on the amount of effort involved in making a sale. For example, commission rates could range from, say, 5 per cent where the product sells easily, to 30 per cent where the effort in selling a product is substantial. An alternative to a flat rate commission is a ramped commission, where the percentage of commission rises as certain targets are met. For example, 10 per cent commission could be paid on the first £25,000 worth of products sold, 15 per cent on the next £25,000 and 20 per cent on anything above £50,000. Ramped commission may also be based on targets, such as a 10 per cent commission on any sales up to a set target, then 20 per cent on any sales after that.

Key term

Piece-rate system (or piecework) Payment based on the number of items each worker produces.

Did you know?

Sometimes workers are paid a small, fixed amount of basic pay, which gives some security, and then a piece rate, which gives them the incentive to increase productivity.

Key term

Commission A sum of money paid to an employee upon completion of a task, usually selling a certain amount of goods or services; commission may be paid as a percentage of sales made or as a flat rate based on sales volume.

Many jobs that use commission-based pay also pay a base salary. The base salary may vary greatly from business to business but is usually designed to help people manage their cash flow and cover basic living expenses. A typical mix is 30 per cent income from base salary and 70 per cent from commission. Often a company with few competitors may choose a 50:50 mix, while a company that wants to really push sales might consider a lower base salary or no base salary at all. Some commission schemes mean that people are paid totally on commission and do not receive a salary or hourly rate.

Advantages of commission-based pay

- From an employee's point of view it enables high performing sales people to earn large amounts in accordance with their efforts and ability.
- From an employer's point of view the use of sales commission acts as an incentive to encourage employees to work hard and therefore increase their productivity. The more sales they make, the more revenue the business makes.
- For employers, payroll costs are related directly to the value of sales revenue achieved (as compared to piece rates, which are a reward for amounts produced, not sold). In a difficult economic climate, a business using a commission system with no base pay can employ a large number of sales people at little cost – particularly valuable if the sales people fail to generate sufficient sales for the business.

Disadvantages of commission-based pay

- Employees, especially those paid on commission with no base pay, have no reliable, regular income to depend upon, and so are in a risky situation if the market in which they are selling products, or the economy, declines.
- There is some suggestion that being paid on a commission basis invites dishonesty in order to earn more. Sales people may cut corners to make sales, by, for example, not explaining the products in enough detail to potential customers. This was a major problem in the recent pensions mis-selling scandal in the UK and is illustrated in the fact file on page 512, on Lloyds Bank and its mis-selling of financial products.
- High commission earnings enjoyed by some of the sales team may be resented elsewhere in the business – particularly if the sales actually depend on a team effort. As a result, other employees may stop working cohesively as a team and may become demotivated.

Recent research suggests that the use of commission is reducing in comparison with the growth of other incentive payment methods.

Salary schemes

Salary schemes are basic rate systems, often known as time-based payment systems. Under a basic rate system, a worker is paid according to a given time period – an hourly rate, a weekly wage or an annual salary. Note that although salaries are quoted in terms of their annual value, they are paid monthly.

The annual salary for the job is usually the established rate for all employees in a particular category who are doing that job, although there are often incremental scales that allow employees to progress to higher salary levels based on experience and skills.

> **Key term**
>
> **Salary schemes** A basic rate payment system where employees are paid an annual salary.

Advantages of salary schemes

- Relatively simple and cheap to administer and allow labour costs to be forecast with accuracy.
- Lead to stability in pay and are easily understood by the workforce, who will be able to more readily predict and check their pay.
- The security provided by salary schemes may motivate workers, according to Maslow's hierarchy of needs.
- There may be fewer disputes and individual grievances than under systems linking pay to performance or results.

Disadvantages of salary schemes

- Do not provide direct incentives to improve productivity or performance and can lead to rigid, hierarchical pay ranges. Individual workers who feel that they put in more than average effort might be demotivated if their own above-average efforts and abilities are not specifically rewarded. (Despite this, employers might prefer to operate simple basic rate systems and improve the design of jobs, so that the job provides the necessary interest, motivation and satisfaction.)
- Payment by time is payment for input rather than output. For example, bank tellers are paid a monthly salary that is not related to the number of customers they serve or enquiries they deal with. Similarly, office workers are paid a monthly salary that is not related to how busy or how productive they actually are. This means that effort is not guaranteed because staff could waste time. (However, appraisal and supervision procedures, the need to achieve targets, or simply completing the responsibilities of the job, can act as a sufficient check.)

Salary schemes are likely to be particularly appropriate in circumstances where:

- the volume or quality of work is difficult or impossible to measure, or the work is complex and involved
- the workflow is uneven and the volume and/or pace of work is outside the workers' control
- high output is not as important as other considerations, such as quality and stable production levels.

Salary schemes are often supplemented by commission (discussed in the previous section) or other performance-related pay schemes, which are discussed in the next section.

Performance-related pay

Performance-related pay (PRP) is usually employed in situations where piece-rate and commission systems are not appropriate because the work cannot be measured in a precise way. Decisions on PRP usually take place following an appraisal that assesses performance and the extent to which individual targets have been met.

> ### Key term
>
> **Performance-related pay** Systems that reward individual employees based on an assessment of their individual performance and usually measured against pre-agreed objectives; this generally takes the form of a bonus or increase in salary awarded for above-average employee performance.

Although PRP is usually financial, it can also be non-financial, for example a day out or a holiday. Sometimes the rise in an employee's annual basic salary is also performance related. For example, where the average pay rise might be 2 per cent, those with above average performance might be given a 5 per cent rise. This can be helpful in retaining employees who are at the top end of the pay scale for their job ranking, but whose performance is still outstanding. Such employees are more numerous in today's flatter organisations, where the opportunities for promotion to a higher rank are fewer than they were in the multi-layered organisations of 20 years ago.

Today, half of all British companies have PRP schemes for at least some of their workforce. Overall, though, such schemes cover only about a quarter of all workers. PRP is also used extensively to reward senior management and chief executive officers.

Advantages of using a system of PRP

- There are direct links between pay and effort.
- It may lead to a reduction in costs as a result of lower levels of supervision, an increase in productivity and an improvement in quality.
- There may be improvements in motivation and a possible reduction in labour turnover and absenteeism.
- It is a useful system for getting staff to work towards company objectives by establishing individual targets at appraisal that are linked to corporate objectives.
- PRP schemes are generally self-funding; the improvement in performance more than pays for the rewards.
- Payments under such schemes are usually made separately from regular salary payments. In this way the recipient appreciates that they are variable, separate and not guaranteed.
- From a firm's point of view, PRP can reduce the influence of trade unions and of collective bargaining, as decisions on pay are related to individuals. (From an individual worker's point of view, this may be a disadvantage.)

Disadvantages of PRP

- It may become a source of conflict among staff who are receiving differential payments for what they perceive to be the same effort.
- The effect on motivation is debatable because PRP usually represents only a small proportion of salary.
- An important question is how performance can be measured, since PRP is often introduced into occupations where it is difficult to measure performance objectively.

Managers often favour PRP because they see it as a means of providing an incentive for staff to improve their performance and commitment, and as a useful control mechanism. However, there is little research evidence to support the benefits claimed for PRP as a system for rewarding individuals, and more emphasis is now put on group PRP.

Fact file

Lloyds Banking Group and their sales incentive scheme

On 11 December 2013, Lloyds Banking Group was fined over £28 million by the Financial Conduct Authority (FCA) for its poorly designed and poorly managed employee incentive scheme, which resulted in serious mis-selling of financial service products. The financial service products involved were investment products, such as share ISAs, and protection products, such as critical illness or income protection insurance.

The FCA's press release states: 'The Financial Conduct Authority (FCA) has fined Lloyds TSB Bank plc and Bank of Scotland plc, both part of Lloyds Banking Group (LBG), £28,038,800 for serious failings in their controls over sales incentive schemes. The failings affected branches of Lloyds TSB, Bank of Scotland and Halifax (which is part of Bank of Scotland). This is the largest ever fine imposed by the FCA, or its predecessor the Financial Services Authority (FSA), for retail conduct failings. The incentive schemes led to a serious risk that sales staff were put under pressure to hit targets to get a bonus or avoid being demoted, rather than focus on what consumers may need or want. In one instance an adviser sold protection products to himself, his wife and a colleague to prevent himself from being demoted.'

The people affected were retail branch sales staff. Usually, in sales teams, base pay is fixed and performance-related pay takes the form of bonuses that are additional to base pay. LBG sales staff did have bonuses – sometimes very large ones – but their base salaries also depended on performance. A poorly-performing branch sales adviser could lose up to 35 per cent of their base pay. At base salaries of around £40,000, a cut of 35 per cent is a severe penalty that would have a significant impact on a household's budget and their ability to pay bills. This goes some way to explaining the pressure that sales advisers were under to sell customers products that they didn't need or that were unsuitable for them.

The bonus schemes created considerable incentives for mis-selling because there were both individual and team bonus schemes, and additional one-off incentive payments in place. There was also collusion between managers and staff over mis-selling. The FCA notes that managers' bonus schemes depended on the performance of their staff, so they had an incentive to encourage mis-selling that inflated the bonuses of their staff or prevented their demotion. The severe financial penalties for under-performance presented a considerable management challenge.

Good customer service may include **not** selling products, if they are unsuitable or not needed. But at LBG, this would have resulted in financial penalties. This created perverse incentives; employees were rewarded for bad service and penalised for good.

The FCA criticised LBG management for their blindness to the risks of such a scheme: 'The root cause of these deficiencies was the collective failure of the firms' senior management to identify remuneration and incentives for advisers as a key area of risk requiring specific and robust oversight ...'

Source: www.fca.org.uk

Author advice

The AQA specification does not require a study of the additional financial methods of motivation discussed in this section. They are included to add more completeness to students' understanding of the major financial methods of motivation available, and to the various schemes available under the PRP umbrella.

Other financial methods of motivation

Performance-related pay includes a number of different approaches to linking an individual's performance in the workplace to the rewards they receive. The following alternative approaches give a flavour of these schemes.

Profit sharing

Profit sharing or profit-related bonuses are financial incentives in which a proportion of a firm's profit is divided among its employees in the form of a bonus paid in addition to an employee's salary.

Advantages of profit sharing

- It may help to reduce problems related to a feeling of 'them and us' between employees and management or shareholders.
- It may lessen resistance to change because the focus is on the profits of the whole organisation rather than an individual's job performance. Financial rewards only result if the organisation as a whole does well.

- If the profit share is large enough, it can provide staff with a personal incentive to work efficiently, provide good customer service, keep costs down and raise productivity in order to improve profits. For example, at John Lewis, the profit share has at times been substantial. It was 20 per cent of annual salary in 2007–08 and 15 per cent in March 2014.

Disadvantages of profit sharing

- Unless the profit share amounts to a reasonable proportion of salary, employees are unlikely to consider it a significant incentive and hence it will have little or no effect on motivation and behaviour.
- As it is not linked to individual performance, it might encourage the free-rider problem, where certain workers put in less effort, knowing that all employees receive the same rewards.
- Large payouts from profits may affect both shareholder dividends and profit retained for investment, with adverse consequences for the firm.

Fact file

Bonuses

Total bonus payments to employees climbed 4.9 per cent to £40.5 billion in the year to April 2014 compared with a year earlier, the Office for National Statistics (ONS) said. This is the highest rate since the same period between 2007 and 2008, which was the year before the financial crisis really took hold.

Bonuses increased to 6 per cent of total pay in the year to April 2014, the highest level since 2008 when bonuses made up 7.1 per cent of pay. In the private sector, payments climbed 5.8 per cent while public sector bonuses fell by 16.3 per cent.

Source: ONS website, www.statistics.gov.uk

Share ownership and share options

Share ownership, in this context, is a financial incentive whereby companies give shares to their employees or sell them at favourable rates below the market price. Share ownership is a means of encouraging workers and managers to identify more directly with company objectives, recognising that their rewards – share value and dividends – are dependent on company performance.

Share options, usually given to chief executives and senior managers, are an option to purchase a fixed number of shares, at a fixed price, by a given date. If the price of the shares on the Stock Exchange rises above this price, it would be in the individual's interest to buy the shares at the fixed price and sell them at the market price.

The benefit of share options is that they are believed to provide senior management with the incentive to perform at their very best. However, there are some problems:

- Some people suggest that it is likely to lead to short-termism, i.e. a focus on improving performance when the share option is due, in order to make a profit from the sale of shares, rather than a long-term commitment to improved performance.

- A criticism that has been prominent in the press is that share options can lead to excessive financial rewards in the boardroom, when the workforce may deserve just as much credit as the directors.

What do you think?

(Note: The following information does not include bonuses and share option data but it does illustrate what might be termed 'excessive financial rewards'.)

Before her move to Apple in April 2014, Angela Ahrendts, the previous Chief Executive Officer of Burberry, was one of the highest paid people in Britain. In 2012, her annual salary was £16.9 million.

In 2014, The High Pay Centre, an independent non-party think tank that monitors pay at the top of the income distribution, published data about top earning business leaders. The following are examples of some of their findings:

- Martin Sorrel, Chief Executive Officer of WPP, the media company, is paid £28.9 million – 780 times more than the average employee in WPP who earns £38,265 per annum.

- Lord Simon Wolfson, Chief Executive Officer of Next, is paid £4.6 million – 459 times more than the average employee at Next who earns £13,248 per annum.
- Andy Harrison, Chief Executive Officer of Whitbread, is paid £6.4 million – 415 times more than the average employee at Whitbread who earns £15,362 per annum.

Such high rewards are based on the assumption that the performance of these individuals is considered a major influence on their company profits and performance. Can any one individual make such a difference to the performance of a company as to justify these huge rewards?

What is the likely impact of such large salaries on the vast majority of the workforce, who in comparison receive very modest salaries?

Fact file

Fringe benefits

Fringe benefits are a way of rewarding employees without actually increasing their wage or salary. Common fringe benefits include discounts when buying a firm's products, subsidised meals, the provision of sports facilities, a company pension scheme, a company car and private medical insurance.

These benefits add to the cost of employing labour, but are expected to pay for themselves by encouraging staff loyalty and commitment and also by reducing labour turnover. Substantial fringe benefits are more common at senior management level, which in turn leads to conflict between workers and management.

Use of money as a motivator

Is money a major motivator? It is obviously important, but most evidence suggests that it does not motivate people particularly well in the long term. Ask yourself why so many wealthy people continue to work when financially they have no need to. Perhaps their reasons are related to Maslow's self-esteem and self-actualisation needs.

Money as a motivator can also lead to serious problems for both individuals and organisations:

- Rewards fluctuate with the performance of the company and this can cause uncertainty in financial planning if employees come to depend upon rewards.

- If financial incentives are high and based firmly on quantity, quality may be sacrificed in the drive to produce or sell more, with serious long-term consequences for organisations. This is easy to understand in a manufacturing situation where actual products are being made, but it is also apparent in the service sector. For example, the substantial monetary incentives provided to salespeople in the financial services sector (pensions, mortgages and insurance) to encourage them to increase the sales of these products has resulted in customers finding, years later, that they had been sold inappropriate products for their particular needs and had as a consequence lost large amounts of money. See the fact file on Lloyds Bank Group on page 512.
- If rewards are based on individual performance, it can cause conflict between employees, especially where an individual employee's contribution cannot be measured objectively and employees are doing the same job.

There are, however, several reasons why financial incentives are used:

- Firms want to overcome or at least reduce resistance to change. By paying bonuses to those who retrain or learn new systems, a firm is likely to be able to implement change more easily.
- Many managers still see money as a major means of control.
- Firms are looking to meet short-term goals, and financial rewards are successful at encouraging what Herzberg termed 'movement'.
- Firms want to reward and recognise individual initiative and effort and employees want to have their initiative and effort recognised and rewarded.

Author advice

Try to consider the reasons for wanting to motivate staff. Is it to increase production or is it to improve job satisfaction? Remember Herzberg said that 'A reward once given becomes a right', meaning that employees can get used to financial rewards and take them for granted.

Practice exercise 2

Total: 40 marks

1 Explain the meaning of 'piece rate' (piecework). *(4 marks)*

2 Identify and explain two problems a business might encounter as a result of using piece rates to pay its employees. *(6 marks)*

3 Explain how commission is used as a financial method of motivation. *(4 marks)*

4 Explain basic rate or time rate schemes and, in doing so, distinguish between wage and salary schemes. *(6 marks)*

5 Explain the term 'performance-related pay'. *(4 marks)*

6 Briefly explain two advantages and two disadvantages to a business of using performance-related pay. *(8 marks)*

7 Identify two other financial methods of motivation. *(2 marks)*

8 Taking one of the methods identified in question 7, explain one advantage and one disadvantage in using this method to motivate employees. *(6 marks)*

Use of non-financial methods of motivating employees

Motivating employees doesn't always have to be about money or financial rewards. The following section explains important non-financial methods of motivating employees.

Job enlargement

Job enlargement means increasing the scope of a job, either by job rotation or job enrichment.

- Job rotation is where the job is expanded horizontally (known as horizontal extension) by giving the worker more tasks, but at the same level of responsibility.
- Job enrichment is where the job is expanded vertically (known as vertical extension) by giving the worker more responsibility.

Each of these approaches is considered below.

Job rotation

Job rotation is a systematic programme of switching jobs to provide greater variety. Essentially, it gives workers more varied work to do, but at a similar level of challenge. For example, a shop worker might spend two hours on the checkout, two hours filling shelves and another two hours in the warehouse.

The employee will thus have a more varied and interesting job compared to doing the same tasks for six hours.

Using job rotation gives a firm several advantages:

- By providing employees with more varied tasks, it is intended to relieve the boredom of the work and provide employees with a more varied working day, so improving motivation. It has the useful side-effect of ensuring that if one person is absent, others can cover the job without difficulty.
- Workers may be more motivated because of their wider range of skills, and they will become more flexible.
- There may be a greater sense of participation in the production process.

However, job rotation has the following disadvantages:

- Retraining costs will increase and there may be a fall in output because there is less specialisation.
- It could be seen as simply involving a greater number of boring tasks, but with a reduction in the social benefits of working, since groups will be constantly changing.

Job enrichment

Job enrichment is a means of giving employees greater responsibility and offering them challenges that allow them to utilise their skills fully. It is closely based on Herzberg's ideas. Herzberg suggested that only job enrichment is likely to provide long-term job satisfaction.

An enriched job should ideally:

- introduce new and more difficult tasks and challenges at different ability levels, some of which might be beyond the employee's experience to date
- give individuals a complete unit of work – in other words, a meaningful task rather than a repetitive part of a larger process, as advocated by Taylor
- provide regular feedback on performance so that the employee knows immediately how well he or she is performing
- remove some of the controls over the employee while retaining accountability
- increase the accountability of the individual for his or her own work.

Such systems have been introduced into many manufacturing organisations, most famously Volvo, Honda and Toyota, all of which completely reorganised their factories so that groups of workers could take charge of producing complete units of work and then check the quality of their own work. Not only did this give workers opportunities to satisfy their social needs, but also, as they were able to manage their own time and work, they had autonomy and responsibility for decision making.

The advantages of job enrichment include the following:

- It develops workers' unused skills and presents them with challenges.
- It allows workers to make greater contributions to the decision-making process.
- It enhances workers' promotional prospects.
- It motivates workers by ensuring that their abilities and potential are exploited, and that individuals gain a high degree of self-control over the setting of goals and the identification of how to achieve those goals.

However, job enrichment has the following problems:

- Although many workers will relish the challenges, others might find the whole process intimidating and may simply feel that it places additional pressure on them that they do not want.
- It could be seen simply as a way to delegate responsibility down through the hierarchy and to reduce the number of employees by delayering (i.e. removing one or more layers of hierarchy from the management structure of the organisation). In this sense, it could be viewed as an attempt to get more out of workers while paying them the same rate.
- It may be costly and benefits may only be achieved in the long term, as when reorganising the shop floor and retraining the workforce in a manufacturing business.
- Not all jobs lend themselves to enrichment. For example, refuse collection offers little scope for greater responsibility and challenges.

Empowering employees

Linked closely to job enrichment is the importance of empowering employees.

Empowerment means giving employees the means by which they can exercise power over their working lives. Whereas delegation might provide the authority for a subordinate to carry out a specific task, empowerment implies a degree of self-regulation and the freedom to decide what to do and how to do it. For example, large retail chains often not only delegate

▲ Some car manufacturers completely reorganised their factories and gave employees more responsibility

responsibility to local store managers, but also empower them to make judgements about what products to promote and what stock to carry.

Empowerment can be achieved through informal systems or through the more formal system of autonomous work groups. These provide workers with autonomy and decision-making powers, and aim to increase motivation while also improving flexibility and quality, thus adding value to the organisation.

Empowerment involves:

- recognising that workers are capable of doing more
- making workers feel trusted and confident to carry out jobs and make decisions without supervision
- recognising workers' achievements
- creating an environment where workers wish to contribute and to be involved.

With such systems in place, empowerment is likely to lead to improved motivation, reduced labour turnover, reduced absenteeism and, in turn, an increase in productivity. However, the cost of training workers to take on responsibility and make decisions could be great, and managers need to be good delegators if the process is to work effectively. In addition, there is a risk for the employer in providing a level of autonomy that may mean employees' actions are difficult to check effectively. There have been many examples of fraudulent activities in financial organisations where employees have been empowered. Nick Leeson and Barings Bank is a classic example of this – see the fact file below. From a more cynical viewpoint, empowerment could be seen simply as a way of delayering and therefore cutting costs, i.e. removing a layer of management and delegating responsibility and authority further down the hierarchy. In a similar manner, it could be argued that workers are being given more responsibility but the same amount of pay.

Working in teams

Teamworking generally means a system where production is organised into large units of work and a group of employees work together in order to meet shared objectives. Teamworking contrasts with systems where individual workers take on smaller, more fragmented processes, characterised by a high division of labour. A team of people working on a larger task, such as making a complete car rather than just a door, will need to be multi-skilled, well trained and motivated by more than the piece-rate rewards received by workers carrying out a single, repetitive task.

By using teamworking, an organisation gets a more motivated, flexible workforce that can cover absences more easily. When accompanied by other techniques such as job rotation and/or job enrichment and some degree of decision making, teamwork can enhance motivation and/or relieve boredom.

Teamworking can be linked to the theories of Mayo (group norms) and Maslow (social needs).

Influences on the choice and assessment of the effectiveness of financial and non-financial reward systems

A successful business will select reward systems (whether financial or non-financial or a mixture) that match the needs of its employees and the nature of their jobs, enable its employees to perform at the highest level and contribute as fully as possible to meeting business objectives. Human resource management must ensure the most appropriate system or systems are selected.

For example, a traditional manufacturing organisation with a fairly authoritarian approach, a tall hierarchy and routine and monotonous work, may find that money is a great motivator, allowing employees to enjoy their social life and home comforts. This supports Taylor's view of what motivates people. It is also likely that in this situation Mayo's informal group influences and Maslow's social needs are important to employees. Ensuring that Herzberg's hygiene or maintenance factors are appropriate will also be vital to avoid dissatisfaction.

On the other hand, in an organisation that employs large numbers of well-educated people with high-level skills, expectations are higher and jobs are more complex. Although rates of pay and working conditions will be important to them, employees will expect more recognition, autonomy, involvement in decision making and empowerment. In other words, they are more likely to be influenced by Maslow's higher-level needs and Herzberg's motivators.

These two scenarios illustrate the fact that a range of factors can influence the choice and assessment of an appropriate reward system. One of the most important influencing factors is organisational design.

Fact file

Added Value Group, global marketing consultancy

On St Valentine's Day 2013, the 85 employees of Added Value Limited, a brand-development and marketing consultancy, boarded a bus to a secret location. First stop was a business meeting, and then the bus took them to Selfridges, where everybody received a £250 voucher.

The business, which provides marketing insights for clients such as Vodafone, Levi's and Santander, became part of the WPP group in 2001 and has expanded into the global Added Value Group with 23 offices in 13 countries.

The original office in Hampton Wick, Surrey, has a predominantly female team and has yet to turn down any request for flexible working. Almost half the staff work flexibly to accommodate family responsibilities or further education. All workers get a month's paid sabbatical every four years (or eight weeks on half pay).

The organisation's values include openness and mutual respect, and everyone is treated fairly. All staff members have performance- and profit-related pay as well as share options, and roughly half the workforce has been employed for more than five years. People don't need to leave to increase their experience, as the firm encourages secondments to offices around the world, as well as periods of six months or more in different UK teams. This ensures departments work well together and people don't feel the consultancy fails to use all their skills.

Source: adapted from *The Sunday Times* 100 Best Small Companies to Work for, 2013 and Added Value Group's website, added-value.com

---

Organisational design

Organisational design, which was examined in detail in Chapter 22, can have a significant influence on how effective different reward systems are likely to be. Some of the issues to consider are explained below.

Levels of hierarchy and spans of control

Whether the organisational structure is tall or flat can influence promotional opportunities, the extent of delegation, the amount of responsibility each employee has, the chain of command and therefore how quickly decisions are made, and the quality of communication. All these factors need to be taken into account by management when deciding on motivational techniques and reward systems to use. For example, in a flat organisation with wide spans of control, effective delegation could empower employees by providing them with more autonomy and responsibility, resulting in improved motivation. In a tall organisation, good communication will be crucial in maintaining high levels of motivation.

Lines of accountability

If lines of accountability are clear, it is much easier to recognise achievement and therefore to reward it, which should lead to improved motivation.

Delegation and empowerment

The process of delegating tasks can be a way of motivating and empowering employees, by allowing them to exercise some power over their working lives and providing them with a degree of freedom to decide what to do and how to do it. However, empowerment can only occur if delegation is effective.

Other influences on the choice and assessment of reward systems

Nature of the job and nature of employees

Although Taylor's view of money as the most important motivator has largely been discredited, it is still followed in a number of organisations. This is often where jobs are routine, low skilled and require little training and where staff are temporary or may not stay long with the employer. In this situation, pay and conditions are likely to be strong motivators and essential to ensure tasks get done on time.

On the other hand, there has been a significant growth in creative, knowledge-driven work. Workers in these jobs expect more and more discretion and autonomy over what they do. In this situation, a different approach to motivating the workforce is required and expected by employees – one that focuses on non-financial factors but also provides incentives to reflect individual contributions.

Research at Harvard Business School found that while external rewards such as PRP, bonuses, etc., may be effective for traditional work that involves instructions and tight structures, such approaches can have a seriously negative impact when applied to work that involves, for example, the solving of novel problems or the creation of products we didn't know we wanted. For example, the fact file in Chapter 4 on Steve Jobs, the co-founder of Apple, notes that Jobs is said to have asked of his employees, 'How do people know what they want until we show them?' The result of such intuition and foresight are evident in Apple products such as the iPod, iPhone and iPad.

For many individuals, their careers are ongoing learning experiences. When individuals are intrinsically motivated in this way, they are interested in their work, find it enjoyable, immensely satisfying and it enables them to achieve and contribute to their own desired goals as well as the goals of the organisation they work for. For these people, financial methods of motivation alone would be inappropriate.

Clarity and nature of business objectives

It is important that employees understand the objectives of their organisation, how their own job contributes to meeting these objectives and how well they are performing their job and hence contributing to the success of the organisation.

Quality of communication

Good communication is important in motivating employees. It can make employees feel valued and an important part of the organisation. Motivational theories recognise the importance of effective communication in raising morale. Any organisation that tries to empower its employees and extend their roles and authority needs to ensure that effective communication systems are in place to support this. Regular feedback on performance, both formal and informal, is an important aspect of employee motivation. By communicating effectively in this area, management is likely to have a much more focused and committed workforce.

Timescale involved

It is easy to motivate people with financial incentives in the short term, or create 'movement' according to Herzberg, but much harder in the longer term.

Organisational culture

Highly bureaucratic organisations with top-down approaches to communications and relationships tend to have very formal structures. Such organisations often find non-financial approaches to motivation, such as job enrichment and empowering employees, difficult because their structures are too rigid to allow for the autonomy and discretion these approaches require.

The recent banking scandals have demonstrated how short-term goals linked to excessive bonuses lead, all too easily, to unethical behaviour and undesirable corporate cultures.

Size of the organisation

Encouraging motivation and engagement can be more of a challenge in larger companies. This is particularly the case if teams are huge and there is little relationship between employees and their supervisors or managers. However, there are many large businesses, for example, Toyota and Honda, which organise their workforce into teams and develop highly effective reward systems using both financial and non-financial elements.

State of the economy and success of an organisation

When the economy is in difficulty and many organisations are focused only on survival, some organisations rely on job insecurity as a motivator, cancelling employee benefits, and increasingly asking for 'more for less' to drive up productivity. Such approaches are unlikely to be successful and may actually be counterproductive.

Research findings

While money is obviously vital for all employees, research suggests consistently that financial rewards alone are not sufficient to create job satisfaction or to improve motivation and productivity.

Being happy with your job seems to depend more on the intangibles: feeling part of a team and being valued and appreciated consistently outrank money when employees are polled about job satisfaction.

Fact file

Beaverbrooks

At Beaverbrooks, the jewellery retailer chain, employees feel valued and respected, and say their suggestions are acted upon. Their managers regularly express appreciation when they do a good job and talk openly and honestly with them, trust their judgement and care about them as individuals.

Staff are impressed by Mark Adlestone, the chain's managing director, and have complete faith in his leadership. They say he knows everybody by name and staff feel comfortable enough to phone him personally with any concerns. In fact, employees are encouraged to have direct contact with any executive by phone or email.

The company develops internal candidates to fill management roles and nearly all managers and assistant managers have been promoted from within. A flexible benefits package includes the option to buy extra holiday, private healthcare for employees and their families, childcare vouchers, life assurance and an employee assistance programme. The family-owned retail jeweller allows staff to take up to five paid days off to do volunteering work.

Beaverbrooks believes customers will get the best service if staff are genuinely happy, so it ensures that they feel rewarded for their efforts and get the support they need from the senior management team. Workers believe they can make a valuable contribution to the success of the organisation and are proud to work there.

The average salary of a consumer consultant is £17,800 for a 32-hour week, and workers feel fairly paid for the work they do relative to others in similar positions within comparable companies and for the responsibilities their job entails.

Source: adapted from *The Sunday Times* 100 Best Companies to Work For, 2014 and www.beaverbrooks.co.uk

Practice exercise 3

Total: 65 marks

1 Explain two problems for a business that might result from a low level of motivation among its employees. *(6 marks)*

2 Explain the terms 'job enlargement', 'job rotation' and 'job enrichment'. *(6 marks)*

3 Explain one advantage and one disadvantage to a business of introducing a system of job rotation. *(6 marks)*

4 Explain two advantages to a business of introducing job enrichment. *(6 marks)*

5 Explain two problems that a business might encounter as a result of introducing job enrichment. *(6 marks)*

6 Explain how job enrichment is linked to the motivation theories with which you are familiar. *(6 marks)*

7 Explain the term 'empowerment'. *(3 marks)*

8 How might empowering its employees benefit a business? *(4 marks)*

9 Explain two benefits of teamworking to a business. *(6 marks)*

10 Discuss the most suitable approach to motivate employees in a business where most of the workforce are unskilled, young and rarely remain with the business for longer than six months and where the tasks they are employed to do are simple and require little training. *(16 marks)*

Case study: TGI Friday's

The chain started life in 1965 in New York, when perfume salesman Alan Stillman decided the best way to meet women would be to open a singles bar. Thank Goodness It's Friday – known as TGI Friday's, or Friday's. It was expanded by Dallas-based Carlson Restaurants and opened in the UK in 1985.

When TGI Friday's UK managing director, Karen Forrester, took over in 2007, the business lacked investment and was seen as tired and dated. She embarked on a people-led strategy that aimed to redefine the culture, engage the employees and improve brand image. The positive impact of these actions is evident. The UK operation is now on a solid financial foundation and is already up to 55 sites and 4,500 employees. It plans to open 20 new restaurants over the next three years, and has just announced plans for the next six. Karen attributes their success to the employees. 'Happy and well-engaged people do a great job.'

Karen's starting point in 2007 was to ensure that all staff were retrained and the company focused on recognising achievement. Getting the right people in the right positions in the company meant that out of 3,000 employees, approximately 12 per cent were sifted out and 20 per cent were identified as needing to improve.

At the end of every October a plan for the next year is set, which is then communicated down to store level so that everyone knows what's going on. That is followed by an annual Team Challenge in November, which sees Karen and her executive team going into every restaurant on a Friday or Saturday night to find people to recognise individually. Top performers are instantly rewarded with gifts, such as iTunes vouchers. Last year, 10 per cent of staff were rewarded over the month. From a business point of view it means all Friday's teams are at their peak as they go into the Christmas and New Year trading period.

Traditionally, one of the most obvious features of TGI Friday's has been the badges worn by staff members. This tradition has been resurrected, but with everyone having to earn their badges or 'medals of honour' as Karen calls them. Although the badges may be an obvious manifestation of recognition, it comes in other ways too, like the team challenge rewards. Friday's has an on-the-spot recognition and reward system for a job well done. The Friday's Legends is another example, where team members are asked to nominate unsung heroes who are then treated to a day

out. There are also financial rewards and 98 per cent of managers received bonuses in 2013.

Of the restaurant managers in training, 70 per cent are internal appointments, and external candidates are only accepted after an intensive 12-week induction programme. No one is appointed as a general manager directly from the outside.

When Conor Hughes, 29, decided to apply for a job at TGI Friday's, he was 'expecting it to be just a job, but, it turned out to be so much more'. A year after applying, he was a shift leader at the company's Stratford restaurant in east London. Working at the company has taken him far. In 2012, Conor was nominated to join the firm's managing director, Karen Forrester, on a trip to Peru, climbing the Inca trail to Machu Picchu to raise money for a youth unemployment charity.

Tom Jennings, 24, now a general manager, started work at Friday's aged 17, serving tables. After graduating from university, he joined full-time. The secret of his success, he says, are the senior staff who coached him. 'I've had a lot of people put a lot of time into teaching me what I know,' he says.

In *The Sunday Times* 100 Best Companies to Work For 2013 survey, employees said their managers were excellent role models and made them feel motivated to give their best every day. They had confidence in their managers' leadership skills and said managers took an active interest in their wellbeing. They felt a strong sense of family in their teams and enjoyed their work. 'I enjoy coming to work,' says 18-year-old door host, Hannah Moore. 'I don't think there's been a shift where I've been bored.'

The majority of people work part-time, with 87 per cent earning less than £15,000 a year. But employees are happy with the pay and benefits they receive and feel they are paid fairly for the work they do relative to their colleagues.

Source: adapted from *The Sunday Times* 100 Best Companies to Work For, 2013 and www.tgifridays.co.uk

Question

Total: 40 marks

1 Identify and explain two approaches to motivation that appear to be successful at TGI Friday's. *(8 marks)*

2 To what extent do the motivation methods used at TGI Friday's suggest that financial incentives are less important than non-financial incentives and how might the effectiveness of the methods used be assessed? *(16 marks)*

3 Discuss how the effectiveness of methods used to motivate staff at TGI Friday's might be assessed. *(16 marks)*

Case study: Richer Sounds

Julian Richer, the founder and chairman, was 19 when he opened his first Richer Sounds shop in 1978. The shop at London Bridge was tiny, but it was passed by 70,000 commuters a day.

He now has more than 50 stores, as well as mail order and internet services. The Richer approach aims to achieve unparalleled customer service through highly motivated staff. Although the company has changed over the years, Richer still maintains a presence and ensures that his employees are kept motivated. 'We all know what we're working for, how our work fits in, and how we can have an impact on the company.'

Communication is excellent, with all staff having ample opportunity to give feedback at seminars, suggestion meetings and branch dinners. The business has a very open communications policy to ensure there is always awareness and discussion among colleagues. Results and performance of stores and of individuals, for example, are regularly measured and examined. This means that colleagues are very much aware of how they are performing and that their efforts are being noticed.

Colleagues are encouraged to take on new responsibilities and promotion from within is the norm; the majority of head office staff have worked on the shop floor. 'The beauty of Richer Sounds is that it is willing to recognise people's potential, and allow them to develop into a role that they may not have previously considered', said one member of staff. Store managers have the independence to set their own reward systems for their staff.

When it comes to motivating staff, Richer is a great believer in measuring performance and then recognising and rewarding achievement. All customers, for example, are asked to rate the quality of the service they have received; salespeople who are rated 'excellent' receive a bonus, while those rated 'poor' are penalised. Each colleague's rating is measured regularly and performance is discussed. Colleagues are also encouraged to contribute to the suggestions scheme, which has a cash bonus for each idea. It has been remarkably successful, producing on average 20 suggestions a year from each employee.

The results of the approach taken by Richer Sounds are impressive: as well as its incredibly high sales per square foot, Richer Sounds has extremely low rates of labour turnover and absenteeism.

It was no surprise to hear Richer, 54, who still holds 100 per cent of the company he started 35 years ago, explain in September 2014, that he had formed a trust for when he dies so that the business becomes a mutual, similar to John Lewis, under which every staff member receives an equal share, with the IT director, Julie Abraham, stepping up to managing director.

The Richer Way, his approach to business and the title of his book (now in its fifth edition) includes: providing free access to holiday homes in the UK and abroad (regardless of sales performance); trips aboard the company jet for those who suggest the best ideas; cash handouts for staff so they can go to the pub and brainstorm; the use of a Bentley for the store which does the best each month. His reasoning is simple: a happy workforce supplies good customer service, boosts sales, decreases complaints, and eradicates theft and absenteeism.

Sources: adapted from *The Sunday Times* 100 Best Companies to Work For, 2013, an article in the *Independent*, 6 September 2014, *The Richer Way* by Julian Richer (5th edition) and www.richersounds.com

Questions

Total: 50 marks

1 Explain one type of financial incentive used by Richer Sounds to motivate its workforce. (*4 marks*)

2 Identify two non-financial incentives used by Richer Sounds to motivate its workforce and explain one of them. (*5 marks*)

3 Analyse possible advantages and disadvantages of giving managers the independence to set up their own reward scheme. (*9 marks*)

4 Financial incentives at Richer Sounds are an important, but not the only, element of the reward system. Evaluate the extent to which it appears that financial incentives are the most effective way for Richer Sounds to motivate its staff. (*16 marks*)

5 Discuss whether it is easier to motivate workers with financial incentives in the short term rather than in the longer term. Use the context of Richer Sounds or any other business you are familiar with. (*16 marks*)

Case study: Honda

Honda, established in Japan in 1948 by Soichiro Honda, is the world's largest manufacturer of motorcycles and engines, and the seventh-largest producer of cars. A British subsidiary was launched in 1965. The head office is in Slough and there is a manufacturing operation in Swindon. Strong team spirit and a can-do attitude are key features of life at Honda UK.

The company's principles are simple. Staff are told, 'Your growth is the key to Honda's growth.' A manager notes, 'Mr Honda's philosophy was that you work first for yourself and then for Honda,' he says. 'We employ people more than specialists, and the global company provides advice and assistance – but delegates decisions to local management.' It is a strong culture with little rigid procedure or hierarchy, but there is a powerful team spirit and sense of empowerment.

At Honda, there is a high degree of motivation for not only personal success, but the collective success of the group – the team and the company.

Honda has given a great deal of thought to their mission, vision and values and they do sincerely strive to put these into practice, providing their employees with a sense of making a contribution, doing something worthy, beyond the pursuit of personal rewards.

Honda's 'Fundamental Beliefs' are divided into 'respect for the individual', which includes equality, initiative and trust and their 'Three Joys' – of buying, of selling and of creating. The 'Three Joys' are each based on how different stakeholders are made to feel by the actions and products of the company.

- The Joy of Buying is achieved through providing products and services that exceed the needs and expectations of each customer
- The Joy of Selling occurs when those who are engaged in selling and servicing Honda products develop relationships with a customer based on mutual trust. Through this relationship, Honda employees, dealers and distributors experience pride and joy in satisfying customers and in representing Honda to the customer.
- The Joy of Creating occurs when Honda employees and suppliers involved in the design, development,

engineering and manufacturing of Honda products recognise a sense of joy in their customers and dealers. The joy of creating occurs when quality products exceed expectations and employees and suppliers experience pride in a job well done.

Work teams at Honda are equivalent to a family unit in society. They are the primary learning organisation, the primary source of bonding with a group, and the primary way employees contribute to the company's mission.

When Honda built plants in the US and later in the UK, it changed the system of motivation from that used in Japan to reflect the characteristics and needs of US and UK employees – acknowledging the importance of individual initiative and individual recognition. The company did not view the Japanese way as best but redesigned its systems to adapt to US and UK cultures. For example, it developed a point system. At award ceremonies, individual employees are awarded with a range of prizes, earned by accumulating points. Every employee earns points by participating in any of the company's improvement processes (e.g. quality circles and suggestion schemes). Points accumulate over an individual's career and can earn a range of items including a Honda car, two weeks off with pay, and flights around the world with spending money. In addition to hourly or salaried basic rate pay, employees participate in profit sharing. Ten per cent of gross profit is shared with employees based on their relative wages and salaries. Good attendance results in another bonus.

Motivation appears to be strong, the workforce is a happy one and the turnover rate is half the industry average. Honda's view is that a highly motivated workforce is not an accident. It is the result of systematic efforts on the part of management to design and apply a system of motivation. The most effective systems balance the encouragement of strong social bonds and strong teamwork and the availability of individual incentives.

Source: adapted from *The Sunday Times* 100 Best Companies to Work for, 2003 and 2005, article by Lawrence Miller, 'The Lean System of Motivation' at www.Industryweek.com, 23 February 2014 and www.honda.co.uk

Questions

Total: 25 marks

1 Analyse how 'a powerful team spirit and sense of empowerment' might benefit Honda UK. *(9 marks)*

2 Using your knowledge of motivation, discuss how effective Honda's approach to its staff is likely to be in producing a successful company. *(16 marks)*

24

Making HR decisions: improving employer–employee relations

This chapter discusses the influences on the extent and methods of employee involvement in decision making. In doing so, it considers methods of employee representation, including trade unions and works councils. How to manage and improve employer–employee communications and relations are then considered. Finally the value of good employer–employee relations is discussed.

Influences on the extent and methods of employee involvement in decision making

Employee involvement in decision making, often known as employee representation, may take many forms, including trade unions, works councils and other employee groups.

Did you know?

Employee representation is also known as employee participation or industrial democracy. Both terms refer to the extent to which employees are involved in the decision-making process. This can take the following forms: worker directors, who are elected to the board of directors by employees from the factory floor; works councils, which are discussed later in this chapter; and workers' co-operatives, where a firm's workers own a majority of its shares, such as in the John Lewis Partnership.

Influences on employee involvement in decision making

- **Organisation size**. All organisations involve employees in decision making to some extent. In very small organisations, this may simply involve employers providing their employees with information and asking for their views. In larger organisations, informing and consulting employees is essential in order to maintain good employer/employee relations and is also a legal requirement. In large organisations, this is likely to involve more formal procedures and methods.

- **External environment**. Government policy and legislation in relation to industrial relations and the role of trade unions is an important influence on the extent of employee involvement in decision making. The state of the economy influences relationships between employers and employees and thus the extent to which employees are involved in decision making. One might assume greater levels of employee involvement during boom periods but there were many examples during the recession of 2008 of businesses involving employees in extensive discussions about the options for survival when revenue and profits were falling. See the fact file on JCB below.
- **Style of leadership**. The more democratic the leadership style in an organisation, the more likely that employees will be involved in decision making. The extent to which employees trust leaders will also influence the extent of employee involvement.
- **Quality of communication**. In organisations with good communications and communications that flow up through the organisation as well as down, it is more likely that employees will be involved in the decision-making process.
- **Organisational culture**. The culture of an organisation will be determined by its mission and vision and will dictate whether, for example, all decisions are made by a small group of individuals at the top of the organisation or whether the style is more participative and empowers employees to take part in decisions that affect their own areas of work and the organisation as a whole.

Fact file

JCB

Like many firms producing capital goods, JCB, maker of bright yellow diggers for muddy building sites, needed to cut jobs as a result of the recession of 2008. It came up with a positive approach following negotiation with the trade union representing most of its workers. The result was that about 2,500 staff agreed to a four-day week and a £50-a-week pay cut. It was an unusual deal. Wages are usually assumed to be 'sticky' and resistance to wage cuts is normally severe. However, a representative of the trade union involved in the negotiations declared: 'I am delighted we have been able to save 350 jobs.'

Methods of employee representation

These include:

- employee groups, such as improvement groups, quality circles and autonomous work groups. Autonomous work groups are teams of people who are given a high level of responsibility for their own work. This might include organising and scheduling their own work, making decisions about the allocation of tasks and, in some cases, recruiting new members of staff
- worker directors, i.e. employees of a company who sit on its board of directors, are involved in decision making at this level and represent the views of the workforce

- suggestion schemes
- a democratic style of management, which encourages employees to contribute to decision making
- trade unions
- works councils.

Trade unions and works councils are considered in more detail below.

Trade unions

Modern **trade unions** tend to be categorised according to whether they have more open or more restricted recruitment policies. The four categories used by the Trades Union Congress (TUC) are:

- unions with members across a range of jobs, employers and sectors, including UNISON, Unite and GMB
- unions with members across a range of jobs and employers but in one broad sector of the economy, including ASLEF (railways), NUM (coalmining)
- unions with members with a particular skill, trade or profession, including Equity (performance), NUT (teaching)
- unions with members who work for a particular employer or closely linked employers, including FDA (senior civil servants).

Functions of trade unions and how they benefit employees

The main functions that trade unions provide for their members are negotiation and representation.

- **Negotiation**. There are often differences of opinion between management and trade union members in relation to issues in the workplace. Negotiation involves the process of finding a solution to these differences. In many organisations, trade unions are formally 'recognised' by the employer, meaning that there is a formal agreement between the trade union and the organisation, giving the trade union the right to negotiate with the employer.
- **Representation**. Trade unions also represent individual union members when they have problems at work. If employees feel they are being unfairly treated, they can ask their trade union representative to help sort out their difficulties with management. If the problems cannot be resolved amicably, they may go to an industrial tribunal, at which individual union members can ask their trade unions to represent them. Trade unions also offer their members legal representation, for example, helping them to get financial compensation for work-related injuries.

In addition to the two main functions of negotiation and representation, trade unions provide information, advice and member services. For example, they can advise on a range of issues, such as employment rights and health and safety issues.

More generally, individual employees have very little power to influence decisions that are made about their jobs. In relation to negotiating pay and conditions, they are in a very weak position compared with a large employer. By joining together with other workers in a trade union, there is more chance of having a voice and therefore having influence. By

529

negotiating with employers on behalf of their members, trade unions are able to improve the lot of their members at work in relation to issues such as rates of pay, work facilities, working conditions, bonuses and targets, job security, contracts, redundancy, dismissal, grievance procedures, job descriptions and job specifications.

Do trade unions benefit employers?

Media reporting tends to suggest that trade unions are something of an irritation to employers, disrupting their operations and preventing them achieving their objectives. However, in general, trade unions benefit employers as well as employees.

- They provide a valuable communication link between senior management and the workforce that has not been filtered by middle managers.
- The presence of a trade union means that management can avoid what would be very time-consuming bargaining and negotiation with each individual employee in relation to their pay and conditions.
- A strong union may encourage management to take workers' needs seriously and may therefore improve employee morale, which in turn may have a positive influence on productivity.
- The presence of a trade union may ease situations that could cause difficulty for a firm, such as relocation, retraining for new technology, downsizing and redundancy, and renegotiation of employment conditions and contracts. Trade union officials can be consulted at an early stage of the decision-making process, which may make the workforce more confident that management is acting properly and thoughtfully.

Industrial disputes and industrial action

Negotiation or collective bargaining is the process whereby workers' representatives meet with employers to discuss and negotiate employment-related issues. Most collective bargaining takes place quietly, away from media attention and with agreements being reached quickly and amicably by the union and the employer. However, disagreements can occur, resulting in an industrial dispute. An industrial dispute is a disagreement between management and the trade union representing the employees, which is serious enough for industrial action to result. An industrial dispute might be resolved by successful conciliation or arbitration. If this does not occur, the union may ballot its members on whether to take industrial action. Industrial action includes measures taken by employees to halt or slow production or disrupt services in order to put pressure on management during an industrial dispute.

Industrial action may include any of the following activities:

- A strike, which involves the complete withdrawal of labour by employees. Strikes are only called as a last resort since both sides have a lot to lose: employers may lose sales revenue because of interruptions to production or services, while employees lose their wages and salaries and may find that their jobs are at risk.
- A work-to-rule, in which employees refuse to undertake any work that is outside the precise terms of their employment contract. In a work-to-rule, the workforce applies the employer's own rules and procedure 'to the letter', thus stopping overtime and many forms of participation and

communication that are accepted practice. This behaviour cannot be criticised by the employer and may lead to considerable delay. Staff may prefer to work-to-rule rather than go on strike because they still receive their basic pay.

- A go-slow, in which employees keep on working, but at the absolute minimum pace required to avoid being subject to legitimate disciplinary action. A go-slow means employees lose any bonuses they might usually earn, but ensures that they receive their basic pay. If conducted at a time of high demand, a go-slow could be successful in applying considerable pressure on an employer.
- An overtime ban aims to disrupt employers' plans while keeping employees' basic wages unaffected. An overtime ban can only be effective if a significant proportion of work in a key section is done on overtime, which is only likely to occur in peak production periods.

Table 24.1 identifies the factors that influence the success of industrial action and the possible problems and benefits for employees and employers.

▼ **Table 24.1** Industrial action

Factors that influence the success of industrial action	Problems of industrial action for employers	Problems of industrial action for employees	Benefits of industrial action
Nature and strength of union	Lost production, reduced revenue and lower profits	Reduced or lost earnings	Resolves ongoing grievances and improves the atmosphere
Workforce concentration (e.g. lots of union members in one firm compared with a few members in many firms)	Continuing poor relationships and grievances with employees, that lead to poor motivation and communication	Closure of the business and redundancies	Often leads to new rules about which all agree (e.g. regarding rates of pay or the need to consult)
Management tactics (e.g. if stocks are available to meet demand during a strike)	Shifts management's focus away from strategic planning for the future	Stress and friction between levels of the hierarchy	Leads to greater understanding of employer/employee positions
Economic climate	Harms the firm's reputation with its customers	If unsuccessful, workers are in a weaker position	
Public support		Support from the public may decline if action affects them	
Legal climate		Must conform to legislation or be liable for damages	

Employers can also take industrial action against their employees, for example, by withdrawing overtime, introducing a lockout (for example, by closing a factory and not allowing employees in to continue working), changing standard and piecework rates, closing the business and dismissing workers.

As Figures 24.1 and 24.2 illustrate, times have changed and industrial unrest in the form of days lost are much less frequent than in the past. Table 24.2 shows the principal causes of working days lost in 2013. By far the main cause of disputes is pay, with other causes, including redundancy and working conditions, being insignificant in comparison.

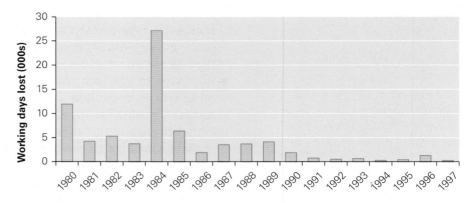

▲ **Figure 24.1** Working days lost in the UK, 1980–97
Source: Office for National Statistics

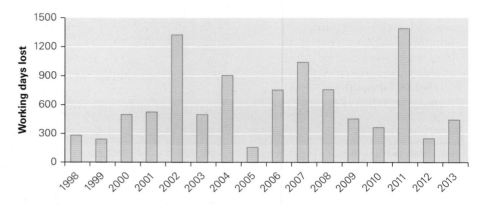

▲ **Figure 24.2** Working days lost in the UK 1998–2013
Source: Office for National Statistics

▼ **Table 24.2** Principal causes of disputes leading to working days lost in the UK, 2013 Source: Office for National Statistics

Principal cause	Days lost in 2013 (000s)	%
Pay	418.7	94.3
Redundancy	14.5	3.3
Working conditions	9.0	2.0
Dismissal and other disciplinary matters	0.8	0.2
Hours worked	0.3	0.1
Staffing issues	0.4	0.1
Total days lost	443.7	

Works councils

Works councils complement the role of trade unions. Bargaining over issues such as wages, terms of employment and productivity levels are excluded from the agenda of works councils, so these issues are left to trade union negotiations.

The role of a works council is essentially to review a company's plans, to provide an opportunity to consult and gain the views of the workforce about these and to contribute these ideas to the decision-making process. A relative weakness of this process is that, because a works council includes representatives from the whole company, it usually lacks the focus of a localised quality circle or improvement group.

Fact file

European Works Councils (EWCs)

As a result of EWCs, about 10 million workers across the EU have the right to information and consultation on company decisions at a European level. Major trade unions representing workers in large companies that operate in two or more EU countries often have extensive involvement in EWCs. For example, GMB (Britain's General Union, which represents employees across a range of jobs, employers and sectors) represents workers in over 130 European Works Councils where it has over 170 seats.

Fact file

EU Information and Consultation Directive

Introduced in April 2005, the EU Information and Consultation Directive gives employees in organisations with 50-plus staff the right to be informed about the business's economic situation and prospects. In effect, the workforce must be notified of all changes that could affect the nature of staff's employment, such as work organisation, contractual relations, redundancies, mergers and takeovers. The law includes a requirement to hold ballots to elect staff representatives and gives staff rights to information and consultation. In the UK, the requirement for national works councils came into force in April 2008.

The European Works Council Directive requires that large companies (with at least 1,000 employees) operating in two or more EU countries must set up European works councils (EWCs). The directive aims to 'improve the right to information and to consultation of employees'. EWCs usually meet once a year and are made up of at least one elected representative from each country plus representatives of central management. EWCs give representatives from the various European countries in which a large multinational company operates a direct line of communication to senior managers. They also ensure that workers in each country receive the same information about policies and plans and at the same time. Areas for discussion include corporate structure, the economic and financial situation, investment, the employment situation, health and safety, cutbacks and closures, acquisitions and new working practices. They provide opportunities for workers' representatives and trade unions in national works councils to consult each other and to develop common European responses to plans that affect them all. Senior managers are required to consider these responses before any plans can be implemented. Single-country issues, including pay and conditions, are not discussed in EWCs. Most commentators agree that the EWC process is worthwhile and encourages good two-way communication between employers (or senior management) and employees.

In addition to trade unions, works councils and other forms of employee participation mentioned earlier, a range of organisations representing the interests of employers and employees aim to help businesses avoid or resolve industrial disputes and thus improve employer–employee relations. These include ACAS, the TUC, employers' associations and the CBI. Each of these is considered briefly in the fact files below.

Fact file

Advisory, Conciliation and Arbitration Service

The Advisory, Conciliation and Arbitration Service (ACAS) was founded in 1975. It aims to improve organisations and working life through better employment relations. It is a non-governmental body that is fully independent, impartial and confidential.

ACAS only becomes involved in a dispute if both sides (employers and employees or their trade union representatives) believe that ACAS can help them make progress in the dispute. As an independent and neutral party, ACAS provides mediation, conciliation and arbitration services. Mediation and conciliation are where it tries to bring both sides of a dispute together to reconcile their differences and reach an agreement. Arbitration is where both sides agree that ACAS will review the evidence and arrive at a decision, which they will accept.

What do you think?

The approach that ACAS takes is: 'Don't get angry – get curious.' Its advice for a first step towards a solution in any kind of dispute is to find out why people are taking the positions they are and why they are angry.

Do you think this is good advice in any dispute in any context? Justify your answer.

Fact file

Trades Union Congress (TUC)

Formed in 1868, the Trades Union Congress (TUC) is the national organisation that represents trade unions in the UK. It has 54 affiliated (member) unions representing nearly 6.2 million working people. Trade unions join the TUC because they know that they can be stronger and more effective if they work together with other unions to protect the rights of working people.

The role of the TUC in relation to improving employer–employee relations includes:

- bringing unions together to draw up common policies
- lobbying the government to implement policies that will benefit people at work
- campaigning on economic and social issues
- carrying out research on employment-related issues
- running training and education programmes for union representatives
- helping unions develop new services for their members
- helping unions avoid clashes with each other.

Fact file

Employers' associations

Just as trade unions represent employees, so employers' associations represent the views and interests of companies within a sector or industry – for example, the Engineering Employers' Federation. They are especially useful for small firms negotiating with large trade unions. Like trade unions, they are financed by members' subscriptions. Their functions

in relation to improving employer–employee relations include:

- providing advice to employers about collective bargaining
- acting as a pressure group influencing government policy in areas of interest to the sector or industry they represent
- providing a negotiating team that can agree minimum pay and conditions with trade unions throughout the industry.

Fact file

Confederation of British Industry (CBI)

The Confederation of British Industry (CBI) was formed in 1965. It performs a similar role for employers to the role the TUC provides for trade unions. It is the main employers' association and includes most of the country's leading firms as members. Its main functions in relation to improving employer–employee relations are to:

- lobby the government in order to influence legislation and economic policies favoured by its members
- provide its members with well-researched reports, such as the CBI's Quarterly Survey of Economic Trends.

The CBI works with the TUC on consultative bodies such as ACAS.

How to manage and improve employer–employee communications and relations

Managing and improving employer–employee communications and relations means understanding the barriers that may need to be overcome and introducing effective strategies to do so.

Issues to consider include the following:

- **Recognising the other side's objectives and needs.** Employee representation means that people come together with very different points of view and conflicting objectives, which may lead to difficulties in arriving at a consensus in decision making. Managers may resent the power and influence of workers and the amount of information they are provided with. Workers, on the other hand, may feel that they do not have enough power or are not provided with enough information. Industrial relations refers to the atmosphere prevailing between an organisation's management and its workforce representatives (i.e. the trade unions). Successful industrial relations result when both employers and trade unions compromise and recognise each other's objectives and needs.

- **Appropriate leadership and culture**. Employees are more likely to have confidence in people they trust and in leadership styles and cultures that encourage their involvement. Appropriate leadership style and organisational culture therefore need to be in place in order to improve employer–employee communication and relations. Successful organisations tend to have leadership styles that are highly committed to including employees. This has given rise to more partnership working, where unions and employees work with leaders and managers to generate positive change and growth for the business.

- **Structural issues including intermediaries and hierarchies**. Intermediaries are individuals or groups within official communication channels through whom messages must be passed in order to reach the intended receivers. The greater the number of intermediaries, and therefore the longer the chain of command, the less effective any communication is likely to be. As Figure 24.3 illustrates, if employee J wants to communicate with manager A, the message has to go via intermediaries F, C and B. This will slow the communication down and may lead to the communication becoming distorted. Even worse, F, C or B may either forget to forward any communication or decide it is not worth passing on. As firms grow in size, they tend to add more layers of hierarchy. This means that communication becomes more difficult because messages moving from the top of the organisation to the bottom have to go through more intermediaries. As well as slowing down the decision-making process, it also means that communication from the bottom to the top of the organisation is more likely to be discouraged. De-layering and flatter hierarchies are increasingly features of successful organisations. Fewer intermediaries exist and more opportunities are available for employers (or senior managers) and employees to communicate and share ideas.

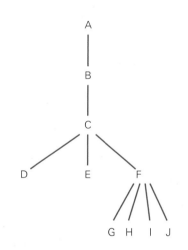

▲ **Figure 24.3** Communication channel with intermediaries

- **Communication and large organisations**. Communication often becomes more difficult as organisations grow. In general, inadequate understanding of corporate objectives, different languages and cultures, different time zones and too many intermediaries all make effective communication much more difficult for larger businesses, especially multinationals, and make it more difficult to manage and improve employer–employee communications and relations. More communication does not always mean better communication. It can lead to communication (or information) overload and adversely affect decision making and employer–employee relations. Possible solutions to the inevitable problems of communication associated with large organisations are delegation and decentralisation. Open communication channels, opportunities for employees to discuss issues that concern them and relay them to senior managers and employee involvement in consultation about major changes are all approaches that can improve communication and thus employer–employee relations.

Value of good employer–employee relations

- **Worker participation**. According to the TUC, a strong sense of worker participation in decisions, often co-ordinated through trade unions, enhances business performance. One study reported that organisations with strong employee involvement were growing more quickly than those without this feature. Other research suggested a positive link between employee representation and productivity.

- **Implementing change**. Good employer–employee relations make it easier to implement change because employees and other stakeholders understand and recognise the need for it. Taking into account the opinions of employees is also likely to encourage greater commitment to the change process.

- **Motivation**. Effective communications and employer–employee relations encourage a more motivated workforce and help to develop commitment to the business from employees at all levels of the organisation. Just as good communication can increase employee motivation, well-motivated employees are likely to communicate more readily with management by suggesting ideas, listening to advice and contributing their opinions, and to be more willing to participate in decision making. Theories of motivation suggest that employees are happier if they feel involved, if they have a part to play in the organisation they work for and if their views are valued by management. More involvement of employees can therefore improve motivation, which in turn may result in lower labour turnover and, often, more innovation and more effective problem solving, all of which may lead to increased productivity.

- **Achieving objectives**. Good communications and employer–employee relations help to ensure that a business is well co-ordinated and that all employees pursue the same corporate objectives. It is important that employees understand the objectives of their organisation, how their own job contributes to meeting these objectives and how well they are performing their job and hence contributing to the success of the organisation.

- **Improving competitiveness**. Good communications and effective employer–employee relations allow the organisation to be more competitive by improving efficiency and identifying opportunities.

- **Decision making**. Problems can arise from employee representation, as involving more people in decision making may slow the whole process down. However, this is not necessarily a bad thing if it causes firms to review situations from different perspectives and therefore make more informed decisions.

Practice exercise 1

Total: 80 marks

1 Explain the term 'employee representation'. *(4 marks)*

2 Explain one advantage and one disadvantage of employee representation for a business. *(6 marks)*

3 What is a trade union? *(3 marks)*

4 Explain three main functions that trade unions carry out on behalf of their members. *(9 marks)*

5 Explain two benefits of trade unions for employers. *(8 marks)*

6 What is a works council? *(3 marks)*

7 Under what circumstances must a business set up a European works council? *(3 marks)*

8 Explain two influences on the level of employee involvement in decision making in a business. *(8 marks)*

9 Explain three benefits to a firm of good communication with its employees. *(9 marks)*

10 Explain two problems that a firm might encounter if it has poor communication with its employees. *(6 marks)*

11 Explain how the number of intermediaries can affect the quality of communication. *(4 marks)*

12 Identify and explain three approaches to making and improving employer and employee communication and relations. *(9 marks)*

13 Identify and explain two examples of the value of good employer–employee relations to a business. *(8 marks)*

Case study: Ragbags

Refer to the case study information on Ragbags on page 472 in Chapter 22 in order to answer the following questions.

Questions

Total: 25 marks

1 Examine the main communication problems facing Ragbags as it has grown from a single-site producer to a multi-site producer. *(9 marks)*

2 Joe Watts recognises that Ragbags needs to manage and improve its employer–employee communications and relations. Discuss why this is important to the business and how it might be achieved. *(16 marks)*

Case study: Thames Water

Thames Water, one of the world's largest water companies, prides itself on its partnership approach to working with trade unions to ensure employees' voices are heard on the issues that matter most to them. Thames Water says that whatever it is reviewing, changing or introducing, it does it all in partnership.

Thames Water works in partnership with its three recognised trade unions – GMB, Unison and Unite. Under its Partnership Agreement, it recognises that its employees and their representatives have key roles to play in the future success of the company. The company actively engages with its trade unions. It has adopted an approach of joint working on key policies and open engagement on strategic plans, key initiatives and business performance to make sure representatives understand the needs of the business and its customers. This approach benefits both employees and the business. Two examples of the benefits illustrate this:

● Pay negotiations: in the past, the annual round of pay negotiations tended to be a prolonged and antagonistic process of offer and counter-offer, with neither side prepared to divulge key information. The partnership approach means that the key information is known to both management and unions as a result of their shared approach to decision making on a day-to-day basis. Negotiations that had previously taken months are now concluded in a few days.

● Shift system: the shift system previously resulted in a huge annual overtime bill for the company.

Thames Water had tried to change the system in the past, but without success because of a complex system of local agreements and a lack of collaboration with employees. By involving shift workers, assisted by union representatives and managers, in discussions about possible changes, a new system was agreed that saved the company money and gave employees more say over the hours they worked.

The business aims to create and provide a positive environment where people are actively engaged, understand their role in the business and the value they add. In both examples above, effective employee involvement, facilitated by constructive trade union support, brought substantial business benefits as well as helping to improve terms and conditions for employees.

During 2013–14, a series of Executive Roadshows visited all sites and offices across London and the Thames Valley, giving more than 4,000 employees an opportunity to ask questions of the leadership team, raise any concerns and highlight any team successes. In addition, a 'workplace listening' initiative was launched that provides opportunities at monthly team meetings for employees to discuss any issues they feel are preventing them from doing their day job effectively.

Source: adapted from Simon Harrison, 'Employee–employer relations in the UK', *Business Review*, November 2003 and www.thameswater.co.uk, September 2014

Questions

Total: 40 marks

1 Explain two methods of employee representation in place at Thames Water. *(6 marks)*

2 Employees at Thames Water belong to one of three trade unions. Explain two possible benefits to employees of belonging to a trade union. *(6 marks)*

3 What does the case study suggest are the benefits of employee representation to:

a) employees of Thames Water *(6 marks)*

b) Thames Water itself? *(6 marks)*

4 To what extent has the partnership approach between the trade unions and Thames Water effectively avoided or resolved potential industrial disputes and improved employee involvement in decision making? *(16 marks)*

Answers to questions

Chapter 1, page 13

Question 1

Variable costs = 2,000 × £6 = £12,000

Fixed costs = £5,000

Total costs = £17,000

Question 2

Variable costs = 900 × £6 = £5,400

Fixed costs = £5,000

Total costs = £10,400

Note that in question 1, although output doubles, total costs increase by less than double their original amount. In question 2, although output falls by 10 per cent, total costs fall by less than 10 per cent. The fact that fixed costs do not change means that total costs will change by a smaller percentage than the change in output.

Chapter 8, page 156

Possible reasons:

- It meets the needs of a market segment (those on low incomes or those not prepared to pay a high price).
- It helps to provide a balanced portfolio.
- There may be less competition in this type of market.
- During a recession, inferior goods may experience rising demand.
- Inferior goods in one country may have greater potential in other countries.

- It makes a profit! This is important. Just because sales are declining, it does not mean that a profit cannot be made. A declining market can be a profitable niche (e.g. pipes for smokers).

Chapter 17

'What do you think?' page 373

The company should stop producing Waterfall. According to Table 17.19, its contribution is negative, so it is not helping to pay for the fixed costs or make a profit. (Alternatively, the company might want to experiment with a price above £18, but this could lead to unsold stock.)

The company should look at Cascade. It provides almost half of the firm's sales volume but contributes less than Fountain and Stream, even though these products sell much lower volumes. (It would be an idea to investigate why these do so well, in order to improve Cascade.) It would also be worth checking to see if the price is set too low.

'What do you think?' page 381

1 The original:
    a) selling price was £5 per unit
    b) variable costs were £1 per unit
    c) fixed costs were £40
2 The amended:
    a) selling price increased to £20 per unit
    b) variable cost increased to £5 per unit
    c) fixed cost increased to £90
3 The original break-even output was 10 units.
4 The final break-even output was 6 units.

Acknowledgements

The Publishers would like to thank the following for permission to reproduce copyright photographs:

Photo credits: **p.1** © Scanrail – Fotolia; **p.3** *t* © Sean Dempsey/PA Archive/Press Association Images; **p.3** *b* © Alex Segre / Alamy; **p.6** © DPA/Press Association Images; **p.10** © Ben Stansall/AFP/Getty Images; **p.11** *t* © SemA – Fotolia; **p.11** *b* © Monkey Business – Fotolia; **p.13** © Andrew Milligan/PA Archive/Press Association Images; **p.17** © photka – Fotolia; **p.18** © Scanrail – Fotolia; **p.20** © auremar – Fotolia; **p.22** © Justin Kase ztwoz / Alamy; **p.23** © Scanrail – Fotolia; **p.26** © Wyn Voysey/AA World Travel Library/TopFoto; **p.29** © Libby Welch / Alamy; **p.30** © Tran-Photography – Fotolia; **p.34** © Scanrail – Fotolia; **p.38** © picturelibrary / Alamy; **p.39** *t* © Kumar Sriskandan / Alamy, *b* © Facundo Arrizabalaga/epa/Corbis; **p.40** © Global Warming Images/REX; **p.50** © nyul – Fotolia; **p.54** © Caro/Photoshot; **p.57** © Colin McConnell/Toronto Star via Getty Images; **p.59** © Konstantin Sutyagin – Fotolia; **p.62** © Kimberly White/Reuters/Corbis; **p.65** © Chris Goodney/Bloomberg via Getty Images; **p.75** © Konstantin Sutyagin – Fotolia; **p.78** © Chris Ratcliffe/Bloomberg via Getty Images; **p.87** © Met Office; **p.92** © Hugh Threlfall / Alamy; **p.94** © Konstantin Sutyagin – Fotolia; **p.95** © Mike Hewitt/Getty Images; **p.96** © Universal Images Group via Getty Images; **p.110** © Scanrail – Fotolia; **p.111** © Newscast / Alamy; **p.112** © Tim Graham/Getty Images; **p.113** © Kzenon – Fotolia; **p.116** © Ingram Publishing Limited; **p.117** © Simon Dawson/Bloomberg via Getty Images; **p.121** © Brent Lewin/Bloomberg via Getty Images; **p.123** © Ian Dagnall / Alamy; **p.125** © Pawel Libera/LightRocket via Getty Images); **p.127** © Jason Alden/Bloomberg via Getty Images; **p.129** © Scanrail – Fotolia; **p.131** © Robert Convery / Alamy; **p.132** © Andres Rodriguez – Fotolia; **p.133** © Monkey Business – Fotolia; **p.134** © Rui Vieira/PA Archive/Press Association Images; **p.144** © Shestakoff – Fotolia; **p.147** © Vanderlei Almeida/AFP/Getty Images); **p.148** © Lucie Lang / Alamy; **p.162** © Scanrail – Fotolia; **p.163** *t* © Purestock, *b* © 1997 Steve Mason/Photodisc/Getty Images; **p.164** © Geoff Tydeman – Fotolia; **p.166** © pumkinpie / Alamy; **p.168** © T.M.O.Buildings / Alamy; **p.170** © Monkey Business – Fotolia; **p.171** © Lenscap / Alamy; **p.172** © Simon Dawson/Bloomberg via Getty Images; **p.174** © Ed Reeve/View/Corbis; **p.176** © Scanrail – Fotolia; **p.179** © Daniel Deme/epa/Corbis; **p.182** © thaifairs – Fotolia; **p.183** © redorbital ./ Demotix/Corbis; **p.185** © Mediablitzimages / Alamy; **p.189** © mark phillips / Alamy; **p.191** © Carolyn Jenkins / Alamy; **p.192** © Martin Williams / Alamy; **p.193** © Tea 42 Restaurants Ltd.; **p.194** © Home Bird / Alamy; **p.195** © aleksey ipatov – Fotolia; **p.197** © Malcolm Fairman / Alamy; **p.199** © Vanoa2 – Fotolia; **p.200** © Nicholas Temple-Fry / Alamy; **p.204** © dinja1 – Fotolia; **p.206** © productsandbrands / Alamy; **p.210** © Tatyana Gladskih – Fotolia; **p.212** © Darren Staples/Reuters/Corbis; **p.213** © studiomode / Alamy; **p.218** © Lam Yik Fei/Bloomberg via Getty Images; **p.227** © seewhatmitchsee / Alamy; **p.228** © Carolyn Jenkins / Alamy; **p.229** © Sergio Azenha / Alamy; **p.230** © ian woolcock – Fotolia; **p.232** © Newscast / Alamy; **p.235** © Konstantin Sutyagin – Fotolia; **p.236** © Jeff J Mitchell/Getty Images; **p.237** © Jack Sullivan / Alamy; **p.239** © Realimage / Alamy; **p.246** © Chris Radburn/PA Archive/Press Association Images; **p.250** © Monkey Business – Fotolia; **p.249** © Konstantin Sutyagin – Fotolia;

p.251 © Rostislav Sedlacek – Fotolia; p.252 © Andres Rodriguez – Fotolia; p.255 © Konstantin Sutyagin – Fotolia; p.262 © templario2004 – Fotolia; p.263 © Imagestate Media (John Foxx); p.269 © Tim Oram/ Photoshot; p.270 © Guy Bouchet/ /Photononstop/Corbis; p.272 © Gill Taylor / Alamy; p.274 © Ingram Publishing Company; p.276 © Konstantinos Moraiti – Fotolia; p.277 © Kim Jae-Hwan/AFP/Getty Images); p.278 © Pavel Losevsky – Fotolia; p.280 © Jan Woitas/DPA/ Press Association Images; p.282 © Simon Dawson/Bloomberg via Getty Images; p.284 *t* © Uwe Annas – Fotolia, *b* © digitallife / Alamy; p.285 'Travel on Tap' Courtesy EE; p.290 © Konstantin Sutyagin – Fotolia; p.291 © Mediablitzimages / Alamy; p.292 © Robert Harding Picture Library Ltd / Alamy; p.294 © Philipp Schmidli/Bloomberg via Getty Images; p.295 © Chris Clark/UPPA/Photoshot; p.302 © Konstantin Sutyagin – Fotolia; p.307 © Rob Ball/Redferns via Getty Images; p.310 © .shock – Fotolia; p.312 © Tomohiro Ohsumi/Bloomberg via Getty Images; p.317 © Monkey Business – Fotolia; p.321 © Jason Knott / Alamy; p.322 © Andrew Michael / Alamy; p.323 © Don Bayley/istockphoto.com; p.325 © Dhiraj Singh/ Bloomberg via Getty Images; p.327 © Monkey Business – Fotolia; p.330 © Scanrail – Fotolia; p.332 © ellisia – Fotolia; p.333 © Louie Psihoyos/ Corbis; p.335 © rrenis2000 – Fotolia; p.344 © wrangler – Fotolia; p.345 *t* © Springfield Gallery – Fotolia, *b* © Chris Ratcliffe/Bloomberg via Getty Images; p.349 © Scanrail – Fotolia; p.350 © Stanislav Komogorov – Fotolia; p.356 © destina – Fotolia; p.357 © Lee Martin / Alamy; p.361 © lesley marlor – Fotolia; p.364 © Kybele – Fotolia; p.367 © graja – Fotolia; p.368 © London Entertainment / Alamy; p.369 © Alexandra Karamyshev – Fotolia; p.371 © 2xsamara.com – Fotolia; p.373 © WavebreakMediaMicro – Fotolia; p.393 © Scanrail – Fotolia; p.394 © NAN – Fotolia; p.395 © Chris Ratcliffe/Bloomberg via Getty Images; p.396 © Oticki – Fotolia; p.400 © Gillian Allen/AP/Press Association Images; p.401 © Rido – Fotolia; p.406 © Anna Khomulo – Fotolia; p.408 © Scanrail – Fotolia; p.409 © Chris Howes/Wild Places Photography / Alamy; p.411 *l* © Newscast / Alamy, *r* © Kadmy – Fotolia; p.416 © seewhatmitchsee – Fotolia; p.420 © Robert Convery / Alamy; p.423 © Konstantin Sutyagin – Fotolia; p.424 © auremar – Fotolia; p.425 © auremar – Fotolia; p.432 © Ulrich Baumgarten via Getty Images; p.437 © Konstantin Sutyagin – Fotolia; p.439 © Alex Segre / Alamy; p.440 © Monkey Business – Fotolia; p.444 © Krisztian Bocsi/Bloomberg via Getty Images; p.450 © Konstantin Sutyagin – Fotolia; p.451 © plus69free – Fotolia; p.456 © tiero – Fotolia; p.462 © Cultura Creative / Alamy; p.478 © CandyBox Images – Fotolia; p.479 © Jeanette Dietl – Fotolia; p.482 © Steven May / Alamy; p.485 © Gina Sanders – Fotolia; p.486 © Justin Kase zninez / Alamy; p.489 © nyul – Fotolia; p.491 © Justin Kase z13z / Alamy; p.494 © Manan Vatsyayana/AFP/Getty Images; p.495 © James Lewis / Alamy; p.497 © Konstantin Sutyagin – Fotolia; p.498 © WavebreakMediaMicro – Fotolia; p.499 © Hulton Archive/Getty Images; p.500 © CandyBox Images – Fotolia, p.501 © Joe Gough – Fotolia; p.503 © Michael Pettigrew – Fotolia; p.504 © Monkey Business – Fotolia; p.510 © RTimages – Fotolia; p.517 © Udit Kulshrestha/Bloomberg via Getty Images; p.518 © Paul McErlane/Bloomberg News via Getty Images; p.527 © Konstantin Sutyagin – Fotolia; p.528 © eye35 / Alamy; p.529 © Nigel Roddis/Reuters/Corbis; p.530 © Christopher Furlong/Getty Images; p.535 © Arno Massee/Science Photo Library.

Every effort has been made to trace all copyright holders, but if any have been inadvertently overlooked the Publishers will be pleased to make the necessary arrangements at the first opportunity.

Index